Professional Java XML Programming with Servlets and JSP

Tom Myers
Alexander Nakhimovsky

Wrox Press Ltd. ®

Professional Java XML Programming with Servlets and JSP

Published by Wrox Press Ltd
Arden House, 1102 Warwick Road, Acock's Green, Birmingham B27 6BH, UK
Printed in USA
ISBN 1-861002-85-8

Trademark Acknowledgements

Wrox has endeavored to provide trademark information about all the companies and products mentioned in this book by the appropriate use of capitals. However, Wrox cannot guarantee the accuracy of this information.

Credits

Authors
Tom Myers
Alexander Nakhimovsky

Editors
Jeremy Beacock
Gregory Beekman

Managing Editor
Paul Cooper

Development Editors
Jeremy Beacock
Timothy Briggs

Project Manager
Sophie Edwards

Index
Marilyn Rowland
Alessandro Ansa
Martin Brooks
Andrew Criddle

Figures/Illustrations
William Fallon

Additional Material
David Megginson

Technical Reviewers
Lee Ackerman
Tim Briggs
Carl Burnham
Jason Diamond
Steven Gould
Paul Houle
Brian Jackson
Jim Johnson
Sergey Kuramshin
Piroz Mohseni
Mark Oswald
Andrew Patzer
Daniel Somerfield
Bryon Vargas
Krishna Vedati

Layout/Production
Tom Bartlett
Mark Burdett
William Fallon
Jonathan Jones
John McNulty

Cover Design
Chris Morris

About the Authors

Alexander Nakhimovsky

Alexander Nakhimovsky received an MA in mathematics from Leningrad University in 1972 and a PhD in general linguistics from Cornell in 1978, with a graduate minor in computer science. He taught general and slavic linguistics at Cornell and SUNY Oswego before joining Colgate's computer science department in 1985. He published a book and a number of articles on theoretical and computational linguistics, several Russian language textbooks, a dictionary of Nabokov's Lolita, and, jointly with Tom Myers, "Javascript Objects", Wrox 1998, and "Professional Java XML Programming with Servlets and JSP", Wrox 1999.

Tom Myers

Tom has a BA (cum laude), St. John's College, Santa Fe, New Mexico ("Great Books" program), 1975 and a PhD in computer science from the University of Pennsylvania, 1980. He taught computer science at the University of Delaware and Colgate before becoming a full-time consultant and software developer. He is the author of "Equations, Models, and Programs: A Mathematical Introduction to Computer Science" Prentice-Hall Software Series, 1988, several articles on theoretical computer science, and two joint titles with Alexander Nakhimovsky: "Javascript Objects", Wrox 1998, and "Professional Java XML Programming with Servlets and JSP", Wrox 1999.

Acknowledgements

We would like to thank the many people who made this book possible.

At Wrox, our editors have been supportive and professional: it was a pleasure to work with Tim Briggs, Jeremy Beacock, Gregory Beekman and Paul Cooper. Our reviewers have caught many errors and made many useful suggestions. David Brownell, whose work is cited in the book, was personally helpful on a couple of specific occasions.

At Colgate, our special thanks again go to the Information Technology Services, especially Ross Miller, Jim Nesbitt, Bill Howell, and all the other good people of SB10. Dylan Strong (Colgate '01) has shown a remarkable perseverance and ingenuity in chasing the demons inside my computer. Charlotte Jablonski, the secretary of the Computer Science department, has been quick and cheerful, as always.

Some of the book's ideas were first tried out in an independent study course in the spring of 1999. The students in the course deserve a special mention: they did a terrific job on the course projects during that semester: the bookstore team of Hui Cheng, Alan Lewis, Sameer Panjwani and Jon Seidman; Dave Blank and Alison Hartwell; Karthik Jayaraman the Java guru; and Matt Seeve and Chris Towt. Armando Singer, Colgate '99, although not a member of that group, was extremely helpful on many occasions and showed remarkable maturity and professionalism in everything he did.

Without our families, nothing would be possible.

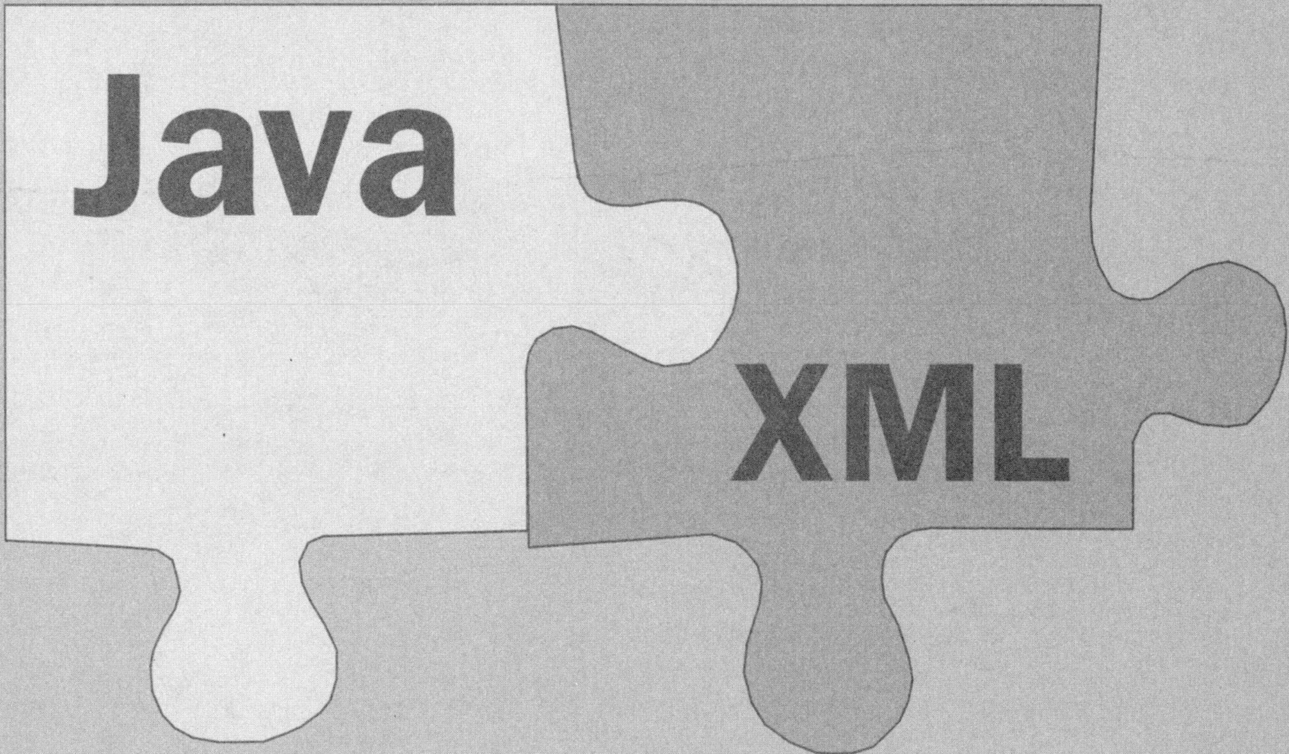
Java
XML

Table of Contents

Chapter 3: A Shell for Three-Tier Applications 85

Chapter 5: XML Beginnings   187

Chapter 6: Entities and DTDs   221

Chapter 7: The DOM, the SAX and the Parser   253

Chapter 8: SAX Processing, the Sun Parser and a Conformance Study 287

Chapter 9: Interpreting XML Mini-Languages 317

Chapter 10: JSPs and JavaBeans 345

Chapter 11: Toward a Many-Legged System: Generic Tools 381

Chapter 12: Toward a Many-Legged System: Specific Constructions   437

Chapter 13: XSLT and XPath   491

Table of Contents

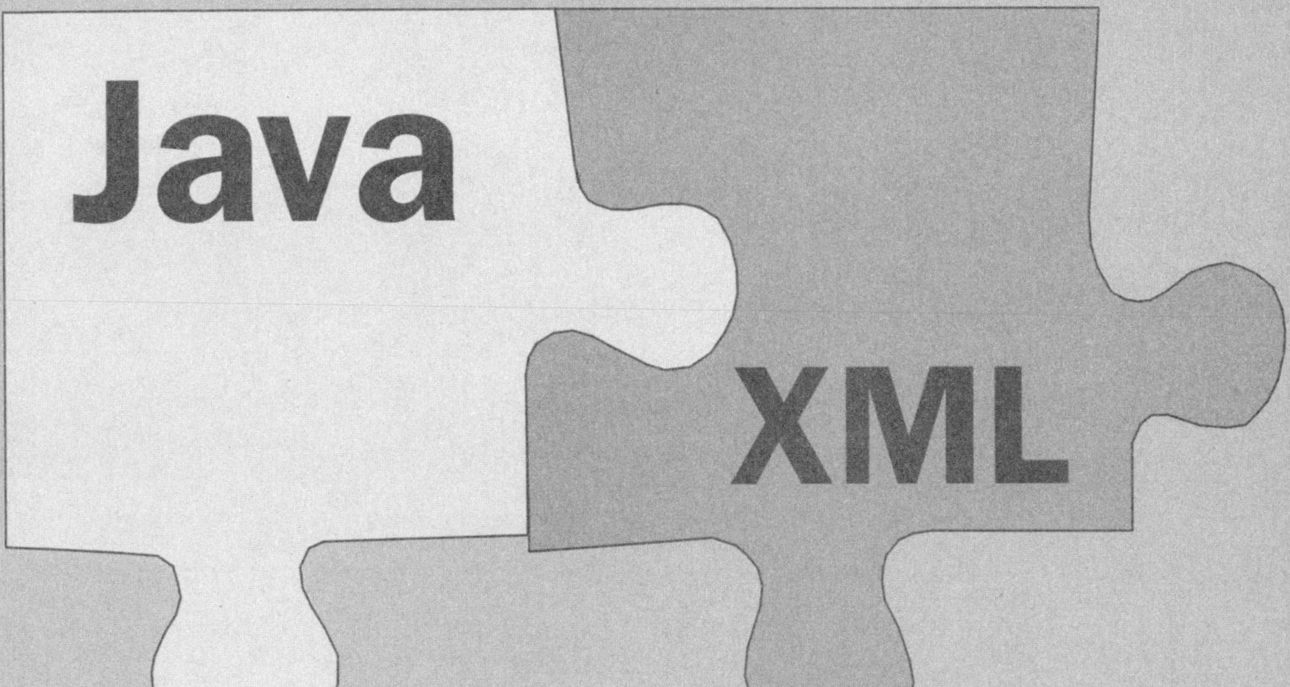
Java
XML

Introduction

What is this Book About?

A single-sentence, sound-bite size answer would go like this:

This book is about three-tier Web applications that are written in Java and use XML languages for configuring the application, exchanging data between its components and providing customizable templates for its HTML output.

For more explanation of what this all means, read on. If you need encouragement, here is what we think about our subject.

- ❑ Distributed Web applications are the most common and best-paid-for kind of applications nowadays.

- ❑ The best way to structure Web applications is as three-tier applications, because this way you neatly separate out the application's three main components: user interface, computational logic and data storage.

- ❑ Java and XML together provide the best tools for creating three-tier applications because, to quote David Brownell from an old interview, **"Java is cross-platform code and XML is cross-platform data"**. Actually, XML is much more than that, as we explain in a moment.

Three-Tier Web Applications

By splitting an application across three tiers, we are able to separate out the three logical components of the application: user interface, computational logic and data storage. Each logical unit can then be developed separately from the others, introducing an enormous degree of flexibility into the design of the application. For example, by separating out the computational logic from the presentation layer, many different kinds of user interfaces can be developed. This allows different groups of users to access the same computational layer (the "work horse" of the application) but with an interface customized for each group's specific needs. The data storage layer can consist of any source of well-structured information, a database or XML documents for example, allowing a complete change to the way the data is stored without ever affecting the application logic or presentation layer.

It is the middle tier that usually benefits most from this three-tier architecture, allowing the computational logic to be developed to any degree of sophistication, itself perhaps containing multiple layers, or to be completely changed, all without affecting the way the user interacts with it. By having the application logic on a single machine that each user must access ensures that any upgrade made to the application software is automatically "enforced" upon all users, and avoids the nightmare of maintaining many different versions of the same application.

In reality, three-tier Web applications generally consist of a Web browser for the user interface, a Web server connected to a "middle tier" application, and a persistent store that is frequently a relational database. In this book, Java is the language of the middle tier. As already noted, the middle tier can be of considerable complexity, and when it gets to be that way it is normal to divide it further, ending up with four, five or N tiers. For simplicity, we always talk about three tiers, with possible subdivisions in the middle.

The diagram below illustrates the three-tier Web application concept:

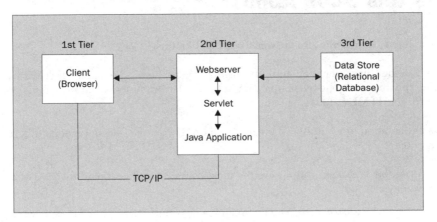

XML

Extensible Markup Language, or XML, is not really a language but rather a meta-language for defining markup languages. For instance, it has been used to define XHTML, a designated successor to HTML. Initially, XML was invented for content-specific markup of documents. Very soon it became clear that it was also an excellent tool for data description, where data is understood broadly to include such things as flow of control or sequence of computations. In this book, we mostly use XML for configuring applications and sending data from one component to another. We rarely display XML files directly in the browser, and always provide an HTML alternative.

How this Book is Different

This book is browser-independent and standards based. It also has a theme: it tries to articulate a certain vision of how Java and XML, working together, can transform the practice of writing Web applications.

Browser Independent

We use JavaScript very sparingly and in browser-independent ways. We do use Cascading Style Sheets (CSS1), and so our applications require a browser that understands them, but otherwise there are no browser restrictions. In particular, all applications in this book can be used with both Internet Explorer 4 and Netscape Communicator 4, as well as with fifth-generation browsers.

Standards Based

Unlike many previous books on XML and related technologies, this book uses only *stable* versions of them: no Working Drafts or beta-releases. This guarantees that the book and its code will remain relevant for a long time, as long as Sun and W3C maintain backwards compatibility with their product releases. In particular, we only use the Recommendations or Proposed Recommendations from W3C, such as:

- XML Path Language (XPath) Version 1.0
- eXtensible Stylesheet Language for Transformations (XSLT) Version 1.0
- XHTML 1.0: The Extensible HyperText Markup Language – A Reformulation of HTML 4.0 in XML
- Associating Style Sheets with XML documents
- Namespaces in XML
- Document Object Model (DOM) Level 1
- XML 1.0

The only Working Draft we discuss at considerable length (but do not use in our code) is XHTML 1.1 – module-based XHTML. Although the details of that specification are still fluid, the principles and mechanisms of modularization have been stable for some time and are unlikely to change. There is no doubt that Web documents of the very near future will start using the modularized version.

For our examples of Document Type Definitions (DTDs), we use such industry standards as DocBook, XHTML and WML (Wireless Markup Language). Where we use JavaServer Pages (JSP) in our code, we only use the stable 1.0 version of it.

The Theme of this Book

Our book develops several substantial applications and covers a good deal of Java, XML, JSP and XSLT. The theme of the book is meta-programming, i.e. writing programs that customize, guide and modify other programs. Meta-programming is not a very new idea (LISP programmers have been doing it for decades) but XML gives it a profoundly new twist. In this brief introduction we can only advance bold claims and wave our hands in their support, but we believe that XML can greatly increase the ability of a Competent User Who is Not a Programmer to exercise control over computer programs by editing human-readable text files. In brief, once .ini files and Notepad are replaced with .xml files and a validating XML editor, the possibilities for controlling programs from text files increase immeasurably, perhaps introducing a new way of programming and a new relationship between the user, the programmer and the program. The theme of our book is this collection of new possibilities; its goal is to help bring about this new relationship.

Another way to describe our Big Idea is to say that we are developing generic programs which know as little as possible about what they are actually being used to do. Instead, their structure and behavior (model, view, and control) are described in domain-specific XML languages with appropriate DTDs, and the programs themselves "interpret" these descriptions. Those familiar with design patterns literature (starting with Gamma et al., *Design Patterns*, Addison-Wesley 1995) will recognize the influence of the "Little Language" pattern which we call Minilanguage and use extensively throughout the book.

Languages and Parsers

In order to use XML for program organization (rather than display) one has to parse XML documents into data structures in memory. We could simply show how to install and use a parser, but we believe that a deeper understanding of the technology is important for using XML effectively. For this reason, we invent a mini-language and write a parser for it before we introduce XML and parsing. The language is not simply a pedagogical device: it is a language for writing template files for HTML output, and we use it to compare the template/mini-language based approach to HTML generation with the JSP approach. Our conclusions are that both approaches have advantages depending on the circumstance, but that the mini-language approach holds definite advantages in those situations where Web developers (Competent Users Who are Not Programmers) do not have the continued support of JSP-proficient tool developers.

A Brief Outline

Throughout, this book has multiple long-term interdependencies and you will get much more reading pleasure from this book if you keep its overall design in mind. Also, it divides into chunks that consist of a couple of chapters each, and those divisions are not obvious from the flat chapter numbering.

Chapters 1 and 2 are preparatory. They introduce the basic plumbing of a Java Web application – servlets (written in Java) and JDBC (Java DataBase Connectivity) – in a step-by-step way, starting with very simple and unstructured examples. By elaborating these initial examples, we gradually evolve the components of the middle tier: the main servlet that acts as a dispatcher, the database connection component, and the HTML-generation component. If you are an experienced three-tier developer, you may find the initial examples offensive to your intelligence because they are not thread-safe, or because they do not use connection pooling, and so forth. However, this sets the scene for later development where such issues will be addressed.

Chapters 3 and 4 are still about Java, apparently with no XML in sight. They develop our first substantial application, a customizable "shell" for three-tier applications. As part of that shell, we develop, in Chapter 4, a substitution mini-language for writing both output template files and initialization/configuration files. This chapter serves two purposes: an obvious one, and a pedagogical one. The obvious purpose is to develop both a mini-language and a parser for it. Although other mini-languages for output templates exist "out there" (and we mention them in the chapter), ours has certain advantages, and we use the XML-ized version of it for serious development. The pedagogical purpose is to prepare you, the reader, for the XML technology. It is our belief that to really understand and effectively use XML, an understanding of formal grammars and parsers is crucial. It is also very useful to become a fluent reader of grammar rules (or "productions") written in EBNF (Extended Backus-Naur Form) because those productions pack a lot of information into very little space.

The next chunk, Chapters 5 and 6, is about XML (including Namespaces), and has no Java at all. We return to Java (but not to three-tier applications!) in Chapters 7 and 8 where we cover XML parsing and the relationship between DOM and SAX specifications. This section leads to a general framework for developing XML mini-languages in Chapter 9: we implement a general mechanism for adding an interpretation to an XML language, and we use it to write a generic converter from XML files to database tables.

We return to three-tier applications in Chapter 10, but with a new twist: instead of servlets, we start using JSP pages. JSP is an amazing technology, and it would be impossible to write a book about mini-languages, output templates, servlets and middle-tier Java applications without covering JSPs because they can be all of the above. This is their greatest weakness: they are just too powerful and flexible, and may easily lead the programmer astray, down the path of large, unstructured lumps of code. We also spend a good deal of time on related architectural considerations: how best to organize JSPs and JavaBeans, working together, into a well-structured application.

Chapters 11 and 12 develop by far the longest and most ambitious application of the book, in which we deliver on our promise to build a generic application that is dynamically configured by an XML configuration file (and additionally customized by user input from an HTML form). The application is a mail client that can be used to send and receive mail and to store mail messages in a relational database. It may not be as powerful as leading commercial software, but it does demonstrate some rather powerful techniques. For example, it configures itself at startup out of JavaBean components that are defined in XML; once configured, the components produce and consume XML data, totally unconcerned as to whether the data is coming from a file, a string variable, a socket, or a database. In other words, it is not only a specific application but also a generic framework for developing distributed applications.

Finally, in Chapter 13 we introduce our last technology for this book, XSLT (including XPath). XSLT is a language for transforming XML documents. It is not a completely general mechanism for XML transformations – there are some things that you can only do with a parser – but XSLT does many things extremely well, in a declarative fashion, and with relatively few lines of code. In addition, XSLT can include extension functions written in Java. The extension mechanism is not yet standardized but it will be, and at that time there will be substantial overlap between XSLT and JSP. XSLT is definitely a tool to be familiar with and to keep an eye on.

If we had had more time and space, we would have developed yet another application. We would have called it an N-topus, an octopus-like creature with N legs and K heads, $K <= N$. Each head would then be either an entry point to the application or a data transformer, and each leg would carry XML-encoded data from one transforming head to another. Some transformers would use XSLT, and others would use XML parsers and custom-designed beans. The entire structure would be dynamically configured by XML files, produced by competent users who are not programmers under the watchful eye of a validating parser. If there is a second edition of this book, we'll write such an application for it and, hopefully, squeeze it in.

Who is this Book for?

This book is for experienced programmers and students of computer science. It assumes that you, the reader, are reasonably comfortable with the basics of Java programming, and specifically the material of the following "basic trails" of Sun's Java Tutorial:

❑   Learning the Java Language
❑   Essential Java Classes.

See http://java.sun.com/books/tutorial/trailmap.html. This material, and much more, is well covered in Ivor Horton's *Beginning Java 2*, WROX Press 1999 (ISBN 1-861002-23-8).

We will also be assuming a more limited familiarity with the basics of

- ❑   HTML, CSS1 and JavaScript
- ❑   HTTP protocol and CGI programming
- ❑   Relational databases
- ❑   SQL syntax and vocabulary

Our HTML and JavaScript are deliberately plain so as not to distract the reader's attention from the main thrust of the book, and to also stay within the capabilities of all current browsers. The assumed limited background in HTTP, CGI, relational databases and SQL is summarized in several Appendices, where references to more extensive treatments are also provided.

What you Need to Use this Book

A distributed Web application, especially one that uses Java and XML, is a complex piece of software that requires an elaborate framework of supporting machinery: a Web browser, a Web server outfitted with a servlet engine, a relational database with a matching JDBC driver, an XML parser and its XSL companion, and, of course, JDK1.2. Amazingly, the entire framework can be installed on a single Win9x machine: most development has been done on a single Windows 98 Pentium II computer. For the Web server and servlets we used two configurations: (1) Microsoft's Personal Web Server with JRun2.3 servlet engine, and (2) Sun's jswdk-1.0. For the data storage, we used the Microsoft Access database and the JDBC-ODBC bridge. For XML and XSLT, we used Sun's XML parser and James Clark's XT, November 5, 1999 release. Appendix A contains detailed instructions on how to install all these components. You will also need to install our supporting code (from the Wrox web site – much easier than typing it all in), a library of utilities that we will gradually introduce as we go along.

Code Conventions

We have used a number of different styles of text and layout in this book to help differentiate between the different kinds of information. Here are examples of the styles we use, and an explanation of what they mean:

Advice, hints, and background information comes in this type of font.

> **Important pieces of information come in boxes like this.**

Important words are in a bold type font.

Words that appear on the screen in menus, like File or Window, are in a similar font to the one that you see on the screen.

Keys that you press on the keyboard, like *Ctrl* and *Enter*, are in italics.

Code comes in a number of different styles. If it's something we're talking about in the text – when we're discussing the `doPost()` method, for example –– it's in a fixed-width font. If it's a block of code from a program, then it's also in a gray box:

```
public void doPost (HttpServletRequest req, HttpServletResponse res)
        throws ServletException, IOException
{
    doGet(req,res);
}
```

Sometimes you'll see code in a mixture of styles like this:

```
<?xml version="1.0" encoding="utf-8"?>
<!DOCTYPE collection [
<!ELEMENT collection (tagpair*, overview?, list)>

<!ELEMENT tagpair EMPTY>
<!ATTLIST tagpair
  xtag CDATA #REQUIRED
  htag CDATA #REQUIRED
>
<!ELEMENT overview (#PCDATA)>

<!ELEMENT list (item+)>
<!ELEMENT item (type, title, description)>
<!ELEMENT type (#PCDATA)>
<!ELEMENT title (#PCDATA)>
<!ELEMENT description (#PCDATA)>
]>
```

The code with a white background is something that we've already looked at and don't wish to examine further.

These formats are designed to make sure that you know exactly what you're looking at. We hope that they make life easier.

Tell Us What You Think

We've worked hard on this book to make it enjoyable and useful. Our best reward would be to hear from you that you liked it and that it was worth the money you paid for it. We've done our best to try to understand and match your expectations.

Please let us know what you think about it. Tell us what you liked best and what we could have done better. If you think this is just a marketing gimmick, then test us out – drop us a line! We'll answer, and we'll take whatever you say on board for future editions. The easiest way is to use email:

feedback@wrox.com

You can also find more details about Wrox Press on our web site. There you'll find the code from our latest books, sneak previews of forthcoming titles, and information about the authors and the editors. You can order Wrox titles directly from the site, or find out where your nearest local bookstore with Wrox titles is located. The address of out site is:

http://www.wrox.com

Customer Support

If you find a mistake in the book, your first port of call should be the errata page on our web site. If you can't find an answer there, send an email to support@wrox.com telling us about the problem. We'll do everything we can to answer promptly. Please remember to let us know the book your query relates to, and if possible the page number as well. This will help us to get a reply to you more quickly.

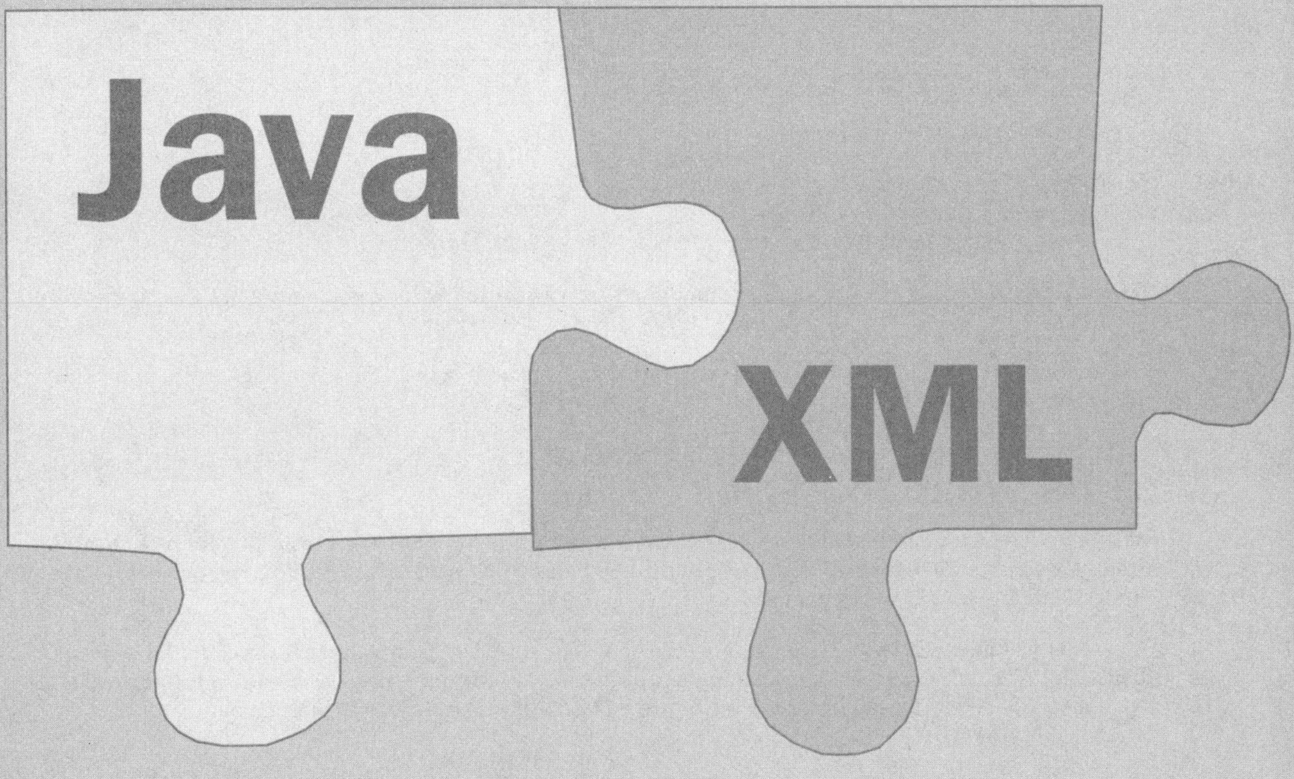
Java
XML

1

Three-Tier Web Applications

This chapter and the next serve as preparation for the rest of the book. Their goal is to make sure we have covered everything we need before really setting off, in Chapter 3. If you are impatient and well prepared, you can skip large parts of these two chapters and come back as needed for the missing details.

What is it that we need? Primarily, three things:

- ❑   an understanding of the structure of three-tier Web applications
- ❑   a familiarity with the Servlet API
- ❑   a familiarity with JDBC

In this chapter, we introduce three-tier applications and discuss a simple example that will lay the basics of this topic: a Phonebook application that can be used to look up phone numbers. Admittedly, this is not the jazziest or coolest application for a book to start with: for a while we were thinking of a database of plants, each with a Latin name, an image and a piece of music appropriate for the plant. However, that would just distract us from the subject and make the two "packing-up-for-the-journey" chapters longer than they need to be. There will be enough excitement before the book is over.

Our introductory Phonebook example is necessarily simple in its assumptions and primitive in its structure but, once the basics have been mastered, we can immediately produce a Better Phonebook that allows a person to have more than one phone number. More importantly, it separates out the different tasks of the middle tier, such as database access and HTML generation, to different classes that can be independently developed without modifying the basic servlet. We also include some utility classes and a useful Logger class. At that point we will have seen two slightly different servlets and will be ready for an overview of the Servlet API 2.1 that rounds off this chapter.

This chapter will cover the following:

- ❑ Three-tier applications
- ❑ Servlet basics, including request-response processing in a servlet
- ❑ JDBC basics: drivers, connections, queries and resultsets
- ❑ Servlet life cycle
- ❑ The Logger class and the advantages of do-it-yourself logging
- ❑ More JDBC: prepared statements
- ❑ The basics of HTML generation
- ❑ An overview of the Servlet API

The last item on this list is rather large. We make it worth its space by providing added value over and above the JavaDoc documentation. We show the logical structure of the API and bring out the most important parts of it. In the end we provide something like an "inverted index" that links common tasks to those parts of the API that are needed to accomplish them.

Three-Tier Applications

A distributed Web application has its different parts spread over different computers on a network. What parts are there? A common design pattern is to divide the application into View, Controller and Model: these are the logical components of the application, and their distribution merely represents the most obvious structuring of the underlying logic.

The Model (or application logic) is the internals of the application which "models" its data. The View and the Controller together form the user interface: the View (or presentation logic) shows the user different parts and aspects of the Model, and the Controller (or business logic) allows the user to modify the values of the Model, or change how the Model is viewed. Often, the user will be unaware that the Controller exists: in its simplest form, it merely handles the communication between the other two tiers. Depending on the constraints of your project, you will see some variance in where the application and business logic reside. In addition to the Model, View and Controller, the application needs a persistent store: some place to save its state between different runs of the application. That store can be a file system or a database.

Think of a familiar application, like Microsoft Excel. The view is a grid of rows and columns that show the numbers and formulas in different parts of the spreadsheet, or perhaps the graph of those numbers and formulas. The controller consists of the buttons on toolbars, menu commands and key shortcuts. The model is a constraint propagation system that ensures that changes in one area of the spreadsheet are propagated throughout the rest of it, so that the constraints expressed by the formulas are maintained. The state of the spreadsheet is saved in a file that has a proprietary `.xls` extension.

Distributed applications usually separate out the user interface and put it on a client computer; that way, many clients can share the same program running on a server. The persistent store can either be on the same or a different server. A generic three-tier application is arranged in three tiers like so:

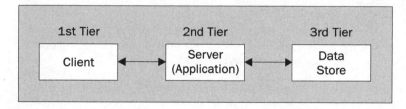

Three-tier applications predate the Web, but the Web has profoundly changed them because a distributed Web application is based on open and widely accepted standards. It uses the Web browser as its user interface. This means that it runs on a TCP/IP network and uses the HTTP protocol to communicate with the server. The HTTP protocol uses HTML and other standard MIME types for the data it passes between the server and the client. The situation on the back end is more complex, but by-and-large, the framework we are using (servlets, JDBC and relational databases) is reasonably close to the open standard ideal (even if it would be hard to work within a subset of SQL that is acceptable to all available databases). A distributed three-tier Web application is arranged in three tiers like so:

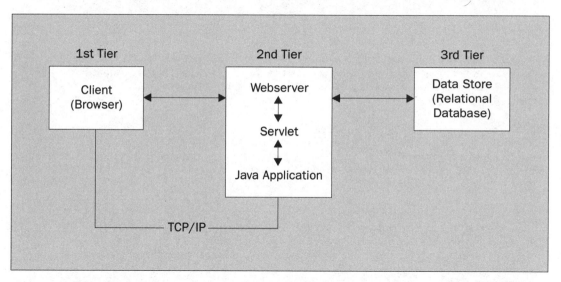

Many variations on this picture are possible, especially if the web page on the client contains a Java applet. For instance, (assuming the security issues are addressed) the applet can open a direct line of communication to the database, or it could open a socket and talk TCP/IP to a dedicated port on a computer somewhere, bypassing the Web server and HTTP. We will investigate these and other possibilities later in the book. For now, our task is to learn the basic framework of the above diagram. This means learning servlet and JDBC programming. This chapter will cover the basics; the next will cover more advanced topics.

A Simple Example

Our first example is a three-tier application that looks up telephone numbers in a database. Execution of the application comprises the following stages:

- ❑ the user enters a name into an HTML form on a browser and submits it as a query
- ❑ the form is then sent to a servlet
- ❑ the servlet queries the database and retrieves the telephone number entered against the name that the user entered
- ❑ the servlet composes the result of the query into a response web page and sends it back to the user's browser

The full code that we have written is given below, but it is also available to download from the Wrox web site at `http://www.wrox.com/`.

> **Some of you will undoubtedly be familiar with the necessary components that need to be installed before this application can be run; for those of you that are unfamiliar with this process, a complete guide to setting up is given in Appendix A.**

After you have installed all the necessary components, you can view the application in action by pointing your browser to `Query0.htm`. Rather than re-type all of the code given below, a much easier solution is to download all the code from the Wrox web site.

> **The code we have written – not just for these introductory chapters but for the entire book – is spread over many different directories and sub-directories: it can only be downloaded from the site as one rather large and, perhaps, complicated structure. However, as we progress through the book, the structure of the code should become more self-evident.**

Once you have guided your browser to the correct file (`MyNa\xml\Query0.htm`), your screen should appear as in the screenshot below:

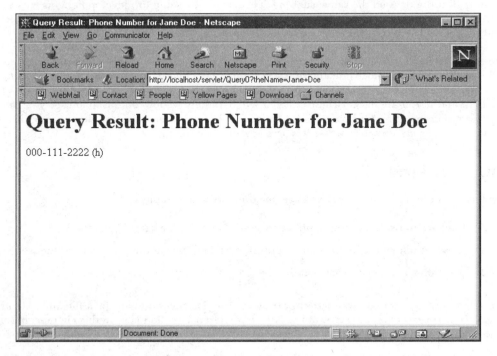

We will now work through this example, spending most of our time on the details of the middle tier.

The Client Side

Web applications are usually set in motion by a user submitting an HTML form via their browser. A simple form is shown below, with an example name entered:

```
<HTML>

<HEAD>
  <TITLE>A Form to Test Servlet</TITLE>
</HEAD>

<BODY>
  <FORM METHOD=GET ACTION="http://localhost/servlet/Query0">
    Enter name to be looked up in phonebook:
    <INPUT TYPE=TEXT NAME="theName" size=50 value="JoeSchmoe">
    <BR>
    <INPUT TYPE=SUBMIT>
  </FORM>
</BODY>

</HTML>
```

Note the details of its ACTION attribute The first part of the ACTION attribute (http://localhost/) shows that we are running both the browser and the web server on the same machine. In fact, we are running all three tiers on the same machine. This is the best setup for development, as we explain in Appendix A. For now just note that http://localhost/ is a default URL for a "loopback" to the local machine. The corresponding reserved IP number is 127.0.0.1.

The second part of the ACTION attribute, servlet/Query0, shows that we are running a servlet. In terms of actual files, it means that there is a compiled Java file, Query0.class, that is sitting in a directory where the web server looks for servlets. You can configure where this directory is and what it is called, and if you are hacker-conscious you will definitely want to do this. (Consult your servlet engine's documentation for how to do it.) In this book, we use the default setting, which for JRun is \JRun\servlets, and for jswdk-1.0 is \jswdk-1.0\examples\servlets.

Servlet Basics

Servlets are little server programs and are, in some ways, like applets:

- ❑ they are not self-standing applications and do not have a main() method
- ❑ they are not called by the user or programmer, but by another application (the web server)
- ❑ they have a life cycle that includes the init() and destroy() stages

In order to create a servlet, we must import two servlet packages into our Java file and extend a servlet class. We will present an overview of the API in a reference section later in this chapter; here, we'll just go though a typical case. Here are the imports:

```
import java.io.*;
import javax.servlet.*;
import javax.servlet.http.*;
import java.sql.*; // for communicating with the database
```

Most servlets process HTTP requests and send back HTTP responses (for a refresher on HTTP, see Appendix C). We thus start by extending the HttpServlet class:

```
public class Query0 extends HttpServlet
```

All the facilities for working with requests and responses are placed into two interfaces, HttpServletRequest and HttpServletResponse. Two objects implementing these interfaces are provided as arguments to the main workhorses of a servlet: the doGet() and doPost() methods:

```
public void doGet (HttpServletRequest req, HttpServletResponse res)
        throws ServletException, IOException
```

with a similar statement for doPost().

We need to implement doGet() or doPost() depending on whether you expect to handle a GET or a POST request. Frequently (or even, always), a sensible thing to do is to implement both, one doing all the work, the other one calling the first. If you need to handle requests other than GET or POST, you have to implement the more general Service() method of the GenericServlet class from which HttpServlet is derived.

In outline, a `doGet()` or `doPost()` method has to go through these steps:

❏ set the content type of the response

❏ get a `PrintWriter` to send the response to

❏ extract information from the request

❏ use the extracted information to perform the database query and retrieval

❏ compose HTML text and send it back down the response stream

Since this is our first example, we've made it easy to read by separating out all the database and HTML material into two distinct function calls. This is not the most efficient organization, and we'll improve on it in `Query1.java`. Here's `Query0.java` (note that this listing, as with most throughout this book, is "interrupted" with explanatory text but, as we've said before, you can download the entire code from the Wrox web site):

```java
// servlet Query0 as first 3tier example

import java.io.*;
import javax.servlet.*;
import javax.servlet.http.*;
import java.sql.*;

public class Query0 extends HttpServlet
{
    public void doGet (HttpServletRequest req, HttpServletResponse res)
        throws ServletException, IOException
    {

        res.setContentType("text/html");
        PrintWriter out = res.getWriter();
        String theName = req.getParameter("theName");
        // theName is the NAME attribute of the input field in submitting form

        String queryResult = lookup(theName);    // does all database work

        String title = "Query Result: Phone Number for " + theName;
        wrapInHTMLPage(out,queryResult,title);    // does all output HTML work
    }

    public void doPost (HttpServletRequest req, HttpServletResponse res)
        throws ServletException, IOException
    {
        doGet(req,res);
    }
```

Note that doGet() and doPost() know nothing about HTML or JDBC. All that knowledge is placed in the wrapInHTMLPage() and lookup() methods that we have written:

```java
public void wrapInHTMLPage(PrintWriter out, String queryResult, String title)
        throws IOException
{
    out.println("<HTML><HEAD><TITLE> " + title + " </TITLE></HEAD>");
    out.println("<BODY> <H1>" + title + "</H1>");
    out.println(queryResult);
    out.println("</BODY></HTML>");
}

public String lookup(String key)
{
    // variables for database work
    String driverName = "sun.jdbc.odbc.JdbcOdbcDriver";
    String dbURL = "jdbc:odbc:PhoneBook";
    String queryString =
        "SELECT THENUMBER FROM PHONEBOOK WHERE THENAME='"
        + key + "';" ;
    // if key is "Jane Doe" then queryString is
    // "SELECT THENUMBER FROM PHONEBOOK WHERE THENAME='Jane Doe'"
    try{
        Class.forName(driverName); // load the driver class
        Connection con =
                DriverManager.getConnection(dbURL, "usr", "pwd");
        Statement stmt=con.createStatement();
        ResultSet rs=stmt.executeQuery(queryString);
        if(null == rs)
        {
            return "db failure on " + key;
        }
        if(!rs.next())
        {
            return "No such name as " + key;    // empty result set
            return rs.getString(1);
        }
    }
    catch (java.lang.Exception ex)
    {
        ex.printStackTrace();
        return null;
    }
}
```

Obviously, the lookup() method needs a lot of explaining, but the rest of the code should be readily understandable. Our next task (after a brief section on JDBC basics) is to rewrite this servlet so that it is both more efficient and more general. We want a servlet *class* that knows as little as possible about HTML and JDBC, and just goes quietly about its servlet business (which is to direct traffic between the requests for information coming from the HTML page and the database providing the information). Once we achieve that, we can replace the subject matter of the application, or improve our HTML generation code, without disturbing the servlet itself.

JDBC Basics

In outline, our JDBC code goes through the following steps:

- ❑ Load the database driver
- ❑ Open a connection to the database
- ❑ Create a statement object
- ❑ Use the statement object to send SQL statements to the database
- ❑ Process the results

We will illustrate the steps with code from `Query0.java`.

Load the Driver

The JDBC API is based on the notion of database-specific drivers that are manipulated by a `DriverManager` object. Drivers come in several shapes and forms, as we explain in Appendix D. Some drivers are freeware or open source; others are commercial products – Appendix B provides a listing of sites from which many of these may be obtained. JDK itself comes with a generic **jdbc-odbc bridge** that passes SQL statements on to an appropriate ODBC driver. This way, a Java application can work with any database for which an ODBC driver is available. Obviously, direct Java drivers for specific databases provide better performance and should be used whenever possible.

A JDBC driver is loaded by calling the **public static native** `forName()` method of the class called `Class`:

```
String driverName = "sun.jdbc.odbc.JdbcOdbcDriver";
...
Class.forName(driverName);
```

Objects of the `Class` class contain information about Java classes, such as the names of their methods and the arguments of their constructors. For each Java class that has been loaded into the Java Virtual Machine there is a `Class` object. You can retrieve that object by calling the `getClass()` method on any instance of your class, or you can simply say `myObj.class`. Once you have obtained the Class object for your class, you have access to a lot of information about it.

The `forName()` method dynamically loads a class that has not yet been loaded. Since a JDBC driver is a Java class, it can be loaded using the `forName()` method. However, the fully-qualified name of the driver must be provided for the `forName()` method to work; in our case, this is `sun.jdbc.odbc.JdbcOdbcDriver`.

Open a Connection.

```
String dbURL = "jdbc:odbc:PhoneBook";
...
Connection con = DriverManager.getConnection(dbURL, "usr", "pwd");
```

Once the driver has been loaded, the `getConnection()` method of the `DriverManager` class will get you a connection to the database. The method takes three arguments: the database "URL" in a driver-specific format, the username and password. The string that identifies the database usually starts with "jdbc" and uses colons to separate its various components. In the case of the JDBC-ODBC bridge, the second ("subprotocol") component is "odbc", and the third component is the ODBC data source name or DSN. A fourth component containing ODBC options may also be present.

Create and Use a Statement

```
String query String =
    "SELECT THENUMBER FROM PHONEBOOK WHERE THENAME='"
    + key + "';";
    // if key is "Jane Doe" then queryString is
    // "SELECT THENUMBER FROM PHONEBOOK WHERE THENAME='Jane Doe';"
...
    Statement stmt = con.createStatement();
    ResultSet rs = stmt.executeQuery(queryString);
```

Ultimately, we want to pass SQL strings to the database and have them executed. This functionality is wrapped in the `Statement` interface and its specialized variants, `PreparedStatement` and `CallableStatement`. Our code shows the simplest approach. In the rest of the book, we'll be mostly using prepared statements because they are more efficient than plain Statements and avoid the pitfalls caused by apostrophes in query strings (such as if the name were O'Grady). Callable statements are for executing stored procedures; since not all databases support stored procedures, we will not be using callable statements much.

If we are executing a SELECT statement that returns data from the database, we run the `executeQuery()` method and place the results into a ResultSet object, as in our code. If we are executing an `INSERT`, `UPDATE` or `DELETE` statement that changes the contents of the database, then we run the `executeUpdate()` method that returns an integer, the count of affected rows. We also use the latter method for executing Data Definition statements, such as `CREATE TABLE` – when used this way, the method returns 0 (zero).

Process the Results

```
if(null == rs)
{
    return "db failure on " + key;
}
if (!rs.next())
{
    return "No such name as " + key;    // empty result set
    return rs.getString(1);
}
```

We make a simplistic assumption that the result set is null, or empty, or contains a single string. Typically, the result set contains multiple rows, and you can iterate through them in a loop: `while(rs.next()) {/* process the next row */}`. Most of the `ResultSet` interface consists of `getXXX()` methods, where `XXX` stands for a data type, such as `String` or `Boolean`. All the `getXXX()` methods take one argument that can be an integer (indicating the column number) or a string (indicating the column name).

A Better Phonebook

Our Query0 does its work but it can certainly stand some improvement, both in functionality and in its structure. Functionally, it makes a simplistic assumption that the result set returned by the query contains only one item. Once this assumption is dropped, we'll have to decide how the result set is incorporated into the response HTML page. Ultimately, we'd like to hand this decision over to the page designer. For now, we'll just put it into an HTML table.

Structurally, Query0 has its entire code in a single class, which makes it difficult to maintain and develop in new directions. Therefore we are going to place the HTML-wrapping and database-querying code into separate classes that we can then transform beyond recognition without touching the servlet class itself. We will also do a number of other additions and improvements:

- ❑ move the initialization code out of the doGet() method and into the init() method of the servlet class to make it more efficient and better structured

- ❑ provide a destroy() method to "clean up" at the end of execution

- ❑ use a prepared statement in database queries to improve efficiency and avoid technical problems with single quotes

- ❑ provide a Logger class, for do-it-yourself logging

- ❑ provide a LookerUpper class, to encapsulate database-related code

- ❑ provide an HtmlWrapper class that partially automates the sometimes tedious task of outputting HTML

Our HtmlWrapper class is a very modest version of this sort of Java utility. We have put it together in order to have a small, self-sufficient application. In the rest of the book, we will be using other approaches, some of them based on the Element Construction Set (ECS), an open source library from http://www.java.apache.org. ECS supports both HTML and XML output, as well as custom-designed markup languages. The whole subject of HTML generation will occupy a separate section of Chapter 2.

The New Servlet Class

The search form for `Query1` is exactly the same as for `Query0`. If we do enter a query, we'll see the results nicely formatted in a table. If we look up phone numbers for Jane Doe, for example, we'll see that she has three of them: home, office and cellular. We will also see her addresses:

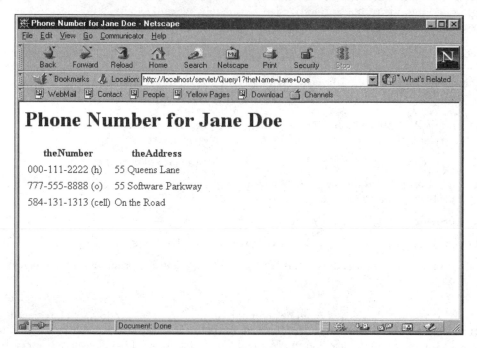

The Import Statements

To see how different the new application is from `Query0`, take a look at the import statements of its servlet class, `Query1.java`. Instead of importing `java.sql` and `java.io` packages, the servlet imports specialized classes from our `MyNa.utils` package. (In case you are wondering, `MyNa` is made up from the first two characters of our names, thus representing code that we have written ourselves.) This means that the servlet itself knows nothing about Java IO or JDBC, which is good because in software, more than anywhere else, it is true that "what you don't know cannot hurt you" (by being a source of bugs resulting from complex interactions between many intimately related things).

```
import javax.servlet.*;
import javax.servlet.http.*;

import MyNa.utils.Logger;      // save admin/debug info to file
import MyNa.utils.LookerUpper; // communicate with database
import MyNa.utils.MiscDB;      // help communicate with database
import MyNa.utils.HtmlWrapper; // send HTML to client

import java.sql.SQLException;  // thrown by LookerUpper
import java.io.IOException;    // thrown by HtmlWrapper
```

Notice that the servlet class no longer imports `java.sql` or `java.io` packages. (It still needs the corresponding exception classes because the code it calls can throw those exceptions.) Instead, it imports four classes from the `MyNa.utils` package: `Logger`, `LookerUpper`, `HtmlWrapper` and `MiscDB`. The first three have already been mentioned; `MiscDB` is one of several classes in the `utils` package that serve as namespaces for a collection of miscellaneous but related utilities. We also have `MiscStrMap`, `MiscDate`, `MiscFile` and others. None of them have constructors; all contain only public static methods.

The code of the servlet is quite brief, about 30 lines. True, we have saved a few lines by taking out the do-nothing `doPost()` method, but we have provided, just this once, a `getServletInfo()` method. It is considered good practice to include a definition of this method (declared in the `Servlet` interface) with a brief description of your servlet. In the rest of our servlets we only provide `doGet()` or `doPost()` methods but not both, and we leave out `getServletInfo()`.

A word of warning for the knowledgeable and the impatient: although this servlet is an improvement on the preceding one, it certainly has problems. In particular, it stores its important parameters, such as `queryString`, `driverName` and `dbUrl` as member variables. This is both unsafe (because of threading) and difficult to modify in porting to other systems. Suspend your displeasure, we will improve further as we go on.

The Shortened Servlet

```java
public class Query1 extends HttpServlet
{
    String queryString =
            "SELECT theNumber,theAddr FROM PHONEBOOK WHERE theName=?;";
    String driverName = "sun.jdbc.odbc.JdbcOdbcDriver";
    String dbUrl = "jdbc:odbc:PHONEBOOK";
    Logger lg=null;
    LookerUpper looker=null;

    public void init(ServletConfig config) throws ServletException
    {
        super.init(config);
        try
        {
            lg = new Logger();
            lg.clearLog();
            lg.logIt("Query1.init()");
            looker = new LookerUpper(driverName,dbUrl,queryString,lg);
        }
        catch(Exception E)
        {
            E.printStackTrace();
        }
    }

    public void destroy()
    {
        //  try to close up.
        lg.logIt("Query1.destroy()");
        looker.close();
    }
```

```
        public void doGet (HttpServletRequest req, HttpServletResponse res)
                throws ServletException, IOException
    {
        res.setContentType("text/html");
        PrintWriter out = res.getWriter();
        String theName = req.getParameter("theName");

        String[][]response =
                MiscDB.resultRowsToStringMatrix(looker.lookup(theName));
        HtmlWrapper hwrap = new HtmlWrapper(out);
        hwrap.wrapTablePage("Phone Number for " + theName, response);
    }

    public String getServletInfo()
    {
        return "A simple 3tier system's servlet";
    }
}
```

Notes on the Servlet Code

This code illustrates the servlet life cycle, about which we'll have more to say in the overview section later. The servlet life cycle begins with the init() method where all the initializations should be made, once per lifetime. The working stage of a servlet's life consists of calls on doGet(), doPost() or some other doXXX() method, in response to requests from the client. (The default behavior is for the servlet engine to run each response in a separate thread.) Eventually, usually after a long period of inaction, the servlet engine will call the destroy() method of the servlet to close up and free resources.

Before we get to init(), we create several non-local, class-level variables. The first three of them are familiar from Query0: the JDBC driver name, the database URL, and the query string. The format of the query string is different from Query0 because we're going to use a prepared statement: the empty slots to be filled by request parameters are indicated by a ?. The other two non-local variables are a Logger object and a LookerUpper. They are initialized in the servlet's init() method. The Logger clears the log file from previous logs and writes a string to it. The LookerUpper object is created to do database work, with four arguments: the driver to use, the database URL, a query string to execute, and the Logger.

By the time you read this, most servlet runners will have implemented the 2.1 version of the Servlet API, and it will be possible to replace the first two lines of init() with a single line:

```
public void init() throws ServletException {    // super(config) not needed
```

This change and the whole mechanism of initialization are more fully explained in the Servlet API overview later in this chapter.

MiscDB Class and its Methods

Most of the actual work in the servlet is done in this line of code:

```
String[][]response = MiscDB.resultRowsToStringMatrix(looker.lookup(theName));
```

As we mentioned, there is a `MiscDB` class in the `utils` package, with a public static `resultRowsToStringMatrix()` method. It takes the output of `LookerUpper`'s `lookup()` method, which is a `ResultSet`, and converts it to a two-dimensional array of strings, ready to be sent to `wrapTablePage()`. Why did we call it `resultRowsToStringMatrix()` rather than `resultSetToStringMatrix()`? The next section explains.

The Row Concept

We would like to think of `ResultSet` as one possible example of a "Collection of Rows", where a Row is an abstract data type of considerable importance to us. Basically, a Row is an ordered set of values, possibly of different data types, that can be accessed either as an array or as an associative array indexed by strings. For example, if R is a Row indexed by "Name", "Address" and "PhoneNumber", with values "Jane Doe", "PO Box 17", and "123-4567", then

```
"Jane Doe" == R.getValue("Name") == R.getValue(0) // Row is 0-based
```

In general, if H is an array of Row headers, then

```
R.getValue(i) == R.getValue(H[i]) // R[i]==R[H[i]] we'd say in JavaScript
```

A JDBC `ResultSet` is almost like our Row with the small difference of being 1-based. We'll deal with this problem when we get to it in the natural order of things; for now, here is the `resultRowsToStringMatrix()` method. In outline, it creates a Vector V of `String` arrays, fills it with data from the `ResultSet`, and converts the Vector of `String` arrays to a two-dimensional array of `Strings`. That conversion is performed by `vectorToStringMatrix()`.

```java
public static String[][] resultRowsToStringMatrix(ResultSet R)
{
    try
    {
        Vector V = new Vector();    // result
        V.addElement(resultSetLabels(R));    // table header line
        while(R.next())
        {
            V.addElement(resultRowValues(R));
            return vectorToStringMatrix(V);
        }
    }
    catch(SQLException E)
    {
        E.printStackTrace();
        return null;
    }
}

public static String[][] vectorToStringMatrix(Vector V)
{
    // V is actually a vector of string-arrays.
    if(V == null || V.size() == 0)
    {
        return null;
    }
}
```

```
        String [][]R = new String[V.size()][];
        for(int i = 0; i < R.length; i++)
        {
            R[i] = (String[])(V.elementAt(i));
            return R;
        }
    }
```

The first element of V is an array of labels that will become the headers of the resulting HTML table. That array of labels is obtained by resultSetLabels(). Similarly, each subsequent element of V is an array of values obtained by resultRowValues(). We will show these methods when we get to the corresponding JDBC material; for now take it on faith that they do what their names suggest, or peek forward into Chapter 2.

The Logger Class

We have been using our own Logger class, both for debugging and administrative purposes, even though the Servlet API provides a log() method of its own. We find several advantages to using do-it-yourself logging:

❑ we can redirect the log to a file of our own choosing

❑ we can have more than one Logger object for different logging purposes

❑ our Logger provides time stamps by using a method from our Misc.Date class in the utils package.

❑ we can set an error level or error mask so that the user can configure the system (eventually, using an XML editor!) to generate or hold back on logging

❑ we can log user information, for various administrative purposes

All in all, your own Logger is a good thing to have around. We will not show logging code in the rest of the book because we have taken all the logIt() and clearLog() calls out of the code we present here to reduce the book's size (they are still included in the code downloadable from the Wrox site, though).

Here is a simplified version of Logger.java; a full-featured version is available from the book's Web site. Unlike the simple version below, the full-featured version is thread-conscious and uses system properties for cross-platform portability.

```
package MyNa.utils; // logger class
import java.io.*;

public class Logger
{
    String fileName;

    public Logger(String fName)
    {
        fileName=fName;
    }
```

```
    public Logger()
    {
        // default log file
        this("C:\\MyNa\\dbLog.log"););
    }

    public void clearLog()
    {
        try
        {
            BufferedWriter f =
                    new BufferedWriter(new FileWriter(fileName,false));
            String S = MiscDate.todaysDate();
            f.write(S, 0, S.length());
            f.newLine();
            f.close();
        }
        catch(IOException e){}
    }

    public void logIt(String S)
    {
        S += '\r';      // so Notepad and such can read it.
        try
        {
            BufferedWriter f = new BufferedWriter(new FileWriter(fileName, true));
            f.write(S, 0, S.length());
            f.newLine();
            f.close();
        }
        catch(IOException e){}
    }

} // end of Logger class
```

The MiscDate class provides utilities for working with dates and calendars. For example, the code for todaysDate() is very straightforward:

```
    public static String todaysDate()
    {
        Calendar C=new GregorianCalendar();
        return C.get(Calendar.MONTH)+"/"
            + C.get(Calendar.DAY_OF_MONTH) + "/"
            + C.get(Calendar.YEAR) + "@"
            + C.get(Calendar.HOUR) + ":"
            + C.get(Calendar.MINUTE) + ":"
            + C.get(Calendar.SECOND) + ":"
            + C.get(Calendar.MILLISECOND)
            + if(Calendar.AM == C.get(Calendar.AM_PM))"AM" else "PM";
    }
```

The LookerUpper Class

In outline, this class consists of:

- ❑ class-level variable declarations: a Logger and variables for database connectivity
- ❑ a constructor that connects to the database
- ❑ the close() method that closes the connection in a finally clause
- ❑ the lookup() method that runs the query and returns the ResultSet

The Constructor and Close()

The code for variable declarations and the constructor is a straightforward re-write of Query0:

```
package MyNa.utils;
import java.sql.*;      // communicate with database

public class LookerUpper
{
    Connection dbConn = null;
    PreparedStatement dbPrepStmt = null;
    String theQueryString = null;
    // "SELECT THENUMBER,THEADDR FROM PHONEBOOK WHERE THENAME=?;";
    String driverName=null;     // initialized in constructor
    String dbUrl=null;          // initialized in constructor
    String theUser = "usr";
    String thePwd = "pwd";
    Logger lg;

    public LookerUpper(String drName, String dbName,
            String queryString, Logger L) throws SQLException
    {
        driverName = drName;
        try
        {
            Class.forName(driverName);
        }
        catch(Exception E)
        {
            E.printStackTrace();
            L.logIt("LookerUpper failed with " + E);
            return;
        }
        dbUrl = dbName;
        theQueryString = queryString;
        lg = L;
        dbConn = DriverManager.getConnection(dbUrl, theUser, thePwd);
        dbPrepStmt = dbConn.prepareStatement(theQueryString);
        lg.logIt("LookerUpper connected to " + dbUrl);
    }
```

The close() method is needed to release the connection without waiting for the garbage collector to get to it, which may not happen for a while if the machine has a lot of memory. By placing the con.close() call in the finally clause we ensure that it will be executed whether or not an exception is thrown.

```
public void close()
{
    // ignore exceptions, try to close up
    lg.logIt("LookerUpper.close()");
    try
    {
        if(dbPrepStmt != null)
        {
            dbPrepStmt.close();
        }
    }
    catch(java.lang.Exception E){}
    finally
    {
        try
        {
            if(dbConn != null)
            {
                dbConn.close();
            }
        }
        catch (java.lang.Exception E){}
    }
}
```

The PreparedStatement

The lookup() method uses a prepared statement. In other words, instead of using the Statement interface, we are using the PreparedStatement interface that extends Statement. The steps to follow in running a query using PreparedStatement are a little different from what you saw in Query0:

❑ In constructing the query string, use question marks as place holders for those SQL parameters that will be filled in later, usually by parameters of the request object.

❑ Once the query string is constructed, give it as an argument to the prepareStatement() method of the connection object.

❑ To fill in the SQL parameters, use the setXXX() methods of the PreparedStatement interface, where XXX stands for Java data types, such as String or Short. All setXXX() methods take two parameters. The first is an integer that indicates the positional number of the question mark to replace (beginning with 1, as in our code); the second provides the value.

❑ Run the PreparedStatement version (with no parameters) of the execute(), executeQuery() or executeUpdate() method.

❑ Get the ResultSet out of the PreparedStatement object using its getResultSet() method.

The Lookup Method

The `lookup()` method takes one argument: a string to be inserted into the prepared statement's query string to replace the question mark. It returns the result of the query as a two-dimensional array of strings. Each row in that array corresponds to a row of the result set, and will become a row in the HTML table.

```
public ResultSet lookup(String V)
{
    // lookup value V
    lg.logIt("looking up: " + V + "; with query = " + theQueryString);
    try
    {
        dbPrepStmt.setString(1,V);      // replace ? with a String value
        if(!dbPrepStmt.execute())
        {
            lg.logIt("no result set");
            return null;
        }
        return dbPrepStmt.getResultSet();
    }
    catch (java.lang.Exception E)
    {
        lg.logIt("lookup: " + E);
        return null;
    }
}
}   // end of LookerUpper class
```

Although readily understandable, some details of this code need discussion, which we will postpone till the general in-depth discussion of JDBC. For now just note that `PreparedStatement` has an `execute()` method that takes no arguments and returns a `Boolean` value indicating success or failure.

The HtmlWrapper Class

Our `HtmlWrapper` class demonstrates one of several possible approaches to providing a structured interface for HTML code generation. We will modify it and compare it to other approaches in a separate section. Here we present a sketch and a motivation. Our motivation is to "outsource" HTML generation from the servlet to an object of an HTML-specialist class. In order to do that, the servlet should hand over to that object a reference to its output stream. This is done at construction time:

```
package MyNa.utils;
import java.io.*;

public class HtmlWrapper
{
    PrintWriter out=null;
    public HtmlWrapper (PrintWriter o)
    {
        out = o;
    }
```

In the servlet's `doGet()` method, as you recall, the constructor is called as follows:

```
PrintWriter out = res.getWriter();
...
HtmlWrapper hwrap = new HtmlWrapper(out);
```

HtmlWrapper Methods

Our `HtmlWrapper` class has specialist methods for outputting HTML elements, including entire pages. For a very general case of a page consisting of a title and a body, it has:

```
public void wrapBodyPage(String title, String body) throws IOException
{
    out.println("<HTML>");
    wrapHead(title);
    out.println("<BODY>");
    wrapHeading(title, 1);      // same title in <H1> element
    out.println(body);
    out.println("</BODY></HTML>");
}
```

Here, `wrapHead(title)` produces the HTML for the `<HEAD>` element with `title` as `<TITLE>`, and `wrapHeading(title, 1)` wraps the same title into `<H1>` tags:

```
public void wrapHead(String title)throws IOException
{
    out.println("<HEAD><TITLE> " + title + " </TITLE></HEAD>");
}

public void wrapHeading(String H,int level)throws IOException
{
    out.println("<H" + level + ">" + H + "</H" + level + ">");
}
```

This method assumes that it receives from the outside fully-formatted bodies of HTML documents.

Wrapping a Table Page

We frequently need a page that has a table in it, to show query results, so we have a variation on the "body page" that receives a two-dimensional array of strings and produces a table:

```
public void wrapTablePage(String title, String[][]tab)
        throws IOException
{
    out.println("<HTML>");
    wrapHead(title);
    out.println("<BODY>");
    wrapHeading(title,1);
    wrapTable(tab);
    out.println("</BODY></HTML>");
}
```

In converting a 2-D array of strings into an HTML table, a utility `stringArrayJoin()` can greatly simplify code. Modeled after the `join()` method of the JavaScript `Array` class, it takes two arguments, an array of strings and a connector string, and outputs a single string in which the elements of the array are run together, with the connector string inserted at the joints. We use it to convert an array of strings to a table row as follows:

```
public void wrapTableRow(String[] R)throws IOException
{
    out.println("<TR>");
    out.println("<TD>" + misc.stringArrayJoin(R, "</TD><TD>")
        + "</TD>");
    out.println("</TR>");
}
```

Similarly, the header row is produced as follows:

```
public void wrapTableHeaders(String[] H)throws IOException
{
        out.println("<TH>" + misc.stringArrayJoin(H, "</TH><TH>")
            + "</TH>");
}
```

Given these two methods, wrapping a table is easy:

```
public void wrapTable(String [][]tab)throws IOException
{
    if(tab == null)
    {
        return;
    }
    out.println("<TABLE>");
    wrapTableHeaders(tab[0]);
    for(int i = 1; i < tab.length; i++)
    {
        wrapTableRow(tab[i]);
    }
    out.println("</TABLE>");
}
```

This is all the `HtmlWrapper` code that is used by `Query1`. Obviously, the class can be made both more complete and more general in several directions.

Possible Improvements

A number of improvements are possible without major philosophical changes in the framework. For instance, both `wrapBodyPage()` and `wrapTablePage()` can have a version with an extra argument that contains a stylesheet and/or a script. The argument would be passed on to `wrapHead()`:

```
    public void wrapTablePage(String title, String[][]tab, String xtra)
        throws IOException
{
    out.println("<HTML>");
    wrapHead(title, xtra);
    ...
}

    public void wrapHead(String title, String xtra)throws IOException
    {
        out.println("<HEAD><TITLE> " + title + " </TITLE>\n"
            + xtra + "</HEAD>");
    }
```

This would improve the appearance of the page; in fact, our screenshot for Query1 was produced using this version. The xtra string can be the stylesheet itself or a reference to a stylesheet file.

A more significant philosophical addition would be to replace raw output code, such as out.println("<BODY>"), with a function call, openBody() which would do the output. This would create several new possibilities. These functions could be called by code outside the package. They could be given string arguments that contain the element's attribute list, e.g.:

```
    public void openBody(String attributes)
    {
        out.println("<BODY " + attributes + " >");
    }
```

Most importantly, given openXXX() and closeXXX() methods for each HTML element, we could start thinking of HTML generation as a recursive process: in order to output an element, we call its openXXX() method, fill in the contents, opening and closing the children elements as needed, and finally call the matching closeXXX() method. You will see this idea implemented shortly, in Chapter 2.

Servlet API Overview

Now that we have seen two slightly different servlets, including a servlet with a full set of init(), doGet() and destroy() methods, it is time to take a broader look at the Servlet API, to see how all its parts fit together. We are presenting the 2.1 version, released on November 6, 1998.

Since this is the first such overview in the book, we would like to outline our approach to API overviews. They are always preceded by a couple of simple examples that show the API in action. We then give a high-level outline showing how various parts of the API fit together and support each other. We try to separate the arcane and rarely-used from the most common, and we only give complete listings after there is a framework into which you can fit the multiple details.

Two caveats may help in avoiding unfulfilled expectations. The first is that some Overview sections are very sketchy. This reflects our judgement that the corresponding material is either well-known (e.g. cookies) or rarely used. The second is that our Overview makes no attempt to cover the specifics of any given servlet engine: you'll have to consult the User Guide that comes with the one you are using.

The Packages

The Servlet API is organized into two packages, `javax.servlet` and `javax.servlet.http`. The first package is more general: it assumes only the basic client-server framework with a stateless request-response protocol. The second package is specific to HTTP: it knows about such things as HTTP methods and headers. To give but one example of the difference between the two packages, `javax.servlet` contains a `GenericServlet` class that implements a `service()` method to process a request-response cycle. The `javax.servlet.http` package has an `HttpServlet` class that implements a number of `doXXX()` methods to process a request-response cycle, where XXX corresponds to various HTTP methods (you have seen the two most common ones, `doGet()` and `doPost()`).

The Main Players

The most important items in `javax.servlet` are the following four interfaces:

- ❑ `Servlet`
- ❑ `ServletConfig`
- ❑ `ServletRequest`
- ❑ `ServletResponse`

`Servlet` is the basic interface that declares the life-cycle methods `init()`, `service()` and `destroy()`. `ServletConfig` declares the methods needed for initialization; the `init()` method takes one argument, a `ServletConfig` object, supplied by the servlet engine. `ServletRequest` and `ServletResponse` declare all the methods that are needed by the `service()` method. The method takes two arguments, a request and a response pair of objects, that implement the two interfaces. The arguments are supplied by the servlet engine.

`javax.servlet` also contains the `GenericServlet` class that provides the default implementation of both the `Servlet` and `ServletConfig` interfaces. Your servlet extends that class, usually not directly but by extending the `HttpServlet` class, which extends `GenericServlet`.

The `HttpServlet` class, together with the `HttpRequest` and `HttpResponse` interfaces, are the most important items of `javax.servlet.http`. They systematically extend the corresponding items of `javax.servlet`.

In summary:

- ❑ class `GenericServlet` implements `Servlet` and `ServletConfig`
- ❑ class `HttpServlet` extends `GenericServlet`
- ❑ interface `HttpRequest` extends `ServletRequest`
- ❑ interface `HttpResponse` extends `ServletResponse`

From this point on, a convenient way of organizing the material is by following the life cycle of a servlet, from the moment it is loaded and instantiated to the moment it is destroyed and removed from memory.

Loading and Instantiation

Servlets are Java classes whose role is to connect a Web server (or several servers) to other computational resources and entities. A servlet is not a self-standing program: it springs into action when a request addressed to it arrives at the server. At that time, the servlet engine calls its custom-designed class loader. The class loader checks to see whether the servlet class is already loaded and whether the loaded version has the same time stamp as the `.class` file. (It finds the `.class` file in the specially designated directory.) If the servlet class is not loaded or is older than the disk file, the engine loads the class into the special JVM provided for that purpose and creates an instance of it. Three entities are thus involved in managing the servlet: the Web server, the servlet engine (perhaps bundled with the server) and the JVM that runs the servlet.

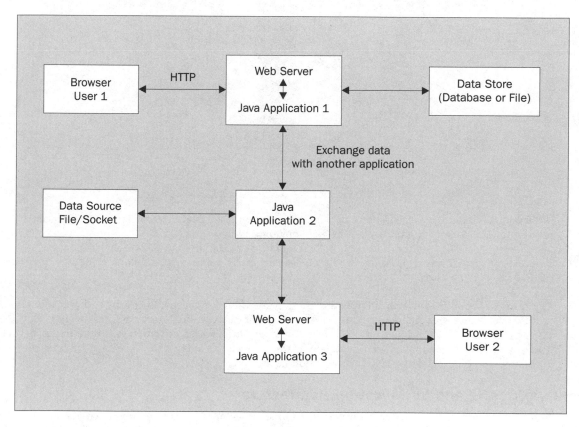

Initialization

Your servlet class (loaded in the previous stage) usually has this pedigree: it extends `HttpServlet`, which in turn extends `GenericServlet`, which implements the Servlet, `ServletConfig` and `Serializable` interfaces.

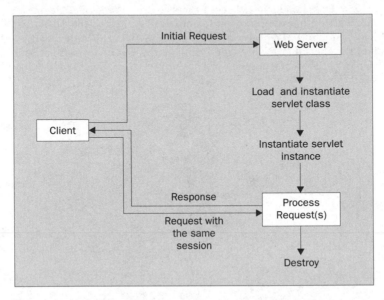

What's in those interfaces? The `Servlet` interface is the most basic: this is what makes a servlet a servlet. It declares four methods: the life cycle methods `init()`, `service()` and `destroy()`, and the `getServletInfo()` method that you have seen in `Query1`. You have also seen `init()` and `destroy()`; `service()` is the method that gets triggered by a request and calls a `doXXX()` method of the `HttpServlet` class.

The only mechanism of initialization is the `init()` method. As you saw in `Query1`, this is a good place to initialize request-independent resources. You can either hard-code those initializations into the `init()` method as we did, or you can provide them as **initialization parameters**, stored in "properties" files of your servlet engine and retrievable by methods declared in the `ServletConfig` interface (see your servlet engine's User Guide for how to edit its property files).

ServletConfig and Initialization Parameters

The `ServletConfig` interface is implemented in an object that the servlet engine creates at instantiation time. For each `instance` of a servlet, there is one and only one such object. In Servlet API 2.0, this object is provided as an argument to the `init()` method. So, in the 2.0 API, the beginning of the `init()` method looks like this:

```
public void init(ServletConfig config) throws ServletException
{
    super.init(config);
    String usrProfile = getInitParameter("usrName"); // a ServletConfig method
```

In Servlet API 2.1, this is simplified because `GenericServlet` itself implements the `ServletConfig` interface. (The implementation is trivial: the new methods of `GenericServlet` simply call identically named methods of the `ServletConfig` object.) As a result, the `init()` method no longer requires an argument, and you can call `ServletConfig` methods directly from your servlet, as below. (The old code also works.)

```
public void init() throws ServletException
{
    String usrProfile = getInitParameter("usrName");
```

As you can see from the last line of code, initialization parameters are name-value pairs where both names and values are `Strings`. They are stored in a text file whose location is implementation-specific. Usually, you can manipulate that file through one of the dialog boxes of your servlet engine's admin utility. In JRun, you want the **ServiceConfig** tab of the **jse** service; the settings go into the `servlets.properties` text file in the `jsm-default/services/jse/properties` directory.

If you have long-term, request-independent information that you as the web site administrator want to make available to your servlets, initialization parameters are good for storing it. The `ServletConfig` interface declares two methods for obtaining initialization parameters:

```
public String getInitParameter(String name);
public Enumeration getInitParameterNames();
```

Do-it-Yourself Init Parameters

In this little section, we are going to jump out from the Servlet API overview to introduce an idea that will be elaborated and used throughout the rest of the book. You can get a better control over initialization by creating your own `initFile.txt` of name-value pairs, and a convenient interface to work with it, for instance:

```
public void writeEnv (Hashtable env, String fileName)
```

Better yet, you can define a class:

```
class Env extends HashTable
```

with a constructor that takes a `String fileName` argument and methods like:

```
public String Env.getPara(String paraName);
public void setPara(String paraName, String paraValue);
public void addPara(String paraName, String paraValue);
public void delPara(String paraName);
```

You can use such a file within servlet initialization. It may be a convenient way to share information between servlets. You can also use an environment class elsewhere, in any situation where you need a mapping from strings to strings or from strings to objects of any kind. We are, in fact going to implement a very similar class and use it extensively (see section on `Env` in the next chapter).

Exception Classes

You've probably noticed that the `init()` method throws a `ServletException` if something goes wrong. There are actually two exception classes defined in the Servlet API:

```
public class ServletException extends Exception
public class UnavailableException extends ServletException
```

If either one of these is thrown, the servlet never advances to its service stage.

ServletContext

The other source of information that you can obtain through `ServletConfig` is a `ServletContext` object that implements the `ServletContext` interface. While `ServletConfig` is available during the initialziation stage, `ServletContext` is available throughout the service stage. There is one instance of `ServletContex` for each servlet running on a server. (The same servlet can run on more than one virtual server, in which case there will be a `ServletContext` object for each server running the servlet.)

`ServletContexts` provide information about:

- ❑ the server and its attributes
- ❑ other loaded servlets
- ❑ MIME types of files on the server
- ❑ real file system paths of any virtual paths, including the servlet root

To give you a few examples of the kind of information that `ServletContext` provides, here are some of its methods, with a brief explanation of what they return:

ServletContext Methods	Description
`public int getMajorVersion()`	The major version of the Servlet API supported by this servlet engine
`public String getMimeType(String file)`	MIME type of the file
`public String getRealPath(String path)`	Converts virtual to real path; inserts system-specific separator
`public URL getResource(String uripath)`	URL object for resource
`public InputStream getResourceAsStream(String uripath)`	Get resource as a stream
`public String getServerInfo()`	Get at least the name and version of the server

Built-in Logging

The `ServletContext` interface also declares a `log()` method that can be used to write to a servlet log file. The method takes a `String` argument and an optional `Exception` argument; if the `Exception` argument is given, the method outputs the stack trace. For some reason, Servlet API 2.0 had the optional argument first in the method's signature:

```
public void log(Exception exception, String msg); // deprecated
```

This has been corrected in 2.1, so the current version is:

```
public void log(String msg, Throwable t);
```

You don't call this method directly because `GenericServlet` class defines its own `log()` method with the same signatures. This method is inherited by `HttpServlet` and therefore by your own servlet class (and of course you can also use our superior `Logger`).

Attributes

There are three methods for working with attributes (name-value pairs) associated with the server and the servlet engine: `getAttribute()`, `getAttributeNames()` and `setAttribute()`. These are of limited usefulness for a servlet writer, unless you want to do something server or servlet-engine specific. The names of attributes follow the same syntax and conventions as package names.

RequestDispatcher

Perhaps the most interesting thing you can get out of `ServletContext` is a `RequestDispatcher`:

```
public RequestDispatcher getRequestDispatcher(String uripath);
```

The `uripath` can refer to any resource that the servlet engine knows about: another servlet, a Java Server Page, a CGI script, etc. `RequestDispatcher`, new in the 2.1 API, is an object that can dispatch the `Request` object to that resource for processing. It has two methods, `forward()` and `include()`. The `forward()` method is used (we quote from Sun's documentation, `Servlet-2.1.pdf`)

"for forwarding a request from this servlet to another resource on the Web server. This method is useful when one servlet does preliminary processing of a request and wants to let another object generate the response. The request object passed to the target object will have its request URL path and other path parameters adjusted to reflect the target URL path of the target object."

Quoting from the same source, the `include()` method is used

"for including the content generated by another server resource in the body of a response. In essence, this method enables programmatic server-side includes. The request object passed to the target object will reflect the request URL path and path info of the calling request. The response object only has access to the calling servlet's `ServletOutputStream` object or `PrintWriter` object."

Class GenericServlet

At this point, we have covered the entire contents of GenericServlet; here is a complete listing of its methods:

```
public abstract class GenericServlet implements Servlet,
        ServletConfig, Serializable;
```

Methods

```
public String getInitParameter(String name);
public Enumeration getInitParameterNames();
public ServletConfig getServletConfig();
    // to get a direct reference to the ServletConfig object
public ServletContext getServletContext();

public void init() throws ServletException;
public void init(ServletConfig config) throws ServletException;
public abstract void service(ServletRequest request, ServletResponse response)
        throws ServletException, IOException;
public void destroy();
public String getServletInfo();

public void log(String msg);
public void log(String msg, Throwable cause);
```

Servlets' Service: Requests and Responses

A servlet's main purpose in life is to receive a request and send back a response. This purpose is fulfilled by the servlet's service method. The more general Servlet interface declares a general service() method, implemented by the GenericServlet class. This method is triggered by a request from the client; in HTTP servlets it calls a doXXX() service method, where XXX stands for an HTTP "method" such as GET or POST. These methods are declared in the HttpServlet interface. In addition to GET and POST, the following HTTP methods are supported: DELETE, HEAD, OPTIONS, PUT and TRACE. (See the Appendix C for reminders of what they do and how they are used.) Each one of those methods has the same signature:

```
protected void doDelete(HttpServletRequest request, HttpServletResponse response)
        throws ServletException, IOException;
```

In order to process requests and responses, the servlet needs:

- ❑ a way to get request parameters out of request
- ❑ a way to get environment-variable information out of request
- ❑ a stream to write a response to
- ❑ a way to serve multiple requests and responses within a single session

Much of this functionality is wrapped into the request and response interfaces that come on two levels: the more general `ServletRequest-ServletResponse` pair, and the more specific `HttpServletRequest-HttpServletResponse` pair. The `HttpServlet` interfaces extend the more general `Servlet` interfaces. The interfaces are implemented in two objects, a request and a response, that the servlet engine passes as arguments to the service method.

Request Parameters

Request parameters are the values of the input elements of the HTML form that submits a request. For instance, if your input form has two fields called "promise" and "performance", and the user typed "great" and "so-so" in them, then you have two request parameters:

	Name	Value
Parameter 1	promise	great
Parameter 2	performance	so-so

Request parameters are accessed by these methods:

```
public String getParameter(String name);
public Enumeration getParameterNames();
public String[] getParameterValues(String name);
```

The last method is for those parameters that have multiple values, such as multiple selections in a SELECT element of the form.

Environment Variables

Most other methods of the request interfaces are for obtaining information traditionally associated with the environment variables of the CGI protocol. Here is a table showing the correspondences between CGI environment variables and the methods of request interfaces:

CGI Environment Variables and Corresponding Servlet Methods	
CGI Environment Variable	**HTTP Servlet Method**
SERVER_NAME	req.getServerName( )
SERVER_SOFTWARE	getServletContext( ) .getServerInfo( )
SERVER_PROTOCOL	req.getProtocol( )
SERVER_PORT	req.getServerPort( )
REQUEST_METHOD	req.getMethod( )
PATH_INFO	req.getPathInfo( )
PATH_TRANSLATED	req.getPathTranslated( )
SCRIPT_NAME	req.getServletPath( )

Table Continued on Following Page

CGI Environment Variables and Corresponding Servlet Methods	
CGI Environment Variable	**HTTP Servlet Method**
`DOCUMENT_ROOT`	`req.getRealPath( " / " )`
`QUERY_STRING`	`req.getQueryString( )`
`REMOTE_HOST`	`req.getRemoteHost( )`
`REMOTE_ADDR`	`req.getRemoteAddr( )`
`AUTH_TYPE`	`req.getAuthType( )`
`REMOTE_USER`	`req.getRemoteUser( )`
`CONTENT_TYPE`	`req.getContentType( )`
`CONTENT_LENGTH`	`req.getContentLength( )`
`HTTP_ACCEPT`	`req.getHeader("Accept")`
`HTTP_USER_AGENT`	`req.getHeader("User-Agent")`
`HTTP_REFERER`	`req.getHeader("Referer")`

Streams

Two specialized abstract stream classes are provided:

```
public abstract class ServletInputStream extends InputStream
public abstract class ServletOutputStream extends OutputStream
```

In addition to these binary streams, servlets can use a `BufferedReader` and a `PrintWriter` for character IO. `ServletRequest` has two methods that return streams:

```
public ServletInputStream getInputStream() throws IOException;
public BufferedReader getReader() throws IOException;
```

Corresponingly, `ServletResponse` also has two methods that return streams:

```
public ServletOutputStream getOutputStream() throws IOException;
public PrintWriter getWriter() throws IOException;
```

A servlet has to open an output stream, either for binary or character output, because the response has to go somewhere. The input streams are rarely used in typical requests because it is more convenient to use `getParameter()` methods. They are used in more specialized situations such as file uploading and servlet chaining.

Content Type and Length

Before beginning to send a response, the servlet must set its content type and, optionally, length. `ServletResponse` has two methods for the purpose that set the corresponding response headers, Content-Type and Content-Length:

```
public void setContentType(String type);
public void setContentLength(int length); // in bytes
```

Content length, if set, allows the browser to display a progress monitor and to maintain a "persistent connection" so it can download both the current page and the pages or images linked into it without resetting the socket connection. The method has to be called before any part of the response body is sent, and the length has to be absolutely precise. The easiest way to achieve this is to use a `ByteArrayOutputStream` as a buffer for output, and to use that array's size as the argument to `setContextLength()`, as in:

```
ByteArrayOutputStream byteArray = new ByteArrayOutputStream(1024); // or whatever
PrintWriter out = new PrintWriter(byteArray, true); // "true" forces flashing

// a number of out.println() statements

res.setContentLength(byteArray.size());
byteArray.writeTo(res.getOutputStream());
```

Request Attributes

There are three methods for working with attributes (name-value pairs) associated with the request object: `getAttribute()`, `getAttributeNames()` and `setAttribute()`. Just as with the server and servlet engine attributes accessible from `ServletContext`, the names of request attributes follow the same syntax and conventions as package names. As an example, the Java Web Server uses request attributes to provide details of an SSL connection, such as peer certificates.

Complete Package Listings

At this point we are now ready to look at the complete listings for the classes and interfaces of `javax.servlet` and `javax.servlet.http`:

Package javax.servlet	
Type	**Name**
Interface	RequestDispatcher
Interface	Servlet
Interface	ServletConfig
Interface	ServletContext
Interface	ServletRequest
Interface	ServletResponse
Class	GenericServlet

Table Continued on Following Page

An empty interface	
Interface	`SingleThreadModel`
Streams and Exceptions	
Class	`ServletInputStream`
Class	`ServletOutputStream`
Class	`ServletException`
Class	`UnavailableException`
Package java.servlet.http	
Interface	`HttpServletRequest`
Interface	`HttpServletResponse`
Class	`HttpServlet`
Session-tracking API	
Interface	`HttpSession`
Interface	`HttpSessionBindingListener`
Interface	`HttpSessionContext (deprecated)`
Class	`Cookie`
Class	`HttpSessionBindingEvent`
Utility methods	
Class	`HttpUtils`

The only items we have not yet covered are the `SingleThreadModel` interface and the session-tracking API. The `SingleThreadModel` interface does not declare any methods; it simply flags a servlet that implements it to indicate that the servlet will not process any two requests in parallel threads; you have your servlet implement the interface if you want that behavior. This usually impairs the servlet's capacity but improves safety, if overlapping threads can interfere with each other. We prefer explicit synchronization, so we won't use this feature much.

Session-tracking API is extensive, and deserves a separate section. Every Web application that includes user authorization or extended interactions with the same user needs some form of session tracking since HTTP is a stateless protocol. We will be using session tracking soon, in our first large application (the Campus Bookstore in Chapters 2 and 3).

Session Tracking

A session is a series of request-response exchanges with *the same client*. Since HTTP is a stateless protocol, identifying the client as "the same" is not a trivial task. Over the many years of CGI programming, several approaches to this task have been developed, using:

- ❑ hidden fields of the submitting form
- ❑ URL rewriting
- ❑ persistent cookies

You can find brief reminders of how these work in Appendix C. Here we present the higher-level session tracking facilities that are included in the Servlet API. Their centerpiece is the `HttpSession` interface. An object implementing that interface is associated with every visitor to the site, and you can store, retrieve and delete arbitrary name-value pairs in that object.

The association between a visitor and a session is established by giving each visiting client a unique session ID, typically a very long string created and maintained by the server. Every time a new request comes in, the client is checked to see whether it has a "valid" ID. If the answer is no, the session is considered "new." If the answer is yes, then the client is in the middle of an ongoing session.

Session-Tracking Methods of HttpServletRequest

To obtain an existing or a new `HttpSession` object use the `getSession()` method:

```
public HttpSession getSession();
public HttpSession getSession(boolean create);
```

If the `boolean create` is true and there is no current session, then a new `HttpSession` object is created and given an ID. If the `boolean` is false, then a new session object is not returned, only an existing one if it does indeed exist. The default is true.

Once you have a session object you can inquire whether or not its ID is saved using a cookie or URL rewriting:

```
public boolean isRequestedSessionIdFromCookie();
public boolean isRequestedSessionIdFromURL();
```

More importantly, you can ask for the ID itself, and whether or not it is valid:

```
public String getRequestedSessionId();
public boolean isRequestedSessionIdValid();
```

In summary, the session object goes through these stages:

- ❑ new
- ❑ valid
- ❑ invalid

Once it is invalid, it is removed from memory, and its session ID on the client becomes invalid. All this is taken care of by the servlet engine; the servlet programmer can sit back and enjoy the comfort.

HttpSession Methods

The methods of `HttpSession` fall into two groups. One has to do with the newness and validity of the session. First off, there is:

```
public boolean isNew();
```

A session is considered new if it has been created by the server and not received from the client as part of the current request. In a situation where you require the user to go through a login procedure, this method should be used to check whether the client has indeed logged in or arrived at your page in some illegitimate way.

If the session is not new but is not valid either, then trying to do anything with it, including asking whether or not it is new, will result in an `IllegalStateException`. If the session is valid, then you can get its ID and ask it various questions about its age and what it's been doing lately:

```
public String getId();
public long getCreationTime();
public long getLastAccessedTime();
public int getMaxInactiveInterval();
```

Invalidating a Session

A session with an ID remains valid until it is invalidated, either by an explicit call on `HttpSession`'s `invalidate()` or if the session remains inactive for a specified period of time. There is usually a default value of about 20-30 minutes for that period. You can find out what that maximum period of inactivity is by `getMaxInactiveInterval()`, and you can change it with `setMaxInactiveInterval()`.

A Session's Values

You can associate any number of name-value pairs with a session object, depending on what you want to do. The name is a `String` and the value is an `Object`. You manipulate them using these methods:

```
public Object getValue(String name);
public String[] getValueNames();
public void putValue(String name, Object value);
public void removeValue(String name);
```

Binding Events and Listeners

We say about value objects that they get bound into, and unbound from, a session. The events of binding and unbinding generate, well, an event:

```
public class HttpSessionBindingEvent extends EventObject
```

This event is communicated to a `HttpSessionBindingListener` whenever the listener is bound to or unbound from a `HttpSession`. The event's source is the `HttpSession`. Binding occurs with a call to `HttpSession.putValue()`, and unbinding occurs with a call to `HttpSession.removeValue()`. Unbinding may also be the result of a session expiring or being invalidated.

HttpSessionBindingEvent and HttpSessionBindingListener

The `HttpSessionBindingEvent` class and the matching listener interface provide support for binding and unbinding events. Their contents are self-explanatory. The event class has a constructor and two methods:

```
public class HttpSessionBindingEvent extends EventObject
{
    public HttpSessionBindingEvent(HttpSession session, String name);
        // constructor takes a session object and the name of a value object
    public String getName();
    public HttpSession getSession();
}
```

The listener interface declares two methods, one for the binding event, the other for the unbinding one:

```
public interface HttpSessionBindingListener
{
    public void valueBound(HttpSessionBindingEvent event);
    public void valueUnbound(HttpSessionBindingEvent event);
}
```

The Cookie Class

In case you want to set up a cookie, for your own session tracking or whatever other reason, the API includes a `Cookie` class. It implements pretty much everything you might want to do with a cookie, as it is defined by the original specification from Netscape as well as RFC 2109. More specifically, it contains a constructor,

```
public Cookie(String name, String value);
```

and a bunch of `getXXX()` and `setXXX()` methods for manipulating cookie properties.

Conclusions

In this chapter, we have worked our way through a simple three-tier application. The first version of the application placed all middle tier code in a single servlet class, separating the tasks of database access and HTML generation into separate methods of that class. This code showed the basics of Servlets and JDBC, the two APIs that provide the essential connectivity of most three-tier applications. We proceeded to rewrite our application in a more modular fashion, placing the tasks of database access and HTML generation into separate classes (and files). This way, our servlet only knows that it has to

- ❏ extract some data from the request object
- ❏ send that data to the database
- ❏ get back some data from the database
- ❏ incorporate that data into an HTML page, to be sent back to the client.

Note how much of this data is text strings: everything except perhaps some of the results of the database query, which have to be converted to strings anyway. (Some of these strings can, of course, refer to binary data.) So, it should be possible to provide parameters for the entire process consisting of just text strings, and this is what we're inching towards, pretty rapidly.

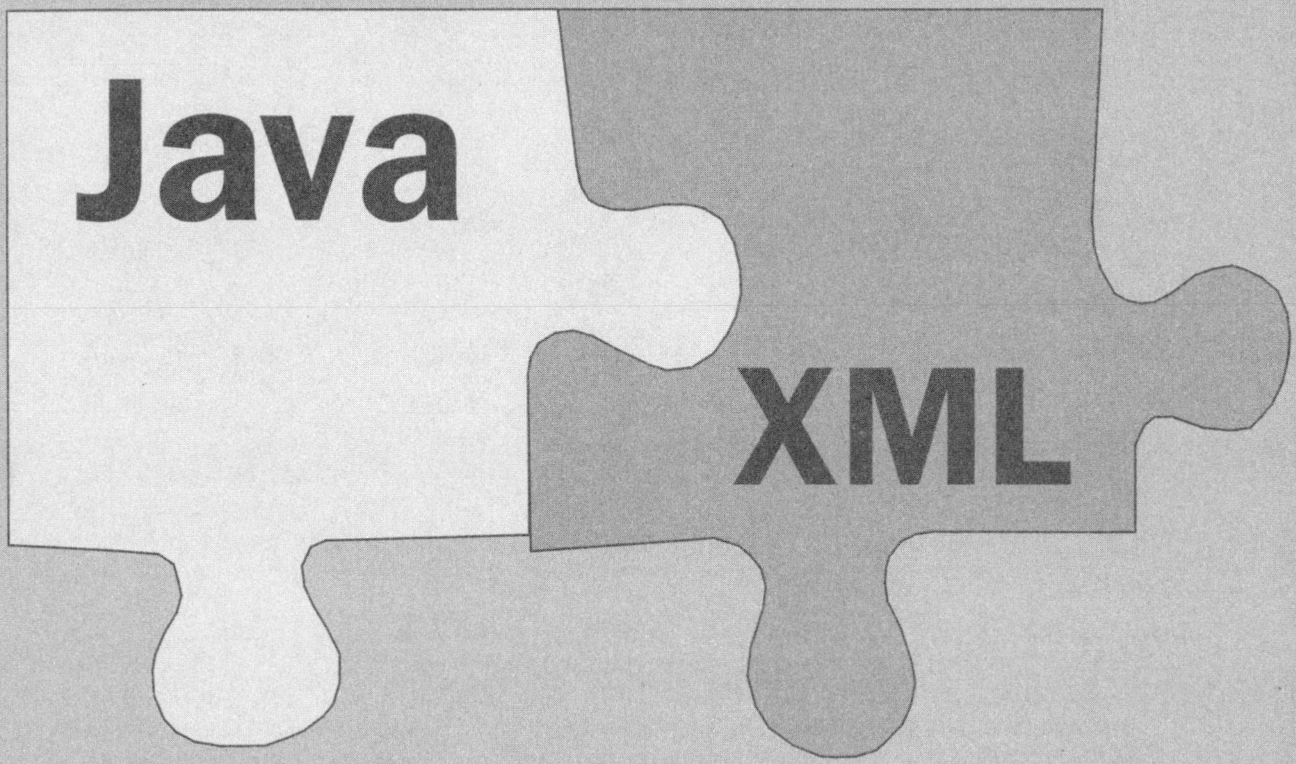
Java
XML

2

Toward a Generic Three-Tier Application

In this chapter, we start the process of generalizing our simple three-tier application into a generic shell for *creating* this type of application. The input to the shell will be a set of configuration parameters that are declarative in nature: text strings and HTML pages. A set of such configuration parameters will determine both the content of the application and its user interface – in other words, the HTML returned by the application.

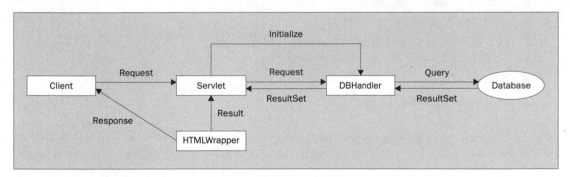

There are two major components that need to be developed: one for handling interactions with the database, and the other for HTML generation. (See the diagram above.) We will develop the database component, DBHandler, in this chapter, and the HTML generator in Chapter 3. In support of DBHandler, we will develop an Env class (derived from Hashtable) that will serve as a general-purpose wrapper around a collection of name-value pairs, with special methods for string values and string array values. All inputs and outputs from DBHandler will be wrapped in Envs, which will mean you could easily plug DBHandler into a variety of architectures:

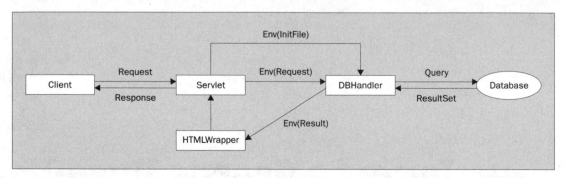

Once the shell is complete, constructing a new application will be mostly a matter of writing SQL queries and HTML pages. In other words, creating a three-tier application will be possible for anybody with SQL and HTML skills, a much larger group of users than Java programmers. (This will not put Java programmers out of work but rather free them for more interesting and/or lucrative pursuits!) We realize that similar functionality is provided by "application servers", but these can easily cost hundreds or thousands of dollars. Our shell is more limited in its aims and capabilities, but it is free and comes with the source code. Even if you never use it for a real-life project (we do), going through the details and understanding what's inside will give you insights valuable to your own development projects.

In outline, the chapter will proceed as follows:

- ❑ design of Query2 and its initialization file
- ❑ implementing the Env class
- ❑ implementing the DBHandler class
- ❑ an overview of several JDBC features for DBHandler: Statement, PreparedStatement, ResultSet and ResultSetMetaData
- ❑ more DBHandler
- ❑ coding the main servlet for Query2

The Java-specific material we will cover in this chapter includes a deeper examination of the JDBC API and the development of an Env (Environment) class that will be used as a general data interchange format throughout the rest of this book.

The Overall Design and Query2

Configuration parameters for a simple three-tier application consist of:

Parameters	Description
database connection parameters	JDBC driver name and database URL
user parameters	user name and password
query parameters	a set of queries that the application makes available to the user

Database and user parameters are obviously string values; how should a query be represented? We use a "named query" abstraction: a query object consists of a name and an SQL statement ready to go into a `PreparedStatement` object. A complete set of configuration parameters can be put into a `Hashtable` object, each query keyed by its name.

The Initialization File

Where would the configuration parameters come from? One possible source is information submitted by a user through a web page on the client. A typical scenario would proceed as follows: the user connects to the application; is presented with the login dialog; submits username and password that are preserved as session variables; runs queries until the session is terminated, either by the user or by the application. This scenario requires session tracking, which we'll discuss in the next chapter. In this chapter, we'll take a simpler approach: we'll put all the configuration parameters in a text file, and have the application read it in at startup. The text file contains keys and values in alternating lines, as in the `Query2.ini` file listed below. (Although we give the file a `.ini` extension, it has nothing to do with Windows `.ini` files.)

```
FileTitle
Query2 Java Servlet Initialization-Environment File
dbDriver
sun.jdbc.odbc.JdbcOdbcDriver
dbName
jdbc:odbc:PHONEBOOK
dbUser
dummyUserName
dbPwd
dummyDBPassword
dbQueries
LOOKUP,RLOOKUP,DELETE,CHANGEVALUE,ADD
LOOKUP
SELECT TheNumber,TheAddr FROM PHONEBOOK WHERE TheName=?;
RLOOKUP
SELECT TheName FROM PHONEBOOK WHERE TheNumber=?;
DELETE
DELETE FROM PHONEBOOK WHERE TheName=?;
CHANGEVALUE
UPDATE PHONEBOOK SET TheNumber=? WHERE TheName=?;
ADD
INSERT INTO PHONEBOOK VALUES(?,?,?);
```

The first pair of lines identifies the file and application; the next four pairs provide initialization and user parameters; these are followed by a comma-separated list of query names; finally, the queries are listed as name-SQL pairs. (RLOOKUP stands for "Reverse LOOKUP", in case you're wondering.) Although somewhat simplistic, this design is perfectly appropriate for an application that doesn't need dynamic user authentication.

Query2 Application

To try out Query2, point your browser to http://localhost/Q2top.htm. You will see a page with two frames, a control frame and a data frame. The data frame is initially empty; the control frame offers a choice of several forms, each corresponding to a database query. Select a query, fill in its input parameters and submit the form. The data frame will show the result of the query. The screenshot below shows the result of RLOOKUP:

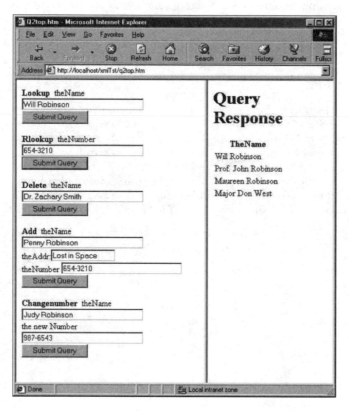

As you read the HTML code for the control frame, look back to Query2.ini to see how it all fits together.

Query2 HTML Code

The frameset document for `Query2` is very simple:

```
<HTML><HEAD><TITLE>Q2top.htm</TITLE></HEAD>
<FRAMESET cols="60%,40%">
  <FRAME name="ctlFrame" src="Q2ctl.htm">
  <FRAME name="dataFrame" src="about:blank">
</FRAMESET></HTML>
```

The data frame will be filled in by the application after it runs the query specified in the control frame:

```
<HTML>
<HEAD>
<TITLE>Q2ctl.htm</TITLE>
</HEAD>

<BODY>
<FORM METHOD=GET TARGET=dataFrame
 ACTION="http://localhost/servlet/Query2">
<B>Lookup</B>
<INPUT TYPE=HIDDEN NAME=dbOperation value=LOOKUP>
theName <INPUT TYPE=TEXT NAME="Parameter1" size=30 value="Will Robinson"><BR>
<INPUT TYPE=SUBMIT>
</FORM>

<FORM METHOD=GET TARGET=dataFrame
 ACTION="http://localhost/servlet/Query2">
<B>Rlookup</B>
<INPUT TYPE=HIDDEN NAME=dbOperation value=RLOOKUP>
theNumber <INPUT TYPE=TEXT NAME="Parameter1" size=30 value="123-4567"><BR>
<INPUT TYPE=SUBMIT></FORM>

<FORM METHOD=GET TARGET=dataFrame
 ACTION="http://localhost/servlet/Query2">
<B>Delete</B>
<INPUT TYPE=HIDDEN NAME=dbOperation value=DELETE>
theName <INPUT TYPE=TEXT NAME="Parameter1" size=30 value="Dr. Smith"><BR>
<INPUT TYPE=SUBMIT></FORM>

<FORM METHOD=GET TARGET=dataFrame
 ACTION="http://localhost/servlet/Query2">
<B>Add</B>
<!-- as this query shows, we can put parameters in any order as long as
     the number matches the field name;
     e.g., theAddr is Parameter3 and precedes Parameter2 -->

<INPUT TYPE=HIDDEN NAME=dbOperation value=ADD>
theName <INPUT TYPE=TEXT NAME="Parameter1" size=30 value="Will Robinson"><BR>
theAddr:<INPUT TYPE=TEXT NAME="Parameter3" size=15 value="Lost in Space"><BR>
theNumber <INPUT TYPE=TEXT NAME="Parameter2" size=30 value="654-3210"><BR>
<INPUT TYPE=SUBMIT></FORM>
```

```
<FORM METHOD=GET TARGET=dataFrame
 ACTION="http://localhost/servlet/Query2">
<B>Changevalue</B>
<INPUT TYPE=HIDDEN NAME=dbOperation value=CHANGEVALUE>
theName <INPUT TYPE=TEXT NAME="Parameter2" size=30 value="Will Robinson"><BR>
the new Number <INPUT TYPE=TEXT NAME="Parameter1" size=30
value="987-6543"><BR>
<INPUT TYPE=SUBMIT>
</FORM>
</BODY>
</HTML>
```

You will notice that each form's ACTION is the same, and is the Query2 servlet. Each form has a hidden field whose NAME is dbOperation; the value of the field is one of the query names specified in Query2.ini. The visible input fields of the form are named "ParameterN", where N is 1,2,... These are for the user to fill in; their values eventually get entered into the PreparedStatement that gets executed by the servlet. The code for the servlet is presented in the last section of the chapter; everything in between explains how it works.

The Env Class for Data Interchange

We have identified at least two possible sources for configuration parameters: a .ini file and the web page on the client; and there will be others (an XML file comes to mind). We need a standard, easily extensible way of receiving information from these sources and packaging it into a Hashtable. The obvious way to do this is to create a class that extends Hashtable and contains whatever additional machinery we need. When a new source of configuration parameters emerges (a JINI device, perhaps) we'll just add a constructor to our class. We call our class Env, short for Environment, because we think of it as providing an environment for evaluating certain frequently-occurring expressions. This class will remain with us for the rest of the book, gradually growing in complexity. By the end of the book we'll have embedded environments and several alternative modes of evaluation.

Declaration and Methods

Looking at its declaration, an Env is simply a hash table (to which specialized methods have been added):

```
class Env extends Hashtable
```

Although we want to be able to save Env object instances as binary files (and we can because Hashtables are serializable), they are primarily intended to handle text: typically, the keys are strings and the values are strings or string arrays. So a typical Env can also be saved as an editable text file. Two specialized methods retrieve a value from an Env object only if it is a string or a string array; otherwise they return null:

```
public String getStr(String key)
{
    Object ob = this.get(key);
```

```
        if (ob instanceof String) return (String)ob;
        else return null;
}
public String[] getStrSeq(String key)
{
    Object ob= this.get(key);
    if(ob instanceof String[]) return (String[])ob;
    else if(ob instanceof String) return new String[]{(String)ob};
    else return null;
}
```

The purpose of `Env` is to serve as a generic "adapter" connecting data flows. For each type of data source, it needs a constructor that takes an object of the corresponding class as an argument. In this chapter, we define constructors from an `HttpRequest` object, a buffered reader and a text file.

Env and HTTP Requests

Since request parameters are name-value pairs whose values are strings or string arrays, constructing an `Env` from an `HttpRequest` is completely straightforward:

```
public Env(HttpServletRequest req)
{
    Enumeration E = req.getParameterNames();
    while(E.hasMoreElements())
    {
        String name=(String)E.nextElement();
        String[]vals=req.getParameterValues(name);
        if(vals.length!=1) // parameter is string array; store it
        this.put(name,vals);
        else this.put(name,vals[0]); // parameter is single string
    }
}
```

We frequently wrap a request into an `Env` object in that way, in order to write code that is independent of the Servlet API: a method can receive a `Hashtable` of values from sources other than a servlet. In fact, we wrap other things in an `Env` object for precisely the same reasons: to make the input/output independent of a specific API. If a method takes an `Env` as an argument and outputs an `Env`, then its input can come from a variety of sources and its output can serve as a generic input to the next stage of processing. Later in this chapter, we'll use `Env` in this way to pass rows of a result set to an HTML generator.

Constructors from a Text File and a Buffered Reader

In order to work with a text file, we need to open a buffered reader stream to it. It makes sense to create a constructor that takes a `BufferedReader` argument, so the filename constructor can delegate all the work to it:

```
public Env(String fName)
{                                    // obtain buffered reader, call constructor
    this(MiscFile.getBufferedReader(fName));
}
```

A `BufferedReader` is constructed from a filename by the general `getBufferedReader()` utility in `MYNa.MiscFile`. It does all the right things, wrapping them in a `try` block and catching possible exceptions. The buffered reader constructor also does a try-catch routine and delegates all initialization work to `addBufferedReader()`. That method can be called from anywhere, not necessarily a constructor. The idea is that an `Env` can always be added to (with proper provisions for name conflicts). So, for each constructor "from" some source, there's an `addXXX()` method, to add name-value pairs from that source.

```
public Env(BufferedReader brin)
{
    try
    {
        addBufferedReader(brin);
    }
    catch(Exception ex){ex.printStackTrace();}
}
public void addBufferedReader(BufferedReader brin)
{
    if(brin==null)return;
    String key;
    String value;
    try
    {
        while(null!=(key=brin.readLine()))
        if(null!=(value=brin.readLine()))
        {
            put(key,value);
        }
        brin.close();
    }
    catch(IOException e)
    {
        try{brin.close();}
    }
    catch(IOException ex)
    {
        ex.printStackTrace ();
    }
}
```

As you can see, `addBufferedReader()` assumes that the source it is reading from consists of an even number of lines that alternate keys and values, as in the `Query2.ini` file above. The method reads the lines two at a time and adds key-value pairs to `Env`.

Other Env Constructors

`Env` also has a default constructor that does nothing (although you can add to the resulting object), and a copy constructor that takes a `Hashtable` argument and does a shallow clone of it. The clone is shallow in the sense that the `Hashtable` is new, but its keys and values are copied by reference (unless they are scalar types):

```
public Env(){}
public Env(Hashtable H)
{
    Enumeration k=H.keys();
    while(k.hasMoreElements())
    {
        Object S=k.nextElement();
        this.put(S,H.get(S));
    }
}
```

Eventually, `Env` will develop more features, but for now that's all we need. However, before we close this section, we would like to address the question of why we use our own `Env` class instead of using the Java `Properties` class.

Env vs. Properties

The Java `Properties` class is simple and familiar to many Java programmers, and it has a `load()` method, which makes it easy to read in definitions in the standard properties-file format:

```
name=value
anothername=anothervalue
...
```

We use the class a lot for specifying environment properties, such as the location of the log file or the name of the XML parser to use. In Chapter 3 we extend it, generating a two-level `PropertyGroups` class from a properties file with a bit of structure in it. (It's a good way to control connection pools, where one application handles a group of similar objects.) However, when it comes to storing and loading configuration parameters for an application, the `Properties` class is inadequate, for at least three reasons. First, a `Properties` collection supports only string values for names, and we need both strings and string arrays because that's what we get from HTML forms. (If your entry field is a group of checkboxes or a multi-value `SELECT` element, you get a `Request` parameter whose value is an array of strings.) Second, many of our configuration parameters are SQL queries that run more than a single line, and the `load()` method does not offer us the flexibility to accommodate them. Third, although we have defined a two-level `PropertyGroup` class, we will eventually need environments of arbitrary depth (that is, an `Env` that contains a `subEnv` that contains a `subEnv`, and so on), where each `Env` describes one of several intercommunicating JavaBeans. In fact, the beans are described by an XML document that gets converted into a structure of embedded `Env`s, and just as XML allows element embedding of arbitrary depth, so does the `Env` class.

DBHandler and the Query Class

The `DBHandler` class is a replacement for the `Query1 LookerUpper` that we discussed in Chapter 1. As the name suggests, `DBHandler` handles interactions with the database: there is a `DBHandler` instance for each database that is used by the application within a user session. Each `DBHandler` operates within a thread allocated to a user session and is not shared across threads.

DBHandler is a large class. The version presented in the book omits a couple of features from the "production version" on the book's web site. (They have to do with data type information for query parameters, and with multi-value request parameters that result from, for example, a group of checkboxes in the HTML page that submits the query.) Even so, the class is too big to present in a single chapter. We will cover most of it here (except for the material having to do with connection pooling), and finish the first version of it in Chapter 3. Eventually, we will revisit it and produce an XML-aware version.

> *DBHandler uses a good deal of JDBC. After much trial and error, we've decided to present the JDBC material all together, in an overview section, because presenting it piecemeal, intermixed with DBHandler material, would lose sight of the inner cohesion of the JDBC API. We've included our JDBC overview as the last section of the chapter, and earlier sections will frequently refer forward to it. One possible reading strategy would be to skim the overview section before reading this one, and returning to the overview after you've seen how it all works together in DBHandler. Another possible strategy is just to read on: we have tried to make this section as self-contained as possible by including parts of the overview within it.*

Structurally, a DBHandler object consists of two parts: the surrounding shell that performs a variety of managerial tasks, and the nucleus that is a Hashtable of Query objects, one for each query that DBHandler can execute. Correspondingly, the class definition consists of two parts: the "outer" DBHandler and the Query inner class.

In more detail, DBHandler consists of:

- ❑ imports, declarations and variables
- ❑ constructors and an initializer method
- ❑ two getQueryXXX() methods: getQueryResult() and getQueryRows()
- ❑ addQuery() and delQuery()
- ❑ a group of three methods for connection pooling
- ❑ a large inner class Query that implements a "named query" abstraction

We present these parts in order in the subsections below. On occasion, when DBHandler uses one of our utilities that we are particularly proud of, we make a detour to present the utility.

Imports, Declarations and Variables

DBHandler imports the sql package and two utility classes, Hashtable and Enumeration. The Enumeration class is needed to work with Hashtable. Hashtable is needed to hold the queries that DBHandler can handle:

```
package MyNa.utils;
import java.sql.*;    // communicate with database
import java.util.Hashtable;
import java.util.Enumeration;
```

Unlike `LookerUpper`, `DBHandler` can handle multiple queries, of both the SELECT and UPDATE varieties. (See the JDBC overview if you need a reminder about the difference.) For ease of reference, each SQL query string that a `DBHandler` object must know about is given a name, and such "named queries" are encapsulated as a private inner class called `Query`. `DBHandler` keeps all its queries (that is, `Query` objects), keyed by their names, in a hash table called `theQueries`. The `currentOp` variable will contain the name of the query currently submitted by the user. It will receive its value from the current request. All the other variables get initialized at construction time.

Otherwise, `DBHandler` has the same variables for database access that you saw in `LookerUpper`: a `Connection` object, and string variables for a JDBC driver, database URL, username and password. In addition, it has two variables for connection pooling that we will not discuss until Chapter 3, and three variables for dealing with dates:

```
public class DBHandler
{
    Hashtable theQueries;    // contains prepackaged queries as Query objects
    String currentOp;        // name of current query
    String driverName;       // e.g., "sun.jdbc.odbc.JdbcOdbcDriver";
    String dbUrl;            // e.g., "jdbc:odbc:PHONEBOOK";
    String theUser;         // e.g., "usr";
    String thePwd;          // e.g., "pwd";

    Connection theConnection;
    DBConnectionManager dbCM;    // one Cache of connection pools
    DBConnectionPool dbCP;       // connection pool for this dbUrl/usr/pwd

    static String defaultDateFormat="yyyy-MM-dd"; // for month,day,year
    String dateFormat;
    java.text.SimpleDateFormat simpleDateFormat;  // reads datestrings
```

DBHandler Constructors

`DBHandler` has two constructors. One receives all the necessary string values as individual arguments, the other receives them in an `Env` object. The two constructors have a lot in common, and we put their common part into the `initDBHandler()` method.

The Two Constructors

The first constructor calls `initDBHandler()` immediately; the second pulls all the arguments out of the `Env` and then calls `initDBHandler()`:

```
public DBHandler(String dbDriver,String dbName,
        String dbUser,String dbPwd,
        String [] qNames,              // names of queries
        String [] qVals)               // values of parameters to be inserted
                                       // into the PreparedStatement
        throws SQLException
{
    initDBHandler(dbDriver,dbName,dbUser,dbPwd,qNames,qVals);
}
```

```
public DBHandler(Env E)throws SQLException,Exception
{
    String dbDriver=E.getStr("dbDriver");
    String dbName=E.getStr("dbName");
    String dbUser=E.getStr("dbUser");
    String dbPwd=E.getStr("dbPwd");
    String dbQueries=E.getStr("dbQueries"); // LOOKUP,DELETE,ADDNUM..
    dateFormat=env.getStr("dateFormat");
    String [] qNames=Misc.stringSplit(dbQueries,',');
    String [] qVals=new String[qNames.length];
    for(int i=0;i<qVals.length;i++)
    {
        qVals[i]=Misc.substLineByTags(env.getStr(qNames[i]),env);
    }
    initDBHandler(dbDriver,dbName,dbUser,dbPwd,qNames,qVals);
}
```

Refer back to the Query2.ini file for the naming conventions and the meaning of various parameters. Note in particular that one of them, dbQueries, is a comma-separated list of query names. It is converted to an array of strings by a utility method Misc.stringSplit().

stringSplit() and the StringSplitter class

There are three easy versions of stringSplit(), all of them creating a StringSplitter object:

```
public static String [] stringSplit(String S,char delim)
{
    Vector V=new Vector();
    StringSplitter SS=new StringSplitter(S,delim);
    while(SS.hasMoreTokens())
    {
        V.addElement(SS.nextToken());
    }
    return vectorToStringArray(V);
}
public static String [] stringSplit(String S,String delim)
{
    Vector V=new Vector();
    StringSplitter SS=new StringSplitter(S,delim);
    while(SS.hasMoreTokens())
    {
        V.addElement(SS.nextToken());
    }
    return vectorToStringArray(V);
}
public static String [] stringSplit(String S)
{                                                   // delim==S[0]
    if(S==null || S.length()==0)return new String[0];
    char delim=S.charAt(0);
    Vector V=new Vector();
    StringSplitter SS=new StringSplitter(S,delim,1);
```

```
        while(SS.hasMoreTokens())
        {
            V.addElement(SS.nextToken());
        }
        return vectorToStringArray(V);
    }
```

Each version of `stringSplit()` creates a corresponding version of a `StringSplitter` object, our in-house version of `java.util.StringTokenizer`. Unlike `StringTokenizer`, our `StringSplitter` allows the delimiter to be a string as well as a character, and it can return an empty token, while `StringTokenizer`, when coming across two delimiters in a row, simply skips both of them. You will find the code for `StringSplitter` in our `utils` package on the Wrox web site for the book.

Initialization Code

`initDBHandler()` puts all the information about the application into `DBHandler` variables. In particular, all queries are made into `Query` objects and put in the hash table, keyed by their names. Recall that `qVals` are parameter values to be inserted into `PreparedStatement`.

```
    public void initDBHandler(String dbDriver,String dbName,
                    String dbUser,String dbPwd,
                    String [] qNames,String [] qVals)
                      throws SQLException
    {
        driverName=dbDriver;
        dbUrl=dbName;
        theUser=dbUser;
        thePwd=dbPwd;
        theQueries=new Hashtable();
        if(null==dateFormat)
            DateFormat=defaultDateFormat;
        try
        {
            checkConnection();                          // connection pooling code
            for(int i=0;i<qNames.length;i++)
            {
                qVals[i]=qVals[i].trim();       // trim whitespace around parameters
                Query Q=new Query(qNames[i],qVals[i]);
                theQueries.put(qNames[i],Q);
            }
            simpleDateFormat=
              new java.text.SimpleDateFormat(dateFormat); //default locale
        }
        catch(Exception ex)
        {
            ex.printStackTrace();
        }
    }
```

Query Processing

DBHandler uses two methods to submit a query and get a result back:

❑ `getQueryResult()`, to return the results of a query as a string matrix;

❑ `getQueryRows()`, to return the result set of a query as a `RowSequence`, where `RowSequence` is a class defined later in this chapter.

Both methods take an `Env` argument, from which they retrieve `dbOperation`, the name of the query to run. They use that name to retrieve the appropriate `Query` from the hash table. The `Query` object does the actual work of contacting the database and running the query.

The `getQueryResult()` method returns all the results together, converted to a string matrix and packaged into an `Env` object. `getQueryRows()` returns the actual `ResultSet` object, wrapped into a `RowSequence` and waiting to be (lazily) evaluated. (If the notion of "lazy evaluation" is new to you, we discuss it in detail in the section on result sets and row sequences below.)

As you read through the code of the two `getXX()` methods, remember that all the necessary information is always packaged into an `Env`, and we typically use `getStr()` to get it out of there.

```
public Env getQueryResult(Env qInfo)throws SQLException
{
    currentOp=qInfo.getStr("dbOperation"); // retrieve name of query from Env
    if(null==currentOp)              // no such dbOperation defined
        return null;
        // use name of query to retrieve Query object from Hashtable of Queries
    Query Q=(Query)theQueries.get(currentOp);
    return Q.getQueryResult(qInfo); // get the Query object to do the rest
}

public RowSequence getQueryRows(Env qInfo)throws SQLException
{
    currentOp=qInfo.getStr("dbOperation");
    if(null==currentOp)
        return null;
    Query Q=(Query)theQueries.get(currentOp);
    return Q.getQueryRows(qInfo); // get the Query object to do the rest
}
```

As you can see, it is the `Query` class that does most of the work. We'll get to it in a moment, after we cover a couple of smaller topics.

addQuery() and delQuery()

`addQuery()` receives enough information to create a `Query` object. It does that, and puts the object into the hash table. `delQuery()` can retrieve a `Query` from the hash table. It does that, closes the query just in case it is open, and removes it from the hash table.

```
public void addQuery(String qNm,String qStr,String qT)
            throws SQLException
{
    theQueries.put(qNm,new Query(qNm,qStr,qT));
}
public void delQuery(String qNm)throws SQLException
{
    Query Q=(Query)theQueries.get(qNm);
    if(null==Q)return;
    Q.close();
    theQueries.remove(qNm);
}
```

Connection Pool Methods

The three methods that manage connection pooling are `checkConnection()`, `freeConnection()` and `gotoSleep()`. The first of them gets a connection out of the pool, the second returns a connection to the pool, and the third is called when a connection is closed or freed. We will discuss all three in the next chapter.

The Query Class

The `Query` class implements the "named query" abstraction. Its constructor receives either an array of two strings (name and query text) or the two strings separately. In either case, its first task is to determine whether this is a `SELECT` query that returns a result set, or an `UPDATE` query that returns an integer, the number of rows affected. Next, it counts the number of arguments for the query by counting the question marks in the query string. Finally, it submits the query string to the `prepareStatement()` method of the `Connection` object.

```
private class Query
{
    public String qName;
    public String qString;
    public PreparedStatement pStmnt;
    public int argCount;
    public int colCount;
    public boolean givesResultSet;

    // two constructors
    public Query(String [] Q)
        {this(Q[0],Q[1]);}
    public Query(String qNm, String qStr)
    {
        try
        {
            qName=qNm; qString=upcaseQueryString(qStr);
                // upcaseQueryString converts SQL operator to upper case
            givesResultSet=qString.startsWith("SELECT");
            argCount=0;
```

```
                for(int i=0;i<qStr.length();i++)
                if(qStr.charAt(i)=='?')argCount++;
                colCount=0;
                pStmnt=theConnection.prepareStatement(qString);
        }
        catch(Exception ex)
        {
                ex.printStackTrace();
        }
    }
}
```

Running the Query

Just like its containing `DBHandler` class, the `Query` class has two `getXXX()` methods, `getQueryResult()` and `getQueryRows()`. Before we look at the code, let's remind ourselves when that code will be run. All the constructors we have discussed so far are part of the initialization process in which a database connection is set up. That process may take place in the `init()` method of the servlet, or in processing the first request of a session. When that process is completed, the next request object to be processed will contain query data. That's when one of the `getXXX()` methods will be called, from within the `doGet()` method of the servlet. The code could look like this:

```
        Env queryData=new Env(req); // create an Env from the request object
        Env result=dbH.getQueryResult(queryData);
```

Whether we return a string matrix or an enumeration, the returned value will go straight into HTML-generating code. You've already seen HTML generated from a string matrix by `wrapTablePage()` in Chapter 1, and in this chapter we are going to reuse it, with slight modification. You will see HTML generated from `RowSequence` in the next chapter, where we present several new options. For now, we concentrate on the mechanics of repackaging the data.

The Env and getQueryResult()

The `getQueryResult()` method demonstrates the flexibility of the `Env` class: the same `Env` object can serve both as a wrapper around request and as a container to hold the result, whether that result is an integer or a two-dimensional array of strings. In the code below, the `Env` returned by the method is the same object as its `qInfo` argument.

As it works through the request parameters, the `getQueryResult()` method makes an important assumption about parameter names, and therefore about the names of some input elements in the form that submits the query. It assumes that those input elements that contain the arguments of the query are named `Parameter1`, `Parameter2`, etc., where the integer in the name reflects the order of the arguments in the query. For instance, if the query is:

```
UPDATE PHONEBOOK SET TheNumber=? WHERE TheName=? AND TheAddr=?
```

then the corresponding form will have three input fields whose names are `Parameter1`, `Parameter2` and `Parameter3`, intended for the phone number, the name, and the address, respectively. This convention is necessary in order to pass the order-of-parameters information from the client to the JDBC code that fills in the parameters of a prepared statement. The convention is potentially dangerous because it establishes an un-localized linkage between database queries and web pages. The dangers can be mitigated by JavaScript form-validating code on the client. In the long run (which may not be all that long), both the input form and the database query will be generated from the same XML structure which is the point of contact between the competent user and the system.

Recall that queries to be run can be of two different kinds: UPDATE queries that modify the data in the database and return an integer, the number of rows affected by the modifications; and SELECT queries that retrieve data from the database without modifying it in any way.

```
public Env getQueryResult(Env qInfo) throws SQLException
{
    argCount=1;
    String V=null;
    // construct ParameterN name, retrieve parameter from qInfo
    // use it to set string value in the prepared statement
    while (null!=(V=qInfo.getStr("Parameter"+argCount)))
        pStmnt.setString(argCount++,V);
    qInfo.put("NumberOfParameters",""+(argCount-1));
    if (givesResultSet)              // it's a SELECT query, returns a ResultSet
    {
        ResultSet R=pStmnt.executeQuery();
        String[][] strMatrix=MiscDB.resultRowsToStringMatrix(R); // as in ch.1
        qInfo.put("ResultTable",strMatrix);
    }
    else // an UPDATE query, returns an integer
    {
        int N=pStmnt.executeUpdate();
        qInfo.put("NumberOfRowsAffected",""+N);
    }
    return qInfo;
}
```

Most of the work is done in the following two lines of the `while` loop:

```
    while (null!=(V=qInfo.getStr("Parameter"+argCount)))
        pStmnt.setString(argCount++,V);
```

The first line extracts the value of a request parameter from `qInfo`. (As explained above, the names of those parameters are standard: `Parameter1`, `Parameter2`, and so on.) The loop stops when that value is `null`, that is, when we have extracted all the parameters. The second line of the loop sets the corresponding IN parameter (indicated by `?`) of the prepared statement. Once all the parameters of the prepared statement are set and we're out of the loop, we run the query and put whatever it returns (a result set or an integer) into `qInfo`.

The code of `getQueryResult()` uses several methods of `PreparedStatement`: `setString()`, `executeUpdate()` and `executeQuery()`. `setString()` fills one of the place holders of the prepared statement with a string value; the first argument of `setString()` identifies the place holder to be filled. The other two methods execute update and select queries, respectively. For more detail, see JDBC overview that has a whole section on `PreparedStatement`.

ResultSet as a Sequence of Rows

The code for getQueryRows() is very similar; the only difference is in the return value:

```
public RowSequence getQueryRows(Env qInfo) throws SQLException
{
    argCount=1;
    String V=null;
    while (null!=(V=qInfo.getStr("Parameter"+argCount)))
    pStmnt.setString(argCount++,V);
    qInfo.put("NumberOfParameters",""+(argCount-1));
    if (givesResultSet)
    {
        ResultSet R=pStmnt.executeQuery();
        return new RowSequence(R,qInfo);
    }
    else
    {
        int N=pStmnt.executeUpdate();
        qInfo.put("NumberOfRowsAffected",""+N);
        return new RowSequence(null,qInfo);
    }
}
```

RowSequence is an Enumeration-like object whose items are Env objects representing the rows of a result set. (We explain how it is different from Enumeration shortly.) Why do we wrap the result set into a sequence of environments? There are at least three advantages to doing this. First, the receiving code doesn't need to know anything about JDBC: it doesn't even import the sql package. Second, and following from the first, the receiving code becomes more generic: the sequence of environments that goes into HTML production can come not only from a JDBC result set but also from a delimited text file, or an XML file, or as a serialized sequence of bytes from a socket somewhere. Finally, RowSequence can pass into the receiving code all sorts of information which are not in the ResultSet: parameter values, user name, session ID and so forth. These are not hypothetical advantages: later projects in the book will utilize them all.

The Rest of Query Class

The rest of Query class (in the book version) consists of:

❑ checkPstmnt() method that makes sure there is a Connection and a PreparedStatement; we'll see it in the next chapter, in the section on connection pooling.

❑ upcaseQueryString() method that makes sure the first word of the query is in upper case, ready for comparison; it's a string manipulation code that uses a StringBuffer for efficiency. (If you use the String class, you generate a lot of objects that need to be garbage-collected. We discuss this matter in greater detail in Chapter 4.)

❑ close() statement that closes everything up. You have both to run the close() method of the JDBC object you are closing and set that object to null.

```
private PreparedStatement checkPstmnt() throws SQLException
{
    if(null==pStmnt)     // get Connection from pool, call its prepareStatement()
    {
        pStmnt=checkConnection().prepareStatement(qString);
    }
    return pStmnt;
}
public String upcaseQueryString(String qStr)
{
    // puts SQL operator, e.g. "Select", into uniform upper case.
    if(null==qStr)return null;
    StringBuffer sB=new StringBuffer(qStr);
    char c;
    for(int i=0; i<sB.length() && Character.isLetter(c=sB.charAt(i)); i++)
      sB.setCharAt(i,Character.toUpperCase(c));
    return sB.toString();
}
public void close()throws SQLException
{
    if(null!=theResult)theResult.close();
    theResult=null;
    if(null!=pStmnt)pStmnt.close();
    pStmnt=null;
}
```

This completes the `Query` class and the entire `DBHandler` class, as far as this chapter is concerned. You will see it again in Chapter 3, where its connection pooling mechanism is presented. For the full-featured version, see the book's web site. There are, in fact, two versions: one in the `utils` directory that expands on the version of this chapter, the other in the `xml` directory that has additional features for handling XML.

Our next challenge is building the `RowSequence` class and understanding the concept of lazy evaluation.

RowSequence and MiscDB Utilities

If you recall, a `RowSequence` is returned by `getQueryRows()` method of the `Query` class, which is a private class within `DBHandler`. `RowSequence` is a kind of adapter class: it represents a result set returned by a database query as a sequence of `Env` objects that is sent to the object that produces HTML output. The main purpose of doing that is to make the receiving code completely generic and independent of its source: the sequence of environments that goes into HTML production can come not only from a JDBC result set but also from a delimited text file, or an XML file, or as a serialized sequence of bytes from a socket somewhere. You will not see all these possibilities realized in this chapter, because, eventually, we will develop an abstract `RowSeq` class from which specific "row sequences" will derive: `DBRowSequence`, `XmlRowSequence`, and so on. The `RowSequence` of this chapter is an introduction to the issues involved and an illustration of several JDBC methods.

As an adapter class, RowSequence must, on the one hand, have the capacity to extract the information it needs from a result set, and on the other hand, provide a generic interface for making its own information available to the receiving code. Extracting information from a result set is mostly done in constructors that make heavy use of our MiscDB utility class. The generic interface consists of two methods, next() and getRow(). We present the material in this order:

❑ declaration and constructors

❑ MiscDB utilities and the ResultSet class

❑ varieties of lazy sequences, or why RowSequence is not an Enumeration

❑ getRow() and next() methods

Declaration and the Constructors

Predictably, RowSequence imports the javax.sql package. It has variables for an Env object, a result set, and several pieces of information about the result set.

```
package MyNa.utils;

import java.sql.*;

public class RowSequence implements Enumeration
{
    Env theEnv; // holds query info, result set info, and current row
    ResultSet theResultSet;
    String [] theColumnLabels;
    String [] theColumnTypes;
    int theNumberOfColumns;

public RowSequence(ResultSet R,Env queryInfo)
    throws SQLException
{
    theResultSet=R;
    theEnv=queryInfo;
    if(R==null)
    {
        theColumnLabels=null;
        theColumnTypes=null;
        theNumberOfColumns=0;
    }
    else
    {        // extract information from ResultSet using MiscDB utilities
        theColumnLabels=MiscDB.resultSetLabels(R);
        theColumnTypes=MiscDB.resultSetTypes(R);
        theNumberOfColumns=theColumnLabels.length;
        for(int i=1;i<=theNumberOfColumns;i++)
        theEnv.put("FieldName"+i,theColumnLabels[i-1]);
    }
}
```

```
public RowSequence(ResultSet R)
    throws SQLException
{
    this(R,new Env());
}
```

We want our `RowSequence` to preserve crucial `ResultSet` information: column labels and their datatypes. We extract this information using utilities from `MyNa.utils.MiscDB`. Those utilities call methods of `ResultSetMetaData` interface of the JDBC API.

MiscDB Utilities and Result Set Metadata

A relational database, as you probably know, contains both data and metadata, that is, both data and information about data. The information is of three kinds:

❑   Information about the entire Relational Database Management System (RDBMS): Does it support transactions? What SQL keywords does it know that are not in the SQL-92 standard? Is the database read-only or read/write? There is a huge amount of detail here.

❑   Information about a specific database: names of tables; within each table, the names of columns (fields) and the data type of each field; the primary keys columns; and much else.

❑   Information about the columns of a result set: the number of columns, their labels and their data types.

The first two kinds of information are encapsulated in the `DatabaseMetaData` interface; the third kind is in the `ResultSetMetaData` interface. You obtain a metadata object for the entire database by calling the `getMetaData()` method of the `Connection` object; you obtain a metadata object for the `ResultSet` object by calling its own `getMetaData()` method. This is what `MiscDB` utilities do.

```
// get column names as a string array
public static String [] resultSetLabels(ResultSet R)
        throws SQLException
{
    ResultSetMetaData rsmd = R.getMetaData();
    String S []=new String[rsmd.getColumnCount()];
    for(int i=0;i<S.length;i++)S[i]=rsmd.getColumnLabel(i+1);
    return S;
}

// get the number of columns in the result set
public static int resultSetColumnCount(ResultSet R)
        throws SQLException
{
    ResultSetMetaData rsmd = R.getMetaData();
    return rsmd.getColumnCount();
}
```

```
// get the data types of columns as a string array
public static String [] resultSetTypes(ResultSet R)
        throws SQLException
{
    ResultSetMetaData rsmd = R.getMetaData();
    String S []=new String[rsmd.getColumnCount()];
    for(int i=0;i<S.length;i++)S[i]=rsmd.getColumnTypeName(i+1);
    return S;
}
```

MiscDB also has methods that have nothing to do with metadata. One of them gets a row of values from the result set using its getString() method.

```
public static String [] resultRowValues(ResultSet R)
        throws SQLException
{
    String S[]=new String[resultSetColumnCount(R)];
    for(int i=0;i<S.length;i++)
        S[i]=R.getString(i+1);    // Java array is 0-based, ResultSet is 1-based
    return S;
}
```

For more detail on both getString() and getMetaData() see the ResultSet section of the JDBC overview. The remaining methods of RowSequence are next() and getRow(), but before we do them, we have to look at ResultSet in more detail.

ResultSet Object as a Lazy Sequence

A ResultSet object can be thought of as a table whose rows satisfy the conditions of the query. The tricky thing about result set rows is that they are not all simultaneously available, and it's important to understand why this is so. Suppose you know that some department has five employees, and you retrieve all and only their records; you still cannot ask the result set for the fifth record, or even for the second record: you have to start with record number 1 and ask for the next one. If you don't know how many records you have retrieved, there is no way to find out other than stepping through them all until the sequence runs out. Whether or not they are actually implemented that way, the ResultSet interface presents result sets as being "lazily evaluated": you get each item (and learn about its existence!) only when you get to it in sequence. This is a common situation that deserves a bit of discussion.

Sequences and Lazy Evaluation

If you have a sequence of objects and you're looking at the first item in the sequence, what do you know about the rest of them? It depends on the sequence. If it's an array of seventeen integers, then you know that all seventeen have already been initialized and are ready for use. But suppose you go to an ATM machine (which operates one request at a time) and ask it: What's your seventeenth input from now? There's no way to find out other than wait for seventeen requests to come in, and you cannot be certain that they will: the machine may get terminally broken and replaced after the next five. (You can, of course, try to make seventeen transactions yourself, but that's cheating, and even so who knows what will happen before they are done?)

Closer to computers, if you are reading a file, and you've read the first line, you don't know whether line 17 exists or not. The only way to find out is to read the first sixteen lines and see whether there's anything left in the file. Until we're prepared to use the seventeenth line, it is not evaluated by the program and its contents, if it indeed exists, are not to be found anywhere in the program memory. This mode of evaluating an element of a sequence only when it is actually needed for some computation is called "lazy evaluation".

If an item in a sequence does not yet exist, it's an excellent reason not to try evaluating it. A stream is the most common example of that sort of lazy evaluation. Think about an input stream that reads data from a sensor that records earthquakes: it would be difficult to ask for the seventeenth item from that sequence until it actually happens. There are also examples in which the items do exist but it's computationally expensive to evaluate them, and so you avoid doing it as long as possible – which is why this mode of evaluation has been called lazy.

*Once you have evaluated such an expensive-to-evaluate item, you want to avoid doing it again. A common trick is to store the result of such a computation in a table, literally "committing it to memory". This process, a form of caching called **memoization** (no r - the word is not memorization), frequently accompanies lazy evaluation.*

Peeking Ahead to the Next Item: Enumeration vs. ResultSet

The `Enumeration` interface of the `java.util` package encapsulates lazy evaluation. It has, as you recall, two methods: `hasMoreValues()` and `next()`. `hasMoreValues()` returns a Boolean, and `next()` returns the next item as a Java object which you cast to the appropriate type. As a side effect, `next()` advances the sequence to the next item.

The `Enumeration` interface assumes that you can determine whether the next item exists without evaluating it. This is the effect of the `hasMoreValues()` method: it peeks ahead to check whether there is another item or not, but it does not return its value. Nor does it have any side effects, such as advancing the cursor to the next element: you can call `hasMoreValues()` as many times as you want and you will get the same result, because the state of the sequence remains the same. If you call `next()` more than once, you will get a different item each time (some of them may have the same value, of course), and sooner or later you'll have an exception thrown because you've run off the end of the sequence. You usually process an `Enumeration` sequence in a loop like this:

```
while(enumSeq.hasMoreValues())
{
  current=(cast to data type of current)enumSeq.next();      // advances the cursor
}
```

The `ResultSet` interface provides a slightly different model of working with a lazily evaluated sequence. It has a `next()` method that returns a Boolean value. You can think of it as advancing a cursor through the result set. In the beginning, the cursor is positioned right before the first item; calling `next()` once, makes the first row the current one; the method returns true. It continues to return true until the cursor is advanced beyond the last row. If `rs` is a result set, you usually process it in a `while` loop, as follows:

```
while(rs.next())
{                      // advances the cursor, returns a Boolean
                       // use getXX() methods to extract values from current row
}
```

What this means is that there is no way to peek ahead in a result set without side effects: the only way to learn whether there is a next item or not is to actually use this item, which advances the cursor and changes the reference of the "next item". This is the reason why we do not represent ResultSets as enumerations of Env objects but rather define our own sequence class, RowSequence, whose next() method has the same semantics as ResultSet.

As for the getXX() methods, ResultSet has a lot of them, for different data types (see JDBC overview) but our RowSequence has only one, getRow(), that returns an Env.

getRow() and next()

getRow() is really trivial; next() does real work of getting values from the result set row and storing them in the Env, indexed by the result set column labels:

```
public Env getRow()
{
    return theEnv;
}

public boolean next()
{
    if(theResultSet==null)return false;
    try
    {
        if(!theResultSet.next())
        {
            theResultSet.close();
            theResultSet=null;
            return false;
        }
        for(int i=1;i<=theNumberOfColumns;i++)
        {
            String S=theResultSet.getString(i);
            theColumnValues[i-1]=S; // array is 0-based, result set is 1-based
            theEnv.put(theColumnLabels[i-1],S);
            theEnv.put("FieldValue"+i,S);
        }
        return true;
    }
    catch(Exception E){}
    return false;
}
```

This completes the RowSequence class. Recall the big picture: our purpose is to make JDBC code for database access completely generic, easily pluggable into many possible contexts. Our main tool in achieving that goal is the Env class, whose role in DBHandler can be illustrated by this diagram, repeated from the Introduction:

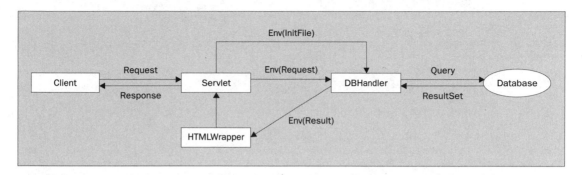

A simple illustration of how it all works together is our `Query2` servlet that uses `DBHandler`.

The Main Servlet

`Query2` has two advantages over `Query1`. One is a direct advantage in functionality: `Query2` can handle multiple queries. The other is a meta-advantage in expandability: to add functionality to `Query1`, you'd have to rewrite its Java code; to add functionality to `Query2`, all you need to do is add (an even number of) lines to the `Query2.ini` file and make corresponding changes to the `Q2ctl.htm` file whose forms invoke the database actions you've defined. The expertise required for revision is not Java but SQL.

The outline of `Query2` is simple: the `init()` method creates a `DBHandler`; `doGet()` runs a query and sends its result to `HtmlWrapper`. The `destroy()` method closes up the `DBHandler`:

```
// servlet Query2 as second 3tier example

import javax.servlet.*;                          // communicate with client
import javax.servlet.http.*;
import java.util.Enumeration;

import MyNa.utils.Env;                            // basic package
import MyNa.utils.DBHandler;                      // communicate with database
import java.sql.SQLException;                     // thrown by DBHandler
import MyNa.utils.HtmlWrapper;                    // send HTML to client.
import java.io.IOException;                       // thrown by HtmlWrapper

public class Query2 extends HttpServlet
{
    DBHandler dbH=null;
    String iniFile = "MyNa/EnvIni/Query2";

    public void init(ServletConfig cfg) throws ServletException
    {
        super.init(cfg);
        try
        {
            Env dbEnv=new Env(iniFile+".ini");
            dbH=new DBHandler(dbEnv);
```

```
        }
        catch(Exception ex){ex.printStackTrace();}
    }

    public void doGet (HttpServletRequest req, HttpServletResponse res)
        throws ServletException, IOException
    {
        HtmlWrapper W=new HtmlWrapper(res.getWriter());
        try
        {
            res.setContentType("text/html");
            Env queryData=new Env(req);              // create an Env from request
            Env result=dbH.getQueryResult(queryData);        // use DBHandler
            W.wrapEnvResultPage(result);             // send result to HtmlWrapper
        }
        catch(Exception ex)
        {
            W.wrapPage("doGet failure",""+ex); return;
        }
    }

    public void destroy()
    {                                                        //  try to close up
        try{if(dbH!=null) dbH.close();}
        catch(SQLException ex)
        {
            ex.printStackTrace();
        }
    }
}                                                            // end of servlet
```

Most of this code should be familiar since the only new element is `wrapEnvResultPage()`. We couldn't use `wrapTablePage()` as we did in `Query1` because we don't know whether the query is going to return a result set or an integer. This is also the reason why we wrap the result in an `Env`, to avoid thinking about it. `wrapEnvResultPage()` simply tests to see what's in `Env` and calls the appropriate method:

```
// an HtmlWrapper method
public void wrapEnvResultPage(Env resEnv) throws IOException
{
    String numRows=resEnv.getStr("NumberOfRowsAffected");
    if(numRows!=null)
        wrapPage ("Rows Affected:",numRows);
    else wrapTablePage("Query Response",
                    (String[][])resEnv.get("ResultTable"));
}
```

`Query2` is, of course, far from perfect. It creates a `DBHandler` when it is initialized rather than for each session, so it can only support one `.ini` file (one kind of functionality) at a time. It has no user authorization, and it can't ask the database to do your username/password authorization because it has to make the database connection before you know who your users will be. It doesn't know about sessions. It isn't thread-safe. And its options for HTML generation are limited to `wrapEnvResultPage()`. We will do all these topics, and more, in Chapter 3. The remaining sections of this chapter are the JDBC overview we promised earlier, and the conclusion.

JDBC Overview: Statement, ResultSet, Metadata

This overview is limited in scope: we will cover most, but not all of JDBC1.1, and we will make only very occasional forays into JDBC 2.0 or the `javax.sql` package. JDBC is a big topic and there are excellent books that cover it, from a couple of very informative chapters in Ivor Horton's *Beginning Java 2*, Wrox Press, 1998 (ISBN 1-862002-23-8) to *JDBC API Tutorial and Reference*, Second Edition, by White et al, Addison-Wesley 1999, ISBN 0-201433-28-1. There are also excellent on-line materials at `http://www.java.sun.com`.

Our purpose is to become thoroughly familiar with those parts of the API that do most of the work in three- or n-tier applications: the `Statement` interface and its descendants, the `ResultSet`, and the metadata facilities. You have already seen all of them in operation, and, except for one call on `DriverManager` to get a connection, we have not had any need for the rest of the API. The same would be true in a setup that uses the advanced features of JDBC 2.0, such as Java Naming and Directory Interface (JNDI) and connection pooling: a connection would be obtained from a `DataSource` object rather than from a `DriverManager`, but once it is obtained, the application code would use the same "core" JDBC API.

Here, we'll discuss `Statement`, `PreparedStatement`, `ResultSet`, and `ResultSetMetaData`, in that order. Whenever possible, the examples are from the code of Chapters 1 and 2. In connection with `PreparedStatement` and `ResultSet`, we will see how Java data types map to SQL data types and vice versa. As before, different sections treat their material at different levels of detail: some are more descriptive, others more cut-and-dried. This again reflects our judgement of the relative importance and difficulty of the material.

The Statement Interface

The `Statement` interface is a mechanism to execute SQL statements over a database connection. You obtain a `Statement` object through the `createStatement()` method of the `Connection` object. After that, you execute SQL statements using one of the following:

```
public abstract ResultSet executeQuery(String qString)
public abstract int executeUpdate(String qString)
public abstract boolean execute(String qString)
```

Methods of Execution

As you may know, SQL consists of two parts, a data definition language (DDL) and data manipulation language (DML). DDL statements actually define and create database tables, while DML statements work with existing tables. DML is further subdivided into those statements that retrieve data and those that modify data. They are called SELECT queries and UPDATE queries, because queries that retrieve data start with the word SELECT while those that modify data start with one of several possible words, none of which is SELECT and one of which is UPDATE. Here are a few examples:

```
DDL:
    CREATE TABLE PHONEBOOK
        (NAME CHAR(20) NOT NULL UNIQUE,PHONENUM CHAR(20))
DML SELECT:
    SELECT PHONENUM FROM PHONEBOOK WHERE NAME='Jane Shane'
DML UPDATE:
    INSERT INTO PHONEBOOK VALUES (Jane Shane,324-5463)
```

In JDBC, you use `executeQuery()` for SELECT queries and `executeUpdate()` for UPDATE queries and DDL statements. `executeQuery()` returns a result set, `executeUpdate()` returns an integer: number of rows affected for UPDATE queries, and zero for DDL statements. (So zero can be ambiguous: it means either "a DDL statement" or "an UPDATE query that didn't change any records".)

Plain execute(), getResultSet(), getUpdateCount(), getMoreResults()

Finally, there's plain `execute()`. It is used in two kinds of circumstance:

- ❑   when you don't know what kind of statement you're going to execute
- ❑   if the statement is going to return more than one result set and/or update count.

Here's an example from Chapter 1; it uses a prepared statement, but the details of the `execute()` method are the same:

```
if (!dbPrepStmt.execute())
{
    lg.logIt("no result set"); return null;
}
return dbPrepStmt.getResultSet();
```

`execute()` returns a Boolean value, indicating success or failure. In case of success, there's possibly more than one item returned, in a "lazily evaluated" sequence: you use `getResultSet()` or `getUpdateCount()` to get the first item, and `getMoreResults()` to advance to the next item; a call on `getMoreResults()` closes the current result set. `getMoreResults()` returns true if the next item is a result set, false if it is an integer. If that integer is non-negative, it's an update count; if it's negative one, you're at the end of the results sequence. In other words, there are no more results if the following is true:

```
(getMoreResults()==false) && (getUpdateCount()<0)
```

Other Methods

The rest of `Statement`'s methods fall into these categories:

Set/get Various Limits.

You can set and get the values of the following properties:

Name	Description
MaxFieldSize	The maximum field size, in bytes, of any field of the returned result set.
MaxRows	The maximum number of rows in a result set.
QueryTimeOut	The number of seconds the driver will wait for the statement to execute.

The methods' signatures follow the standard conventions:

```
int getMaxRows() throws SQLException
void setMaxRows(int max) throws SQLException
```

close()

Use it to free the resource by closing the database connection.

Deal with Warnings

Databases issue both warnings and error messages that arrive in your Java program as objects of the classes SQLWarning and SQLException. (SQLWarning extends SQLException which in turn extends java.lang.Exception). Although both classes derive from Exception (directly or indirectly), their behavior is different: SQLException objects are thrown and caught, while SQLWarning objects are silently chained to the objects whose methods caused the warnings, so you have to poll them to see if there are any warnings. Executing a statement flushes the warnings from the preceding statement so they don't build up.

The two classes have very similar content. Both have:

❑   a description of the warning or error, a string

❑   SQL state, a string code identifying the condition, following the X/Open SQLState conventions

❑   an error code, an integer specific to the database vendor

❑   a link to the next warning retrieved by getNextWarning() or getNextException()

If there is a warning, or several warnings, returned by the statement, you get the first one by calling the getWarnings() method of Statement, and the rest of them, if any, by calling the getNextWarning() method of the current warning. You get rid of the warnings by calling clearWarnings().

Miscellaneous

❑   The cancel() method of a Statement object can be called from another thread to cancel the execution of the statement.

❑   setCursorName() creates a named cursor for positioned updates and deletes. If the database doesn't support positioned updates and deletes, the method does nothing.

❑ setEscapeProcessing(): this method takes a Boolean argument to enable or disable escape substitution in SQL statements. This has to do with the escape keyword in SQL that allows you to specify an escape character. See the SQL literature for details.

This concludes our discussion of Statement and we'll look at PreparedStatement next.

PreparedStatement Extends Statement

A prepared statement contains an SQL statement that has already been compiled. That pre-compiled SQL statement may contain one or more placeholders for parameters that have not been specified when the statement was compiled, and must be specified before it can be executed. (They are called IN parameters.) Prepared statements are very good for situations when the same statement needs to be executed many times with minor variations; for instance, in a loop.

You obtain a PreparedStatement object by the prepareStatement() method of Connection. The method takes one argument, a query string, with question marks as placeholders for IN parameters.

PreparedStatement modifies some of the methods it inherits from Statement, and adds methods for setting and clearing the values of IN parameters.

Modifications

All three execute methods are used without arguments in PreparedStatement because the SQL string is already there, compiled at creation time.

Additions

The additional methods all have to do with IN parameters. A number of setXXX() methods are used for setting their values, and the clearParameters() methods un-sets whatever values have been set.

The XXX in setXXX() stands for a Java data type which the driver will map to a JDBC data type and send to the database where it will be converted to the corresponding SQL data type. In order to understand setXXX() methods of PreparedStatement (and getXXX() methods of ResultSet), we'll have to take a little detour on Java-JDBC-SQL data type conversions.

Data Types

There are two problems in converting values between SQL and Java datatypes. First, Java and SQL datatype systems are not identical. Second, different database systems may support somewhat different sets of SQL datatypes, and may give different names to the same datatypes. In order to get away from the second problem, JDBC defines a special set of generic SQL datatypes. They are called JDBC types and defined as public static final variables of the Types class in java.sql package. The class doesn't serve any other purpose, and is never instantiated.

From Java Types to JDBC Types and Back

In choosing the appropriate XXX in getXXX() and setXXX() methods, Java programmers do not have to think of the specific datatype of the database they're working with: they only need to consult the tables of correspondences between Java and JDBC datatypes. These tables are given below. The only time when the specific database datatypes have to be used is in the CREATE TABLE statement; consult the database documentation if you have to do that.

Suppose you have a result set and you're not sure which `getXXX()` method to apply to a particular column. If you know its JDBC data type, you look up the answer in the table. What if you don't know the JDBC data type? You can find out what it is from `ResultSetMetaData`, as we explain in the Metadata section.

JDBC Types Mapped to Java Types	
JDBC Type	**Java Type**
CHAR	String
VARCHAR	String
LONGVARCHAR	String
NUMERIC	java.math.BigDecimal
DECIMAL	java.math.BigDecimal
BIT	boolean
TINYINT	byte
SMALLINT	short
INTEGER	int
BIGINT	long
REAL	float
FLOAT	double
DOUBLE	double
BINARY	byte []
VARBINARY	byte []
LONGVARBINARY	byte []
DATE	java.sql.Date
TIME	java.sql.Time
TIMESTAMP	java.sql.Timestamp

getObject(), setObject()

The tables above will tell you which `getXXX()`/`setXXX()` method to choose if you know what type to expect from the database: if you know a `DATE` is coming, use `getDate()`, and use `setDate()` to set a `DATE` value. What if you have no idea? This may happen if you write generic code and, at compile time, you don't know what kind of values will be inserted into your prepared statement or extracted from the result set. In this case, use the `get/setObject` methods which take a Java object as an argument or return it as value, and cast it automatically to the appropriate type. Note that in this case, instead of scalar data types like `boolean` or `int`, you will get the corresponding wrapper classes `Boolean` and `Integer`. (See a Java book, such as Ivor Horton's Beginning Java 2, for an explanation of wrapper classes and how to get values out of them.) The tables below show how Java objects are cast to the appropriate Java and JDBC data types:

JDBC Types Mapped to Java Object Types	
JDBC Type	**Java Object Type**
CHAR	String
VARCHAR	String
LONGVARCHAR	String
NUMERIC	java.math.BigDecimal
DECIMAL	java.math.BigDecimal
BIT	Boolean
TINYINT	Integer
SMALLINT	Integer
INTEGER	Integer
BIGINT	Long
REAL	Float
FLOAT	Double
DOUBLE	Double
BINARY	byte[]
VARBINARY	byte[]
LONGVARBINARY	byte[]
DATE	java.sql.Date
TIME	java.sql.Time
TIMESTAMP	java.sql.Timestamp

setXXX() Methods of PreparedStatement

We're now ready to look at the setXXX() methods in detail. Most of them follow this pattern:

```
void setBoolean(int parameterIndex, boolean bValue)
    throws SQLException   // declaration
pstmt.setBoolean(2, true); // example of use: set second IN parameter to true
```

The method takes two arguments: the integer index of the IN parameter (starting from 1, not 0) and the value to set that parameter to. Other data types provided for are:

Byte, Short, Int, Long, Float, Double, BigDecimal, String, Bytes (i.e., byte[]), Date, Time, Timestamp, Object.

To get the name of the appropriate method, concatenate `get` or `set` with the name of the appropriate data type from this list: "get"+"BigDecimal"=="getBigDecimal". Note that `Date`, `Time` and `Timestamp` are the names of classes in `java.sql` package; their fully qualified names are `java.sql.Date`, `java.sql.Time` and `java.sql.Timestamp`.

In addition to this group of methods, there is also a `setNull()` method to set a parameter value to `NULL`, and three methods to associate a parameter with a stream. `setNull()` has this signature:

```
void setNull(int parameterIndex, int jdbcType) throws SQLException
```

As you can see, even though you set the value to `NULL`, you still have to provide the JDBC datatype.

Set-to-stream Methods

The three set-to-stream methods have the self-explanatory names `setAsciiStream()`, `setUnicodeStream()` and `setBinaryStream()`. They are useful when the value of a parameter contains large amounts of data and you want to send it in chunks. Suppose you have an `Employee` table that contains images, and one of them just had a new picture taken. You can update her record as follows:

```
// assume import java.io.*; import java.sql.*;
PreparedStatement psmt
    =con.prepareStatement("UPDATE Employee SET photo=? where name=?");

File fileObj=new File("images/JaneS.jpg");
int nBytes=fileObj.length();
InputStream fileIn=new FileInputStream(fileObj);
pstmt.setBinaryStream(1,fileIn,nBytes);
pstmt.setString(2,"Jane Shane");
pstmt.executeUpdate();
```

Note that you have to provide the third argument, the precise amount of data to be sent, because many databases require this piece of information before data transfer can begin.

This concludes our discussion of `PreparedStatement`; on to result sets!

ResultSet

`ResultSet` methods are numerous but repetitive, and many of them parallel the methods of `Statement` and `PreparedStatement` that you have just seen. They fall into these groups:

❏ `next()` and `close()` methods

❏ methods for accessing results by column number

❏ methods for accessing results by column label

❏ `getMetaData()`

❏ `findColumn()`

❏ methods for dealing with warnings, as in `Statement`

❏ `getCursorName()` (compare `setCursorName()` in `Statement`)

The most commonly used methods are in the first three categories: `next()`, `close()` and `getXXX()` are used virtually every time you use a record set. `getMetaData()` is used every time you need information about data tables, which will happen often in the rest of the book. So we'll concentrate on these methods that we use often; for the rest of them, consult *JDBC API Tutorial and Reference* from Addison-Wesley or Sun's online documentation.

The most numerous group of methods is `getXXX()`; if you thought `PreparedStatement` had too many of them, `ResultSet` has exactly twice that number because they all come in pairs like this one:

```
boolean getBoolean(int colNumber) throws SQLException
boolean getBoolean(String colName) throws SQLException
```

This includes all the methods you've seen in `PreparedStatement`, including

❑ `getDate()`, `getTime()`, and `getTimestamp()` for getting `javax.sql` package datatypes;

❑ `getObject()`: used in applications that try to be generic;

❑ `getYYStream()`, where YY is Ascii, Unicode or Binary: used for associating a large value with a stream.

The stream methods may be used less often now that JDBC 2.0 has introduced two new classes, `Blob` and `Clob`. Many databases implement specialized datatypes for large objects, `BLOB` (Binary Large Object) and `CLOB` (Character Large Object). The new classes are designed to deal with those large objects; in particular, they have `getYYYStream()` methods themselves.

Finally, `getMetaData()` returns a `ResultSetMetaData` object. It's used like this (`rs` is a `ResultSet`):

```
ResultSetMetaData rsmd=rs.getMetaData();
```

Once you have such a metadata object, what do you do with it? The best way to find out is to look inside.

Metadata Interfaces of JDBC

The `DataBaseMetaData` interface is huge, easily the largest in the entire API. In addition to the usual `getXXX()` methods, it has a large number of `supportsXXX()` methods that take no arguments and return a Boolean, for instance:

```
boolean supportsFullOuterJoins() throws SQLException
```

This is all we are going to say about `DataBaseMetaData`; refer to online documentation or *JDBC API Tutorial and Reference* from Addison-Wesley or Sun's online documentation for more information.

ResultSetMetaData

While `DataBaseMetaData` is huge, `ResultSetMetaData` is compact and can be covered in its entirety. With the exception of `getColumnCount()` which takes no arguments, all the methods of the interface take one argument, `int column`. The names of the methods begin either with `get` (returns an integer or a string) or `is` (returns a Boolean). The rest of the name describes what it is you're getting or the property you're checking, for instance

```
public abstract int getColumnCount() throws SQLException
public abstract String getColumnLabel( int column) throws SQLException
public abstract boolean isCaseSensitive( int column) throws SQLException
```

As you can see, the names can be self-explanatory. In the complete listing below, we omit the words "public abstract" in the beginning of each declaration and the words "(int column) throws SQLException;" at the end:

Type	Method Name	Description
String	getCatalogName	Fully qualified name of a table is `catalog-name.schema-name.table-name`; returns the catalog name for the table from which the column was taken.
String	getColumnClassName	New in 2.0: for use with object-oriented databases.
int	getColumnDisplaySize	Gets the maximum width (in characters) for the column.
String	getColumnLabel	Label to use for printing and display.
String	getColumnName	The actual name of the column in the database.
int	getColumnType	Returns the JDBC type for the value stored in the column.
String	getColumnTypeName	Returns the datatype for the value stored in the column.
int	getPrecision	Returns a value dependent on the type: maximum number of decimal digits for numbers; maximum characters for character and string types; maximum length (in bytes) for binary values.
int	getScale	Gets the number of digits to the right of decimal point for values in column.

Table Continued on Following Page

Type	Method Name	Description
String	getSchemaName	Gets the schema name from which the column's table was derived.
String	getTableName	Gives the table names, or returns "" when there is no single table, such as in a join.
boolean	isAutoIncrement	Finds whether the table is automatically numbered, and thus read-only.
boolean	isCaseSensitive	Self-explanatory.
boolean	isCurrency	Checks whether values in the column are cash.
boolean	isDefinitelyWritable	Checks whether a write will definitely succeed.
int	isNullable	See below; checks whether the column will allow storage of NULL values.
boolean	isReadOnly	Self-explanatory.
boolean	isSearchable	Whether or not values can be used in WHERE clauses.
boolean	isSigned	Whether values in columns are signed.
boolean	isWritable	Checks whether writing to the column is possible.

You will notice that there is one method that begins with is but returns an integer: isNullable(). The reason is that there are three possible answers: yes, no, and unknown. The answers are represented as integer constants:

```
public final static int columnNoNulls; = 0
public final static int columnNullable; = 1
public final static int columnNullableUnknown; = 2
```

This completes our discussion of ResultSetMetaData and the overview of JDBC. If you're unfamiliar with JDBC, this should probably give you a stronger understanding of how DBHandler, RowSequence and MiscDB classes work.

Conclusions

To review this chapter, let's take a second look at the diagram that opened it:

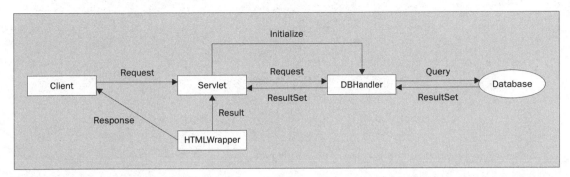

In this chapter, we have made two important steps towards a generic shell for three-tier applications. First, we developed a general-purpose Env class for data interchange among the components of such an application. Second, our DBHandler class has taken over all interactions with the database: a direct path has been constructed from a plain-text initialization file with very simple syntax to a DBHandler object, via an Env object. Another information path leads from the DBHandler, via an Env object or an enumeration of such objects, to the HTML generator.

In terms of Java API coverage, we have reviewed the following:

❑ several key interfaces of the java.sql package: Statement, PreparedStatement, ResultSet and ResultSetMetaData;

❑ a number of smaller classes and interfaces of the package: SQLWarning, Date, Time, and TimeStamp;

❑ mappings between Java datatypes and JDBC datatypes;

❑ interfaces for lazy evaluation in Enumeration and ResultSet.

We need one more chapter to further develop the information flows through the system. There are three main joints of the system – client to servlet, servlet to database, and servlet back to client – and all three are in need of improvement. First, we want to be able to receive user data from the web browser, separately from the queries. This will require session tracking on the servlet. Second, we want to make the system more robust and scalable by maintaining a pool of connections. Third, we would like to have a more flexible and sophisticated subsystem of HTML generation. These three projects will occupy us in Chapter 3.

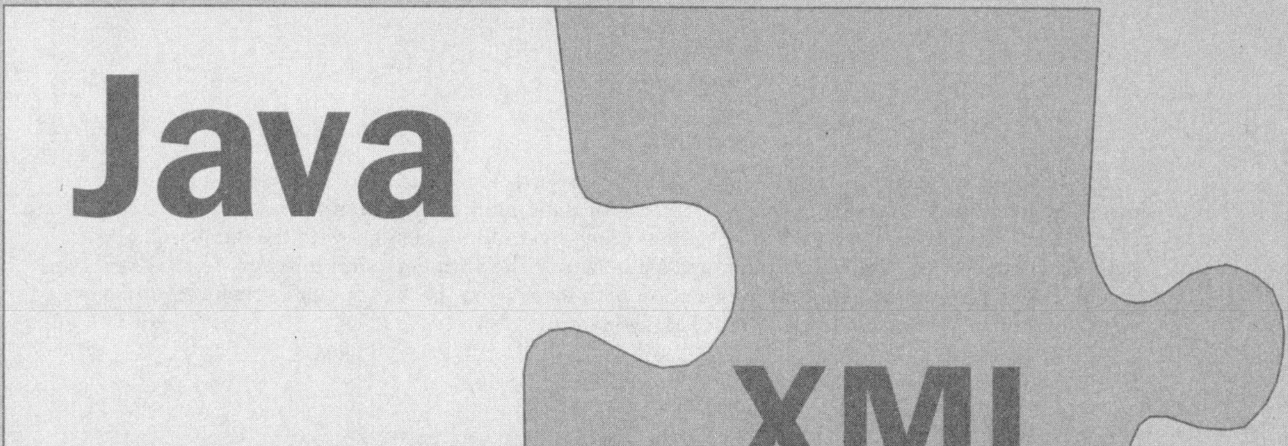
Java
XML

3

A Shell for Three-Tier Applications

In this chapter, we revise our Query2 until it becomes a shell (or standard template) for creating three-tier applications. Most of the work is in two areas: initialization, which fills in all the application-specific details, and output, which puts out all the application-specific HTML pages. In the end, we have a fairly general tool for creating simple three-tier web applications without writing any Java code.

For initialization, we use three sources of information: the user, the servlet's init() parameters, and the initialization file as in Query2:

❑ from the user comes their username and password, not yet encrypted

❑ from the init() parameters comes the directory path to the application-specific files, such as the initialization file (see the later section, *Application-Specific Files*)

❑ from the initialization file comes the database information and its queries

For HTML generation, we compare two different approaches: generating output in Java vs. embedding Java into a "template" HTML file. We present several options for both approaches, including the Element Construction Set (ECS) from the Apache project. We also briefly discuss JavaServer Pages (JSP) from Sun, postponing their in-depth treatment until Chapters 10-12.

With the HTML component in place, we turn our attention to the unfinished business of connection pooling. The last (and longest) section of this chapter presents our implementation of connection pooling, as an example of using a general-purpose Cache class.

In outline, this chapter proceeds as follows:

❑ a step-by-step approach to the process of creating *new* applications by using `Query2` as a template file

❑ using `init()` parameters to improve the above process

❑ improving the process further by separating out user login from the rest of the initialization process, and introducing session tracking, which completes the initialization part of the chapter (our application is now called `Query3`, but the servlet itself contains no application-specific information: it is all in application-specific files, none of which are Java files)

❑ using ECS for HTML output, in combination with our code from Chapter 2

❑ comparing our template files for output with JSPs

❑ `Query3` renamed as `QShell`; summary of steps needed to create an application of your own, using `QShell` as a starting point

❑ the general purpose `Cache` class and its use in connection pooling

❑ `DBHandler` and the entire `QShell` completed, except for mini-language implementation

Do-it-Yourself Three-Tier, Version 1

Before we start upon our three-tier shell improvement, let's remind ourselves – via an example – of what we already have. Suppose you know a system administrator who needs a simple three-tier application for their users. Having installed the `Query2` software, you can then tell the system administrator that they can create the application themselves. However, what instructions do we need to give them to allow them to do this?

Version1a: Edit Query2

To be specific, let's assume that you are on an NT server and using JRun as the servlet engine. The database is a small bookstore inventory. One of its tables (`Bookdata`) contains these fields: `ISBN`, `Author`, `Title`, `Publisher`, `Year`, and `ListPrice`. The task of creating an application concerns creating three files:

❑ a frameset Web page with two frames

❑ a page for the control frame

❑ a `.ini` file

Instead of creating new files let's further assume, for simplicity, that our system administrator will be editing the existing `Query2` files. Let's start with the initialization file, `Query2.ini`, which we repeat here in an abbreviated form:

```
FileTitle
Query2 Java Servlet Initialization-Environment File
dbDriver
sun.jdbc.odbc.JdbcOdbcDriver
dbName
jdbc:odbc:PHONEBOOK
dbUser
dummyUserName
dbPwd
dummyDBPassword
dbQueries
LOOKUP,RLOOKUP,DELETE,CHANGEVALUE,ADD
LOOKUP
SELECT TheNumber,TheAddr FROM PHONEBOOK WHERE TheName=?;
... (more queries)
```

Proceeding line by line, the following should be observed in order to create a new application:

- ❑ edit `FileTitle` as desired (the second line in the file)
- ❑ `dbDriver` remains the same (line four)
- ❑ `dbName` (line six) has to be replaced: the system administrator needs to create a DSN for their database using the ODBC control panel, and then replace PHONEBOOK (currently entered in the file as the `dbName`) with it
- ❑ `dbUser` (line eight) and `dbPwd` (line ten) remain dummies
- ❑ the list of `dbQueries` and query contents have to be replaced (line twelve onwards)

Adding a Query

Modifying the initialization is, as we saw above, relatively straightforward and needs to be done only once. Let's concentrate on what it takes to add a query to the initialization file. To add support for the query:

```
SELECT AUTHOR,TITLE,LISTPRICE FROM Bookdata WHERE ISBN = <some input data>
```

proceed as follows:

- ❑ give the query a meaningful name, such as `LookupATP` (standing for `Lookup Author, Title, Price`)
- ❑ add this name to the comma-separated list under the `dbQueries` line of the `.ini` file
- ❑ add the following two lines to the list of queries in the `.ini` file:

```
LookupATP
SELECT AUTHOR,TITLE,LISTPRICE FROM Bookdata WHERE ISBN=?
```

This adds support for the query in the `.ini` file. Next we need a matching form in `Q2ctl.htm`. The following conventions need to be observed:

❑ for each query, there must be a form in the control page – each one of these forms has a hidden field whose NAME is `dbOperation`, and whose value is the query name for this form

❑ the fields for data entry are named `Parameter1`, `Parameter2`, an so on, in the order in which they appear in the SQL statement

❑ the action for these forms is the same `Query2` servlet

In our example, the added form in `Q2ctl.htm` will be as follows:

```
<FORM METHOD=GET TARGET=dataFrame
 ACTION="http://localhost/servlet/Query2b">
  <B>Look up Author, Title, ListPrice by ISBN number</B>
  <INPUT TYPE=HIDDEN NAME=dbOperation value=LookupATP>
  ISBN Number<INPUT TYPE=TEXT NAME="Parameter1" value="Enter ISBN"><BR>
  <INPUT TYPE=SUBMIT>
</FORM>
```

Simply repeat this process for all the queries that need to be supported.

Finishing Touches

This file, `Q2top.htm`, can be edited as often as desired. When done, the `.ini` file must then be placed in the `JRun\jsm-default\MyNa\EnvIni\` folder. Place the two `.htm` files wherever you want your users to find them. The newly-created application is then complete.

The obvious drawback of this "shell" is that it only allows one application at a time: in order to create a new application, the current one must be destroyed. The main reason for this is that the location of the `.ini` file is fixed (by the string `iniFile`) in the servlet:

```
public class Query2 extends HttpServlet
{
    DBHandler dbH = null;
    String iniFile = "MyNa/EnvIni/Query2";

    public void init(ServletConfig config) throws ServletException
    {
        super.init(config);
        try
        {
            Env dbEnv = new Env(iniFile + ".ini");
            dbH = new DBHandler(dbEnv);
        }
        catch(Exception ex)
        {
            ex.printStackTrace();
        }
    }
}
```

To get round this limitation, we need to give each application its own .ini file (and a matching control web page). This is the perfect place to make use of a servlet's init() parameters. With .ini file specified separately for each application, new ones can be created by copying and renaming Query2. Although this is a bit simplistic, it is workable, and allows us to have as many applications as needed.

Version1b: Copy and Customize Query2

In terms of code, all we need to do is insert five simple lines into the init() method:

```java
public class Query2 extends HttpServlet
{
    DBHandler dbH = null;
    String iniFile = "MyNa/EnvIni/Query2";

    public void init(ServletConfig config) throws ServletException
    {
        super.init(config);

        // five new lines follow
        String fName = getInitParameter("iniFile");
        if(fName != null)
        {
            iniFile = fName;
        }

        try
        {
            Env dbEnv = new Env(iniFile + ".ini");
            dbH = new DBHandler(dbEnv);
        }
        catch(Exception ex)
        {
            ex.printStackTrace();
        }
    }
}
```

If the init() parameter, iniFile, is not defined then the name will remain as it was in Query2.java, so the book code will still work even if you do nothing. If that parameter is defined, the servlet will read the new .ini file that defines the new application.

To create a second application, we need to modify our instructions for creating a new application as follows:

❑   start by making a copy of Query2.class and rename it (NewApp.class, say) as desired; keep it in the servlets directory

❑   make a copy of the .ini file and rename it as desired

❑   add the name, without the .ini extension, as an initialization parameter of the NewApp servlet

❑   edit the .ini file as described above

❑ edit the control page as described above, with one additional change: the ACTION attribute of all the query forms should be "http://localhost/servlet/NewApp"

...and a new application is complete.

You may be wondering why we don't put all the initialization material into the init() parameters of the servlet and dispense with the .ini file altogether. The main reason for this is that it's much easier for a system administrator, or any other individual, to edit a text file than it is for them to edit initialization parameters. Other advantages to using text files are:

❑ they are portable from one server system to another

❑ their portability allows cut-and-paste copy techniques between files

❑ they can be backed up as visible/checkable units

❑ text file initialization can be made cumulative – they can be given whatever properties we want it to have, because it's under our control

Very soon, we'll get into a situation where we want our .ini file pre-processed by some Java code before it is used to initialize the servlet; we couldn't do that within init() parameters. So, we put the information on how to find the initialization file into (servlet-engine dependant) init() parameters, but put the rest of the initialization into a simple text initialization file.

Another possible source of initialization information is, of course, the user. Earlier, we divided that information into three categories: database information, user information, and application information (queries). It would be possible to put all of it on the client and let the user type SQL statements into input text boxes. More likely, the system administrator would prefer to keep the database and application information on the server, but obtain the username and password from the user. This is the version of the shell that we are going to develop next; it will require session tracking. We're going to call it Query3, but 3tshell may be a better name because there will be literally nothing in the Java code that is specific to Phonebook Queries. All application-specific information will reside in the initialization file and other application-specific files, none of them Java files.

Query3: Three-Tier with Sessions

We are going to change the basic specifications for the system. In Query2, the interactions between the user and the system follow this sequence:

User	System
1. Connect to application URL	Display frame page, data frame blank
2. Submit query (repeat as needed)	Display the result of query or error message in data frame

This is going to change to:

User	System
1. Connect to application URL	Display username and password page/dialog
2. Enter username and password	If authenticated, display frame page, data frame blank
3. Submit query (repeat as needed)	Display the result of query or error message in data frame
4. Logout	Terminate session

In Step 2, on the system side, we can use any one of several authentication schemes. For now, we are simply going to pass the user data to the database for authentication (see security considerations later in this chapter). Step 4 is optional; if the user doesn't log out, the session will be terminated automatically after a specified timeout period.

Application-Specific Files

Our list of application-specific files looks like this:

❑ **The login page.** This could be the front page of the application, or the user may arrive at it after some preliminary pages, but it's the first page to invoke the servlet and create a session. This page must contain a login form, with fields for username and password, and a hidden field whose name is dbOperation and whose value is InitDBHandler.

❑ **The frameset page.** This page must contain at least two frames, one for the control page, the other for displaying query results.

❑ **The control page.** This page contains query forms, as in Query2. Later in this section, we'll go over the format of the query forms one more time.

❑ **The initialization file.** This file is the same as in Query2, with the addition of one more name-value pair: the name is templateFile, and the value is the name of the frameset page, which in the case of Query3 is Q3top.htm.

Where are these files located and how does the servlet find them? The login page can be anywhere: it needs to know where the servlet is, but the servlet doesn't need to go back to it. The other three files . are best placed in the same directory that is specific to the application, but many other arrangements are possible. Remember that there are three channels of communication that the system administrator may use to communicate application-specific data to the servlet. One channel is the request from the client: for instance, the login page may contain a field specifying the directory path to application-specific files. This may not be a good idea for security reasons. The best channel for this kind of sensitive data is the servlet's initialization parameters. One of them should specify the location of the initialization file, which is the third channel of communication. Once the initialization file is found, all sorts of application-specific data can be communicated through its name-value pairs.

Communication Options

In Query3, we have structured these options as follows. Every application is associated with a specific directory, defined by a file path. This path is relative to the system-specific and servlet-engine-specific default path to the directory where servlets are directed to look for files (in the case of JRun, the specific path is C:\JRun\jsm-default).

The locations of the three application files are specified relative to the file path. All specifications are stored as String variables: filePath, iniFileName, topFileName and ctlFileName. All four variables have defaults, hard-coded into Query3, so again, if you download the code from www.wrox.com, you won't have to do anything to run it. These defaults are overridden if any of the following are defined:

❑ a servlet initialization parameter

❑ a request parameter (i.e. an input field in a form) whose name is the same as the name of the variable

❑ a name-value pair in the initialization file

Although there are three items on this list, the last two items – request parameters and initialization file pairs – are stored in the same Env object, so there are just two places to check. If both return null, the default is used. This process is implemented as a setStr() method of the servlet. This is a difficult method that performs a number of intricate steps. We illustrate it with an example in the next section: you may want to work through the example after the first reading of the code, then come back to re-read the code. The setStr() method will be used a lot in the remainder of the book:

```
public String setStr(Env env, String resultingName, String preName, String name,
        String default)
{
    //set env[resultingName] to preName+(getInitParameter(name) or env[name] or
default)
    String val = getInitParameter(name);                    // try init parameter
    // if null, try env that has request or .ini file info
    if(null = val)
    {
        val = env.getStr(name);
    }
    if(null = val)
    {
        val = default;                                      // if null, use default
    }
    env.put(resultingName, preName + val);
    return preName + val;
}
```

In the context of Query3, preName is a directory path and name is a file name. We want to concatenate them and put the result in env, indexed by resultingName. If we cannot find a value for name anywhere, we use the default. Often, resultingName and name are the same string, so we have a shorter version with four arguments:

```
public String setStr(Env env, String name, String preName, String default)
{
    //sets env[name] to preName+(getInitParameter(name) or env[name] or default)
    return setStr(env, name, preName, name, default);
}
```

An Example: Overriding the Defaults of Query3

As an example, the code of Query3 starts out with setting up the default values for file names:

```
public class Query3 extends HttpServlet
{
    String filePath = "MyNa/Query3/";      // C:\JRun\jsm-default\MyNa\Query3
    String iniFileName = "Q3.ini";         // defaults for servletRequest
    String topFileName = "Q3top.htm";      // or override with getInitParam
    String ctlFileName = "Q3ctl.htm";
```

Then, in the doInit() method we have several setStr() calls such as these:

```
filePath = setStr(E, "filePath", "", filePath);
String ini = setStr(E, "iniFileName", filePath, iniFileName);
```

Let's examine these in detail because setStr() is a bit complex. The key is to keep clear in your mind the distinction between filePath, which is the name of an argument to the procedure, and "filePath" which is the value of such an argument. (Compare the second and fourth arguments in both calls.)

In the first line, the init() parameters are searched for the value indexed by "filePath" (the second argument, a string); if a value is not found, the E object is then searched, with the same key. If both the init() parameters and the Env return null for that key, the current value of filePath (i.e. the fourth argument) is used. This value is concatenated with the third argument (an empty string, in this case), and the result added to E as the value for which "filePath" (the string value of the second argument) is key.

(We note, parenthetically, that this is not thread-safe; however, the final QShell will be, because filePath will be declared final, and no class variables will be changeable, only those inside the session, such as the DBHandler.)

In the second line, the init() parameters are searched for the value of "iniFileName"; if a value is not found, the E object is then searched. If neither contains such a value, the current value of iniFileName is used. This value is then concatenated with the value of the third argument (filePath), and the result added to E as the value of "iniFileName".

In both of these examples, the name to look up ("filePath" in the first example) and the name used in the name-value pair that gets added to Env are the same, so we use the second version of setStr().

Our next task is to understand how these files work together to define a three-tier application. The best place to start is with the servlet. You have already seen the beginning of it; immediately following is the doPost() method.

Overview of the Query3 Servlet

One major difference between `Query2` and `Query3` is that there is no `init()` method in `Query3`: all action, including `getInitParameter()`, takes place in the `doPost()` method. Another, smaller, difference is that `doGet()` has been replaced with `doPost()`. The reason for this is that we don't want the user information to be visible in the URL, although putting it – virtually unencrypted – into the request body is not much better. On the other hand, nothing is to prevent you from using SSL (Secure Socket Layer), nowadays increasingly known as TLS (Transport Layer Security). The Servlet API does not care whether you use `http://` or `https://` (the latter indicating an SSL site), even though it can tell the difference: `getScheme()` will return `"https"` for SSL sites. Implementing SSL has recently become much easier (for North Americans), with Sun's release of the Secure Socket Extension Library on Oct. 14, 1999.

The code of `doPost()` consists of six parts, the last four of which correspond to possible values of the `dbOperation` parameter:

- **Part1**: create an `HtmlWrapper` object and a session object

- **Part2**: create an `Env` object from the request object, and add the URL of the servlet to it (the URL may have been rewritten, as explained below)

- **Part3**: when the value of `dbOperation` is `"InitDBHandler"`, we obtain the username and password from the request, read in the `.ini` file and try to create a `DBHandler` for the session

- **Part4**: when the value of `dbOperation` is `"null"`, display a page with two frames, as in `Query2`

- **Part5**: when the value of `dbOperation` is `"Logout"`, we invalidate the session and exit with a message to the user

- **Part6**: when the value of `dbOperation` is a query name, runs the specified query and returns the result

As you can see, `doPost()` expects to find a `dbOperation` parameter in every request except one, and that particular request, as you will see, does not come from a form submission. In other words, all submitted forms must have an input field whose name is `dbOperation`. The parameter has these possible values: `"InitDBHandler"`, `"null"`, `"Logout"`, or the name of a query from the query list.

The trickiest part of it is dealing with session tracking, and specifically with URL rewriting. Recall what URL rewriting does: it adds session information to the servlet's URL and, for the duration of the session, it is the expanded URL that has to be used to access the servlet. Thus, the URL we add to `Env` may be different from the one specified in the initial request. This expanded URL is unknown until the session is initialized in response to the initial request. The main consequence of this is that our control page cannot be static, as in `Query2`, because the `ACTION` attribute of the forms has to be the rewritten URL of the servlet.

doPost() Code

As we just explained, the code is in six parts, flagged in the comments. Some of them are just function calls:

```
public void doPost (HttpServletRequest req, HttpServletResponse res)
        throws ServletException, IOException
{
    res.setContentType("text/html");
    HtmlWrapper W = new HtmlWrapper(res.getWriter());        // Part1
    HttpSession sess=req.getSession(true);

    try
    {

        Env E = new Env(req);                                // Part2
        String myURL = res.encodeURL(req.getRequestURI());
        E.put("dbServlet", myURL);
        String dbOperation = E.getStr("dbOperation");

        if("InitDBHandler".equals(dbOperation))
        {
            doInit(sess, E, W);                              // Part3
        }
        else
            if(dbOperation == null)
            {
                sendCtl(E, W);                               // Part4
            }
        else
            if("Logout".equals(dbOperation))
            {
                doEnd(sess, W);                              // Part5
            }
        else
            doQuery(sess, E, W);                             // Part6

    }
    catch(Exception ex)
    {
        W.wrapPage("doPost failure", "" + ex);
    }
}
```

Parts 1 and 2 of the above code are quite straightforward, but `doInit()` goes into some interesting material.

Parts 3 and 4: doInit() and sendCtl()

```
public void doInit(HttpSession sess, Env E, HtmlWrapper W)
        throws Exception,SQLException
{
    // the URL may appear outside a form, so _must_ have an argument;
    // FRAME src="/servlet/Query3" does not invoke the servlet
    // whereas src="/servlet/Query3?dummyField=dummyVal" does

    filePath = setStr(E, "filePath", "", filePath);
    String ini = setStr(E, "iniFileName", filePath, iniFileName);
    E.addBufferedReader(MiscFile.getBufferedReader(ini));
    setStr(E, "templateFile", filePath, "topFileName", topFileName);

    String myURL = E.getStr("dbServlet");
    if(myURL.indexOf('?') < 0)
    {
        // URL must have query arguments
        E.put("dbServlet",myURL+"?dummyField=dummyVal");
    }
    sess.putValue("theDBHandler", new DBHandler(E));
    W.wrapEnvPage(E);       // the Env defines output
}
```

You have already seen the first two lines of doInit(): the first sets the value of filePath; the second finds the initialization file. Once it is found, we add its contents to our Env object by calling addBufferedReader(). The last call on setStr() adds one more name-value pair to Env: the name is "templateFile" and the value is the name of the frameset page. The notion of a template file is explained under *HTML Generation* later in this chapter. For now, just assume that, with the template file specified, wrapEnvPage() does the right thing and outputs the frameset page as intended.

The frameset page loads the control page into its control frame. This is where we have to make sure that the forms of the control file have the appropriately rewritten URL for session maintenance. The sendCtl() method does that:

```
public void sendCtl(Env E, HtmlWrapper W)
{
    setStr(E, "templateFile", filePath, "ctlFileName", ctlFileName);
    W.wrapEnvPage(E);
}
```

In the same pattern as before, we specify the template file for the control page and call wrapEnvPage(). With the template file specified, it does the right thing and outputs the control page as intended.

Parts 5 and 6: doQuery() and doEnd()

This code is much the same as it was in `Query2`. The small additions have to do with session management (explained below):

```java
public void doQuery(HttpSession sess, Env E, HtmlWrapper W)
        throws SQLException,IOException
{
    // process user query
    dbH = (DBHandler) sess.getValue("theDBHandler");
    if(dbH == null)
    {
        W.wrapPage("doPost Failure", "No dbhandler in sess " + sess.getId());
    }
    else
    {
        Env result = dbH.getQueryResult(E);    // use DBHandler
        W.wrapEnvResultPage(result);      // send result to HtmlWrapper
    }
}

public void doEnd(HttpSession sess, HtmlWrapper W)
        throws IOException,SQLException
{
    DBHandler dbH=(DBHandler)sess.getValue("theDBHandler");
    if(null != dbH)
    {
        dbH.close();
    }
    sess.invalidate();
    W.wrapPage("Session Ends","come back soon");
}
```

The output statements, `wrapPage()` and `wrapEnvResultPage()`, are exactly the same as in `Query2`.

Creating and Using a Session in Query3

We have been presenting `Query3.java` piece by piece; it's time now to see how all the pieces fit together. Here's `Query3` in outline:

```java
// import statements
public class Query3 extends HttpServlet
{
    String filePath = "MyNa/Query3/"; // default for path to application
    String iniFileName = "Q3.ini";    // defaults for application files
    String topFileName = "Q3top.htm"; //
    String ctlFileName = "Q3ctl.htm"; // or override with getInitParam()
```

```
    public void doPost() {}     // calls the other methods
    public void doInit() {}     // override defaults; create DBHandler
    public void sendCtl() {}    // output control file into control frame
    public void doQuery() {}    // run specified query
    public void doEnd() {}      // terminate session
    public String setStr() {}   // for overriding defaults; two versions
}
```

Session tracking is spread through the methods of Query3 as follows. A session object is provided by a request's getSession() method at the very beginning of doPost(). At this point, if the session is maintained using URL rewriting, the modified URL can be obtained by getRequestURI(). We then submit it to the encodeURL() method of response and place the result into Env:

```
String myURL = res.encodeURL(req.getRequestURI()); // in doPost()
E.put("dbServlet", myURL);
```

The DBHandler, once it is created in doInit(), becomes a property of the session:

```
sess.putValue("theDBHandler", new DBHandler(E)); // in doInit()
```

We retrieve it from there when we need to process a query:

```
dbH = (DBHandler)sess.getValue("theDBHandler"); // in doQuery()
...
Env result = dbH.getQueryResult(E); // use DBHandler
```

Also in doQuery(), we use getId() in an error message. Finally, in doEnd(), we call invalidate() to terminate the session.

We have now presented all of Query3 except for the HTML output. There are three different output statements for this in Query3: wrapPage(), wrapEnvResultPage() and wrapEnvPage(). All three are methods of the HtmlWrapper class. They reflect different approaches to HTML generation. We'll start with the approaches you have already seen, then build upon them.

HTML Generation

There are three basic approaches to HTML:

❑ just do it

❑ use a library

❑ use template files with pre-processing

The first approach is where you simply do it with println() statements. Examples in the literature are abundant, including our very first servlet.

The second approach is what we have been doing in Query2, except that our library is rudimentary: there are much more elaborate alternatives, and we will present one of them shortly.

The third is the approach of ColdFusion, Active Server Pages (ASP) and JavaServer Pages (JSP). Instead of embedding HTML in Java or some other programming language, you embed Java or some other programming or scripting language into HTML. There is a pre-processing stage when the embedded code is executed on the server and the results of the computation are integrated into the page before it is sent to the browser. In this chapter and the next, we will take this approach and compare our (modest but useful) contribution with JSP.

Building Pages Out of Elements: wrapPage()

Our `wrapPage()` method takes two strings (a title and a body) and outputs a page. It consists of a layer of Java code over a sequence of `out.println()` statements. The primitives used in that layer of code are `wrapElement()`, `openElement()` and `closeElement()` methods, which we have implemented for some but not all elements:

```
public void wrapPage(String title, String body) throws IOException
{
    wrapHeader(title);
    openBody();
    wrapHeading(title,1);
    out.println(body);
    closeBody();
    out.close();
}
```

To complete this approach, we'd have to write many more such methods, which is not difficult but a little tedious. An alternative is to use an already implemented, complete and Open Source package called Element Construction Kit or ECS, available from `http://java.apache.org/ecs/`. Here is how `wrapPage()` would appear after using ECS:

```
public void wrapPageECS(String title, String body) throws IOException
{
    Html thePage = new Html()
        .addElement( new Head()
            .addElement( new Title(title) )
        )
        .addElement( new Body()
            .addElement( new H1(title) )
            .addElement(body)
        );
    out.println(thePage.toString());
    out.close();
}
```

In the next two sections we go over the basics of using the ECS package, and detail a possible approach to extending it for the needs of your application.

ECS Basics

The ECS package, patterned after a commercial product called htmlKona from WebLogic, is very easy to use. Here is a slightly edited example from their Web site; it adds to our example by showing how to set attributes:

```
Html html = new Html()
    .addElement( new Head()
        .addElement( new Title("Demo") )
    )
    .addElement( new Body()
        .addElement( new H1("Demo Header") )
        .addElement( new H3("Sub Header:") )
        .addElement( new Font().setSize("+1").setColor(HtmlColor.WHITE)
            .setFace("Times")
            .addElement("The dog & the cat chased each other.")
        )
    );
out.println(html.toString());
```

For each HTML element, ECS has a class whose name is the same as the name of the element. All these element classes are derived from the ConcreteElement class. Each one of them has one or more constructors and several addElement() methods. Each addElement() method returns its owner object (i.e. the last line of its code is return(this)). As a result, addElement() method calls can be chained as in the examples above. Similarly, for each attribute there is a setXXX() method, where XXX stands for the name of the attribute; each one of those methods also concludes with return(this). With proper indentation, ECS code is very pleasant both to read and to write.

addElement() and Related Methods

All element classes inherit two private fields from ConcreteElement. One is h_element, a hashtable that holds all the elements added to its owner element. The other is v_element, a Vector that holds all the keys of that hashtable. The two fields are altered by an addElementToRegistry() method of ConcreteElement. There are several slightly different versions of the method, but the basic one, which others call, is:

```
public Element addElementToRegistry (String hashcode, Element element)
{
    h_element.put(hashcode, element);
    v_element.addElement(hashcode);
    return(this);
}
```

addElement() also has more than one version (four, to be precise), but all of them essentially have the same two lines of code: the first calls the appropriate version of addElementToRegistry(); the other is simply return(this). Since addElement() is the most important tool of the package, it's useful to see what its versions are:

```
public Table addElement(String hashcode, Element element)
public Table addElement(String hashcode, String element)
public Table addElement(Element element)
public Table addElement(String element)
```

The first version is the most straightforward. The second allows you to add a text string element that is not wrapped in tags by the code. If you don't provide `hashcode`, the ECS method creates an integer hash code using the `hashCode()` method of `Object`, coverts it to `String` and calls one of the two-argument methods.

There are many useful features of the package that are beyond the scope of our book; in particular, it's very easy to add your own tags or create XML elements. Our interest is in extending the package for use in programs that need to combine information from more than one source to create an HTML page.

As you work with ECS, it is important to remember that although `addElementToRegistry()` is inherited, `addElement()` is not – it is defined in each element class to return an object of that class. (Otherwise, you'd have to cast the output of `addElement()` to the right class before you could chain it.) What it means for a programmer who writes code using ECS is that if you want your code to apply to different element classes without keeping track of what those classes are you have to call `addElementToRegistry()` directly, rather than use `addElement()`.

Extending the ECS Package

The `Table` class of ECS provides only the default constructor. As we have seen, we frequently need to create a table from a string matrix. It would be wasteful to repeat the code that does that every time the need arises. One possible way to encapsulate that code would be to extend `Table` with our own class (e.g. `MyNaTable`) that has a constructor with a `String[][]` argument. Another way is to augment the ECS class with a `makeTableECS()` method that creates an empty table and initializes it:

```
public Table makeTableECS(String[][] tab)
{

    Table theTable = new Table();
    TR heads = new TR();

    for(int i = 0; i < tab[0].length; i++)
    {
        heads.addElement( new TH().addElement(tab[0][i]) );
    }
    theTable.addElement(heads);

    for(int j = 1; j < tab.length; j++)
    {
        TR theRow = new TR();
        for(int k = 0; k < tab[j].length; k++)
        {
            theRow.addElement( new TD().addElement(tab[j][k]) );
        }
        theTable.addElement(theRow);
    }

    return theTable;

}
```

We show in the next subsection how this method can be used.

101

Outputting Pages of Specific Types

ECS is a great help in constructing pages out of elements, but it doesn't address the need to output pages of specific type on the basis of some specific data. To continue with the table example, it is a common task in three-tier applications to output a page with a table in it on the basis of a result set returned by a query. Whether you use ECS or our own wrap-open-close approach, we need a separate method to output such a page. You have already seen our `wrapTablePage()` in Chapter 2; here's a version using ECS and its extension from the preceding section:

```
public void wrapTablePageECS(String title, String[][]tab) throws IOException
{
    Html thePage = new Html()
            .addElement( new Head()
                .addElement( new Title(title) ) )
            .addElement( new Body()
                .addElement( new H1(title) )
                .addElement( makeTableECS(tab) ) );
                //.addElement(new MyNaTable(tab))) if we extended Table class
    out.println(thePage.toString());
    out.close();
}
```

This is fine as far as it goes, but it would be tedious to write such methods for every possible kind of page we might need. Worse yet, this approach puts the task of HTML generation entirely into the lap of an expensive Java programmer, while most of the required expertise is HTML. Consider our problem with the control page for `Query3`. In `Query2`, as you recall, the control page looks like this:

```
<HTML>

  <HEAD>
    <TITLE>Q2ctl.htm</TITLE>
  </HEAD>

  <BODY>
  <FORM METHOD=POST TARGET=dataFrame ACTION="http://localhost/servlet/Query2">
    <B>Lookup</B>
    <INPUT TYPE=HIDDEN NAME=dbOperation value=LOOKUP>
      theName
    <INPUT TYPE=TEXT NAME="Parameter1" size=30 value="Will
    Robinson"><BR>
    <INPUT TYPE=SUBMIT>
  </FORM>

...many more such forms

  </BODY>

</HTML>
```

For `Query3`, we need exactly the same page with one small difference: the `ACTION` attribute of the forms has to be replaced with a specified string, the rewritten `URL`. Instead of writing a long `wrapControlPage()` method, most of which would be outputting existing HTML, we need a substitution mechanism that would allow us to, given a template HTML page and a list of substitutions, make those substitutions and output the page.

In order for this to work, we need two things: a data structure to store substitutions, and a set of conventions to identify those elements of the page that require substitution. The first item is easy: we can use `Env`. The second requires a notational convention in the template file.

Template Files

In our specific problem, `Query3` has these two lines of code:

```
String myURL = res.encodeURL(req.getRequestURI());
E.put("dbServlet", myURL);
```

A little further down, we have a `sendCtl()` method:

```
public void sendCtl(Env E, HtmlWrapper W)
{
    setStr(E, "templateFile", filePath, "ctlFileName", ctlFileName);
    W.wrapEnvPage(E);
}
```

You can probably guess what's going on. The `Env` object has a `"templateFile"` key, whose associated value is the name of the control file. The `wrapEnvPage()` method finds the template file, substitutes all occurrences of `"dbServlet"` with the rewritten `URL` of the servlet, and outputs the file. How does it know to substitute `"dbServlet"`? Because we place that string between some delimiters that tell the program to use what's between them as a key to retrieve a value from the same `Env` object, and substitute it for the key. Here's what the control file for `Query3` looks like:

```
<HTML>
  <HEAD>
    <TITLE>Q2ctl.htm</TITLE>
  </HEAD>

  <BODY>


    <FORM  METHOD=POST TARGET=dataFrame
      <myna:SUBST>ACTION="|dbServlet|"></myna:SUBST>
      <B>Lookup</B>
      <INPUT TYPE=HIDDEN NAME=dbOperation value=LOOKUP>
      theName <INPUT TYPE=TEXT NAME="Parameter1" size=30 value="JoeSchmoe"><BR>
      <INPUT TYPE=SUBMIT>
    </FORM>

...many more such forms

  </BODY>

</HTML>
```

As you can see, we have tried to use a convention that would blend well with HTML markup. The tradition of inventing pseudo-tags for preprocessing is by now well established. Ours simply says: in the content of the `<myna:SUBST>` element, substitute all strings between the delimiters with their values in Env. Here's the code for `wrapEnvPage()` in `HtmlWrapper`:

```
public void wrapEnvPage(Env E)
{
    String fName = E.getStr("templateFile");
    String fValue = MiscFile.substFile(fName, E);
    out.println(fValue);
    out.close();
}
```

All the real work is done in `MiscFile.substFile()`. We are not going to look at that code until the next chapter because our "little language" of pseudo-tags is a bit more sophisticated than that we used in `Query3`, and requires something of a parser. We will thus discuss `substFile()` in the context of other "little languages" and their grammars and parsers. For now, let's trace how it happens that the control file is loaded into the control frame of `Q3top.htm`. You may want to review the servlet's code before proceeding to the next section.

Template Files and HTML Output in Query3

The frameset page of `Query3` looks like this before it is processed by the servlet:

```
<HTML>

  <HEAD>
    <TITLE>Q3top.htm</TITLE>
  </HEAD>

  <FRAMESET cols="60%,40%">
  <myna:SUBST delim="$">
    <FRAME name="ctlFrame" src="$dbServlet$">
  </myna:SUBST>
    <FRAME name="dataFrame" src="about:blank">
  </FRAMESET>

</HTML>
```

This file, as you recall, is output by the `doInit()` method of `Query3`. To remind you of the code, it sets the value of `templateFile` to (the value of) `topFileName` concatenated with `filePath`, and sends the Env thus amended to `wrapEnvPage()`:

```
setStr(E, "templateFile", filePath, "topFileName", topFileName);
...
W.wrapEnvPage(E);    // the Env defines output
```

The `wrapEnvPage()` method performs the required substitutions within the template file and sends it to the browser. As the page is loaded into the browser, it generates a request for a servlet page (with the rewritten URL): that is the one call on the servlet that does not come from a form. The value of `dbOperation` is therefore null, and the servlet calls its `sendCtl()` method – `sendCtrl()` changes the value of `"templateFile"` to `Q3ctl.htm`, and sends the Env object to `wrapEnvPage()` one more time.

Template Files vs. JavaServer Pages

There are already several technologies that have introduced specialized pre-processing tags into HTML pages. For Java programmers, the most important such technology is JavaServer Pages (note that JavaServer is one word), or JSPs, and this is the only one we're going to discuss, in quite some detail, including an API overview and extended examples. We will postpone this discussion, however, until the next chapter; here we explain why we haven't used JSP in Query3. The reason is that JSP assumes a different cast of users, and a different mode of interaction between them, from what we would like to provide for.

In a nutshell, JSPs provide a very powerful mechanism that sets up a structured framework for cooperation between programmers and non-programmers within a joint project. This is how the JSP White Paper describes that cooperation:
(http://java.sun.com/products/jsp/whitepaper.html)

> *"Using JSP technology, web page developers use HTML or XML tags to design and format the results page. They use JSP tags or scriptlets to generate the dynamic content on the page (the content that changes according to the request, such as requested account information or the price of a specific bottle of wine). The logic that generates the content is encapsulated in tags and JavaBeans components and tied together in scriptlets, all of which are executed on the server side. If the core logic is encapsulated in tags and Beans, then other individuals, such as web masters and page designers, can edit and work with the JSP page without affecting the generation of the content."*

To get a sense of the kind of expertise that "web page developers" will need, consider an example page from the same white paper:

```
<HTML>
<%@ page language="java" imports="com.wombat.JSP.*" %>

<H1>Welcome</H1>

<P>Today is </P>
<jsp:useBean id="clock" class="calendar.jspCalendar" />
<UL>
<LI>Day: <%=clock.getDayOfMonth() %>
<LI>Year: <%=clock.getYear() %>
</UL>

<% if (Calendar.getInstance().get(Calendar.AM_PM) == Calendar.AM) { %>
Good Morning
<% } else { %>
Good Afternoon
<% } %>
<%@ include file="copyright.html" %>

</HTML>
```

In summary, the following JSP tags are used in this page:

```
<%@ page       for various "page directives"
<%@ include    for including files to be processed
<jsp:useBean   for including javabeans
<%             for including Java code
<%=            for including Java expressions to be evaluated
```

You will notice that in order to use JSP tags or scriptlets, one pretty much has to be a Java programmer. The overall picture seems to be as follows: " web page developers" are Java programmers who also "design and format the results page". After they are done, "other individuals, such as web masters and page designers" can get to work on that page. Presumably, if they want to change the placement or formatting of the results of preprocessing, they will bounce the page back to the programmers. Alternatively, the programmers may introduce some changes in the code while the page designers are working on its HTML content and style.

Our motivation in designing our several tags is to reduce the demands on the skill-set of web page developers. Our assumption is that 80% of dynamically generated pages can be done with several simple tags that have clear semantics and familiar HTML syntax. This is what our little language of several substitution tags will try to achieve. (An open-source package called Webmacro pursues similar goals; see html://www.webmacro.org.)

The JSP White Paper seems to agree that embedded Java code constitutes a problem, for it proceeds to say:

> *"Web page developers are not always programmers familiar with scripting languages. The JavaServer Pages technology encapsulates much of the functionality required for dynamic content generation in easy-to-use, JSP-specific XML tags. Standard JSP tags can access and instantiate JavaBeans components, set or retrieve bean attributes, download applets, and perform other functions that are otherwise more difficult and time-consuming to code.*
>
> *The JSP technology is extensible through the development of customized tag libraries. Over time, third-party developers and others will create their own tag libraries for common functions. This lets web page developers work with familiar tools and constructs, such as tags, to perform sophisticated functions. "*

This passage agrees that web page developers need "familiar tools and constructs" and promises tag libraries as a solution. It is quite possible that, when the mechanism of tag libraries is in place, JSP will become a very good template meta-language, a standard mechanism for associating XML tags with executable content. It will not be the only one: XSL will probably develop an alternative mechanism, and we develop a fairly general one in Chapters 8 and 9. In the meantime (December 1999), tag libraries are not here yet, and even when they are, the question of what kind of mini-languages we want is pertinent. This is our concern at this "pre-XML" stage of the book: we define a mini-language suitable for three-tier applications and implement it as an HTML add-on in Chapter 4. This will both complete the QShell application and serve as an introduction to the XML technology.

The pros and cons of JSP vs. mini-languages are the subject of occasional flare-ups on the JSP-interest list (JSP-interest@java.sun.com). November 1999 witnessed a particularly passionate one, in which Justin Wells, the creator of WebMacro, battled several proponents of JSP. We will have more to say about this argument in the XML part of the book. In the meantime, we're going to use a simple mechanism of a few <myna:SUBST> tags processed by a small parser because it gives us a good deal of flexibility at relatively little cost.

Using Query3 to Create an Application

We conclude this section by listing the procedure for creating simple three-tier applications using Query3.

We assume the following have already been done:

❑   all the utility classes installed

❑   Query3.class placed into the servlets directory

❑   a database program with a matching JDBC driver installed

❑   a database for the new application created, including the queries available to the users

Procedure:

❑   **Step 1**. Make a copy of Query3.class and give it a name appropriate for your application. (You also have to rename the class and recompile.)

❑   **Step 2**. Create a login page. Give it a name and a directory path appropriate for your application. The ACTION attribute of the login form is the servlet created in *Step 1*.

❑   **Step 3**. Create the frameset page and the control page for your application, probably by editing the existing frameset and control pages. These are plain HTML pages except for <myna:SUBST> elements that can be left unchanged from the existing pages. Place them in the servlet's "working directory," or its subdirectory. Let's call the relative path from the servlet's working directory to the directory that holds application files "the application directory".

❑   **Step 4**. Create the .ini file, probably by editing the existing file. It should contain the following information:

   ❑   dbDriver and dbName

   ❑   a list of dbQueries

   ❑   a name-SQL pair for each query

   ❑   the name of the current templateFile, which is the frameset page

❑   **Step 5**. Enter the application directory and the name of the .ini file as initialization parameters of the servlet.

The application is now complete.

From Query3 to QShell

The procedure above is simple and workable... perhaps it is time to rename Query3 as QShell and think of its possible uses. Suppose that a shell similar to the one we have been describing, with added security features, is a reality (and it will be before the book is over.) This will turn three-tier applications into a product that can be packaged and marketed in new ways. Here are some possible business scenarios.

Scenario 1: ISP

You're an Internet Service Provider running a Linux server with Apache JServ and MySql. If you can install QShell on your server, you can offer your customers very inexpensive three-tier applications. An application, in this context, will consist of:

❑   a MySql database

❑   a list of queries

❑   a .ini file

❑   a bunch of web pages, some of them with `<myna:SUBST>` tags

If you're running an NT server with IIS4.0, JRun and MS SQL Server, substitute an MS SQL database for a MySql database.

Given the modularity of the system, you can be very flexible in how the work is divided between you and your clients. If the client has in-house web page designers, you can let them create their own pages. If the client has an in-house database person who can do SQL or at least QBE (Query By Example), you can also delegate query creation to the client.

Scenario 2: Networking Specialist and System Integrator

Your business is in networking small organizations and providing intranets for them. Your typical install includes a web server and a database management system. You can greatly enhance your services if you, in addition, install a JDBC driver for the database, a servlet runner, and QShell. You can then offer a variety of three-tier applications, with rapid installation and customization, and all the flexibility mentioned in the preceding section.

Of course clients will want extra features, sooner or later (mostly sooner). To the extent that you (or your Java programmer) can incorporate these features into the shell structure (by making sure that they are controllable from an `Env` object, and reportable through an `Env`) they will be immediately transferable from the clients who requested them to other clients who haven't thought of them yet.

Other scenarios are possible; the underlying theme of them all is that with QShell, three-tier applications can become a commodity, and their creation a retail business with minor customizations.

Is This an Application Server?

Can we claim that QShell is a very (VERY) modest but useable application server? While looking for an answer to this question, we did a web search and came up with an article whose title confirmed our suspicions: "Application server eludes definition" by Mike Ricciuti, Staff Writer, CNET News.com, August 24, 1998. One definition it mentions, quoting Ted Schadler, an analyst with Forrester Research, goes like this: "a software server that supports thin clients with an integrated suite of distributed computing capabilities". At this level of detail, QShell will qualify, especially since, before the book is over, it will become thoroughly XML-ized and add support for sockets, and therefore RMI. However, further research has shown that, for many writers, transaction management is a necessary part of an application server. We do not do transaction management in this book, but there is no reason why it cannot be added to QShell. With such an addition, QShell would probably do very well in the category of free, open source and expandable application servers.

Connection Pooling and the Rest of DBHandler

There are two large areas of QShell that have not yet been covered. One is the implementation of the mini-language; this will be covered in Chapter 4. The other is database connection management using connection pooling; this will be done here and now.

What is the Problem? Scalability and Performance

What is the problem that connection pooling tries to solve? It has to do with performance and scalability. Many database management systems limit the number of connections that can be open to a database at any given time. For that reason, the simple approach of "give a dedicated connection to each user (session)" will not scale to systems with a lot of users. The actual time of running a query and retrieving the result takes a small fraction of the time that the session remains alive, but the connection stays open throughout a session.

Another simple solution is to open a connection for each query, and close it as soon as the query is done. This is also untenable because it will severely degrade performance: opening a connection is a very time-consuming operation.

Here is how the connection pool approach solves this problem. We create a pool of connections that all share access to the same database, with the same JDBC driver and list of queries. When a user needs to run a query, the connection manager obtains a connection from the pool and gives it to the user for the duration of the query; once the query returns, the connection is returned to the pool. Only if all the connections in the pool are busy serving other customers will the manager create another connection and add it to the pool.

Security and Thread-Safety

Any connection pooling scheme has to solve two technical problems (at least): database security and thread-safety.

Database Security

If different users with different database access privileges use connections from the same pool, we obviously have a security problem: if Jane uses a connection with Joe's access profile she has access to all the same data that Joe has. There are two approaches to fixing this: a coarse-grained one and a fine-grained one. The coarse-grained approach is simply to have several or multiple pools such that all connections in the same pool have the same user profile. This is adequate for many intranet situations. However, imagine a shop-cart situation in which all customers have the same kind of profile but each must be provided with a private shop-cart and transactions record. In this case, a more fine-grained approach can be deployed that shifts the task of private-data protection from the user profile to individual query. It goes roughly like the following.

We keep a password datatable, and when Jane Rochester signs on, we find the row in that datatable that matches the given dbURL/name/password triple. From that row, we extract a substitute name (e.g. "Customer25743") and a substitute password (e.g. "i#%^xyA429\!-urfledO0p"). These substitutes have the desired user profile, and a Connection is fished out of, and then returned to, the appropriate pool. Now think about John Smith, who signs on as "JSmith394", has exactly the same database permissions, and gets exactly the same Connection that Jane has just used: can he get to Jane's private data? Not if our queries are carefully constructed: they should all be constructed for the individual HttpSession with

```
WHERE CustID='|dbUser|'
```

as a protective clause. These distinct queries will be stored in their `HttpSession` objects, so they will not have access to one another's data, and yet they do have the same database permissions so they can share Connections.

We do not provide a database with these ideas implemented, but rest assured that with reasonable care, it is quite possible to implement connection pooling without violating users' security.

Thread-Safety

Connections in pools are shared among different user sessions, each running in its own thread; unless precautions are taken, they are not thread-safe. The precautions are two-fold. First, the `DBConnectionManager`, which controls access to connections, is designed so that it has no more than a single instance at any given time. (In other words, it implements the Singleton pattern, identified in the 1985 Gamma et al. book.) Second, all the methods that access connections are declared "synchronized", which blocks access by others during the method call. Both of these will become clear as we look at the implementation.

Connection Pools and Caching

Where do all these connections and connection pools live? We have been talking of them as "checked out" and "returned"; returned where? There are really just two possible local candidates, the hard drive and memory, and we obviously want them in memory because the whole idea is to make access to them as fast as possible. An area in memory where computationally expensive resources are stored for fast access is called a cache, and the technique is called caching, so connection pooling and caching clearly go together. What we would like to emphasize is that connection pooling is one of many possible uses of caching: we might also want to cache parsed template pages (just as JSPs are cached once processed), tree representations of XML documents (DOM trees, discussed in Chapter 7), or simply results of expensive computations. (Recall our discussion of memoization in Chapter 2, in connection with lazy evaluation.)

Since caching is such a general problem, and connection pooling is an instance of it, we are going to reflect this relationship in our design, by developing a general Cache class, from which `DBConnectionManager` is derived, as well as all the other classes that might use caching. We would declare `Cache` an abstract class except the methods that really need to be overridden (`getInstance()`, `freeInstance()` and `close()`) cannot be declared abstract because they have to be static and synchronized.

We can now present the overall design of the connection pool subsystem.

Overall Design and Order of Exposition

The design is presented in the diagram below. `Cache` is a parent class that holds in its belly a private hash table that all its children inherit. Both `Cache` and its children are Singleton classes, so at any given time there is only one instance of that private hash table for any one of the derived classes.

One of those derived classes is `DBConnectionManager`. In addition to the inherited hash table in which it stores connections, it also contains an `Enumeration` of connection pools and a hash table of JDBC drivers. An individual connection pool is implemented as a `DBConnectionPool` class.

Finally, there is an initialization component that consists of a `PropertyGroups` class. It extends `Hashtable`, just as the `Properties` class does, and it gets initialized from a property file of a special format that allows it to build a hash table that contains sub-tables for individual pools.

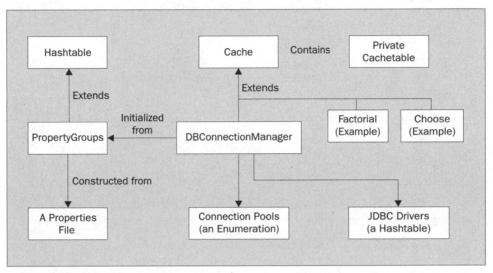

The most important part of this material is the `Cache` class and its extensions, so we shall start with it. To show how extension is done, we will first illustrate it on the simple case of memoizing the results of expensive computations. The examples we show are factorials and binomial coefficients. Factorials are just a simple pedagogical example, but in the case of binomial coefficients, memoization turns a simple but hopelessly time-consuming algorithm into one that works. Finding the number of ways to select 25 items out of 50 would take decades on a 450MHz Pentium II; the same method, supplemented with a clause that says "if you've already calculated this sub-problem, then just use the answer" finishes the problem in less than a second.

Once the mechanism of extending the `Cache` class is explained, we present `DBConnectionManager`, beginning with its initialization component and the `PropertyGroups` class. After that, we present the class that implements an individual connection pool, `DBConnectionPool`. Finally, we show the operation of the entire system, by reviewing those methods of `DBHandler` that make use of it. (We skipped over them in Chapter 2.)

The Cache Class

`Cache` is not to be instantiated but extended, and the extended class must be a Singleton, allowing only a single instance at any given time. The extended class must also tightly control access to the protected hash table it contains. These considerations determine the access modifiers on the variables and methods of `Cache`: the constructor, `init()` methods and the internal hash table are protected; the three public methods to be overridden in derived classes are static, and so are the variables "instance" (which holds the singleton) and "clients" (which holds a count of instance's users). After we go through the code, we will indicate the ways in which the public methods get overridden, and proceed to examples.

Declarations, the Constructor and init()

```
package MyNa.utils;
import java.util.*;
public class Cache
{

    public static synchronized Cache getInstance()
    {
        return null;
    }

    public static synchronized int freeInstance()
    {
        return 0;
    }

    public static synchronized boolean close()throws Exception
    {
        return false;
    }

    protected Cachetable cache = null;
    // the cache for answers; this is the only actual instance variable

    protected Cache()
    {
        init();
    }    // constructor only called internally

    protected void init()
    {
        cache = new Cachetable();
    }    // set up cache
```

Since the constructor is protected, the only way to get an instance is to call the public static
getInstance() method. In a derived class, its code will be similar to:

```
public static synchronized Cache getInstance()
{
    if(null == instance)
    {
        instance = new Cache(); // "Cache" -> subclass name
    }
    clients++;
    return instance;
}
```

The only difference is that instead of "new Cache()" you would say "new
DBConnectionManager()" – or whatever other class you are developing.

Public Methods for Access to Inner Table

These methods are for working with the protected inner hash table. The `get()` and `put()` methods call the identically-named methods of `Cachetable` which override and overload the identically-named methods of `Hashtable`. (`Cachetable` extends `Hashtable`.) We have to override `get()` and `put()` of `Hashtable` because we want to be able to use "null" as a key; we overload them because we want multiple-argument versions of `get()` and `put()` that use more than one key. For instance, a connection pool is identified by three items: username, password and database URL.

```java
public boolean freeItem(Object ob)
{
    return true;
    // called by freeSpace; override if you need to do anything here.
}

// release the first numToFree items
public int freeSpace(int numToFree)
{
    return cache.freeSpace(numToFree);
}

public Object get(Object k)
{
    // k's are for keys
    return cache.get(k);
}

public Object get(Object k1, Object k2)
{
    return cache.get(k1,k2);
}

public Object get(Object k1, Object k2, Object k3)
{
    return cache.get(k1, k2, k3);
}

public Object put(Object k, Object v)
{
    // v is for value
    cache.put(k, v);
    return v;
}

public Object put(Object k1, Object k2, Object v)
{
    cache.put(k1, k2, v);
    return v;
}

public Object put(Object k1, Object k2, Object k3, Object v)
{
    cache.put(k1, k2, k3, v);
    return v;
}
```

These are public access methods; the actual work is done in `Cachtable`.

The Cachetable Class

`Cachetable` has a do-nothing constructor, a `freeSpace()` method, and `put()` and `get()` methods. The important thing to remember is that a `Cachetable` may contain sub-tables. When there are two keys, the first key retrieves a subtable, while the second key and the value form a name-value pair in the subtable. With three keys, there are two levels of embedding.

```java
class Cachetable extends Hashtable
{

    public Cachetable(){}

    public synchronized int freeSpace(int numToFree)
    {
        // returns leftover
        Enumeration enum = keys();
        while(enum.hasMoreElements() && numToFree>0)
        {
            Object k = enum.nextElement();
            Object v = get(k);
            if(v instanceof Cachetable)
            {
                Cachetable sub = (Cachetable) v;
                numToFree = sub.freeSpace(numToFree);
                if(numToFree>0)
                {
                    remove(k);
                    // didn't free enough, sub must be empty.
                }
            }
            else
            {
                freeItem(v);
                remove(k);
                numToFree--;
            }
        }
        return numToFree; // this many still not freed
    }

    public synchronized Object put(Object k, Object v)
    {
        if(null == k)
        {
            k="";
        }
        return super.put(k,v); // use Hashtable method
    }

    public synchronized void put(Object k, Object k2, Object v)
    {
```

```
        // k retrieves a sub-table; k2 and v form name-value pair in sub-table
        Cachetable subCache = (Cachetable) get(k);
        if(null==subCache)
        {
            put(k, subCache = new Cachetable());
        }
        subCache.put(k2, v);
    }

    public synchronized void put(Object k, Object k2, Object k3, Object v)
    {
        Cachetable subCache = (Cachetable) get(k);
        if(null == subCache)
        {
            put(k, subCache = new Cachetable());
        }
        subCache.put(k2, k3, v);
    }

    public synchronized Object get(Object k)
    {
        return super.get(null == k?"":k);
    }

    public synchronized Object get(Object k, Object k2)
    {
        Cachetable subCache = (Cachetable) get(k);
        if(null == subCache)
        {
            return null;
        }
        return subCache.get(k2);
    }

    public synchronized Object get(Object k, Object k2, Object k3)
    {
        Cachetable subCache = (Cachetable) get(k);
        if(null == subCache)
        {
            return null;
        }
        return subCache.get(k2, k3);
    }

} // end of Cachetable inner class

} // end of Cache class (started some pages back)
```

Overriding Cache

In creating a class that extends `Cache` you have to override the following:

- ❑ two static variables, because they have to be the static variables of the derived class, not the parent class
- ❑ three public static synchronized methods

We will show how it works on a very simple example: factorials of large integers. This example does not use sub-tables.

Cache Example 1: Factorial

The obvious factorial function would go like this:

```
public int fact(int n)
{
    return n == 0 ? 1 : n*fact(n-1);
}
```

However, the numbers get very big very fast: `fact(50)` is

```
30414093201713378043612608166064768844377641568960512000000000000
```

This is not an "`int`", it's a "`BigInteger`", a Java class for huge integers that has its own methods to do arithmetic. To deal with huge integers, we rewrite the simple factorial as follows:

```
public BigInteger biV(int n)
{
    // convert int to BigInteger
    return BigInteger.valueOf(n);
}

public BigInteger fact1(int n)
{
    // traditional recursive answer.
    if(n == 0)
    {
        return biV(1);
    }
    return biV(n).multiply(fact1(n-1));
}
```

Suppose you compute `fact1(50)` and then discover you need `fact1(60)`. With the simple-minded factorial you have to redo all the work, but with `FactCache` you can reuse it:

```java
package MyNa.utils;
import java.math.BigInteger;
import java.util.*;

public class FactCache extends Cache
{

    public BigInteger biV(int n)
    {
        // convert int to BigInteger
        return BigInteger.valueOf(n);
    }

    public BigInteger fact(int n)
    {
        BigInteger biN = biV(n);
        BigInteger R = (BigInteger) cache.get(biN);
        // see if the result is already cached
        if(null != R)
        {
            // if so, return it
            return R;
        }
        if(n == 0)
        {
            // otherwise, compute, save and return
            return saveFact(biN, biV(1));
        }
        return saveFact(biN, biN.multiply(fact(n-1)));
    }

    private synchronized BigInteger saveFact(BigInteger n, BigInteger factN)
    {
        // save and return
        cache.put(n, factN);
        return factN;
    }

    // override block for Cache variables and methods
    private static Cache instance = null; // the one and only class instance
    private static int clients = 0;        // how many are asking us?

    protected void init(){super.init();}  // e.g., register, init logger

    public static synchronized Cache getInstance()
    {
        // implement Singleton pattern
        if(null == instance)
        {
            instance = new FactCache();
        }
        clients++;
        return instance;
    }
}
```

```
    public static synchronized int freeInstance()
    {
        if(null == instance)
        {
            return 0;
        }
        clients--;
        if(clients==0)
        {
            close(); // all gone, and the cache with it
        }
        return clients;
    }

    public static synchronized boolean close()
    {
        clients = 0;
        instance = null;
        return true;
    }
}// end of FactCache
```

To test cached and uncached factorials, we have also provided `Fact.java` that does `BigInteger` factorials without caching, and two servlets, `FactServlet` and `FactCacheServlet`. To test, type something like

```
http://localhost/servlet/factservlet?n=100
```

into the location window. Try a sequence of inputs like 20, 50, 30, 100 on both and observe the difference in behavior. Here is the `doPost()` of `FactCacheServlet`:

```
public void doPost (HttpServletRequest req, HttpServletResponse res)
        throws ServletException, IOException
{
    res.setContentType("text/html");
    HtmlWrapper W  =new HtmlWrapper(res.getWriter());
    HttpSession sess = req.getSession(true);
    try
    {
        Env E = new Env(req);
        String S = E.getStr("n", "0");
        // get value of "n" from Request via Env
        int n = Integer.parseInt(S);
        FactCache fact = (FactCache)FactCache.getInstance();
        W.wrapPage("factorial of " + n, fact.fact(n).toString());
        // compute and send
    }
    catch(Exception ex)
    {
        W.wrapPage("Fact.doPost failure: " + ex);
    }
}
```

Cache Example 2: Binomial Coefficients

In this example, we calculate the function `Choose(n, k)`, the number of ways to choose k items out of n. Here is some math first:

```
choose(n, k) = 0, if(k>n or k<0)
             = 1, if(n==k or k==0)
             choose(n-1,k) + choose(n-1,k-1) otherwise
```

(A quick reminder: the reason for line 1 is that you can't choose k=5 (say) items from n=3 (say), or -1 items from anything; the reason for line 2 is that there's just one way of choosing all or none; the reason for line 3 is that if you want to choose a k that is less than n, then you can either choose item 1 (say) to be one of your k items, or not; if you do choose it, then you're left with choosing the remaining k-1 items from the n-1 items that are left, and if you skip it you still have to choose all k of your items from the n-1 items that are left.)

A direct rewriting of the math into Java produces:

```java
public BigInteger choose1(int n, int k)
        throws ArithmeticException
{
    // traditional recursive answer.
    if(n < k || k < 0)
    {
        return biV(0);
    }
    if(n == k || k == 0)
    {
        return biV(1);
    }
    return choose1(n-1, k).add(choose1(n-1, k-1));
}
```

This is a terrible algorithm because it repeats the same calculation over and over: to do `choose1(6, 3)`, you will call `choose1(6, 2)` and `choose1(5, 3)`, and both of them, independently, will call `choose1(5, 2)`. The calculation `choose1(25, 10)` takes 46 seconds to produce 3,268,760, and the browser times out on `choose1(30, 10)`. If it didn't time out, the time would be about seven minutes. For `choose1(50, 25)`, the time would be somewhat more than half a century. Meanwhile, `choose(50, 25)`, using a cache, takes less than a second, as does `choose(100, 50)`, which without caching, would take more than a hundred billion times the estimated age of the universe on a Pentium II 450. For testing, as before, type into the browser location window:

```
http://localhost/servlet/ChooseServlet?n=100&k=50&cache=yes
```

The main point of this example is that we have to store results by two keys, n and k, and therefore need to use sub-tables.

```java
package MyNa.utils;
import java.math.BigInteger;
import java.util.*;
public class Choose extends Cache
{

    // same public BigInteger biV(int n) as in FactCache

    public BigInteger choose(int n,int k)
            throws ArithmeticException
    {
        BigInteger biN = biV(n);
        BigInteger biK = biV(k);
        BigInteger R = (BigInteger)get(biN,biK); // get with two keys
        if(null != R)
        {
            // if result found, return it
            return R;
        }
        if(n < k || k < 0)
        {
            R = biV(0);
        }
        else
        {
            if(n == k || k == 0)
            {
                R = biV(1);
            }
        }
        else
        {
            R = choose(n-1, k).add(choose(n-1, k-1));
        }
        return (BigInteger)put(biN, biK, R);// put with two keys, and return
    }

    // the override block
    private static Cache instance = null; // the one and only class instance
    private static int clients = 0;       // how many are asking us?

    protected void init(){super.init();}  // e.g., register, init logger

    public static synchronized Cache getInstance()
    {
        // same as in FactCache except for the name of subclass
        if(null == instance)
        {
            instance = new Choose();
        }
        clients++;
        return instance;
    }
```

```
    public static synchronized int freeInstance()
    {
        // same as in FactCache
        if(null == instance)
        {
            return 0;
        }
        clients--;
        if(clients == 0)
        {
            close(); // all gone, and the cache with it.
        }
        return clients;
    }

    public static synchronized boolean close()
    {
        clients = 0;
        instance = null;
        return true;
    }
}// end of Choose
```

The example above shows how to run `ChooseServlet`. If you type `cache=no`, the uncached version will be run (but trying `n=100&k=50&cache=no` would be impractical).

We are ready to tackle `DBConnectionManager` now, starting with how it gets initialized from a properties file.

Properties Files and PropertyGroups

A properties file is an extremely convenient mechanism for initializing class instances. It is a text file in which all lines have the same format:

```
propAname=propAvalue;
propBname=propBvalue;
...
```

The file must be given the extension `.properties`, and placed anywhere on the classpath. An object of any class whatsoever can get to such a file and store its name-value pairs in an object of the `Properties` class, which is an extension of `Hashtable`. The code to read a properties file into a `Properties` object goes like this:

```
InputStream is = getClass().getResourceAsStream("/db.properties");
    Properties dbProps = new Properties();
    try
    {
        dbProps.load(is);
    }
```

121

```
catch (Exception e)
{
    System.err.println("Can't read the properties file. " +
        "Make sure db.properties is in the CLASSPATH");
    return;
}
```

Most of the action is in the first line. `getClass()` is a method of `Object`, inherited by objects of every other class; it returns an object of class `Class` associated with the object that calls the method. The `Class` class has a method called `getResourceAsStream()` that can open a stream to a variety of resources. Finally, the `Properties` class has a `load()` method that converts a properties file into a `Properties` hash table.

The code above has been quoted from Hans Bergsten's article on connection pooling at `http://www.webdevelopersjournal.com/columns/connection_pool.html`. The article has influenced our implementation, as you can see from perusing it. Our code has two major differences in structure and one major advance in functionality. The two structural differences are:

❑ We have abstracted `Cache` into a separate mechanism that can be used in a variety of caching situations.

❑ We have developed a `PropertyGroups` class, an alternative to `Properties`, that can contain both `Strings` and `Properties` objects as values. The motivation is that a `DBConnection` manager must contain several connection pools, each associated with its own Properties object.

In terms of functionality, Bergsten's design creates all connection pools at initialization and allows access to them only by names also created at initialization. We allow dynamic creation of new connection pools as needed, and they are accessed by their defining characteristics, i.e. `dbUrl`, username and password. This is related to the fact that, in Bergsten's design, connection pools are inner objects, and his program returns individual connections, while in our design, connection pools are separate objects managed by a `Cache`, and the program returns connection pools.

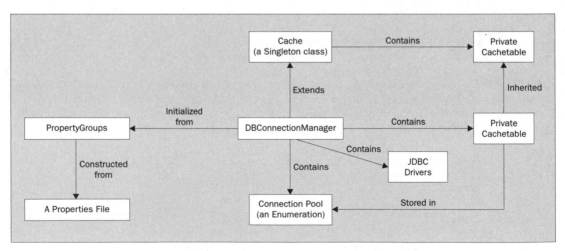

PropertyGroups

We would like to use the standard properties loading mechanism because it is so convenient; on the other hand, we would like to have `Properties`-like tables with sub-tables so we can have access by more than one key. `PropertyGroups` is the answer. It extends `Hashtable`, and it opens a stream to a properties file, just like the Properties class does. However, it has its own custom-designed `load()` method that parses the names of properties and creates sub-tables as indicated by those names.

The convention we follow is that if a property name has an underscore in it, then everything preceding the underscore is the name of a sub-table, and everything following the underscore is the property name for that sub-table. For instance, suppose we have the following property file:

```
alpha_zip=1111
beta_zip=2222
gamma_zip=3333
alpha_zap=uggle
simpleA=wing
beta_zap=wuggle
simpleB=zing
```

Our `load()` method of `PropertyGroups` would create three `Properties` objects, alpha, beta and gamma. The `alpha` `Properties` object will contain two name-value pairs, zip-1111 and zap-uggle; `beta` will also contain two pairs, and gamma will contain one. In addition to those `Properties` objects, the `PropertyGroups` object will also have two simple name-value pairs itself: simpleA-wing and simpleB-zing.

To access all those values, a `PropertyGroups` object has the following methods (we show the results they would return in our example):

```
Enumeration propertyKeys()                // [alpha,beta,gamma]
Enumeration simpleKeys()                  // [simpleA,simpleB]
Properties getProperties("alpha")         // a Properties object
String getProperty("simpleA")             // "wing"
String getProperty("simpleX", "defaultVal") // "defaultVal"
String getProperty("alpha", "defaultVal")  // "defaultVal"
```

It is an error to define a key both as a `Properties` name and as a simple property name. It is not an error to ask for a simple property whose name is the name of a `Properties` property: you simply get a null back.

We are not going to go through the code of `PropertyGroups` because it would distract us too much from the main topic. The code is available on the book's web site. Let's look at it in operation, with a sample `DBConnMgr.properties` file in mind:

```
admin.log=/C:/MyNa/DBadmin.log
err.log=/C:/MyNa/DBerr.log
dbUser=
dbPwd=
dbTimeout=100
dbInitSize=3
dbMaxSize=4
```

```
driver_sun.jdbc.odbc.JdbcOdbcDriver=true
phones_dbUrl=jdbc:odbc:PHONEBOOK
phones_dbUser=
phones_dbPwd=
phones_dbTimeout=200
phones_dbInitSize=2
phones_dbMaxSize=0
flowers_dbUrl=jdbc:odbc:BIRTHDAYS
flowers_dbUser=JaneSchmoe
flowers_dbPwd=v1ryS2cr3t4v5
flowers_dbTimeout=200
flowers_dbInitSize=1
flowers_dbMaxSize=3
```

As you can see, DBConnectionManager contains two of our Logger objects, which we are going to show in the code. It also contains default values at the top level, which can be used or overridden by properties of the same names at the lower level, within individual DBConnectionPool objects. (See the section on the DBConnectionPool class below.) If, during the run of the program, a need arises for a new connection pool, these defaults, rather than the properties file, will be used to start it up.

DBConnectionManager

The code of DBConnectionManager largely falls into two parts: initialization using PropertyGroups and overriding Cache variables and methods (there is some overlap and leftover, but mostly that's what it is).

Declarations and Constructor

```java
package MyNa.utils;
import java.util.*;
import java.sql.*;

public class DBConnectionManager extends Cache
{
    //singleton class

    static private PropertyGroups pG;
    static private Hashtable drivers;

    static Logger errLg, adminLg;

    static String dbUser = null, dbPwd = null, dbUrl = null; //defaults
    static int dbTimeout = 100, dbInitSize = 2, dbMaxSize = 3; // more defaults

    protected DBConnectionManager()throws Exception
    {
        // construct PropertyGroups from a properties file
        pG = new PropertyGroups("/DBConnMgr.properties");

        // extract simple string properties into class-level variables
        // use defaults as default arguments to getProperty()
        adminLg = new Logger(pG.getProperty("admin.log", "DBadmin.log"));
```

```
        errLg = new Logger(pG.getProperty("err.log", "DBerr.log"));
        dbUrl = pG.getProperty("dbUrl", dbUrl);
        dbUser = pG.getProperty("dbUser", dbUser);
        dbPwd = pG.getProperty("dbPwd",dbPwd);

        // use topIntProp() to extract and convert integer properties
        dbTimeout = topIntProp("dbTimeout", dbTimeout);
        dbMaxSize = topIntProp("dbMaxSize", dbMaxSize);
        dbInitSize = topIntProp("dbInitSize", dbInitSize);

        // get Properties objects from PropertyGroups
        // one for drivers, the rest for connection pools
        initDrivers(pG.getProperties("driver"));
        Enumeration pools = pG.propertyKeys();

        while(pools.hasMoreElements())
        {
            String name = (String)pools.nextElement();
            if(!"driver".equals(name))
            {
                initPool(name,pG.getProperties(name));
            }
        }
    }
```

The constructor calls `topIntProp()`, `initDrivers()` and `initPool()`. The `topIntProp()` method and its helper, `intKey()`, are just utilities that handle integer conversions and catch exceptions.

Integer Utilities

```
private int topIntProp(String key, int def) throws Exception
{
    String S = pG.getProperty(key);
    if(null == S)
    {
        return def;
    }
    return intKey(key, S);
}

private int intKey(String key, String intStr) throws Exception
{
    try
    {
        return Integer.parseInt(intStr);
    }
    catch(Exception ex)
    {
        String msg = "DBConnectionManager: integer key " + key
                + "='" + intStr + "'";
```

```
            errLg.logIt(msg);
            throw new Exception(msg);
        }
    }
```

`intKey()` is also called by `getInt()` that is used in pool initializations:

```
private int getInt(Properties p, String key, int def)throws Exception
{
    int res = def;
    // get string value from p; use pG.getProperty(key) as default
    String S = p.getProperty(key,pG.getProperty(key));
    if(null != S)
    {
        return intKey(key, S);
    }
    return res;
}
```

initPool()

This method is called in the constructor inside the loop that initializes all connection pools:

```
Enumeration pools = pG.propertyKeys();
while(pools.hasMoreElements())
{
    String name = (String)pools.nextElement();
    if(!"driver".equals(name))
    {
        initPool(name, pG.getProperties(name));
    }
}
```

As you can see, the arguments to `initPool()` are a name and a `Properties` object. The name is just used for administrative purposes; internally, a connection pool has a name constructed out of the `dbUrl` and user name. The method extracts all the information from `Properties`, creates a connection pool object, and stores it in the `Cachetable` object of `DBConnectionManager` (inherited from `Cache`, of course). It uses the `put()` method of `Cache` with three arguments: `dbUrl`, username and password:

```
private void initPool(String poolName, Properties props)
        throws Exception
{
    String url = props.getProperty("dbUrl", dbUrl);
    if(null == url || url.length() == 0)
    {
        String msg = "No dbUrl for connection pool " + poolName
                + " in " + props;
        errLg.logIt(msg);
        throw new Exception(msg);
    }
```

```
        // extract string and integer properties
        String usr = props.getProperty("dbUser", dbUser);
        String pwd = props.getProperty("dbPwd", dbPwd);
        int timeout = getInt(props, "dbTimeout", dbTimeout);
        int maxSize = getInt(props, "dbMaxSize", dbMaxSize);
        int initSize = getInt(props, "dbInitSize", dbInitSize);
        // create DBConnectionPool object with name url--usr
        DBConnectionPool cP = new DBConnectionPool(url + "--"
                + usr, url, usr, pwd, timeout, initSize, maxSize, errLg, adminLg);
        // the big step: store connection pool in Cachetable
        put(url, usr, pwd, cP);
        adminLg.logIt("created pool " + poolName + " for " + url + "--" + usr);
    }
```

initDrivers()

initDrivers(), with the help of addDriver(), creates a Properties object that holds JDBC drivers:

```
    protected void initDrivers(Properties drivernames) throws Exception
    {
        drivers = new Hashtable();
        Enumeration names = drivernames.keys();
        while(names.hasMoreElements())
        {
            addDriver((String)names.nextElement());
        }
    }

    public void addDriver(String name) throws Exception
    {
        if(null == name || name.length() == 0 || null != drivers.get(name))
        {
            return;
        }
        try
        {
            Driver driver = (Driver)Class.forName(name).newInstance();
            DriverManager.registerDriver(driver);
            drivers.put(name,driver);
            adminLg.logIt("Registered JDBC driver: " + name);
        }
        catch(Exception ex)
        {
            errLg.logIt("can't register JDBC driver: " + name);
            throw new Exception("can't register JDBC driver: " + name);
        }
    }
```

Now that we have connection pools, we want to be able to get one of them out.

getConnectionPool()

This method uses get() with three arguments. If get() comes back empty, a new connection pool is created, installed in the Cachetable and returned:

```
public DBConnectionPool getConnectionPool(String url,
        String usr, String pwd) throws Exception
{
    if(null == url || url.length() == 0)
    {
        url = dbUrl;
    }
    if(null == url || url.length() == 0)
    {
        throw new Exception("no dbUrl for connection pool");
    }
    DBConnectionPool cP = (DBConnectionPool)get(url, usr, pwd);
    if(null != cP)
    {
        adminLg.logIt("retrieved pool for " + url + "--" + usr);
    }
    if(null != cP)
    {
        return cP;
    }
    cP = new DBConnectionPool(url + "--" + usr, url, usr, pwd,
            dbTimeout, dbInitSize, dbMaxSize, errLg, adminLg);
    put(url, usr, pwd, cP);
    adminLg.logIt("created new pool " + url + "--" + usr);
    return cP;
}
```

The remaining methods override the methods of Cache, in familiar ways. Only the last of them, close(), presents interesting problems and will be commented upon.

Inherited Methods

```
public boolean freeItem(Object ob)
{
    // called by freeSpace; override if you need to do anything here.
    if(!(ob instanceof DBConnectionPool))
    {
        errLg.logIt("non-connectionpool in DBConnectionManager cache!" + ob);
        return false;
    }
    DBConnectionPool cP = (DBConnectionPool)ob;
    cP.close();
    return true;
}

private static Cache instance = null; // the one and only class instance
private static int clients = 0;       // how many are asking us?
```

```
protected void init()
{
    super.init();  // e.g., register, init loggers
}

public static synchronized Cache getInstance()
{
    try
    {
        if(null == instance)
        {
            instance = new DBConnectionManager();
        }
        clients++;
        adminLg.logIt("added new ConnectionManager instance");
        return instance;
    }
    catch(Exception ex)
    {
        ex.printStackTrace();
        return null;
    }
}

public static synchronized int freeInstance()
{
    if(null == instance)
    {
        return 0;
    }
    adminLg.logIt("freed instance of connectionmanager");
    clients--;
    if(clients == 0)
    {
        try
        {
            close(); // all gone, and the cache with it.
            adminLg.logIt("closed connection manager");
        }
        catch(Exception ex)
        {
            errLg.logIt("freeInstance ",ex);
        }
    }
    return clients;
}

public static synchronized boolean close()throws Exception
{
    clients = 0;
    while(0 == instance.freeSpace(10000)); // succeeded in freeing that many!
    {
        instance = null;
    }
    Enumeration enum = drivers.keys();
    while(enum.hasMoreElements())
```

```
    {
        String key = (String)enum.nextElement();
        try
        {
            DriverManager.deregisterDriver((Driver)drivers.get(key));
            adminLg.logIt("Deregistered driver " + key);
        }
        catch(Exception ex)
        {
            String msg = "failed to deregister driver " + key;
            errLg.logIt(msg);
            throw new Exception(msg); // or return false, or just skip it
        }
    }
    return true;
}

} // end of DBDriverManager
```

And the last remaining class for connection pooling is, of course, `ConnectionPool`.

The ConnectionPool Class

We maintain unused connections in a `Queue`: a free connection is retrieved from the head of the queue, and freed connections are added to the end of the queue so that they all have a chance to be used. (In a stack, those closer to the bottom would often time out before getting a chance to serve.)

The most difficult part of connection pooling is what to do when your connections have run out: you have to put the request for connection on a timer so it wakes up after a timeout interval and tries again. This is what the timeout variable is for. The rest of the variables are fairly straightforward and explained in code comments:

Imports and Declarations

```
package MyNa.utils;

import java.util.Date; // to set the wakeup moment as current date+timeout
import java.sql.Connection;
import java.sql.SQLException;
import java.sql.DriverManager;

public class DBConnectionPool
{
    int maxSize;  // maximum size of pool
    int initSize; // initial size of pool
    int inUse;    // how many are in use
    int timeout;
    // String variables from PropertyGroups
    String poolName;
    String dbUrl; String dbUser; String dbPwd;
    Queue Q; // the queue of connections
    Logger errLg; Logger adminLg; // two loggers
```

Constructor and Initialization

The constructor initializes the variables and calls `preload()`, which creates the initial number of connections, itself calling on `newConnection()` to create each one.

```
public DBConnectionPool(String nm, String url, String usr, String pwd,
        int timeout, int initSize, int maxSize,
        Logger er, Logger adm) throws Exception
{
    poolName = nm;
    dbUrl = url; dbUser = usr; dbPwd = pwd;
    this.maxSize = maxSize;
    this.initSize = initSize;
    this.timeout = timeout;
    errLg = er; // same as in DBConnectionManager
    adminLg = adm;
    Q = new Queue();
    inUse = 0;
    adminLg.logIt("DBConnectionPool init for " + poolName);
    preload(initSize);
}

public void preload(int N) throws Exception
{
    for(int i = 0; i < N; i++)
    {
        Connection con = newConnection();
        if(null == con)
        {
            throw new Exception("connection failure in " + dbUrl);
        }
        Q.append(con); // append to the end of queue
    }
}

private Connection newConnection()
{
    adminLg.logIt("new connection for pool " + poolName);
    try
    {
        if(null == dbUser || dbUser.length() == 0)
        {
            return DriverManager.getConnection(dbUrl);
        }
        else
        {
            return DriverManager.getConnection(dbUrl, dbUser, dbPwd);
        }
    }
    catch(SQLException ex)
    {
        errLg.logIt("no newConnection for " + dbUrl, ex);
        return null;
    }
}
```

Getting a Connection

Getting a connection is a two-step process: first you pop it off the queue, and, if successful, you actually get it; if not, you try to create a new one, and if successful, you get it; otherwise, you return null:

```
public synchronized Connection getConnection()
{
    Connection con = popConnection();
    if(null == con)
    {
        if(maxSize < 0 || inUse < maxSize)
        {
            con = newConnection();
        }
    }
    if(null != con)
    {
        inUse++;
    }
    return con; // can be null
}
```

The `popConnection()` method tries to pop the first available connection that has not been closed. If a closed connection is found on the queue, both logs register the event and the loop continues until an open connection is found or the queue is finished:

```
public synchronized Connection popConnection()
{

    while(!Q.isEmpty())
    {

        try
        {
            Connection con = (Connection)Q.next();
            if(!con.isClosed())
            {
                return con; // might be closed by dbase
            }
            adminLg.logIt("REJECT: connection in " + poolName + " was closed");
        }
        catch(Exception ex)
        {
            errLg.logIt("DBConnectionPool.popConnection: ", ex);
        } // continue with loop

    } // end of while loop

    return null;

}
```

From the outside, we can call three `getConnection` methods: `getConnection()`, `getConnection(int timeout)`, or `getConnectionTimeout()`. The first has just been covered. The second tries the first, and, in case of failure, goes to sleep:

```
public Connection getConnection(int timeout)
{
    long waitUntil = new Date().getTime() + timeout;
    Connection con;
    while(null == (con=getConnection()) // try to get a connection
            && waitUntil > new Date().getTime())
    {
        try
        {
            wait(timeout);
        }
        catch(InterruptedException ex){}
    }
    return con;
}
```

Finally, the third `getConnection` method is a one-liner that calls the second with the default value of timeout:

```
public Connection getConnectionTimeout()
{
    getConnection(timeout);
    // timeout is class-level variable set at construction
}
```

close() and freeConnection()

The `close()` method, surprise-surprise, closes up:

```
public synchronized void close()
{
    Connection con;
    while(!Q.isEmpty())
    {
        if(null == (con=popConnection()))
        {
            continue; // already closed
        }
        try
        {
            con.close();
            adminLg.logIt("closed connection in " + poolName);
        }
        catch(SQLException ex)
        {
            errLg.logIt("err in closing " + poolName, ex);
        }
    }
```

```
        if(inUse > 0)
        {
            errLg.logIt("close " + poolName + " with " + inUse
                    + " still connected");
        }
    }
```

Next, the `freeConnection()` method puts the connection on the end of the queue and uses the `notifyAll()` method of the `Object` class to notify every waiting thread in its thread group that something has happened and it may be time to wake up:

```
public synchronized void freeConnection(Connection con)
{
    Q.append(con);
    inUse--;
    notifyAll(); // wake up anyone waiting in getConnection(timeout);
}

}// end of ConnectionPool class begun some pages back
```

This completes the code for connection pooling. We can finally go back to `DBHandler` and review the three methods that make use of it.

Use of Connection Pooling in DBHandler

The three methods involved are presented below. Recall that `DBHandler` has a `DBConnectionManager` variable and a `DBConnectionPool` variable:

```
protected Connection getConnection()throws SQLException
{
    return checkConnection();
}

protected Connection checkConnection() throws SQLException
{
    if(null != theConnection)
    {
        return theConnection;
    }
    try
    {
        if(null == dbCM)
        {
            dbCM = (DBConnectionManager)DBConnectionManager.getInstance();
        }
        dbCM.addDriver(driverName);
        if(null == dbCP)
        {
            dbCP = dbCM.getConnectionPool(dbUrl, theUser, thePwd);
        }
        theConnection = dbCP.getConnection();
        if(null == theConnection)
        {
            throw new SQLException(dbUrl + ", driver " + driverName
                    + " null connect");
        }
```

```
            return theConnection;
        }
        catch(Exception ex)
        {
            throw new SQLException(dbUrl + ", driver " + driverName +
                    " failed to connect " + ex);
        }

    }


    protected void freeConnection()
    {
        // called on close or gotosleep.
        if(null == theConnection)
        {
            return;
        }
        dbCP.freeConnection(theConnection);// call ConnectionPool method
        theConnection = null;
    }
```

As you can see, `DBHandler` just calls `DBConnectionManager` and `DBConnectionPool` for all its connection needs.

Conclusions

This has been a long chapter. It was both an exercise in system design and a lot of practical, down-to-earth code development. It is our hope that whether or not you find a use for `QShell` (or its XML version), that `Cache`, `PropertyGroups` and perhaps our entire connection pooling mechanism can join other tools in your toolbox.

Our design goal was to separate, as cleanly as possible, the skills required for different components of the system, and to make the interfaces between the components accessible to a competent user (the system administrator). For instance, we tried to separate out code from the presentation in the output component not only because it is a good design principle that makes life easier for the programmer, but also because two very different people are likely to work on code and presentation, and we want to make their cooperation as effortless as possible.

In terms of Java coverage, we have done more work with servlets, including initialization parameters and session tracking. We have covered a useful ECS package and introduced the first example of JSP. In contrast to JSP, we have started developing template files that use our simple `<myna:SUBST>` mini-language. In the last section, we completed our work on `DBHandler` by developing a substantial connection pooling component that can be used in many different contexts. As part of this component, we developed two classes, `Cache` and `PropertyGroups`, which can be considered truly general-purpose utilities.

In the next chapter, we will further develop that mini-language in the context of a general discussion of mini-languages and their role in programming. This will complete the `QShell` code. At the same time, much of what we say there will be directly relevant for the XML part of the book.

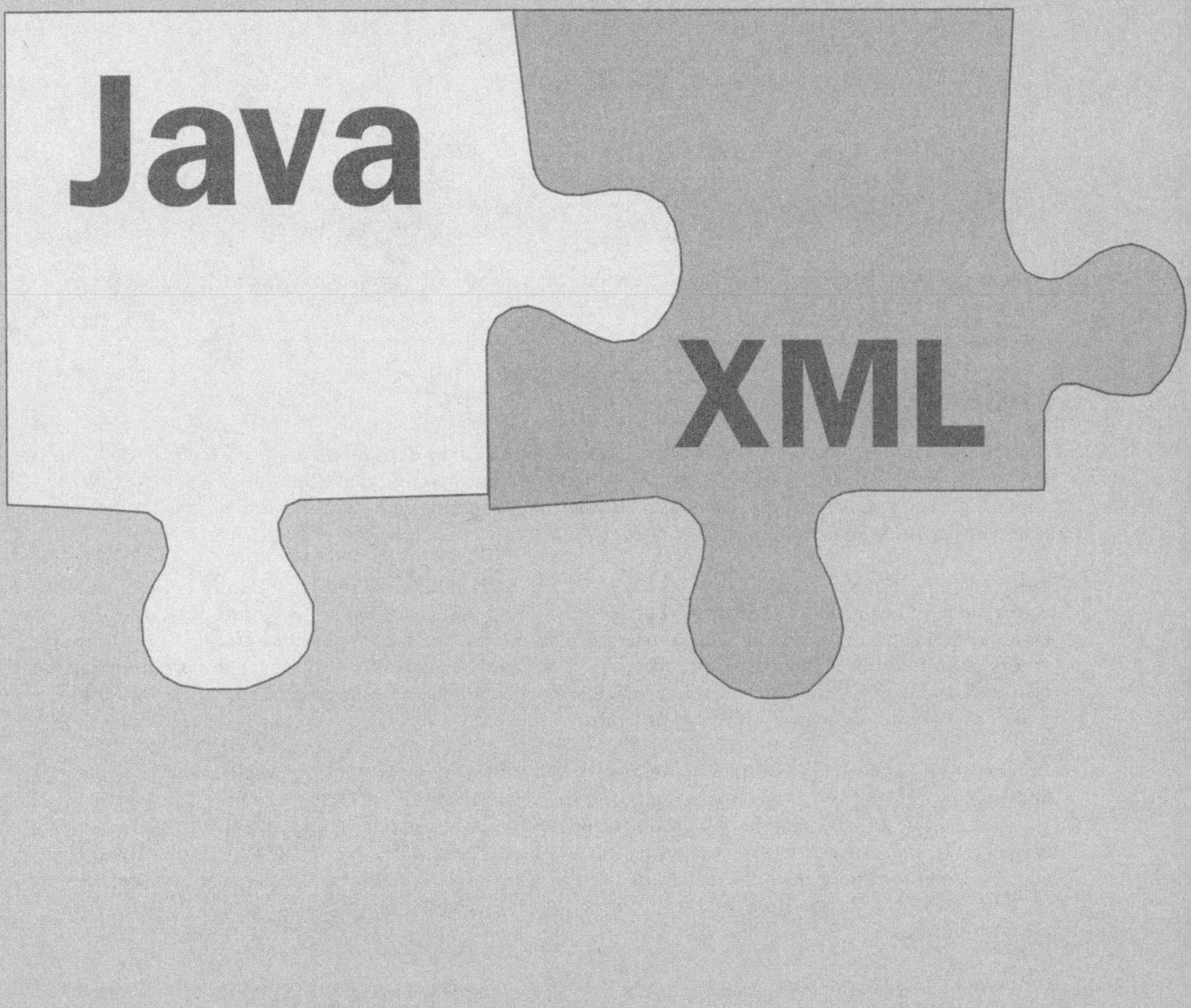
Java
XML

4

Languages, Grammars and Parsers

This chapter is the linchpin of the book: it completes the QShell application of the first part of the book, it introduces the ideas that are essential for understanding XML, and it shows how to implement a mini-language. On the one hand, XML will make the latter less necessary because if you build your mini-languages using XML, you don't have to write a parser for them. On the other hand, it is our firm conviction that in order to make good use of XML, XML DTDs and XML parsers, it is essential that you work your way through a grammar for a formal language and a parser that's based on it.

In the preceding chapter, as part of the QShell functionality, we used template files with <myna:SUBST> tags in order to produce a control page for the user input. We did not explain how the tags worked but promised to do so in this chapter. Before we get to that explanation, we're going to add another level of flexibility to QShell by allowing template files also to be used in the query output and in the initialization files. This will require three more tags, but the overall explanation will remain the same. It boils down to this: we're going to treat template files containing our custom tags as a formal language and write a grammar, a parser and a lexical analyzer for it.

This may seem like a lot of heavy machinery, but the payoff is worth it. First, a little background in formal languages and grammars will be very useful when we get to XML because XML is, in effect, a mechanism for defining formal languages and grammars for them. Second, a grammar, a parser and a lexical analyzer work together to implement a mini-language. Creating a mini-language for a set of related tasks is a well-known and very powerful design pattern, and worth knowing.

We'll conclude this chapter by showing that even the small mini-language that we will have implemented is flexible enough to create a variety of three-tier applications without any application-specific Java programming. We illustrate the point by building a small shopping cart application using only an initialization file and template files.

In outline this chapter will proceed as follows:

❑ Template files for query output: what's involved and some examples

❑ Start detour: formal languages and grammars, with examples from English and earlier chapters of the book

❑ End detour: template files as a formal language, and a grammar for it

❑ The parser, the parse tree and the lexical analyzer, implemented as `ParseSubst`, `ParseTree` and `MyNaLex`

❑ The payoff: a shopping cart application without any Java code that is specific to the application – all the application-specific information is in the `.ini` file and the template pages for the application

To view the shopping cart, point your browser at `MyNa\xml\QShellLogin.htm` (assuming you've downloaded the code from the Wrox web site). You will see a form with three fields: username, password, and a SELECT box with four options.

Select the "basic shopcart" option. Log in as Joe Schmoe, password JSchmoe. The application assumes the context of a college bookstore. Since Joe is a registered student, you will be able to log in and view the books for those courses in which Joe has registered. You can review Joe's shopping cart and add or delete items to it:

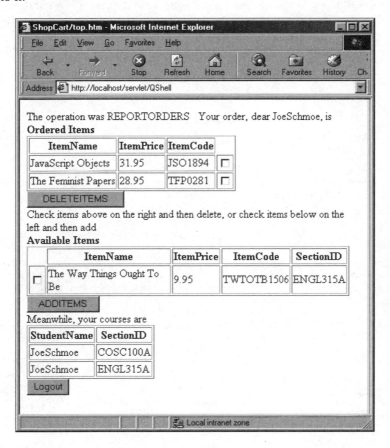

Template Files for Query Output

In the preceding chapter, we used template files with <myna:SUBST> tags in order to produce the control file for the user input. In this chapter, we're going to add another level of flexibility to QShell by allowing template files for query output. The page designer for a three-tier application can create a custom page for each query, using the same <myna:SUBST> tag, and also <myna:SUBSTROW> or <myna:SUBSTROWLIST> tags for query results. A simple query output page may look like this:

```
<HTML>
  <HEAD>
    <TITLE>LOOKUP.htm</TITLE>
  </HEAD>

<BODY>

<myna:SUBST>
  For this query, the user was |dbUser|, the requested operation was
  |dbOperation|, and its query string was:

  <P>|dbQueryString|</P>

  The number of parameters was |NumberOfParameters| (which ought to be "1"),
  and the value of parameter 1 was |Parameter1|. The value of parameter 2, as
  you might expect, is "|Parameter2|". The template file (this file) is
  |templateFile|. All these values come from the Env object that was passed
  as an argument to the wrapEnvPage() method of HTMLWrapper.
</myna:SUBST>

Now, let's look at a result table for that query.

<myna:SUBST>
  <TABLE BORDER="1"><TR><TH>
  |FieldName1|</TH><TH>|FieldName2|
  </TH></TR>
</myna:SUBST>
<myna:SUBSTROWLIST>
  <TR><TD>|FieldValue1|</TD><TD>|FieldValue2|</TD></TR>
</myna:SUBSTROWLIST>
</TABLE>
This table of responses was filled in by substituting values from the query
result for FieldValue place holders.

</BODY>

</HTML>
```

When used with our Phonebook application, this page produces the following output:

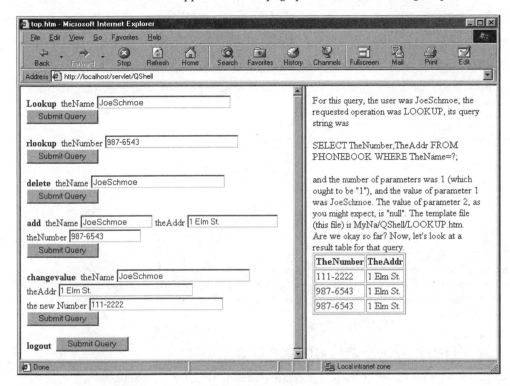

The Mini-Language of Substitutions

Our template files use a mini-language to produce dynamic output without programming. The language consists of the following elements:

- ❑ four tags that look like HTML tags, but with a `myna:` prefix to avoid name conflicts
- ❑ one attribute, `delim`, shared by all four tags
- ❑ a predefined vocabulary of identifiers

Here is how a template file is processed. All text outside the four mini-language tags is left untouched. Within a mini-language tag (i.e. between one of our custom tags and its matching end tag), if a predefined identifier is found between delimiters then it is replaced by the value of that identifier in the "current environment", i.e. a dictionary-like object that contains values indexed by names. (As you might have guessed, we'll implement it as an `Env` object.) The entire substitution process assumes that there is always a current environment; the four mini-language tags differ in where that environment comes from:

- ❑ the `<myna:SUBST>` tag simply assumes that there is a current environment for substitutions

- ❑ the `<myna:SUBSTROW>` tag simply takes the next record from the database and makes it the current environment

- ❑ the `<myna:SUBSTROWLIST>` tag runs a query and uses each row of the result, in turn, as the current environment – this tag is, in effect, a loop through the result set

- ❑ the `<myna:SUBSTERR>` tag is for the page designer to output error messages, if such are desired

The predefined vocabulary of identifiers consists of these items:

- ❑ `dbServlet`

- ❑ `dbUser`, `dbOperation` and `dbQueryString`

- ❑ `FieldName1`, `FieldName2`, ...

- ❑ `FieldValue1`, `FieldValue2`, ...

This is a small language for a narrowly defined purpose, but it covers a large part of database interactions while completely insulating the page designer from programming concepts, such as function calls, assignments or loops. It does assume that the page designer is familiar with the structure of the database, however.

Code for Query Output Templates

The extra flexibility provided by output template files requires only one change in the code of Query3, specifically in the doQuery() method. In Chapter 3, doQuery() called wrapEnvResultPage() to send query results, as a string matrix, to HtmlWrapper. We now replace that output call with three new lines of code, so it looks as below. You may want to review doQuery() from Chapter 3, before proceeding:

```
public void doQuery(HttpSession sess, Env env, HtmlWrapper W)
        throws SQLException, IOException
{
    dbH = (DBHandler) sess.getValue("theDBHandler");
    if(dbH == null)
    {
        W.wrapPage("doPost Failure", "No dbhandler in sess " + sess.getId());
    }
    else
    {
        Env result = dbH.getQueryResult(env);      // use DBHandler
        setStr(env, "templateFile", fP, env.getStr("dbOperation") + ".htm");
        RowSequence rows = dbH.getQueryRows(env);
        W.wrapRowsPage(rows, env); // again the Env defines output.
    }
}
```

The first of the new lines sets the template file name in the environment. The default, which can be overridden by the submitted request, is to concatenate `filePath` with the name of the query as the file name and `.htm` as the extension. The second line runs the query and returns the result as a sequence of Env objects, each corresponding to a row of the result set. (We discussed such `RowSequences` in Chapter 2. A query that returns an integer results in a `RowSequence` that contains a single Env containing a single name-value pair.) Finally, the last line sends the `RowSequence` to output using `wrapRowsPage()`.

`HtmlWrapper.wrapRowsPage()` is very similar to `wrapEnvPage()` that you have already seen in Chapter 3. Both methods are listed below; both pass all the work to (two different versions of) a general `fileSubst()` method in the `MiscFile` utility class:

```
// from HtmlWrapper
public void wrapRowsPage(RowSequence dbRows, Env rqEnv)
{
    String fName = rqEnv.getStr("templateFile");
    String fValue = null;
    try
    {
        fValue = MiscFile.fileSubst(fName, dbRows);
    }
    catch(Exception ex)
    {
        ex.printStackTrace(out);
        return;
    }
    out.println(fValue);
    out.close();
}

public void wrapEnvPage(Env E)
{
    String fName = E.getStr("templateFile");
    String fValue = null;
    try
    {
        fValue = MiscFile.fileSubst(fName, E);
    }
    catch(Exception ex)
    {
        ex.printStackTrace(out);
        return;
    }
    out.println(fValue);
    out.close();
}
```

The two versions of `fileSubst()` differ in that the second argument of one takes an Env argument and the other a `RowSequence` argument. That difference corresponds to the distinction between the `<myna:SUBST>` tag that uses the current environment for substitutions, and the `<myna:SUBSTROW>` and `<myna:SUBSTROWLIST>` tags that expect to retrieve their substitution environment from a `RowSequence` of environments. Usually, the source of the `RowSequence` is a result set, but it doesn't have to be, and nothing in the code depends on where the environments come from. They can just as well come from an XML file, or from the properties of a Java bean.

Both versions of `fileSubst()` are brief because they pass all the work to the `ParseSubst` class. More precisely, they read the template file into a string buffer, then use that string buffer to construct a `ParseSubst` object. That object performs all substitutions and writes the resulting text to a string:

```
// from MiscFile
public static String fileSubstByTag(String fName, RowSequence rowSeq)
        throws Exception
{
    StringBuffer sBuff = fileToStringBuffer(fName);
    if(sBuff == null)
    {
        throw new Exception("no file for " + fName);
    }
    ParseSubst pS = new ParseSubst(sBuff);
    return pS.toString(rowSeq);
}

public static String fileSubst(String fName, Env env)
        throws Exception
{
    StringBuffer sBuff = fileToStringBuffer(fName);
    ParseSubst pS = new ParseSubst(sBuff);
    return pS.toString(env);
}
```

As you can see from the `return.pS.*` lines in the above code listing, the `Env-RowSequence` duality continues in `ParseSubst`, which has two `toString()` methods. `ParseSubst`, at last, is a substantial piece of code that introduces new ideas: a formal language and a parser for it. In brief, we treat template files with `<myna:SUBST>` tags as a mini-language and process them accordingly. Before we look at `ParseSubst` (and the accompanying `ParseTree` and `SubstLexAnalyzer`), we will go over the notion of a formal language in a general way, using a simpler example. This material will be useful not only for the code of `ParseSubst`, but also for understanding the workings of JavaServer Pages and XML.

Formal Languages and Grammars

A formal language is simply a set of strings. What makes it a language is a set of grammar rules that tell us which strings are in the language (grammatical) and which are not (ungrammatical). In the case of a programming language, ungrammatical strings are **programs** that do not compile. In XML literature, we call them invalid **documents**. In a natural language like English, when we approach it as a formal language for which we want to construct a (formal) grammar, we talk of grammatical and ungrammatical **sentences**. Whether we call it a program, a document or a sentence, a grammatical string has to be produced by grammar rules according to this simple (meta) rule:

> **To produce (or derive) a grammatical string using grammar rules, start with a designated start-symbol and use the rules to expand it.**

More precisely, a grammar of a formal language defines four things:

- ❏   a vocabulary out of which the strings of the language are constructed (**terminal vocabulary**)
- ❏   another vocabulary that is used to formulate grammar rules (**non-terminal vocabulary**)
- ❏   the rules themselves, also known as **productions**. Every rule has a left-hand side and a right-hand side. The meaning of a rule is that you can substitute its right-hand side for its left hand side
- ❏   a designated start symbol

There is usually another whole component of **lexical rules** that specify how the terminal vocabulary is constructed out of an alphabet of characters, but we will disregard this complication until after we look at some examples.

English Examples

Let's consider some examples from English. English has an element called **Noun Phrase**, **NP** for short. Some examples of NPs are:

- ❏   "bread"
- ❏   "sour milk"
- ❏   "a glass"
- ❏   "a tall clean transparent glass"
- ❏   "the central station"

Here, bread, milk, glass, and station are all nouns (N); sour, tall, and central are adjectives (A); the words "a" and "the" are called **articles** (Art) in grammar books. We can cover our examples with these rules:

```
1. NP-> Art NPWA
2. NP-> NPWA
3. NPWA-> A NPWA
4. NPWA-> N
5. Art-> a
6. Art-> the
7. N->bread
8. N->milk
9. A->sour
...
```

Read these rules as follows (each explanation is followed by an example)

- ❑ **Rule 1:** a noun phrase may consist of an article and a noun-phrase-without-an- article (NPWA) (e.g. "a glass")

- ❑ **Rule 2:** it may have no article at all (e.g. "sour milk")

- ❑ **Rule 3:** NPWA can add any number of adjectives (or no adjectives at all) to its beginning using a **recursive rule** that defines NPWA in terms of itself. As a result, an NP (with or without an article) can have any number of adjectives in it (e.g. "a tall clean transparent glass" or "crunchy wholesome bread")

- ❑ **Rule 4:** sooner or later, after producing zero or more adjectives, NPWA has to become a noun

- ❑ **Rules 5-9:** articles, nouns and adjectives rewrite themselves as lexical items

In these productions, the words "bread", "sour", "the", and so on, are the **terminal symbols**, or **terminals**, because we cannot re-write them any further: there are no rules that have them on the left-hand side. They form the first of the two vocabularies of the grammar. The symbols NP, NPWA, N, A, and Art are **non-terminal symbols**, or **non-terminals**, because we can re-write them: there are rules that have them on the left-hand side. They form the second of the two vocabularies of the grammar.

We can now repeat the definition of a grammatical sentence (or a program that compiles, or a valid XML document): a sentence is grammatical if it can be produced by a series of rewritings such that

- ❑ it starts with the start symbol
- ❑ it uses grammar rules to get from one rewriting to the next
- ❑ it does not contain any non-terminals

Such rewritings are called **derivations**. For a certain kind of grammar (we'll explain what kind it is in a moment), derivations can be neatly described by a tree structure which is called, sensibly enough, a **derivation tree**.

Grammars and Parsers

One way to decide whether a string is grammatical or not is to start deriving all possible strings until we get the one we want. If the grammar is such that the left-hand side of a rule is always shorter than the right-hand side then we can use this method and stop either when the string is found or we start getting strings that are longer than our string. Even for such grammars, the method is not very practical.

> **What usually happens instead is that the string is submitted to a program called a parser that checks the string for grammatical correctness (and perhaps other conditions).**

Very commonly the parser operates by running the grammar rules in reverse, from right-hand side to left-hand side, until the string is collapsed into a single non-terminal (the start symbol) or an error is found.

Context-Free and Context-Sensitive Grammars

Look back at our little grammar for English noun phrases. All its rules share the property: the left-hand side consists of a single non-terminal symbol. It doesn't have to be the case: one can imagine a grammar for pulp fiction with rules like:

```
his A muscles->his bulging muscles
```

The rules state: in the context "his __ muscles" always re-write A as "bulging". Grammars that allow such "context-sensitive" rewritings are called **context-sensitive grammars**. Grammars that allow only a single non-terminal **and nothing else** on the left-hand side of a rule are called **context-free**.

Context-free grammars are great. They have these nice properties: their derivations are completely described by tree structures, and their parsers are easy to write, much easier than parsers for context-sensitive grammars. In fact, there are programs that take a context-free grammar on input and output the code for the corresponding parser. Such parser-generators are called, for historical reasons, compiler compilers, and there are a lot of them by now. The earliest of the famous ones is YACC (Yet Another Compiler Compiler) produced at Bell labs where a lot of compiler theory was invented. The GNU version of YACC is called Bison. There are several Java versions, including Sun-sponsored JavaCC, to be found at `http://www.suntest.com/JavaCC/`.

A Little History

Formal grammars in general, and especially context-free and context-sensitive grammars, were first studied by a linguist, Noam Chomsky, in the 1950s. He observed that a good deal of English grammar could be described by context-free rules. (He also observed that a lot more of the English grammar could be described by simple transformations of context-free rules, which is why his theory was called "transformational grammar".) In collaboration with other people he proved several important facts about formal grammars, such as:

- ❑ There are languages that can be fully described by a context-sensitive grammar, but for which there can be no possible context-free grammar

- ❑ You can parse a sentence in a context-free language in one pass from left to right without lookahead using a stack. The result of the parse is a tree structure

Chomsky invented the notation for grammars that we used in the examples above: they are said to be in "Chomsky Normal Form". In the 1960s, Chomsky's work influenced John Backus at IBM who realized that programming languages are mostly context-free. He used context-free grammars to describe the syntax of programs, and developed what we now call the BNF notation. BNF initially meant "Backus Normal Form", until another gentleman, Peter Naur, revised it, and acquired the middle letter of the acronym for himself. It has since been further revised and extended, so nowadays programming language specifications, including the XML specification, are written in EBNF, Extended Backus-Naur Form.

EBNF Notation

The two most noticeable differences between EBNF and the Chomsky-style rules are:

- ❏ EBNF uses : : = instead of ->
- ❏ EBNF combines several rules into one by using regular-expression notation

For example, consider again the rules we used to describe our small sample of English noun phrases. In summary, they say that an English NP can start with one or zero articles followed by any number (including zero) of adjectives, followed by a noun. In EBNF, this would be written as a single rule:

```
NP ::= Art? A* N
```

Even if you are not familiar with regular expressions, you must have seen ? and * used as "wild-card characters" in filenames; the usage is basically the same: ? means "0 or 1 repetitions", and * means "0 or any number of repetitions".

Historically, it so happened that linguists continued with the Chomsky Normal Form, while EBNF was mostly used to write rules like these:

```
Statement ::= SingleStatement | CompoundStatement
SingleStatement ::= AssignmentStatement | WhileStatement | DoStatement | ....
CompoundStatement ::= "{" Statement* "}"
WhileStatement ::= "while" "(" Expression ")" Statement
DoStatement    ::= "do" Statement "while" "(" Expression ")"
```

An Example: the .ini File as a Formal Language

Our initialization file format has certain constraints that can be expressed by context-free grammar rules. We'll try several versions, to explore the power and limitations of context-free grammars. Think of these rules as leading to a validating parser that would help system administrators to catch errors in their initialization files. Such a parser could, in turn, be incorporated into an authoring tool for system administrators that they could use interactively to create initialization files. The tool would provide both a fill-in-the-blanks interface and an error checker based on a validating parser (based on our grammar rules).

The easiest constraint to express is that a .ini file must have an even number of lines. Here are the rules:

```
IniFile  ::= LinePair+
LinePair ::= NameLine ValLine
NameLine ::= Text EOLN
ValLine  ::= Text EOLN
Text     ::= any text as long as it doesn't contain EOLN
EOLN     ::= LF | CR | LF CR
```

These rules say that a .ini file consists of one or more LinePairs, where each LinePair consists of a NameLine and a ValLine. Although we give them names that are indicative of their function (they contain a name and a value, respectively) we don't really say anything about their content beyond the simple fact that they consist of some text followed by a system-dependent end-of-line marker EOLN. The last two rules are **lexical rules** whose right-hand sides show the terminal elements, actual characters or patterns of characters that constitute Text or EOLN. We show terminal elements in bold. In the case of Text, we have inserted a descriptive comment instead of a regular expression that would express the same meaning in a formal and precise way.

Our .ini file (or IniFile) certainly has more structure than this first version of its grammar suggests. We can capture more of it by making the grammar more detailed:

```
IniFile ::=
    FileTitlePair dbDriverPair dbNamePair dbQueriesPair dbQueryPair+ templFilePair
FileTitlePair ::= FileTitle EOLN Text EOLN
dbDriverPair  ::= dbDriver EOLN Text EOLN
dbNamePair    ::= dbName EOLN Text EOLN
dbQueriesPair ::= dbQueries EOLN CommaList EOLN
dbQueryPair   ::= QueryName EOLN SQLText EOLN
templFilePair ::= templateFile EOLN FileName EOLN
Text          ::= any text as long as it doesn't contain EOLN
CommaList     ::= comma-separated list of QueryNames
QueryName     ::= a single word in capital letters
FileName      ::= a file name with .htm or .html extension
SQLText       ::= an SQL query with quesion marks for some parameters
```

Instead of an undifferentiated LinePair, this version of the grammar has non-terminals for several different kinds of line pairs (FileTitlePair, dbDriverPair, etc.). It specifies the order in which those line pairs must appear in the file, and for several line pairs it specifies the precise terminal element that must appear in them. It also introduces several varieties of Text: CommaList, QueryName, FileName and SQLText.

Grammar Rules, Semantic Constraints and Lexical Rules

The next step in improving our grammar would be to replace the comments in italics with something more precise. We can relatively easily do that for all of them except the last one. Providing formal specification for the last line would mean writing a SQL grammar, clearly an unreasonable thing to do. So, we're going to replace the last line with the one that simply says:

```
SQLText ::= Text
```

However, it still makes sense to have the SQLText non-terminal, because we can use it to specify the rule informally, as a **semantic constraint**. Attached to the grammar as comments, such constraints explain the meaning of its elements to the human reader. Semantic constrains will not be captured by automatic parser generators, but a manually-produced parser can incorporate them.

For a specific example, consider another semantic constraint on initialization files that our grammar has not yet captured: the comma-separated list of query names contains those and only those names that appear on the first lines of dbQueryPairs (the grammar rule that defines query name and SQL text combinations – see the IniFile grammar code above). Here's the corresponding portion of the .ini file from Chapter 3:

```
dbQueries
LOOKUP,RLOOKUP,DELETE,CHANGEVALUE,ADD
LOOKUP
SELECT TheNumber,TheAddr FROM PHONEBOOK WHERE TheName=?;
RLOOKUP
SELECT TheName FROM PHONEBOOK WHERE TheNumber=?;
DELETE
DELETE FROM PHONEBOOK WHERE TheName=?;
CHANGEVALUE
UPDATE PHONEBOOK SET TheNumber=? WHERE TheName=? AND TheAddr=?;
ADD
INSERT INTO PHONEBOOK VALUES(?,?,?);
```

This semantic constraint can easily be captured by a piece of Java code that processes the file, even though it would be difficult to describe it declaratively in a grammar rule. As a general principle, if a constraint can be expressed by a context-free rule then it's good to do so because it will be captured and enforced by the general parsing process, and programming it will not require any *ad hoc* procedures (apart from the general and well-understood process of transforming grammar rules into parser code). On the other hand, there are borderline situations when the tradeoffs are not so clear.

Going back to our grammar, the rest of the rules that contain comments are not semantic constraints but lexical rules that can be formalized using regular expressions:

```
QueryName::= [A-Z]+
CommaList ::= ^QueryName(,QueryName)*$
Text      ::= [^LF CR]+
FileName  ::= ^[A-Za-z_][A-Za-z0-9]+\.[hH][tT][mM]([lL])?
```

The `FileName` production is not to be taken too seriously: it's way too restrictive, allowing only ASCII alphanumeric characters and the underscore. The right way to do it would be to define several classes of characters (such as letters and digits) and define allowable names in terms of those classes. That's the way it's done in the XML Recommendation: peeking ahead, we find (productions are numbered):

```
[4]  NameChar ::=  Letter | Digit | '.' | '-' | '_' | ':' | CombiningChar |
                   Extender
[5]  Name ::=  (Letter | '_' | ':') (NameChar)*
[6]  Names ::=  Name (S Name)*
[7]  Nmtoken ::=  (NameChar)+
```

Name character `NameChar` is defined as `Letter` or `Digit` or `CombiningChar` or `Extender` (plus the three specific characters '.', '-' and '_'). These character classes are defined in Appendix B of the XML 1.0 Specification (see *Appendix H*), where `Letter` is additionally defined as `BaseChar` or `Ideographic`, and those are listed individually or in contiguous stretches. With character classes defined, `Name` and the more restrictive `NameToken` are defined. In a later `Namespaces Recommendation`, in which the colon character was assigned the special role of separating the `Namespace` prefix from the name proper, a new category of names, `NCName` (No-Colon-Name), was defined. As the label suggests, `NCName` is exactly like `Name`, except it does not contain colons. We'll have much more to say about all this in the next chapter.

This completes the description of the `.ini` file as a formal language. The next step would be to write a parser for it. We are not going to do that for `.ini` files. Instead, we will give a complete formal language treatment to our template files, including a grammar, a parser and a lexical analyzer. Writing a parser and a lexical analyzer for `.ini` files is a much easier task.

Template Files as a Formal Language

We are going to approach our template files as a formal language: we'll write a grammar for it, then a parser based on that grammar. This will show a common technique for parser writing called **recursive descent parsing**.

The Grammar

The first rule of the grammar says that our document consists of any number of pieces, where each piece is either Text or Subst followed by more text:

```
Root ::= (Subst | T)*
```

Here T can be any sequence of characters, including the empty string, that does not contain any of our four mini-language tags. This rule is easy to say and easy to program in a parser but rather hard to express as a regular expression, so we won't bother writing it out in a formal way. Nor shall we write into the grammar the additional constraint that T elements are always of maximal length: the parser will never produce two T elements in a row. It's possible to have a file which starts with Subst, or which consists of Subst, Subst, Subst, T, Subst. It is not, however, possible to have a file which consists of Subst, T, T; the lexical analyzer would produce the two T's joined as one.

We could express this precisely by saying

```
Root ::= T? (Subst T?)*
```

This says that the document may optionally begin with a text block; after that, it consists of zero or more Subst elements, each optionally followed by a text block. Our Root rule, however, does not guarantee that there will be no sequence T, T, T, T; we only know this because we know the specification of the lexical analyzer, which takes longest-matches. It's a common way to do matching.

The Subst Production

The most involved rule is Subst. To make it more manageable, we'll use two supporting productions. One defines S as a sequence of zero or more space characters. Space characters are Space, Tab, LF and CR – the hexadecimals 20, 9, A and D:

```
S ::= (#x20|#x9|#xA|#xD)+
```

The other supporting production defines Eq as an equal sign, possibly with spaces around it:

```
Eq ::= S? "=" S?
```

In addition to these abbreviations, we're using a non-context free convention in the rule: we attach the = character to some of the non-terminals used in the rule to indicate that they must have the same value in the right-hand side. For instance, in the sample line below, we want to make sure that the same string is used as a value of the delim attribute and in all the delimited sequences that need to be processed:

151

```
<myna:SUBST delim="$">some text $FieldName1$ more text </myna:SUBST>
Subst ::=
  "<myna:" =SubTag (S "delim" Eq  =D)? S? ">" T (=D TnD =D T)* "</" =SubTag ">"
```

Here, D stands for `Delimiter`, T for `Text`, and `TnD` for `Text-with-no-Delimiters-in-it`.

Strictly speaking, our `Subst` rule is not a rule but a **rule schema**. (A grammar of XML would also have to have a rule schema of this kind.) To get the actual rules, we would replace =D with each one of the delimiter strings we use (in our practice just two single-character strings, "|" and "$"), and =SubTag with each one of the substitution tags we use (four so far). For each delimiter, we would also write a TnD production saying that TnD can be any text that does not contain the delimiter. If ND is the number of delimiter strings and NS the number of substitution tags, the schema above corresponds to ND*(NS+1) context free rules, so the language generated by our grammar is still context free.

For reasons of flexibility, we don't want to commit to a specific limit on the number or length of our delimiters and tags – it's easier to have a parser that doesn't care – and so in the formal sense our grammar is not context-free. However, the structure of the parser will be very similar to a typical "recursive-descent" parser for a context free grammar. The reason such parsers are called "recursive-descent" is because they have a procedure or method for each grammar rule, and recursive rules come out as recursive procedures that keep calling themselves (descending down the tree) until they bottom out at a non-recursive rule.

The `Subst` production and the structure of the parsing program may actually be clearer if we rewrite it as two rules:

```
Subst ::= StartTag(tag,d) T (Delim(d) T(d))* EndTag(tag);
Delim(d) ::= d T(d) d;
```

Read this as follows: `Subst` begins with a `StartTag` (defining the actual tag and `Delim` to be used), and ends with a matching `EndTag` (so `<myna:SUBST>` will end with `</myna:SUBST>`). In between we have initial text, then zero or more repetitions of a `Delim` followed by more text. Finally, we see that a `Delim` begins and ends with the defined delimiter, and has plain text, not containing the delimiter, in between.

Together with the `Doc` production and the `T` production which we never wrote, this completes our grammar. Armed with these productions, we can move on to writing a parser.

The Parser Overview

Recall from earlier in this chapter that the work of processing a template file is done in the `fileSubst()` methods of the `MiscFile` utility class. Let's take another look at one of them:

```
// from MiscFile
public static String fileSubst(String fName, Env env)
        throws Exception
{
    StringBuffer sBuff = fileToStringBuffer(fName);
    ParseSubst pS = new ParseSubst(sBuff);
    return pS.toString(env);
}
```

We can understand this code a little better now. The two arguments of the method are: a file to process and the "current environment", which is an `Env` object. The method reads the template file into a string buffer and uses the buffer to construct a `ParseSubst` object. That object has a `toString()` method that takes an `Env` as an argument and writes the `ParseSubst` object to string while performing all substitutions. The other `fileSubst()` method is very similar, except it has a `RowSequence` argument instead of an `Env`; the corresponding `toString()` method retrieves the next `Env` object from that `RowSequence` before doing substitutions.

In a narrow sense, a parser is a program that takes some text on input and produces a data object that represents the syntactic structure of that text, usually a tree. The main components of a parser are:

❑ an input stream or buffer

❑ a lexical analyzer that gets the next token from input and feeds it into the parser proper

❑ a parser that attaches the new token to the emerging tree

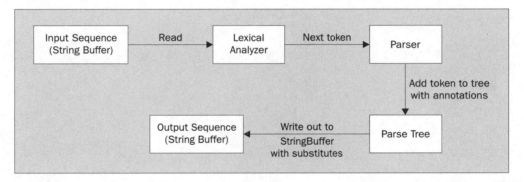

Many parsers, after constructing a tree, do something with it. For instance, an optimizing compiler will rearrange parts of the tree to make the program more efficient. In our case, the parser constructs a tree in which each node is "decorated" with additional information about whether or not its content contains substitutions, and of what kind. In the end, this tree is written to a string, with all substitutions performed. In terms of Java objects, the main components of `ParseSubst` are:

❑ input: `StringBuffer theBuff`

❑ lexical analyser: `MyNaLex lex`

❑ parse tree: `ParseTree theTree`

❑ output: `StringBuffer outBuff`

Note on Strings and StringBuffers

We use string buffers for input and output for reasons of efficiency, having to do with garbage collection. Java `Strings` are "immutable objects" in the sense that a `String` cannot be modified in place. There is no `setCharAt()` method, and all `String` methods that return a `String` return a modified copy of the original string. Manipulating `String` objects usually results in a good deal of memory usage and garbage collection. String buffers are much more efficient; for instance, you can refer to a sequence of characters within a buffer without creating a copy of them. By contrast, every time you say `substring()`, a new `String` object is created.

It is true that `StringBuffer` lacks some of the useful methods that `String` has. However, it has a `toString()` method which, in effect, wraps a `String` object around it without making a copy of the character data. As long as you don't use `String` methods that return `Strings`, no new memory is allocated. This is the way that `Strings` and `StringBuffers` are used in our parser: the parse tree it constructs does not contain text strings in its nodes but rather two integers, `lo` and `hi`, that indicate where the corresponding text begins and ends in the input `StringBuffer`.

An Example

Time for an example. Suppose our input text is:

```
"The time <myna:SUBST> has come, |speaker1| said, to |communicateAbout| many
</myna:SUBST> things, of <myna:SUBST delim="$"> $topicA$ and $topicB$, of $topicC$
and $topicD$ </myna:SUBST>; of why the sea is boiling hot, and whether pigs have
wings."
```

This text, when parsed, will produce the following tree:

```
<ROOT>
    <TEXT>The time </TEXT>
    <myna:SUBST>
        <TEXT> has come, </TEXT>
        <DELIM>speaker1</DELIM>
        <TEXT> said, to </TEXT>
        <DELIM>communicateAbout</DELIM>
        <TEXT>  many </TEXT>
    </myna:SUBST>
    <TEXT> things, of </TEXT>
    <myna:SUBST delim="$">
        <TEXT> </TEXT>
        <DELIM>topicA</DELIM>
        <TEXT> and </TEXT>
        <DELIM>topicB</DELIM>
        <TEXT>, of </TEXT>
        <DELIM>topicC</DELIM>
        <TEXT> and </TEXT>
        <DELIM>topicD</DELIM>
    </myna:SUBST>
    <TEXT>; of why the sea is boiling hot, and whether pigs have wings.</TEXT>
```

Assuming that the `Env` has all the right definitions, such as:

```
speaker1->the Walrus
topicC->cabbages
```

the tree will be written out as the familiar text. We are ready to get into the code of the application.

The Parser, the Tree and the Lexical Analyzer

The three classes that make up our application are ParseSubst, ParseTree and MyNaLex (the lexical analyzer). ParseSubst consists of two distinct parts: one constructs a ParseTree object and the other writes the tree to a string. We will go through the code in the following order: the parser part of ParseSubst, the ParseTree, the tree-to-string procedures and, finally, the lexical analyzer.

The Parser

ParseSubst has several private variables that contain references to all its supporting objects. The constructor initializes them.

```java
package MyNa.utils;
import java.io.*;
import java.util.*;

public class ParseSubst
{
    StringBuffer theBuff;    // input text
    String theString;        // same as String
    MyNaLex lex = null;        // lexical analyzer
    ParseTree theTree = null; // tree to be constructed
    Env theEnv = null;         // environment for substitutions
    RowSequence theRowSequence = null; // RowSequence of environments
                                       // (ResultSet)
    boolean substFailure;    // needed for control structures
    StringBuffer outBuff;    // output text

public ParseSubst(StringBuffer sB) throws Exception
{
    if(sB == null)
    {
        throw new Exception("can't parse null string buffer");
    }
    theBuff = sB;
    theString = sB.toString(); // no new memory is allocated
    lex = new MyNaLex(theBuff);
    substFailure =false;
    theTree = parseRoot();
}
```

The last line of the constructor calls the parseRoot() method that implements the first of our grammar productions. This is the most straightforward way to "derive" a parser from a grammar: for each grammar production there is a parser method that "consumes" a token that corresponds to the non-terminal on the left-hand side of the production, makes it into a tree node and, if it's not the root, attaches that node to the tree. In the case of the root the resulting node is the entire tree.

parseRoot()

The production for parseRoot() is:

```
Root ::= (Subst | T)*
```

The * in the production corresponds to a while loop in the code. Otherwise, the code of parseRoot() shows a good deal of the functionality of the lexical analyzer and ParseTree:

```java
public ParseTree parseRoot() throws Exception
{
    ParseTree root = new ParseTree("ROOT",0,theString.length());
    int tokType = lex.getToken();
    while(MyNaLex.endAllToken!=tokType)
    {
        if(tokType == MyNaLex.noToken)
        {
            throw new Exception("ERROR: Bad token at parseRoot:\n "
                    + lex.context());
        }
        int lo = lex.startToken();
        int hi = lex.endToken();

        if(tokType == MyNaLex.textToken)
        {
            root.addChild(new ParseTree("TEXT", lo, hi));
        }
        else
        {
            if(tokType == MyNaLex.mynaToken)
            {
                root.addChild(parseSub(lo,hi));
            }
        }
        else
        {
            throw new Exception("ERROR: Bad token at beginning:\n "
                    + lex.context());
        }
        tokType = lex.getToken();
    }
    return root;
}
```

Starting with the lexical analyzer, we notice that it has these methods: getToken(), startToken() and endToken(). The getToken() method returns an integer that indicates the current token's type. Three such types appear in the code: noToken, textToken and mynaToken. Judging by the references, they are static variables of the MyNaLex class. The startToken() and endToken() methods return the lo and the hi of the current token, i.e. their start and end indices in the string buffer.

The `ParseTree` constructor is used twice in the code, to create the ROOT node and TEXT nodes:

```
ParseTree root = new ParseTree("ROOT", 0, theString.length());
...
if(tokType == MyNaLex.textToken)
{
    root.addChild(new ParseTree("TEXT", lo, hi));
}
...
```

As you can see, the `ParseTree` constructor takes three arguments: a label, and the start and end positions of the corresponding token. The start and end of the ROOT token are 0 and `theString.length()`. As promised, we use the `String` class method to extract various pieces of information about the buffer while being careful not to use methods that return a string.

In addition to the constructor, `ParseTree` has an `addChild()` method. If the token type is `textToken` then a new `subtree` is created and immediately added to the tree. If the token type is one of the `<myna:...>` tokens then the child tree is created by a call on `parseSub()`, corresponding to the next grammar production.

parseSub()

This method implements both of the remaining productions:

```
Subst ::= StartTag(tag,d) T (Delim(d) T(d))* EndTag(tag);
Delim(d) ::= d T(d) d;
```

The * in the production again corresponds to a while loop in the code, and the loop condition is directly derived from the production. Since the token contains an element with an attribute, the tree node has a new component, a `hashtable`, to contain it. (In principle, the parser can process a mini-language that allows any number of attributes on elements.) The `hashtable` is created by the `getTokenProps()` method of the lexical analyzer and given as an argument to the `ParseTree` constructor. As you can see, there are at least two different constructors, one with three arguments, the other with four; the forth argument, a hash table, is required for `<myna:SUBST>` nodes because they may have attributes on them.

As you read through the code, keep in mind that both TEXT nodes and DELIM nodes result from tokens whose `tokType` is `textToken`. The lexical analyzer closes one text token and starts another one at the `Delimiter` string. The while loop in the code, corresponding to the * sub-expression in the production, processes two text tokens and attaches the first as a TEXT node, and the second as a DELIM node to the tree. If a non-`textToken` is found, then it means we've encountered the closing `<myna:SUBST>` tag and the loop is broken.

```
public ParseTree parseSub(int lo, int hi) throws Exception
{
    // the current token is a mynaToken, or we wouldn't be here.
    // first consume the rest of the opening tag: attributes, if any
    Hashtable tokProps = lex.getTokenProps();
    String tagName = theString.substring(lo, hi);
    ParseTree pS = new ParseTree(tagName, lo, hi, tokProps);
    int tokType;
```

```
    while(MyNaLex.textToken == (tokType=lex.getToken()))
    {
        //first text token
        pS.addChild(new ParseTree("TEXT", lex.startToken(), lex.endToken()));
        if(MyNaLex.textToken != (tokType=lex.getToken()))
        {
            // second token; is it text?
            break; // found the closing myna:SUBST tag
        }
        pS.addChild(new ParseTree("DELIM", // add second textTok as DELIM node
                lex.startToken(), lex.endToken()));
    }

    String closeTag = null;
    if(tokType != MyNaLex.endMynaToken // it should be the closing tag
        || !tagName.equals(closeTag=lex.theTokenString()) )
    {
        throw new Exception("ERROR: expected [" + tagName +
                "], found [" + closeTag + "]");
    }
    return pS;
}
```

This concludes the parsing-and-tree-building part of `ParseSubst`; let's take a look at the tree it builds.

The ParseTree class

This class is relatively simple. The parse tree doesn't really need to know much; it doesn't even know how to write itself to a string: this is done in the `ParseSubst` class that has access to the original text.

The private variables of `ParseTree` are already familiar, except for the Vector of children:

```
package MyNa.utils;
import java.io.*;
import java.util.*;

public class ParseTree
{
    int lo = 0;               // boundaries of corresponding text in
    int hi = 0;               // StringBuffer
    String tagName = null;    // label on the root of this tree, e.g., TEXT
    Hashtable props = null;   // the attributes, if any
    Vector children = null;
```

The constructors initialize the variables from arguments. Only the tag name is a required argument; the rest have default values, 0 or null, as appropriate:

```
public ParseTree(String tag, int L,int H,Hashtable tab)
{
    tagName = tag;
    lo = L;
    hi = H;
    props = tab;
}

public ParseTree(String tag)
{
    this(tag, 0, 0, null);
}

public ParseTree(String tag, int L)
{
    this(tag, L, L, null);
}

public ParseTree(String tag, int L, int H)
{
    this(tag, L, H, null);
}

public ParseTree(String tag, int L, Hashtable H)
{
    this(tag, L, L, H);
}
```

For setting tagName, lo and hi, there are appropriate getXXX() and setXXX() methods:

```
public String getTagName()
{
    return tagName;
}

public int getLow()
{
    return lo;
}

public int getHigh()
{
    return hi;
}

public void setTagName(String tag)
{
    tagName = tag;
}
```

```
public void setLow(int i)
{
    lo = i;
}

public void setHigh(int i)
{
    hi = i;
}
```

There are two methods to manipulate the hash table of properties:

```
public Object get(Object key)
{
    if(props == null)
    {
        return null;
    }
    else
    {
        return props.get(key);
    }
}

public Object put(Object key, Object val)
{
    if(props == null)
    {
        props = new Hashtable(1);
    }
    props.put(key, val);
    return val;
}
```

Finally, there are three methods to work with the Vector of children:

```
public int numChildren()
{
    if(children == null)
    {
        return 0;
    }
    else
    {
        return children.size();
    }
}

public ParseTree child(int i)
{
    if(numChildren() <= i)
    {
```

```
        return null;
    }
    return (ParseTree)children.elementAt(i);
}

public void addChild(ParseTree pT)
{
    if(children == null)
    {
        children = new Vector(1);
    }
    children.addElement(pT);
}
```

And that's all there is to the `ParseTree` class.

Writing the Tree to a String

Now that the structure of `ParseTree` is familiar, let's go back to `ParseSubst` and see how it is written out to a string. Unwinding from the beginning, here are the `toString()` methods that get called in `substFile()` with an `Env` or a `RowSequence` argument:

```
public String toString(Env env) throws Exception
{
    theEnv = env;
    outBuff = new StringBuffer();
    toStringBuffer(theTree);
    return outBuff.toString();
}

public String toString(RowSequence rows) throws ParseSubstException
{
    theRows = rows;
    if(null == rows)
    {
        throw new ParseSubstException("empty RowSequence in toString");
    }
    theEnv = theRows.getRow();
    outBuff = new StringBuffer();
    toStringBuffer(theTree);
    return outBuff.toString();
}
```

In both cases, an `Env` object provides the bindings to use in substitutions. In the first version, the `Env` is given as an argument; in the second, we retrieve the next `Env` from the `RowSequence`. As you can see, in either case all the work is done in the `toStringBuffer()` method that operates on the parse tree. The code checks the tag name of the tree and does whatever is right for each:

```
public void toStringBuffer(ParseTree T) throws Exception
{
    if(T == null)
    {
        return;
    }
    int N = T.numChildren();
    String tag = T.getTagName();
    if(tag.equals("ROOT"))
    {
        for(int i = 0; i < N; i++)
        {
            toStringBuffer(T.child(i));
        }
    }
    else
    {
        if(tag.equals("TEXT"))
        {
            outText(T);
        }
    }
    else
    {
        if(tag.startsWith("myna:"))
        {
            substStringBuffer(tag, T);
        }
    }
    else
    {
        throw new Exception("expected ROOT or 'myna:', found " + tag);
    }
}
```

If the tag is ROOT then the method gets recursively called on each sub-tree in order. If the tag is TEXT, then the text of the tree is appended to the buffer without any processing:

```
public void outText(ParseTree T)
{
    int low = T.getLow();
    int high = T.getHigh();
    if(low >= high)
    {
        return;
    }
    outBuff.append(theString.substring(low, high));
}
```

Finally, if the tag starts with "myna:", both the tag and the tree are dispatched to substStringBuffer() for substitutions. Here, another set of possibilities presents itself. If the tag is <myna:SUBST> then the substitutions are done with the current environment. If the tag is <myna:SUBSTROW>, we get the next Env before doing the substitutions. If the tag is <myna:SUBSTERR>, we check to see whether indeed we are in an error condition, and if so output whatever error message was provided, with substitutions. Finally, if the tag is <myna:SUBSTROWLIST>, we go through a while loop:

```
public void substStringBuffer(String tag, ParseTree T)
        throws ParseSubstException
{
    newQuery(T);
    if(tag.equals("myna:SUBST"))
    {
        outSubVals(T);
    }
    else
    {
        if(tag.equals("myna:SUBSTROW"))
        {
            if(substFailure || null == theRows || !theRows.next())
            {
                substFailure = true; return;
            }
            else
            {
                theEnv = theRows.getRow();
                outSubVals(T);
            }
        }
    }
    else
    {
        if(tag.equals("myna:SUBSTERR"))
        {
            if(substFailure)
            {
                outSubVals(T);
            }
        }
    }
    else
    {
        if(tag.equals("myna:SUBSTROWLIST"))
        {
            if(substFailure || null == theRows)
            {
                return;
            }
            while(theRows.next())
            {
                theEnv = theRows.getRow();
```

```
                    outSubVals(T);
                }
            }
        }
        else
        {
            if(tag.equals("myna:SUBSTDEF"))
            {
                doDef(T);
            }
        }
        else
        {
            throw new ParseSubstException("unrecognized tag " + tag);
        }
    }
```

All branches of substStringBuffer() end up by calling outSubVals() with an argument tree that has alternating TEXT and DELIM sub-trees. The job of substStringBuffer() is to go through those sub-trees and dispatch each either to outText() or outVal() as appropriate:

```
public void outSubVals(ParseTree T)
{
    int N = T.numChildren();
    for(int i = 0; i < N; i++)
    {
        if(T.child(i).getTagName().equals("DELIM"))
        {
            outVal(T.child(i));
        }
        else
        {
            outText(T.child(i));
        }
    }
}
```

We have already seen outText(); outVal() does the actual lookup and substitution:

```
public void outVal(ParseTree T)
{
    int low = T.getLow();
    int high = T.getHigh();
    if (low >= high)
    {
        return;
    }
    outBuff.append(theEnv.getStr(theString.substring(low, high)));
}
```

This concludes the `ParseSubst` class. The last class to look at is the lexical analyzer. It is long and does a good deal of grunt work as it plows its way through the buffer. We'll present an overview and a couple of representative samples; the rest is left for your individual reading pleasure.

The Lexical Analyzer

A common way to organize a lexical analyzer is to have a number of `getXXX()` methods, each of which consumes a sequence of characters that have a specific property and advances the "current location" past the end of that sequence. In `MyNaLex`, if the method consumes an entire token then it returns the token's type, an integer; if the method consumes a component of a token, it returns a boolean to indicate success or failure.

getWhiteSpace()

As a simple example, consider the `getWhiteSpace()` method. We defined whitespace in the grammar as one of four characters, space, tab, LF or CR:

```
S ::= (#x20|#x9|#xA|#xD)+
```

Correspondingly, we define `isWhiteSpace()` and `getWhiteSpace()`:

```java
boolean isWhiteSpace(char c)
{
    return c=='\u0020' || c=='\u0009' || c=='\u000A' || c=='\u000D';
}

public boolean getWhiteSpace()
{
    if(curLoc >= sBuffLength)
    {
        return false;
    }
    char c = sBuff.charAt(curLoc);
    if(!isWhiteSpace(c))
    {
        return false;
    }
    while((++curLoc<sBuffLength) && (isWhiteSpace(sBuff.charAt(curLoc))))
        ; // consume white space by advancing curLoc
    return true;
}
```

The sequence to be consumed may be defined by a property other than one belonging to a character class. For instance, we may want to match a quoted string, as in `<myna:SUBST delim="$">`:

```java
public boolean getQStr()
{
    int start = curLoc;
    if(curLoc >= sBuffLength)
    {
        return false;
    }
```

```
    char qChar = sBuff.charAt(curLoc++);
    while (curLoc < sBuffLength && qChar != sBuff.charAt(curLoc))
    {
        curLoc++;
    }
    if(curLoc >= sBuffLength)
    {
        curLoc = start; return false; // unmatched quote character
    }
    curLoc++;                          // step past the matching quote character;
    return true;
}
```

There are a number of such supporting functions, including:

```
public boolean getLetter()                  // a-zA-Z
public boolean getChar(char c)              // specific character
public boolean getCharRange(char lo, char hi) // characters in specific range
public boolean getStr(String s)            // specific String
```

and several others. All of them serve in support of methods that consume entire tokens. In addition to advancing curLoc, these methods set the found token's properties and return its type. Before we look at the methods, let's become familiar with token properties and token types, which are represented as variables of the MyNaLex class.

MyNaLex Variables1: Token Types and Properties

Token types are represented as static final integers:

```
public static final int noToken = -1;
public static final int textToken = 0;
public static final int mynaToken = 1;
public static final int endMynaToken = 2;
public static final int endAllToken = 3;
```

A token is completely characterized by four items: its start and end points in the buffer (tokenStart and tokenEnd), its type (tokenType), and its tokenProps hash table, which is null for all tokens except those mynaTokens that have attributes.

```
private int tokenType; // these four properties are current token
private int tokenStart;
private int tokenEnd;
private Hashtable tokenProps = null;

public static String[]tokTypeNames = //noToken==-1
  new String[]
    {"noToken", "textToken", "mynaToken", "endMynaToken", "endAllToken"};
```

MyNaLex Variables2: Other Variables

In addition to token types and properties, `MyNaLex` has:

```
public static String defaultDelim = "|";

private StringBuffer sBuff = null; // the buffer to process
private String theString = null;   // theString is a reference to sBuff

private int sBuffLength;
private int curLoc;                // curLoc advances through sBuff as we read

private String currentDelimiter; // null when not in range of any delimiter
private Stack delimStack;         // for multiple nested delimiters
```

These are fairly self-explanatory. The final set of variables has to do with pushback.

MyNaLex Variables3: Pushback

It is common for a lexical analyzer to have a one-item-deep memory for those situations where, in order to make sure that we have reached the end of the current token, we have to match the next one. For instance, suppose we find the beginning of a `mynaToken`, as in

```
some text<myna:SUBST>
```

Since we allow unescaped `'<'` characters in our text, when the lexical analyzer comes across one of them, it cannot be sure that it is, indeed, the beginning of a `myna` token. In order to find out, it has to parse the next token before returning the current one. In order not to waste that work, the next token is saved in `MyNaLex` "pushback" variables and retrieved by the next call on `getToken()`. The pushback variables are:

```
private int pushbackTokenType; // these four are a token which has
private int pushbackTokenStart; // been recognized but not yet yielded
private int pushbackTokenEnd; // as in "some text<myna:SUBST>..." where
private Hashtable pushbackTokenProps; // we produce "some text", save SUBST
```

We're ready to look at the main methods of the analyzer, `getToken()` and `setToken()`, now.

setToken()

As you may remember from `ParseSubst`, the method that gets called from the outside is `getToken()`. It sets `lo` and `hi` of the next token and returns its type. Internally, `getToken()` calls `setToken()` to set the next token's properties. The only property that require any work is the delimiter, which is set in `mynaToken`, and unset in `endMynaToken`:

```
public int setToken(int lo, int hi, int tType, Hashtable tProps)
{
  tokenStart = lo;
  tokenEnd = hi;
  tokenType = tType;
```

```
   tokenProps = tProps;
        // delimiters are set by mynaToken, unset by endMynaToken
   if(tokenType == endMynaToken)
   {
     // set delimiter to null
     currentDelimiter = null;
   }
   else
   {
     if(tokenType == mynaToken)
     {
       // look up delimiter in the hashtable
       String delim;                 // if not found, set to default
       if(tProps != null && null != (delim=(String)tProps.get("delim")))
       {
         currentDelimiter = delim;
       }
       else
         currentDelimiter = defaultDelim;
     }
   }
   return tokenType;
}
```

This version of setToken() is actually a little simplified somewhat, compared to the actual code. The version in the .jar file allows for the possibility of embedded myna tags with different delimiters as in this example:

```
<myna:SUBST delim="|">
   one potato |x| two potato
   <myna:SUBSTROW delim="*">
     three potato *y* the verticalbar "|" is not a delim here
   </myna:SUBSTROW>
     but here verticalbar is a delimiter again, 'cos we've lifted scope
</myna:SUBST>
```

To accommodate such examples, MyNaLex needs one more variable, a delimiter stack, and slightly more verbose code in setToken(). For instance, the endMyNaToken clause becomes:

```
   if(tokenType == endMynaToken)
   {
       if(delimStack == null || delimStack.empty())
       {
           currentDelimiter = null;
       }
       else
       {
           currentDelimiter = (String)delimStack.pop();
       }
   }
```

and similarly in the mynaToken clause. No other methods are affected.

getToken()

This is the most important top-level method that gets called from the outside – it is the method that advances the current location and returns the type of the next token. Before it gets to the general case, `getToken()` checks three easy possibilities:

- ❑ the next token has already been matched and pushed back
- ❑ the current location is beyond the length of the buffer and we're done
- ❑ we're at the very beginning but the buffer does not contain any `<myna:` elements at all

Here's the beginning of the code:

```
public int getToken()
{
    tokenProps = null;
    if(pullforthToken())
    {
        return tokenType; // previously matched
    }
    if(curLoc >= sBuffLength)
    {
        return tokenType = endAllToken; // nothing there
    }
    if(curLoc == 0)
    {
        // initial call manual optimization (check empty case)
        // does not affect the actual result
        int firstLoc = theString.indexOf("<myna:");
        if(firstLoc < 0)
        {
            return setToken(0, curLoc = sBuffLength, textToken, null);
        }
    }
}
```

If we drop through these initial tests, we arrive at the main case, which is a `while` loop that tries to find the next token until the current location goes past the end of the buffer. Within the loop, we call specialized methods to check whether we are at the beginning of a `mynaToken` or a delimiter. If we are, the corresponding action is taken; if not, we advance by a single character:

```
int oldCurLoc = curLoc;      // save location at start of attempted match
while(curLoc < sBuffLength)
{
    char c = sBuff.charAt(curLoc); // another manual optimization;
    if(c != '<' &&      // if these tests fail, so would matching below.
            (currentDelimiter == null || c != currentDelimiter.charAt(0)) )
    {
        curLoc++;
        continue;
    }                                // end manual optimization section
```

```
        int startMatch = curLoc;            // location as we start trying to match.
        if(getMynaToken())
        {
            return pushbackToken(oldCurLoc, startMatch, textToken, null);
        }
        if(getEndMynaToken())
        {
            return pushbackToken(oldCurLoc, startMatch, textToken, null);
        }
        if(getStr(currentDelimiter))
        {
            return setToken(oldCurLoc, startMatch, textToken, null);
        }
        curLoc++;
    }                                       // end while loop
    return setToken(oldCurLoc, sBuffLength, textToken, null); // final text token
}
```

As we mentioned before, when a `MyNaToken` or `EndMyNaToken` is matched, the token is pushed back for later use. Here is the `pushbackToken()` method, together with its `pullforth` partner.

pushbackToken() and pullforthToken()

This complementary pair save a token and retrieve a token. The code is straightforward:

```
public void pushbackToken()
{
    pushbackTokenStart = tokenStart;
    pushbackTokenType = tokenType;
    pushbackTokenEnd = tokenEnd;
    pushbackTokenProps = tokenProps;
    tokenProps = null;
}

public int pushbackToken(int lo, int hi, int tt, Hashtable tp)
{
    pushbackToken();
    return setToken(lo, hi, tt, tp);
}

public boolean pullforthToken()
{
    if(pushbackTokenType == noToken)
    {
        return false;
    }
    setToken(pushbackTokenStart, pushbackTokenEnd,
            pushbackTokenType, pushbackTokenProps);
    pushbackTokenType = noToken; // mark as unavailable.
    return true;
}
```

The Matching Methods and Grammar Productions

Taking a broader look at the organization of `getToken`, we can see that the lexical analyzer is also based on grammar productions. For instance, `getToken()` itself is based on this rule:

```
Token ::= TextToken | MyNaToken | EndMyNaToken | Delimiter
```

For each possible kind of token except the default `TextToken` there is a `getXXX()` method that matches it. For `Delimiter`, the method is `getStr()` which simply matches the string it is given. For the remaining two types, the methods are `getMynaToken()` and `getEndMynaToken()`. These are also based on grammar productions. For instance, the production for `getMyNaToken()` (the more complex of the two because it has to worry about attributes) is as follows:

```
MyNaToken ::= "<myna:" Id S? (Def S)* ">"
```

Read this as follows: a `myna` token consists of the initial `"myna:"` sequence, followed by the token's ID (such as `SUBST` or `SUBSTROW`) followed by an optional whitespace, followed by zero or more attribute definitions separated by whitespace, followed by the closing bracket. More grammar rules define the structure of `Id` and `Def`. (We have already shown the rule for `S`.) It's a fair bet that the implementation of `getMyNaToken()` will contain calls on `getId()`, `getDef()` and `getWhiteSpace()`, and indeed, if you check the code you'll find all of them there.

```
public boolean getMynaToken()
{                                                               // ""
    int startTok = curLoc;
    if(!getStr("<myna:"))
    {
        return false;
    }
    int startId = curLoc;
    if(!getId())
    {
        curLoc = startTok;
        return false;
    }
    int endId = curLoc;
    if(getWhiteSpace())
        while(getDef())
            while(getWhiteSpace());
    if(!getChar('>'))
    {
        curLoc = startTok;
        lg.logIt("gMT failed 1" + context());
        return false;
    }
    setToken(startTok + 1, endId, mynaToken, tokenProps);   // skip "<"
    return true;
}
```

This is a very common way to organize a lexical analyzer. Also typical is the use of pushback for some tokens. The use of setToken() to set the start and end points of the token is less common; many lexical analyzers simply return strings. Our design is motivated, as we explained earlier, by considerations of efficiency: we didn't want to do a lot of string copying which would require garbage collection.

This completes our parsing support for template files. We recommend that you try to modify our three main classes, ParseSubst, ParseTree and MyNaLex, to provide the same support for .ini files. In the meantime, we're going to *use* template files in a more substantial application.

The Payoff: a Small Shopping Cart

It's been a good deal of work to implement the SUBST mini-language, but the payoff is substantial. First, we've learnt general techniques of implementing a mini-language. Second, now that we have a general purpose parser and lexical analyzer, it will be relatively little work to add more features to the language. For instance, we could add more tags, or make our delimiter strings into a pair of start and end tags (perhaps <% and %>), and give them attributes to further specify the kind of processing they require. Finally, even without any extensions to the mini-language, we can implement a variety of three-tier applications without any application-specific Java programming. In this section, we're going to illustrate the range of possibilities by building a small shopping cart application simply by changing the .ini file and the template files.

A College Bookstore

The main business of a college bookstore is selling the required books for various courses. Every semester, students register for specific sections of specific courses, and each section has several required and recommended book titles associated with it. The bookstore receives this information after students register for their courses and professors select books for them. Possession of that information is the only competitive advantage that a small college bookstore has against the likes of Amazon.com or Borders, so restricted access is important.

To simplify things, we will temporarily assume that all relevant information is kept in four tables of the same database, as follows:

- ❑ REGISTRATION (StudentName, SectionID): records the registration of specific students in specific sections of courses

- ❑ COURSEBOOKS (SectionID, ItemCode): records that a given item (usually a book) is required or recommended for a particular section.

- ❑ INVENTORY (ItemCode, ItemName, ItemPrice): keeps information about books and other items on sale in the bookstore

- ❑ ORDERS (StudentName, ItemCode) contains shopping cart contents

Clearly, there is more information on courses, students and bookstore items elsewhere in the database, but it will be easy to add later. A typical scenario of use proceeds as follows:

User	System
1. Log in	2. Display required books for courses that the user is registered for, separating already-ordered from not-yet-ordered.
3. Make changes (add/delete) to the list of courses for which books are shown.	4. Record and show changes.
5. Add books to order, delete from order.	6. Record and show changes.
7. Submit order.	8. Send email confirmation.

In this section we will only implement steps 1 through 6.

New Code for Env.addBufferedReader()

To create an application, in our framework, is to create a `.ini` file and template files for output. Let's start with the `.ini` file. Its application-specific content consists of database queries. In the case of the shopping cart, these queries must mention the user, because we want each user to be able to see that user's shopping cart and nobody else's. Looks like we have a problem: there is only one `.ini` file, created at design time, while there are many users whose identity is not known until run time. The solution is to allow substitution elements in the `.ini` file, just as we allow them in template files. This new functionality will require a change to the `addBufferedReader()` method of the `Env` class. In Chapter 2, you saw its code as:

```
public void addBufferedReader(BufferedReader brin)
{
    if(brin == null)
    {
        return;
    }
    String key;
    String value;
    try
    {
        while(null != (key=brin.readLine()))
        {
            if(null != (value=brin.readLine()))
            {
                put(key, value);
            }
        }
        brin.close();
    }
    catch(IOException e)
    {
        try
        {
            brin.close();
        }
```

```
        catch(IOException ex)
        {
            ex.printStackTrace();
        }
    }
}
```

When we first presented this method, we honestly admitted that this version was simplistic, for two reasons. First, it assumes that the value stored in Env comes directly from the text source, without any intermediate processing. Second, it only allows values that can fit on a single line. We made a promise at the time to present the 'real' version in Chapter 4. Since Chapter 4 is almost over, it is time to redeem this promise. We'll make, in total, three changes:

❑   The contents of the .ini file will go through the same parsing and substitution process that template files go through

❑   Long lines can be broken into several lines, using the "\" character to escape EOLN. This will be particularly helpful in writing SQL queries

❑   Since some lines will be constructed out of several lines, we'll place them in a string buffer rather than a string, to minimize garbage collection

The new addBufferedReader() will use the parser and so may throw a ParseSubstException. However, the Env constructor that calls addBufferedReader() was written to catch any Exception whatsoever, and thus needs no change.

Here's the result:

```
public void addBufferedReader (BufferedReader brin)
        throws ParseSubstException
{
    if(brin == null)
    {
        return;
    }
    String key;
    String line;
    StringBuffer value = new StringBuffer();
    try
    {
        while((key = brin.readLine()) != null)
        {                                               // read in key
            if((line = brin.readLine()) != null)
            {
                // read in the first line of value
                value.setLength(0);                 // reset buffer for value
                while(line != null && line.endsWith("\\")
                        && !line.endsWith("\\\\"))
                {
                    // escape EOLN with \; escape \ with another
                    value.append(line);
                    value.setCharAt(value.length()-1, '\n');
                    line = brin.readLine();
                }
```

```
                    if(line != null)
                    {
                        value.append(line);
                    }
                    // add to Env, with substitutions
                    put(key, Misc.substLine(value.toString(), this));
                }
            }
            brin.close();
        }
        catch(IOException ex)
        {
            lg.logIt("addBufferedReader: ", ex);
        }
    }
```

The following line packs a lot of action:

```
    put(key, Misc.substLine(value.toString(), this));
```

First, we convert the `value` `StringBuffer` to `String` and submit it as the first argument to `substLine()`. The `substLine()` method does exactly the same processing to a text string that `substFile()` does to a text file, i.e. creates a `SubstParse` object from it, and then outputs it with substitutions to another buffer, via a `ParseTree`. The result becomes the second argument of the `put()` method. Note the dual role of the `Env` object: it serves both to provide substitutions for `substLine()` and to store the new name-value pair.

With `addBufferedReader()` fixed, we can move on with the bookstore application.

The .ini File

The `.ini` file now contains references to `dbUser` that will be substituted at run time with the appropriate `Env` value, whose source is the `Request` object:

```
FileTitle
The Bookstore's ShoppingCart Initialization-Environment File
dbOperation
InitDBHandler
dbDriver
sun.jdbc.odbc.JdbcOdbcDriver
dbName
jdbc:odbc:PHONEBOOK
dbQueries
REPORTORDERS,ADDITEMS,DELETEITEMS,SETUPADD,SETUPDELETE
REPORTORDERS
SELECT O.ItemCode,ItemName,ItemPrice \
    FROM ORDERS O,INVENTORY I \
    WHERE O.ItemCode=I.ItemCode \
      AND <myna:SUBST> CustomerName='|dbUser|'</myna:SUBST> \
    ORDER BY ItemName;
ADDITEMS
```

```
INSERT INTO ORDERS \
  <myna:SUBST> VALUES('|dbUser|',?); </myna:SUBST>
DELETEITEMS
DELETE FROM ORDERS \
  <myna:SUBST>\
    WHERE CustomerName='|dbUser|' AND ItemCode=?; \
  </myna:SUBST>
SETUPDELETE
  <myna:SUBST>|REPORTORDERS|</myna:SUBST>
SETUPADD
SELECT Reg.SectionID,CBooks.ItemCode,ItemName,ItemPrice \
  FROM  COURSEBOOKS CB,INVENTORY I,REGISTRATION R \
  WHERE CB.ItemCode=I.ItemCode AND \
        R.SectionID=CB.SectionID AND \
        <myna:SUBST> R.StudentName='|dbUser|';</myna:SUBST>
```

The SQL of these queries is fairly straightforward, but their meaning within the application can only be understood in the context of the overall design. In three-tier applications, database queries have a strong relationship to the application's user interface.

User Interface and Template Files

The user interface after login consists of the familiar two frames, a control frame and a data frame. You have seen it in the beginning of the chapter:

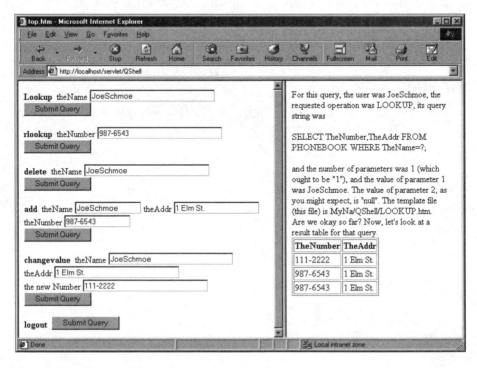

The interface is created by two files, `top.htm` and `ctl.htm`.

The Top File

Our minimal top file has two parameters to substitute, `filePath` and `dbServlet`:

```
<HTML>
  <HEAD>
    <TITLE>
      top.htm
    </TITLE>
  </HEAD>

  <FRAMESET cols="60%,40%">
  <myna:SUBST delim="$">
      <FRAME name="ctlFrame" src="$dbServlet$?filePath=$filePath$">
  </myna:SUBST>
      <FRAME name="dataFrame" src="about:blank">
  </FRAMESET>
</HTML>
```

`dbServlet`, as you recall, contains the rewritten URL; `filePath`, set by an initialization parameter for the servlet, points to the directory that contains all the application's files.

The Control Page

The control page contains four forms corresponding to four (out of six) queries defined in the `.ini` file:

```
<HTML>

<HEAD>
  <TITLE>
    ShopCart/ctl.htm
  </TITLE>
</HEAD>

<BODY>

<FORM  METHOD=POST TARGET=dataFrame
<myna:SUBST delim="$">ACTION="$dbServlet$"></myna:SUBST> >
<B>View shopping cart</B>
<INPUT TYPE=HIDDEN NAME=dbOperation value=REPORTORDERS>
<INPUT TYPE=SUBMIT VALUE="View Cart"></FORM>

<FORM  METHOD=POST TARGET=dataFrame
<myna:SUBST delim="$">ACTION="$dbServlet$"></myna:SUBST> >
<B>Delete some items</B>
<INPUT TYPE=HIDDEN NAME=dbOperation value=SETUPDELETE>
<INPUT TYPE=SUBMIT VALUE="Go to Delete"></FORM>

<FORM  METHOD=POST TARGET=dataFrame
<myna:SUBST delim="$">ACTION="$dbServlet$"></myna:SUBST> >
<B>Add some items</B>
<INPUT TYPE=HIDDEN NAME=dbOperation value=SETUPADD>
<INPUT TYPE=SUBMIT VALUE="Go to Add">
</FORM>
```

```
<FORM  METHOD=POST TARGET=dataFrame
<myna:SUBST delim="$">ACTION="$dbServlet$"></myna:SUBST> >
<B>Logout</B>
<INPUT TYPE=HIDDEN NAME=dbOperation value=Logout>
<INPUT TYPE=SUBMIT VALUE="Logout">
</FORM>

</BODY>

</HTML>
```

The output of the queries (except LOGOUT) is defined by template files. For REPORTORDERS, the template file is very straightforward:

```
<HTML>

<HEAD>
  <TITLE>
    REPORTORDERS.htm
  </TITLE>
</HEAD>

<BODY>
For <myna:SUBST> |dbUser| </myna:SUBST>
we have the following items ordered:
<UL><myna:SUBSTROWLIST>
    <LI>|FieldValue2| (item |FieldValue1|),
        costing |FieldValue3|)</LI>
    </myna:SUBSTROWLIST>
</UL>
</BODY>

</HTML>
```

This generates a list of items in the shopping cart, as in the following screen shot:

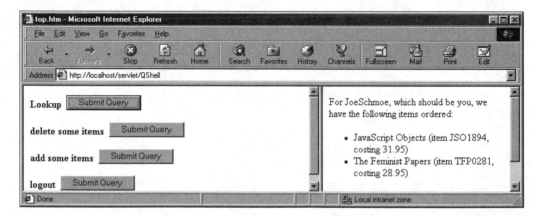

For the other two queries, SETUPADD and SETUPDELETE, the story is a bit more complicated, because their output is, in turn, a form asking the user to submit a query. We trace what happens with SETUPADD and ADDITEMS; the story of SETUPDELETE and DELETEITEMS is similar.

Setup for Adding Items to Shopping Cart

The output of SETUPADD is determined by the SETUPADD.htm template file. As you read through the file, keep these two new ideas in mind. First, this template file is both the result of a query, and thus contains elements of the SUBST mini-language, and also of an input to the next query, and thus contains input elements with names like Parameter1; their values will become parameters of the prepared statement run by the next query. Second, the input element whose name is Parameter1 happens to be a collection of checkboxes because we want the user to be able to add several items at once. Its value will not be a string but a collection of strings. Fortunately, we will not need any new programming to accommodate the new kind of parameter: it is supported by the Request object from which the Env is constructed, and, with amazing foresight, we have built support for string array values both in the Env class and in the dbHandler class that uses an Env to initialize its Query object.

The SETUPADD.htm file may be easier to read with the SETUPADD query in front of you: here it is, repeated from the .ini file:

```
SELECT Reg.SectionID,CBooks.ItemCode,ItemName,ItemPrice \
  FROM  COURSEBOOKS CB,INVENTORY I,REGISTRATION R \ .
 WHERE CB.ItemCode=I.ItemCode AND \
       R.SectionID=CB.SectionID AND \
       <myna:SUBST> R.StudentName='|dbUser|';</myna:SUBST>
```

From this query, you can see that in the template file below, we'll make the following substitutions:

- ❏   FieldValue1: the name of the section
- ❏   FieldValue2: the item code of the checked-off book
- ❏   FieldValue3: the book's title
- ❏   FieldValue4: the book's price

The file must generate a list of items with checkboxes next to them, to indicate items to be added to a shopping cart.

```
<HTML>

<HEAD>
  <TITLE>
    SETUPADD.htm
  </TITLE>
</HEAD>

<BODY>

<FORM METHOD=POST
  <myna:SUBST>ACTION="|dbServlet|"></myna:SUBST> >
<B>Checked Items Will be Added to Your Order!</B>
<INPUT TYPE=HIDDEN NAME=dbOperation value=ADDITEMS><BR>
```

```
<myna:SUBSTROWLIST>
  <INPUT TYPE=CHECKBOX NAME="Parameter1" value="|FieldValue2|">
  |FieldValue3| costs |FieldValue4|; it's item |FieldValue2|,
  for course |FieldValue1| <BR>
</myna:SUBSTROWLIST>
<INPUT TYPE=SUBMIT>
</FORM>
</BODY>

</HTML>
```

The result of this query places a form in the data frame that looks like this:

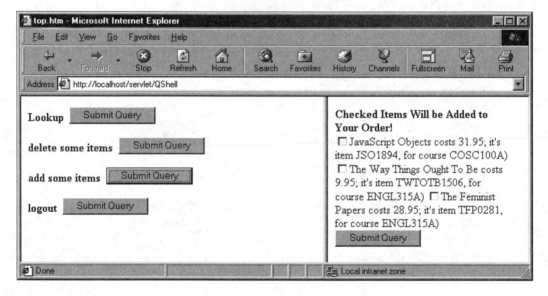

To indicate the various possibilities, only minor changes in the HTML will produce the same list of items arranged in a table:

```
<HTML>

<HEAD>
  <TITLE>
  SETUPADD.htm
  </TITLE>
</HEAD>

<BODY>
<FORM METHOD=POST
  <myna:SUBST>ACTION="|dbServlet|"></myna:SUBST>
<B>Checked Items Will be Added to Your Order!</B>
<INPUT TYPE=HIDDEN NAME=dbOperation value=ADDITEMS><BR>
  <TABLE BORDER="1">
<myna:SUBST>
    <TR><TH></TH><TH>|FieldName3|</TH><TH>|FieldName4|</TH>
        <TH>|FieldName2|</TH><TH>|FieldName1|</TH></TR>
```

```
    </myna:SUBST>
<myna:SUBSTROWLIST>
  <TR><TD>
  <INPUT TYPE=CHECKBOX NAME="Parameter1"
     value="|FieldValue2|" > </TD>
     <TD>|FieldValue3|</TD><TD> |FieldValue4| </TD>
     <TD>|FieldValue2|</TD><TD> |FieldValue1|</TD></TR>
</myna:SUBSTROWLIST>
  </TABLE>
<INPUT TYPE=SUBMIT>
</FORM>
</BODY>

</HTML>
```

The query result will now look like this:

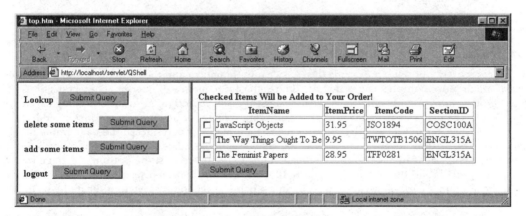

Whatever the looks, the user is all set up to check off items to add.

Adding Items

With the ADDITEMS form set up, the user can check off items to add to the shopping cart, then click submit. This runs the ADDITEMS query:

```
INSERT INTO ORDERS \
  <myna:SUBST> VALUES('|dbUser|',?); </myna:SUBST>
```

The output of this query is determined by ADDITEMS.htm:

```
<HTML><HEAD><TITLE>ADDITEMS.htm</TITLE></HEAD><BODY>
  <myna:SUBST delim="$">
    Item $Parameter1$ added to the order for $dbUser$;
    and the number of items added is $NumberOfRowsAffected$.
  </myna:SUBST>
</BODY></HTML>
```

This results in the following output (notice that `Parameter1` is replaced by a list):

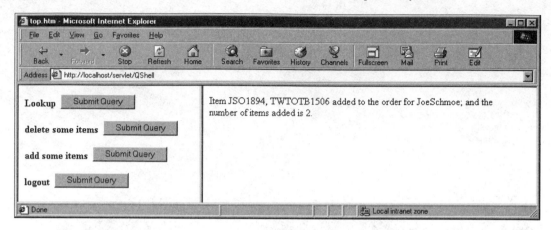

Chaining Queries

This section is strictly optional: it extends the SUBST mini-language and the QShell application into the area of much more complex pages that are the result of a sequence of queries. The extension is motivated by the following idea. In the current design, in order to add items to the shopping cart and view the results, the user has to go through three different screens. A better user interface would probably allow the user to add and delete items from the same page and refresh the page immediately to reflect the changes. For instance, the page could show the books currently in the shopping cart at the top, with a checkbox next to each book to indicate items to be deleted. At the bottom, the page would show "currently available" books that are required for the courses that the user requested to see, but are not yet in the shopping cart; a checkbox next to an available item would serve to indicate items to be added to the shopping cart. There will be thus only one frame visible at any given time. To clarify how it works, we have provided a version that puts successive partial fill-ins into frames ordered from left to right. To view this version, go back to the QShell login page and select the javascript-passing shopcart option.

Here is what it looks like (normally, only the rightmost frame will be visible):

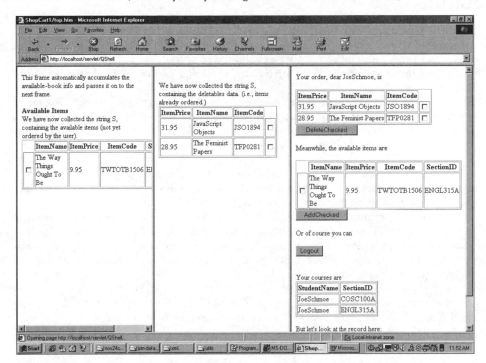

In order to implement this interface, we have to be able to combine several queries in such a way that the output of one is immediately used as the input to another. For instance, the result of SETUPADD is immediately fed into ADDITEMS and from there into REPORTORDERS. We have implemented this capability within the SUBST/QShell framework in two ways. One way leaves the Java code unchanged but complicates the .ini file and template pages; in particular, template pages contain (very simple) JavaScript. The other way (whose output is shown in the screenshot above) leaves the .ini file and template pages largely intact but adds more functionality to the Env and DBHandler classes.

In slightly more detail, the main idea of the first implementation is that a template page çan contain simple JavaScript code that constructs an HTML string which is the result of one of the queries in a chain; this string is loaded, using onload(), into an invisible frame, and the resulting (invisible) page is used as a starting point of the next query. The main idea of the second implementation is to add a few lines to DBHandler, placing the DBHandler itself in the Env or RowSequence it produces, and ask it to run another query. For complete detail, see the code in ShopCart2 (remember, it's all freely available from http://www.wrox.com/) and the comments we've put there.

Conclusions

In this chapter we have made two major advances, one more practical, the other more theoretical. On the practical side, we have completed the implementation of QShell: this is as far as we're going to take it before converting everything to XML. Although limited in scope, the shell is flexible enough to produce a variety of three-tier applications, such as the shopping cart in the final section of the chapter.

On the theoretical side, we have learned the basics of formal grammars and parsing. This material is useful in several ways. First, it has provided a very general and easily extensible implementation of QShell and template files. Second, it is important for understanding XML. Third, it forms the basis of a powerful design pattern. We will build on this basis in the next and subsequent chapters.

In the next chapter, we will go a little more deeply into software engineering, by presenting UML-based design diagrams and the concept of design patterns. We will give examples of several patterns, concentrating especially on the Little Language (or Mini-Language) pattern and its implementations. This next will be the last chapter of Part 1 of the book. In Part 2, after we absorb the basics of XML, we'll put this material to use, as we develop more substantial applications, including a fully-fledged implementation of College Bookstore. As you work through those chapters, you will see a number of design diagrams and design patterns; you will also see more Java material, having to do with security, email, connection pooling, and other practical matters.

You can read the next chapter now, or you can go straight to the first chapter of Part 2 and start learning about XML. This chapter has given you all the necessary background.

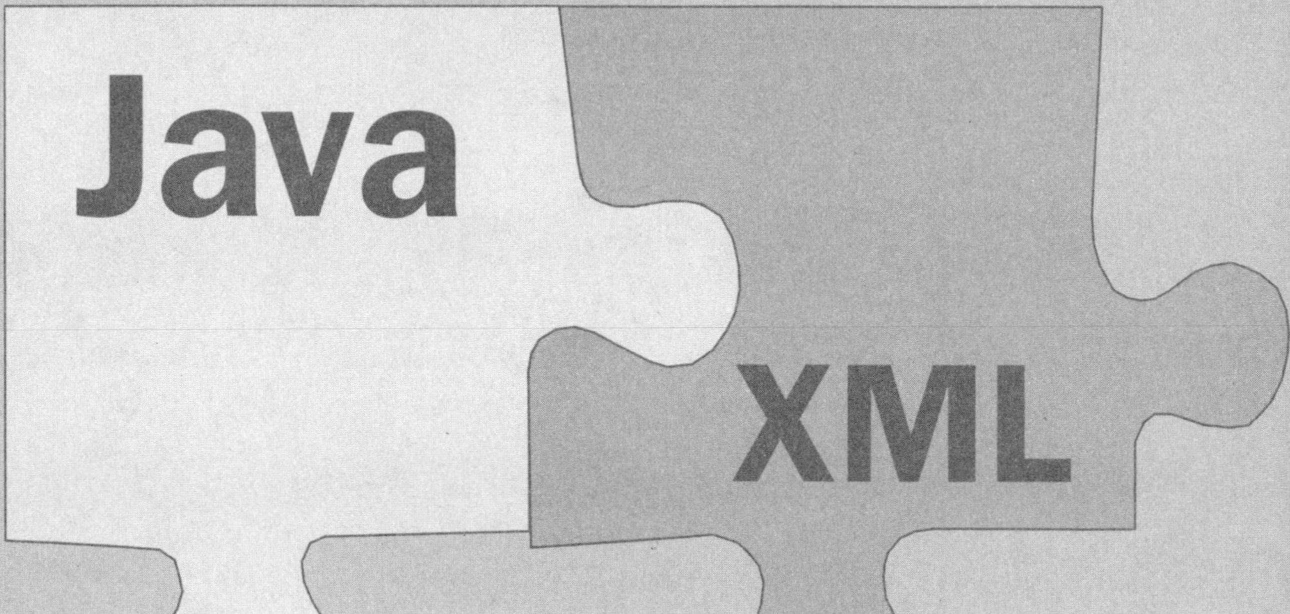
Java
XML

5

XML Beginnings

In this chapter, we're taking our first look at XML, the eXtensible Markup Language. Although called a language, XML is really a tool for defining languages, where a language is a set of tags and attributes with various constraints on them. For instance, XML has been used to define a successor to HTML called XHTML. Many examples in this chapter and the next are from the XHTML specification.

XML is not a single technology, but a bundle of several related technologies. Since XML allows you to define your own element tags and attributes, it follows that you have to have a style sheet, to specify how your elements are to be displayed. You need a mechanism for associating your document with the style sheet. You also need a mechanism for preventing name conflicts between your tags and somebody else's somewhere on the Web.

When XML was first released, all those additional technologies and mechanisms were still in the draft stages. Unavoidably, the first wave of XML books had to use draft specifications that have since been revised beyond recognition. To give just one example, the eXtensible Style Language, XSL, has split into two languages, one for transforming XML documents (XSLT), the other for displaying them (the formatting part of XSL, which has comparable features to Cascading Style Sheets). XSLT specification has been issued as a recommendation, while the formatting part is still in a working draft stage.

This book is one of the first that use only established standards: **all the specifications described in this book have been issued as Recommendations by W3C**. In particular, we cover the contents of the following documents (all of them to be found at `http://www.w3.org/TR/`):

Recommendation	Date approved
HTML 4.01	August 1999 (Proposed)
XML 1.0	February 1998
Namespaces in XML	January 1999
Associating Style Sheets with XML Documents	June 1999
XHTML 1.0	August 1999 (Proposed)
XSLT 1.0	November, 1999
XPath 1.0	November, 1999

In a book on Java and XML, we could not possibly cover all this material in complete detail. We're looking for the bigger picture, and to understand the features of XML that make it so important for processing both documents and data. However, you can use our chapters for reference also, together with W3C specifications. After this chapter, you should be able to read W3C specifications fluently, including EBNF (the Extended Backus-Naur Form for defining grammars that we discussed in Chapter 4). The XML specification and other W3C documents use EBNF productions to describe syntactic constructions, and we will quote those productions often because, once you know how to read them, they pack a lot of content into very few lines.

This chapter and the next are about the core XML specification. In this chapter, we go over:

- ❏ A brief tour of XML
- ❏ Differences between XML and SGML, shown through differences between XHTML and HTML 4.0
- ❏ XML document syntax
- ❏ XML Namespaces

The next chapter is about XML DTDs, the physical organization of XML documents, and the relationship between the XML Recommendation and XML processors. Processors themselves make their appearance in the chapter after that. If you are already familiar with XML, you may want to skip to Chapter 7, to see how it is used in a Java application. If you are new to XML, use this chapter and the next as references: don't try to absorb all the details on first reading but rather get the main ideas and the general picture, and return to these chapters as needed.

Our first task is to explain what makes XML so important.

A Brief Tour of XML

There's so much hype about XML that the natural reaction is to be a bit suspicious. Or maybe it was a natural reaction, the first year or so. Now, it's clear that XML is an important development, with wide ranging ramifications. The main points, which we will elaborate in the subsections that follow, are these:

- ❑ XML is a tool for defining languages.

- ❑ XML languages are easy to read and learn.

- ❑ There is a large body of HTML users who can move to XML languages easily. SGML users can move to XML languages even more easily.

- ❑ XML languages are easy for computers to process, exchange and display.

- ❑ XML processors are ubiquitous, free and conform to established standards.

This combination of technical features and practical circumstance makes XML a major enabling technology for standardization of data and document formats. Standardization leads to rapid progress in electronic interchange of data and documents, among and between computer programs and human agents.

XML is Easy to Read

Suppose you have a database of book records, containing, for instance:

```
Title: Javascript Objects
Authors:
    Author:
        Last: Myers
        First: Tom
    Author:
        Last: Nakhimovsky
        First: Alexander
Publisher: Wrox Press, Ltd.
Year: 1998
List price: 39.95
ISBN:1-861001-8-49
cover: paper
```

If you were asked to represent this information in HTML, you could use a table row for each data record:

```
<tr><td>Javascript Objects</td>…</tr>
```

Or, you could use <DIV> for each record, <H1> for the title within each record and paragraphs for the remaining fields:

```
<DIV><H1>Javascript Objects</H1>…</DIV>
```

Whatever the choice, the markup has nothing to do with the content of the record, which makes it hard to organize and search for data. If you use an XML language, however, you can write:

```
<book cover="paper">
    <title>Javascript Objects</title>
    <authors>
        <author><last>Myers</last><first>Tom></first></author>
        <author><last>Nakhimovsky</last><first>Alexander></first></author>
    </authors>
    ...
    <isbn>1-861001-8-49</isbn>
</book>
```

The structure and meaning of the database record are clearly reflected in XML markup, because in XML you are free to define your own markup languages tailored for the specific kind of information your document contains.

XML is a Tool for Defining Markup Languages.

Simplifying a bit, a markup language is a set of tags and a set of attributes for each tag. You don't have to write a formal definition in order to start using an XML markup language: you can simply decide in your mind what tags and attributes you need and start using them, just as we did with our book records. XML also contains a tool for defining markup languages formally. A language, in this context, is:

- ❑ a set of tags, each specifying an **element** of the language. For instance, the definition of HTML specifies all the tags that it can use: HEAD, BODY, P, and so on.

- ❑ structure rules: what other elements, if any, an element can contain. For instance, BODY can contain P, but HEAD cannot contain P, and P cannot contain BODY.

- ❑ a set of **attributes** defined for each element. For instance, BODY can have an onload attribute but P can't.

We will call a language defined in XML "an XML language" or "an XML application". The syntax of an XML language is the familiar HTML syntax of tags and attributes. Traditionally, an XML language is called "document type", and a grammar for such a language is called "Document Type Definition" or DTD. Texts that conform to a DTD (equivalent to grammatical English sentences or syntactically correct programs) are called **valid documents**.

DTDs and CFGs

DTDs serve the same function as context free grammars, but their syntax is different. For instance, to define our book-language markup, we would say:

```
<!DOCTYPE book [
    <!ELEMENT book (title,authors,publisher,year,listprice,isbn)>
    <!ATTLIST book
        cover (hard|paper) "hard" <-- "hard" is the default -->
    >
    <!ELEMENT title (#PCDATA)     -- Parsed Character Data -->
    <!ELEMENT authors (author +) -- one or more authors    -->
    <!ELEMENT author (last,first)>
    <!-- and so on -->
]>
```

Don't worry about the details for now; the main point to notice is that, apart from attributes, DTDs are very similar to formal grammars. The first rule, for the book element, would be rewritten in EBNF as:

```
book::= title authors publisher year listprice isbn
```

Here are some analogies between formal grammars and XML/SGML DTDs:

Formal Grammars	SGML/XML
grammar	DTD
language	document type
non-terminals	elements
start symbol	root element
sentence	document
grammar rule	element declaration
right-hand side of a rule	element content model

A major difference between an XML document and an English sentence or a computer program is that an XML document always contains its non-terminal symbols (tags), and can also contain its grammar (DTD). Constructing a parse tree for an English sentence or a computer program is a complex task, while constructing a parse tree for an XML document is very easy: the document contains its own parse tree in the form of element tags.

XML Documents Describe Their Own Syntax

Addressing our theme from the previous chapters, one of the great things about XML documents is that they are self-describing, in two ways:

❑ Each document is marked up to show its parse tree.

❑ A document may contain its grammar (DTD), or a reference to it. The parser can check whether or not the document conforms to the grammar.

This makes it easy for non-programmers to produce grammatically correct documents. Add to this the ubiquity of parsers, including validating parsers embedded in XML editors, and you get a great tool for defining mini-languages that initialize and customize programs. In fewer, if more technical, words, XML is well suited to support meta-programming, programs that create or modify or customize other programs.

XML can be Displayed in a Browser

Like HTML documents, documents written in any XML language can be displayed in a browser. The difference is that, out of the box, browsers know how to display HTML elements, such as <H1> or <UL>. You can override browser defaults using a style sheet, but style sheets are optional. In XML, you define your own tags, and the browser has no idea how to display them unless you provide a style sheet. Given a style sheet (either CSS or XSL), 5th generation browsers, such as Internet Explorer 5.0 or the Mozilla project, can display .xml files directly. Moreover, since XML tags can and should contain only structural information, the same XML file can be outfitted with different style sheets for different occasions; some of them may specify, for instance, how to "display" the file as a sound or video stream.

What about earlier browsers that don't know about XML files or even style sheets? For those, we'd have to arrange to have the XML file parsed into a parse tree and displayed by traversing the tree; or we can convert the XML file to HTML and then display it. Beginning with Capter 7, we will show examples of how this can be done.

XML is a Serialization Format for Objects

Serialization is the process of encoding an arbitrary graph of inter-related objects (such as Java objects) into a linear sequence. This is essential for being able to save the state of an object-oriented program to a file for later retrieval, or for sending objects over a network connection. Traditionally, serialization is performed by converting to a binary format, but there's no reason why characters cannot be used. Character-based serialization is likely to require more disk space and/or bandwidth, but it has its advantages.

XML provides, in effect, a serialization format with a very attractive combination of properties: it follows a standard non-proprietary syntax; it uses Unicode, just as Java does; it is human-readable; software for parsing, transforming and synthesizing data in XML formats is ubiquitous and free; and finally, XML-ized data can always be coupled with a style sheet and presented to a human user in a variety of modes and formats. It's not surprising that using XML for data interchange, although less prominent initially, is rapidly overtaking the use of XML for document authoring and presentation.

XML is a Good Glue for Multi-Tier Applications

Since XML can be both displayed in the browser and used to encode objects to be passed from one application component to another over the network, it is becoming widely used in multi-tier applications. On the client, it is used for display and simple processing. In the middle tier, it is used to serialize and exchange data. A multitude of companies, including both Microsoft and Sun, have published white papers showing multi-tier diagrams with components sending XML to each other and to the browser.

XML is a Major Enabling Technology

XML has become a major enabling technology for standardization of data and document formats. Hardly a day passes by without an announcement such as this one (quoted from Robin Cover's SGML/HTML page at `http://www.oasis-open.org/cover/xfrmlAnn.html`):

NEW YORK, NY. August 30, 1999.

The `<http://www.aicpa.org/>`American Institute of Certified Public Accountants (AICPA), six information technology companies, and the five largest accounting and professional services firms are developing an XML-based specification for the preparation and exchange of financial reports and data. The announcement was made today by the AICPA.

Through this project, these organizations are seeking to improve access and lower distribution costs for financial information.

The specification, which is currently called XFRML (for "XML-based Financial Reporting Markup Language"), will be the digital language of business. This is a framework that will allow the financial community a standards-based method to prepare, publish in a variety of formats, exchange and analyze financial reports and the information they contain. XFRML, which will be freely licensed, will also permit the automatic exchange and reliable extraction of financial information among various software applications.

In addition to the AICPA, the project working group now includes the five largest accounting and professional services firms (Arthur Andersen LLP, Deloitte & Touche LLP, Ernst & Young LLP, KPMG LLP and PricewaterhouseCoopers LLP); two accounting software market-related companies (FRx Software Corporation, Great Plains); the e-content company, a division of Interleaf, Inc., and a leader in the delivery of XML-based content management solutions for e-business applications; `FreeEDGAR.com`, Inc./EDGAR Online, Inc., leading distributors of financial information over the Internet; and The Woodburn Group, a middle-market business information-systems consultant. In addition, Microsoft Corporation, developer of the BizTalk framework, is a member of the working group.

A great number of similar initiatives are in various stages of development; you can find references to them at Robin Cover's page. Everyone has understood the need for standardization for a long time, but XML provides a format in which standards can be easily formulated, discussed and agreed upon. There's also a big incentive: once an XML-based standard is in place, the implementation comes for free, in the form of all those XML parsers and browsers that can process and display your standard documents. Standardization, in turn, leads to rapid progress in electronic document and data interchange both between organizations and between computer programs.

We're not going to get into financial reports, but two other recent XML languages are so important that we felt we should use them as examples and cover in some detail. One is **XHTML**, the successor of HTML that will take over the Web in a couple of years. The other is **WML**, **Wireless Markup Language**, that will bring the Web to small devices, such as cellular phones, pagers and PDAs. WML is part of a suite of specifications known as **WAE** (Wireless Applications Environment), developed by WAP forum. (See `http://www.wapforum.org` for all the exciting stuff.)

XML and SGML; XHTML and HTML

XML is a descendant of SGML, simplified and streamlined for use in distributed environments. SGML stands for Standard Generalized Markup Language, a standard invented in the 1980s for the publishing industry. What we said about XML applies to SGML as well: it's not really a language, but a tool for defining languages. In fact, SGML is even more a definition tool than XML, because an XML document can be useful even without a DTD, while in SGML, each document must have a DTD, so it must belong to a formally defined document type. During the years of SGML existence, many excellent document types have been created and used for publishing and other needs. By far the best-known of them is HTML.

From the beginning, HTML was intended to be a SGML language, but a formal DTD had to wait until there was an established authority to author a DTD and make it stick. The first version to have a DTD is HTML 4.0, adopted as a Recommendation in December 1997. In fact, it has three of them: a forward-looking "strict DTD", a backward-looking "transitional DTD" that makes concessions to the accumulated body of bad HTML habits, and a separate DTD for frameset documents.

When XML first appeared, one frequently heard the question: "What's the difference between HTML and XML?" The question is not very good because it mixes levels; it's a little bit like asking: "What's the difference between this cookie and that cookie cutter?" XML is a tool for defining languages, and you could use it to define (a new version of) HTML. That's exactly what happened: in 1999, the three HTML 4.0 DTDs were superceded by a corresponding triple of XHTML DTDs, written in XML.

This obviously suggests the question "What are the differences between HTML 4.0 and XHTML 1.0?" Section 4 of the XHTML specification answers precisely this question. It lists 10 differences, but, in fact, only one of them is really major. Two others follow from it, and the rest are minor details. We'll start with the major one.

The Well-formedness Constraint

In quick summary, HTML elements in a page can contain other elements, and this containment hierarchy forms a tree. The root of every HTML document tree is the `<HTML>` element. Being the root means that all other elements in the page are its children or more distant descendants: it contains all other elements, and it does not itself have a parent element. Every other page element has one and only one parent. This is what it means to form a tree: every element except the root has one and only one parent. The single-parent requirement, in turn, means that elements cannot partially overlap: either they do not overlap at all, or one of them properly contains in the other.

This is the most basic **well-formedness constraint** on all documents in all SGML and XML languages, including HTML: no partial overlap. For non-empty elements that are properly outfitted with both start and end tags, the no-overlap constraint is easy to state in terms of tags: for no two tags A and B is it legal to have:

```
<A>...<B>...</A>...</B>
```

Another way of stating this constraint is to say that we are going to pair up start and end tags in the last-in first-out order: an end tag is paired up with the last start tag that is still single. Under this procedure, our example has tags that do not match: we have `<B>...</A>` and, enclosing them, `<A>...</B>`.

If all elements have start and end tags, the well-formedness constraint is very easy to check in a single pass over the document, using a stack: as you encounter a start tag, push it on stack; as you encounter a matching end tag, pop the start tag off the stack. If in the end the stack is empty then the document is well-formed. If at any time during the pass, you come across an end tag that does not match the start tag at the top of the stack, the document is not well-formed. If you reach the end of the document and there are still some start tags sitting on the stack, the document is not well-formed either. Note a very important fact: we don't need a DTD in order to check for well-formedness in this way.

This brings us to the most important difference between XHTML (and other XML languages) and HTML (and other SGML languages): **an XHTML document can be checked for well-formedness using the procedure just described, and without using a DTD**. This is the major difference between XTHML and HTML that we were talking about. There are two aspects to it: first, XML is different from SGML in its requirements; second, the existing HTML browsers are lax in enforcing even the requirements that are common to XML and SGML. As the specification puts it:

Well-formedness is a new concept introduced by XML. Essentially this means that all elements must either have closing tags or be written in a special form (as described below), and that all the elements must nest.

Although overlapping is illegal in SGML, it was widely tolerated in existing browsers. (Section 4.1)

Over-indulgent browsers aside, the two syntactic differences between XHTML and HTML, which are really general differences between XML and SGML are as follows:

- ❑ In XTHML, all non-empty elements must have an end tag. In HTML, many elements don't have to.

- ❑ In XHTML, empty elements may have an end tag. If they don't, they use an abbreviated syntax that combines a start-end tag pair in a single tag: `<BR/>`.

Let's look at an example.

An HTML/XHTML/XML Page

Here's a very simple HTML page with all its start tags neatly matched by the corresponding end tags:

```
<html><head><title>HTML Example</title></head>
<body>
   <p>a paragraph followed by a list</p>
   <ul>
    <li>item one</li>
    <li>item two</li>
   </ul>
   <p>Another paragraph with a line break <BR></BR>in the middle.</p>
</body></html>
```

This is both a legal HTML document and a legal XHTML document: you could precede it with either of the following two declarations:

```
<!DOCTYPE HTML PUBLIC "-//W3C//DTD HTML 4.0 Strict//EN"
    "http://www.w3.org/TR/REC-html140/strict.dtd">

<!DOCTYPE html PUBLIC "-//W3C//DTD XHTML 1.0 Strict//EN"
    "http://www.w3.org/TR/xhtml1/DTD/strict.dtd">
```

> **Note that the DOCTYPE is HTML (in capitals) in the HTML file, but could also be in lowercase. In the XHTML file, the DOCTYPE is in lowercase and has to be that way. XML is case sensitive, and requires that all tags and attribute names must be in lower case.**

The same page is also a valid XML document, and so you could put exactly the same content in a `.xml` file, with the following declaration:

```
<?xml version='1.0' encoding='us-ascii'?>
<!DOCTYPE html SYSTEM "http://www.w3.org/TR/xhtml1/DTD/strict.dtd">
```

For a `.xml` file, you would have to provide a style sheet, in order to specify how the elements are displayed. In a `.html` file, the browser can use the default style specifications that come with the browser.

With respect to markup, in XHTML, the `<BR></BR>` sequence would likely be replaced by `<BR/>`, but no other changes are possible or necessary. An HTML document would probably omit a number of end tags:

```
<html><head><title>HTML Example</title></head>
<body>
  <p>a paragraph followed by a list
  <ul>
    <li>item one
    <li>item two
  </ul>
  <p>Another paragraph with a line break <BR>in the middle.
</body></html>
```

This is still a legal HTML 4.0 document. However, leaving out `</UL>` would violate the DTD. How do we know that? Let's look at the grammar rule – that is, element declaration – for `UL`.

An SGML Element Declaration

The `UL` element is declared in the HTML 4.0 strict DTD as follows:

```
<!ELEMENT UL - - (LI)+ -- unordered list -->
```

This rule consists of the following components:

- ❑ **<!ELEMENT**: the tag in the DTD language that introduces element declarations
- ❑ **UL**: the name of the element to be defined. Corresponds to the left-hand side of a context-free grammar rule. In HTML 4.0, the tag is in the upper case, although it's not case sensitive.
- ❑ **- -**: indicate that both start and end tag are required. Optional tags are indicated by an O.
- ❑ **(LI)+** : the element's "content model". Corresponds to the right-hand side of a grammar rule. The + means "one or more", as usual.
- ❑ **-- unordered list** --: a comment
- ❑ **>**: the closing bracket. There are no end tags in the DTD language.

With the exception of an optional comment, these are the components of all element declarations in SGML. Let's look at another one:

```
<!ELEMENT P - O (%inline;)* -- paragraph -->
```

This says that a `<P>` element has a required start tag but an optional end tag, and it may consist of 0 or more repetitions of something called `inline`. To refer to `inline` you place it between a percent sign and a semicolon: `%inline;`. This is an example of an **entity reference**, and `inline` is an example of an entity name. Entity names are like abbreviations, or macros that need to be expanded. We are not going to trace inline back to its declaration (but you're welcome to: the HTML DTD makes very good reading). The main point for us is that a `<P>` element doesn't have to have an end tag, and, as a result, the parser cannot construct the document tree without consulting the DTD.

End Tags, Empty Elements and the Parser

Getting back to our example, what is the parser to do after seeing this sequence:

```
<p>a paragraph followed by a list <ul> ... </ul>
```

If this were an XML parser, it would immediately assume that the overall structure is like this:

```
<p>... <ul>...</ul>...</p>
```

In other words, the parser would assume that the UL element is a child, not a sibling, of P. An HTML parser has to consider the additional possibility that P and UL are siblings. In order to decide on the right structure, the parser has to consult the DTD, to see whether a `<UL>` is allowed inside a `<P>`. In other words, it has to track down all those entity definitions; or else it has to consult a table that, for each possible ordered pair of elements states whether the second element terminates the first in the absence of an end tag. A similar problem arises with empty elements, such as `<BR>`, whose end tag (in HTML) is always optional:

```
<!ELEMENT BR - O EMPTY -- forced line break -->
```

SGML was developed in the 1980s, for the publishing industry. It predates both the Internet and authoring tools. Its designers were trying to minimize keystrokes, and didn't hesitate to make the parser's job more difficult because the parser was supposed to reside on a powerful mainframe. SGML's mutation into XML, and the XHTML re-write of HTML 4.0, were motivated by an opposite set of concerns. On a wide-open Web, a DTD may or may not exist, and even if it does, it may reside on a different – and sometimes inaccessible – computer. The "user-agent" that interprets the file may be on a very small computing platform, like a Palm Pilot. At the same time, authoring tools have largely automated the task of tag-typing. For these reasons, XML languages have been designed to be easy to parse, and to yield a unique parse tree even in the absence of a DTD. In particular, there are no optional tags: the XHTML declarations for UL and BR are:

```
<!ELEMENT ul (li)+>
<!ELEMENT BR EMPTY -- forced line break -->
```

Extensibility

As an additional bonus, if an XML language does have a DTD, it is easier to modify and extend than an SGML-based DTD. If you want to add a new element to an SGML language, you have to specify how its tags interact with other elements' tags. Under XML rules, since every subtree is well-formed and properly nested, you simply add an element. Here's how the XHTML specification puts it:

"XHTML is designed to be extensible. This extensibility relies upon the XML requirement that documents be well-formed. Under SGML, the addition of a new group of elements would mean alteration of the entire DTD. In an XML-based DTD, all that is required is that the new set of elements be internally consistent and well-formed to be added to an existing DTD. This greatly eases the development and integration of new collections of elements.(http://www.w3.org/TR/1999/xhtml1-19990505/#why)"

The modularized and easily-extensible version of XHTML is a separate document that is still in draft form (http://www.w3c.org/TR/xhtml-modularization). We will see its DTD in the next chapter.

Parsers and Discipline

XHTML differs from HTML 4.0 not only in technical detail but also in its philosophical attitude towards grammatical errors. As you well know, existing browsers will bend over backwards to display a page even if it's riddled with grammatical mistakes. Our example page can be stripped to almost nothing, as below, and both Netscape and Microsoft browsers will still show it as if it were a full grammatical document:

```
<p>a paragraph followed by a list
    <li>item one
    <li>item two
```

Yes, this is the entire page, there's nothing else in the file. As you can imagine, this means a lot more work for the parser writers, and for the parsers themselves. This is fine if you have a powerful desktop and a multi-megabyte browser, but what if you want to view your page from a Palm Pilot? Here's again what the XHTML specification has to say:

"XHTML is designed for portability. There will be increasing use of non-desktop user agents to access Internet documents. Some estimates indicate that by the year 2002, 75% of Internet document viewing will be carried out on these alternate platforms. In most cases these platforms will not have the computing power of a desktop platform, and will not be designed to accommodate ill-formed HTML as current user agents tend to do. Indeed if these user agents do not receive well-formed XHTML, they may simply not display the document."(http://www.w3.org/TR/xhtml1/#why)

What it boils down to is that XHTML processors are going to enforce grammar rules more vigorously than current browsers do. Does this mean that a lot of sloppy HTML documents out there are going to become unusable? Yes and no. They will become unusable in later browsers unless you tidy them up using a program such as TIDY. This is what the specification has to say about it:

"HTML Tidy" is a tool for detecting and correcting a wide range of markup errors prevalent in HTML. It can also be used as a tool for converting existing HTML content to be well formed XML. Tidy is being made available on the same terms as other W3C sample code, in other words, free for any purpose, and entirely at your own risk. It is available from http://www.w3.org/Status.html#TIDY. A Windows version of Tidy is available, as part of a larger package, HTML-Kit, from www.chami.com/html-kit.

HTML vs. XHTML: Summary of Differences

We can now inspect section 4 of the XHTML 1.0 specification that gives a 10-point summary of differences between HTML 4.0 and XHTML 1.0. Here's the section almost in full, with a couple of examples and explanations omitted, and a couple of explanations of our own inserted in square brackets:

4. Differences with HTML 4.0

Due to the fact that XHTML is an XML application, certain practices that were perfectly legal in SGML-based HTML 4.0 must be changed.

4.1 Documents must be well-formed

Well-formedness is a new concept introduced by XML. Essentially this means that all elements must either have closing tags or be written in a special form (as described below), and that all the elements must nest.

Although overlapping is illegal in SGML, it was widely tolerated in existing browsers.
`<snip/>`

4.2 Element and attribute names must be in lower case

XHTML documents must use lower case for all HTML element and attribute names, [because that's how they are defined in the XHTML DTD]. XML is case-sensitive e.g. `<li>` and `<LI>` are different tags.

4.3 For non-empty elements, end tags are required

In SGML-based HTML 4.0 certain elements were permitted to omit the end tag; with the elements that followed implying closure. This omission is not permitted in XML-based XHTML [because it violates the well-formedness constraint]. All elements other than those declared in the DTD as EMPTY must have an end tag.
`<snip/>`

4.4 Attribute values must always be quoted

All attribute values must be quoted, even those which appear to be numeric.
`<snip/>`

4.5 Attribute Minimization

XML does not support attribute minimization. Attribute-value pairs must be written in full. Attribute names such as compact and checked cannot occur in elements without their value being specified.

CORRECT: unminimized attributes

```
<dl compact="compact">
```

INCORRECT: minimized attributes

```
<dl compact>
```

199

4.6 Empty Elements

Empty elements must either have an end tag or the start tag must end with />. For instance, <br/> or <hr></hr>. See HTML Compatibility Guidelines for information on ways to ensure this is backward compatible with HTML 4.0 user agents.

```
<snip/>
```

4.7 White space handling in attribute values

In attribute values, user agents will strip leading and trailing white-space from attribute values and map sequences of one or more white space characters (including line breaks) to a single inter-word space (an ASCII space character for western scripts). See Section 3.3.3 of [the XML Recommendation].

4.8 Script and Style elements

In XHTML, the script and style elements are declared as having #PCDATA content. As a result, < and & will be treated as the start of markup, and entities such as < and & will be recognized as entity references by the XML processor to < and & respectively. Wrapping the content of the script or style element within a CDATA marked section avoids the expansion of these entities.

```
<script>
<![CDATA[
... unescaped script content ...
]]>
</script>
```

CDATA sections are recognized by the XML processor and appear as nodes in the Document Object Model, see Section 1.3 of the DOM Level 1 Recommendation.

An alternative is to use external script and style documents.

4.9 SGML exclusions

SGML gives the writer of a DTD the ability to exclude specific elements from being contained within an element. Such prohibitions (called "exclusions") are not possible in XML.

```
<snip/>
```

4.10 The elements with 'id' and 'name' attributes

HTML 4.0 defined the name attribute for the elements a, applet, frame, iframe, img, and map., for backward compatibility with HTML 3.2. HTML 4.0 also introduced the id attribute. Both of these attributes are designed to be used as fragment identifiers.

In XML, fragment identifiers are of type ID, and there can only be a single attribute of type ID per element. Therefore, in XHTML 1.0 the id attribute is defined to be of type ID. In order to ensure that XHTML 1.0 documents are well-structured XML documents, XHTML 1.0 documents MUST use the id attribute when defining fragment identifiers, even on elements that historically have also had a name attribute. See the HTML Compatibility Guidelines for information on ensuring such anchors are backwards compatible when serving XHTML documents as media type text/html.

Note that in XHTML 1.0, the name attribute of these elements is formally deprecated, and will be removed in a subsequent version of XHTML.

Discussion

As we said, the biggest change is the principle that XHTML documents must be well formed, and their well-formedness must be verifiable in the absence of a DTD. This is Difference 4.1. Differences 4.3 and 4.6 follow from it. The rest are relatively minor details. Many of them require a familiarity with XML that we haven't yet reached, but they will be revisited as we go along.

Tidy will take care of misplaced or missing end tags and quotes around attribute values. It will not completely convert your HTML document to XHTML. However, the XHTML Recommendation contains a very useful "Appendix C. HTML Compatibility Guidelines" that explains how to make your pages both good XML and recognizable by HTML browsers. We will go over that appendix in the next chapter, after we cover all the XML detail that it discusses.

XML Documents

The central information unit of XML is an XML document. As with any other complex piece of software, an XML document has physical content and logical structure. Although the distinction sounds neat, in practice it is hard to talk about logical structure without mentioning physical entities, such as characters, strings and files. (A generic name for all of them in XML specifications is "entity".) We are going to present the logical organization first, but there will be a number of times when we'll have to refer forward to the entities section.

Documents, Processors and Applications

Another general picture to bear in mind is how documents function within an overall system. The XML Recommendation assumes that there is a separate software module, called the processor or the parser, that converts the physical content of the document into a data structure or a sequence of events and callbacks. The output of the processor is made available to a larger application (which may or may not be a web browser). The interactions between the processor and the application are codified in two specifications: **Document Object Model (DOM)** and **Simple API for XML (SAX)**. We will characterize them very briefly here, but will look at them in depth in Chapters 7, 8 and 9.

DOM, developed by W3C, specifies interfaces between the application and the internal representation of the document created by the processor. A typical DOM method is `getFirstChild(Node n)`.

SAX does not create an internal representation of the document. It specifies a sequence of standard events and callbacks that the application can use to interact with the processor. A typical SAX application defines event handlers such as `startDocument()`, `endDocument()`, `startElement()`, `endElement()`. SAX was developed by David Megginson (`www.megginson.com`), outside W3C, as a result of discussions on the xml-dev list. The package name for SAX is `org.xml.sax`.

Most parsers, including Sun's, implement both DOM and SAX interfaces. We'll have much more to say about them in the chapters to follow.

Validating and Non-Validating Processors

Without access to a DTD, the best a processor can do is check the document for well-formedness and construct its element tree. This is pretty good, and there are several reasons why the processor wouldn't go any further:

❏ There is no DTD.

❏ The processor doesn't have access to it.

❏ The processor is such that it doesn't know what to do with a DTD.

❏ The processor is instructed to ignore the DTD, for reasons of efficiency.

If none of these hold, the processor can go further and check the document against its grammar rules. This is called "validating"; the processor that knows how to do it is called a "validating parser", and a document that checks out is called "valid".

The Main Data Types: CDATA and PCDATA

Ultimately, XML documents consist of characters, or "character data" (CDATA). It comes in two flavors: CDATA that may contain markup and needs to be parsed (PCDATA), and plain CDATA that is not going to be parsed for markup. Elements consist of PCDATA, while attribute values consist of CDATA. A separately recognized data type is NMTOKEN, a string of "name characters" defined by the XML Recommendation.

Note that PCDATA is "data that is going to be parsed", not "data already parsed". A subject of frequent concern is how to escape markup characters in PCDATA. There are five characters that need to be escaped: `<`, `>`, `"`, `'<`, `&`. To insert them as data, you can either refer to them by their number or by a special predeclared name:

Character	Number	Name
<	60	lt ("less-than")
>	62	gt ("greater-than")
"	34	quot
'	39	apos
&	38	amp

In order to refer to the character, you place its name or number within the `&...;` delimiters; the number is preceded by #. So, to refer to the `&` character, you can say `&amp;` or `&#138;`. We'll have much more to say about these subjects in the next chapter.

The Logical Structure

Logically, an XML document consists of the following five kinds of components:

Kind of component	Delimited by
declarations in the DTD	`<!DOCTYPE[...]>` `<!ELEMENT...>`
	`<!ATTLIST...>`
	`<!ENTITY...>` `<!NOTATION...>`
elements in the document proper	*<tag ...>... </ tag >* or *<tag .../>*
CDATA sections	`<![CDATA[...]]>`
comments	`<!-- -->`
processing instructions (PIs)	`<?...?>`

The main parts are declarations that form the DTD and elements that form the content of the document. The rest are minor players, three flavors of unparsed text. In this chapter, we'll do documents that do not contain a DTD, so we don't have to worry about the information in the first row of the table.

Documents have to have element content, but everything else is optional. Here is an example of a very simple, complete and well-formed document:

```
<greeting>Hello, XML!</greeting>
```

In order to compose more complex documents we need to know the rules of composition. Frequently, we will present them as EBNF productions followed by examples and explanations. All EBNF productions are quoted from the XML specification and other W3C documents where they are carefully numbered. Production 1 defines the document:

The Document Syntax

```
[1]   document ::=  prolog element Misc*
```

This says that a document is composed of a prolog, followed by the root element, followed by optional miscellaneous material. For instance:

```
<?xml version='1.0' encoding='us-ascii'?>
   <!-- this was xml declaration; nothing can come before it, not even a comment
   -->

<!DOCTYPE html SYSTEM "http://www.w3.org/TR/xhtml1/DTD/strict.dtd">
   <!-- this was Document type declaration;
        everything up to here, including this comment, constitutes the prolog
   -->
```

```
<html>
  <!-- the root element has started; must be the same as DOCTYPE -->
  <body>This looks like HTML, but it's XML</body>
</html><!-- end of root element -->
  <!-- you can add miscellaneous comments or processing instructions in the end
    -->
```

The Document's Prolog

`Prolog` is composed of optional elements, as follows: an optional XML declaration, followed by `Misc*`, followed by an optional DTD, again with `Misc*` thrown in:

```
[22]  prolog ::=  XMLDecl? Misc* (doctypedecl Misc*)?
```

It's not hard to figure out what `XMLDecl` and `doctypedecl` are; what's `Misc*`? It's any sequence, including possibly an empty sequence, of comments, PIs (processing instructions), and whitespace. Here's the `Misc` production:

```
[27]  Misc ::=  Comment I PI I  S
```

Remember the `S` non-terminal from Chapter 4? We didn't tell you at the time, but we lifted it, together with `Eq` and several others, from the XML specification.

The XML Declaration

Although optional, an XML declaration should always be included in an XML document. It's considered to be good form, and it gives you an opportunity to specify important attributes of the document.

```
[23]  XMLDecl ::=  '<?xml' VersionInfo EncodingDecl? SDDecl? S? '?>'
[24]  VersionInfo ::=  S 'version' Eq (' VersionNum ' I " VersionNum ")
[25]  Eq ::=  S? '=' S?
[26]  VersionNum ::=  ([a-zA-Z0-9_.:] I '-')+
```

Once you've decided to include an XML declaration, you must include the version number. You can also include the encoding and the standalone attributes. Here's a complete set:

```
<?xml version="1.0" encoding='us-ascii' standalone='yes'?>
```

The encoding attribute has to do with the character set and how it is encoded in bits and bytes. We will have a section on that when we get to the physical content of XML files. The standalone attribute is an optimization feature: if your document does not depend on declarations in external entities then you can set the attribute to 'yes', hoping that the parser will notice and optimize its behavior accordingly. This is less useful than it sounds: if there is no external DTD, then standalone is assumed to be "yes" by default; if there is an external DTD then it is likely to contain declarations.

The Document Type Declaration

Document type declarations are defined by production [28] shown here reformatted and with some optional whitespace (S?) removed for ease of reading:

```
[28]   doctypedecl ::=   '<!DOCTYPE' S Name
    (S ExternalID)?
    ('[' (markupdecl | PEReference | S)* ']')?
                    '>'
        [  VC: Root Element Type ]
```

The first line shows the opening literal string followed by a Name. The Validity Constraint at the bottom says that the Name must be the same as the name of the root element. The lines in between show two optional elements: `ExternalID` and a sequence, in square brackets, of two more elements, in any number or order, separated by whitespace. The two elements are `markupdecl` (declarations) and `PEReference` (Parameter Entity Reference). These will have to wait till the next chapter.

Comments, CDATA Sections, and PIs

Comments and PIs, together with CDATA sections, are three different flavors of unparsed character data in which markup characters are ignored: the parser suspends its normal operation and only looks for the end marker (`-->`, `?>` or `]]>`). They differ in their intent and in what the processor does when the end marker is found.

Comments

XML comments are exactly like HTML/SGML comments. Many XML parsers ignore them and exclude them from the resulting representation. DOM provides for Comment nodes in the resulting document structure, but you cannot count on it. Even if Comment nodes are there, you cannot control where in the tree they will appear: there is no established relationship between comments and XML elements. If you want to say something to the human reader of your document, use a comment. If you have character data that you don't want parsed but do want passed on to the application, use other options. They include PIs and CDATA sections.

CDATA Sections

Suppose, to take a concrete example, you want to include some Java code in your XML file. You can put your code in an element, e.g., `<java>...</java>`, and it will be very easy for the processor to find it and separate it for special treatment. The problem is that element content is `PCDATA`, and if your code has a line like `while(a>b && b<a)` you'll have to enter it as:

```
while(a&gt;b &amp;&amp; b&lt;a)
```

To avoid this chore, you can put the content of your `<java>` elements into CDATA sections whose content is left unparsed:

```
<java>
    <![CDATA[
        while(a>b && b<a)
        doIt();
    ]]>
</java>
```

Every CDATA section forms a node in the DOM tree, a child of the node for the element that contains the CDATA section.

You have to make sure that your code does not contain a]]> sequence as in:

```
if(arr[indexArr[4]]>5) ...
```

If it does, insert a space between]] and >, or separate the]]> sequence into two CDATA sections.

Processing Instructions

Processing instructions are for invoking some application other than the XML processor to do some computation on a part of your document. For instance, suppose you have an equation-solving program and you want to invoke it in the middle of your XML document. You say:

```
<?SolveIt equation="3*x+4=10" ?>
```

It is up to your application to find the processing instruction, separate it into meaningful tokens and perform whatever action it calls for.

PIs are SGML legacy that is not treated warmly in the XML community. Their drawbacks are:

❑   They use non-standard syntax (PIs are not elements).

❑   There is no connection between XML content and PIs. You cannot nest a PI within a specific element or otherwise control where it will appear in the resulting data structure.

❑   As a minor annoyance, the processor will strip all the leading whitespace.

PIs are used, at least for now, to link style sheets into documents (see below). We will also use PIs as a pretext to practice EBNF, because PI productions contain some very common EBNF idioms, frequently found in XML Recommendation.

EBNF Practice: PI and Name

In defining the syntax of processing instructions, we want to say something like: "start with the start marker; continue with any text that does not contain the end marker; finish with the end marker". Given that the end marker is ?>, the set of all strings that contain the end marker is defined by:

```
(Char* '?>' Char*)
```

Accordingly, the set of all strings that do NOT contain the end marker is defined by:

```
(Char* - (Char* '?>' Char*))
```

This is a very common idiom in the XML Recommendation. You can say it in English as "any sequence of characters that does not contain any sequence of characters that contains ?>". (You should be reminded of a similar rule in our minilanguage grammar of Chapter 4.) Once you understand this idiom, the PI production becomes clear:

```
[16]   PI ::=  '<?' PITarget (S (Char* - (Char* '?>' Char*)))? '?>'
```

There are four parts to this expression: the opening literal <?, the PITarget, an optional part in parentheses, and the closing literal. The optional part consists of some whitespace followed by the expression we have just discussed: anything that does not contain the end marker.

PITarget is intended to be the name of the program to be invoked. It can be any legitimate XML name other than the sequence "xml", in any capitalization pattern. This is another common idiom in the XML Recommendation.

```
[17]   PITarget ::=  Name - (('X' | 'x') ('M' | 'm') ('L' | 'l'))
```

What's in a Name? This is a separate area, related to the subject of Namespaces.

XML Names

A Name is a sequence of Unicode characters that starts with a letter, an underscore or a colon, and continues with any NameChar.

```
[4]   NameChar ::=  Letter | Digit | '.' | '-' | '_' | ':' | CombiningChar |
                     Extender
[5]   Name ::=  (Letter | '_' | ':') (NameChar)*
```

Letter, Digit, CombiningChar and Extender are groups of Unicode characters defined in the XML spec (productions 84-89). In brief:

❑ Letter includes both letters from all alphabets and also ideographic characters from the Chinese-Japanese-Korean writing systems.

❑ Digit includes our familiar digits but also the ten digits used in Tibetan writing.

❑ Combining characters and Extenders are "decorations" that appear on base characters, like accents on some French vowels (á) or umlauts on some German vowels (ö).

Name is an important class of identifiers in XML: not only PITarget, but also element tags and attribute names must be Names. Although the production allows Name to contain a colon or even begin with a colon, in practice, colon was from the beginning "reserved for experimentation with name spaces" (Section 2.3). The Namespace Recommendation redefines the Name production to restrict the use of colon; as a result, several key productions that depend on Name are also redefined. We'll have much more to say about Names in the section on Namespaces.

PIs for Linking Style Sheets into XML Documents

As we said, PIs are SGML legacy and rarely used in XML. You should use the <? ...?> pair of brackets in only two circumstances: for XML declarations (which are not really PIs) and for linking a stylesheet into your document. This is the only time a PI is recommended in a W3C spec, and the recommendation is not exactly enthusiastic:

"The use of XML processing instructions in this specification should not be taken as a precedent. The W3C does not anticipate recommending the use of processing instructions in any future specification." (http://www.w3.org/TR/xml-stylesheet)

In a separate Rationale section, the Recommendation explains: " There was an urgent requirement for a specification for style sheet linking that could be completed in time for the next release from major browser vendors. Only by choosing a simple mechanism closely based on a proven existing mechanism could the specification be completed in time to meet this requirement."

The "proven existing mechanism" is the HTML 4.0 LINK tag. Here are some examples of its use, together with the equivalent XML examples, all borrowed from the xml-stylesheet Recommendation:

```
<LINK href="mystyle.css" rel="stylesheet" type="text/css">
<?xml-stylesheet href="mystyle.css" type="text/css"?>

<LINK href="mystyle.css" title="Compact" rel="stylesheet "type="text/css">
<?xml-stylesheet href="mystyle.css" title="Compact" type="text/css"?>

<LINK href="mystyle.css" title="Medium" rel="alternate stylesheet"
type="text/css">
<?xml-stylesheet alternate="yes" href="mystyle.css" title="Medium"
type="text/css"?>
```

These examples all show CSS stylesheets. XSL stylesheets are linked in exactly the same way. The only difference is that their type is "text/xsl".

Alternatives to PIs

If PIs are shunned, then we should consider alternatives. Remember that the purpose of PIs is to pass information from an XML document, via an XML processor, to an application. There is no reason why such information cannot be passed using standard XML syntax of elements and attributes. There are two main options with subdivisions:

- ❑ Put the information into elements. The application will do the right thing on the basis of the elements' tags.

- ❑ Put the information into attribute values. The application will do the right thing on the basis of the attribute names, or on the basis of special delimiters within attribute values that separate XML data from "processing instructions".

Both approaches are used in such XML languages as XSLT stylesheets, the Wireless Markup Language, and JavaServer Pages. (By the time you read this, JSPs should become fully compliant XML documents.) All three will be discussed at length in the remainder of the book, but here are a couple of examples.

Processing Information in Elements

JSPs have an element <jsp:usebean> whose content is calls on javabean methods. WML has an element <go> that is used for changing location. It can contain <setvar> elements whose attributes are the name and value of a variable. When the application encounters a <go> element, it follows the link to the new location, and, upon arrival, changes the values of the variables.

Processing Information in Attributes

Also in WML, variable names, prefixed by the $ character, can be inserted into an attribute value, and the name will be evaluated by the application. The name can be put in parentheses in case it contains whitespace. A sequence of two dollar signs ($$) represents a single dollar sign character. We use a similar convention in our Subst mini-language.

The Document Proper and Namespaces

The two main parts of an XML document are the DTD (if any) and the document proper, i.e., the root element and everything it contains. While the DTD is less commonly known, the syntax of the document proper is the familiar HTML syntax of tags and attributes. However, since we're now in the business of defining languages, rather than all using the same language, we need a mechanism to prevent name conflicts. This mechanism is called Namespaces. We will present it both through examples and EBNF productions.

About Productions

Now that you have seen several productions from the XML spec, we can give you a couple of general facts about them. They fall into two groups: those that use regular expressions to define groups of characters or character sequences (such as Letter or Name) and those that define context-free grammar productions (such as document or prolog). The productions in the first group are non-recursive, those in the second group are recursive. As a notational convention, the lhs non-terminals in the first group are capitalized, while those in the second group are all lower-case.

Some productions are accompanied by **Well-Formedness Constraints** (**WFC**) and/or **Validity Constraints** (**VC**). WFCs are those constraints that can be checked by a parser that doesn't use the DTD. The most important WFC is the Basic Well-Formedness constraint about matching start and end tags and non-overlapping elements, but there are others, such as: names must be declared before they are used. You will see a number of WFCs below. Validity constraints are those that rely on a DTD and a validating parser that can use it.

The Element Production

The main production for document proper is element:

```
[39] element ::=  EmptyElemTag | STag content ETag
                [  WFC: Element Type Match ][  VC: Element Valid ]

[44] EmptyElemTag ::=  '<' Name (S Attribute)* S? '/>'
[40] STag ::=          '<' Name (S Attribute)* S? '>'
[41] Attribute ::=  Name Eq AttValue
[42] ETag ::=  '</' Name S? '>'
```

These should be very familiar, both from Chapter 4 and from your HTML experience. The Empty Element Tag is exactly like the Start Tag, with a "/" character added. The WFC "Element Type Match" is the Basic Well-Formedness Constraint: the Name in STag must be the same as the Name in ETag. The VC says that the root element will be valid if all the elements it contains are valid.

These element and tag productions are from the 1998 XML 1.0 spec. Like all productions that use the `Name` non-terminal, they were revised in the Namespace recommendation. The revisions replace `Name` with `QName` (qualified name): `Name` qualified by a namespace prefix, to avoid name conflicts.

Namespaces in Programming

All programming languages have some conventions to confine a set of names to an enclosed namespace, so that the same names can peacefully coexist in different namespaces without a conflict. In Java, a package is a namespace for its classes and interfaces, a class is a namespace for its variables and methods, and a method is a namespace for its local variables. So, you can have:

```java
class Author
{
    static public String adj="Dear ";
    String name;
    String title;   // e.g., Mrs., Mr., Miss, Ms., Dr., etc
    ...
}
class Book
{
    Author author;
    String title;
    String adj="boring";
    int nPages;
    public String formLetter()
        {
            String adj=nPages>1000?"too long":this.adj;
            String S=Author.adj+author.title+author.name+":";
            S+="Your book, "+title+" has been remaindered and discontinued"
            S+=" because it is "+adj;
            return S;
        } ...
}
```

You can see that `author.title` can coexist with `book.title`, and the `adj` that is local to `formLetter()` coexists with `this.adj` and `Author.adj`. The local name, in fact, blocks a direct unqualified reference to `this.adj` and `Author.adj`: you have to use their **fully-qualified names**. A fully-qualified name, you notice, consists of the **namespace prefix**, followed by some separator ("." in most object-oriented languages), followed by the unqualified name that is local to the namespace.

In C and C++, you have in addition a "global" namespace, which really means "in the same file but outside any function or class definition". (That was before the Internet and the Web, when the words "global" and "universal" didn't have quite the same literal ring to them.) C and C++ programs don't have to worry about name conflicts with other programs somewhere else on the globe, or even on the same computer. An XML document has exactly that worry, and, until XML Namespaces came along, no remedy for it.

Name Conflicts in XML

A DTD for your document can come from several sources. Suppose you want to have an XHTML document with a few additional tags for book records, as in our little DTD in the beginning of the chapter. You would combine them as follows:

```
<?xml version='1.0' encoding='us-ascii'?>
<!DOCTYPE html SYSTEM "http://www.w3.org/TR/xhtml1/DTD/strict.dtd">
[
    <!ELEMENT book (title,authors,publisher,year,listprice,isbn)>
    <!ATTLIST book
        cover (hard|paper) "hard" <-- "hard" is the default -->
    >
    <!ELEMENT title (#PCDATA)    -- Parsed Character Data -->
    <!ELEMENT authors (author +) -- one or more authors    -->
    <!ELEMENT author (last,first)>
    <!-- and so on -->
]>
```

Now you can write pages that combine elements from both sources:

```
<html><head><title>Books with descriptions</title></head><body>
<p>This book is described elsewhere.</p>
<book cover="paper">
    <title>Javascript Objects</title>
    <authors>
        <author><last>Myers</last><first>Tom</first></author>
        <author><last>Nakhimovsky</last><first>Alexander</first></author>
    </authors>
    ...
    <isbn>1-861001-8-49</isbn>
</book>
<p>This book is ... </p><book>...</body></html>
```

The XML terminology for this arrangement is that your DTD has an **external subset** and an **internal subset**. The problem is that both define a `title` element and, in fact, the second definition will be ignored. In this particular case, no harm results because in both cases title is defined as (`#PCDATA`), but you can easily imagine different and conflicting definitions.

In the initial XML model, all XML names are, in effect, local names in a single namespace. As long as each document belongs to a single DTD, this is not a problem. Once we start thinking of modularizing DTDs and freely combining the modules, the single-namespace model becomes untenable.

A Prefix Solution

We could use the device introduced in Chapter 4 and add a prefix to each tag in our small internal subset:

```
<html><head><title>A list of books</title></head><body>
<ul>
<li>
    <bk:book cover="paper">
    <bk:title>Javascript Objects</bk:title>
    <bk:authors>
        <bk:author><bk:last>Myers</bk:last><bk:first>Tom</bk:first>
        </bk:author>
        <bk:author><bk:last>Nakhimovsky</bk:last><bk:first>Alexander</bk:first>
        </bk:author>
    </bk:authors>
    ...
    <bk:isbn>1-861001-8-49</bk:isbn>
    </bk:book>
</li>
<li><bk:book>...</ul></body></html>
```

However, any such prefix-based notation would be incomplete without additional provisions because we need a way to make sure that our prefix is unique on the Web, now and in the future. That's a tall order.

Fully-Qualified Names for the Web

Fortunately, there is already a mechanism in place for giving unique names to Web resources; it's called the **Uniform Resource Identifier** (**URI**). So, the Namespace Recommendation follows this strategy:

❏ An element within an XML document can be assigned to a globally-unique namespace.

❏ A namespace is uniquely identified by a URI. Beyond the general requirement that it should be unique and persistent, there are no assumptions made about that URI. For instance, it does not have to contain the list of all the names in the namespace. In other words, **it takes no part in the validation process**. This is the greatest weakness of the Namespace mechanism as it now stands.

❏ URIs are too long to use as a prefix, and they do not conform to XML Name syntax. So, within a given document, a short prefix, conforming to XML syntax, is associated with the URI that identifies the desired namespace.

❏ After the document is parsed, the prefix is mapped to the URI, to provide globally-unique fully-qualified names.

In our XHTML-book example, we would add a special attribute to the `<book>` element:

```
<li><bk:book xmlns:bk="http://www.mynamultimedia.com" cover="paper">
```

This associates the prefix `bk:` with a unique URI. (The `xmlns` attribute is reserved by W3C for this purpose.) **After the document is parsed and its element tree built,** in a separate layer of processing, the prefix can be replaced with the URI to obtain names that are guaranteed to be unique, as long as the URIs are unique. This solves our problem: we have unprefixed names that belong to an undeclared "local" namespace, and we have prefixed names that belong to a declared "global" namespace, identified by a URI.

The Scope of the Namespace Declaration

Notice that we declare the namespace prefix only for the `book` element, not for its descendants. The namespace prefix is inherited: if the processor encounters an element with a prefix but without an `xmlns` attribute, it goes to the parent, then grandparent, and so on, until the namespace declaration is found. If it's not found, a **NameSpace Constraint** (**NSC**) is violated. Note that it's not a validity constraint: validity is checked earlier, if at all.

Default Namespace

Namespace inheritance saves a bit of typing. You can save even more typing by declaring a **default namespace**. In other words, the namespace of unprefixed identifiers doesn't have to be local and undeclared: you can associate it with a global namespace identified by a URI. The syntactic convention is to use the `xmlns` attribute without the trailing colon-prefix part:

```
<fin xmlns ='http://ecommerce.org/schema'>
    <!-- the namespace identified by http://ecommerce.org/schema
        is the default namespace for the fin element-->
    <!-- 'price' and 'x-rate' are in that namespace -->
    <price units='Euro'>32.18</price>
    <x-rate>0.97</x-rate>
</fin>
```

In this version, the declared namespace becomes the default for the element in which it is declared and its descendants. Unqualified local element names are assumed to belong to that namespace.

Setting `xmlns` to the empty string is equivalent to having no `xmlns` attribute at all. Suppose you have two elements, `outer` and `inner`, in a page like this:

```
<outer xmlns="http://www.outerspace.com">
    <elt>some element, in outerspace</elt>
    ...
    <inner xmlns="">
        <elt>same element name, different (local) namespace</elt>
    </inner>
    ... back in outer space
</outer>
```

For the beer lover and/or Anglophile, here's an example from the Recommendation:

```
<?xml version='1.0'?>
<Beers>
    <!-- the default namespace is HTML -->
    <table xmlns='http://www.w3.org/TR/REC-html40'>
        <th><td>Name</td><td>Origin</td><td>Description</td></th>
        <tr>
            <!-- no default namespace inside table cells -->
            <td><brandName xmlns="">Huntsman</brandName></td>
            <td><origin xmlns="">Bath, UK</origin></td>
            <td>
                <details xmlns=""><class>Bitter</class><hop>Fuggles</hop>
                    <pro>Wonderful hop, light alcohol, good summer beer</pro>
                    <con>Fragile; excessive variance pub to pub</con>
                </details>
            </td>
        </tr>
    </table>
</Beers>
```

Namespaces and Attribute Names

So far, we have been talking exclusively about element names (or tags). What about attributes? Here things get a little trickier because attribute names are already partitioned into namespaces by elements: it is perfectly common for two different elements to have attributes with the same name. So, in a default namespace, attribute names without prefixes are treated differently from element names without prefixes: they are assumed to be just local names. This is sometimes described by saying that an XML namespace is not just one flat thing the way namespaces are in programming languages, but rather consists of three sub-spaces: element names, attribute names with prefixes and attribute names without prefixes. Each of these three parts forms a namespace in the traditional sense.

What this means in practice is that, if you're using a default namespace with unqualified local names then your attribute will not come from that default namespace: they will simply be local names. The only way to have your attributes to belong to a global namespace, is to declare a prefix for it and use that prefix to qualify your attribute names.

Here's an example to illustrate the point. As you know, it is illegal for a tag to have two attributes with identical names and different values. In the example, the default namespace is the same as the namespace associated with the prefix n1. However, the document is legal because the default namespace does not apply to attribute names:

```
<!-- http://www.w3.org is both the default and bound to n1 -->
<x xmlns:n1="http://www.w3.org"
   xmlns="http://www.w3.org" >
  <bad a="1"
       a="2"/><!-- cannot have two attributes with the same name -->
  <good a="1"
        n1:a="2"/><!-- unprefixed 'a' is in the local, not default namespace
                      it does NOT have an expanded name with a URI prefix -->
</x>
```

If both namespaces had prefixes associated with them, the document would be illegal, as in:

```
<!-- http://www.w3.org is bound to n1 and n2 -->
<x xmlns:n1="http://www.w3.org"
   xmlns:n2="http://www.w3.org" >
   <bad n1:a="1"
        n2:a="2"/><!-- both map to the same expanded name -->
</x>
```

Namespaces and DTDs

Default namespaces do much more than save keystrokes: they make it possible to use namespaces **without rewriting the DTDs**. Remember the big problem: namespaces and DTDs are totally unrelated. When the parser checks prefixed names for validity, it is totally unaware of the significance of the prefix-colon convention. If the DTD declares an `<author>` element, and the document uses `<bk:author>`, the document is not valid. David Megginson (the creator of SAX, among other things) invented useful terminology to describe the current situation with names in XML documents: there is an XML 1.0 perspective and a Namespace perspective, and they are very tenuously related. Megginson's "19 Short Questions about Namespaces (with Answers)" is an excellent summary. We give two long quotes, but read it in full at `http://www.megginson.com/docs/namespace-questions.html`.

Megginson's Q&A on Namespaces

Background

This brief review uses James Clark's notation for writing names that contain both a URI part and a local part. For example, if the URI part of a name were `http://www.foo.com/` and the local part were `a`, the name would be written:

`{http://www.foo.com/}a`

This is purely a convenience notation for the sake of documentation; it is not defined by any known specification, and is unlikely to be recognized by any processor.

Chapter Two. The Namespaces Perspective

[Example 2a]

```
<z:a z:b="x" c="y" xmlns:z="http://www.foo.com/"/>
```

[Q] What is the name of the element in the example above?
[A] The name is z:a from the XML 1.0 perspective, or `{http://www.foo.com/}a` from the Namespaces perspective.
[Q] What is the name of the first attribute in the example above?
[A] The name is z:b from the XML 1.0 perspective, or `{http://www.foo.com/}b` from the Namespaces perspective.
[Q] What is the name of the second attribute in the example above?
[A] The name is c from both the XML 1.0 and the Namespaces perspectives.
[Q] What is the name of the third attribute in the example above?
[A] The name is xmlns:z from the XML 1.0 perspective; from the Namespaces perspective, this attribute is a declaration.

[Q] What do the names mean?

[A] The application determines the meaning of the names.

[Q] What does the namespace URI `http://www.foo.com/` mean?

[A] It has no defined meaning.

[Q] How do you write a DTD declaration describing the structure of this element?

[A] DTDs use the XML 1.0 perspective:

```
<!ELEMENT z:a EMPTY>
<!ATTLIST z:a
  z:b CDATA #IMPLIED
  c CDATA #IMPLIED
  xmlns:z CDATA #FIXED "http://www.foo.com">
```

[Example 2b]

```
<a b="x" c="y" xmlns="http://www.foo.com/"/>
```

[Q] What is the name of the element in the example above?

[A] The name is a from the XML 1.0 perspective, or `{http://www.foo.com/}`a from the Namespaces perspective.

[Q] What is the name of the first attribute in the example above?

[A] The name is b from both the XML 1.0 and the Namespaces perspectives.

[Q] What is the name of the second attribute in the example above?

[A] The name is c from both the XML 1.0 and the Namespaces perspectives.

[Q] What is the name of the third attribute in the example above?

[A] The name is xmlns from the XML 1.0 perspective; from the Namespaces perspective, this attribute is a declaration.

[Q] What do the names mean?

[A] The application determines the meaning of the names.

[Q] What does the namespace URI `http://www.foo.com/` mean?

[A] It has no defined meaning.

[Q] How do you write a DTD declaration describing the structure of this element?

[A] DTDs use the XML 1.0 perspective:

```
<!ELEMENT a EMPTY>
<!ATTLIST a
    b CDATA #IMPLIED
    c CDATA #IMPLIED
    xmlns CDATA #FIXED "http://www.foo.com">
```

Are Namespaces of Any Use?

The key fact in all of this is that namespace URIs are purely formal devices that have no defined meaning; in particular, they take no part in validation. Why is this so? James Clark explains in `http://www.w3.org/XML/#9902clark-ns`:

"It would of course be very useful to have namespace-aware validation: to be able to associate each URI used in a universal name with some sort of schema (similar to a DTD) and be able to validate a document using multiple such URIs with respect to the schemas for all of the URIs. The XML Namespaces Recommendation does *not* provide this. The reason is is that DTDs have many other problems and missing features in addition to lack of namespace-awareness. So the plan is to come up with a new schema mechanism that fixes the problems with DTDs and, as part of this, provides namespace-awareness. This work is being done by the XML Schema Working Group."

Ultimately, Namespaces and their URIs will probably be used to associate an XML language (a set of tags and attribute names) with its intended interpretation, although there is an ongoing debate about whether they should be used that way, and how "interpretation" should be described. In the meantime, Namespaces are essential for understanding the workings of several important XML languages, such as JSP (covered in chapters 10-12), XSLT (covered in Chapter 13) and RDF (not covered in this book. The best way to use them in your own languages is probably with embedded default namespaces, to avoid DTD rewriting. However, if you have a namespace-ready DTD with names already prefixed, then you can certainly use its elements without concern for name conflicts.

Supporting Variants with Namespaces

Suppose your DTD already has a set of prefixed names intended to be used with a namespace declaration. You can maintain several versions of your DTD by simply assigning them to different namespaces. This seems to be Microsoft's plan for maintaining both their initial implementation of XSL, based on an early draft, and the standard XSL, based on the W3C Recommendation. As you may know, an XSL style sheet is an XML document in which all names have the `xsl:` prefix. The names and their meanings are slightly different in the draft and the Recommendation; by associating the stylesheet with different URIs, the author can indicate to the Microsoft browser which version is intended. This is very clever, but also creates multiple opportunities for confusion and mischief. We'll have more to say about this in the XSL chapter.

XML Schema and Alternative Proposals

XML Schema is a W3C project whose goal is to develop a more structured alternative to DTDs. XML Schemas will have a better developed system of data types, a better mechanism for combining them, and perhaps some form of inheritance. The project is still in working draft and fairly far from completion. The latest drafts can be found at:

```
http://www.w3.org/TR/xmlschema-1/ (XML Schema Part1: Structures) and
http://www.w3.org/TR/xmlschema-2/ (XML Schema Part 1: Data types
```

There are also alternative ideas on how to revise or replace DTDs and integrate namespaces with validation. See, for example:

```
http://www.oasis-open.org/cover/xslAsValidator19990124.html
http://www.mulberrytech.com/xsl/xsl-list Digest V2 #286
```
(Oren Ben-Kiki's "Crazy idea")
```
http://www.w3.org/People/Raggett/dtdgen/Docs/.
```

New Productions and Changes in XML 1.0 Productions

Because of Namespaces, several productions in the initial XML Recommendation have become superceded by the new namespace-aware productions of the Namespace Recommendation. This section goes over these and related productions.

This is how the Namespace declaration mechanism is summarized in the first four productions of the Namespace specification:

```
[1]  NSAttName ::=  PrefixedAttName | DefaultAttName
[2]  PrefixedAttName ::=  'xmlns:' NCName [ NSC: Leading "XML" ]
[3]  DefaultAttName ::=  'xmlns'
[4]  NCName ::=  (Letter | '_') (NCNameChar)* /*  An XML Name, minus the ":" */
```

This says that the NSAttName can be prefixed or default. The default name is simply xmlns; the prefixed name is xmlns: followed by an NCName ("no-colon-name"), which is the local prefix for the namespace. There is a **NameSpace Constraint** (**NSC**) that the local prefix cannot contain the 'xml' sequence of characters in any case combination because it is reserved by W3C.

Another group of productions defines the notion of **qualified name** or QName. Notice that a name can be qualified by default, and therefore the prefix part is optional:

```
[6]   QName ::=   (Prefix ':')? LocalPart
[7]   Prefix ::=   NCName
[8]   LocalPart ::=   NCName
```

Since new non-terminals, NSAttName, NCName and QName, have been introduced, some of the key productions of XML 1.0 have to be revised to use the new kinds of names instead of older plain names:

```
[ 9]   STag ::=   '<' QName (S Attribute)* S? '>'  [ NSC: Prefix Declared ]
[10]   ETag ::=   '</' QName S? '>'
[11]   EmptyElemTag ::=   '<' QName (S Attribute)* S? '/>'

[12]   Attribute ::=   NSAttName Eq AttValue | QName Eq AttValue
```

The change from the original version is that all occurrences of Name have been replaced with a QName or, in one instance, with NSAttName. The new names can contain a namespace prefix. There is also a namespace constraint (in each production, but we only show it once) that the prefix must be declared before use.

Expanded Element and Attribute Names

As a useful tool for visualizing namespace-qualified names, an appendix to the Recommendation defines **expanded names**, expressed as empty XML elements. Here are the definitions from Appendix A.3:

[Definition:] An **expanded element type** is expressed as an empty XML element of type ExpEType. It has a required type attribute which gives the type's LocalPart, and an optional ns attribute which, if the element is qualified, gives its namespace name.

[Definition:] An **expanded attribute name** is expressed as an empty XML element of type ExpAName. It has a required name attribute which gives the name. If the attribute is global, it has a required ns attribute which gives the namespace name; otherwise, it has a required attribute eltype which gives the type of the attached element, and an optional attribute elns which gives the namespace name, if known, of the attached element.

An example illustrates:

```
<!-- 1 --> <RESERVATION xmlns:HTML="http://www.w3.org/TR/REC-html40">
<!-- 2 --> <NAME HTML:CLASS="largeSansSerif">Layman, A</NAME>
<!-- 3 --> <SEAT CLASS="Y" HTML:CLASS="largeMonotype">33B</SEAT>
<!-- 4 --> <HTML:A HREF='/cgi-bin/ResStatus'>Check Status</HTML:A>
<!-- 5 --> <DEPARTURE>1997-05-24T07:55:00+1</DEPARTURE></RESERVATION>
```

RESERVATION	`<ExpEType type="RESERVATION" />`
NAME	`<ExpEType type="NAME" />`
HTML:CLASS	`<ExpAName name="CLASS" ns="http://www.w3.org/TR/REC-html40" />`
SEAT	`<ExpEType type="SEAT" />`
CLASS	`<ExpAName name="CLASS" eltype="SEAT"/>`
HTML:CLASS	`<ExpAName name="CLASS" ns="http://www.w3.org/TR/REC-html40" />`
HTML:A	`<ExpEType type="A" ns="http://www.w3.org/TR/REC-html40" />`
HREF	`<ExpAName name="HREF" eltype="A" elns="http://www.w3.org/TR/REC-html40" />`
DEPARTURE	`<ExpEType type="DEPARTURE" />`

Notice how the local CLASS attribute, in its expanded form, doesn't have an ns attribute, but does have an elns attribute because it belongs to the local namespace of its element. HTML:CLASS, in its expanded form, does have an ns attribute and does not have an elns attribute, because it belongs to a global namespace identified by a URI. The constraint that attribute names must be unique within an element can be simply expressed by saying that no two attributes of the same element can have the same expanded form.

Summary

In this chapter, we have covered a good deal of XML. First, we had a brief tour of XML features; the main point is that it is a tool for defining languages tailored for the specific needs of your application. The language has a self-describing syntax of tags and attributes, largely inherited from SGML and familiar to most through HTML.

Second, we have shown many examples of XML in the context of a comparison between HTML 4.0 (an SGML language) and XHTML 1.0 (an XML language). The main point here is that XML documents must be well-formed and can be checked for well-formedness in the absence of a DTD. As you will see in the chapter on XML processors, this makes it possible to process an XML document using exclusively standard events and callbacks (the SAX processing model). Such a model would not be possible with HTML documents (or any other SGML documents that allow optional end tags).

With XHTML background, we could present the formal definition of the syntax of XML documents, using XHTML as a source of examples. We have discussed the prolog, comments, processing instructions, and CDATA sections. We have left the most interesting part: DTDs, entities and element-attribute declarations for the next chapter.

Finally we covered the recent Namespaces Recommendation, with all its clever but controversial ideas. This is one area where changes are very likely when the XML Schema Recommendation is ready.

With a good deal of XML behind us, we're ready to move on to DTDs.

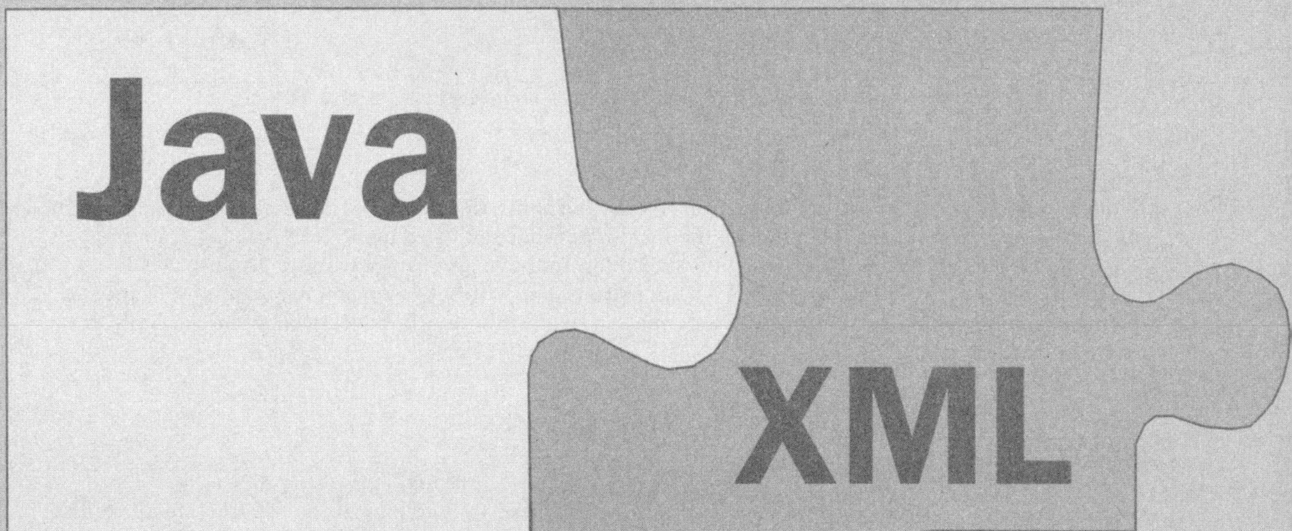
Java
XML

6

Entities and DTDs

Introduction

The XML *Recommendation* makes a distinction between the physical content and logical structure of an XML document. Although the distinction seems fairly obvious, in practice it is hard to talk about logical structure without mentioning physical entities, entity names and entity references. When it comes to DTDs, separating the two kinds of structures is completely impossible because DTDs define both elements and attributes (that form the logical structure) and entities (that form the physical structure). So, we'll present entities first, then element and attribute declarations, then interactions between entities on the one hand and elements and attributes on the other.

We will draw most of our examples from well-known DTDs such as XHTML Strict and WML (Wireless Markup Language). Studying well-known DTDs is useful both because they show good design and because they can be reused, perhaps in a customized form. There are many outstanding DTDs already written, some originally in XML, others converted from SGML. Appendix B provides links to the most important DTD repositories.

Physical Entities

Physically, an XML document consists of text characters. These characters are contained in "storage units" called **entities**. The terminology of entities sometimes gets confusing because they are classified along several dimensions, and the names for some categories are not very intuitive. Here's a summary diagram:

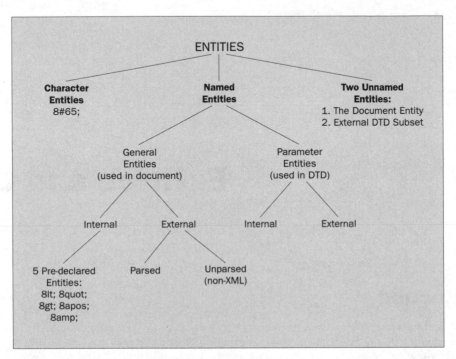

The first difference is between **character entities**, referred to by the character Unicode number, and **named entities**, referred to by name. (The term "named entities" is our invention.) With the exception of the five pre-declared single-character entities, named entities have to be declared in the DTD before they are used. The declaration specifies whether the entity is to be used in the DTD or in the document. Character entities do not need a declaration. References to character entities can be used either in the DTD or in the document.

References to Character Entities

We have already seen character entities; they look like this:

```
&#65;    <!-- capital A, using the decimal numeric code -->
&#x41;   <!-- same in hex -->
&#x0041; <!-- this is also ok -->
```

The numbers are Unicode numbers, with or without the leading zeros (the first 128 Unicode characters, you will recall, are identical to the ASCII sequence). We will see many more examples in the DTDs as we progress through this chapter.

Parameter and General Entities

Named entities are specified, at declaration time, to be solely for use in the DTD or in the document, but never for use in both. If the entity reference is to be used in the DTD, it is called a **parameter entity**; if the entity reference is to be used in the document, it is called a **general entity**. It is an error to put a parameter entity reference in the document. It is not an error to use a general entity reference in the DTD in defining the value of a parameter entity, but that reference will not be "resolved" (i.e. replaced with the entity value) until it is used in the document. For more detail, see *Entity Reference Replacement Process* towards the end of this chapter.

Entity Declaration and Reference

The syntax of declaration and reference is a little different for general entities (GEDecl) and parameter entities (PEDecl):

```
[70]    EntityDecl ::=  GEDecl | PEDecl
[71]    GEDecl ::=   '<!ENTITY' S Name S EntityDef S? '>'
[72]    PEDecl ::=   '<!ENTITY' S '%' S Name S PEDef S? '>'
```

The main difference to note is that there's an extra % character literal in the parameter entity declaration, to indicate that it is a parameter entity, not a general one, that is being declared. The same % character serves as the start delimiter for the parameter entity reference, rather than the & character used for general and character entities. The end delimiter is the semicolon in all cases:

```
[67]    Reference ::=   EntityRef | CharRef
[68]    EntityRef ::=  '&' Name ';'
[69]    PEReference ::=  '%' Name ';'
```

There are well-formedness and validity constraints (WFCs and VCs), most of which we discussed in the last chapter: names have to be declared before use, and PE references can only be used in the DTD. Another WFC prohibits recursive entity definitions, both for parameter and general entities.

Here is a minimal example of entity declaration and reference:

```
<!-- within the DTD -->

<!ENTITY GenEntity "I am general">
<!ENTITY % ParEntity "I am parameter">
%ParEntity; <!-- parameter entity reference, replaced by its value -->

<!-- DTD has ended, document has started -->

&GenEntity; <!-- general entity reference in the document,
                replaced by its value -->
```

This example shows internal entities whose definitions are string values.

Entity Definition: Internal and External Entities

Named entities are either strings (**internal entities**) or files (**external entities**). Correspondingly, an entity definition can be either a string, the **value** of an internal entity, or an **identifier** for an external entity.

```
[73]   EntityDef ::=  EntityValue | (ExternalID NDataDecl?)
[74]   PEDef ::=  EntityValue | ExternalID
```

External general entities can be **parsed** or **unparsed**. Unparsed general entities contain either binary data (e.g. a JPEG image), or character data that is not XML (e.g. a TeX document). An unparsed general entity definition would be followed by an `NData` declaration that specifies the data format of the entity. This is an obscure feature; we'll discuss how to use it, and how to avoid using it, in a separate section on unparsed entities later in this chapter. Without that additional complication, the productions for entity definitions would look identical for general and parameter entities: the entity definition can be either a string value or an external identifier.

External Identifiers: SYSTEM and PUBLIC

External identifiers begin with a keyword, `SYSTEM` or `PUBLIC`. The `SYSTEM` keyword is followed by a system-specific identifier, which is a directory path & filename, or a URI. The `PUBLIC` keyword is followed by two identifiers. The first is a **public identifier**, also known as a Formal Public Identifier or FPI; the second is a system identifier (without the `SYSTEM` keyword). Here is the production and an example from XHTML Strict:

```
[75]   ExternalID ::=   'SYSTEM' S SystemLiteral
                       | 'PUBLIC' S PubidLiteral S SystemLiteral

<!ENTITY % HTMLlat1 PUBLIC
   "-//W3C//ENTITIES Latin1//EN//HTML"
   "http://www.w3.org/TR/xhtml1/DTD/HTMLlat1x.ent">
%HTMLlat1; <!-- the declared entity is immediately referenced,
                so its text is included in the DTD -->
```

System identifiers are nothing mysterious: they are either file names or URLs. Both of these options have the drawback of being dependent on the actual location of the entity: if the file is moved to a different directory, the system identifier is no longer valid. If there are multiple links all over the web pointing to this resource, all those links will become broken, and there is no easy way to find and fix them all. Public identifiers were invented to remedy this problem. The concept is simply to associate a resource with a constant identifier that does not change over time. In a registry somewhere, that identifier is associated with a physical location. If the physical location changes, there's only one place (the registry) where the change needs to be registered.

Public identifiers are part of SGML where they are known as Formal Public Identifiers or FPIs. For FPIs to work, there has to be a central authority that would create and maintain the registry, or establish standards for multiple, mutually-supportive registries. As of this writing, no such authority or standard yet exists, even though they are being vigorously developed (see the next section). In the meantime, **XML requires that if you provide an FPI you must provide a system identifier also**.

Current Work on Registry Standards

Work on registry standards is carried out by OASIS (Organization for the Advancement of Structured Information Standards), a non-profit organization that has been an SGML authority for a long time, and is very active in XML affairs as well. Two notable facts about OASIS are that it maintains DocBook, a well-known SGML DTD for computer documentation, and it provides a home for Robin Cover's SGML/XML Pages, the single most important source of current information on XML. If you have not yet done so, you should `visit http://www.oasis-open.org` and `http://www.oasis-open.org/cover`.

In 1998, the *OASIS Registry and Repository Technical Committee* declared its intent to (`http://www.oasis-open.org/html/techpubs.htm#tech`):

> *"...specify operation of a registry for some set of XML-related entities, including but not limited to DTDs and schemas, with appropriate interfaces, that enable searching on the contents of a repository of those entities. The OASIS Registry and Repository shall interoperate and cooperate with other registries and repositories compliant with this specification and respond to requests for entities by their identifiers. This specification, which is the primary deliverable, is to be implemented in a prototype registry and repository."*

The latest version of the specification can be found at `http://www.oasis-open.org/html/spec.htm`.

The Syntax of Public Identifiers

Public identifiers for DTDs follow certain conventions that can be summarized as EBNF rules (the productions of the XML *Recommendation* are not very helpful here):

```
pubid ::= standards_org Delim owner Delim title Delim language
Delim ::= "//"
standards_org ::= "ISO" | "+" | "-"
```

As can be seen above, a public identifier consists of four fields (`standards_org`, `owner`, `title`, and `language`) separated by a delimiter:

❑ The first field is: "ISO" for ISO-approved documents, "+" for documents approved by some other standards body, and "-" for everything else. (Note that W3C uses "-" for itself because it is not a standards body but an industry consortium, even though, in practice, their recommendations are pretty much the law of the Web.)

❑ The second and third are owner and title fields, which contain text.

❑ The last field is the language code, and is a two-letter string following the ISO-639 standard. (This standard is also used elsewhere in XML, as values of the `lang` and `xml:lang` attributes, for instance). Clearly, 676 codes are not enough to specify all languages in the world, and alternative schemes have developed, which we present in the section on attributes.

External Entitites for Non-XML Data: Notations

XML allows external general entities to contain non-XML data, either binary or non-XML character data. These are called **unparsed entities**. References to them can appear only in attribute values. There are no examples of their use in our "model DTDs", an indication that we're getting into rarely-used material here. Here's a made-up example: you can declare a `.gif` file as an external entity like this:

```
<!ENTITY portrait SYSTEM pict.gif NDATA gifimage>
```

The keyword NDATA indicates that the data is not XML; the identifier that follows (gifimage in our example) has to be pre-declared as a NOTATION:

```
<!NOTATION gifimage PUBLIC "-//IETF// O SGML Media Type image/gif//EN"
"http://www.isi.edu/in-notes/iana/assignments/media-types/image/gif">
```

This example includes both a public and a system identifier. The system identifier here can be omitted; the NOTATION declaration is the only place in an XML document where a public identifier can appear alone:

```
[82]  NotationDecl ::=  '<!NOTATION' S Name S (ExternalID |  PublicID) S? '>'
```

Notice that if you use this approach to show GIF images, you'll have to declare each image in the DTD as an unparsed entity! That's a lot of work, and that's not how it is done in HTML 4.0 or XHTML, as we show below.

MIME to the Rescue

The purpose of notation declarations is to inform the processor, so that it can inform the application, about the format of non-XML data. The application would then most likely call a helper application to process the data and integrate it with the rest of the document. To quote the *Recommendation, Section 4.7*:

> *"Notation declarations provide a name for the notation, ... and an external identifier for the notation which may allow an XML processor or its client application to locate a helper application capable of processing data in the given notation."*

There is a more general and commonly used method for doing that: the MIME standard *(RFC2046: Multipurpose Internet Mail Extensions (MIME) Part Two: Media Types*, N. Freed and N. Borenstein, November 1996). If you can assume that your application knows MIME, and that's a reasonable assumption to make, then you don't ever need to use NOTATION declarations. Here is how it is done in XHTML. First, a parameter entity called ContentType is declared:

```
<!ENTITY % ContentType "CDATA">
    <!-- media type, as per [RFC2045] -->
```

ContentType is just another name for character data, to remind the human reader and, perhaps, the validating processor, what the characters should mean. The attribute list for the object element (where arbitrary non-XML data can appear) contains a type attribute whose "attribute type" is ContentType. The processor, perhaps after checking for correct MIME syntax, passes the value of that attribute to the application. The application will either know what to do with the type or it will complain (or crash your machine, as the case may be).

Five Pre-Declared and Two Unnamed Entities

To recapitulate, all non-character entities used in a document are referred to by a name that the author has to explicitly declare in the DTD. There are two kinds of exceptions to the general "declare-before-use" procedure for named entities that we discuss next: five pre-declared internal general entities that can be used without a declaration, and two entities that do not have a name.

Five Pre-Declared Entities

These are the same for all documents in all XML and SGML languages, and they can appear in documents that don't have a DTD. Their names are: amp, lt, gt, apos, quot. You have probably seen them in HTML. They stand for the five most important characters: &, <, >, ', and ". Since they are general entities, their references look like this: '. Although the values of these entities are single characters, they are *not* character entities, but rather general named entities whose values happen to be single-character strings.

If you want to be backward-compatible with SGML, or if you expect to run into a processor that is not fully compliant with XML 1.0, you may want to declare these five entities anyway. There is a little catch here: the entity text for < and & has to produce those characters escaped, because they cannot appear in a well-formed XML document. So, you end up inserting an extra #38; literal, as in this quote from wml.dtd (http://www.wapforum.org):

```
<!ENTITY amp   "&#38;#38;"> <!-- ampersand -->
<!ENTITY lt    "&#38;#60;"> <!-- less than -->
<!ENTITY gt    "&#62;"> <!-- greater than -->
<!ENTITY apos  "&#39;"> <!-- apostrophe -->
<!ENTITY quot  "&#34;"> <!-- quotation mark -->
```

What happens in the first line of these declarations is that the processor discovers a character entity, &, and converts it to its value, the ampersand character. At that moment, the string "&#38;" becomes "&", which is an entity reference, and is left alone until the general entity & is referenced in the document. At that time, the entity reference is resolved, the character entity is converted to its value, and the ampersand character is appended to the string to be passed from the processor to the application.

Two Unnamed Entities

There are two entities that do not have a name: the **document entity**, which is the entire document, and that part of the DTD that resides in an external file (the **external DTD subset**). The document entity has some system-specific name that the application would use to refer to it, but it doesn't have a name, and it cannot be referred to, from within itself. The external subset of the DTD, like any other external entity, has a system identifier and an optional public identifier. Both are specified in the DOCTYPE declaration, not in an entity declaration. It is common practice to provide the identifiers in the introductory comment.

DOCTYPE Declarations

DTDs use the `<!DOCTYPE...>` "pseudo-empty-tag" for defining the document type. The tag can appear only once per document. If the DTD is internal, the tag is followed by square brackets that contain the rest of the declarations, as in this little example repeated from Chapter 5:

```
<!DOCTYPE book [
  <!ELEMENT book (title authors publisher year listprice isbn)>
  <!ATTLIST book
    cover (hard|paper) "hard" <-- "hard" is the default -->
  >
  <!ELEMENT title (#PCDATA)    -- Parsed Character Data -->
  <!ELEMENT authors (author +) -- one or more authors   -->
  <!ELEMENT author (last first)>
  <!-- and so on -->
]>
```

For DTDs of substantial size, or any DTDs that can be reused in more than one document, it is much more common to have an external DTD. Consider the introductory comment to the XHTML Strict DTD, quoted in full:

```
<!--
Extensible HTML version 1.0 Strict DTD
This is the same as HTML 4.0 Strict except for
changes due to the differences between XML and SGML.
Namespace = http://www.w3.org/TR/xhtml1/strict
For further information, see: http://www.w3.org/TR/xhtml1
Copyright (c) 1998-1999 W3C (MIT, INRIA, Keio),
All Rights Reserved.
This DTD module is identified by the PUBLIC and SYSTEM identifiers:
PUBLIC "-//W3C//DTD XHTML 1.0 Strict//EN"
SYSTEM "http://www.w3.org/TR/xhtml1/DTD/strict.dtd"
-->
```

This means that an XHTML document should open with these lines:

```
<?xml version="1.0" ?>
<!DOCTYPE html PUBLIC "-//W3C//DTD XHTML 1.0 Strict//EN"
"http://www.w3.org/TR/xhtml1/DTD/strict.dtd">
```

although this opening is also legitimate:

```
<?xml version="1.0" ?>
<!DOCTYPE html SYSTEM "http://www.w3.org/TR/xhtml1/DTD/strict.dtd">
```

Internal and External Subsets

Even if you have an external DTD, you can add internal definitions. So if you want to extend the XHTML DTD with an element of your own, we could write:

```
<?xml version='1.0' encoding='us-ascii'?>
<!DOCTYPE html SYSTEM "http://www.w3.org/TR/xhtml1/DTD/strict.dtd"
  [<!ELEMENT myElement (#PCDATA)>
]>
```

Your DTD now consists of an **external** and an **internal subset**. By itself, this is not particularly helpful because your own element is not integrated in any way with the elements of the external subset: you couldn't make it bold, for instance, by placing it inside `<B>...</B>` unless you extend the definition of `<B>` to include your element. As long as the external subset is a large monolithic piece with many internal interdependencies, this will be a daunting project. This is why the modularization of XHTML, currently still in a working draft at W3C, is so important. It introduces various ways of using entities to modularize DTDs, breaking them into independently-reusable files. The next section illustrates this and other uses of entities.

Examples of Using Entities

In this section we present several common examples of how entities should be used. The examples come from XHTML, DocBook, WML, and other well-known DTDs.

Mnemonic Names for CDATA

DTDs are not very good at data types: there is no mechanism even to declare that something is an integer. All we have to work with is PCDATA for element content and CDATA for attribute values. (There is also NMTOKEN, a slightly restricted character string type for attribute values, similar to Name.) Even so, it is often useful to give a mnemonic name to a specific use of character data, describing to human readers (including the author of the DTD) semantic constraints that we cannot express as grammar rules. Recall how in Chapter 4, in discussing a grammar for initialization files, we characterized some non-terminals as SQL, even though, in our grammar, it was just a synonym for Text. A similar device is very often used in both HTML 4.0 and in the XHTML DTD.

"Imported Names" in XHTML Strict

XHTML Strict has a whole section labeled *Imported Names*, with the following declarations (although the list is rather long, each one is slightly different and illustrates different possibilities):

```
<!--================== Imported Names =============================-->

<!ENTITY % ContentType "CDATA">
    <!-- media type, as per [RFC2045] -->

<!ENTITY % ContentTypes "CDATA">
    <!-- comma-separated list of media types, as per [RFC2045] -->

<!ENTITY % Charset "CDATA">
    <!-- a character encoding, as per [RFC2045] -->

<!ENTITY % Charsets "CDATA">
    <!-- a space separated list of character encodings, as per [RFC2045] -->

<!ENTITY % LanguageCode "NMTOKEN">
    <!-- a language code, as per [RFC1766] -->

<!ENTITY % Character "CDATA">
    <!-- a single character from [ISO10646] -->
```

```
<!ENTITY % Number "CDATA">
    <!-- one or more digits -->

<!ENTITY % LinkTypes "CDATA">
    <!-- space-separated list of link types -->

<!ENTITY % MediaDesc "CDATA">
    <!-- single or comma-separated list of media descriptors -->

<!ENTITY % URI "CDATA">
    <!-- a Uniform Resource Identifier, see [RFC2396] -->

<!ENTITY % UriList "CDATA">
    <!-- a space separated list of Uniform Resource Identifiers -->

<!ENTITY % Datetime "CDATA">
    <!-- date and time information. ISO date format -->

<!ENTITY % Script "CDATA">
    <!-- script expression -->

<!ENTITY % StyleSheet "CDATA">
    <!-- style sheet data -->

<!ENTITY % Text "CDATA">
    <!-- used for titles etc. -->

<!ENTITY % FrameTarget "NMTOKEN">
    <!-- render in this frame -->

<!ENTITY % Length "CDATA">
    <!-- nn for pixels or nn% for percentage length -->

<!ENTITY % MultiLength "CDATA">
    <!-- pixel, percentage, or relative -->

<!ENTITY % MultiLengths "CDATA">
    <!-- comma-separated list of MultiLength -->

<!ENTITY % Pixels "CDATA">
    <!-- integer representing length in pixels -->
```

All these CDATA synonyms are used in declaring attribute data types; for instance, the table element has an attribute width whose type is %Length;. For the parser, it's just quoted characters, but for the human reader it's a reminder that only digits and the percent sign are allowed. Eventually, when DTDs develop more data type sophistication (or, more likely, when they get replaced by some mechanism that includes data types), it will be easier to convert existing DTDs to the new kind.

Core Data Types in WML

WML specification has a section called *Core WML Data Types* that lists both the basic XML data types (CDATA, PCDATA, NMTOKEN) and parameter entity declarations:

```
<!ENTITY % length "CDATA">
  <!-- [0-9]+ for pixels or [0-9]+"%" for percentage length -->
<!ENTITY % vdata "CDATA">
  <!-- attribute value possibly containing variable references -->
<!ENTITY % HREF "%vdata;">
  <!-- URI, URL or URN designating a hypertext node.
    May contain variable references -->
<!ENTITY % boolean "(true|false)">
<!ENTITY % number "NMTOKEN">
  <!-- a number, with format [0-9]+ -->
```

Variable references (mentioned in the comments) are WML variable references, specific to WML. They are introduced by the $ character in attribute values, as we mentioned in the section on placing code in XML documents in the preceding chapter.

Mnemonic Names for Characters

All three XHTML DTDs – strict, transitional and frameset – declare a great number of "character mnemonic" entities that give names to characters in the upper end of the ASCII character set, and to various special characters. The names, for the most part, are not new but have been borrowed from the SGML standard (ISO 8879). When a Unicode character does not have a name in ISO 8879, a new name is introduced, chosen not to conflict with any of the existing SGML names. Each declaration is followed by a comment that gives the Unicode number in hexadecimal; XML character references use the same number in decimal. Here are a few examples:

```
<!ENTITY nbsp    " "> <!-- non-breaking space, U+00A0 ISOnum -->
<!ENTITY iexcl   "&#161;"> <!-- inverted exclamation mark, U+00A1 ISOnum -->
<!ENTITY cent    "&#162;"> <!-- cent sign, U+00A2 ISOnum -->
<!ENTITY pound   "&#163;"> <!-- pound sign, U+00A3 ISOnum -->
<!ENTITY Alpha   "&#913;"> <!-- greek capital letter alpha, U+0391 -->
<!ENTITY omicron "&#959;"> <!-- greek small letter omicron, U+03BF NEW -->

<!ENTITY quot    "&#34;"> <!--  quotation mark = APL quote,  U+0022 ISOnum -->
<!ENTITY amp     "&#38;"> <!--  ampersand, U+0026 ISOnum -->
<!ENTITY lt      "&#60;"> <!--  less-than sign, U+003C ISOnum -->
<!ENTITY gt      "&#62;"> <!--  greater-than sign, U+003E ISOnum -->

<!ENTITY lrm     "&#8206;"> <!-- left-to-right mark, U+200E NEW RFC 2070 -->
<!ENTITY rlm     "&#8207;"> <!-- right-to-left mark, U+200F NEW RFC 2070 -->
```

With these declarations included in the DTD, all XHTML documents can use, for instance, £ to refer to the pound symbol.

Included Files

The mnemonic character names are not placed in the DTDs directly, for two good reasons: they would clutter the DTDs, and you would have to repeat them in each of the three DTDs. Instead, they are collected into three files named:

❏ `HTMLlat1x.ent` (Latin1 characters from 160 to 255)

❏ `HTMLspecialx.ent` (some commonly used Unicode characters that are not in Latin1)

❏ `HTMLsymbolx.ent` (Greek letters and mathematical symbols).

Each file has an introductory comment that makes good reading; here's the one from `HTMLspecialx.ent`:

```
<!-- Special characters for HTML -->

<!-- Character entity set. Typical invocation:
<!ENTITY % HTMLspecial PUBLIC
"-//W3C//ENTITIES Special//EN//HTML"
"http://www.w3.org/TR/xhtml1/DTD/HTMLspecialx.ent">
%HTMLspecial;
-->

<!-- Portions (C) International Organization for Standardization 1986:
Permission to copy in any form is granted for use with
conforming SGML systems and applications as defined in
ISO 8879, provided this notice is included in all copies.
-->

<!-- Relevant ISO entity set is given unless names are newly introduced.
New names (i.e., not in ISO 8879 list) do not clash with any
existing ISO 8879 entity names. ISO 10646 character numbers
are given for each character, in hex. values are decimal
conversions of the ISO 10646 values and refer to the document
character set. Names are Unicode names.
-->
```

The files are declared as external entities in the DTDs and immediately referenced for inclusion:

```
<!ENTITY % HTMLlat1 PUBLIC
"-//W3C//ENTITIES Latin1//EN//HTML"
"http://www.w3.org/TR/xhtml1/DTD/HTMLlat1x.ent">
%HTMLlat1;
```

External Files for Boiler-Plate Text

External text files are also useful if you have frequently-reused boiler-plate text. Suppose you have a copyright notice, `cpright.txt`, that you insert into all your documents, for example. You can declare it as an entity within the DTD:

```
<!-- entity declaration within the DTD -->
<!ENTITY copyright SYSTEM "../includes/cpright.txt">...
```

The declaration says that there is a file out there whose system-specific name is such-and-such; we hereby declare that its name within the document is "copyright". To include the file in the document, we refer to it thus:

```
<!-- external general entity reference within the document -->
The use of these ideas is free as long as you keep this copyright in mind:
&copyright;
```

External Parameter Entities as Modules

External parameter entities are a main tool for modularizing DTDs. The DocBook DTD for software documentation is a primary example. Its main "driver" file consists exclusively of entity declarations and references. The introductory comment recommends a procedure for customizing the DTD: create your own driver file and include the DocBook driver file as an external parameter entity:

```
<!-- ................................................................ -->
<!-- DocBook DTD V3.1 ............................................... -->
<!-- File docbook.dtd .............................................. -->
<!-- Copyright 1992, 1993, 1994, 1995, 1996, 1998, 1999 HaL Computer
Systems, Inc., O'Reilly & Associates, Inc., ArborText, Inc., Fujitsu
Software Corporation, and the Organization for the Advancement of
Structured Information Standards (OASIS).
$Id: docbook.dtd 3.1 1999/02/02 11:54:12 nwalsh Exp $
Permission to use, copy, modify and distribute the DocBook DTD and
its accompanying documentation for any purpose and without fee is
hereby granted in perpetuity, provided that the above copyright
notice and this paragraph appear in all copies. The copyright
holders make no representation about the suitability of the DTD for
any purpose. It is provided "as is" without expressed or implied
warranty.
If you modify the DocBook DTD in any way, except for declaring and
referencing additional sets of general entities and declaring
additional notations, label your DTD as a variant of DocBook. See
the maintenance documentation for more information.
Please direct all questions, bug reports, or suggestions for
changes to the davenport@berkshire.net mailing list. For more
information, see http://www.oasis-open.org/docbook/.
-->

<!-- ................................................................ -->

<!-- This is the driver file for Version 3.1BETA1 of the DocBook DTD.
Please use the following formal public identifier to identify it:
"-//OASIS//DTD DocBook V3.1//EN"
For example, if your document's top-level element is Book, and
you are using DocBook directly, use the FPI in the DOCTYPE
declaration:
<!DOCTYPE Book PUBLIC "-//OASIS//DTD DocBook V3.1//EN" [...]>
Or, if you have a higher-level driver file that customizes DocBook,
use the FPI in the parameter entity declaration:
<!ENTITY % DocBookDTD PUBLIC "-//OASIS//DTD DocBook V3.1//EN">
%DocBookDTD;
```

```
The DocBook DTD is accompanied by an SGML declaration.
See the documentation for detailed information on the parameter
entity and module scheme used in DocBook, customizing DocBook and
planning for interchange, and changes made since the last release
of DocBook.
-->
```

Following this comment, the driver file contains multiple declarations of, and references to, external files, such as:

```
<!-- Document hierarchy .............-->
<!ENTITY % dbhier PUBLIC
"-//OASIS//ELEMENTS DocBook Document Hierarchy V3.1//EN">
%dbhier;
<!-- ............................................... -->
<!-- Other general entities ............................................. -->
<!ENTITY % dbgenent PUBLIC
"-//OASIS//ENTITIES DocBook Additional General Entities V3.1//EN">
%dbgenent;
<!-- End of DocBook DTD V3.1 ............................................. -->
<!-- ............................................... -->
```

Modularized XHTML

The XHTML 1.0 *Recommendation* adopted in August 1999 consists of three monolithic DTDs that include only the three files with mnemonic character names. There is also an XHTML draft (`http://www.w3.org/TR/xhtml-modularization`) that breaks those DTDs into modules and puts them back together again by combining the modules in three different ways. Many of the modules can also be included, independently of the others, into customized DTDs, and user-defined modules can be added to the modularized XHTML. This is still a draft, but very much worth watching. Section 6 is particularly useful for DTD developers:

```
6. Developing DTDs with defined and extended modules
6.1. Defining additional attributes
6.2. Defining additional elements
6.3. Defining a new module
6.4. Defining the content model for a collection of modules
6.4.1. Integrating a stand-alone module into XHTML
6.4.2. Mixing a new module throughout the modules in XHTML
6.5. Creating a new DTD
6.5.1. Creating a simple DTD
6.5.2. Creating a DTD by extending XHTML
6.5.3. Creating a DTD by removing and replacing XHTML modules
6.6. Using the new DTD
```

Conditional Sections and External Parameter Entities

Modularized XHTML makes heavy use of a DTD's **conditional sections**. (This is a good example of how it's impossible to talk about DTDs without bringing in entities, and vice versa.) The syntax of conditional sections is similar to CDATA sections, with these differences:

❑ Conditional sections appear in the DTD, not in the document

❑ The keywords are INCLUDE and IGNORE

❑ Conditional sections can be nested: you can have an IGNORE section inside an INCLUDE section, and it will be ignored (but not the other way around: INCLUDE doesn't override IGNORE)

❑ Conditional sections may contain internal parameter references, and they will be properly expanded

Here's a simple example of conditional sections, without using parameter entities:

```
<![INCLUDE [
<!ELEMENT editorialcomment (#PCDATA)>
]]>
```

If you change the keyword to IGNORE, the declaration will, in effect, disappear. You may want to be able to do that with several declarations at once. This is where a parameter entity can help:

```
<!ENTITY % editorials "INCLUDE">
<![%editorials; [
<!ELEMENT editorialcomment (#PCDATA)>
]]>
```

By redefining editorials to be IGNORE, you will make all your editorial elements disappear.

Conditional Sections and Modularization

Modularized XHTML uses conditional sections very systematically to break the DTD into modules. All declarations are divided into modules according to their meaning and function. For instance, all declarations having to do with applets go into the applet module, and all declarations having to do with lists go into the list module, and so on. Each such module of related declarations is collected into an external file with a .mod extension. (For instance, the imported names file is XHTML1-names.mod.) There are thirty three such files in the XHTML Draft. For each such file, there is also an *internal* parameter entity whose name ends in .module. The value of the entity would be, as you can guess, either INCLUDE or IGNORE.

In the DTD, you create (or copy) a block like this for each module:

```
<!-- Common Names Module .............................. -->
<!ENTITY % XHTML1-names.module "INCLUDE" >

<![%XHTML1-names.module;[
<!ENTITY % XHTML1-names.mod
PUBLIC "-//W3C//ENTITIES XHTML 1.0 Common Names//EN"
"XHTML1-names.mod" >

%XHTML1-names.mod;
]]>
```

In this block of code, XHTML1-names.mod is both the name of the file that contains the module's declarations and the name of the *external* parameter entity that refers to that file. To turn a module "on", set its .module parameter entity to INCLUDE; to turn it "off", set it to IGNORE. This is very useful feature, and works equally well for both W3C and user-defined modules.

Internal Parameter Entities as Macros

Another common use of a parameter entity is to abbreviate often-repeated strings. XHTML DTDs offer many examples. Consider font style elements, such as typewriter or italic:

```
<!ENTITY % fontstyle "tt | i | b | big | small">
```

A reference to fontstyle then appears in several other declarations, including inline:

```
<!ENTITY % inline "a | %special; | %fontstyle; | %phrase; | %inline.forms;">
```

inline is then used to define Inline (XML is case sensitive):

```
<!ENTITY % Inline "(#PCDATA | %inline; | %misc;)*">
```

This says that Inline is a mix, in any order, of parsed character data, inline entities and misc entities. This is what spans, paragraphs, headers, inline quotes and many other things are made of:

```
<!ELEMENT span   %Inline;>
<!ELEMENT p      %Inline;>
<!ELEMENT h1     %Inline;>
<!ELEMENT h2     %Inline;>
<!ELEMENT q      %Inline;><!-- and so on -->
```

There's more to entities, especially to their interaction with the logical structure of the document. That's what we're going to look at next.

Element and Attribute Declarations

To review what we have done so far, take another look at the table we presented in Chapter 5 that lists all the components of an XML document, and all types of declarations that can be found in a DTD:

Kind of component	Delimited by
Declarations in the DTD	`<!DOCTYPE[...]>` `<!ELEMENT...>`
	`<!ATTLIST...>`
	`<!ENTITY...>` `<!NOTATION...>`
Elements	`<tag ...>... </tag >` or `<tag .../>`
Comments	`<!-- -->`
CDATA sections	`<![CDATA[...]]>`
Processing instructions (PIs)	`<?...?>`

We have already covered most of this table: we are left with the fun part, declarations of elements and attributes. This is where you really define your language.

Element Declarations

An **element declaration** consists of the name of the element and a **content specification**:

```
[14]   elementdecl ::=  '<!ELEMENT' S QName S contentspec S? '>'
```

This production comes from the Namespace spec; it replaces production [45] from the initial XML 1.0. As a general rule, all XML 1.0 productions using Name are superceded by Namespace productions using QName (standing for "Qualified Name", a name qualified by a namespace prefix).

What's "contentspec"? There are four kinds, illustrated by four examples:

```
[46]   contentspec ::=  'EMPTY' | 'ANY' | Mixed | children
```

```
<!ELEMENT br EMPTY>
<!ELEMENT container ANY>
<!ELEMENT p (#PCDATA|a|ul|b|i|em)*> <!-- Mixed content -->
<!ELEMENT greeting (greet-word mid-punct address end-punct)><!--children only-->
```

EMPTY is self-explanatory: there is no content. ANY is a kind of mixed content that allows both parsed character data and all possible types of children elements, in any order. It is common to specify the root element type as ANY, but for most other elements it should be possible to be more specific, using either a Mixed or a children specification.

Mixed Element Content

The difference between Mixed and children is that a Mixed element can contain a mixture of children elements and character data, as in this HTML fragment:

```
<p>This is a paragraph element with <em>some</em> but not <big>all</big> of its
content contained in children elements.</p>
```

In specifying a Mixed element content, you have to list #PCDATA first:

```
[16]   Mixed ::=  '(' S? '#PCDATA' (S? '|' S? QName)* S? ')*'
                 | '(' S? '#PCDATA' S? ')'
```

This is much easier to read with all the optional whitespace (S?) removed:

```
[16]   Mixed ::=   '(#PCDATA' ('|' QName)* ')*'
                 | '(#PCDATA)'
```

As you're reading this, remember that we're quoting context-free productions of the general XML grammar that themselves *define* the format of context free rules for a specific XML language. Both "meta" rules and "target" rules use the same regular expression conventions: parentheses for grouping, vertical bar for choice, ?, + and * for the repetition factor. So you have to count the quotes carefully to see which of these meta-characters are in the production describing XML syntax and which are in the element declaration of an XML language like XHTML. The first line of production 16 states:

*You can have the literal "(#PCDATA" followed by any number of alternating '| ' and QNames, followed by the literal sequence ") * ".*

Here are two examples from XHTML Strict, both conforming to that rule:

```
<!ELEMENT p (#PCDATA|a|ul|b|i|em)*>
<!ELEMENT object (#PCDATA | param | %block; | form | %inline; | %misc;)*>
```

The second line of production 16 states that you can simply have (#PCDATA) as in:

```
<!ELEMENT title (#PCDATA)>
```

Elements Consisting of Children Elements

To define the children content specification, we need the notion of a **content particle** (cp). A content particle is, at its simplest, a QName. This is the base case. The rest is highly recursive: a cp can also be a choice of cp's (cp's separated by vertical bars) or a sequence of cp's (cp's separated by commas). Finally, a cp can conclude with an optional repetition factor character, '+', '*' or '?':

```
[15]   cp ::=  (QName | choice | seq) ('?' | '*' | '+')?

/* next two productions have S? removed */

[49]   choice ::=  '(' cp ('|' cp)* ')'
[50]   seq ::=  '(' cp (',' cp )* ')'
```

The children content specification itself is a choice or a sequence, followed by an optional repetition factor character:

```
[47]   children ::=  (choice | seq) ('?' | '*' | '+')?
```

What this all boils down to is that you can construct truly complex element declarations of arbitrary depth. What happens in practice is that, if a declaration becomes very complex, parts of it are split off into internal parameter entities, especially if those parts are reused in more than one element. This is certainly very common in XHTML 1.0 (and in HTML 4.0 before that). We'll work through an example in a moment.

Content Specifications and the Treatment of Whitespace

In summary, the elements content specification allows only other elements as children; the Mixed content specification allows parsed text to be interspersed with children elements. The difference roughly corresponds to the distinction between data and documents. When XML is used to represent the structure of data, it is uncommon to allow text nodes to appear in arbitrary positions in the parse tree. When XML is used to represent the structure of a document, text nodes are likely to appear exactly like that, in arbitrary positions in the document. This is not a hard-and-fast rule, just as the distinction between documents and data is not a hard-and-fast distinction, but in general this correspondence holds.

The difference between `children` and `Mixed` has implications for how whitespace is treated by the parser. If an element is defined with a `children` (or `EMPTY`) production, the whitespace within it is ignored because it is assumed to be there just for readability of the code. If it is defined with a `Mixed` (or `ANY`) production, the whitespace is assumed to be character data and is preserved, even if no other character data is there. Consider, for example, an element `suppertime`, with nothing in it except a few space characters:

```
<suppertime id="17">                    </suppertime>
```

Such an element could have been defined with any of the four possible content specifications:

```
<!-- 1 --><ELEMENT! suppertime 'EMPTY'>
<!-- 2 --><ELEMENT! suppertime 'ANY'>
<!-- 3 --><ELEMENT! suppertime (#PCDATA | relief-expletive | other-expletive)*>
<!-- 4 --> <ELEMENT! suppertime (relief-expletive | other-expletive)* >
```

In cases 1 and 4, the node of the tree corresponding to suppertime 17 will have no children. In cases 2 and 3, it will have a child `Text` node containing whitespace. The amount of whitespace depends on the value of the `xml:space` attribute. If it is defined to be "preserve" then the entire white space is preserved. If it is defined to be "default" (or left out altogether), the whitespace `Text` node is "normalized" to contain only a single space. (As with everything else, this requirement may or may not be respected by the processor implementing the XML Recommendation.)

> **According to some recollections, the XML committee spent more time on whitespace than on any other single issue. The reason was that one of their principles was "don't try to second guess the user" but, when it comes to whitespace, that's exactly what you have to do: guess whether it is intended for code formatting or for content.**

We will come back to whitespace after the Attributes section.

Attribute-List Declarations

To define an attribute list for an element, start with the `ATTLIST` tag followed by the name of the element (which can be a Qualified Name), followed by any number of **attribute definitions**. An attribute definition consists of an attribute name, followed by a **type declaration** and a **default declaration**:. The attribute name can be qualified by a namespace prefix, or it can be the literal `xmlns` that is used to declare the prefix:

```
[17]  AttlistDecl ::=  '<!ATTLIST' S QName AttDef* S? '>'
[18]  AttDef ::=  S (QName | NSAttName) S AttType S DefaultDecl
```

Here is an example that illustrates several attribute types and default declarations:

```
<!ELEMENT kitchensink 'EMPTY'>
<!ENTITY % URI "CDATA">
    <!-- a Uniform Resource Identifier, see [RFC2396] -->
<!ATTLIST kitchensink
  name      CDATA        #REQUIRED      <!-- StringType -->
```

```
    ISBN      ID            #REQUIRED      <!-- one of TokenizedTypes -->
    ref2id    IDREF         #IMPLIED       <!-- another TokenizedType -->
                                           <!-- IMPLIED means 'optional' -->
    penname   NMTOKEN       #IMPLIED       <!-- yet another TokenizedType -->
    authors   NMTOKENS      #REQUIRED      <!-- yet another TokenizedType -->

    answer    (YES|NO)            "NO"     <!-- EnumeratedType, default is "NO" -->
    method    CDATA         #FIXED "GET"   <!-- StringType, fixed as "GET" -->
    goto      (%URI;|THEMOVIES) #REQUIRED  <!-- EnumeratedType -->
  >
```

These are probably self-explanatory; let's look at the productions and validity constraints.

Attribute Types

As the examples suggest, there are three kinds of attribute types. By far the most common is CDATA, a string of characters.

```
[54]  AttType ::=  StringType | TokenizedType | EnumeratedType
[55]  StringType ::=  'CDATA'
```

As you will remember from previously, QName is a Name possibly qualified by a namespace prefix, and NSAttName is the attribute name that is used to define namespaces (the literal xmlns, either by itself or followed by a colon and the prefix being defined).

Tokenized Types and Validity Constraints

Tokenized types are described by this production:

```
[56]  TokenizedType ::=   'ID'        [  VC: ID ]
                                       [  VC: One ID per Element Type ]
                                       [  VC: ID Attribute Default ]
                        |  'IDREF'     [  VC: IDREF ]
                        |  'IDREFS'    [  VC: IDREF ]
                        |  'ENTITY'    [  VC: Entity Name ]
                        |  'ENTITIES'  [  VC: Entity Name ]
                        |  'NMTOKEN'   [  VC: Name Token ]
                        |  'NMTOKENS'  [  VC: Name Token ]
```

There are numerous Validity Constraints here, all of them quite reasonable:

❑ ID must be unique per element type per document. If you have a book element, and its ISBN attribute is declared to be of type ID then the validating parser will check that no two instances of book have the same ISBN

❑ an attribute of type ID must be #REQUIRED or #IMPLIED; it cannot have a default value, whether fixed or not fixed

❑ an IDREF attribute must have a value that is an existing ID in the document

❑ an attribute of type ENTITY must have as its value the name of a declared external unparsed entity

❏ the values of ID, ENTITY and NMTOKEN must all satisfy constraints on the possible character content of an ID, an ENTITY and a NameToken, respectively. We'll leave it to you to trace all those regular expressions through the specification, when the need arises

❏ the "plural" types (IDREFS, ENTITIES, NMTOKENS) must consist of whitespace-separated lists of the corresponding "singular" types (IDREF, ENTITY, NMTOKEN)

Enumerated Types

An attribute of an enumerated type is a list of NOTATIONs or a list of NMTOKENs; a list of NOTATIONs is preceded by the literal 'NOTATION'. In the productions below, multiple instances of optional whitespace (S?) have been removed for readability:

```
[57]  EnumeratedType ::=  NotationType | Enumeration
[58]  NotationType ::=  'NOTATION' S '(' Name ('|' Name)* ')'
                         [ VC: Notation Attributes ]
[59]  Enumeration ::=  '(' Nmtoken ( '|'  Nmtoken)* ')' [ VC: Enumeration ]
```

The validity constraint on the NotationType is that the Names listed in the value must be declared notations. The validity constraint on Enumeration has to do with backward compatibility with SGML. NotationType is rarely seen, but Enumeration is quite common. Whenever the possible values of an attribute are few and known, Enumeration is an obvious choice. In the example below, three possible values of srctype are listed as an Enumeration:

```
<!ELEMENT datablock (#PCDATA)>
<!ATTLIST datablock
  srctype       (xmlfile|txtfile|dbtable)     #IMPLIED
  ...
>
```

It frequently happens that the same disjunction of possible values repeats in more than one element's attribute list. In that case, it makes sense to declare it as a parameter entity. This is common practice in XHTML:

```
<!-- vertical alignment attributes for cell contents -->
<!ENTITY % cellvalign
  "valign      (top|middle|bottom|baseline) #IMPLIED"
  >
...
<!ATTLIST thead
  %attrs;
  %cellhalign;
  %cellvalign;
  >
```

This parameter entity, together with cellhalign, is reused in the attribute lists of tfoot, tbody, tr, th, and td. The attrs entity contains multiple attribute declarations that repeat with many more elements. We'll show them momentarily.

Default Declarations

Default declarations provide answers to these two questions:

❑ Does the attribute have to have a value?

❑ Does the attribute have to be defined in the document?

If an attribute does not have to have a value, then, clearly, it will not necessarily be defined in the document. The corresponding default declaration is #IMPLIED. (If this use of the word "implied" puzzles you, you're not alone.) If an attribute must have a value then there are two possibilities: there is a default or there is no default. If there is no default, the default declaration is #REQUIRED. If there is a default then the default declaration is that default. For instance, the FORM element in HTML has a METHOD attribute that *must* have a value. If the attribute is not defined in the document, it is given the default value "POST".

In other words, if an attribute is not explicitly defined in the document, it may mean two different things:

❑ the attribute is optional and has no value

❑ the attribute is required but has a default value

To distinguish between these two possibilities, the parser has to look at the default declaration of the attribute and retrieve the default value, if present. Even a non-validating parser will check the internal DTD subset for default attributes. However, non-validating parsers may or may not go out to external entities, so if your attributes have default values specified in external entities, and the parser doesn't validate, your attributes may be left without a value. (See below on the expected behavior of validating and non-validating processors.)

Default Declaration Production and Examples

```
[60]  DefaultDecl ::=  '#REQUIRED' | '#IMPLIED' | (('#FIXED' S)? AttValue)
```

The possible values of default declaration are #REQUIRED, #IMPLIED or simply the default value of the attribute. The default value may be preceded by the keyword #FIXED, indicating that the default value is the only value possible. This is a minor optimization that saves the parser a little work.

The script element in XHTML DTD illustrates various default declarations:

```
<!ELEMENT script (#PCDATA)>
<!ATTLIST script
  charset     %Charset;       #IMPLIED
  type        %ContentType;   #REQUIRED
  src         %URI;           #IMPLIED
  defer       (defer)         #IMPLIED
  xml:space   CDATA           #FIXED      "preserve"
  >
```

This attribute list presents several interesting features. First, it shows various default declarations. Second, it shows three different attribute types: CDATA, an enumerated list with only one value (defer), and parameter entities. Finally, one of the attribute names is qualified by the xml: prefix. Its default value, which cannot be overridden, specifies that script elements in all XHTML documents must preserve the whitespace characters (i.e. the original formatting).

The "Generic Attributes" of XHTML

As an example of design and a reference, consider the *Generic Attributes* section of XHTML Strict, slightly abbreviated. It ends with the definition of the `attrs` entity that is used in many attribute list definitions:

```
<!--==================== Generic Attributes ===================================-->

<!-- core attributes common to most elements
  id        document-wide unique id
  class     space separated list of classes
  style     associated style info
  title     advisory title/amplification
-->
<!ENTITY % coreattrs
 "id            ID          #IMPLIED
  class         CDATA       #IMPLIED
  style         %StyleSheet; #IMPLIED
  title         %Text;      #IMPLIED"
  >


<!-- internationalization attributes
  lang          language code (backwards compatible)
  xml:lang      language code (as per XML 1.0 spec)
  dir           direction for weak/neutral text
-->
<!ENTITY % i18n
 "lang          %LanguageCode; #IMPLIED
  xml:lang      %LanguageCode; #IMPLIED
  dir           (ltr|rtl)     #IMPLIED"
  >

<!-- attributes for common UI events
 ...
-->
<!ENTITY % events
 "onclick       %Script;       #IMPLIED
  ondblclick    %Script;       #IMPLIED
  onmousedown   %Script;       #IMPLIED
  onmouseup     %Script;       #IMPLIED
  onmouseover   %Script;       #IMPLIED
  onmousemove   %Script;       #IMPLIED
  onmouseout    %Script;       #IMPLIED
  onkeypress    %Script;       #IMPLIED
  onkeydown     %Script;       #IMPLIED
  onkeyup       %Script;       #IMPLIED"
  >

<!-- attributes for elements that can get the focus
  accesskey     accessibility key character
  tabindex      position in tabbing order
  onfocus       the element got the focus
  onblur        the element lost the focus
-->
```

```
<!ENTITY % focus
 "accesskey      %Character;      #IMPLIED
  tabindex       %Number;         #IMPLIED
  onfocus        %Script;         #IMPLIED
  onblur         %Script;         #IMPLIED"
  >

<!ENTITY % attrs "%coreattrs; %i18n; %events;">
```

Almost every element in HTML 4.0/XHTML has attributes collected in attrs; many elements have no other attributes:

```
<!ELEMENT body %Block;>
<!ATTLIST body
  %attrs;
  onload             %Script;    #IMPLIED
  onunload           %Script;    #IMPLIED
  >

<!ELEMENT div %Flow;>  <!-- generic language/style container -->
<!ATTLIST div
  %attrs;
  >

<!ELEMENT p %Inline;>
<!ATTLIST p
  %attrs;
  >
```

This is pretty much all there is to know in order to design and implement a DTD. The rest is practice and study of well-designed examples, such as those mentioned in this and the preceding chapter.

Beyond DTDs

DTDs are a great invention; they have been used and will continue to be used to define extremely useful and powerful languages. However, there are two major things wrong with them. First, they do not use XML syntax, and so cannot be processed and validated by the standard XML tools. Second, they were designed primarily for document markup, not data interchange, and as a result they:

❑   don't have any notion of data types other than text

❑   are not modular: the closest thing to a module is an external parsed entity, equivalent to an include file in C

❑   are not easy to extend and reuse

In brief, DTDs themselves are not like objects, and neither are the structures they define. The momentum to replace DTDs with something more like objects in an object-oriented programming language is very strong. The name of the replacement is XML Schema, a W3C project. *XML Schema Requirements*, a W3C Note dated February 15, 1999 stated the design goals for the project as follows.

The XML schema language shall be:

1. more expressive than XML DTDs;

2. expressed in XML;

3. self-describing;

4. usable by a wide variety of applications that employ XML;

5. straightforwardly usable on the Internet;

6. optimized for interoperability;

7. simple enough to implement with modest design and runtime resources;

8. coordinated with relevant W3C specs (XML Information Set, Links, Namespaces, Pointers, Style and Syntax, as well as DOM, HTML, and RDF Schema).

The XML schema language specification shall:

1. be prepared quickly;

2. be precise, concise, human-readable, and illustrated with examples.
   (http://www.w3.org/TR/1999/NOTE-xml-schema-req-19990215)

For Java programmers working with XML, XML Schema will be an extremely useful tool. *XML in the Java Platform*, a presentation at the 1999 JavaOne conference, shows XML Schemas as central to data binding within Java programs. While DTDs will remain with us for a long time as an established way of defining XML languages, XML Schema will rapidly grow in importance for XML-based data processing and interchange.

Documents, Processors and DTDs

Let's review what the processor (an XML parser) is supposed to do with a document, and how it would use the DTD in doing that. In the absence of a DTD, the best a parser can do is check the document for well-formedness and construct the document tree. If the DTD is present, the parser, whether validating or non-validating, can do much more.

Non-Validating Parsers

It would be natural but wrong to assume that non-validating parsers ignore the DTD. The non-validating parser is required to read the document entity, including the internal DTD subset and use its information for the following tasks:

❑ normalize attribute values

❑ include the replacement text of internal entities

❑ supply default attribute values

Attribute Value Normalization

To normalize an attribute value means to process all character and entity references, and to replace all whitespace characters with the space character #x20. (If a "#xD#xA" sequence is found in a parsed entity it is replaced with a single #x20.) If the attribute type is not CDATA, then the XML processor will further discard leading and trailing space characters, and replace sequences of space characters by a single such character. If a non-validating parser doesn't know what the attribute type is, it must treat it as CDATA and leave space characters untouched.

Non-Validating Parsers and Parsed Entities

How can it happen that a non-validating parser doesn't know the attribute type? Remember, non-validating processors are not required to read any external entities, including the external DTD subset. If a non-validating processor does not process external entities, it will stop reading the DTD as soon as an external entity reference is encountered, because that external entity may have an impact on later declarations in the internal DTD subset. If the same element, attribute or entity is declared twice, the first declaration takes precedence, but that first declaration may be in the external parameter entity that the non-validating processor has not seen.

This has ramifications for entity processing within the document. Suppose an entity is declared in a DTD external subset, and the non-validating processor has not seen it. What is it supposed to do when it comes across a reference to an entity that, as far as it knows, has never been declared? The answer is that if the document is declared as "standalone='yes'" then the processor reports an error, but if the document is not so declared then the processor ignores the reference and continues. (The standalone declaration may appear in the XML declaration line at the very beginning of the prolog.)

Document Normalizaton

Because of these problems, if you have to use a non-validating processor you may want to normalize your documents before submitting them to the parser. Normalization here means expanding all external entity references and merging adjacent text nodes. The XML specification stipulates that it should be possible to perform such an expansion "algorithmically", i.e. by use of a computer program. James Clark has a sgmlnorm utility that expands all external entities in a document. (See http://www.jclark.com/sp/index.htm.)

Differences Among Non-Validating Parsers

The *Recommendation* does not say that they **must not** read external entities, only that they are not required to. So, for instance, Sun's XML parser will read them, as Sun's XML Tutorial proudly declares:

> *"All non-validating parsers are not created equal! Although a validating parser is required to process all external entities referenced from within the document, some of that processing is optional for a non-validating parser. With such a parser, an externally stored section of the DTD that is "included" in the current document using an entity reference might not be processed. In addition, a non-validating parser is not required to identify ignorable whitespace (although a validating parser must). In that case, whitespace which can legitimately be ignored would be returned as part of the normal character stream. The non-validating parser in Sun's Java XML library implements both of these optional behaviors – it processes all external entities and it identifies ignorable whitespace (http://java.sun.com/xml/tutorial_intro.html)."*

This clearly raises the danger of parser wars, with different parsers trying to outdo each other in providing mutually-incompatible features. To stave off the danger, Sun is undertaking to define a "Java API for XML Parsing (JAXP)", implemented as a `javax.xml` package. The package includes Java bindings for SAX and DOM, and the basic interfaces and classes that a Java XML parser must implement. The package, in first public draft as of this writing, can be found at `http://www.java.sun.com/xml`. The software is said to offer "100% conformance to the XML 1.0 Specification, SAX 1.0, DOM Level 1 Core and XML namespaces." We'll say more about it in the next chapter.

Validating Parsers

Unlike non-validating parsers, validating ones are highly predictable: they process all external parseable entities and always read through the entire DTD. Their entity replacement process and whitespace handling follow standard procedures. We review these procedures in the remaining two sections of this chapter.

Whitespace Handling

White space is treated differently by the processor depending on where it is found:

- ❑ in the document between elements
- ❑ in element content
- ❑ in an attribute value
- ❑ in markup and DTD
- ❑ in processing instructions, comments and CDATA sections

While the details are many, there are only two basic attitudes: normalize, or pass on to the application. The main principle is that **all whitespace within the document is passed on to the application**. The processor must inform the application whether or not the whitespace is part of the element content.

Element Content

Consider a document fragment:

```
<a><b>inside b 1</b>
    <b>inside b 2</b>
</a>
```

Possible declarations for `<a>` include:

```
<!ELEMENT a (b*)><!-- children only -->
<!ELEMENT a (PCDATA|b)*><!-- Mixed -->
```

With the first declaration, but not with the second, the whitespace between the two instances of `<b>` is outside the element content. If the processor is non-validating and DTD-ignorant, it has to assume that all whitespace is part of the element content.

xml:space

Consider the following declaration and document fragment:

```
<!DOCTYPE poem [
<!ELEMENT poem (verse+)>
<!ATTLIST poem
  xml:space (preserve|default) "preserve"
...
]>
<poem>
<verse>Telemachos, my son!  The Trojan war</verse>
<verse>  is over. Who won, I can't remember.</verse>
<verse>I bet the Greeks. Who else except the Greeks</verse>
<verse>  would leave so many dead so far from home?</verse>
...
</poem>
```

In the poem element, the whitespace is not part of the content. However, the xml:space attribute can be set to "preserve" to signal to the application that it is desirable to have the whitespace preserved. The only other possible value of this attribute is "default", meaning that the application's default policy toward whitespace should be appropriate. This value can be used to block children elements from inheriting the "preserve" value. If the xml:space attribute is not specified then its default value, which is "default", is assumed to apply to all elements except the root element. For the root element, no assumptions are made.

In truth, the xml:space attribute is probably of limited importance. If the application is going to display the document to a human user, the document will be accompanied by a style sheet, whose instructions can format the output much more precisely than the whitespace in the document's content. However, the attribute is useful for preserving the format of code, traditionally formatted using indentation and other whitespace. As you recall, the <script> element of XHTML has the xml:space attribute fixed at "preserve".

End-of-Line Handling

One instance where the XML processor abandons its "hands-off" policy towards whitespace in document content is the treatment of end-of-lines. As you know, different operating systems use different ways of indicating end of line, as follows:

OS	EOLN marker	Hex code
Unix	Line Feed (LF)	"#xA"
Mac	Carriage Return (CR)	"#xD"
DOS/Windows	LF CR sequence	"#xA #xD"

To make life easier for the applications, whether they want it or not, the XML processor is mandated to replace all EOLN markers with a single occurrence of the LF character. As the *Recommendation* observes:

"[t]his behavior can conveniently be produced by normalizing all line breaks to #xA on input, before parsing."

Documents are typically read line-by-line into a data structure for processing, and the normalization can take place during that reading process.

Whitespace Within the DTD, Markup and Attribute Values

Whitespace within the DTD and markup is normalized, as follows:

❑ every tab, LF and CR is replaced by the space character, "#x20" (the LF-CR sequence is replaced by a single space character)

❑ all leading and trailing space characters are removed, and all remaining sequences of space characters are collapsed into a single such character

In attribute values, if the attribute is not CDATA then it is also normalized. This makes sense: if the type is not CDATA then it has to be, ultimately, a Name, an NMTOKEN or a sequence of such. Neither a Name nor an NMTOKEN can contain whitespace, so the only whitespace needed is a single #x20 to separate items in a sequence.

As usual, if the processor is DTD-ignorant, it takes the conservative attitude and preserves everything.

Whitespace normalization is part of the process of normalizing attribute values. During that process, the processor also replaces character and entity references with their replacement values. More on this in the next section.

Entity Reference Replacement Process

Replacing a general entity reference in the document is fairly straightforward: replace the reference with the entity text, recursively replacing character and entity references in it, if any. All the recursive replacements take place at the same time, in a FirstIn-FirstOut order.

Replacing internal parameter entity references in the DTD can be quite tricky because only character and parameter entities are replaced at the time: general references are preserved in the replacement text, together with the delimiting characters around them. Here's a relatively simple example from *Section 4.4* of the *Recommendation*:

```
<!ENTITY % pub "&#xc9;ditions Gallimard" >
<!ENTITY rights "All rights reserved" >
<!ENTITY book "La Peste: Albert Camus,
&#xA9; 1947 %pub;. &rights;" >
```

The *Recommendation* distinguishes between the **literal entity value**, which is the quoted string in the entity declaration, and the actual **replacement text**, in which all and only character references and parameter references have been replaced with their values. The literal entity value of the book entity contains character, parameter and general entities; the parameter entity pub, in turn, contains a character reference to an accented French vowel. As the DTD is processed, the character and parameter entities all get replaced yielding the following replacement text:

```
La Peste: Albert Camus,
© 1947 Éditions Gallimard. &rights;
```

The general-entity reference `&rights;` will get expanded in the process of expanding the general reference `&book;` when a document instance is constructed.

Additional complexities result when the replacement text of a general entity contains characters that need to be escaped. *Appendix D* of the *Recommendation* provides a nice tongue twister:

```
<!ENTITY example "<p>An ampersand (&#38;#38;) may be escaped
numerically (&#38;#38;#38;) or with a general entity
(&amp;amp;).</p>" >
```

This DTD fragment defines a general entity `example`. When the DTD fragment is parsed, the character references, but not the general references, are processed. The resulting replacement text for the example entity becomes:

```
<p>An ampersand (&#38;) may be escaped
numerically (&#38;#38;) or with a general entity
(&amp;amp;).</p>
```

In the tricky second line of the example entity, the first `#38` in the triple is left alone because it's inside a general entity reference; the second is replaced with `&`, making the rest of the text in parentheses a general entity reference. Thus `(&#38;#38;#38;)` becomes `(&#38;#38;)`. When in a document, a general entity reference of the form `&example;` is encountered, it becomes:

```
An ampersand (&) may be escaped
numerically (&#38;) or with a general entity
(&amp;).
```

As the specification itself observes, with a touch of self-irony, the seemingly simple rules for entity reference replacements can have complex interactions. *Appendix D* of the *Recommendation* provides yet another example that contains both parameter references within general entity definitions and multiply escaped characters. Those who like doing puzzles may find it good fun to put together several such examples, process them by hand and compare the results to what a conforming processor would do.

Summary of Entities and Contexts

A table in Section 4.4 of the XML 1.0 specification provides an excellent summary of the processor action in response to an entity name or reference, depending on the context and the type of entity. Rather than reproduce that information here, we refer you to *Appendix H*, which reproduces the specification in full.

Conclusions

As we said in the beginning, we cannot possibly pack every detail of several very tightly packed specifications into two chapters. We have left some odds and ends out, including, most notably:

- ❑ precise definitions of character classes (see *Appendix B* of the XML 1.0 *Recommendation*)
- ❑ many productions (you should read them all)
- ❑ language codes
- ❑ character encoding and their auto-detection by the processor

We do believe that we have covered all the major features of several recent specifications, especially XML 1.0 and Namespaces (the specification of both of these are reproduced in *Appendices H* and *I*, respectively). These two specifications form the basis of the latest version of HTML, which has become an XML application. They also make it possible to define multiple other XML languages, both for more expressive documents, and for data description and manipulation. To indicate the possible range of uses for XML, consider that XSLT (the style-and-transformation language for XML), JSP (JavaServer Pages), and MathML (language for presenting mathematical formulae) are all XML applications, as well as languages for news stories, financial analysis, and multiple other industry or domain specific languages. Our main interest in the forthcoming chapters will be in using XML as a data interchange format, for moving data between relational databases and application components.

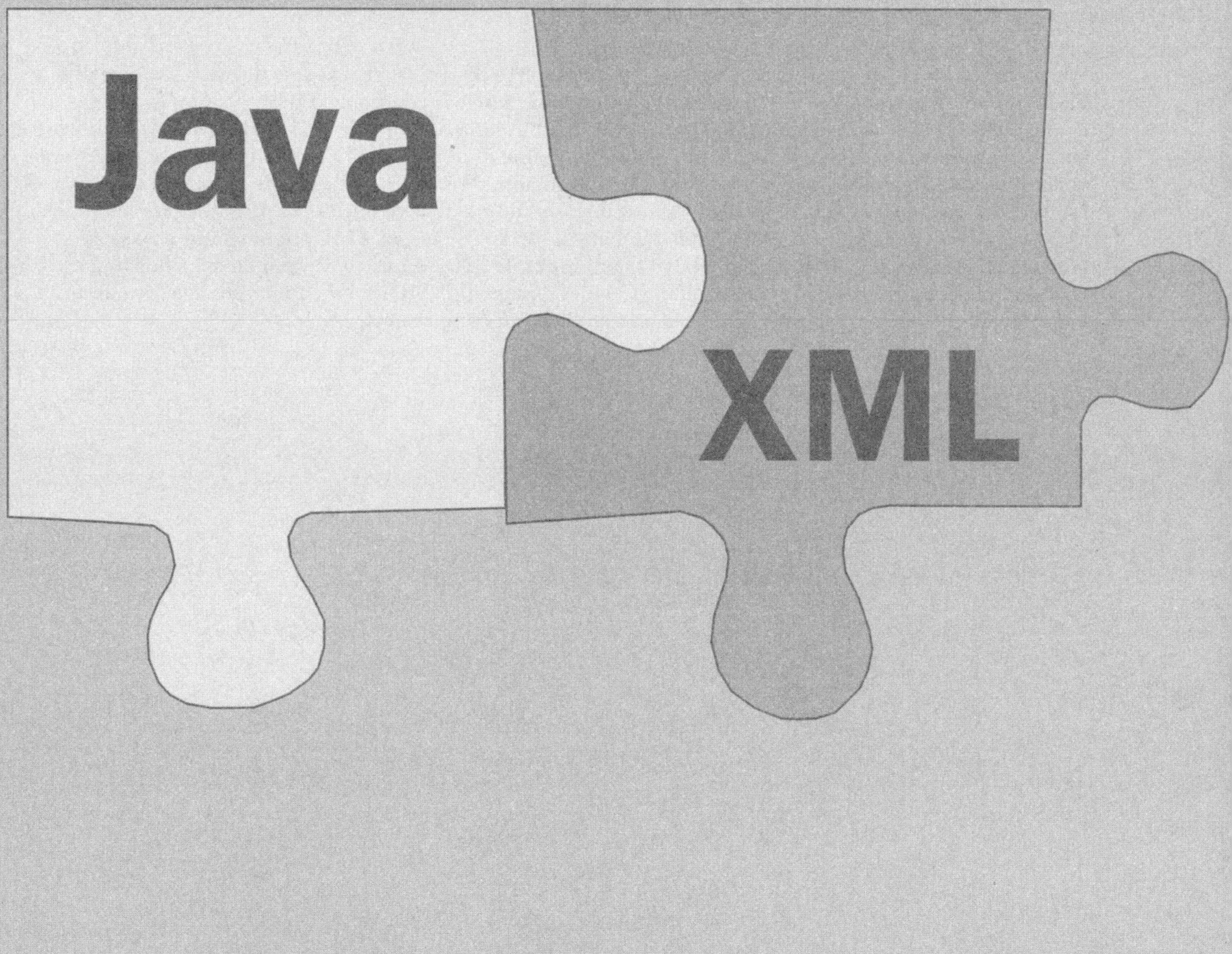
Java
XML

7

The DOM, the SAX and the Parser

Now that we know how to write an XML document, with or without a DTD, how are we going to work with them? There are two toolsets which can help: one lays out the document in time, the other in space. SAX, the Simple API for XML, associates an event with each tag (opening or closing) and with each block of text. You just write the event handlers and sit back to watch the document pass by. DOM, the Document Object Model, describes the document as a tree. You can traverse it, edit it, do what you please with it, as long as you can store it all at once.

Note that either could be implemented using the other: you could generate the SAX events by traversing a DOM object (it would be silly, but you could do it) and you could generate the DOM object by appropriate SAX event handlers (that's not silly at all, and in fact you can already get it done for you; the Sun toolkit for example, uses this process to generate DOM structures.)

Why choose one over the other? It's the usual time/space programmer's problem, where a time-structure saves on space but space-structure adds flexibility. SAX can deal with arbitrarily large documents, and lets you begin a response as soon as the document starts up. DOM lets you move back and forth, up and down, and over into parts of the document which you just inserted.

This chapter is mostly about DOM, dealing with SAX only in so far as it is used to build a DOM object. (The next chapter is mostly about SAX, and also about the Sun toolkit-specific extensions to both DOM and SAX.) In outline, this chapter proceeds as follows:

- ❑ parsing an XML file; SAX and DOM comparison
- ❑ a DOM application (`DocWalker`)
- ❑ extended `DocWalker`: `XmlManipulator` (copy-cut-paste a node)
- ❑ DOM in detail.

Parsing an XML document

Let us begin with the larger picture. The purpose of parsing an XML document is to make some interfaces available to an application that needs to make use of the document; using those interfaces, the application can inspect, retrieve and modify the document's contents. The XML parser thus sits in the middle between an XML document and an application that uses it.

The relationship between the parser and the application is specified in two places. First, XML 1.0 Recommendation has various things to say about how a "conformant processor" must or may or should respond to various aspects of the document. (We reviewed those requirements in the chapter before this.) Second, SAX and DOM spell out the Java interfaces that an application can expect from the parser. These are just interfaces that have to be implemented, and they cover many, but not all, aspects of converting a document into events or data structures that an application can use.

The rest of the picture comes from the parser. The relationship of the parser to XML 1.0 is in terms of conformance, from "very conformant" to "terribly non-conformant". In the next section, we summarize a very thorough recent study of conformance levels of most currently available parsers, published in http://www.xml.com/pub/1999/09/conformance/summary.html.

The relationship of the parser to SAX and DOM is twofold. First, it implements SAX and DOM interfaces. In the process, new classes are defined, and the interfaces may be extended. Second, the parser fills in the gaps that SAX and DOM are silent about. In particular, SAX and DOM say nothing about how an application obtains an instance of the parser class, and how that instance gets access to the document that it is called upon to parse.

As we already pointed out in last chapter, this picture could clearly result in a "parser war", in which various parsers compete to provide seductively powerful and mutually incompatible features. This is not to suggest that different parsers should not try out different things, but it ought to be possible to write a complete application that would be completely portable between installations that use different parsers. This is not possible today: even if you have two parsers that guarantee "100% conformance to the XML 1.0 Specification, SAX 1.0, DOM Level 1 Core and XML namespaces", you'll have to change some code if you replace one with the other in your application.

Fortunately, this is likely to change because Sun is undertaking to define a "Java API for XML Parsing (JAXP)", implemented as javax.xml package. The package includes Java interfaces from SAX and DOM, and the basic interfaces and classes that a Java XML parser must implement. The package, in first public draft as of this writing, can be found at java.sun.com/xml. The quote in the last paragraph about 100% conformance is from the documentation.

What parsers are there, and which one do we use?

There are at least a dozen non-validating parsers and about half that many validating ones. They are all listed in the Resources appendix and also in the conformance study that we present in the next chapter. The best come from the usual suspects: Sun, Oracle, IBM and James Clark.

We chose to use Sun's parser, Technical Release 2 (TR-2), available at java.sun.com/xml. When we made that choice, Java API for XML Parsing was only a distant promise, but we expected it to be close to the technical release, and indeed, it turned out to be so. Only minor changes, mostly renamings, will be needed to convert our code to use javax.xml. In other respects, also, we have been pleased with our choice: the parser is easy to install, fast, and provides good diagnostics. According to the study, it is them most conformant of available parsers.

An important consideration in choosing a parser is whether there is a matching XSL processor. (If you know nothing about XSL, wait till Chapter 13 with all your questions.) As of now, Sun's parser doesn't have one, but we have successfully configured James Clark's xt to work with TR-2, both from the command line and as a servlet. We have also used xt with James Clark's parser, xp.

With these preliminaries out of the way, we can move on to a detailed discussion of DOM and SAX. We will mostly be talking about parsing and modifying existing documents, a task that can be performed using either of the two sets of interfaces. To create a document from scratch, you have to use DOM (but, as you will see, you may still need a SAX parser).

DOM and SAX

To process an existing document, you need an "input source" that delivers the document's contents. Once an input source is in place, the lexical analyzer can convert its sequence of characters into a sequence of tokens, and the parser can get to work. The application that uses the parser wants to access various components of the document for the purpose of displaying or modifying or rearranging them (or whatever else it needs to do). The parser can provide access to the document's components in two ways (at least):

❑ It can build an internal representation of the document, a tree of nodes. The parser then gets out of the way, and the application works with the internal representation. This is the DOM way.

❑ It can provide access to the tokens as they are encountered in a pass through the document, without constructing an internal representation of the document. This is the SAX way

More on SAX

To elaborate on SAX first, we usually don't know or care how the parsing process unfolds and in what order lexical analysis and production rules are applied. However, we can *visualize* that process as a steady progression through the text that sends notifications of certain important events: the document has started, an element has started, an element has ended, a character sequence between two elements has been found, and so on. SAX provides standard names for callback functions that are triggered by these events. Writing a SAX application mostly consists of implementing those callbacks. Here are some of their declarations, from the `org.xml.sax.DocumentHandler` interface:

```
void characters(char[] ch, int start, int length)
     //  Receive notification of character data.
void endDocument()
     //  Receive notification of the end of a document.
void endElement(java.lang.String name)
     //  Receive notification of the end of an element.
void processingInstruction(java.lang.String target, java.lang.String data)
     //  Receive notification of a processing instruction.
void startElement(java.lang.String name, AttributeList atts)
     //  Receive notification of the beginning of an element.
```

When you use SAX, you have to think in terms of an unfolding process, a sweep through the text to be parsed. If you come across an element or an attribute list that you want to use later, you have to save a persistent reference to it, because it is not yet part of any data structure.

More on DOM

By contrast, DOM is all about a data structure: DOM provides standard interfaces to the document's representation that has resulted from the parsing process. Suppose you want to decrease the list price of every paperback in your book inventory by 10%. With SAX, you say things like: "For every book element that passes by, if its type attribute has the value "paperback" then reduce the value of the next price element by 10%". With DOM, you say things like: "For every book element that is a descendant of the root, if its type attribute has the value "paperback" then reduce the value of its child price element by 10%". With SAX, there are no parents and children, which is both a weakness and a strength: you don't have to parse the entire document before doing something to its first element, and you don't have to hold a representation of the entire document in memory at the same time.

DOM and SAX history

DOM was the first to be standardized: W3C released its DOM Level 1 Recommendation in October 1998. As people started using it for document processing, some drawbacks of the DOM approach have become obvious. It takes a good deal of time, and a lot of memory space, to construct a representation for a very large document. Until it is constructed, you cannot do anything with it. For instance, if you want to do a little fix on the second child of the root node and nothing else, you still have to parse the entire document and construct a huge tree before you can get to your little fix. When we shift from conventional documents to databases, the "document" may fill gigabytes, and the DOM approach is simply not practical.

SAX came about in response to these and similar criticisms that were frequently voiced on the xml-dev list. The person who actually got it done is David Megginson, www.megginson.com. (You have already seen his name in connection with the Namespaces Q&A in Chapter 5; he is involved in several XML projects, including a co-chairmanship of W3C Core XML Working Group.) SAX is even less of a formal standard than W3C Recommendations – it is not backed by any consortia – but it's very widely accepted, both by individual developers and by the likes of Sun and IBM, and so its stability is insured, especially since it is included, in total, in the `javax.xml` package.

An Input Source and a Document Object

To recapitulate, the first thing an application needs is an input source. With an input source in hand, you can either say `parser.parse(input)` and get yourself a sequence of SAX events, or you can say `createXmlDocument(input, false)` and produce a DOM document object. (This will run the non-validating parser; set the second argument to `true` if you want to use the validating one.)

Input Source and the Resolver Class

In Sun's Project X – see `http://java.sun.com/xml/xml-side1.html` – the way you create an input source is the same whether you are writing a DOM or a SAX application: you use a `createInputSource()` method of the `Resolver` class. There are several such methods, with different configurations of arguments; all of them return an `InputSource` object.

The `InputSource` class is declared in the SAX package. It has several constructors (from a file name, an input byte stream, an input character stream, and so on), but they are not used because they expect that all the entity references are already resolved. That's what the "factory methods" of the `Resolver` class do: they take a file name or a URL as an argument and produce an input source with all external entities resolved and the encoding correctly identified so the lexical analyzer can get to work, converting sequences of characters into tokens. We'll have more to say about `Resolver` in the SAX section; for now, we continue with DOM.

Skeleton of a DOM Application

Apart from two small utility packages, Sun's XML toolkit consists largely of four packages:

- ❏ `com.sun.xml.parser` (implements and extends SAX)
- ❏ `com.sun.xml.tree` (implements and extends DOM)
- ❏ `org.w3c.dom`
- ❏ `org.xml.sax`

A DOM application that parses an existing document (rather than creating one from scratch) uses all four of them. More precisely, in order to create a DOM object, the application will minimally use:

- ❏ `InputSource` and exception classes from the `sax` package
- ❏ `Resolver` from the `parser` package
- ❏ `XmlDocument` from the `tree` package

Assuming that the input source is created from an XML file specified on the command line, the program can obtain a DOM object this way:

```
org.xml.sax.InputSource input;
com.sun.xml.tree.XmlDocument doc;

try
{
    input = com.sun.xml.parser.Resolver.createInputSource (new File (argv [0]));
    doc = XmlDocument.createXmlDocument (input, false);
    // use DOM API to process the document
    ...
}
catch (SAXParseException err)
{
    ...                                                    // parser errors
}
catch (SAXException e)
{
    ...                              // other SAX errors, e.g., in creating a parser
}
catch (IOException t)
{
    ...                              //IO errors in creating an input source
}
```

`XmlDocument` implements or inherits all the methods you need to work with a DOM object. Once you have an instance of `XmlDocument` you're ready to go.

Elaborations on the Skeleton

Two actions need to be performed to start a DOM application: create an input source and parse it to create a DOM object. In the skeletal code above, those two actions are performed by two lines of code. Both of those lines allow elaborations and extensions that provide additional functionality but are also more toolkit-specific. We briefly mention the additional functionality here and give examples later in this chapter and the next.

Resolver and InputSource

The `Resolver` class provides methods for creating an input source from a file, a URL, a public ID or an input stream. The format of the incoming data can specified using MIME or, if you don't trust the server, you can ignore the MIME information and use the built-in auto-detection algorithm to identify the character encoding.

XmlDocument Object

The code above uses the static `createXmlDocument()` method of `XmlDocument`, with an `InputSource` object as an argument, to construct a DOM object. Other variants of that method bypass the `Resolver` class services and construct a DOM object directly from a stream or a URL. These should be used with care, since they can't cope with relative URLs.

Instead of a static method of `XmlDocument`, you can use an `XmlDocumentBuilder` object, as follows (assume, as before, that the XML file name is specified on the command line):

```
// turn the filename into a fully qualified URL
//
uri = "file:" + new File (argv [0]).getAbsolutePath ();
XmlDocumentBuilder builder;
Parser parser;

builder = new XmlDocumentBuilder ();
parser = new com.sun.xml.parser.Parser ();
parser.setDocumentHandler (builder);
parser.setErrorHandler (new MyErrorHandler ());
builder.setParser (parser);
builder.setDisableNamespaces (false);
parser.parse (uri);
doc = builder.getDocument ();
```

If you go this route, you can customize error handling, and you can ask the parser to enforce namespace syntax rules for you (going beyond the DOM specification). The price to pay is that the code becomes more toolkit-specific. Since the toolkit is going to be a JDK standard extension, the price may not be too high in this case, but it depends very much on how much control you have over distribution.

An Example Application: DocWalker

Walking a tree is a well-known pastime; there are many programs that do that. Usually, the walk is not random but follows one of three patterns: **preorder**, **inorder** or **postorder**. In preorder, you visit the root before you (recursively) do a complete walk of its subtrees; in inorder, you visit the root after walking the left sub tree and before walking the rest of them; in postorder, you visit the root after walking all its subtrees. The package `com.sun.xml.tree` includes a `TreeWalker` class that does a preorder walk of the DOM tree.

Our application puts the user in control. Its control frame has buttons for Parent, FirstChild, LastChild, PreviousSibling and NextSibling. The data frame shows the entire contents of the current node, together with some additional information about it. To try the application, double-click on `DocWalker.htm` from the code samples available from `www.wrox.com`.

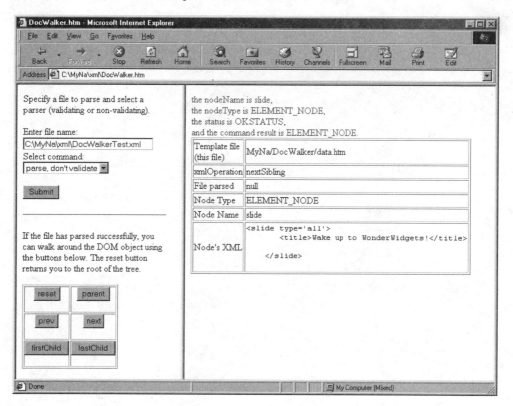

The Structure of the Application

The application is organized into the Document-View-Controller pattern we discussed in Chapter 1. The control and the data frames of `DocWalker.htm` represent the controller and the view, respectively. `DocWalker.class` in the `Utils` directory represents the model. `DocWalkerServlet.class` mediates between the web page and the model, relaying user commands to the model and sending the contents of the changed model back.

In more detail, the source file for the control frame, `DocWalkerCtl.htm`, has a form in which the user specifies the next action to take. The `Request` submitted by that form becomes an `Env` object in the servlet. That object is set by the servlet to be the `Env` of the `DocWalker` class as well. The `DocWalker` carries out the command specified by the user, places several items in the shared `Env`, and returns the result of the command (which may be the node type of the current node or an error message) to the servlet. The servlet places more stuff in the `Env` and gives it to the `HtmlWrapper` object. `HtmlWrapper` uses a template file, `data.htm`, to generate the output (the changed "view") that goes into the data frame of `DocWalker.htm`.

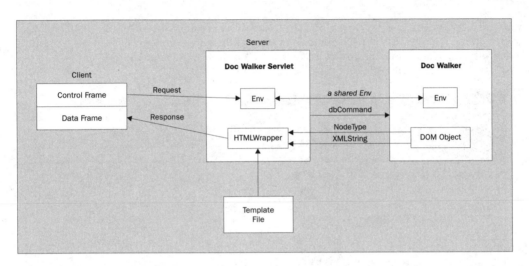

DocWalkerServlet

The servlet imports all the usual suspects, in addition to the `DocWalker` class that does all the DOM work.

```
// servlet DocWalkerServlet, which sets up commands for the DocWalker class

import javax.servlet.*;          // communicate with client
import javax.servlet.http.*;

import MyNa.utils.Env;
import MyNa.utils.MiscFile;
import MyNa.utils.HtmlWrapper; // sends HTML to client.
import java.io.IOException;     // thrown by HtmlWrapper

import MyNa.xml.DocWalker;      // the DOM-aware class, does all the work

public class DocWalkerServlet extends EnvServlet
{
    String filePath = "MyNa/DocWalker/";
        // C:\JRun\jsm-default\MyNa\DocWalker
        // (location of template file for output)
}
```

doPost() and doCommand()

The two important methods are doPost() and doCommand(). In doPost(), we obtain a session object and an HtmlWrapper, before setting up an Env with all the request information, including the command from the user. If there is no command, we send a usage message and return. If the command is "Logout", we terminate the session and return:

```
public void doPost (HttpServletRequest req,
                    HttpServletResponse res)
           throws ServletException, IOException
{
    res.setContentType("text/html");
    HtmlWrapper W=new HtmlWrapper(res.getWriter());
    HttpSession sess=req.getSession(true);

    try
    {
        Env E=new Env(req);
        String myURL=res.encodeURL(req.getRequestURI());
        E.put("xmlServlet",myURL);
        setStr(E,"filePath","",filePath);
        String xmlOperation=E.getStr("Command");
        if(xmlOperation==null){sendCtl(E,W); return;}
        if("Logout".equals(xmlOperation)){doEnd(sess,W); return;}
```

If we get this far, then we need a DocWalker object. First we check to see if there is one already in the session. If there isn't we create a new one, and save it as a session attribute. After that, we call doCommand():

```
        DocWalker dWalker=(DocWalker)sess.getValue("dWalker");
        if(null==dWalker)
        {
            dWalker=new DocWalker();
            sess.putValue("dWalker",dWalker);
        }
        doCommand(dWalker,E,W); // this is where all the work is done
    }
    catch(Exception ex)
    {
        W.wrapPage("doPost failure",""+ex);
    }
} // end of doPost()
```

The three arguments to doCommand() are: a DocWalker, an Env that has all the information the DocWalker needs, and an HtmlWrapper for output. The first action of doCommand() is to make the servlet's Env also the Env variable of DocWalker, thus establishing a channel of communication between the two classes. DocWalker uses its Env to execute the command. The command's output and the XmlString are returned to the servlet directly, and added to the Env within the servlet. Finally, we pass the Env, together with the template file, to HtmlWrapper to produce the desired output:

```
public void doCommand(DocWalker dW,Env env,HtmlWrapper W)
     throws IOException
{                                               // process user query
   dW.setDefs(env);
   String cmdResult=dW.doCommand(); // node type or error message
   String xmlString=dW.writeNode(); // current node linearized in XML
   env.put("cmdResult",cmdResult);  // place command result in Env
   env.put("xmlString",xmlString);  // and xmlSting also

   String fName="data.htm";                 // default template file name
   setStr(env,"templateFile",filePath,fName);// place template file name in Env
   W.wrapEnvPage(env);             // the Env and the template file define output
}
```

Note that `DocWalkerServlet` doesn't know anything about DOM, it just mediates between `Request`, `DocWalker`, and `HtmlWrapper`. All DOM knowledge is in the `DocWalker` class. The `DocWalker` class, on the other hand, knows absolutely nothing about servlets, as you will see from its imports.

DocWalker

`DocWalker` is a case study in using the DOM constructs. Later in the chapter, we will extend it to `XmlManipulator`, a preliminary form of an XML editor. We won't use it directly outside this chapter, but it will prepare you to work with DOM-based code in the `XmlConfig` classes of Chapter 11. Not in the book, but included with the code on the book's web site, is the `TreeSubst` class which is an XML version of our `ParseSubst` from Chapter 4. It didn't quite make it into the book because it involves no new concepts, but it brings them together fairly nicely, and it uses DOM extensively.

Like most programs that work with trees, `DocWalker` is highly recursive, because a tree is a recursive data structure. A program that needs to perform an operation on every node of a tree typically proceeds as follows:

- ❑ if the root of the tree is null, return

- ❑ do to the root whatever needs to be done to each node of the tree

- ❑ recursively repeat this procedure with every child of the current root as the root

You will see a lot of this sort of programming in `DocWalker` and other programs that use the DOM.

Main Components of DocWalker

`DocWalker` consists of four fairly independent parts: initialization, parsing, node-to-XML echoing, and the actual walking, that is, changing the current node in response to a user command. The operation of `DocWalker` can be summarized as follows:

- ❑ Obtain request information from the servlet by getting a copy of its `Env`. Start executing commands.

- ❑ If the user command is `parseFile` or `parseValidateFile`, then parse the XML file specified by the user and create a DOM object whose root is the current node.

❏ If the user command is reset, make the root the current node.

❏ Otherwise, change the current node as the user instructs and return the type of the new current node.

❏ Upon request, write out the current node as pretty-printed XML.

In addition to its action, each command produces some output, either the type of the new current node or an appropriate error message. That output, as you recall, is one of two items that the servlet retrieves from its `DocWalker` object; the other one is the XML-linearized contents of the current node (including all subnodes). The servlet uses its `HtmlWrapper` object to send the two items to the browser, via its `Env` object. The servlet's `Env` object, as before, determines the browser output.

Imports and Setup

The list of `DocWalker` imports is instructive. Apart from the usual general Java classes and our utilities, it has several DOM classes, three classes from SAX to do basic parsing, and two `com.sun.xml` classes: the `Resolver` and the `XmlDocument`. This is a typical set:

```
package MyNa.xml;

import MyNa.utils.*;
import java.io.*;
import java.util.*;

import org.w3c.dom.Node;
import org.w3c.dom.Element;
import org.w3c.dom.Attr;
import org.w3c.dom.DocumentType;
import org.w3c.dom.NamedNodeMap;

import org.xml.sax.InputSource;
import org.xml.sax.SAXException;
import org.xml.sax.SAXParseException;

import com.sun.xml.parser.Resolver;
import com.sun.xml.tree.XmlDocument;
```

The variables are fairly self-explanatory. The constructor creates instances of the variables. The `Env` variable is used for communicating with the servlet. The request data is passed to `DocWalker` by setting the servlet's `Env` to be `DocWalker`'s `Env`, via the `setEnv()` method:

```
public class DocWalker
{
    Env defs;                      // to communicate with the Env of the servlet
    Node theNode;                  // the current node
    Node originalNode;             // used in reset() to restore original

    public DocWalker()
    {                              // start out new, get values from setup
        defs=new Env();
        theNode=null;
```

```
            originalNode=null;
        }
    }
    public void setDefs(Env e)
    {
        defs=e;
    }                                   // to refer to the servlet's Env
```

With the request information in, `DocWalker` can start executing commands.

Executing the User Command

User commands fall into four groups, corresponding to two parts of the control frame. Commands in the first group have to do with parsing and creating a document. Commands in the second group have to do with walking around.

```
public String doCommand()
{
    String cmd=defs.getStr("Command");
    if(null==cmd)return addNodeData("No 'Command' given");

                        // two document parsing commands call the same method

    if(cmd.equals("parseFile"))
        return initFile(defs.getStr("theFile"),false);
    if(cmd.equals("parseValidateFile"))
        return initFile(defs.getStr("theFile"),true);

                        // the rest are "walking" commands

    if(cmd.equals("firstChild"))return getFirstChild();
    if(cmd.equals("parentNode"))return getParentNode();
    if(cmd.equals("nextSibling"))return getNextSibling();
    if(cmd.equals("previousSibling"))return getPreviousSibling();
    if(cmd.equals("lastChild"))return getLastChild();
    if(cmd.equals("reset"))return reset();
    return addNodeData("Command '"+cmd+"' not understood");
}
```

Parsing and Creating a Document

This is the familiar skeleton of a DOM application, fleshed out with exception-handling code. We also provide for two possible input sources, local system files and URLs:

```
public String initFile(String fileName,boolean validate)
{
    InputSource  input;
    XmlDocument  doc;
    if(null==fileName)return addNodeData("cannot initFile of null");
    theNode=originalNode=null;
```

```
    try
    {
        try
        {
            if(fileName.startsWith("http:"))
            {
                URL uri=new URL(fileName);
                input=Resolver.createInputSource(uri,true);
            }
            else
            {
                File inFile=new File(fileName);
                input=Resolver.createInputSource(inFile);
            }
            doc = XmlDocument.createXmlDocument (input, validate);
            theNode=originalNode=doc;
            return addNodeData(theNode);
        }
        catch (SAXParseException err)
        {
            return addNodeData(""+err);
        }
        catch (SAXException e)
        {
            Exception x = e.getException ();
            ((x == null) ? e : x).printStackTrace ();
            return addNodeData(""+e);
        }
    }
    catch (IOException t)
    {
        t.printStackTrace (); return addNodeData(""+t);
    }
}
```

Node Type and Node Name

Now we are finally entering DOM territory: the rest of `DocWalker` is not toolkit-specific. For each node, we return its node type and node name. Node types are defined in the DOM and correspond closely to the familiar components of XML document as specified in the XML 1.0 Recommendation. The only node type that does not have a parallel in XML 1.0 is DOCUMENT_FRAGMENT_NODE. Document fragment is a more recent specification, `http://www.w3.org/TR/WD-xml-fragment`. We'll cover it in the DOM overview later in the chapter.

Node Types in IDL and Java

DOM uses the same **Interface Definition Language** or **IDL** as CORBA for specifying its APIs. It also provides translations from IDL into Java and into JavaScript. We give more background on the IDL and its translations in the DOM overview; in the case of node types, the translation is trivial. Node types are integer constants. The data type of an integer constant is "const unsigned short" in IDL and " public static final short" in Java. So, the node types are declared in IDL as:

```
// NodeType
const unsigned short        ELEMENT_NODE        = 1;
const unsigned short        ATTRIBUTE_NODE      = 2;
const unsigned short        TEXT_NODE           = 3;
const unsigned short        CDATA_SECTION_NODE  = 4;
```

```
const unsigned short      ENTITY_REFERENCE_NODE = 5;
const unsigned short      ENTITY_NODE        = 6;
const unsigned short      PROCESSING_INSTRUCTION_NODE = 7;
const unsigned short      COMMENT_NODE       = 8;
const unsigned short      DOCUMENT_NODE      = 9;
const unsigned short      DOCUMENT_TYPE_NODE = 10;
const unsigned short      DOCUMENT_FRAGMENT_NODE = 11;
const unsigned short      NOTATION_NODE      = 12;
```

In the Java translation, this comes out as:

```
// NodeType
public static final short            ELEMENT_NODE = 1;
// and so on
```

Mapping Node Type to its String Name

To map a node type to a string that names it, we put the strings in a static array:

```
static final String[] NODETYPENAMES=
{
    "ELEMENT_NODE","ATTRIBUTE_NODE","TEXT_NODE","CDATA_SECTION_NODE",
    "ENTITY_REFERENCE_NODE","ENTITY_NODE","PROCESSING_INSTRUCTION_NODE",
    "COMMENT_NODE","DOCUMENT_NODE","DOCUMENT_TYPE_NODE",
    "DOCUMENT_FRAGMENT_NODE","NOTATION_NODE"
};
```

Given a node type, we subtract 1 and use the result as an index into the array because array indices start at 0 while node types start at 1. If an error condition arises, we return a string suitable for display in a web page.

```
public String getNodeTypeName(Node theNode)
{
    if(null==theNode)
        return "null node has no type";
    short nT=theNode.getNodeType();                        // a DOM-defined method
    if(0<nT && nT<=NODETYPENAMES.length)
        return NODETYPENAMES[nT-1];  // array index starts at 0, node types at 1
    return "invalid Nodetype "+nT+" for node";
}
```

Node Name

The node's type determines what constitutes the node's name and the node's value, according to the following table (DOM):

Node Type	nodeName	nodeValue
Element	tagName	null
Attr	name of attribute	value of attribute
Text	#text	content of the text node

Node Type	nodeName	nodeValue
CDATASection	#cdata-section	content of the CDATA Section
EntityReference	name of entity referenced	null
Entity	entity name	null
ProcessingInstruction	target	entire content excluding the target
Comment	#comment	content of the comment
Document	#document	null
DocumentType	document type name	null
DocumentFragment	#document-fragment	null
Notation	notation name	null

In IDL, the Node interface contains the following declaration:

```
readonly attribute DOMString nodeName;
```

IDL's "attribute" corresponds to a Java variable. However, the Java translation does not insist that the class implementing the interface must have a nodeName variable; it only specifies that the Java interface Node declares a getNodeName() method that returns a string. The "readonly" modifier of IDL is expressed in Java indirectly, by the absence of a setNodeName() method.

In DocWalker, the getNodeName() method is used within addNodeData() that adds several items to Env, for future use by the servlet and, eventually, by HtmlWrapper.

Adding Node Data to Env

There are four items we might want to add to Env for eventual display on the client: an error message, the current node's name, the current node's type, and the "status" which may have one of three possible values:

- ❑ OKSTATUS: current node changed successfully, new node type returned;

- ❑ NULLSTATUS: the requested node is NULL (for example, the first child of a node with no children);

- ❑ ERRSTATUS: an error occurred; e.g., the validating parser found the document invalid, for example.

On the client, we use the status value to give different styles to different values. (The error message is red.)

Many methods, including all the methods that change the current node, call `addNodeData()` to retrieve the values from `Node` and store them in `Env`. The actual work of putting the values in `Env` is done by `addErrNameTypeStat()`:

```
public String addNodeData(Node theNode, String errMess)
{
    // sets Error, nodeName,nodeType,status in defs;
    if(null==theNode)
            return addErrNameTypeStat("Null Node","NULL","NULL","NULLSTATUS");
    if(null==errMess)errMess="";
    String theName=theNode.getNodeName();
    String theType=getNodeTypeName(theNode);
    String theStatus=(0==errMess.length())?"OKSTATUS":"ERRSTATUS";
    return addErrNameTypeStat(errMess,theName,theType,theStatus);
}
public String addErrNameTypeStat(String errMess, String theName,
                 String theType,String theStatus)
{
    defs.put("Error",errMess);
    defs.put("nodeName",theName);
    defs.put("nodeType",theType);
    defs.put("status",theStatus);
    if(0==errMess.length())return theType;
    return errMess;
}
```

Frequently, we want to call `addNodeData()` with just one argument. The default node is `theNode`, which is the variable of `DocWalker`; the default error message is the empty string:

```
public String addNodeData(Node theNode)
{
    return addNodeData(theNode,"");
}
public String addNodeData(String err)
{
    return addNodeData(theNode,err);
}
```

You will see `addNodeData()` used a lot in the section below entitled "Walking the Tree".

Echoing a Node

To echo a node, we ultimately have to go through a switch statement of node type cases. For nodes with children, we call `echoChildren()` that recursively calls `echoNode()`:

```
public void echoChildren(Node theFirst, Writer out)
throws IOException
{
    while(null!=theFirst)
    {
        echoNode(theFirst,out);
```

```
                theFirst=theFirst.getNextSibling();
    }
}

public void echoNode(Node theNode,Writer out)
                    throws IOException
{
    if(null==theNode){
      return;
    }
    short code=theNode.getNodeType();
    switch(code)
    {
        case Node.ATTRIBUTE_NODE:
            Attr at=(Attr)theNode;
            out.write(" ");
            out.write(at.getName());
            out.write("='");
            out.write(at.getValue());
            out.write("'");
        return;
        case Node.CDATA_SECTION_NODE:
            out.write("<CDATA[[");
            out.write(theNode.getNodeValue());
            out.write("]]>");
        return;
        case Node.COMMENT_NODE:
            out.write("<!-- ");
            out.write(theNode.getNodeValue());
            out.write("-->\n");
        return;
        case Node.DOCUMENT_FRAGMENT_NODE: // we can't reconstitute this; dump it
        case Node.DOCUMENT_NODE:
            echoChildren(theNode.getFirstChild(),out);
        return;
        case Node.DOCUMENT_TYPE_NODE:
            DocumentType dT=(DocumentType)theNode;
            echoDTD(dT,dT.getName(),out);
        return;
        case Node.ELEMENT_NODE:
            out.write("<"); out.write(theNode.getNodeName());
            echoAttributes(theNode.getAttributes(),out);
            Node kid=theNode.getFirstChild();
            if(kid==null) out.write("/>\n");
        else
        {
            out.write(">");
            echoChildren(kid,out);
            out.write("</");
            out.write(theNode.getNodeName());
            out.write(">\n");
        }
        return;
        case Node.ENTITY_NODE:
            out.write("<ENTITY: ");
            out.write(theNode.getNodeName());
```

```
                out.write(">");
                out.write("</");
                out.write(theNode.getNodeName());
                out.write(">\n");
        return;
        case Node.ENTITY_REFERENCE_NODE:
                out.write("<ENTITY_REF: "); out.write(theNode.getNodeName());
                out.write("/>\n");
        return;
        case Node.NOTATION_NODE :
                out.write("<NOTATION: "); out.write(theNode.getNodeName());
                out.write("/>\n");
                return;
        case Node.PROCESSING_INSTRUCTION_NODE:
                out.write("<? "); out.write(theNode.getNodeName());
                out.write(" "); out.write(theNode.getNodeValue());
                out.write(" ?>\n");
        return;
        case Node.TEXT_NODE:
                out.write(theNode.getNodeValue());
        return;
        default:return;
    }
}
```

There isn't much one can do with the DTD using DOM 1.0 and SAX 1.0, because of the unsettled situation with namespaces. To quote the DocumentType page from Sun's TR-2 JavaDoc documentation: "The DocumentType interface in the DOM Level 1 Core provides an interface to the list of entities that are defined for the document, and little else because the effect of namespaces and the various XML scheme efforts on DTD representation are not clearly understood as of this writing." This situation should improve soon, in the meantime, we restrict ourselves to writing out the doctype:

```
public void echoDTD(DocumentType theDTD,String theName,Writer out)
                throws IOException
{
// sun implementation does not provide full access,
// so we just produce the name.
    out.write("<!DOCTYPE "); out.write(theName);
    out.write(" />\n");
}
```

For attributes, DOM provides a data type called NamedNodeMap, an associative array of name-value pairs indexed by strings:

```
public void echoAttributes(NamedNodeMap attrs,Writer out)
                throws IOException
{
    int N=attrs.getLength();
    for(int i=0; i<N; i++)echoNode (attrs.item(i),out);
}
```

Walking the Tree

This is pure DOM, including our `addNodeData()` that is completely DOM-based. Each of the methods below uses a DOM method to change the current node. It returns the new node's type as a string or an error message in case of failure.

```
public String getFirstChild()
{
    if(null==theNode)return addNodeData("cannot getFirstChild of null");
    Node kid=theNode.getFirstChild();
    if(null==kid)return addNodeData("cannot getFirstChild of node");
    theNode=kid;
    return getNodeTypeName(theNode);
}

public String getParentNode()
{
    if(null==theNode)return addNodeData("cannot getParentNode of null");
    Node kid=theNode.getParentNode();
    if(null==kid)return addNodeData("cannot getParentNode of node");
    theNode=kid;
    return getNodeTypeName(theNode);
}

public String getNextSibling()
{
    if(null==theNode)return addNodeData("cannot getNextSibling of null");
    Node kid=theNode.getNextSibling();
    if(null==kid)return addNodeData("cannot getNextSibling of node");
    theNode=kid;
    return getNodeTypeName(theNode);
}

public String getPreviousSibling()
{
    if(null==theNode)return addNodeData("cannot getPreviousSibling of null");
    Node kid=theNode.getPreviousSibling();
    if(null==kid)return addNodeData("cannot getPreviousSibling of node");
    theNode=kid;
    return getNodeTypeName(theNode);
}

public String getLastChild()
{
    if(null==theNode)return addNodeData("cannot getLastChild of null");
    Node kid=theNode.getLastChild();
    if(null==kid)return addNodeData("cannot getLastChild of node");
    theNode=kid;
    return getNodeTypeName(theNode);
}
public String reset()
{
    theNode=originalNode;
    return getNodeTypeName(theNode);
}
```

Writing Out an XML String

The methods that walk the DOM tree return the current node type (or an error message), but they do not return the text content of the node. This is done by the `writeNode()` method, called, as we saw a while ago, from the servlet:

```
String xmlString=dWalker.writeNode(); // the contents of current node
```

We already have all the `echoXX()` methods we need to write a node to a stream, but we want a string. The easiest way to get it is to "filter" a stream through a `StringWriter` that has a `toString()` method. This is how it works:

```
public String writeNode() throws IOException
{
    StringWriter sW=new StringWriter();
    PrintWriter pW=new PrintWriter(sW);
    try
    {
        echoNode(theNode,pW);
    }
    catch (IOException t) {t.printStackTrace (pW);}
    return sW.toString();
}
```

This completes the `DocWalker` code. Now that we have seen the innards of both `DocWalkerServlet` and `DocWalker`, it will be useful to take a look at the output template file. It shows how `Env` values, filtered through the `subst` mini-language processor we developed over Chapters 3 and 4, can be used to control output within HTML, CSS and JavaScript.

The Template File

The template file sets up a very simple style sheet and uses very simple JavaScript to control the color of the command output depending on the value of the status field in `Env`:

```
<!DOCTYPE HTML PUBLIC "-//W3C//DTD HTML 4.0 Transitional//EN">
<html>
<head>
<title>
data.htm
</title>

<style>
 div.OKSTATUS {color:green}
 div.NULLSTATUS {color:yellow}
 div.ERRSTATUS {color:red}
</style>
</head>

<body>
<myna:SUBST>
<div class="|status|">
```

```
<script>
  if("|status|"!="OKSTATUS")
    document.write("the Error message is |Error|,<BR>");
</script>
the nodeName is |nodeName|,<BR>
the nodeType is |nodeType|,<BR>
the status is |status|,<BR>
and the command result is |cmdResult|.<BR>
</myna:SUBST>
```

The rest of the template file displays these values and the XML contents of the current node in tabular format:

```
<table border="1" width="80%">
<tr>
<td>Template file<BR>(this file)</td>
<td><myna:SUBST>|templateFile|</myna:SUBST></td>
</tr><tr>
<td>xmlOperation</td>
<td><myna:SUBST>|Command|</myna:SUBST></td>
</tr><tr>
<td>File parsed</td>
<td><myna:SUBST>|theFile|</myna:SUBST></td>
</tr><tr>
<td>Node Type</td>
<td><myna:SUBST>|nodeType|</myna:SUBST></td>
</tr><tr>
<td>Node Name</td>
<td><myna:SUBST>|nodeName|</myna:SUBST></td>
</tr><tr>
<td>Node's XML</td>
<td><myna:SUBST><XMP>|xmlString|</XMP></myna:SUBST></td>
</tr>
</table>
</center></div></body></html>
```

As you can see, a combination of the Env data structure, the subst mini-language, and the client-side technology of HTML, CSS and JavaScript, provides a good deal of flexibility for a competent user who is not a Java programmer. It seems to divide the work between such a user (who can do HTML, CSS and simple JavaScript) and the Java programmer along the right lines.

Returning to DOM, the DocWalker application has demonstrated a good deal of DOM functionality. One aspect of DOM that has been left out is document and node creation: DOM declares a number of createXX() methods that make it possible to create a node of any type, and three methods to insert new nodes into a document: appendChild(), insertBefore() and insertAfter(). We are not going to write a full-fledged editor that can insert textual materials into new nodes, but we will extend the DocWalker class to make it capable of simple editing actions: copy, cut and paste an existing node.

XmlManipulator: Cut, Copy and Paste

This application is structured exactly the same way as DocWalker. The servlet class, XmlManipServlet, is identical to DocWalkerServlet, except that it uses an instance of XmlManipulator rather than DocWalker. The XmlManipulator class is derived from DocWalker in a straightforward way.

The Assumptions of the Program

The program needs a "clip node" to store the node that has been cut. We give the user the ability to specify whether the cut node is to be pasted once or multiple times. If the pasting is to be done more than once, then we keep a deep clone of the node in the clip node for future use. Otherwise, we set the clip node to null after the first paste.

The Imports, Variables and the Constructor

The imports of XmlManipulator are exactly the same as those of DocWalker, so we don't repeat them here. The only two variables are clipNode and multiplePaste:

```
public class XmlManipulator extends DocWalker
{
    Node clipNode=null;
    boolean multiplePaste=false;
}
public XmlManipulator()
{
    super();
}
public void setMultiplePaste(boolean mp)
{
    multiplePaste=mp;
}
public void checkMultiplePaste()
{
    String ok=defs.getStr("multiplePaste");
    if(null==ok)return;
    if(ok.equals("yes"))multiplePaste=true;
    else if(ok.equals("no"))multiplePaste=false;
}
```

doCommand()

We're ready for doCommand(). If the command is one of the new ones that XmlManipulator knows about, then the appropriate action is taken. Otherwise, the command is bounced up to DocWalker:

```
public String doCommand()
{
    String cmd=defs.getStr("Command");
    if(null==cmd)return addNodeData("No 'Command' given");
    addError("");
    if(cmd.equals("copy"))return copy();
    if(cmd.equals("cut"))return cut();
    checkMultiplePaste();
```

```
    if(cmd.equals("pasteAfter"))return pasteAfter();
    if(cmd.equals("pasteBefore"))return pasteBefore();
    if(cmd.equals("pasteUnder"))return pasteUnder();
    else return super.doCommand();
}
```

copy(), cut(), paste()

The code is self-explanatory. We provide pasting as a sibling (before or after the current node) or as the last child. The methods use:

❑ addNodeData() from DocWalker

❑ the familiar getXX() methods from DOM

❑ cloneNode(), removeChild(), appendChild(), insertBefore() and insertAfter() from DOM

```
public String copy()
{
    if(null==theNode)return addNodeData("cannot copy null");
    clipNode=theNode.cloneNode(true);                        //deep copy
    return addNodeData(theNode);
}

public String cut()
{
    if(null==theNode)return addNodeData("cannot cut null");
    clipNode=theNode;
    Node parent=theNode.getParentNode();
    Node next=theNode.getNextSibling();
    if(null==next)next=parent;
    if(null!=parent)parent.removeChild(theNode);
    theNode=next;
    return addNodeData(theNode);
}

public String pasteUnder()
{                                                          //add as last child
    if(null==clipNode)return addNodeData("cannot paste null");
    if(null==theNode)theNode=clipNode;
    else theNode.appendChild(clipNode);
    if(multiplePaste)
      clipNode=clipNode.cloneNode(true);
    else clipNode=null;              // cannot append object more than once
    return addNodeData(theNode);
}
public String pasteBefore()
{
    if(null==clipNode)return addNodeData("cannot paste null");
    if(null==theNode)return addNodeData(theNode=clipNode);
    Node parent=theNode.getParentNode();
    if(null==parent)return addNodeData("cannot pasteBefore without parent");
    parent.insertBefore(clipNode,theNode);
```

```
        if(multiplePaste) clipNode=clipNode.cloneNode(true);
        else clipNode=null; // cannot append object more than once
        return addNodeData(theNode);
    }
    public String pasteAfter()
    {
        if(null==clipNode)return addNodeData("cannot paste null");
        if(null==theNode)return addNodeData(theNode=clipNode);
        Node parent=theNode.getParentNode();
        if(null==parent)return addNodeData("cannot pasteAfter without parent");
        parent.insertBefore(clipNode,theNode.getNextSibling());
                            // this is fine even if getNextSibling() is null
        if(multiplePaste) clipNode=clipNode.cloneNode(true);
        else clipNode=null; // cannot append object more than once
        return addNodeData(theNode);
    }
```

This completes the `XmlManipulator` application. We are ready for a systematic overview of DOM.

DOM Interfaces

The notion of Document Object Model, or DOM, first reached wide-spread attention on the release of 4th generation browsers, as part of Dynamic HTML. Within that context, DOM meant a set of naming conventions and APIs for working with objects in the web page. Its area of application was the web browser.

Although DOM was supposed to be language independent and standard across browsers, in practice the two major browsers simply implemented their DOMs as they wanted them to be, in JavaScript and, in the case of Microsoft, also in VBScript. A more narrowly defined HTML DOM, without an event model, was codified by W3C as DOM Level 0 in late 1997. The IE4 DOM is very close to that specification; the NC4 DOM, released a few months earlier, is substantially different. In the future, both IE and NC are expected to be in compliance with the current and forthcoming levels of DOM.

DOM Level 1

The current DOM is Level 1, released in October 1998. Its coverage includes both XML (that is, all XML languages) and HTML 4.0. Since XML can be used for data interchange between applications anywhere, DOM is not just for browsers any more.

DOM Level 1 consists of two parts: Core DOM and HTML DOM. Core DOM is further subdivided into fundamental interfaces and extended interfaces. Fundamental interfaces must be implemented by all DOM-compliant processors, including XML parsers and HTML browsers: they specify the structure and behavior of `Document`, `Node`, and other fundamental structural elements of any SGML/XML document. Extended interfaces specify those items that are never found in an HTML document but can be part of an XML document: DTD, processing instructions, entities and entity references, and so on. A compliant XML processor must implement Core DOM in its entirety. A compliant HTML processor must implement the fundamental interfaces of the Core and the HTML DOM. In summary:

```
DOM == Core + HTML
Core == Fundamental + Extended
For XML: all Core
For HTML: Fundamental + HTML
```

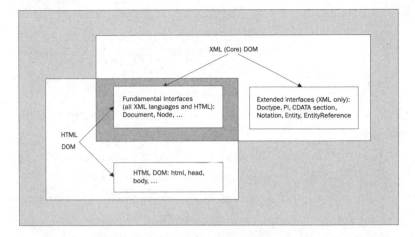

XML, DOM and Language Bindings

Core DOM ultimately goes back to the XML specification. It is the first step from the specification to a computer program that can create or process documents that conform to the XML specification.

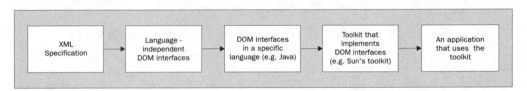

DOM specifies interfaces that are eventually implemented in some programming language. The interfaces imply an abstract data structure of a tree that consists of nodes. DOM tree is not the same as a tree of document elements: for instance, it contains nodes for comments and processing instructions, and the text content of an element is wrapped in a separate text node that is a child of the element's node.

DOM does not specify data structures; it specifies objects, their containment relationships and their collaborations (e.g., an object may have a method that returns another object). This said, it is still useful to visualize the Document object as a tree consisting of nodes, where each node is itself a tree. Whether or not it is implemented as a tree or some other way is up to the program that implements the DOM; in our case, an XML parser.

Node Types in DOM

Here's a complete list of node types in DOM (quoted from `http://www.w3.org/TR/REC-DOM-Level-1/level-one-core.html`). Twelve types of node are recognized; they are listed below together with the sub-nodes they can contain

Node type	Can contain
Document	Element (maximum of one), ProcessingInstruction, Comment, DocumentType
DocumentFragment	Element, ProcessingInstruction, Comment, Text, CDATASection, EntityReference
DocumentType	no children
EntityReference	Element, ProcessingInstruction, Comment, Text, CDATASection, EntityReference
Element	Element, Text, Comment, ProcessingInstruction, CDATASection, EntityReference
Attr	Text, EntityReference
ProcessingInstruction	no children
Comment	no children
Text	no children
CDATASection	no children
Entity	Element, ProcessingInstruction, Comment, Text, CDATASection, EntityReference
Notation	no children

With the exception of `DocumentFragment`, these are, of course, the familiar components of an XML document and correspond directly to the productions. Notice that the document type declaration, comments, CDATA sections, and the parsed text of the mixed element model all become nodes in the resulting tree.

DOM Features that are not in XML 1.0 Specification

Since DOM is a step closer to processing than the XML specification, it includes several features that meet computational needs. They are:

❑ An exception, `DOMException`, which contains standard names and numerical codes for several common error conditions.

❑ A `DOMImplementation` interface, for providing information about the implementation, via the `hasFeature()` method. You can also find out the DOM version on which the implementation is based.

❑ `NodeList` and `NamedNodeMap`, two interfaces for dealing with collections of nodes.

❑ `DocumentFragment`, a "lightweight" interface that extends `Node` and represents a piece of the document that can be cut and pasted and otherwise moved around.

On Document Fragments

`DocumentFragment` nodes do not have to be well-formed XML documents. For example, a document fragment might have only one child that is a Text node. No XML production allows such a structure, but it may be quite useful in an application. A `DocumentFragment` may also contain several top nodes (that is, form a forest of trees) that can be moved around together and inserted as siblings.

As of this writing, `DocumentFragment` is a Working Draft, `http://www.w3.org/TR/WD-xml-fragment`. However, the Status section of the draft says:

"The XML Fragment Working Group, with this 1999 June 30 Working Draft considers its charter discharged. This is the XML Fragment WG's W3C Working Draft as revised to reflect comments received during Last Call review. This draft is technically ready to go to Proposed Recommendation, but the WG decided to hold at this stage to await some implementation experience and to allow possibly related work in other WGs to progress further before submitting this draft for PR."

As with many other current W3C projects, the "related work" that is holding back the Fragment recommendation certainly includes XML Schemas, intended as a replacement for DTDs. It would be useful to be able to validate a fragment, but DTD declarations, which do not follow XML syntax, are difficult to embed in a specific document or its fragment. The June 30 Working Draft prominently displays (in red italics) their decision to stay away from inline inclusion of DTD declarations (Section 4, Fragment Context Information Set).

In practical terms, it is unlikely that you will see many Fragment Nodes for a while. To the best of our knowledge, the DOM interface `DocumentFragment` has not been implemented in any existing Java XML processors.

DOM Bindings

DOM is programming-language-independent. However, in addition to English prose (translated into several other languages), it has to be specified in some formal notation. That notation is, in fact, yet another language, designed for specifying interfaces in a programming-language-independent way. That language is called, reasonably enough, Interface Definition Language or IDL. There are several such languages in existence, including one that Microsoft uses to specify COM interfaces, and another one from Object Management Group (OMG) that is used to specify CORBA interfaces. W3C uses the OMG language but makes it clear that the choice does not imply any kind of taking sides in the COM-CORBA contest.

So, DOM interfaces are twice removed from the actual implementation. To get to an implementation, you first have to choose a programming language and translate DOM interfaces into the appropriate constructs of that language: abstract classes in C++, interfaces in Java, objects and properties in JavaScript, and so on. This process is called **language binding**: the language-independent interfaces of DOM are bound to constructs in a specific language. No actual code is written in the process, only declarations. In the second stage of implementation, the language-specific constructs, such as Java interfaces, are implemented in actual working code. That code is used in application programming.

To insure that different DOM implementations in at least some languages are broadly compatible with each other, W3C itself provides the first stage of implementation – language binding – for two languages, Java and JavaScript (ECMA Script). This is how it is all laid out in the appendices to the specification (quoted from the extended table of contents, http://www.w3.org/TR/REC-DOM-Level-1/expanded-toc.html):

We will spend most of the time looking at the Java binding, but one example of an interface definition in IDL is in order.

An Example of IDL and Java Bindings

The central concept of DOM is a **node**. We think of it as a node in a tree, so that the entire tree is a node, and every node within it is a (sub)tree. The DOM recommendation defines a Node interface from which other, more specific interfaces are derived: for instance, Document derives from Node. The Node interface itself is too big to serve as an example, but let's look at the Document:

Document Interface in IDL

```
interface Document : Node
{
    readonly attribute  DocumentType        doctype;
    readonly attribute  DOMImplementation   implementation;
    readonly attribute  Element             documentElement;

    Element                 createElement(in DOMString tagName)
                                    raises(DOMException);
    DocumentFragment        createDocumentFragment();
    Text                    createTextNode(in DOMString data);
    Comment                 createComment(in DOMString data);
    CDATASection            createCDATASection(in DOMString data)
                                        raises(DOMException);
    ProcessingInstruction   createProcessingInstruction(in DOMString target,
                                            in DOMString data)
                                        raises(DOMException);
    Attr                    createAttribute(in DOMString name)
                                    raises(DOMException);
    EntityReference         createEntityReference(in DOMString name)
                                        raises(DOMException);
    NodeList                getElementsByTagName(in DOMString tagname);
};
```

IDL uses the term "attribute" where we would say "variable" in Java or "data member" in C++. As you can see, DOM specifies that a `Document` object must have three "attributes", several factory methods for manufacturing various objects, and a method to retrieve all descendants with a specified tag name. Most of this material goes back to the XML specification and its productions. For instance, the XML specification says that a document can have a DTD and a single element, and this is reflected in the attributes declared in the interface.

Java Binding for the Document Interface

DOM says absolutely nothing about the data types or data structures: `DocumentType` can be a string, an integer or an enumerated type; `Element` can be a tree, a hash table, or (in FORTRAN) an array. All these decisions are up to the implementor, and the Java binding provided by W3C, while making some choices, tries to leave most of them to the implementor also. For instance, the Java interface does not declare any variables to correspond to IDL attributes, but only declares access methods that return the appropriate objects. (This is the way it should be, really, because variables should be private, access methods public, and the programmer should program to public interfaces.)

```java
package org.w3c.dom;

public interface Document extends Node
{
    public DocumentType       getDoctype();
    public DOMImplementation  getImplementation();
    public Element            getDocumentElement();
    public Element            createElement(String tagName)
                                        throws DOMException;
    public DocumentFragment   createDocumentFragment();
    public Text               createTextNode(String data);
    public Comment            createComment(String data);
    public CDATASection       createCDATASection(String data)
    public ProcessingInstruction createProcessingInstruction(String target,
                                                 String data)
                                                 throws DOMException;
    public Attr               createAttribute(String name)
                                        throws DOMException;
    public EntityReference    createEntityReference(String name)
                                          throws DOMException;
    public NodeList           getElementsByTagName(String tagname);
}
```

Note how an IDL's `attribute` corresponds to a `public getXXX()` method, not to a specific data type. The `readonly` qualifier of IDL simply means that there is no corresponding `setXXX()` method. Of the three `getXXX()` methods, the first two don't do much.

The Structure of the Java Binding

DOM Core Java binding (Fundamental and Extended together) is only 210 lines of code, and makes easy reading. It consists of one class and seventeen interfaces.

DOMException

The only class in the Java binding is DOMException. It extends RuntimeException and defines a number of public static codes for different error conditions. These are copied directly from IDL (where they are called const unsigned short):

```
public static final short        INDEX_SIZE_ERR        = 1;
public static final short        DOMSTRING_SIZE_ERR    = 2;
public static final short        HIERARCHY_REQUEST_ERR = 3;
public static final short        WRONG_DOCUMENT_ERR    = 4;
public static final short        INVALID_CHARACTER_ERR = 5;
public static final short        NO_DATA_ALLOWED_ERR   = 6;
public static final short        NO_MODIFICATION_ALLOWED_ERR = 7;
public static final short        NOT_FOUND_ERR         = 8;
public static final short        NOT_SUPPORTED_ERR     = 9;
public static final short        INUSE_ATTRIBUTE_ERR   = 10;
```

Java Binding Interfaces

Among the interfaces, four are top-level (DOMImplementation, Node, NodeList and NamedNodeMap), and the remaining thirteen are subinterfaces of Node. Node is by far the most important interface; it is Node's methods (such as getFirstChild() or insertBefore()) that do most of the work in accessing and changing the components of a document (as you saw in DocWalker and XmlManipulator).

The Node interface and its descendants arrange themselves into a tree as follows:

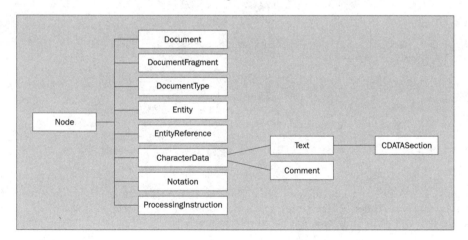

CharacterData

CharacterData, which groups together Text and Comment nodes, is not given a separate node type; the rest are exactly the twelve types of node that you have seen used in DocWalker and XmlManipulator.

The reason text nodes, comments and CDATA sections are grouped together is because they all need the same methods for access and editing:

```
public interface CharacterData extends Node
{
    public String              getData()
                                  throws DOMException;
    public void                setData(String data)
                                  throws DOMException;
    public int                 getLength();
    public String              substringData(int offset,
                                        int count)
                                        throws DOMException;
    public void                appendData(String arg)
                                     throws DOMException;
    public void                insertData(int offset,
                                     String arg)
                                     throws DOMException;
    public void                deleteData(int offset,
                                     int count)
                                     throws DOMException;
    public void                replaceData(int offset,
                                     int count,
                                     String arg)
                                     throws DOMException;
}
```

These are the methods you would use if you decided to implement an XML editor.

NodeList and NamedNodeMap

NodeList defines an ordered sequence of nodes, indexed by integers, zero based. In order to work with such a sequence, you need to know its length, and you need to be able to access a node by its index in the sequence. Those are the two methods of the interface:

```
int getLength()
        // Returns the value of the length property.
Node item(int index)
        // Returns the indexth item in the map.
```

NodeList is read-only; NamedNodeMap is read-write. NamedNodeMap defines an associative array of "named items" that can be accessed by name. There are three methods for working with them, get, set and remove:

```
Node getNamedItem(java.lang.String name)
        // Retrieves a node specified by name.
Node removeNamedItem(java.lang.String name)
        // Removes a node specified by name.
Node setNamedItem(Node arg)
        // Adds a node using its nodeName attribute
```

`NamedNodeMap` does not extend `NodeList`, and `NamedNodeMaps` are not maintained in any particular order. However, `NamedNodeMap` does have a `getLength()` and an `item()` methods, with the same signatures as in `NodeList`. This makes it possible to do a for-loop on the elements of a `NamedNodeMap`, as in our code for `echoAttributes()`, repeated here:

```
public void echoAttributes(NamedNodeMap attrs,Writer out)
                    throws IOException
{
    int N=attrs.getLength();
    for(int i=0; i<N; i++)echoNode(attrs.item(i),out);
}
```

Attributes are frequently stored in a `NamedNodeMap` variable because the `Node` interface has a `getAttributes()` method that returns the node's attributes as a `NamedNodeMap`.

DOMImplementation

This is a one-line interface that allows you to check availability of features in versions:

```
public interface DOMImplementation
{
    public boolean hasFeature(String feature, String version);
}
```

This concludes our discussion of DOM. For further details, read the DOM Java binding. It's just 210 lines of code that can be found in Appendix J of this book. It is, of course, available on the Web at W3C, and it is included, in javadoc format, in the Sun XML toolkit API. All the links are in the Resources appendix.

Conclusion

In this chapter, we moved from XML specification to XML processing in Java. Java XML processing is codified by two standards, DOM and SAX. Both standards are language independent, and have been implemented in different languages, but both have standard "Java binding", encapsulated in two packages, `org.w3c.dom` and `org.xml.sax`. Both are implemented in Sun's XML toolkit. In this chapter, we briefly described both standards before going more deeply into DOM. First, DOM was shown by example, in two small applications; then in a more systematic overview.

In the next chapter, we will cover SAX in greater detail, following the same order of presentation: first, an example, then an overview. The example will be more substantial, having to do with constructing database tables from XML documents in a completely generic way. We will also give an overview of Sun's XML toolkit. Although SAX and DOM codify many aspects of XML processing, both are still in their 1.0 versions and incomplete in many details. Any application has to go beyond them into some toolkit-specific material.

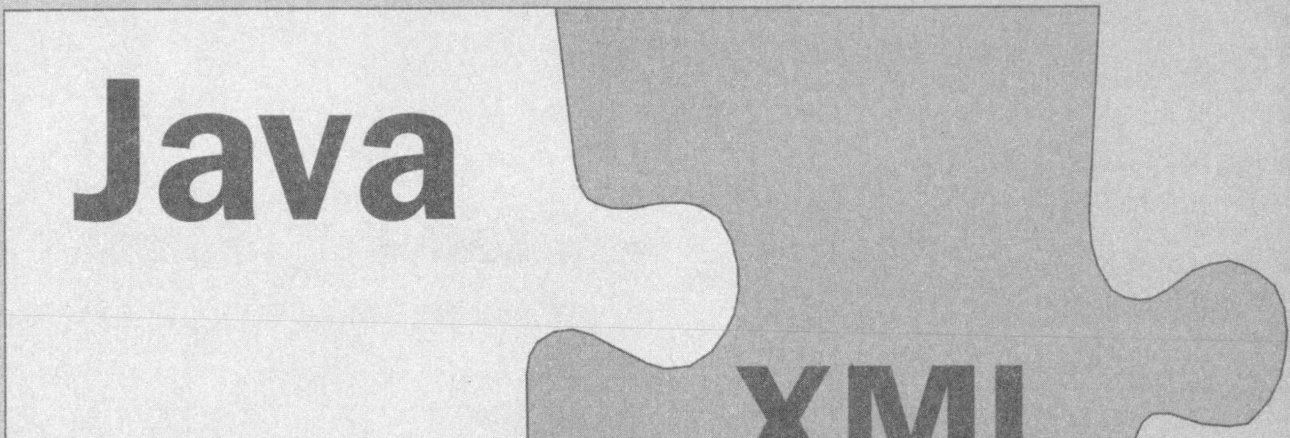
Java
XML

SAX Processing, the Sun Parser and a Conformance Study

In this chapter, we will become thoroughly familiar with SAX (Simple API for XML), first by working through two examples, then looking at its documentation in some detail. The first (and very brief) example will come from Sun's Java-XML tutorial; the second and much lengthier one will use SAX to convert XML to XHTML in user-customizable ways.

After the examples, we will present an overview of the SAX packages and the entire Sun toolkit. Although not yet a product, it has made clear commitments to several major features on which we concentrate.

In outline, this chapter will proceed as follows:

- ❑ `EchoAsHtml`: an application which uses SAX to convert XML to HTML
- ❑ A simple `Echo` example from Sun's Java-XML tutorial
- ❑ SAX in detail
- ❑ Sun's TR-2 toolkit in detail
- ❑ Java parsers compared for conformance (`http://www.xml.com/pub/1999/09/conformance`)

EchoAsHtml

Our first, largely pedagogical application uses SAX to read an XML file and echo it back as legal HTML; for instance, `<employee> ... </employee>` becomes `<span class="employee">` `... </span>`. If you provide CSS stylesheet information for "employee", that information will be used; otherwise the class attribute will be ignored by the browser and the output will be a plain span. If you want some XML element to come out as an HTML element other than span (you want each employee record to be a `DIV` or a `P`) for example, you can specify the HTML element to use in the XML document. The details are explained as we go through the code.

In order to demonstrate the effects of including a DTD, we provide two sample XML files for processing (`Echo.xml` and `EchoDTD.xml`) that are identical except that one of them contains an internal DTD. The user can control from the input form which parser, validating or non-validating, gets invoked. Remember that you can invoke a non-validating parser on a document with a DTD, but you cannot invoke a validating parser on a document without a DTD.

The `EchoAsHtml` application is structured in the same three-tier Model-View-Controller style as the `DocWalker` example we looked at in the previous chapter. In order to run the application, point your browser to `EchoAsHtml.htm` (after downloading the code for this book from `http://www.wrox.com` if you haven't already done so); use the **SELECT** element in the control frame to choose between a validating and a non-validating parser.

> Obviously, if you try to run a *validating* parser on a document *without* a DTD, a parser error will be generated.

We list the code for `EchoDTD.xml` below:

```
<?xml version="1.0" encoding="utf-8"?>
<!DOCTYPE collection [
<!ELEMENT collection (tagpair*, overview?, list)>

<!ELEMENT tagpair EMPTY>
<!ATTLIST tagpair
  xtag CDATA #REQUIRED
  htag CDATA #REQUIRED
>
<!ELEMENT overview (#PCDATA)>

<!ELEMENT list (item+)>
<!ELEMENT item (type, title, description)>
<!ELEMENT type (#PCDATA)>
<!ELEMENT title (#PCDATA)>
<!ELEMENT description (#PCDATA)>
]>

<collection>
    <!-- tagpairs are one of several ways to set up mappings
```

```
            between XML elements and XHTML elements -->
    <tagpair xtag="list" htag="ul" />
    <tagpair xtag="item" htag="li" />
    <tagpair xtag="title" htag="h3" />
    <tagpair xtag="description" htag="p" />

<overview>
This is a listing of accidental items found in the attic of an old house. The
items were just lying around but each was carefully described, including date
of creation or purchase.

<![CDATA[
This paragraph appears within a <![CDATA[]] > section.
]]>
</overview>

<list>
  <item><type>slide</type>
        <title>fall leaves</title>
        <description>Fall in New England, Oct.1999</description>
  </item>
  <item><type>utensil</type>
        <title>tea kettle</title>
        <description>Purchased accidentally, summer 1982</description>
  </item>
  <item><type>painting</type>
        <title>Breakfast on the grass</title>
        <description>Painted by somebody in the family a long time
                     ago</description>
  </item>
</list>
</collection>
```

If we run the validating parser on `EchoDTD.xml`, we get the screenshot below:

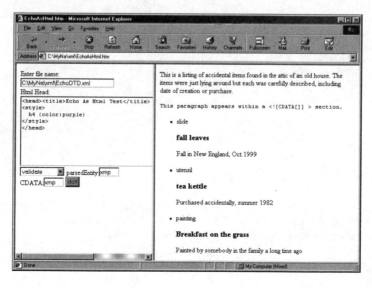

The HTML source of the data frame looks as shown below. It is slightly abbreviated, as indicated by the ... comments, but the whitespace is unchanged:

```xml
<?xml version='1.0' encoding='UTF-8'?>
<!DOCTYPE html PUBLIC '-//W3C//DTD XHTML 1.0 Strict//EN'
'http://www.w3.org/TR/xhtml1/DTD/strict.dtd'>
<html xmlns='http://www.w3.org/TR/xhtml1/strict' xml:lang='en' lang='en'>
<head>
<title>Echo As Html Test</title>
<style>
  h3 {color:purple}
</style>
</head>

<body>

  <span class='collection'>
  <!--  tagpairs are one of several ways to set up mappings
          between XML elements and XHTML elements -->

    <span class='tagpair'
    >
  ... three more tagpair spans

    <span class='overview'>
    This is a listing of accidental items found in the attic of an old house. The
items were just lying around but each was carefully described, including date of
creation or purchase.

<xmp>
This paragraph appears within a <![CDATA[]] > section.
</xmp>
    </span>
    </span><ul class='list'>
      <li class='item'>
        <span class='type'>
        slide
        </span>
        <h3 class='title'>
        fall leaves
        </h3>
        <p class='description'>
        Fall in New England, Oct.1999
        </p>
      </li>
      ... two more li items
    </ul>
  </span></body></html>
```

This output results from running Echo01 with a validating parser. If you have it invoke a non-validating parser on the DTD-less version of the same file (Echo.xml), the same output will be produced in the browser, but a lot more whitespace will appear in the source code.

Sun's Java XML Tutorial

For the basic echoing functionality, implemented as a local application, we borrow material from Sun's Java XML tutorial, `http://java.sun.com/xml/docs/tutorial/TOC.html`.
This excellent tutorial allows its material to be copied and modified as long as its copyright notice accompanies it. We show the notice below, as part of the `Echo01.java` example. The example is copied from the tutorial, broken into sections and expanded with additional comments.

Copyright and Imports

```
/*
 * @(#)Echo01.java     1.5 99/02/09
 *
 * Copyright (c) 1998 Sun Microsystems, Inc. All Rights Reserved.
 *
 * Sun grants you ("Licensee") a non-exclusive, royalty free, license to use,
 * modify and redistribute this software in source and binary code form,
 * provided that i) this copyright notice and license appear on all copies of
 * the software; and ii) Licensee does not utilize the software in a manner
 * which is disparaging to Sun.
 *
 * This software is provided "AS IS," without a warranty of any kind. ALL
 * EXPRESS OR IMPLIED CONDITIONS, REPRESENTATIONS AND WARRANTIES, INCLUDING ANY
 * IMPLIED WARRANTY OF MERCHANTABILITY, FITNESS FOR A PARTICULAR PURPOSE OR
 * NON-INFRINGEMENT, ARE HEREBY EXCLUDED. SUN AND ITS LICENSORS SHALL NOT BE
 * LIABLE FOR ANY DAMAGES SUFFERED BY LICENSEE AS A RESULT OF USING, MODIFYING
 * OR DISTRIBUTING THE SOFTWARE OR ITS DERIVATIVES. IN NO EVENT WILL SUN OR ITS
 * LICENSORS BE LIABLE FOR ANY LOST REVENUE, PROFIT OR DATA, OR FOR DIRECT,
 * INDIRECT, SPECIAL, CONSEQUENTIAL, INCIDENTAL OR PUNITIVE DAMAGES, HOWEVER
 * CAUSED AND REGARDLESS OF THE THEORY OF LIABILITY, ARISING OUT OF THE USE OF
 * OR INABILITY TO USE SOFTWARE, EVEN IF SUN HAS BEEN ADVISED OF THE
 * POSSIBILITY OF SUCH DAMAGES.
 *
 * This software is not designed or intended for use in on-line control of
 * aircraft, air traffic, aircraft navigation or aircraft communications; or in
 * the design, construction, operation or maintenance of any nuclear
 * facility. Licensee represents and warrants that it will not use or
 * redistribute the Software for such purposes.
 */

import java.io.*;

import org.xml.sax.*;
import org.xml.sax.helpers.ParserFactory;
import com.sun.xml.parser.Resolver;
```

As you can see, in this initial application, almost all the imports are from the SAX API. The only toolkit-specific class is the `Resolver`, to create an input source.

The SAX API itself consists of two packages: `sax` proper and `sax.helpers`. The helpers package contains three utility classes that

> "help programmers get started using the SAX APIs"

as the documentation says. The most commonly used class is `ParserFactory` because it has static methods for dynamically loading SAX parsers.

Main Class Declaration and the Main() Method

SAX interfaces, as you will recall, declare a number of callbacks that a SAX application has to implement. A convenience class, HandlerBase, provides a default do-nothing implementation of all those callbacks. A typical SAX application extends HandlerBase and overrides the default implementations as needed, as this example shows:

```java
public class Echo01 extends HandlerBase
{
    static private Writer out;

    public static void main (String argv [])
            throws IOException
    {
        InputSource input;
        if (argv.length != 1)
        {
            System.err.println ("Usage: cmd filename");
            System.exit (1);
        }

        try
        {

            // Set up output stream
            out = new OutputStreamWriter (System.out, "UTF8");

            // Turn the filename into an XML input source
            input = Resolver.createInputSource (new File (argv [0]));

            // Get an instance of the non-validating parser.
            Parser parser;
            parser = ParserFactory.makeParser ("com.sun.xml.parser.Parser");
            parser.setDocumentHandler ( new Echo01() );

            // Parse the input, generate SAX events
            parser.parse (input);

        }

        catch (Throwable t)
        {
            t.printStackTrace ();
        }

        System.exit (0);

    }
```

Much of this code should be familiar from `DocWalker`: the author uses the `Resolver` class to create an input source, obtain a parser instance, and call its `parse()` method to generate a sequence of SAX events. A new detail is the way in which the parser is created, by the static `makeParser()` method of `ParserFactory`. This method can be used with a string argument that provides the name of the `Parser` class, or it can be used without an argument, relying on the value of the `org.xml.sax.parser` system property. In the Sun toolkit, if you have not configured your system properties and did *not* provide an argument to the `makeParser()` method either, then the `com.sun.xml.parser.Parser` parser (the non-validating one) will be used.

Once the parser is created, you use its `setDocumentHandler()` method to connect the parser to your class that extends `HandlerBase`. Now you can start using SAX callbacks.

SAX DocumentHandler Methods

Sun's tutorial provides two helper methods for echoing: `emit()` and `nl()`. The first of these takes a string argument and writes it to the `OutputStreamWriter`; the second starts a new line in a system-independent way. We'll see them in a moment; for now, here's the essence of SAX:

```
public void startDocument () throws SAXException
{
    emit ("<?xml version='1.0' encoding='UTF-8'?>");
    nl ();
}

public void endDocument () throws SAXException
{

    try
    {
        nl ();
        out.flush ();
    }

    catch (IOException e)
    {
        throw new SAXException ("I/O error", e);
    }


}

public void startElement (String name, AttributeList attrs)
        throws SAXException
{

    emit ("<" + name);

    if (attrs != null)
    {
        for (int i = 0; i < attrs.getLength (); i++)
        {
            emit (" ");
            emit (attrs.getName(i) + "=\"" + attrs.getValue (i) + "\"");
        }
```

```
        }

        emit (">");

    }

    public void endElement (String name) throws SAXException
    {
        emit ("</"+name+">");
    }

    public void characters (char buf [], int offset, int len)
            throws SAXException
    {
        String s = new String(buf, offset, len);
        emit (s);
    }
```

Helper Methods: emit() and nl()

Finally, the helpers. The `emit()` method performs two functions: it makes sure that the stream is flushed, and wraps its I/O exceptions in `SAXExceptions` because that's what SAX callbacks throw. The `nl()` method simply ensures that the correct line separator is written to the stream:

```
    private void emit (String s) throws SAXException
    {
        try
        {
            out.write (s);
            out.flush ();
        }
        catch (IOException e)
        {
            throw new SAXException ("I/O error", e);
        }
    }

    private void nl () throws SAXException
    {
        String lineEnd =  System.getProperty("line.separator");
        try
        {
            out.write (lineEnd);
        }
        catch (IOException e)
        {
            throw new SAXException ("I/O error", e);
        }
    }

} // end of Echo01 class
```

Enhancements to EchoAsHtml

We are going to develop this example in several directions at once:

❑ introduce more features of SAX and `com.sun.xml.parser` (as in Sun's tutorial)

❑ turn it into a three-tier GUI application

❑ make it output HTML

❑ include an option to allow the user to switch between documents and parsers

EchoAsHtml, Three-Tier Version

This application consists of the following components (similar to `DocWalker`):

❑ On the client, `EchoAsHtml.htm` (a two-frame document) and `EchoAsHtmlCtl.htm` (the control frame)

❑ `EchoAsHtmlServlet`, mediating between the control-view and the model

❑ `EchoAsHtml`, the working class that does the actual echoing

The first two components of the application will be very much the same as the corresponding components of `DocWalker`. If anything, they will be simpler because there are no commands to execute, no session to control and no template file – only the initial setup needs to be performed. The third component, `EchoAsHtml`, will introduce a good deal more of SAX and `sun.com.xml.parser` functionality.

EchoAsHtmlServlet

This servlet is very simple: all it has is a `doPost()` method, and a do-nothing `doGet()` method that refers to it. The imports are minimal `EnvServlet` imports, plus the `EchoAsHtml` class that does all the work:

```
import javax.servlet.*;
import javax.servlet.http.*;

import MyNa.utils.Env;
import MyNa.utils.EnvServlet;
import MyNa.utils.HtmlWrapper;    // sends HTML to client.
import java.io.IOException;       // thrown by HtmlWrapper
import java.io.PrintWriter;       // for res.getWriter();

import MyNa.xml.EchoAsHtml;       // does all the XML work
```

The servlet will fill out the fields of its `Env` object and share it with the SAX-aware class. That class will then do all the work. The resulting HTML is output to the data frame. We don't need any template files, and the template file directory is not involved at all:

```
public class EchoAsHtmlServlet extends EnvServlet
{
    // the do-nothing doGet() goes here

    public void doPost (HttpServletRequest req, HttpServletResponse res)
            throws ServletException, IOException
    {
        res.setContentType("text/html");
        PrintWriter out = res.getWriter();
        HtmlWrapper W = new HtmlWrapper(out);
        try
        {
            Env E = new Env(req);
            String myURL = res.encodeURL(req.getRequestURI());
            String theXmlData=E.getStr("XmlData");
            if(null == theXmlData)
            {
                W.wrapPage("EchoAsHtml error", "no Xml Data Source specified");
                return;
            }
            /* place input file name and output stream reference into Env
             * create an EchoAsHtml object
             * share the Env with it
             * tell it to do it
             */
            E.put("echo_inputFileName", theXmlData);
            E.put("echo_out", out);
            EchoAsHtml eah = new EchoAsHtml();
            eah.setEnv(E);
            eah.doIt();
        }
        catch(Exception ex)
        {
            W.wrapPage("EchoAsHtml doPost failure", "" + ex);
        }
    }
}
```

EchoAsHtml Class

The `EchoAsHtml` class converts an XML file into a generic, user-customizable, cross-browser XHTML file, viewable by 4th generation browsers. The conversion is driven by an `Env` object that contains parameters such as `echo_inputFileName`, `echo_indentSpace`, and so on, but may also contain tag mappings. By default, each XML tag `<xyz>` becomes the class of a span: `<span class='xyz'>`, and the closing tag `</xyz>` becomes `</span>`. However, if the `Env` object defines xyz as 'h3', then we get `<h3 class='xyz'>` and the closing tag becomes `</h3>`. This is not applied to `CDATA` blocks or parsed external general entities, which are simply wrapped in `<xmp>` tags. Comments are wrapped in the `<!--` and `-->` tag pairs and placed in the resulting document. The output HTML source is nicely printed, using proper indentation, as you can see by going to View Source in your browser.

It would be easy to improve the conversion by requiring that every XML element must have an attribute whose value can be either "block" or "inline". The output would use a `<div>` or a `<span>`, correspondingly.

The head is produced as

```
"<head><title>" + inputFileName + "</title></head>"
```

unless the `Env` object contains a definition for `echo_head`, which would be used instead.

`EchoAsHtml` consists of three parts. The setup part includes constructors, `setXXX()` methods and the `doIt()` method. The `DocumentHandler` part includes `DocumentHandler` callbacks. In addition, it includes Sun-specific `LexicalEventListener` callbacks that respond to events generated by comments, `CDATA` sections and parsed general entities. Finally, we use our own `ErrorHandler` class, installed by the `setErrorHandler()` method. We present the three parts in that order.

Imports, Constructors and Other Setup

The imports are obvious enough. The only feature that deserves comment is the importation of `Class` and `Constructor` classes that are able to load a named class and create an instance of it. Since SAX provides a `processingInstruction()` method, these two classes can be used to create an instance of a Java class that is the target of a processing instruction. (Later chapters will show two other ways of invoking Java code from XML: the XSLT extension mechanism and JSP pages.)

```
import MyNa.utils.*;
import java.io.*;

// SAX and com.sun.xml.parser imports
import org.xml.sax.*;
import org.xml.sax.helpers.ParserFactory;
import com.sun.xml.parser.Resolver;
import com.sun.xml.parser.LexicalEventListener;

// for working with ProcessingInstruction whose target is a class name
import java.lang.Class;
import java.lang.reflect.Constructor;
```

Declarations and Constructors

Declarations are as transparent as imports. Note that `indentLevel` and `indentSpace` are for ensuring correct layout in the printing of the HTML output. You can see their effect by viewing the source in your browser, but they have no effect on the appearance of the HTML document.

Constructors initialize the variables and do nothing else:

```
public class EchoAsHtml extends HandlerBase implements LexicalEventListener
{

    // variables for selecting the parser
    String nonValidatingParserName = "com.sun.xml.parser.Parser";
    String validatingParserName = "com.sun.xml.parser.ValidatingParser";
    String parserName;
    boolean validation;     // comes from the client

    // the Env and variables for input and output
    Env defs;
    PrintWriter out;
    String inputFileName; // comes from the client

    // variables for pretty printing of the source
    String lineEnd; // system specific
    int indentLevel;
    String indentSpace;

    // variables for working with CDATA and parsed entities
    String cDATAWrap;        // HTML tags to put around CDATA and entities
    String parsedEntityWrap; // such as PRE or (deprecated) XMP
    boolean inCDATA;
    boolean inParsedEntity;

    // two constructors
    public EchoAsHtml()
    {
        defs = null;
        out = null;
        indentSpace = "    ";
        inputFileName = null;
        indentLevel = 0;
        lineEnd = ystem.getProperty("line.separator");
        parserName = nonValidatingParserName;
        validation = false;
        cDATAWrap = "xmp";
        parsedEntityWrap = "xmp";
        boolean inCDATA = false;
        boolean inParsedEntity = false;
    }

    public EchoAsHtml(PrintWriter o)
    {
        this();
        setOut(o);
    }
```

We use the completely deprecated <XMP> tag as the default wrapper for CDATA sections and parsed entities because it's the only one that protects its insides from parsing. It's still a source of puzzlement for us that HTML 4.0 doesn't provide an equivalent.

setXXX() Methods

These methods perform two functions: they change the values of the variables, and they store the new values in the Env object. As you will see in the code, the Env code is used by several methods to access the state of the EchoAsHtml class.

```
public void setOut(PrintWriter o)
{
    out = o;
    defs.put("echo_out", o);
}

public void setInputFileName(String S)
{
    inputFileName = S;
    defs.put("echo_inputFileName", S);
}

public void setIndentSpace(String S)
{
    indentSpace = S;
    defs.put("echo_indentSpace", S);
}

public void setIndentLevel(int N)
{
    indentLevel = N;
    defs.put("echo_indentLevel", "" + N);
}

public void setParserName(String S)
{
    parserName = S;
    defs.put("echo_parserName", S);
}

public void setCDATAWrap(String S)
{
    cDATAWrap = S;
    defs.put("echo_CDATAWrap", S);
}

public void setParsedEntityWrap(String S)
{
    parsedEntityWrap = S;
    defs.put("echo_ParsedEntityWrap", S);
}

public void setValidation(boolean B)
{
    validation = B;
    defs.put("echo_validation", "" + B);
    if (B)
        setParserName(validatingParserName);
    else
        setParserName(nonValidatingParserName);
}
```

The setEnv() Method

setEnv() allows control by servlet, applet or main; we can create a new Env, fill out its fields with values obtained from the user, and give it as an argument to setEnv(), in the following fashion:

```
Env e = new Env();
E.put("echo_out", new OutputStreamWriter(System.out, "UTF8"));
E.put("echo_inputFileName", "file:///C:/MyNa/xml/test.xml");
E.put("echo_indentSpace", "    ");
E.put("echo_indentLevel", "4");
E.put("echo_nonValidatingParserName",....)
E.put("echo_validatingParserName",...);
E.put("echo_validation", "true");
E.put("echo_head", "<head><title>Narcissus&Echo</title></head>");
EchoAsHtml eAH = new EchoAsHtml();
eAH.setEnv(e);
```

The method itself sets the local Env (that is, defs) to the new Env, and systematically extracts all the variable values from it. If the value is non-null, the appropriate setXXX() method is called to reset the variable:

```
public void setEnv(Env E)
{
    defs = E;
    if(null == defs)
        return;

    Object o = defs.get("echo_out");
    if(o instanceof PrintWriter)
    {
        out = (PrintWriter)o;
    }

    String S = defs.getStr("echo_inputFileName");
    if(null != S)
        setInputFileName(S);

    S = defs.getStr("echo_indentSpace");
    if(null != S)
        setIndentSpace(S);

    S = defs.getStr("echo_indentLevel");
    if(null != S)
        indentLevel = (new Integer(S)).intValue(); // "5"|"12"|..

    S = defs.getStr("echo_nonValidatingParserName");
    if(null != S)
        nonValidatingParserName=S;

    S = defs.getStr("echo_validatingParserName");
    if(null != S)
        validatingParserName=S;
```

```
        S = defs.getStr("echo_parserName");
    if(null != S)
        setParserName(S);

    S = defs.getStr("echo_validation");  // "true" or "false"
    if(null != S)
        setValidation((new Boolean(S)).booleanValue());
}
```

The doIt() Method for Parsing

Finally, we are going to see some XML processing. The doIt() method creates an input source and a parser, and gives the former to the latter to generate a SAX stream:

```
public void doIt()throws IOException
{
    // doIt() is called with no arguments by the servlet
    // obtain input file name from class variable, ultimately from Env
    doIt(inputFileName);
}

public void doIt(String inputFileName) throws IOException
{
    InputSource input;

    try
    {

        if(null == out)
            out = new PrintWriter(new OutputStreamWriter(System.out, "UTF8"));

        input = Resolver.createInputSource(new File(inputFileName));
        // could also create input source from a URL, URN or input stream

        Parser parser = ParserFactory.makeParser(parserName);
        parser.setDocumentHandler(this);
        parser.setErrorHandler( new EchoErrorHandler() ); // our own
        parser.parse (input); // generates SAX events
        // event handling, as in Echo01

    }
    catch (SAXParseException err)
    {
        ...
    }
    catch (SAXException e)
    {
        ...
    }
    catch (Throwable t)
    {
        ...
    }

}
```

Unless an exception has been thrown, we now have a stream of SAX events to work with. The handlers are overridden methods of the `HandlerBase` class (which itself implements the `DocumentHandler` interface).

HandlerBase Methods

Some of these methods will be familiar from `Echo01.java`, but many are new, such as those having to do with the `Locator` object.

Locator

`Locator` is a SAX interface for associating a SAX event with a specific location in the source document. A location is a pair of integers that represent line and column numbers, both 1-based. The "locations" that are returned by the `Locator` object are valid only during the scope of each document handler method. It makes no sense to call the methods of a `Locator` in any other context.

In order to get a `Locator`, you have to override the `setDocumentLocator()` method of `HandlerBase` which, by default, does nothing.

In addition to identifying locations within a document, a `Locator` can identify the document itself: it has methods that return the document's public and system identifiers. Relative URLs are resolved in the process. That's all we use our `Locator` for:

```
public void setDocumentLocator (Locator L)
{
    // Save this to resolve relative URIs or to give diagnostics.
    defs.put("echo_locator", L.getSystemId());
}
```

startDocument() and endDocument()

The `startDocument()` method outputs XHTML declarations, including the head element and the start body tag; the default header is the input file name. In contrast, the `endDocument()` does the expected closing XHTML tags. Flushing the stream is a must:

```
public void startDocument() throws SAXException
{
    out.println("<?xml version='1.0' encoding='UTF-8'?>");
    out.println("<!DOCTYPE html PUBLIC '-//W3C//DTD XHTML 1.0 Strict//EN'");
    out.println(" 'http://www.w3.org/TR/xhtml1/DTD/strict.dtd'>");
    out.println("<html xmlns='http://www.w3.org/TR/xhtml1/strict'
            xml:lang='en' lang='en'>");

    String hd = defs.getStr("echo_head");
    if(null == hd)
    {
        out.print("<head><title> ");
        out.print(inputFileName);
        out.println(" </title></head>");
    }
```

```
    else
      {
          out.println(hd);
      }

      out.println("<body>");
}

public void endDocument ()throws SAXException
{
      out.println("</body></html>");
      out.flush ();
}
```

startElement()

The `startElement()` method checks for an output HTML tag within the `Env` object. If one is not found, `startElement()` outputs a `<span>` tag, and uses the input XML tag as the (stylesheet) class name of the output element. To output end-of-lines, a modified version of Sun's `nl()` method is called. We'll show its code shortly; for now, just note that our `nl()` can take a string buffer argument and output to that buffer:

```
public void startElement (String name, AttributeList attrs)
        throws SAXException
{
      indentLevel++;
      String tag = defs.getStr(name);
      if(null == tag)
          tag="span";
      StringBuffer buff = new StringBuffer();
      nl(buff);
      buff.append("<");
      buff.append(tag);
      buff.append(" class=\'");
      buff.append(name);
      buff.append("\'");
      if(null != attrs && 0 < attrs.getLength())
          startAttrs(attrs,buff);
      buff.append(">");
      out.print(buff);
}
```

There are several ways to associate XML input tags with HTML output tags in the `Env` object. One of them is to place `xtag-htag` pairs in the beginning of the XML file, within tag-pair elements declared as:

```
<!ELEMENT tagpair EMPTY>
<!ATTLIST tagpair
    xtag NMTOKEN #REQUIRED
    htag NMTOKEN #REQUIRED
>
```

The `startAttrs()` method will check for the `xtag-htag` attributes and use them to add associations to the `Env` object. Note that tag-pair elements themselves will be echoed to the output as spans, but their style can be set to `display:none`.

startAttrs()

Apart from `xtag-htag` attributes, `startAttrs()` copies input to output, with appropriate error checking:

```java
public void startAttrs(AttributeList attrs, StringBuffer buff)
        throws SAXException
{

    for(int i = 0; i < attrs.getLength(); i++)
    {

        String name = attrs.getName(i);
        String val = attrs.getValue(i);

        if(!"xtag".equals(name))
        {

            nl(buff);
            buff.append(name);
            buff.append("=\'");
            buff.append(val);
            buff.append("\'");

        }

        else

        {

            i++;
            if(i >= attrs.getLength() || !"htag".equals(attrs.getName(i)))
            {
                throw new SAXException("xtag " + val +
                        " with no matching htag");
            }

            defs.put(val,attrs.getValue(i));

        }

    }

    nl(buff);

}
```

endElement() and characters()

These are completely straightforward and do not require any comment:

```java
public void endElement (String name) throws SAXException
{
```

```
        StringBuffer B = new StringBuffer();
        nl(B);
        String endTag = defs.getStr(name);
        if(null == endTag)
            endTag="span";
        B.append("</");
        B.append(endTag);
        B.append(">");
        out.print(B);
        indentLevel--;
    }

public void characters (char buff[], int offset, int len)
        throws SAXException
    {
        // if(inCDATA) then we're in a CDATA block.
        nl();
        out.write(buff, offset, len);
    }
```

ignorableWhitespace()

This callback receives notification of ignorable whitespace in element content. (As you recall from the XML chapters, if an element's content model is "children-only" rather than "mixed" then all whitespace in its content is ignorable.) Validating parsers must use this method to report each chunk of ignorable whitespace to the application. Non-validating parsers don't have to be capable of parsing and using content models, but Sun's non-validating parser is so capable, and proud of it. ("Not all non-validating parsers are created equal" says the documentation.) This is one of several instances where a non-validating parser uses the DTD.

In this particular application, ignorable whitespace is, indeed, ignored:

```
public void ignorableWhitespace (char buf [], int offset, int len)
        throws SAXException
    {
        // ignore it!
    }
```

processingInstruction()

As you recall, the contents of processing instructions consist of a target string that names the application, followed by some character data that does not contain the closing PI tag. The character data may be empty:

```
[16]   PI ::=  '<?' PITarget (S (Char* - (Char* '?>' Char*)))? '?>'
[17]   PITarget ::=  Name - (('X' | 'x') ('M' | 'm') ('L' | 'l'))
```

Appropriately, processingInstruction() receives two arguments, target and data:

```
public void processingInstruction (String target, String data)
        throws SAXException
    {
```

Just for fun, and for the sake of an example, consider the possibility that the target is a Java class name. Let's assume that the class has two constructors that take one or two arguments, depending on whether the data string in the XML source is empty. Both constructors take an Env argument so they can communicate with other parts of the system. Given these assumptions we can load the class and use the Reflection API to obtain and call an appropriate constructor. The constructor presumably will do some non-trivial processing that we are interested in:

```
public void processingInstruction (String target, String data)
       throws SAXException
{
    try
    {
        Class C = Class.forName(target);
        boolean empty = (null == data || 0 == data.trim().length());

        // create arrays of parameter types and parameter values
        // the types are String (if data non-empty) and Env
        // the values are data (if non-empty) and defs
        // use Reflection getConstructor() method to get constructor object
        // use its newInstance() method to create instance

        if(!empty)
        {
            Class[] paramTypes = {Class.forName("java.lang.String"),
                    Class.forName("MyNa.utils.Env")};
            Object[] paramVals = {data,defs};
            Constructor cons = C.getConstructor(paramTypes);
            Object ob = cons.newInstance(paramVals);
        }
        else
        {
            Class[] paramTypes = {Class.forName("MyNa.utils.Env")};
            Object[] paramVals = {defs};
            Constructor cons = C.getConstructor(paramTypes);
            Object ob = cons.newInstance(paramVals);
        }
    }
    catch(Exception ex)
    {
        throw new SAXException("" + ex);
    }
}
```

An Example of Using Java-Class PI

Instances of our PI class have access to the Env object, and the Env object contains a reference to the output stream. It follows that we can use PIs to insert content into the output. Since PIs can receive data from the XML file, we can add that data to Env and massage it in various ways before outputting it. For instance, we can format our PI data as an initialization file (the following code is from EchoPI.xml):

```
<!-- PROCESSING INSTRUCTION -->
    <?MyNa.utils.AddDefs title
This is a list of definitions to be added to the env
bibliography
ul
item
li
title
em
subject
span
echo_outputlist
<h4>The parser is:,echo_parserName,</h4><h5>validate=,echo_validation,</h5>
?>
```

The data part of this `PI` is:

```
title
This is a list of definitions to be added to the env
bibliography
ul
...
echo_outputlist
<h4>The parser is:,echo_parserName,</h4><h5>validate=,echo_validation,</h5>
```

The Java class that is the target of the `PI` will know to use the initial line pairs to create bindings between XML and XHTML tags; the last pair will be used for output. Here is a screen shot of `EchoPI.xml` processed by `EchoAsHtml`; the second line of the output is produced by the processing instruction:

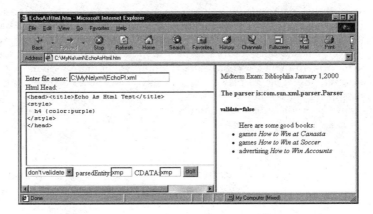

An XML File with a Java-Class PI

The complete text of `EchoPI.xml` is below:

```
<?xml version="1.0" encoding="utf-8"?>
<test>
  <title>Midterm Exam:
    <subject>Bibliophilia</subject>
    <date>January 1,2000</date>
  </title>
    <!-- PROCESSING INSTRUCTION -->
    <?MyNa.utils.AddDefs title
This is a list of definitions to be added to the env
bibliography
ul
item
li
title
em
subject
span
echo_outputlist
<h4>The parser is:,echo_parserName,</h4><h5>validate=,echo_validation,</h5>
?>
  <bibliography>Here are some good books:
    <item><subject>games</subject><title>How to Win at Canasta</title></item>
    <item><subject>games</subject><title>How to Win at Soccer</title></item>
    <item><subject>advertising</subject><title>How to Win Accounts</title></item>
  </bibliography>
</test>
```

If we convert the lines of the "data" section to a `BufferedReader` (via `StringReader`), we can use the `addBufferedReader()` method of the `Env` class to add them as name-value pairs to the `defs` object. The PI's target can use them in a meaningful way. For instance, it can interpret the value of `echo_outputlist` as a comma-separated list of strings, make it into an array, and use each element of the array as a name to look up in `defs`. If no value is found, we output the name itself, otherwise we output its value. In our example, the strings `echo_parserName` and `echo_validation` are indeed associated with values in `defs`, as you can see from the screen shot above. (Note `echo_validation` gets there from the `Request` object: it's the name of the select element in the form; `echo_parserName` is set by the Java code.)

PI's Target, AddDefs.class

Here is the code for the target of the PI, `AddDefs` class in the `MyNa.utils` package:

```
package MyNa.utils;
import java.io.*;

public class AddDefs
{
    public AddDefs(String data, Env defs)throws ParseSubstException
    {
```

```
            StringReader sr = new StringReader(data);
            BufferedReader brin = new BufferedReader(sr);
            defs.addBufferedReader(brin);
            // the definitions from data are now in defs

            String nameListStr = defs.getStr("echo_outputlist");
            if(null == nameListStr)return;
            String[] nameList = Misc.stringSplit(nameListStr, ',');
            defs.remove("echo_outputlist");     // output only once.
            PrintWriter out = (PrintWriter)defs.get("echo_out");
            if(null == out)
                throw new ParseSubstException("no output stream");
            for(int i = 0; i < nameList.length; i++)
            {
                String val = defs.getStr(nameList[i]);
                if(null == val)
                    out.print(nameList[i]);
                else
                    out.print(val);
            }
        }
    }
```

This concludes our parade of `DocumentHandler` methods. The Sun toolkit additionally provides a `LexicalEventListener` interface that provides access to lexical data: comments, CDATA sections and general parsed entities. `EchoAsHtml` implements the interface.

LexicalEventListener Methods

These methods set the Boolean variables to indicate state, and use the `xWrap` variables as tags for outputting CDATA sections and parsed entities. We use the deprecated XMP as default because the recommended PRE puts its contents through the parser rather than render them literally. Comments are rendered as comments:

```
public void comment(java.lang.String text) throws SAXException
{
    // Receive notification that a comment has been read.
    nl();
    out.write("<!-- ");
    out.write(text);
    out.println("-->");
}

public void startCDATA() throws SAXException
{
    // Receive notification that the CDATA section started.
    inCDATA = true;
    if(null != cDATAWrap && cDATAWrap.length()>0)
    {
        nl();
        out.write("<");
        out.write(cDATAWrap);
        out.write(">");
    }
}
```

```
public void endCDATA() throws SAXException
{
    // Receive notification that the CDATA section finished.
    inCDATA = false;
    if(null != cDATAWrap && cDATAWrap.length()>0)
    {
        out.write("</");
        out.write(cDATAWrap);
        out.write(">");
    }
}

public void startParsedEntity (java.lang.String name) throws SAXException
{
    // Receive notification that the named entity is being included
    // in document content (not attributes).
    inParsedEntity = true;
    if(null != parsedEntityWrap && parsedEntityWrap.length()>0)
    {
        nl();
        out.write("<");
        out.write(parsedEntityWrap);
        out.write(">");
    }
}

public void endParsedEntity (java.lang.String name, boolean included)
        throws SAXException
{
    // Receive notification that entity inclusion into document finished.
    inParsedEntity = false;
    if(null != parsedEntityWrap && parsedEntityWrap.length()>0)
    {
        out.write("</");
        out.write(parsedEntityWrap);
        out.write(">");
    }
}
```

nl() revised

As we mentioned, our `nl()` helper function is not quite the same as in `Echo01`. First, it does nothing if the output comes from a CDATA section of a parsed entity. Second, we have a version that takes a `StringBuffer` argument and outputs to that buffer:

```
// Start a new line and indent the next line appropriately

private void nl()throws SAXException
{
    if(inCDATA || inParsedEntity)
        return;
    out.write (lineEnd);
    for (int i = 0; i < indentLevel; i++)
        out.write(indentSpace);
}
```

```
private void nl(StringBuffer B)throws SAXException
{
    if(inCDATA || inParsedEntity)
        return;
    B.append(lineEnd);
    for (int i = 0; i < indentLevel; i++)
        B.append(indentSpace);
}
```

This completes the code of the `EchoAsHtml` application.

Summaries and Overviews

Now that we've seen an extended SAX example, it is a good time for a systematic overview of the SAX standard distribution. After that, we can take a broad look at the entire Sun package, and summarize a recent study that compares all the major Java-XML toolkits in terms of their conformance to the XML specification.

SAX Overview

The standard SAX Java distribution consists of two packages containing eleven classes and interfaces in the `org.xml.sax` package and another three classes in the `org.xml.sax.helpers` package. (There are also five demonstration classes showing example applications.) The two packages are included in the Sun toolkit and properly documented in its JavaDoc-generated documentation.

The SAX classes and interfaces fall into these groups (quoted, with changes, from the file `roadmap.txt` that comes with the SAX distribution):

- **interfaces implemented by the parser:** `Parser` and `AttributeList` (required), and `Locator` (optional)

- **interfaces implemented by the application:** `DocumentHandler`, `ErrorHandler`, `DTDHandler`, and `EntityResolver`. These are all optional. `DocumentHandler` is the most important one for typical XML applications, but instead of implementing it directly, applications usually extend the `HandlerBase` class and override its methods

- **standard SAX classes:** `SAXException`, `SAXParseException`, `InputSource`, and `HandlerBase`. These are all fully implemented by SAX, and you have seen them all in the examples of the last two chapters. (The two `Exception` classes and the `InputSource` class are used in DOM applications because, as you know, Sun's toolkit uses a SAX parser to construct a DOM object.)

- **optional Java-specific helper classes in the `org.xml.sax.helpers` package:** `ParserFactory`, `AttributeListImpl`, and `LocatorImpl` (these are all fully implemented by the SAX Java distribution)

An Overview of Sun's Toolkit

As of this writing, Sun's Java-XML toolkit is in *Technical Release 2*, and comes with the warning that it is not a supported product: theoretically, everything in it may change. However, the overall structure and some major classes, especially those covered in the tutorial, are probably stable.

The TR-2 distribution consists of six packages, as follows:

- ❑ two SAX packages, just mentioned
- ❑ `com.sun.xml.parser` package that extends and implements SAX classes and interfaces
- ❑ `org.w3c.dom` package, based on the DOM Java binding
- ❑ `com.sun.xml.tree` package that extends and implements DOM classes and interfaces
- ❑ a small `com.sun.xml.utils` package

A general strategy is to extend the interfaces provided by SAX and DOM and implement the extended interfaces. Corresponding to `AttributeList`, `Document`, `Element`, and `Node`, there are `AttributeListEx`, `DocumentEx`, `ElementEx`, and `NodeEx`. Many of the extensions are there to support namespaces. `AttributeList` is extended to provide better integration between SAX and DOM. The extended `Document` interface provides support for printing, localization, and moving nodes between two different DOMs.

The two classes that are used in every XML application, whether SAX or DOM, are `Resolver` and `Parser`. `Resolver`, as you recall, produces `InputSource` objects from a variety of sources: file, URL, and MIME. It has several useful features; the major ones being:

- ❑ Support for character encoding. All the character encodings specified in the XML documentation are correctly identified. You can turn off the MIME specifications that come from the server and rely on the built-in auto-detection of the encoding.

- ❑ Support for a local catalog of names (public identifiers) mapped to URIs or Java resources. The local catalog is consulted before anything else. You can use this feature to minimize network traffic by, for instance, creating a local cache of commonly used DTDs.

The `Parser` class provides a non-validating parser that does everything such a parser can do, including much that it doesn't have to, including processing of external parsed entities. You can configure it to support namespaces by providing a `DtdEventListener`. As you saw in `EchoAsHtml`, the parser "supports some features (exposing comments, `CDATA` sections, and entity references) that are allowed by DOM but not required to be reported by conformant XML processors" (quoted from the documentation).

The Conformance Study of XML Processors

As regards conformance, Sun's documentation claims that their parser "strictly adheres to the XML 1.0 specification." A comparative study of Java XML processors published in `http://www.xml.com` in September 1999 supports that claim. It should be mentioned that the study was done by David Brownell who also wrote Sun's TR-2 Java-XML package. However, the study is clearly objective and fair (even if Sun comes out on top). It is also easily reproducible because it is based on freely available tools. All the quotes in this section are from Brownell's study.

The main tool is the Conformance Test Suite, a database of test cases usable with XML processors with APIs in any programming language. The suite, thoroughly documented, has been developed by a working group at OASIS (the *Organization for Advancement of Structured Information Systems*), the same organization that is working on standardizing Public Identifier catalogs (see Chapter 6). In addition to the suite, the working group has produced:

> "*a valid XML document acting as a **test database**, describing each test in terms of:*
> *(a) what part of the XML specification it tests;*
>
> *(b) any requirements it places on the processor, such as what types of external entities it must process;*
>
> *(c) an interpretation of the intent of that test; and*
>
> *(d) a test identifier, used to uniquely identify each test.*"

The database can be used in two kinds of applications. In conjunction with an XSL stylesheet (also developed by the OASIS group) it generates test documentation; in conjunction with a test driver (publicly available and included with the study) it generates a **testing report**. We summarize the main findings of the report; for more details, see the original publication at
`http://www.xml.com/pub/1999/09/conformance/`.

Non-Validating Processors

The processors tested, their scores and brief summary judgements are brought together in the following table:

Processor Name and Version	Passed Tests	Rating	Summary
Ælfred 1.2a (July 2, 1998)	865	***	If you want to trade off some correctness to get a very small parser, look at this one.
DataChannel XML Java Parser (April 15, 1999)	327	*	Don't even consider using this package until its bugs are fixed.
IBM XML4j 2.0.15 (August 30, 1999)	832	***	Two notable bugs are the root cause of most of the errors detected in this processor.
Lark 1.0beta (January 5, 1998)	923	****	More of the current generation of processors should be as conformant as this one!

Processor Name and Version	Passed Tests	Rating	Summary
Oracle XML Parser 2.0.0.2 (August 11, 1999)	904	****	This new entry on the processor scene is quite promising, despite rough edges where it should learn from its validating sibling.
Silfide XML Parser (SXP) 0.88 (July 25, 1999)	731	**	Better choices are available for standalone XML processors.
Sun "Java Project X" TR-2 (May 21, 1999)	1065	*****	No conformance violations detected.
XP 0.5beta (January 2, 1999)	1050	*****	This processor is all but completely conformant.

Validating Processors

There aren't nearly as many validating processors as non-validating ones. The field is narrowed to just four contenders, all of them very big companies. There seem to be no Open Source validating processors supporting the SAX API. The table below is quoted from the article; our explanatory comments are in brackets:

Processor Name and Version	Passed Tests	Rating	Summary
IBM XML4j 2.0.15 (August 30, 1999)	832	***	This has the problems of its non-validating sibling, and does not permit validity errors to be continued.
Microsoft MSXML JVM 5.00.3186 (August 24, 1999)	615	*	It's curious that this was bundled into Microsoft's Java VM without fixing its well-known conformance bugs. Avoid using it. [See below on the other MS parser.]

Processor Name and Version	Passed Tests	Rating	Summary
Oracle XML Parser 2.0.0.2 (August 11, 1999)	871	***	If this just permitted continuation of validity errors [i.e. continued processing rather than terminating after non-fatal errors], it would be a top contender.
Sun "Java Project X" TR-2 (May 21, 1999)	1065	*****	No conformance violations detected.

In addition to the parser bundled with Microsoft's Java VM, there is also a parser that comes with IE5. It is distributed as a DLL, and it does not support SAX, so it required a special "test harness" to be tested. As a result of cooperation between David Brownell and Microsoft, that testing was done, and David reported the results in the November 1999 issue of XML.org. In a one-sentence summary, that parser is much more conformant and earned four starts on the same test suite, both in its validating and non-validating modes. For details, see
`http://www.xml.com/pub/1999/11/parser/summary.html`.

In conclusion, it should not be surprising that Sun's parser is conforming: this was the design goal, and the OASIS test suite was presumably used during development. However, as Brownell observes, a large subset of the OASIS suite (the XMLTEST set) has been widely available since the early days of XML, and yet few of the parsers worked correctly even on those. One would hope that an official test suite from OASIS will put some pressure on the vendors to become more uniform in their implementations.

Conclusion

In this chapter, we have covered the SAX specification and the main features of Sun's Java-XML toolkit. We have also summarized the results of a conformance study that compares most of the currently available Java-XML processors.

This is the last of the four chapters (5 through 8) that have covered the foundations of XML and Java XML processing. The applications in these chapters have been mostly pedagogical in nature, designed to illustrate the technology. We are ready to move on to more substantial projects whose goal is to investigate the wide-open possibilities resulting from the happy marriage of Java and XML.

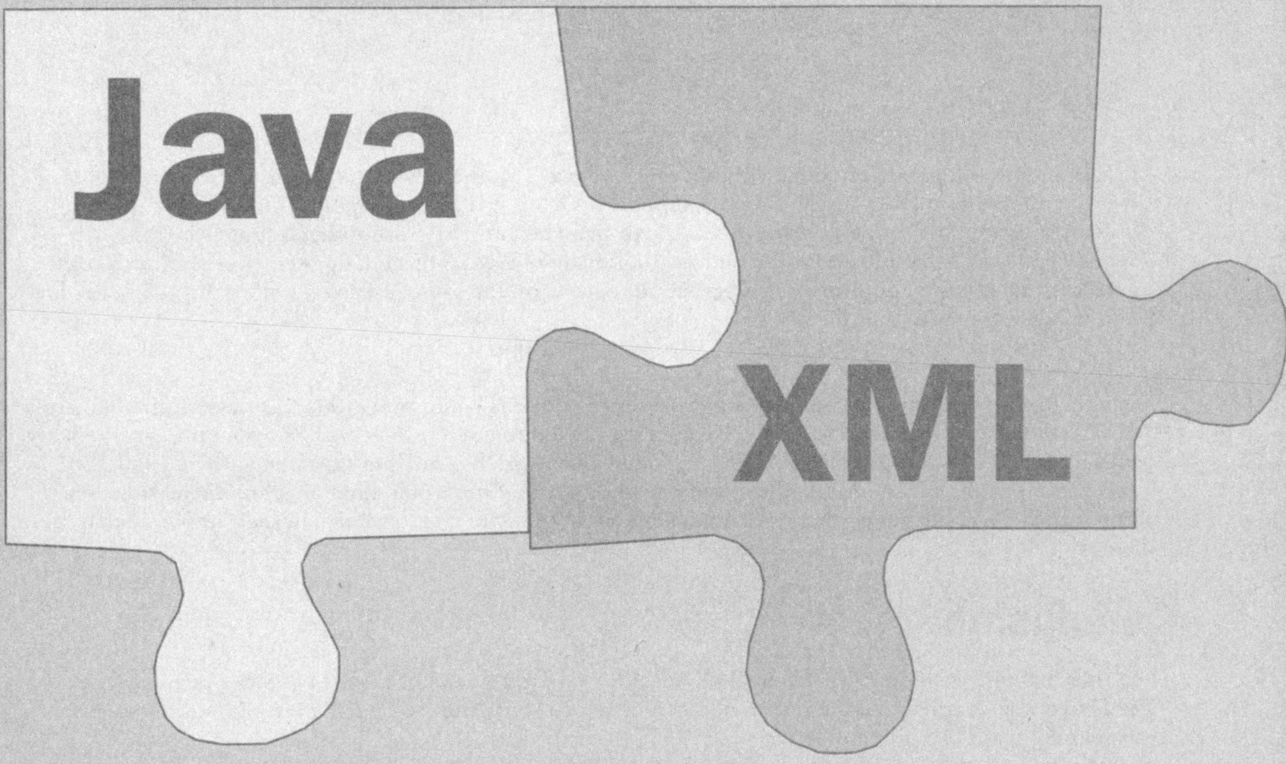
Java
XML

Interpreting XML Mini-Languages

In this chapter, we will go deeper into SAX and develop a more substantial XML/Java application. SAX, as you recall, is great for those situations when you have a big XML file and you don't need to hold all of it in memory at the same time. One such situation is when you have relational database data written out to an XML file, and you want to put it back into a database.

One obvious possible source of such XML files is another database, queried by our `DBHandler` to produce a series of `ResultSet`s that are then processed by `ParseSubst` and inserted into template files. The `ParseSubst` idea can be implemented, in a more efficient and extensible way, by using XML syntax, borrowing some code from the `XmlManipulator` of Chapter 8. This is the `TreeSubst` project that is not covered in the book but included with the code on the book's web site. Perhaps the most interesting and encouraging part of that project is that it doesn't introduce any really new ideas, which is why it is simply included with the code. Think of it as a worked exercise, and try to think through your own answer before you look at it. You really do have all the pieces you need for your own specialized template mini-language defined as an XML language.

At this point we should probably spell out what has been implicit in our talk about mini-languages: a mini-language is a language that is given an **interpretation**. The SUBST collection of tags from Chapter 4 is a mini-language because each tag "means" something. The meaning can be very simple; for the plain myna:SUBST tag it is "use the text between delimiters to retrieve the corresponding value from the Env; replace the text with that value". For myna:SUBSTROWLIST, the meaning is quite complex and involves complex computations. In either case, there is an interpretation associated with each tag. This is what distinguishes a mini-language from a "formal language" like XML languages: formal languages have a syntax defined by a grammar, but they have no interpretation, until it is provided by a separate mechanism. ParseSubst is such a mechanism for the SUBST mini-language, and TreeSubst is a much more general mechanism for associating meaning with an XML language. In this chapter, we are developing a different, SAX-based approach to associating an interpretation with an XML language.

"Interpretation", as you can see, is the central notion of this chapter: in order to convert an XML document into a database we need to **interpret** what it says in a specific way. The word "interpret" is used here in a non-technical way: we don't mean to suggest that these are interpreted (rather than compiled) languages. (We simply follow the usage of a well-known book title, *Structure and Interpretation of Computer Programs*, by Abelson and Sussman, ISBN: 0-070004-84-6.)

What does it mean to interpret a language, and how does one go about it? In the case when a language consists of **expressions** that have a **value** (such as 23+10, with the value of 33), the "meaning" of the expression is its value, and to interpret an expression is the same as to **evaluate** it, or compute its value. We will start with a very simple language of arithmetic expressions and work through a paper-and-pencil example of how its interpretation function may work. On the basis of that example, we will develop a generic SAX mini-language interpreter, such that interpreters for specific languages can be built by extending the generic one. Our first specific example will be an interpreter for arithmetic expressions. Our second and final example will be a mini-language application that converts XML documents to database tables in a completely generic fashion. Unlike multiple other efforts, ours is "meta-model driven": our DTD defines a mini-language for describing database structure, rather than mirroring the structure of a specific database. We will give a detailed explanation in the end of the chapter, after you have seen the code.

In outline, this chapter will proceed as follows:

- ❑ arithmetic expressions as an XML mini-language
- ❑ SAXMinilanguage processor
- ❑ an interpreter for arithmetic expressions in XML
- ❑ Xml2DBTables as an XML mini-language

SAXMinilanguages

An XML language with a DTD is a formal language, but it's not *really* a language, in the sense that it does not provide an interpretation function: what does a document mean? Consider this example:

```
<add>
  <num>23</num>
  <num>10</num>
</add>
```

It is obvious to a human reader that this XML fragment "means" 23+10, or 33. However, there is nothing in XML itself that would provide such an interpretation. Our task in this chapter is to create a program that will provide interpretation to XML languages. To do this, we'll create a number of Java methods that operate on XML elements according to the intended rules of interpretation. Since we expect to work with large documents, our machinery will operate within the SAX framework: the interpretation function for each element will be a callback triggered by the end tag of that element. We will call such functions **end handlers**.

Arithmetic Expressions Language

Our first task is to define the XML language of our example more precisely. The language will consist of two kinds of elements. One is the element <num> that has no child elements, only character data. The only thing that its end handler will need to do is convert its character data to a number, for example, a float. The other kind will consist of elements that have child-only content models: add, sub, mul, div. As you can guess from their names, they stand for arithmetic operations, and the required action is to apply the operation to its arguments. The arguments are the child elements, already evaluated. We will allow arithmetic operations to have any number of arguments greater than 0. Here's a DTD:

```
<!DOCTYPE arithexp [
<!ENTITY % exp "(num|add|sub|mul|div)">
<!ELEMENT arithexp %exp;>
<!ELEMENT add (%exp;)+>
<!ELEMENT sub (%exp;)+>
<!ELEMENT mul (%exp;)+>
<!ELEMENT div (%exp;)+>
<!ELEMENT num (#PCDATA)>
]>
```

This DTD defines the context-free syntax of XML-ish arithmetic expressions. Now we are going to approach these expressions as computer programs that say: evaluate me and return the result.

Two-stack Approach

A common approach to interpreting programs that have context-free syntax is to create two stacks, one for expressions that are opened but not yet evaluated, the other for values that have been computed but not yet used by their parent operation. Since we're thinking of each open expression (that is, XML element) as a procedure call that is waiting for its arguments, we will refer to the first stack as "the call stack", and to the second stack as "the value stack". In addition to the name of the operation (that is, the tag of the element being evaluated), the call stack will all hold the number of its arguments that have been evaluated. When the time comes to apply the operation to its arguments, that many values will be popped off the value stack.

An Example and a Trace

The reason we need stacks is because our expressions can contain sub-expressions, as in 5+((5-2)*7). In XML, it comes out as:

```
<add>
    <num>5</num>
    <mul>
    <sub>
        <num>5</num>
        <num>2</num>
    </sub>
    <num>7</num>
    </mul>
</add>
```

How will this work out with the stacks? We start with the stacks empty and a single `<arithexp>` element on input. (In the trace below, `arithexp` is abbreviated to capital A.) We end when there is nothing on input, nothing but A on the call stack and a single number on the value stack; that value is the answer. Here's the trace:

Input	Call stack (items separated by ;)	Val stack
A		
`<add>`	A;add,0	
`<num>`	A;add,0;num,0	
5	A;add,0;num,1	"5"
`</num>`	A;add,1	5
`<mul>`	A;add,1;mul,0	5
`<sub>`	A;add,1;mul,0;sub,0	5
`<num>`	A;add,1;mul,0;sub,0;num,0	5
5	A;add,1;mul,0;sub,0;num,1	5,"5"
`</num>`	A;add,1;mul,0;sub,1	5,5
`<num>`	A;add,1;mul,0;sub,1;num,0	5,5
2	A;add,1;mul,0;sub,1;num,1	5,5,"2"
`</num>`	A;add,1;mul,0;sub,2	5,5,2
`</sub>`	A;add,1;mul,1	5,3
`<num>`	A;add,1;mul,1;num,0	5,3
7	A;add,1;mul,1;num,1	5,3,"7"
`</num>`	A;add,1;mul,2	5,3,7
`</mul>`	A;add,2	5,21
`</add>`	A	26

Outline of Procedure

In algorithmic outline, this is what we need our SAX code to do:

❑ In response to `characters()`, push the accumulated string on the `ValStack`; this is the most basic value structure.

❑ In response to a start tag, put the tag name on the call stack. Process attributes, if any, and place them also in the same item on the call stack.

❑ In response to an end tag, use the tag name to find the right function to apply to the values of the element's children; use the number of children to get their values from the value stack.

❑ To compute the value of an `<num>` element, simply convert its character data to number. To compute the value of a child that is an element with children, apply this whole procedure again to the child.

It would be easy enough to write SAX-based code that implements our interpretation/evaluation procedure. We will aim for a more general solution from which specific mini-languages can be derived. We will define a class that sets up the stacks and provides general-purpose methods and defaults. To define a specific mini-language, the user will:

❑ define the XML language (that is, tags and attributes; a DTD is useful but optional)

❑ derive a class from our generic mini-language processor

❑ override end handlers.

The language can be an expression-oriented language whose interpretation consists of evaluating expressions, or it can be a procedure-oriented language whose interpretation consists of creating some side effects, with multiple gradations in between. After our generic language processor is defined, we will derive two specific languages from it. One will be an expression-oriented language of arithmetic expressions. The other will be a procedural language that converts XML documents to database tables.

Functions and Objects

An essential step in our procedure is to find the function to invoke, based on the element's tag, a string. In many languages (C, C++, Lisp, JavaScript) strings can be associated with functions in a direct way: you can look up a function in a table. Java does not provide functions (or function pointers) in the same way; all you have is classes and objects. So, our end-handlers will have to be objects of classes that all derive from the `EndHandler` class. That class encapsulates the common functionality of all end-handlers; derived classes override its `doIt()` method to implement the specific function required by the application. So, we cannot, in Java, associate the string "add" with an `Add()` function object, but we can associate it with `EndAddHandler.doIt()`, which works just as well.

SAXMinilanguage

So, we are going to define a class that can do SAX (that is, extends `HandlerBase`), and give it two stack variables, `theCallStack` and `theValStack`. Before we can do that, we have to import everything we need, including `java.util.Stack`:

```
package MyNa.xml;
import MyNa.utils.Env;

import java.io.*;
import java.util.Stack;
import java.util.Hashtable;
import java.util.Enumeration;
import java.net.URL;

import org.xml.sax.*;
import org.xml.sax.helpers.ParserFactory;
import com.sun.xml.parser.Resolver;

public class SAXMiniLanguage extends HandlerBase
{
    private PrintWriter out;
    Stack theCallStack=null;
```

```
Stack theValStack=null;
String theFileName=null;
Env theEnv=null;
HandlerSet theHandlerSet; // keeps track of end-handlers for tagnames
```

Everything here should look familiar, with one exception: what's `HandlerSet`?

Inner Classes of SAXMiniLanguage

`HandlerSet` is one of three inner classes that `SAXMiniLanguage` will contain. The reason we use inner classes is because they need access to the private stacks of `SAXMiniLanguage`, and making them separate classes would result in much more verbose code. Since the SAX methods of `HandlerBase` make frequent references to the inner classes, we should become familiar with them first. The classes are: `HandlerSet`, `CallStackItem`, and `EndHandler`.

HandlerSet

`HandlerSet` is just a collection of `EndHandler`s indexed by tags and maintained as a `Hashtable`. There is a constructor and two methods, `put()` and `get()`. There is also a default `EndHandler` that is returned if the `Hashtable` comes up empty:

```
class HandlerSet
{
    Hashtable table;
    EndHandler defaultHandler;

    public HandlerSet()
    {
        defaultHandler=new EndHandler();
        table=new Hashtable();
    }
    public void put(String tagName,EndHandler eH)
    {
        table.put(tagName,eH);
    }
    public EndHandler get(String tagName)
    {
        EndHandler eH=(EndHandler)table.get(tagName);
        if(eH==null)return defaultHandler;
        return eH;
    }
} // end of HandlerSet class
```

CallStackItem

Items that are placed on the call stack have internal structure: they must contain

- ❑ the tag name of the element being processed
- ❑ the number of its children
- ❑ the set of its attributes (if any)

Each `CallStackItem` has a name. By default, this name is the tag name of the corresponding element. If the user wishes to identify a `CallStackItem` by an item-specific name, he/she can supply such a name as the value of the "name" attribute. The "name" attribute, if present, becomes the value of the name variable of `CallStackItem`; the rest of the attributes are stored in a hash table called `attrs`:

The `CallStackItem` class consists of just four variables and a constructor that fills them in.

```
public class CallStackItem
{
                                    // helper/holder class, conceals nothing
    public String tagName;      // the <tagname> for the xml item
    public String name;         // the value of "name" attr if present
                                    // else same as tagName
    public int kidNum;          // number of children on ValStack
    public Hashtable attrs;     // attributes, not including name

    public CallStackItem(String tag,AttributeList aL)
    {
        kidNum=0;
        tagName=tag;
        int N=aL.getLength();
        int nonName = N; // number of attributes other than "name"
        name=aL.getValue("name");
        if(name==null) name=tag; else nonName--;
        if(nonName==0)
        {
            attrs=null; return;
        }
        attrs=new Hashtable(nonName);
        for(int i=0;i<N;i++)
        {
            String key=aL.getName(i); if("name".equals(key))continue;
            String val=aL.getValue(i);
            attrs.put(key,val);
        }
    }
} // end CallStackItem helper class
```

EndHandler

This is where all the action takes place, the rest are props and helpers. The `EndHandler` class provides

❑ general-purpose methods for manipulating the stacks

❑ methods for transferring data to the `Env` object `Hashtable` of attributes

❑ a default implementation of the `doIt()` method that needs to be redefined in derived classes

In working with `java.util.Stack` objects, remember that they store objects of class `Object`. When you pop or peek into one of them, you have to cast it to their actual type before use. The `peek()` method allows you to take a look at the top stack item without removing it from the stack.

```
public class EndHandler
{
    public EndHandler(){}  // nothing to do in initialization

                             // pop children element values off the Value stack
    public void popAll(CallStackItem cSI)
    {
        for(int N=cSI.kidNum;N>0;N--)theValStack.pop();
    }

  // push value on Val stack; increment children count in the item below
  // the item below corresponds to parent element of the top item
    public void pushVal(Object v)
    {
        theValStack.push(v);
        ((CallStackItem) theCallStack.peek()).kidNum++;
    }

  // store attributes in the Env object
    public void addAttrsToEnv(CallStackItem cSI)
    {
        Hashtable H=cSI.attrs;
        if(H!=null) theEnv.addHashtable(H);
    }

                        // associate Call stack item with a String on Val stack
    public void assocVal(CallStackItem cSI)
    {
        theEnv.put(cSI.name,(String)theValStack.peek());
    }
```

The Default doIt()

The default doIt() proceeds as follows:

❑ Pop call stack; if there is only one child element, add a name-value pair to Env

❑ Store attributes, if any, in Env

❑ Pop all associated values off value stack.

```
    // default doIt(): pop Call stack, move data to Env, pop Val stack
    public void doIt() throws SAXException
    {
        CallStackItem cSI=(CallStackItem)theCallStack.pop();
        if(cSI.kidNum==1)assocVal(cSI);
        addAttrsToEnv(cSI);
        popAll(cSI);
    }
} // end EndHandler class
```

Attributes are added to the `Env` in the obvious "name-value" fashion. The case of one child deserves a comment. If you look up at `assocVal()`, you will see that it creates a name-value pair and adds it to `Env`. The name in the pair is the name of the `CallStackItem`, which is the tagname of the element. The value in the pair is the value of the one-down-from-top item on the value stack, which is the value of the one and only child.

Suppose you have an document fragment `<uname>J. Doe</uname>`; what happens when it is processed by the default `doIt()`? The `<uname>` element has one child, a text node, whose value is the String "J. Doe". (See `characters()` method below.) The pair "uname" - "J. Doe" gets added to the `Env` object.

SAXMiniLanguage Constructor and Methods

In outline, the code for `SAXMiniLanguage` consists of three parts:

❏ package and import statements, declaration and variables

❏ constructor and methods

❏ three inner class definitions

We have seen the first and the last part. Time to look at the actual code of the class: constructor and methods.

The Constructor and doIt()

The constructor initializes the variables. Most of them are freshly minted, and the only argument needed is the name of the file to process:

```
public SAXMiniLanguage (String fileName)
{
    theCallStack=new Stack();
    theValStack=new Stack();
    theFileName=fileName;
    Hashtable H=new Hashtable();
    theEnv=new Env();
    theHandlerSet=new HandlerSet();
}
```

Once an object is created, it is set in motion by its `doIt()` method. Even though its code is quite different from the `doIt()` methods of end handlers, it shares with them two important characteristics: first, it receives and returns `void`; second, the method that calls it (a servlet method, in this case) does not do anything else after the call, but completely transfers the continuation of the computation to the `doIt()` method. We have developed a habit of giving the name `doIt()` to all methods with these two characteristics.

This particular `doIt()` goes through the familiar motions of creating an input source and parsing the file, generating a stream of SAX events:

```
public void doIt()
{
    InputSource in=null;
    try
    {
        if(theFileName.startsWith("http:"))
        {
            URL uri=new URL(theFileName);
            in=Resolver.createInputSource(uri,true);
        }
        else
        {
            File inFile=new File(theFileName);
            in=Resolver.createInputSource(inFile);
        }
        Parser parser=ParserFactory.makeParser("com.sun.xml.parser.Parser");
        parser.setDocumentHandler(this);
        parser.parse(in);
    }
    catch (SAXParseException t)
    {
        t.printStackTrace();
    }
    catch (Throwable t)
    {
        t.printStackTrace();
    }
}
```

SAX Callbacks

`startDocument()` and `endDocument()` do not do anything except log their passage, so we don't even show them. `startElement()` pushes an item on the call stack; `endElement()` retrieves the appropriate end handler from the `HandlerSet` and calls its `doIt()` method:

```
public void startElement (String tag, AttributeList attrs)
    throws SAXException
    {
        theCallStack.push(new CallStackItem(tag,attrs));
    }

public void endElement (String tag) throws SAXException
    {
        theHandlerSet.get(tag).doIt();
    }
```

Finally, `characters()` pushes a string on the value stack and increments the number-of-children counter of the parent element (which is the item right below the top of the call stack):

```
public void characters (char buf [], int offset, int len)
    throws SAXException
    {
        String s = new String(buf, offset, len);
        theValStack.push(s);
        CallStackItem cSI=(CallStackItem)(theCallStack.peek());
        cSI.kidNum+=1;
    }
```

This completes the `SAXMinilanguage` class. The language of arithmetic expressions comes out of it as a fairly simple extension.

Arithmetic Expressions Minilanguage

As we said a few pages earlier, in order to define a specific mini-language, we need to do three things:

❑ define the XML language (that is, tags and attributes; a DTD is useful but optional)

❑ derive a class from our generic mini-language processor

❑ override end handlers.

We have already defined a DTD, so we can go right ahead and derive a class. The whole thing is less than 80 lines long, with plenty of repetitions.

Imports, Declarations and a Method

In deviation from the usual order, we start with imports, declarations and the `getFloatResult()` method. (The constructor is coming up.) `XmlArithEval` operates by building the result in the `floatResult` variable, and in the end returning it:

```
package MyNa.xml;
import MyNa.utils.Env;
import java.io.*;
import java.util.Stack;
import java.util.Hashtable;
import java.util.Enumeration;
import org.xml.sax.*;
import org.xml.sax.helpers.ParserFactory;
import com.sun.xml.parser.Resolver;

public class XmlArithEval extends SAXMiniLanguage
{
    String floatResult="";

    public String getFloatResult()
    {
        return floatResult;
    }
```

The Constructor

The constructor calls the parent constructor, then populates the `HandlerSet` with end handlers for num, add, sub, mul and div elements, in addition to the root (arithexp) element:

```
public XmlArithEval (String fileName)
{
    super(fileName);
    theHandlerSet.put("num",new EndNumHandler());
    theHandlerSet.put("add",new EndAddHandler());
    theHandlerSet.put("mul",new EndMulHandler());
    theHandlerSet.put("div",new EndDivHandler());
    theHandlerSet.put("sub",new EndSubHandler());
    theHandlerSet.put("arithexp",new EndArithExpHandler());
}
```

As pointed out to us by a reviewer, it would be good to put this kind of association, linking a name to a class, into a file. That's true; it would increase the generality of SAXMinilanguage greatly if we had it read an XML configuration file at startup, one which linked tagnames with classnames and performed other initializations. That's exactly the kind of functionality that we will provide with our XmlConfig interface in Chapter 11.

End Handlers

End handlers for add, sub, mul and div have a lot in common: they all proceed as follows:

❑   pop the top item from the call stack

❑   pop the top item from the value stack

❑   repeat

❑   apply the appropriate operation to the top value item and the next one

❑   store the result in the top item

❑   until the right number of arguments has been popped

❑   push the top item back on the value stack

As before, the only way to encapsulate this common functionality in Java is to define a class with a public method that does it:

```
class EndOpHandler extends EndHandler
{

  // just to define this function, shared by add,sub,div,mul:

    public void floatOp(String op) throws SAXException
    {
        CallStackItem cSI=(CallStackItem)theCallStack.pop();
        int kidNum=cSI.kidNum;                          // can be any number >= 1
        float arg2=((Float)theValStack.pop()).floatValue();
                                                        // top Val stack item
```

```
        for(int i=1;i<kidNum;i++)
        {                                 // just once if there are two arguments
            float arg1=((Float)theValStack.pop()).floatValue();
            if("add".equals(op))arg2=(arg1+arg2);
            else if("mul".equals(op))arg2=(arg1*arg2);
            else if("sub".equals(op))arg2=(arg1-arg2);
            else if("div".equals(op))arg2=(arg1/arg2);
            else throw new SAXException("ArithExp error, op=='"+op+"'");
        }
        pushVal(new Float(arg2));
    }
}                                          // end of EndOpHandler class
```

End handlers for the operations extend this new class and define `doIt()` in a trivial way:

```
class EndAddHandler extends EndOpHandler
{
    public void doIt() throws SAXException {floatOp("add");}
}
class EndMulHandler extends EndOpHandler
{
    public void doIt() throws SAXException {floatOp("mul");}
}
class EndSubHandler extends EndOpHandler
{
    public void doIt() throws SAXException {floatOp("sub");}
}
class EndDivHandler extends EndOpHandler
{
    public void doIt() throws SAXException {floatOp("div");}
}
```

The remaining two methods extend `EndHandler` directly. `EndNumHandler` pops the two stacks and tries to convert the `String` value to `float`. If successful, it pushes the numeric value back on the value stack. Finally, `EndArithExpHandler` does the opposite conversion: it retrieve the `Float` that is the result of the entire computation, converts it to `String`, and places it into the `floatResult` variable:

```
class EndNumHandler extends EndHandler
{
    public void doIt() throws SAXException
    {
        CallStackItem cSI=(CallStackItem)theCallStack.pop();
        String floatRep=(String)theValStack.pop();
        Float f;
        try
        {
            f=new Float(floatRep);
        }
        catch(Exception ex)
        {
            throw new SAXException("invalid float '"+floatRep+"'");
        }
        pushVal(f);
```

```
        }
    }
    class EndArithExpHandler extends EndHandler
    {
        public void doIt() throws SAXException
        {
            CallStackItem cSI=(CallStackItem)theCallStack.pop();
            floatResult=((Float)theValStack.pop()).toString();
        }
    }
} // end XmlArithEval
```

That's all there is to XmlArithEval. We hope you agree that it falls out of the general
SAXMiniLanguage in a straightforward and pleasing manner.

The Drivers: Client and Servlet

In order to test XmlArithEval, we need the client-server infrastructure of a web page with a form and
a servlet. That infrastructure is by now so familiar that we will present it very briefly. As usual, the user
has a form with a textbox to type a file name or a URL in. The action of the form is
ArithExpServlet, and name of the input field is XmlData.

When the user clicks "submit", XmlData travels to ArithExpServlet. The servlet gives it as an
argument to the constructor of XmlArithEval. Once an XmlArithEval object is constructed, its
doIt() method can be called into action, and its result (the value of the arithmetic expression) sent to
the output. Here is the doPost() method of the servlet:

```
public void doPost (HttpServletRequest req,
                    HttpServletResponse res)
        throws ServletException, IOException
{
    res.setContentType("text/html");
    HtmlWrapper W=new HtmlWrapper(res.getWriter());
    try
    {
        Env E=new Env(req);
        String myURL=res.encodeURL(req.getRequestURI());
        E.put("xmlServlet",myURL);
        String theXmlData=E.getStr("XmlData");
        if(null==theXmlData)
        {
            W.wrapPage("XmlArithEval error","no Xml Data Source specified");
            return;
        }
        XmlArithEval xae=new XmlArithEval(theXmlData);
        xae.doIt();
        String floatResult=xae.getFloatResult();
        W.wrapPage("XmlArithEval ","produced "+floatResult+" from
                "+theXmlData);
    }
    catch(Exception ex)
```

```
        {
            W.wrapPage("doPost failure",""+ex);
        }
    }
}
```

The screen shot below shows an XML file with an arithmetic expression in it, and `XmlArithEval` doing the arithmetic right.

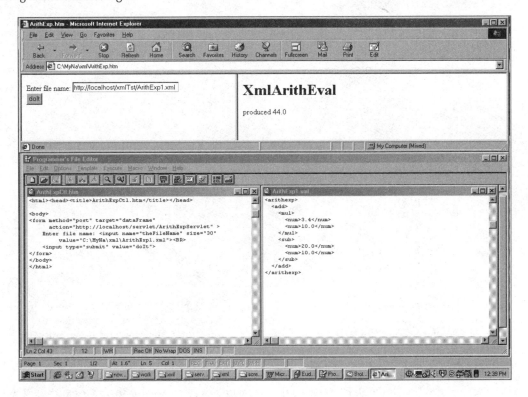

Xml2DBTables

Our task is to develop a SAX mini-language for representing database tables as XML files. As before, the syntax of the mini-language is defined by a DTD, and its semantics are defined by a Java class that extends `SAXMiniLanguage`. The class will "interpret" the documents written in the mini-language by converting them to database tables. Here is the DTD.

DTD for Xml2DBTables

We use attributes for several pieces of information. In particular, we use an attribute for a field data type, in order to be able to list all possible values. The values listed are those of JDBC data types; the default value is "`VARCHAR`", corresponding to Java `String`.

```
<!ELEMENT dbdata (jdbc_info, user-info, table*)>
<!ELEMENT jdbc_info EMPTY>
<!ATTLIST jdbc_info
    driver CDATA "com.sun.jdbc.odbc"
    db_url CDATA "YourFavoriteDB"
>
<!ELEMENT user-info (uname?, upass?)>
<!ELEMENT uname (#PCDATA)>
<!ELEMENT upass (#PCDATA)>

<!ELEMENT table (headers, row*)>
<!ATTLIST table
    name CDATA #REQUIRED
    reset (true|false) "false"
>

<!ELEMENT headers (header+)>
<!ELEMENT header EMPTY>
<!ATTLIST header
    name CDATA #REQUIRED
    fieldType
(CHAR|VARCHAR|LONGVARCHAR|NUMERIC|DECIMALBIT|TINYINT|SMALLINT|INTEGER|
BIGINT|REAL|FLOAT|DOUBLE|BINARY|VARBINARY|LONGVARBINARY|DATE|TIME|TIMESTAMP)
        "VARCHAR" >

<!ELEMENT row (field*)>              <!-- number of field <= number of headers -->
<!ELEMENT field (#PCDATA)>
<!ATTLIST field
    name CDATA #REQUIRED
>
```

As you can see, we assume that, in addition to database tables, the XML file will also store all the information that is needed to connect to the database: user ID and password, a reference to the database, and a reference to the JDBC driver to use. In many situations, it would be an impossible security lapse to place the login information into an XML file. For this reason, we made the user information optional, allowing for the possibility that it may be obtained by the application from some other source, such as a login dialog. To accommodate this feature, all we'd need to do is give SAXMiniLanguage (and therefore its derived classes) another constructor that takes an Env argument. That Env would contain all the Request object information, including the username and password.

To illustrate the DTD, here's a small example:

```
<?xml version="1.0" encoding="us-ascii"?>
<!DOCTYPE dbdata SYSTEM "dbdata.dtd">
<dbdata>
<jdbc_info driver="sun.jdbc.odbc.JdbcOdbcDriver"
   db_url="jdbc:odbc:BIRTHDAYS" />
<user-info>
    <uname>JoeSchmoe</uname>
    <upass>orgleborgle</upass>
</user-info>
<table name="Birthdays" reset="true">
```

```
        <headers>
            <header name="Who"  fieldType="VARCHAR" />
            <header name="When"  fieldType="DATE" />
            <header name="Addr"  fieldType="VARCHAR" />
        </headers>
        <row>
            <field name="Who">Martin Van Buren</field>
            <field name="When">12/5/1782</field>
            <field name="Addr">mvburen@whitehouse.gov</field>
        </row>
        <row>
            <field name="Who">Walt Disney</field>
            <field name="When">12/5/1901</field>
            <field name="Addr">wdisney@disney.com</field>
        </row>
    </table></dbdata>
```

Now that the syntax is clear, let's go on to the interpretation, performed by Xml2DBTables.

Xml2DBTables Class

Xml2DBTables extends SAXMiniLanguage and imports all the same packages and classes that its parent does. In addition, it imports java.sql.* because it needs to communicate with databases. For the same reason, its variables include a Connection, a Statement and a PreparedStatement. The Statement creates tables; the PreparedStatement inserts rows in them.

```
public class Xml2DBTables extends SAXMiniLanguage
{
    Connection theDBConnection=null;
    Statement theCreateTableStatement;
    PreparedStatement theInsertPreparedStatement;
```

The constructor, just like the XmlArithEval constructor, takes one argument, a String that is the name of an XML file. That argument is given to the parent constructor, after which the HandlerSet is populated with the appropriate EndHandlers.

```
public Xml2DBTables (String fileName)
{
    super(fileName);
    theHandlerSet.put("user-info",new EndUser_Info());
    theHandlerSet.put("header",new EndHeaderHandler());
    theHandlerSet.put("headers",new EndHeadersHandler());
    theHandlerSet.put("row",new EndRowHandler());
    theHandlerSet.put("table",new EndTableHandler());
    theHandlerSet.put("dbdata",new EnddbDataHandler());
}
```

It is the EndHandlers that do all the work, in their doIt() methods. We'll take them up one by one.

EndUser_Info

If you look back at the DTD, you'll see that by the time endElement() callback is fired on the user_info element, the parser will already have seen the jdbc_info element and the child elements (uname and upass) of user_info. What happens to them and their data?

Default Processing of db_info and user_info

Let's look back at how endElement() is implemented in the parent class, SAXMiniLanguage:

```
public void endElement (String tag) throws SAXException
{
    theHandlerSet.get(tag).doIt();
}
```

For those elements that do not have custom EndHandlers in this class, the endElement() retrieves an instance of the default EndHandler from the parent class. That default's doIt(), as you recall, adds name-value pairs to Env and pops the stacks. (See the EndHandler section for more details and an example.) In our case here, as a result of default processing, the following material is added to Env: the attributes of db_info (driver, db_url) and their values, "uname" and its text content, and "upass" and its text content. This sets up the stage for the custom user_info EndHandler to try and connect to the database.

EndUser_Info and its doIt()

This class takes us all the way back to earlier chapters and database connections. The only difference is that it has to wrap ClassNotFoundException and SQLException into SAXExceptions, and re-throw:

```
class EndUser_Info extends EndHandler
{
    public EndUser_Info(){}                     // nothing to do at construction
    public void doIt() throws SAXException
    {
        CallStackItem cSI=(CallStackItem)theCallStack.pop();
        String driver=theEnv.getStr("driver");
        String db_url=theEnv.getStr("db_url");
        String uname=theEnv.getStr("uname");
        String upass=theEnv.getStr("upass");

        try
        {
            Class.forName(driver);
            theDBConnection= DriverManager.getConnection(db_url,uname,upass);
            theCreateTableStatement=theDBConnection.createStatement();
        }
        catch(ClassNotFoundException e)
        {
            throw new SAXException ("driver not found error", e);
        }
        catch(SQLException e)
        {
            throw new SAXException ("SQL error", e);
        }
    }
}                                               // end of EndUser_Info class
```

As you can see, we expect that at this point the user name and password are in the Env object. If they were in the XML document, this will indeed be the case.

EndHeaderHandler

At this point, we are connected to an existing database and ready to transfer content from an XML file to database tables. The content consists of tables, tables consist of a header row and multiple data rows, and the header row consists of headers. We take them all in turn, beginning with individual headers:

```
class EndHeaderHandler extends EndHandler
{
    public EndHeaderHandler(){}
    public void doIt() throws SAXException
    {
        CallStackItem cSI=(CallStackItem)theCallStack.pop();
        cSI.attrs.put("name",cSI.name);  // attrs never null for header
        pushVal(cSI.attrs);
    }
}
```

If you check the DTD, you will see that the header element is empty but has two required attributes (well, one #REQUIRED, the other provided with a default). The first attribute's name is "name". This attribute is not processed the same way as others: its value is transferred to be the official name of the CallStackItem, instead of the element's tag name. (See the CallStackItem constructor on how this happens.) The other attribute is "type" and its value is one of JDBC data types. The handler adds the "name" attribute to the attrs Hashtable, where it should have been to begin with, and pushes the entire Hashtable onto the value stack.

EndHeadersHandler

By the time EndHeadersHandler comes along, all headers have been processed by EndHeaderHandler, and the value stack has a Hashtable of attributes for each header. The call stack has the <headers> item on top, and right underneath it the <table> item. That item contains the name attribute of the table (the intended table name) and the "boolean" reset attribute. So, EndHeadersHandler has all the information it needs to create a table and a prepared statement that will be used to create rows. The two tasks of creation are relegated to two methods with appropriately descriptive names, createTable() and createInserter(). Both assume that field names and field datatypes have been extracted from those individual Hashtables and packaged into two arrays. The methods receive the arrays as arguments when they are called from doIt() where the arrays are constructed.

In summary, the class consists of a do-nothing constructor, the doIt() method and two creation methods. We present them in that order.

doIt()

The code of doIt() is quite transparent; we leave it to code comments to tell the story.

```
class EndHeadersHandler extends EndHandler
{
    public EndHeadersHandler(){}
```

```
public void doIt() throws SAXException
{
    CallStackItem cSI=(CallStackItem)theCallStack.pop();
    int N=cSI.kidNum;
    // create string arrays of field names and datatypes
    String[]header_names=new String[N];
    String[]header_types=new String[N];
    for(int i=N-1;i>=0;i--)
    {
        Hashtable aL=(Hashtable)theValStack.pop();
        header_names[i]=(String)aL.get("name");
        header_types[i]=(String)aL.get("fieldType");
    }
    // peek to get the table name
    CallStackItem tableCSI=(CallStackItem)(theCallStack.peek());
    String tableName=tableCSI.name;
    // store everything in Env
    theEnv.put("header_names",header_names);
    theEnv.put("header_types",header_types);
    theEnv.put("tableName",tableName);
    // reset? or not to reset?
    Hashtable attrs=tableCSI.attrs;
    String reset=(null==attrs?null:(String)attrs.get("reset"));
    boolean doReset="true".equals(reset);
    // finally, doIt!
    createTable(tableName,header_names,header_types,doReset);
    createInserter(tableName,header_names,header_types);
}
```

createTable() and createInserter()

Both of these methods start by constructing an SQL query string that does the right thing. In
createTable(), the query string is given to theCreateTableStatement to execute. In
createInserter(), the query string is given to theInsertPreparedStatement to create a
PreparedStatement:

```
public void createTable(String name,String[]fldnames,
                        String[]fldtypes,boolean doReset)
{
    // construct query String such as
    // "CREATE TABLE COURSEBOOKS (SectionID TEXT, ItemCode TEXT)";
    try
    {
        int N=fldnames.length;
        String createStr="CREATE TABLE "+name+" (";
        if(N>0)createStr+=fldnames[0]+" "+fldtypes[0];
        for(int i=1;i<N;i++)
        {
            createStr+=", "+fldnames[i]+" "+fldtypes[i];
        }
        createStr+=");"; // SQL and Java get a semicolon each
        try
        {
            theCreateTableStatement.execute(createStr);
        }
```

```
                     catch(SQLException e)
                     {
                         e.printStackTrace();
                     }
                                     // even if table creation fails,
                                     // we may continue with a different query string
                     if(doReset)
                     {
                         String delStr="DELETE * FROM "+name+";";
                         theCreateTableStatement.execute(delStr);
                     }
                 }
             catch(SQLException e){e.printStackTrace();
         }
     }

     public void createInserter(String name,String[]fldnames,String[]fldtypes)
             throws SAXException
     {
         // build strings like insertStr="INSERT INTO COURSEBOOKS VALUES (?,?);"
         try
         {
             int N=fldnames.length;
             String insertStr="INSERT INTO "+name+" VALUES (";
             if(N>0)insertStr+="?";
             for(int i=1;i<N;i++)insertStr+=", ?";
             insertStr+=");";
             theInsertPreparedStatement=theDBConnection.prepareStatement
                     (insertStr);
         }
         catch(SQLException e)
         {
             e.printStackTrace();
             throw new SAXException("createInserter error",e);
         }
     }
```

We are all set to insert rows into the table.

EndRowHandler

EndRowHandler pops the call stack, gets the header names from Env, and uses them to populate the prepared statement. The statement gets executed and its parameters cleared.

```
class EndRowHandler extends EndHandler
{
    public EndRowHandler(){}
    public void doIt() throws SAXException
    {
        CallStackItem cSI=(CallStackItem)theCallStack.pop();
```

```
        try
        {
            String [] names=(String[])theEnv.get("header_names");
            for(int i=1;i<=names.length;i++)
            theInsertPreparedStatement.setString(i,
                    (String)theEnv.get(names[i-1]));
            theInsertPreparedStatement.executeUpdate();
            theInsertPreparedStatement.clearParameters();
        }
        catch(SQLException e)
        {
            throw new SAXException ("SQL error", e);
        }
    }                                                   // end of doIt()
}                                            // end of EndRowHandler class
```

Note that we use setString() for setting the prepared statement parameters, without regard for the actual data type stored in the header_types array, itself stored in the Env. The strings will undergo automatic conversion on their way to the database. We have been pleased with the results of those conversions in our practice. If your JDBC driver and database do not understand the format of your string data, you will have to provide the conversion yourself, as described in Chapter 2, section on setObject().

Closing operations: EndTableHandler and EnddbDataHandler

EndTableHandler's doIt() pops the call stack and closes the PreparedStatement. EnddbDataHandler's doIt() pops the call stack and closes the other Statement and the entire connection.

```
class EndTableHandler extends EndHandler
{
    public EndTableHandler(){}
    public void doIt() throws SAXException
    {
        try
        {
            CallStackItem cSI=(CallStackItem)theCallStack.pop();
            theInsertPreparedStatement.close();
        }
        catch(SQLException e)
        {
            throw new SAXException ("SQL error", e);
        }
    }
}
class EnddbDataHandler extends EndHandler
{
    public EnddbDataHandler(){}
    public void doIt() throws SAXException
    {
        try
        {
            CallStackItem cSI=(CallStackItem)theCallStack.pop();
            theCreateTableStatement.close();
```

```
                theDBConnection.close();
        }
        catch(SQLException e)
        {
                throw new SAXException ("SQL error", e);
        }
    }
}
// end Xml2DBTables class
```

This completes the `Xml2DBTables` class. The next question is "what is it good for?" In part, that question is really "Where do the XML tables come from?" The most likely source is some process that originates with some other database table or tables somewhere. In other words, we need a tool to turn `ResultSets` into XML documents in the `dbdata.dtd` format. We do exactly that with `TreeSubst`, an XML variant on `ParseSubst` that we mentioned in the Introduction to this chapter. `TreeSubst` just does a recursive traversal of a DOM tree looking to see what substitutions or loops it should do; apart from substitutions, it writes out the tree as XML in exactly the same way as `XmlManip` does. Together, `Xml2DBTables` and `TreeSubst` can serve to exchange data, as a `dbdata` XML document, between any two relational databases.

It is time to take a broader look and XML and databases.

XML and Relational Datatables

The subject of XML and datatables has attracted a lot of attention. An excellent review can be found at

```
http://www.informatik.tudarmstadt.de/DVS1/staff/bourret/xml
                                              /XMLAndDatabases.htm.
```

Its author, Ronald Bourret, is also the developer of XML-DBMS, a collection of Java classes for transferring data between a relational database and an XML document. We summarize the main points of the review and place our efforts in Bourret's overall context. (Neither the review nor this book extends the topic to include object databases or object-relational databases.) All the quotes are from the 9/23/1999 version; we give section numbers in parentheses.

XML and Databases: a Review

XML-database software falls into three groups: Middleware, XML Servers and Content Management Systems, characterized as follows: "as a general rule, middleware is software you use with an existing database, an XML server is a database and middleware together, tuned for data storage and application development, and a content management system is a database and middleware together, tuned for document storage (6)".

Data Transfer: Template-driven Approach

Our `Xml2DBTables` clearly belongs in the middle tier, and specifically in that component that handles data transfer between the database and XML. There are two approaches to the task of data transfer, template-driven and model-driven. (4.2) "In a template-driven mapping, there is no predefined mapping between document structure and database structure. Instead, you embed commands in a template that is processed by the data transfer middleware". (4.2.1) Bourret offers this example:

```
<?xml version="1.0"?>
  <FlightInfo>
    <Intro>The following flights have available seats:</Intro>
      <SelectStmt>SELECT Airline, FltNumber, Depart, Arrive FROM Flights
      </SelectStmt>
    <Conclude>We hope one of these meets your needs</Conclude>
  </FlightInfo>
```

When processed by the middleware, the SELECT statement is replaced by the query result, yielding something like:

```
<?xml version="1.0"?>
  <FlightInfo>
    <Intro>The following flights have available seats:</Intro>
    <Flights>
      <Row>
        <Airline>ACME</Airline>
        <FltNumber>123</FltNumber>
        <Depart>Dec 12, 1998 13:43</Depart>
        <Arrive>Dec 13, 1998 01:21</Arrive>
      </Row>
      ...
    </Flights>
    <Conclude>We hope one of these meets your needs</Conclude>
  </FlightInfo>
```

According to Bourret, as of the time of his writing (September 1999), "template-driven mappings are available only for transferring data from a relational database to an XML document." (4.2.1) We should point out that our DBHandler-ParseSubst combo, which fits into this category, can be used to generate XML (as well as plain text) from relational databases.

Data Transfer: model-driven Approach

"In a model-driven mapping, a data model of some sort is imposed on the structure of the XML document and this is mapped, either implicitly or explicitly, to the structures in the database and vice versa... Two models for viewing the data in an XML document are common. The first of these, which is used by many of the middleware packages for transferring data between an XML document and a relational database, models the XML document as a single table or set of tables. That is, the structure of the XML document must be similar to the following, where the <database> element does not exist in the single-table case:

```
<database>
    <table>
        <row>
            <column1>...</column1>
            <column2>...</column2>
            ...
        </row>
        ...
    </table>
    ...
</database>
```

where the term "table" is loosely interpreted to mean a single result set (when transferring data from the database to XML) or a single table or updateable view (when transferring data from XML to the database)." (4.2.2)

Inserting a comment of our own, when Bourret says that "the structure of the XML document must be similar" to the code above, he means that it will be a concrete model, with application-specific tag names for database, table, row and column. The code shown is a **meta-description** of the actual code. What we have done is create a DTD and a Java processor that put the meta-description into an XML document. The concrete model is not encoded as markup, but as the document's content. As is often the case, a meta-linguistic approach has a number of advantages which we will discuss shortly.

The other common model is a tree of objects, "in which elements generally correspond to objects and attributes and PCDATA correspond to properties. This model maps directly to object-oriented and hierarchical databases and can be mapped to relational databases using traditional object-relational mapping techniques or SQL 3 object views. Note that this model is *not* the Document Object Model (DOM); the DOM models the document itself, not the data in the document." (ibid.)

Data transfer: Mini-Language Approach

How does Xml2DBTables fit in? It is different from the other approaches because it uses, in effect, an XML metalanguage for describing a database. The meta-language document can serve both as a model, in the sense of Bourret's model-driven approach, and a template, for receiving the results of the query. It thus combines the best features of both approaches: it has the flexibility of the template approach and the simplicity of the model approach. In particular, in order to specify input, the user only has to create an XML document conforming to a given DVD.

We are not going to develop a complete middleware system in this book (although we will come pretty close). We do believe that a combination of our SAXMinilanguage approach for creating XML-based mini-languages and our SubstMinilanguage approach, when properly XML-ized, together create a foundation of a simple and flexible middleware system for transferring data between XML documents and several kinds of data stores, including relational databases. Since the system is easy to use, it also provides a means for initialization and customization based on XML files you can validate. We will continue this line of development in the remaining chapters.

Conclusion

In this chapter, we have moved from learning new technologies to extending them. XML documents and SAX parsers are great tools, but they don't themselves tell you how to use them in creating applications. There are obviously many good ways, but we particularly favor the meta-linguistic, minilanguage approach: use them to create a language for the application and express the application in that custom-designed language.

Since all such languages and their processors have a lot in common, we started by designing a generic SAXMiniLanguage processor, implemented as a Java class. To design a minilanguage for specific problems and problem domains, you extend this class and write domain-specific handlers for domain-specific XML languages. Our two examples in this chapter are arithmetic expressions and a minilanguage for describing XML documents that contain database data. Note that although Xml2DBTables is a specific SAXMiniLanguage for a specific domain, it is itself a meta-language for that domain, with all the resulting advantages in generality and flexibility.

A natural thing to do now would be to design a specific application using Xml2DBTables, so that we finally have something concrete we can roll out and play with. However, before we do that we would like to bring in another Java and XML technology. This technology is **JavaServer Pages**, or **JSP**, and it is the subject of the next chapter.

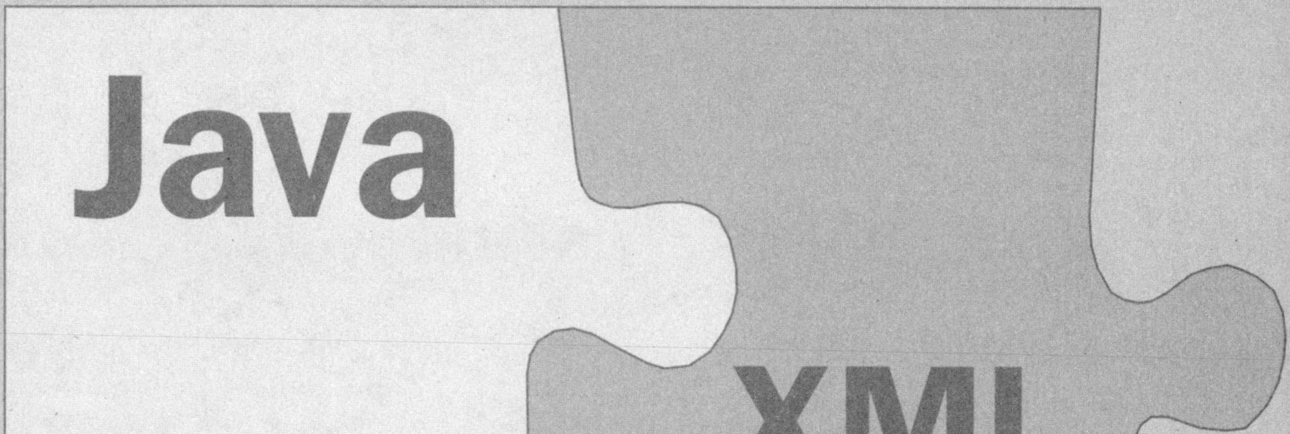
Java
XML

10

JSPs and JavaBeans

Introduction

JavaServer Pages, or JSP, is a technology that is certain to be very widely used. It has been a little slow in spreading because it has not had a stable release until recently, and pre-release versions were not clear about their overall direction. Clarity had to wait until the release of the XML and Namespace Recommendations by W3C (see Appendices H and I). With that release, JSP started a rapid transition to XML. As with several other technologies, including the XSLT recommendation, in this book we're among the first to use an official stable release, JSP 1.0. We refer to the specification, which we quote often, as JSP 1.0.

A JSP page is an HTML or XML page that contains JSP elements. JSP elements are delimited by JSP tags. Some of these tags have standard XML/Namespaces syntax, others have JSP-specific syntax reminiscent of Processing Instructions. Beginning with version 1.0, all non-XML tags have equivalent XML tags defined in the JSP DTD, so that **a JSP page can be a valid XML page**. JSP 1.0-compliant processors are not required to accept JSP pages in XML syntax, but JSP 1.x-compliant processors are required to, in effect, incorporate a validating XML parser. They are also required to accept definitions of namespaces from a JSP (the `taglib` feature), in addition to the default `jsp:` namespace.

The largest challenge of JSP, as you will see throughout the chapter, is to find a good way to structure the application into components: a JSP page is so versatile that it is easy to try to make it do too much. JavaBeans are a big help here. Instead of mixing Web content with unstructured stretches of Java code, a JSP page can try to isolate its procedures into a compiled Java bean, and use its JSP elements mostly to create and manipulate an instance of such a bean. This is a clear direction of JSP evolution from version 0.92 to versions 1.0 and 1.1.

Combining the two changes together, we can say that JSP pages are moving towards becoming XML pages that have servlet functionality and allow the incorporation of Java code. Apart from JSP (and also the SAXMiniLanguage), there is one more way to incorporate Java code in XML pages: through the "extension" mechanism of an XSLT style sheet (see Chapter 13 for more details and an example). Although not yet standardized, it is definitely on its way to becoming a standard; once this happens, there will be a significant area of functional overlap between XML+XSLT+(Java code) and JSP-as-XML. The version 1.1 specification, in an appendix entitled "Future", makes it clear that its authors are aware of the converging lines of development; the XML-Java team and the JSP team are working closely together.

In outline, this chapter proceeds as follows:

- ❑ Major features of JSP
- ❑ A JSP example and the servlet it generates
- ❑ Overview of JSP syntax and semantics
- ❑ Design considerations
- ❑ An example of a circular conversation between a page, a bean and a browser
- ❑ An application with JavaMail, JSP and a database

In addition to an overview section in this chapter, *Appendix F* contains the syntactic summary of JSP. As you will see, the syntax of JSP is small and intuitive, and its semantics are easy to grasp for those who have a background in servlets. The main challenge, with respect to JSPs, is to find good uses for their impressive functionality. This is what this chapter will concentrate on.

Major features of JSP

Throughout this book, our distributed applications have had at least these four separate components:

- ❑ a servlet, to receive a request and map it to a response
- ❑ some backend code that the servlet invokes to do backend work, e.g. run a database query
- ❑ an `HtmlWrapper` class that produces the output
- ❑ a template file for output that contains both static template material and dynamic elements filled in by the servlet and backend code

The great advantage of a JSP is that it can be all those components at once. It has access to the same `Request`, `Response` and `Session` objects that a servlet does, and it has a `PrintWriter` that writes to `Response`. It can contain arbitrary amounts of Java code, and it can dynamically load Java beans. At the same time, it is an HTML or an XML page with JSP elements inserted in it; beginning with version 1.0, those JSP elements may themselves be well-formed XML, so the entire JSP is a well-formed XML document, which can be validated against the JSP DTD.

What Does it Look Like?

You have already seen a short example of JSP in Chapter 3; here is another one, combined from examples in the GNU JSP 1.0 distribution and our own embellishments:

```html
<html>
<head>
<title>JSP example page</title>
    <%! int i=5,j=2; %>                          <!-- a declaration -->
    <%@ page import="java.util.Date" %>          <!-- a directive -->
</head>
<body>

<h1>The Famous JSP Hello Program</h1>
        <% String s = "GNU"+"JSP"; %>            <!-- a code fragment -->

The following line should contain the text "Hello GNUJSP World!".
<br>If thats not the case start debugging ...
<p>Hello <%= s %> World!<br>                     <!-- an expression -->
The current date is <%= new Date() %>.<br>       <!-- another expression -->
The integer value is <%= ++i+j %>               <!-- another expression -->

<% if(i<12){ %>              <!-- code fragment -->
<br>less than a dozen        <!-- template data -->
<% }else %>                  <!-- code fragment -->
<br>a dozen or more          <!-- template data -->
<% ; %>                      <!-- code fragment -->

</body>
</html>
```

If you have this document served to you by a JSP-enabled server (i.e. a server that has a **JSP engine**) then this is what you will see:

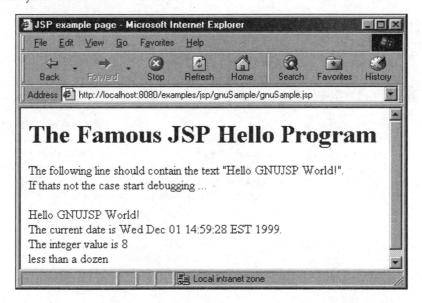

Click the **Reload/Refresh** button several times, and you will reach the point where the message changes. Our next task is to understand how this comes about. We are not aiming for a systematic coverage at this point, but note that a JSP file consists of template data, which is just HTML, and JSP elements of various kinds. The file above shows a declaration, a directive, and several code fragments and expressions. Each kind is indicated by a specific JSP tag.

How Does it Work?

JSP pages work within a request-response, client-server protocol, such as HTTP. Although JSP 1.0 talks about JSP engines implementing other protocols, for now it is HTTP that JSP engines implement, and that is the context we assume: when we say "request" or "response", we mean HTTP versions.

When a request for a JSP page comes from a client to a JSP-enabled server (whether as a URL to load or a form action to execute), the server passes it on to its JSP engine. The JSP engine delivers requests from a client to a JSP page, and responses from the JSP page to the client. Theoretically, JSP engines are free to implement "request" as they wish, but in practice, this is what happens: deep down inside, a JSP page is a servlet, and requests and responses are Java objects of type `HttpServletRequest` and `HttpServletResponse`.

How and when does a JSP page become a servlet? This is an optimization trick that is not codified in a definitive way: the translation of JSP text into servlet code can happen (to quote the specification)

> "at any time between initial deployment of the JSP page into the runtime environment of a JSP engine, and the receipt and processing of a client request for the target JSP page." (1.4)

Typically, during the "receipt and processing" of the first request, the servlet class is compiled and loaded, so subsequent requests return much faster than the first one. The class is not recompiled until changes to the JSP pages are made, which may be a problem for pages that dynamically load Java beans because if a bean is changed and recompiled, the system won't notice unless you also "touch up" the JSP page to force recompilation of the servlet.

Translating JSP into Servlet

Simplifying quite a bit, the translation process boils down to this: the Java code of the page becomes the Java code of the underlying servlet, while the template data gets rewritten as `out.println()` statements. The way it is done depends on the JSP engine; we illustrate by going through the code generated by jswdk-1.0 from the example above. We found reading the code instructive.

Our JSP page is in the directory `jswdk-1.0 \examples\jsp\`; the Java code file is generated in `jswdk-1.0\work\%3A8080%2Fexamples`. (In the text below, we will sometimes refer to the `jswdk-1.0` directory as `JSP_ROOT`.) In addition to the code file, the translation process also generates a binary data file in the same directory. That file, as we will see shortly, contains the text of the JSP file, saved as a two-dimensional array of characters. It also contains some data structure, probably a Vector, that holds array indices for the beginning and end of each JSP element.

In outline, the generated code consists of:

- ❏ package and import statements
- ❏ declarations
- ❏ an initialization method
- ❏ a service method

We will look at each of these in turn.

Package and Import Statements

The name of the package is generated from the path to the directory containing the JSP page and, depending on your directory structure, will look something like:

```
package D_0003a.jswdk_0002d_00031_0005f_00030.examples.jsp.ch_00031_00030;
```

The import statements show what JSP pages need to function. We have rearranged their order to group related ones together, but we have not moved the last one because its position is not random: this is the only one in this example that has been generated from a directive in the page:

```
import javax.servlet.*;
import javax.servlet.http.*;
import javax.servlet.jsp.*;
import com.sun.jsp.runtime.*;
import com.sun.jsp.JspException;

import java.io.PrintWriter;
import java.io.IOException;
import java.io.FileInputStream;
import java.io.ObjectInputStream;
import java.util.Vector;
import java.beans.*;

import java.util.Date; // generated from a page directive
```

As you can see, there is a new kid on the block, the `javax.servlet.jsp` package. Let's take a quick look at it.

javax.servlet.jsp

The package consists of two interfaces and four classes, all of them abstract. The implementations and non-abstract extensions of them all are in `com.sun.jsp.runtime`. We will see glimpses of them as we read through the code.

- ❏ Interfaces: `HttpJspPage`, `JspPage`
- ❏ Classes: `JspEngineInfo`, `JspFactory`, `JspWriter`, `PageContext`

The JavaDoc API documentation explains what these do, and we will see examples in the code. The main point is that the JspPage interface extends javax.servlet.Servlet, and HttpJspPage extends JspPage. The servlet class generated from a JSP page extends HttpJspBase, which implements HttpJspPage.

Declarations

Next come declarations, a null constructor, and a couple of static variables. Note how every time Java code is extracted from JSP text, two automatically generated comments indicate the beginning and end of the extraction. (The `// begin` comment unfortunately wraps around on a book page.)

```
public class exa3_jsp_1 extends HttpJspBase
{
    static char[][] _jspx_html_data = null;
    // begin [file="D:\\jswdk1.0\\examples\\jsp\\ch10\\exa3.jsp";
                                              from=(3,11);to=(3,25)]
        int i=5,j=2;    // both lines above are part of the //begin comment
    // end

    public exa3_jsp_1( ) {}

    private static boolean _jspx_inited = false;
```

The static two-dimensional array of char represents the text of the JSP file: rows are lines, and columns are columns. The array is put to immediate use to copy the declarations of two integer variables. The preceding `// begin` comment gives the beginning and end point (from=(3,11);to=(3,25)) of where the declarations occur. If you check our JSP file, you will see that, indeed, the two integer variables are declared on line 4, beginning at character 12 and end on the same line at character 25.

The private static boolean is to keep track of initialization. It is set to true once the initialization method is called from the service method.

Initialization

The _jspx_init() method is final: except for the name of the data file, it is the same for all applications. Its main task is to open an ObjectInputStream to the data file that contains the two-dimensional array of char, and read that array into a variable, _jspx_html_data:

```
public final void _jspx_init() throws JspException
{
    ObjectInputStream oin = null;
    int numStrings = 0;
    try
    {
        FileInputStream fin = new
                FileInputStream("work\\%3A8080%2Fexamples
                    \\D_0003a.jswdk_0002d_00031_0005f_00030.
                        examples.jsp.ch_00031_00030exa3.dat");

        oin = new ObjectInputStream(fin);
        _jspx_html_data = (char[][]) oin.readObject();


    }
```

```
    catch (Exception ex)
    {
        throw new JspException("Unable to open data file");
    }
    finally
    {
        if (oin != null)
        try
        {
            oin.close();
        }
        catch (IOException ignore)
        {
        }
    }
}
```

This method is called from the service method that does all the work.

Service

The service method is public, and it looks very much like a servlet's service method:

```
public void _jspService(HttpServletRequest request, HttpServletResponse
        response) throws IOException, ServletException
{
```

The method starts by declaring and initializing all its local variables, and running the _jspx_init()
method if it has not been run yet:

```
        JspFactory _jspxFactory = null;
        PageContext pageContext = null;
        HttpSession session = null;
        ServletContext application = null;
        ServletConfig config = null;
        JspWriter out = null;
        Object page = this;
        String _value = null;
        try
        {
            if (_jspx_inited == false)
            {
                _jspx_init();
                _jspx_inited = true;
            }
```

The next thing we need is a pageContext object. This is generated by a JspFactory:

```
            _jspxFactory = JspFactory.getDefaultFactory();
            response.setContentType("text/html");
            pageContext = _jspxFactory.getPageContext(this, request,
                    response, "", true, 8192, true);
```

With a `pageContext` in hand, we obtain the remaining objects we need:

```
application = pageContext.getServletContext();
config = pageContext.getServletConfig();
session = pageContext.getSession();
out = pageContext.getOut();
```

Now we can start writing to `out`, generating the response. If a line has only template material, we output it as is. If there are JSP elements involved, they are dealt with appropriately, according to their type. Every time a JSP element is processed, `//` `begin` and `//` `end` comments are generated:

```
out.print(_jspx_html_data[0]);
out.print(_jspx_html_data[1]);
out.print(_jspx_html_data[2]);
// begin [file="D:\\jswdk-1.0\\examples\\jsp\\ch10\\exa3.jsp";
                                     from=(9,3);to=(9,28)]
    String s = "GNU" + "JSP";
// end
out.print(_jspx_html_data[3]);
// begin [file="D:\\jswdk-1.0\\examples\\jsp\\ch10\\exa3.jsp";
                                     from=(13,12);to=(13,15)]
    out.print( s );
// end
out.print(_jspx_html_data[4]);
// begin [file="D:\\jswdk-1.0\\examples\\jsp\\ch10\\exa3.jsp";
                                     from=(14,23);to=(14,35)]
    out.print( new Date() );
// end
out.print(_jspx_html_data[5]);
// begin [file="D:\\jswdk-1.0\\examples\\jsp\\ch10\\exa3.jsp";
                                     from=(15,25);to=(15,32)]
    out.print( ++i+j );
// end
out.print(_jspx_html_data[6]);
// begin [file="D:\\jswdk-1.0\\examples\\jsp\\ch10\\exa3.jsp";
                                     from=(17,2);to=(17,13)]
if(i < 12)
{
    // end
    out.print(_jspx_html_data[7]);
    // begin [file="D:\\jswdk-1.0\\examples\\jsp\\ch10\\exa3.jsp";
                                     from=(19,2);to=(19,9)]
}
else
// end
out.print(_jspx_html_data[8]);
// begin [file="D:\\jswdk-1.0\\examples\\jsp\\ch10\\exa3.jsp";
                                     from=(21,2);to=(21,6)]
    ;
// end
out.print(_jspx_html_data[9]);
```

```
        }
        catch (Throwable t)
        {
            if (out.getBufferSize() != 0)
            {
                out.clear();
            }
            throw new JspException("Unknown exception: ", t);
        }
        finally
        {
            out.flush();
            _jspxFactory.releasePageContext(pageContext);
        }
    }
}
```

Implicit Objects and Scope

One conclusion to draw from this is that a JSP page has some implicit objects associated with it. They are: Request, Response, a Writer, a PageContext, a session, a ServletConfig, and an application, which is a ServletContext. If an exception is thrown but not caught by the implementing class of a JSP page, and a special error page is specified by a page directive (see below), that exception becomes an implicit object in the error page, referred to by the name exception.

In addition to implicit objects, JSP page code can create other objects as needed, or dynamically load objects; loading JavaBeans is particularly easy. Section 1.4.1 of JSP 1.0 states: "The created objects have a scope attribute defining where there is a reference to the object and when that reference is removed." (In other words, it's both the scope and the temporal extent.) The following scopes are supported (we quote from Section 1.4.1):

- ❑ page – Objects with page scope are accessible only within the page where they are created. All references to such an object shall be released after the response is sent back to the client from the JSP page or the request is forwarded somewhere else. References to objects with page scope are stored in the PageContext object (see Chapter 2, *Implicit Objects*).

- ❑ request – Objects with request scope are accessible from pages processing the same request where they were created. All references to the object shall be released after the request is processed; in particular, if the request is forwarded to a resource in the same runtime, the object is still reachable. References to objects with request scope are stored in the request object.

- ❑ session – Objects with session scope are accessible from pages processing requests that are in the same session as the one in which they were created. It is not legal to define an object with session scope from within a page that is not session-aware (see Section 2.7.1, "The page Directive"). All references to the object shall be released after the associated session ends. References to objects with session scope are stored in the session object associated with the page activation.

- ❑ application – Objects with application scope are accessible from pages processing requests that are in the same application as the one in which they were created. All references to the object shall be released when the runtime environment reclaims the ServletContext. Objects with application scope can be defined (and reached) from pages that are not session-aware (see Section 2.7.1, "The page Directive"). References to objects with application scope are stored in the application object associated with a page activation.

JSP Syntax and Semantics

JSP syntax is quite straightforward and compact: it all fits on a double-page syntax card available from Sun at `http://java.sun.com/products/jsp/syntax.pdf` (see also *Appendix F*). A JSP page consists of template data and JSP elements. Template data is just HTML or XML; the JSP processor passes it on to output untouched. JSP elements fall into the following groups: **directives**, **scripting elements**, **comments**, and **actions**. Scripting elements are further subdivided into **declarations**, **expressions** and **code fragments**, or **scriptlets**.

The first three groups have always been part of JSP and they have non-XML syntax, as well as alternative XML/Namespace syntax. The "actions" group is more recent and has only XML/Namespace syntax.

Non-XML Syntax

Non-XML syntax of directives, scripting elements and comments is summarized in the table below. You have seen all of them used in our simple example

Type of Element	Syntax Description	Example
Directives	<%@ directive %>	`<%@ page language="java" %>`
Scripting elements		
Declarations	<%! declarations %>	`<%! int i=0, j=5; %>`
Expressions	<%= expression %>	`<%= i+7 %>`
Code fragments	<% code fragment %>	`<% if(i < j-4 { %>`
Comments	<%-- comment --%>	`<%-- not for the client --%>`

Alternative XML Syntax

A JSP page that is also a valid XML document opens with the following declarations:

```
<! DOCTYPE root
   PUBLIC "-//Sun Microsystems Inc.//DTD JavaServer Pages Version 1.0//EN"
    "http://java.sun.com/products/jsp/dtd/jspcore_1_0.dtd">
<jsp:root xmlns:jsp="http://java.sun.com/products/jsp/dtd/jsp_1_0.dtd">
```

XML alternatives to older, non-XML syntax are summarized in the following table:

Type of Element	Non-XML Syntax	XML Tag
Directives	<%@ directive %>	`<jsp:directive.page ... />` `<jsp:directive.include ... />`
Scripting elements		

Declarations	<%! declarations %>	`<jsp:declaration>`
		`...`
		`</jsp:declaration>`

Expressions	<%= expression %>	`<jsp:expression>`
		`...`
		`</jsp:expression>`

Code fragments	<% code fragment %>	`<jsp:scriptlet>`
		`...`
		`</jsp:scriptlet>`

Comments	<%-- comment --%>	`<%-- not for the client --%>`

Directives are EMPTY elements that take a number of attributes. Scripting elements have no attributes, and only PCDATA content. That content will often contain special characters, such as <, & and quotes. These have to be escaped, or else the entire body of the scripting element has to be made into a CDATA section. The same consideration applies to action elements, see below.

To us, writing extensive scripting elements seems like an error-prone process in precisely the complex cases where it really matters. It is possible that good "lint"-style tools will appear that will catch a forgotten closing bracket. A better approach is never to write a scripting element that is longer than a line or two, and use Java beans instead.

The taglib Directive

The one remaining JSP element, the taglib directive, is not mentioned in the table because it does not translate into an XML element, but rather results in a change of namespace. The purpose of the taglib directive is to introduce an additional library of tags. That library is identified by a namespace uri and a namespace prefix, as in:

```
<%@ taglib uri="http://www.mytaglibs.com/tags" prefix="private" %>
```

In the XML document corresponding to JSP pages, the taglib directive is represented as a Namespace attribute (xmlns:name-of-tag-library).

The taglib directive is not part of JSP 1.0 but JSP 1.1, so this whole little section may seem premature. The reason we included it is because we believe that, once the directive is implemented, it will become an extremely powerful tool for creating mini-languages.

Semantics in Brief

- **Directives** are addressed to the JSP engine. They do not produce any output.

- Within scripting elements, **Declarations** are exactly that, Java declarations and, perhaps, initializations. Declarations do not produce any output.

- **Expressions** are Java expressions; they are evaluated and their values are inserted into the output stream.

- **Code fragments** are stretches of Java code. They don't have to be complete statements or valid expressions.

- **JSP comments** are not sent to the client; they are strictly for documenting code.

- You can also use standard XML comments in a JSP page and they will be treated like regular XML comments. You can even include non-XML JSP content in XML-style comments, and it will be treated as part of comments, i.e. ignored.

The semantics of scripting elements are easy to understand; it's just Java code. Directives and their attributes require a little more discussion.

JSP Directives

There are three directives: `page`, `include` and `taglib`. However, `taglib` is not implemented in version 1.0, so we only use `page` and `include`.

Page Directive

The page directive has a number of attributes; the easiest way to show them all is to quote the DTD definition of the `jsp.directive.page` element:

```
<!ELEMENT jsp:directive.page EMPTY>
<!ATTLIST jsp:directive.page
  language CDATA "java"
  extends CDATA #IMPLIED
  contentType CDATA "text/html; ISO-8859-1"
  import CDATA #IMPLIED
  session (true|false)"true"
  buffer CDATA "8kb"
  autoFlush (true|false)"true"
  isThreadSafe(true|false)"true"
  info CDATA #IMPLIED
  errorPage CDATA #IMPLIED
  isErrorPage(true|false)"false"
>
```

Let us go through them in order.

Directive	Description
language	Specify the language of scripting elements; currently only Java is supported.
extends	Allows you to specify a parent class for the servlet that is automatically generated from the JSP page. It is rarely used because it prevents the engine from doing some optimizations.
contentType	Specifies the MIME type and encoding; one per page.
import	Specifies Java packages and classes to be imported.
session	If `true`, then the implicit variable named `session` of type `javax.servlet.http.HttpSession` references the current/new session for the page; otherwise, that variable is unavailable.
buffer	Controls the size of the buffer associated with the `JspWriter`. If you want unbuffered output, set it to `none`.
autoFlush	Specifies whether the buffered output should be flushed automatically (`true` value) when the buffer is filled, or whether an exception should be raised (`false` value) to indicate buffer overflow.
isThreadSafe	If `false`, the JSP page implementation will implement `javax.servlet.SingleThreadModel`, so that all requests sent to that instance will be delivered serially to the `service()` method of the page implementation class. Synchronization issues are complex; consult JSP 1.0 for a detailed discussion.
info	Provides an information message about your JSP page; it becomes the return value of the `Servlet.getServletInfo()` method of the implementation class.
errorPage	Specifies a relative URL of the local page to which any Java programming language `Throwable` object(s) thrown but not caught by the page implementation are forwarded to for error processing.
isErrorPage	Specifies whether this is or is not an error page.

Here is an example of using page from the Birthdays application (presented in full later in this chapter):

```
<%@ page import="java.util.*, MyNa.utils.*" errorPage="errorpage.jsp" %>
```

Action Elements

Action elements fall into three groups as follows:

❑ actions having to do with beans: useBean, getProperty, setProperty

❑ include and forward actions, corresponding to the include() and forward() methods of the RequestDispatcher interface in the javax.servlet package (see Chapter 1)

❑ the plugin action, for downloading a plug-in to the client (we don't use it in this book – see the documentation for more details)

All action tags appear with the `jsp:` namespace prefix. Some action elements are EMPTY, with a number of attributes; others have content. When action elements appear in a JSP page that is intended to be a well-formed and valid XML document, their content frequently has to be wrapped in a CDATA section.

Beans and Properties

Here is an example of using action elements from the Birthdays application which we develop later in this chapter:

```
<jsp:useBean id="bbean" scope="session" class="birthday.BirthdayBean" />
```

The `id` attribute of `useBean` specifies the name of the bean within the application. The scope attribute can have one of the values we discussed above: `page`, `request`, `session`, or `application`. Finally, the class attribute gives the fully-qualified class name of the bean. As the DTD says:

```
<!ELEMENT jsp:useBean %jsp.body;>
<!ATTLIST jsp:useBean
id ID #REQUIRED
class CDATA #REQUIRED
scope (page|session|request|application) "page"
>
```

You will notice from the first line that the DTD specifies `useBean` as having `%jsp.body;` content. That content can be empty, as in our example, but it may not be. If there is content, it is usually `setProperty` elements that customize the bean. Alternatively, `setProperty` elements may follow the `useBean` element.

Here is an example of using `setProperty`:

```
<jsp:setProperty name="bbean" property="*" />
```

To set a property, one needs a property name and a value. There are two sources for values. One is the attributes of a `setProperty` element:

```
<jsp:setProperty name="abean" property="prop1" value="value1" />
```

More often, the values come from `Request` parameters, ultimately, from form inputs on the client. In this case, instead of value, you specify the name of the parameter whose value is to be used:

```
<jsp:setProperty name="abean" property="prop1" param="param1" />
```

If the name of the bean property is the same as the name of the request parameter, then you don't have to specify the parameter name. If you want all request parameters copied to bean properties of the same name, you code `property="*"`, as in the first example we looked at, above.

The Include Action

Here's an example that illustrates the `include` action. The action is performed only if the condition in the preceding scriptlet holds true:

```
<% }else if("change".equals(select)){ %>
    We have changed <%= bbean.getNumberAffected() %> rows.
    <%@ include file="continue.jsp" %>
<% }else if("msgsent".equals(select)){ %>
...
```

Two Include Mechanisms

Including material from other files is an important tool for breaking up JSP pages into manageable components. There are two mechanisms for inclusion, a directive and an action. Their properties are:

What	Syntax	Phase	Parsed?
directive	`<%@ include file=... %>`	translation-time	yes
action	`<jsp:include page=... />`	request-time	no

We have found the include directive very useful in structuring JSP applications, as you will see in the example later in this chapter.

We hope you agree that, with the possible exception of synchronization issues, the syntax and semantics of JSP pages are quite clear and intuitive. (This does not mean that the current generation of JSP engines always behave in clear and intuitive ways.) The main challenge, as we said in the introduction, is in large-scale structuring of JSP applications. This is what we are going to work on now. In the next section we present two possible approaches, then illustrate one of them in a larger example application.

Design Considerations

JSP syntax is compact and uses the familiar format of tags and attributes, so learning JSP on the level of syntactic correctness is easy. The challenge is to find good ways of using JSPs in the overall system: the technology is very young and good practices have not yet been established. Paradoxically, the versatility of JSPs may hinder, rather than promote, good system design. There is a natural temptation to use a JSP page simultaneously as a servlet, a backend processor, and a template file for output, simply because you can. This can easily result in monolithic JSP pages that are difficult to understand, debug and maintain.

One evidently correct practice is to unload the backend processing part to Java beans, minimizing the amount of code fragments (`scriptlets`) in the page. Going a step further, it is also possible to separate the servlet functionality from the template file functionality, using the JSP page only as an output template. This idea has been very clearly articulated by Craig McClanahan, a frequent contributor to the JSP-INTEREST list; some of his contributions end up as entries in the JSP FAQ at `http://www.esperanto.org.nz/jsp/`. We advise you to have a look at it.

Conversations with the Client

We are, however, interested in the opportunities offered by the JSP page that functions both as a servlet and an output template. In particular, this combination allows for a very compact and elegant conversation between the JSP page and the client. The idea is that a JSP page functioning as a servlet uses `include` directives to include output template pages, while each output template page contains a form whose `ACTION` attribute is the JSP page functioning as a servlet.

Here is how it works in the Birthday application. The main page of the application, `Birthday.jsp`, uses a bean, `BirthdayBean`, whose properties include `bbcmd` and `jspcmd`:

```
String bbcmd=null; //BirthdayBeanCommand from JSP specifies action
        // login; dodb; send; logout;
String jspcmd=null; // JSPCommand from BirthdayBean specifies display
        // birthdaylist; list; msgsent; change; error; logout
```

`Birthday.jsp`, at some point, calls the `doCommand()` method of the bean, whose operation depends on the value of `bbcmd`. The `doCommand()` method sets the `jspcmd` property. That property determines which of several supporting JSP files gets included in the response page. If the `jspcmd` is not `logout` and does not result in an error, then the response includes a form, which includes a select element whose name is `bbccd`. That value of that select element becomes the value of the `bbcmd` property of the bean. We've come full circle and are ready to call `doCommand()` again:

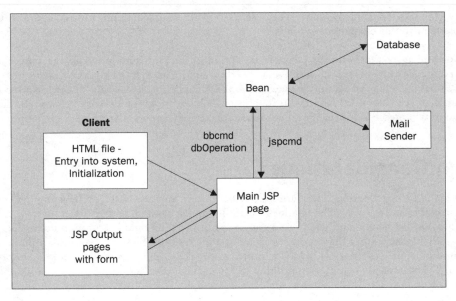

At this point, you might be interested in what the Birthday application does with all of this. Given the preceding content of the book, it shouldn't be surprising that it accesses a database and makes the results available to human users. The new element (apart from JSP pages and beans) is that the results are made available via electronic mail.

Birthday Announcements with JSP and JavaMail

This is a toy application that has, we believe, the potential to get grown-ups interested. Suppose you have a group of people working together, and you want to build a spirit of community among them. One way to do that is to make sure that if today is someone's birthday then you let everyone know and send congratulations via email. So, you put together a table in your database that has everyone's name, birthday and email address. Every morning a friendly demon submits a form, and if there is a birthday on that day, everybody gets an email. (As you well know, it's very easy to overdo these things, and get everybody extremely annoyed at you for too much friendly email.)

The entry point to the application is `birthdays.htm`. It sets up the initial parameters, two of them in hidden input elements: `bbcmd` is set to `login` and `dbOperation` to `BIRTHDAYLIST`. Visible inputs can be used to customize the application in much the same way an initialization file is used in the `QShell` application we developed in the first chapters of the book. This is what `birthdays.htm` looks like:

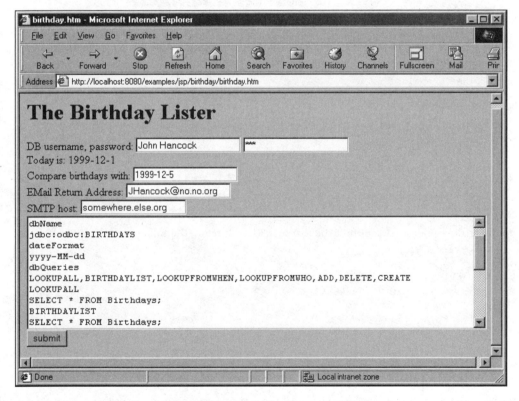

After the initial form gets submitted, control is passed to the main JSP page, `birthdays.jsp`. It creates the `BirthdayBean` and sets its properties. One of those properties is `bbcmd`. That property determines what the bean will do. If the command is `sendMail`, the bean will send email, using the parameters set by the user in the form on the client. If the command is `dbOperation`, the bean will create a `DBHandler` object (unless it has already been created) and run the `dbOperation`. (Do you still remember DBHandler? That's the guy that handles all the interactions with the database using internal `Query` objects. It's still with us, after all these chapters, and is as useable out of a bean as it is out of a servlet.)

Suppose the user has submitted a database query asking for December 8 birthdays. The screen shot below shows the results returned by the database, and the email parameters set by the user:

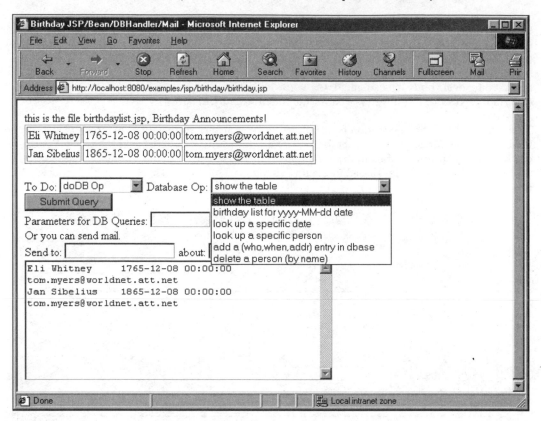

If the user now selects and submits the `sendMail` command, the following email will be sent:

```
X-POP3-Rcpt: sasha@cs
Return-Path: <tomm@tommyers.colgate.edu>
Date: Thu, 28 Oct 99 09:05:43 -0400
From: tomm@tommyers.colgate.edu
To: sasha@cs.colgate.edu
Subject: December 8 Birthdays

Eli Whitney     1765-12-08 00:00:00     tom.myers@worldnet.att.net
Jan Sibelius    1865-12-08 00:00:00     tom.myers@worldnet.att.net
```

The bean also sets its `jspcmd` property, and the rest of the application operates in a circle described in the preceding section. The `jspcmd` property determines the page returned to the user. If it is not an error or logout, then the page returned to the user contains a form; the user can specify the command to perform and submit the form, and so on. Our task now is to understand how it all works together. We will start with the client, move on to the JSP page, visit the bean, and follow its database and email connections. As we meander through the application, the following bean-centric diagram, showing the bean's inputs and outputs, may be useful in keeping track of where we are in the overall scheme of things:

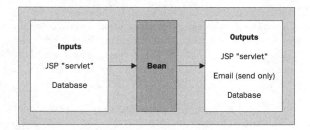

Entry Point: birthday.htm

The entry point to the system is an HTML file that consists entirely of a single form.

```
<html><head><title>birthday.htm</title></head><body bgcolor="lightblue">
<h1>The Birthday Lister</h1>
<form name=theForm type=POST action="birthday.jsp">
```

Within that form, there are the following divisions:

- ❑ two hidden inputs for bbcmd and dbOperation
- ❑ two inputs for the database: username and password
- ❑ a simple piece of JavaScript code to generate an input for Date with the value of the current date
- ❑ two inputs for sending mail: return address and SMTP host
- ❑ a textarea element with initialization data, in the same format as a QShell initialization file

The first of these divisions have already been mentioned; the second is completely trivial:

```
<input type=hidden name="bbcmd" value="login">
<input type=hidden name="dbOperation" value="BIRTHDAYLIST">
DB username, password:
<input type=text name="dbUser" value="name"><br>
<input type=password name="dbPwd" value="pwd">
```

The JavaScript code is a sequence of document.write() statements, to make it cross-browser. It creates a Date object that holds the current date and converts it to String in the yyyy-mm-dd format that Java likes:

```
<script>
    function dw(x){document.write(x);}
    var today=new Date();
    var todayStr=today.getFullYear()+"-"+
            (1+today.getMonth())+"-"+
            today.getDate();
    dw(todayStr);
    dw("<br>Compare birthdays with: ");
    dw("<input type=text name=when value=\"");
    dw(todayStr);
    dw("\">");
</script>
```

The inputs having to do with e-mail are, in a sense, self-explanatory; the way they work in JavaMail code will be discussed later. These two inputs create a great opportunity for mischief: imagine an immature and mean-spirited hacker writing a little program that submits the form 100 times using the e-mail of somebody they hate and 20 different SMTP servers. There are, and probably there will always be people like that among us, so in any kind of serious application, a JSP page that receives such a form should be password-protected.

Finally, the initial content of the textarea element contains initialization data in the familiar format. One new entry there is `dateFormat` so users can specify their own input date format, if necessary. (The output format will not be affected: it will always be JDBC "escape format", as defined in `java.text.SimpleTextFormat`.)

```
<br>EMail Return Address: <input type=text name=retaddr value="">
<br>SMTP host: <input type=text name=smtphost value="cs.colgate.edu">
<br>
<textarea name="initdefs" rows="5" cols="40">
dbDriver
sun.jdbc.odbc.JdbcOdbcDriver
dbName
jdbc:odbc:BIRTHDAYS
dateFormat
yyyy-MM-dd
dbQueries
LOOKUPALL,BIRTHDAYLIST,LOOKUPFROMWHEN,LOOKUPFROMWHO,ADD,DELETE,CREATE
...
CREATE
CREATE TABLE Birthdays(Who VARCHAR, When DATE, Addr VARCHAR);
</textarea>
<input TYPE=submit name="submit" value="submit">
</form></body></html>
```

The main thing to remember about all these input elements is that our `BirthdayBean` has properties with identical names, and at some point the main JSP page will say:

```
<jsp:setProperty name="bbean" property="*" />
```

As we discussed above, if you want all request parameters copied to bean properties of the same name, you code it as `property="*"`.

The Main JSP page: birthday.jsp

You have already seen the beginning of `birthday.jsp`:

```
<html>
<head>
<title>Birthday JSP/Bean/DBHandler/Mail</title>
</head>
<body>

<%@ page import="java.util.*, MyNa.utils.*" errorPage="errorpage.jsp" %>
<jsp:useBean id="bbean" scope="session" class="birthday.BirthdayBean" />
<jsp:setProperty name="bbean" property="*" />
```

Since `birthday.jsp` is our main servlet for the application, we unload all processing to the bean, in order to keep the structure of the servlet clear. In particular:

❑ we process the request in the bean, by calling its public `processRequest()` method

❑ we have the bean process the current command, on the basis of the `docmd` property set in the user input

❑ we produce output based on the value of the `jspcmd` property set by the bean. If the required output is more than a couple of lines long, we put it into an include file

Since much of `birthday.jsp` code has already been discussed, we show the rest of it in one piece:

```jsp
<% bbean.processRequest(request); %>
<%
    bbean.doCommand(); // usually, this is all we need after setting properties
    String msgtext="";  // accumulate messages here, if needed.
    String select=bbean.getJspcmd();

    if("logout".equals(select))
    {
%>
Goodbye, come again soon.
<%
    }
    else if("error".equals(select))
    {
%>
Something went wrong: <%= bbean.getErrorString() %>
Click your back button and try again, or tell us.
<%
    }
        else if("change".equals(select))
    {
%>
    We changed <%= bbean.getNumberAffected() %> rows.
    <%@ include file="continue.jsp" %>
<%
    }
    else if("msgsent".equals(select))
    {
%>
    Congratulations, you sent a message.
<%@ include file="continue.jsp" %>
<%
    }
    else if("list".equals(select)){ %>
    <%@ include file="listall.jsp" %>
<%
    }
```

```
          else if("birthdaylist".equals(select))
          {
%>
          <%@ include file="birthdaylist.jsp" %>
<%
          }
          else
          {
%>
          Unimplemented command [<%= select %>]; how did this happen?
<%
          }
%>
</body>
</html>
```

The possible values of `select` (i.e. of `jspcmd`) are: `logout`, `error`, `change`, `msgsent`, `listall` and `birthdaylist`. The difference between the last two is that `listall` lists the entire contents of the birthdays table in the database, while `birthdaylist` lists only the records matching the specified date. The corresponding output files both include the file `continue.jsp`. Let's take a look at the output.

Output Template Files

Apart from `error.jsp`, there are three output files, `birthdaylist.jsp`, `listall.jsp` and `continue.jsp`. The first two are very similar: they show a typical JSP loop to output a table. Here is `birthdaylist.jsp`:

```
this is the file birthdaylist.jsp,
<%
    String[][]rows=bbean.getResultTable();
    if(rows.length==0){
%>
    Sorry, nobody has a birthday coinciding with <%= bbean.getWhen() %>.
<%
    }
    else
    {
%>
        Birthday Announcements!<br>
        <table border="1">
<%
        for(int i=0;i<rows.length;i++)
        {
%>
    <tr>
<%
        String[] row=rows[i];
        for(int j=0;j<row.length;j++)
        {
            msgtext+=row[j]+"\t";
%>
            <td><%= row[j] %></td>
<%
        }
```

```
%>
    </tr>
    <% msgtext+="\n"; } %>
    </table>
<%
    }
%>

    <%@ include file="continue.jsp" %>
```

Continue.jsp

This file outputs a form whose ACTION is birthday.jsp, to complete the circle. It's almost completely HTML; the only JSP element is an expression, <%= msgtext %>, that we place in the textarea as a possibly helpful hint to the user. Otherwise, it's just an HTML form with two SELECT elements and several text inputs; the SELECT elements are for bbcmd and dbOperation. We precede the form with a simple JavaScript function to validate its input values before sending them to the server.

In outline, then, continue.jsp consists of two large sections:

```
<script>
    <!-- two Javascript functions, including onsub() -->
</script>
<form name="theForm" action="birthday.jsp"
        method="post" onsubmit="return onsub()">
    <!-- the form as described -->
</form>
```

We present the two sections in order.

Two Javascript Functions

The onsub() method checks two conditions: that the toaddr and subject inputs are filled, and that database queries have the right number of parameters. For each condition, there is a supporting function that checks it. In order to check the right number of arguments, we set up a JavaScript object argCount, which associates a query name with the number of arguments for that query. (As you may know, Javascript objects can be used as associative arrays. For more details, see our *JavaScript Objects*, Wrox Press 1998, ISBN: 1861001894.)

```
<script>
    var argCount={LOOKUPFROMWHEN:1,LOOKUPFROMWHO:1,ADD:3,DELETE:1};
    function onsub()
    {
        var theForm=window.document.theForm;// get reference to the form
        var theCmd=theForm.bbcmd.value;     // get the value of bbcmd
        if(theCmd=="logout")return true;    // if logout, submit the form
        if(theCmd=="send")
          return sendOk(theForm);// check sendOk condition
        return doDBOk(theForm);  // it's a db query:check doDBOk condition
    }
```

```
    function sendOk(theForm)
    {
        if(""==theForm.toaddr.value)
        {
            alert("must fill in toaddress");
            return false;
        }
        if(""==theForm.subject.value)
        {
            alert("must fill in subject");
            return false;
        }
        return true;
    }
    function doDBOk()
    {
        var theOp=theForm.dbOperation.value;
        var N=argCount[theOp]; // retrieve number of arguments
        if(!N)N=0; // if null, set it to 0
        theForm.ParameterMax.value=N;
        for(var i=1;i<=N;i++)
        {
            if(""==theForm["Parameter"+i].value)
            {
                alert("must fill in Parameter"+i);
                return false;
            }
        }
        if(theOp=="BIRTHDAYLIST") // param passed as "when"
            theForm.when.value=theForm.Parameter1.value;
        return true;
    }
</script>
```

The Form

And here is the form; its onsubmit attribute is a call on onSub(). As we said, the only JSP element in it (and the entire page) is an expression inside the text area:

```
<form name="theForm" action="birthday.jsp"
        method="post" onsubmit="return onsub()">
<input type=hidden name=ParameterMax value="0">
<input type=hidden name=when>

Select a BirthdayBean Command:
<select name=bbcmd size=1>
<option value="dodb" selected>doDB Op</option>
<option value="send">send message</option>
<option value="logout">logout</option>
</select>
<br>
```

```
Select a Database Op:
<select name=dbOperation size=1>
<option value="LOOKUPALL" selected>show the table</option>
<option value="BIRTHDAYLIST">birthday list for yyyy-MM-dd date</option>
<option value="LOOKUPFROMWHEN">look up a specific date</option>
<option value="LOOKUPFROMWHO">look up a specific person</option>
<option value="ADD">add a (who,when,addr) entry in dbase</option>
<option value="DELETE">delete a person (by name)</option>
</select>
<br>
<input type=submit>
<br>
Parameters for DB Queries:
<br><input type=text name=Parameter1 size=10 value="">
<br><input type=text name=Parameter2 size=10 value="">
<br><input type=text name=Parameter3 size=10 value="">
<br>
Or you can send mail. <br>
Send to: <input type=text name=toaddr value="" size=20><br.
about: <input type=text name=subject value="" size=20>
<br>
<textarea name=msgtext rows=10 cols=50>
<%= msgtext %>
</textarea></form>
```

This concludes `continue.jsp`. We have now seen all the inputs and outputs, and the entry point and the main JSP "servlet page". What we have not seen is the Java code that makes it all work. Time to open up the bean.

Inside the Bean: BirthdayBean.java

The bean works with the familiar components, `Env` and `DBHandler`, to do database access, and with new email components that are tucked away in `MyNa.utils.MiscMail.java`. For now, let's concentrate on the overall structure. We have, as usual:

- ❑ imports and declarations
- ❑ a null constructor, `getXXX()` and `setXXX()` methods
- ❑ `processRequest()` and `doCommand()` methods called by the JSP page
- ❑ "command methods": `doLogout()`, `sendMessage()` and `doDB()` (with `pruneResults()`)

We take them up in order.

Imports and Declarations

Imports are self-explanatory, but remember that `MyNa.utils.*` now includes `MiscMail`:

```
package birthday;

import javax.servlet.http.*;
import java.util.Vector;
import java.io.BufferedReader;
import java.io.StringReader;
import java.util.Enumeration;
import javax.mail.MessagingException;
import MyNa.utils.*;

public class BirthdayBean
{
    String bbcmd = null; //BirthdayBeanCommand from JSP specifies action
    String jspcmd = null; // JSPCommand from BBean specifies display

    // variables for databases: the fields of the table are WHO, WHEN and RETADDR
    String who = null;
    String when = null;
    String retaddr = null;

    // variables for mail connection
    String toaddr = null;
    String smtphost = null;
    String mailuser = null;
    String subject = null;
    String msgtext = null;

    // variables for Env and DBHandler; initdefs comes from client
    String initdefs = null;
    Env env = null;
    DBHandler dbh = null;

    // outputs
    String errorString = null;
    String[][] resultTable = null;
    String numberAffected = null;     // if query returns a number
```

The first two declarations, `bbcmd` and `jspcmd`, have been explained earlier.

Constructor, Getters and Setters

Most of this is fairly trivial code, but some of it sets `jspcmd`:

```
public BirthdayBean()
{
}

public void setBbcmd(String S)
{
    bbcmd = S;
}
```

```
public void setWhen(String S)
{
    if(null != S)
    {
        when = S;
    }
}

public void setRetaddr(String S)
{
    retaddr = S;
}

public void setToaddr(String S)
{
    toaddr = S;
}

public void setSmtphost(String S)
{
    smtphost = S;
}

public void setSubject(String S)
{
    subject = S;
}

public void setMsgtext(String S)
{
    msgtext = S;
}

public void setInitdefs(String S)
{
    initdefs = S;
}

// set methods that also set jspcmd
public void setNumberAffected(String S)
{
    jspcmd = "change";
    numberAffected = S;
}

public void setResultTable(String[][] S)
{
    jspcmd = "list";
    resultTable = S;
}

public void setErrorString(String S)
{
    errorString = S;
```

```
        if(null != S && S.length() > 0)
        {
            jspcmd = "error";
        }
    }


// get methods
public String getErrorString()
{
    return errorString;
}

public String getNumberAffected()
{
    return numberAffected;
}

public String getWhen()
{
    return when;     // to a new jsp page
}

public String[][] getResultTable()
{
    return resultTable;
}

public String getJspcmd()
{
    return jspcmd;
}

public Env getEnv()
{
    return env;
}

public boolean shouldDoDB()
{
    return "login".equalsIgnoreCase(bbcmd) || "dodb".equalsIgnoreCase(bbcmd);
}
```

processRequest() and doCommand()

What processRequest() does depends on the value of bbcmd. The possible values are:

- ❑ login (sent from the entry HTML page)
- ❑ dodb
- ❑ sendmsg
- ❑ and logout (sent from the continue.jsp page)

If the value of `bbcmd` is `sendmsg` or `logout` then the `processRequest()` method does nothing. With either of the first two options, the bean will have to do database access, either to establish a connection and a login (for "`login`"), or to run a query (for "`dodb`"). You will see from the second last line of the code above that `shouldDoDB()` returns exactly the boolean value of the disjunction (in English) "`bbcmd` equals '`login`' or `bbcmd` equals '`dodb`'".

So, in either of those two cases we have to process a new `Request`, which means re-initializing the `Env` that holds request information. This is what is done in the first part of the method: a new `Env` is created from `Request`, and information from `initdefs` is added, if it is not null. (It will be non-null only if we are processing the initial HTML file that has an `initdefs` textarea element.)

```
public void processRequest(HttpServletRequest request)
{
    try
    {
        if(shouldDoDB())
        {

            // set up env with Request and initdefs info
            try
            {
                env = new Env(request);
            }
            catch(java.lang.NullPointerException e)
            {
                setErrorString("null in Env init");
                return;
            }
            // end create Env from Request

            if(null == env)
            {
                setErrorString("can't initialize env from request");
            }

            else
            {
                if(null != initdefs)
                {
                    // add initdefs to Env
                    StringReader sr = new StringReader(initdefs);
                    BufferedReader brin = new BufferedReader(sr);
                    env.addBufferedReader(brin);
                }
                // end add initdefs to Env
            }

        }      // end shouldDoDB
```

If we are, indeed, doing the "login" command then we also have to establish a database connection and initialize queries, all of which is wrapped into a DBHandler object, created from the Env:

```
        try
        {
            if("login".equalsIgnoreCase(bbcmd))
            {
                // login to database
                dbh = new DBHandler(env);
            }
        }

        catch(java.lang.NullPointerException e)
        {
            setErrorString("null in DBHandler init");
            return;
        }   // end create DBHandler

    } // end try

    catch(ParseSubstException e)
    {
        setErrorString("bad initdefs" + e);
    }

    catch(Exception e)
    {
        setErrorString("dbhandler failure: " + e);
    }

}
```

The doCommand() method does not really do any commands itself, just dispatches the action to the right method:

```
public void doCommand()
{
    if("logout".equalsIgnoreCase(bbcmd))
    {
        doLogout();
    }
    else
    {
        if("send".equalsIgnoreCase(bbcmd))
        {
            sendMessage();
        }
    }
    else
    {
        if(shouldDoDB())
        {
            doDB();
        }
    }
```

```
        else
        {
            setErrorString("unrecognized command [" + bbcmd + "]");
        }
    }
```

These two methods are public and called from the outside by the JSP page. The rest are the bean's internal affairs.

Command Methods

The methods that do specific commands have one thing in common: they set the `jspcmd` variable, so the JSP page knows what to include for output. Otherwise, they each do their own tasks. The `doLogout()` method closes the `DBHandler`:

```
public void doLogout()
{
    jspcmd = "logout";
    try
    {
        if(dbh != null)
        {
            dbh.close();
        }
    }
    catch(java.sql.SQLException e)
    {
        setErrorString("query failure: " + e);
    }
}
```

Note that the `sendMessage()` method does a fairly sophisticated thing, but it is hidden in the static `sendMail()` method of our `MiscMail` utility class. The method takes five arguments, all of them strings: a mail host name (such as `"center.colgate.edu"`), and four components of the message: from, to, subject and body.

```
public void sendMessage()
{
    try
    {
        MiscMail.sendMail(smtphost, retaddr, toaddr, subject, msgtext);
        jspcmd = "msgsent";
    }
    catch(MessagingException e)
    {
        setErrorString("send failure: " + e);
    }
}
```

Finally, doDB() goes to the database and comes back either with an integer or a table of results, stored in the Env. It starts by clearing previous values, if any, then runs the query. For the BIRTHDAYLIST query, an additional pruning action is necessary, as explained below:

```
public void doDB()
{
    env.remove("NumberOfRowsAffected");
    env.remove("ResultTable");

    try
    {
        dbh.getQueryResult(env);
    }
    catch(java.sql.SQLException e)
    {
        setErrorString("query failure: " + e);
    }

    String n = env.getStr("NumberOfRowsAffected");
    if(null != n)
    {
        // an update query
        setNumberAffected(n);
        return;
    }

    setResultTable((String[][])env.get("ResultTable"));
    if("BIRTHDAYLIST".equalsIgnoreCase(env.getStr("dbOperation")))
    {
        pruneResults();
    }
}
```

Pruning the Results

In our Birthdays database, the "when" field is of Date data type, converted from String by DBHandler. Because of this, we cannot query on month and day in database-independent ways. (Database-dependent solutions are certainly available, e.g. the use of embedded Visual Basic in Access queries.) So, if the query is BIRTHDAYLIST, we return the entire table and have the bean prune it by pruneResults():

```
public void pruneResults()
{
    // "when" field is a String in yyyy-mm-dd format, e.g. 1999-03-25
    // we prune the result table so that only birthday matches survive.

    jspcmd = "birthdaylist";
```

```
        if(resultTable.length == 0)
        {
            return;
        }
        String monthDay = when.substring(4); // "-03-25 "
        Vector v = new Vector();

        for(int i = 0; i < resultTable.length; i++)
        {
            String S = resultTable[i][1]; // the "When" field;
            if(null == S)
            {
                continue;
            }
            if(S.indexOf(monthDay) != 4)
            {
                continue;
            }
            v.addElement(resultTable[i]);
        }

        resultTable = new String[v.size()][];
        for(int i = 0; i < v.size(); i++)
        {
            resultTable[i] = (String[])v.elementAt(i);
        }
    }

}                                               // end of BirthdayBean class
```

Obviously, this pruning solution can only work for small tables; for a table of unknown (and possibly huge) size, we would have to move the pruning up the food chain, either all the way to the database, or to the RowEnumeration process. In order to move the pruning to the database, we would split the Date field into three number fields, year, month and day, and query on month and day. Alternatively, we could prune the rows emitted from the ResultSet, by extending our RowEnumeration class to PrunedRowEnumeration:

```
public RowEnumeration pruneEnum(RowEnumeration re, String when)
       throws SQLException
{
    // when == "1999-03-25", march 25 1999, jdbc escape format;
    String monthDay = when.substring(4);    // "-03-25";
    return new PrunedRowEnumeration(re, "When", monthDay, 4);
}

public class PrunedRowEnumeration extends RowEnumeration
{
    String fieldName;
    String match;
    int offset;
    // we produce only those elements of re where fieldname
    // matches match beginning at offset.
```

```
    public PrunedRowEnumeration(RowEnumeration re, String fieldName,
        String S, int N) throws SQLException
{
    super();
    initFromRowEnumeration(re);
    this.fieldName = fieldName;
    this.match = S;
    this.offset = N;
}

public boolean hasMoreElements()
{
    boolean gotAnother = true;
    while((gotAnother = super.hasMoreElements()))
    {
        String val = ((Env)nextElement()).getStr(fieldName);
        if(val.substring(offset).startsWith(match))
        {
            continue;
        }
    }
    return gotAnother;
}
}
```

The JSP presentation code would then loop through a `RowEnumeration`, completely unaware that it was actually a `PrunedRowEnumeration`. Generalizations of this solution to include regular-expression matching and filtering are quite possible but outside the scope of this book.

From Here...

This concludes the Birthday application. Its main point is not the content of the commands it can carry out, but rather the overall structure: the main JSP page that acts as a servlet; a bean that carries out its commands and sets up a selector for output; included template JSP pages for output that contain a form whose action takes us back to the main JSP page. We will reproduce this structure, with more meaningful content, in the application of the next chapter.

You may feel a little disappointed that we have said nothing about how JavaMail works. Not to worry: the next application will use JavaMail in a more comprehensive way, and we'll show you all the details.

JSP vs. SUBST Mini-Language for Output Templates

Before we close this chapter, we would like to draw some comparisons between JSP pages and our `SUBST` mini-language. You probably have customers who could generate new `QShell` applications; in other words, they could copy and modify HTML or XML templates in some limited language like the `SUBST` mini-language we developed earlier, and they are comfortable with defining new database queries. It is not at all obvious that they will be able and willing to work with something like:

```
<% bbean.doCommand(); String msgtext="";
    String select=bbean.getJspcmd();
    if("logout".equals(select))
    {
%>

    Goodbye, come again soon.

<%
    }
    else if("error".equals(select))
    {
%>
```

Even if willing to give it a try (after all, you might just suggest that they change the text in between `%>` and `<%` marks) will they persevere after the first time that a typo evoked a Java compiler error message? This is an empirical question, and the answer can only come from experience with using JSP in products that are delivered to end users. In the meantime, we remain a little skeptical. JSP is great stuff for Java programmers. It is a big timesaver when you are developing servlets. It can be wonderful for joint projects involving non-programmers. However, it is an open question whether or not it is a good tool for the development of specialized languages in which non-programmers can express their specialized knowledge.

Conclusions

In this chapter, we have learned JSP: JavaServer Pages. We have looked at their syntax and discussed the meaning of their basic constructs. The point we have emphasized throughout is that they are construction material of outstanding flexibility and versatility that requires a conscious design effort in order to be put to good use. Two uses we have emphasized are: the main servlet of the application, and output template files. We strongly recommend against using JSP pages as containers for back-end code.

In terms of the Model-View-Controller pattern, think of JSP as presentation logic, ignorant (as much as possible) of the underlying model but carrying all of the view information and some of the controller. As a project grows, we suggest that the bean takes the role of control, the model is confined to the classes controlled by the bean, and JSP is purely view, including view of the controller.

One component of the design that is conspicuously absent from this chapter is XML. We have shown how a JSP file can be a valid XML file (and thus produced and validated by an XML editor), but the relationship between JSP and XML is much deeper than that, we believe. One major use of JSPs is to manage an associated JavaBean (or several beans). The beans themselves can serve as processors of incoming and outgoing streams of information. XML, as you know, is ideally suited for encoding streams of information, and Java has the best tools for processing XML. Putting the two together, it is natural to organize an application as a network of JSP pages and associated beans that produce and consume XML streams. The initial source of an XML stream may be a database or an email store or anything else, as long as it is XML. This is what we will do in the next chapter.

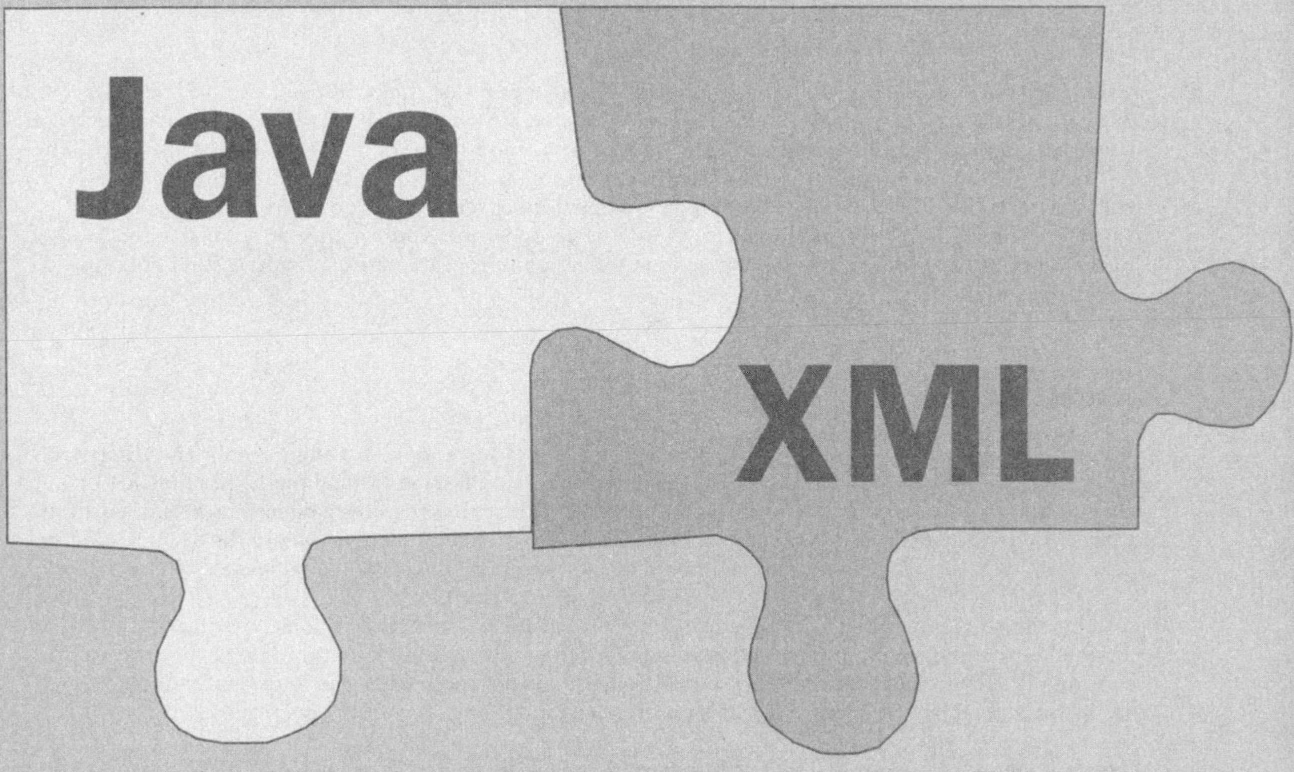
Java
XML

Towards a Many-Legged System: Generic Tools

Introduction

In the Introduction chapter, we spoke of an N-topus, "an octopus-like creature with N legs and K heads, K <= N. Each head would be either an entry point to the application or a data transformer, and each leg would carry XML-encoded data from one transforming head to another. Some transformers would use XSLT, and others would use XML parsers and custom-designed beans. The entire structure would be dynamically configured by XML files, produced by competent users who are not programmers under the watchful eye of a validating parser." We are not going to produce a complete N-topus in this book, but, in this chapter and the next we will build a substantial application that will come pretty close.

In this chapter and the next, we will build a large application that brings together several earlier topics from the book:

- ❏   JSP servlets
- ❏   relational databases
- ❏   JavaMail
- ❏   `RowSequence` **and** `Env`
- ❏   XML

Our emphasis is still on architectural questions: how does one build systems out of such components, and how do the components interact? However, the scale of our architectural efforts will be considerably larger in these two chapters than in the preceding ones because of the extra complexity involved in linking these separate technologies together.

Apart from a brief overview of JavaMail, we will not be introducing any new technologies or specifications. The main goal here is to develop an ability to think in terms of abstract and general flows of information. Consider, for example, the similarity between database rows in a table and email messages in an email folder. A database row can be defined as a collection of fields, each with a data type and a value. An email message can be thought of as such a row, with fields like "sender", "subject", "content", and so on.

Our goal is to create an application which saves and sends email without actually knowing whether the server it talks to is a conventional email server (POP3 or IMAP), or a database (accessed via a JDBC driver). To achieve this result, we consider both a database table and an email folder to be an abstract sequence of rows, so that mail folders and database tables become equivalent sources of row sequences. Whatever the nature of the source, we can open and close it, search it repeatedly, and delete items as needed. We should also be able to output the contents of our sources as new data tables or XML files or as email.

When you define abstract structures that have to do concrete things (like sending email), the main question is: "At what point, and how, does the abstract structure take a concrete form?" We'll define a fairly ambitious configuration mechanism that uses arbitrarily-nested XML files to instantiate and configure a collection of beans that are used by the application's main JSP page. The application's concrete functionality depends on which beans get instantiated; a bean can be instantiated within this framework as long as it implements our XmlConfig interface. As usual, configuration parameters defined by an XML file on the server can be overridden by user input from an HTML form.

In outline, this chapter will proceed as follows:

- ❑ An overview of the "many-legged" system
- ❑ The RowSeq class and its derivatives
- ❑ RowViewSource, an editable view of RowSeqs
- ❑ The new, recursive, Env that can contain other Envs
- ❑ The XML configuration subsystem

The next chapter will complete the application by going over

- ❑ Two smaller beans
- ❑ The ViewSource beans
- ❑ The main bean and the main JSP page
- ❑ The entry points and the JSP pages for output

Overview of the Application

The structure of the XmlMail application that we will develop in this chapter is similar to that of the Birthdays application we developed in the last chapter. A user logs in from a web browser and submits some initialization parameters for the back end. The back end consists of, as before, a JSP page acting as the main servlet, a number of JSP pages for output, and a bean that is both instantiated and initialized by the servlet page. The bean and the servlet repeatedly cycle through the same conversation:

- ❑ a bean command goes from the servlet to the bean

- ❑ the bean executes the command and sets up the jspcmd for the servlet

- ❑ the servlet selects an output page to include in output on the basis of jspcmd

- ❑ this include page contains a form whose ACTION is the main JSP servlet

There are two new features in this picture, compared to the Birthdays application.

One is that the bean first gets initialized from an XML initialization file. The file has a DTD and can be validated, thus reducing, if not eliminating, the possibility of initialization errors. The settings coming from the XML file can be overwritten by the form input, so we have the same kind of layered initialization as in QShell. In support of bean-configuration-by-XML, we have upgraded the Env class to provide a "recursive Env" that can contain subEnvs.

The second departure from the preceding chapter is that the bean is both capable of doing much more and less aware of what it is doing. This is because the bean itself is generic and delegates all the work to any number of sub-beans (of which there are four in this instance). We should make it clear that sub-beans are not sub-classes or inner classes of the main bean but free-standing independent classes. The relationship between them and the main bean is that of one-directional collaboration: the main bean instantiates its sub-beans and uses their services. If a sub-bean has sub-beans of its own, they will stand in the same relationship to their "parent" bean. The tree structure of beans and sub-beans is established by that relationship of one-directional collaboration.

The sub-beans are highly specialized code units that perform pre-defined tasks; there is no overlap between the sub-beans in the work that they do:

- ❑ the mailSource sub-bean sends material into the (parent) bean from a mail store

- ❑ the databaseSource sub-bean sends material into the (parent) bean from a database

- ❑ the msgSender sub-bean sends emails

- ❑ the msgComposer sub-bean aids in the writing of email messages

Each sub-bean must then be coded with the following knowledge:

- ❑ mailSource: protocols for email storage and retrieval (e.g. POP3, IMAP4)

- ❑ databaseSource: JDBC, tables and PreparedStatements

- ❑ msgSender: SMTP protocol for sending email

- ❑ msgComposer: messages, message headers and message parts

This information is illustrated diagrammatically below:

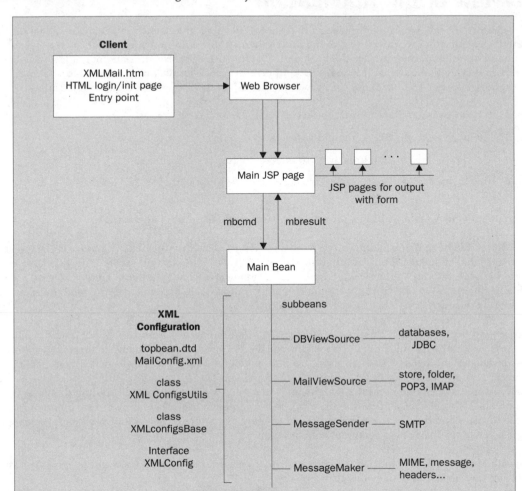

As you can see from looking at the above diagram, this is a larger application than the earlier ones, with over a thousand lines of code. It is important that, as it unfolds, we keep track of where we are in it. Fortunately, it is easy to carve it up into four fairly independent subsystems:

❑ The first subsystem is XML-based configuration.

❑ The second subsystem is the new RowSeq class and its derivatives, one of which, DBRowSequence, is a replacement for the old RowSequence that was defined in Chapter 2.

❑ The third subsystem consists of the main bean and its four sub-beans. Each bean can be configured from an XML file and therefore implements the XmlConfig interface. In addition, those sub-beans that serve as views of data sources implement the RowViewSource interface and contain a RowSeq object.

❑   Finally, the fourth subsystem is the three-tier structure from the preceding chapter, consisting of the entry page, the main JSP page, output template pages, and the information channels between the main JSP page and the main bean.

In the remainder of this *Overview* section we will briefly characterize the new subsystems of this chapter and the JavaMail API. In the sections that follow, we will look at each subsystem in detail, before assembling them all together.

Try it Out

Right now, the best way to proceed may be to try the application and see what it can do. (Remember that all the source code can be downloaded from the books web site at `http://www.wrox.com`.) You might want to perhaps send a test message to yourself or your friends, just to get a feel for it.

We provide three slightly different versions of the entry page to try out different aspects of the application; however, the underlying form that submits the data is the same in each case. First, try `xmlMail.htm` in the `xmlMail` directory. It shows fields for the parameters of a simple mailer, filled in with suggestive but not-quite-real names. (The configuration file is real, though, and has defaults that will be respected for any fields left empty.)

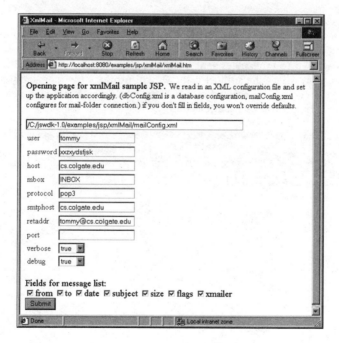

Simply type in the actual user, password, host, folder and so forth. Remember that INBOX is the only folder supported by the JavaMail POP3 provider. The default port will normally be fine. This will produce something like:

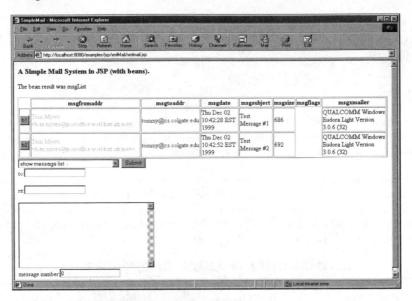

This screen shot shows two test messages sent from one address to another, and one advertisement. By clicking on the b1 button, where the subject is mm2, will produce the message fields including content mm2 body; note that the content is echoed into the textarea element for message composition (these are the fields whose names begin with messageMaker_).

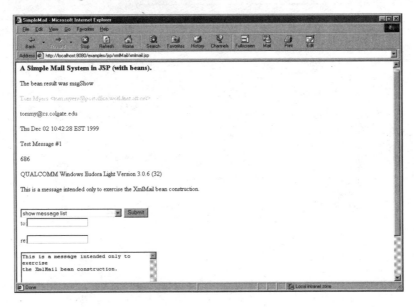

Now choose a command from a simple `<select>` menu element: delete message:

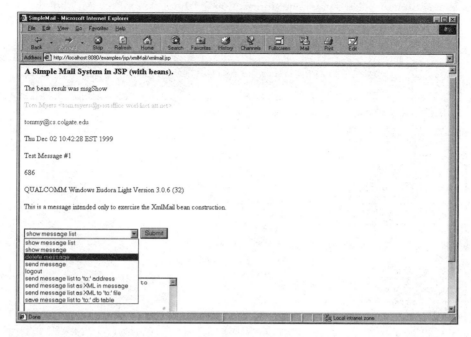

Submit the command, and the message is marked for deletion (which will take effect when you logout). Other commands are:

- ❑ show the list as we've already seen it
- ❑ show the message
- ❑ send a message (using the "to" and "re" fields we just saw, and the textarea element as content)
- ❑ logout

The extended command list shows the contents of the "to" field:

- ❑ it can be an address to which we forward all the email, or
- ❑ it can, in effect, be a table name in the now-familiar syntax of the Xml2DBTables system (`dbdata.dtd`)

The resulting XML, a stored representation of the message list as a database table, can be

- ❑ placed into the message body itself as a single message, or
- ❑ can be saved as a file, or
- ❑ can be sent directly to a database

Next connect to `xmlMailDB.htm`, and you will see the database configuration. The return address and SMTP host are still mail-related (these are information for the `MessageSender`) but the rest are database parameters:

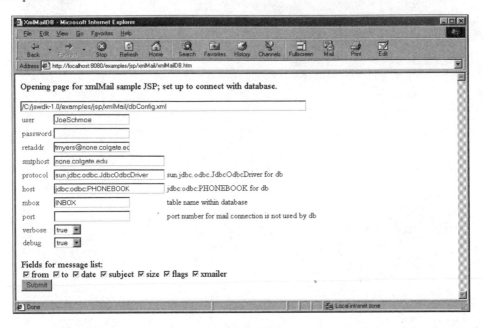

The remaining screens are identical, because the top level program which generates them is the same; it doesn't know what's going on underneath. You can do either set of functions from the same generic page, `xmlMailDefault.htm`:

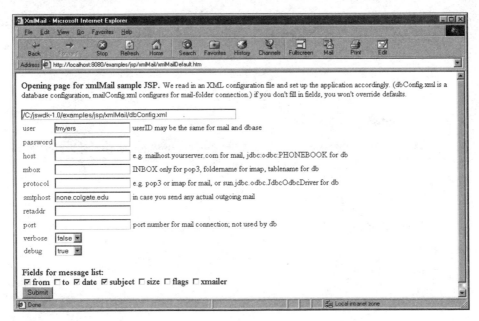

The XML-Configuration Subsystem

This subsystem consists of an interface, called `XmlConfig`, and two classes, `XmlConfigUtils` and `XmlConfigBase`:

❑ `XmlConfigUtils` provides a collection of static methods that help in implementing `XmlConfig`: the methods do the actual work of parsing the XML file, instantiating the beans, and exchanging data between DOM trees and `Envs`.

❑ `XmlConfigBase` provides a minimal default implementation of `XmlConfig`: if your beans don't have to extend some other class, they can simply extend `XmlConfigBase` rather than implement `XmlConfig` directly.

Sequences and Data Sources

As the bottom part of the diagram below indicates, `MailViewSource` and `DBViewSource` both implement the `RowViewSource` interface. Among other methods, `RowViewSource` declares `getRowList()`, a method that returns an object of the abstract `RowSeq` class. However, abstract classes don't have instances, so each implementation must return an object of a class that extends `RowSeq`. In `MailViewSource`, `getRowList()` returns `MailSequence`; in `DBViewSource`, it returns `DBRowSequence`. Both `MailSequence` and `DBRowSequence` extend the abstract `RowSeq` class.

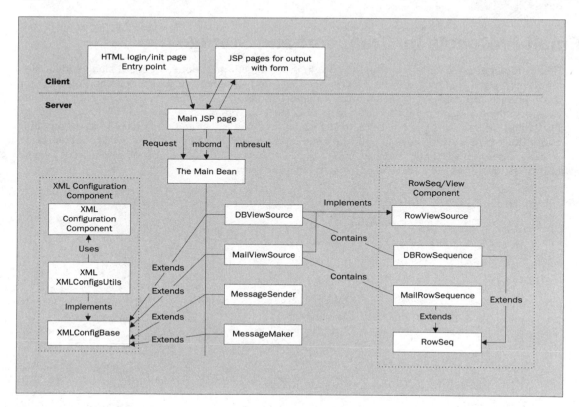

One thing to notice here is that the good old `RowSequence` class that's been with us since Chapter 2 is now gone. It has been divided up between `RowSeq`, which is common to all sources of row sequences, and `DBRowSequence`, which is more focused and specialized on databases. So, we'll have to revisit the subject of lazy evaluation of a sequence of rows, each represented by an `Env` object – especially since the `Env` class has also had a facelift in order to be able to cope with XML inputs and bean initialization.

Notice also that the method that returns a `RowSeq` object is called `getRowList()`, not `getRowSeq()`. This is to suggest that the classes that implement `RowViewSource` contain and manage something that is not a lazily-evaluated sequence, but rather a finite list that represents a limited view of such a sequence. The sequence itself (a `ResultSet` from a database or a collection of messages from an email store) may be large and unwieldy; the object returned by `getRowList()` is all contained in memory, and we can reset it, delete from it, and, if enough information is provided, add to it. Think of it as a live view of a database table that allows us to edit the original in a limited way.

The Beans and the JavaMail API

The bean-sub-beans component can be further subdivided according to the services a sub-bean performs. The database sub-bean stands separate: it extends the `DBHandler` class and knows nothing about email. The other three sub-beans use different parts of JavaMail, corresponding to the different components of an email system and the different protocols they implement.

We place an overview of JavaMail right here but you can skip it now and return when we get to the beans.

Email Protocols for Transport and Storage

Electronic mail is a client-server application: in order to get things done, an email client connects to an email server and requests services. The services fall into two broad categories: send and receive or, in more precise and commonly used terms, **Transport** and **Store**. There are several protocols in either category; the most common, and implemented in the JavaMail package, are SMTP for `Transport`, and POP3 and IMAP4 for `Store`. The big claim about JavaMail is that you don't have to know anything about those protocols in order to build JavaMail applications, and your authors are proof that this claim is indeed true. This is a major achievement, and rests on a well-designed abstraction layer of Java classes hiding the details of the underlying protocols from the user:

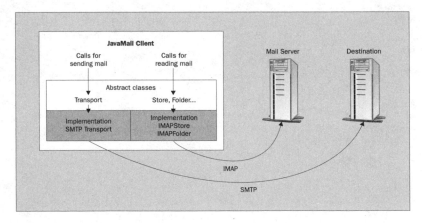

As the diagram above shows, the abstract layer contains Java classes that encapsulate the functionality of the protocols. The implementation of those classes can change without affecting any applications that use JavaMail. In fact, in transition from 1.0 to 1.1, the implementation of the two key classes, `Transport` and `Store`, changed rather drastically (both became subclasses of an abstract `Service` class) without affecting the use of the classes themselves or any of their subclasses defined in specific applications.

The Structure of JavaMail

JavaMail is large: it consists of four substantial packages, with many interfaces and classes in them. The most important abstract classes are (quoted from the *JavaMail Guide for Service Providers*, August 1998):

❑ **Message**: Abstract class that represents an electronic mail message. JavaMail implements the RFC822 and MIME Internet messaging standards. The `MimeMessage` class extends `Message` to represent a MIME-style email message.

❑ **Store**: Abstract class that represents a database of messages maintained by a mail server and grouped by owner. A `Store` uses a particular access protocol.

❑ **Folder**: Abstract class that provides a way of hierarchically organizing messages. Folders can contain messages and other folders. A mail server provides each user with a default folder, and users can typically create and fill subfolders.

❑ **Transport**: Abstract class that represents a specific transport protocol. A `Transport` object uses a particular transport protocol to send a message.

Another important class is `Session`, whose instance is used to manage the configuration options and user authentication information. It is from a `Session` object that an application obtains its instances of `Transport` and `Store`.

Starting a Session

Here is how the system starts up:

❑ One of the options of the `doCommand()` method of the main bean is "login"

❑ In response, the bean calls its `doLogin()` method

❑ `doLogin()` calls `initBeanTree()`

❑ `initBeanTree()` creates the sub-beans, including `MessageSender`

❑ `initBeanTree()` then calls its `startSession()` method to create a session

```
public void startSession()
{
    // a method of MessageSender bean
    Properties props = System.getProperties();
    props.put("mail.smtp.host", getSmtphost());
    session = Session.getDefaultInstance(props, null);
    session.setDebug(debug);
}
```

Note the role of `System` properties here: JavaMail expects that an applications that uses its APIs will set the values of some system environment properties, especially:

❏ `mail.store.protocol`

❏ `mail.transport.protocol`

❏ `mail.host`

❏ `mail.user`

❏ `mail.from`

(In our application, these properties are set from bean properties that are themselves set from data in the XML configuration file and can be modified from the input form.) The code of `startSession()` shows a typical way system environment properties are manipulated in a Java program – by using static methods of the `System` class and get/put methods of the `Properties` class. (The `Properties` class extends `Hashtable`.)

Appendix A of the JavaMail specification (see `http://java.sun.com/products/ javamail/`) lists all the system properties that are used by its APIs. We will see this code again in action when we get to see the beans in detail.

RowSeq and its Derivatives

`RowSeq` is a new abstract class that defines much of the functionality of the "sequence of rows" abstract data structure. The essential features of a sequence of rows are:

❏ It is a lazily-evaluated sequence that provides access to its elements only through these two methods: `next()` and `getRow()`.

❏ The elements of the sequence are `Env` objects each of which is a mapping from field names to field values. In addition, each field has an associated data type.

Although abstract, the class has quite a bit of substance to it: the objects it constructs know how to write themselves to a database, an XML file, a mail message or simply to a `Writer`. At this level, however, they don't know what's being written. `RowSeq` manages sequences, but it does not know what they are sequences of. For an actual construction we need a concrete class, `DBRowSequence` or `MailSequence`. Think of the abstract class as providing a pipeline, while the concrete classes provide the stuff that flows through it.

There are also two "general purpose" derived classes: `FilterRowSeq` that filters a row sequence by applying a predicate to each row, and `MapRowSeq` that maps a function over a row sequence.

All these classes rely heavily on the `Env` class in which we had to develop some new functionality in order to cope with all the new demands placed on it. After we show `RowSeq` and its descendants, we will go over the new functionality of `Env`; in the meantime, please suspend your disbelief when you see `Env` doing surprising things.

RowSeq

RowSeq consists of:

- imports, declarations and constructors
- initialization routines
- output methods

We take them up in order.

Imports, Declarations and Constructors

RowSeq imports packages for JDBC and JavaMail as well as MyNa.utils. Its variables support the Row abstraction:

```
import java.util.*;
import java.io.*;
import java.sql.*;             // for database access

import javax.mail.*;          // JavaMail
import javax.mail.internet.*;  // JavaMail
import javax.activation.*;     // for JavaMail

import MyNa.utils.*;

public abstract class RowSeq
{
    // leaves the nextElement() method for subclass implementation,
    // because only a subclass will know what an element (row) contains.
    Env theEnv;
    String [] theColumnLabels;  // {"Name","Birthdate","LifeStory"...}
    String [] theColumnTypes;   // {"VARCHAR","DATE","LONGVARCHAR"...}
    String [] theColumnValues;  // {"JoeSchmoe","9/9/99","I was born ..."..}
    String [] theFieldValueNum; // {"FieldValue1","FieldValue2",...}

    int theNumberOfColumns;
```

This implementation of the row abstraction is deliberately redundant, in that a row is represented both by arrays of strings and in the Env; moreover, references to those arrays of strings are also stored in the Env. The payoff is that we can refer to the value in the second field of the current row as any one of the following:

```
theColumnValues[1]
theEnv.getStr("FieldValue2")
theEnv.getStr(theFieldValueNum[1])
theEnv.getStrSeq("FieldValue")[1]  // getStrSeq() retrieves an array of strings
```

The following *equalities* also hold:

```
theEnv.getStr(theColumnLabels[i]) == theColumnValues[i]
theEnv.getStr("FieldName1") == theColumnLabels[0],
. . . and so on
```

We could prune the implementation making it slightly more efficient, but the gains would be minuscule compared to the main expense of retrieving the next element of the sequence.

The constructor takes an `Env` object with all the required information in it:

```
public RowSeq (Env seqInfo) throws Exception
{
    theEnv = seqInfo;
    if( !findStrSeqs(false) )
    {
        return;
    }
    setInitEnv();
}

public RowSeq()throws Exception
{
    this(new Env());
}
```

(There are also all the requisite `getXXX()` and `setXXX()` methods but we are not reproducing them here.) As you can see, the real work of initializing an object is relegated to `findStringSeqs()` and `setInitEnv()`.

Initialization Routines

The `findStrSeqs()` method tries to retrieve `columnLabels` and `columnTypes` from the `Env`. In case of failure, it consults the value of the `mustWork` flag: if true, the method throws an exception; otherwise, it returns false. In the constructor, this method is called with the `mustWork` flag set to false, so the method always returns a boolean value:

```
public boolean findStrSeqs(boolean mustWork)throws Exception
{

    String[] colL = theEnv.getStrSeq("columnLabels");
    String[] colT = theEnv.getStrSeq("columnTypes");

    if(null != colL)
    {
        theColumnLabels = colL;
    }

    if(null == theColumnLabels)
    {
        if(mustWork)
        {
            throw new Exception("missing columnLabels");
        }
        else
        {
            return false;
        }
```

```
    }

    if(null != colT)
    {
        theColumnTypes = colT;
    }

    if(null == theColumnTypes)
    {
      if(mustWork)
      {
          throw new Exception("missing columnTypes");
      }
      else
      {
          return false;
      }
    }

    return true;

}
```

If `findStrSeqs()` returns true, we call `setInitEnv()` which sets the values of the remaining variables, and then copies the values from the (successfully found) string arrays to the `Env`. This is the redundancy we mentioned earlier, but it makes it possible to fold all the information about a `RowSeq` into its `Env`:

```
public void setInitEnv() throws Exception
{
    // call with columnLabels,columnTypes found

    if(null == theEnv)
    {
        throw new Exception("null Environment in RowSeq.setInitEnv");
    }

    findStrSeqs(true);

    theNumberOfColumns = theColumnLabels.length;
    theColumnValues = new String[theNumberOfColumns];

    theEnv.put("NumberOfColumns", "" + theNumberOfColumns);
    theEnv.put("FieldName", theColumnLabels);
    theEnv.put("FieldType", theColumnTypes);
    theEnv.put("FieldValue", theColumnValues);

    theFieldValueNum = new String[theNumberOfColumns];

    for(int i = 1; i <= theNumberOfColumns; i++)
    {
        theEnv.put("FieldName" + i, theColumnLabels[i-1]);
        theFieldValueNum[i-1] = "FieldValue" + i;
    }

}
```

In addition to initializations from an Env, there is also the equivalent of a copy constructor called shallowClone() that initializes one RowSeq from another. A reference to the argument RowSeq is stored as a local variable so we can retrieve its elements as needed; in addition, references to string arrays are also copied. Note that the copy is "shallow" and therefore shares structure: the original and the copy share a reference to a lazily-evaluated sequence, and a call on next() in one of them advances the sequence for both:

```
public void shallowClone(RowSeq re)
{
    theEnv = (Env) re.next();
    theColumnLabels = re.getColumnLabels();
    theColumnTypes = re.getColumnTypes();
    theColumnValues = re.getColumnValues();
    theFieldValueNum = re.getFieldValueNum();
}
```

Output Methods

The output methods of RowSeq send their contents to a database, an XML file or a mail message, assuming that they have all the necessary details. The details are actually provided in derived classes.

toDB()

There are two methods for writing to a database. One expects the database information as arguments, and the other looks for it in the Env object; if the information is found, the first version of the method is called:

```
public void toDB(Connection conn, String tableName, boolean reset)
        throws Exception
{
    Statement stmnt = conn.createStatement();

    MiscDB.createTable(stmnt, tableName,
            theColumnLabels,theColumnTypes,reset);

    stmnt.close();

    PreparedStatement ps =
            MiscDB.createInserter(tableName, theColumnLabels, conn);

    while(next())
    {
        for(int i = 0; i < theColumnLabels.length; i++)
        {
            ps.setString(i + 1, theColumnValues[i]);
        }
        ps.executeUpdate();
    }

    ps.close();
}
```

```
public void toDB() throws Exception
{

    String tableName = theEnv.getStr("tableName", "ROWENUM");
    String resetStr = theEnv.getStr("reset", "false");

    boolean reset = (new Boolean(resetStr)).booleanValue();

    String dbDriver = theEnv.getStr("dbDriver",
            "sun.jdbc.odbc.JdbcOdbcDriver");

    String dbUrl = theEnv.getStr("dbUrl", "jdbc:odbc:PHONEBOOK");
    String dbUser = theEnv.getStr("dbUser", "JohnSmith");
    String dbPwd = theEnv.getStr("dbPwd", "password");

    Class.forName(dbDriver);
    Connection conn = DriverManager.getConnection(dbUrl, dbUser, dbPwd);
    toDB(conn,tableName, reset);
    conn.close();

}
```

toXML()

In a similar pattern, toXML() either receives the necessary information as arguments or looks for it in the Env. Its output conforms to our dbdata.dtd that we used in Xml2DBTables in Chapter 9. In other words, the XML that is output from a RowSeq is ready to be fed into a database table. This sets the stage for sending the contents of an email folder to a database, or for exchanging data between databases:

```
public void toXML(Writer out, String tableName, boolean reset)
        throws Exception
{

    String lineSeparator = "\n";

    out.write("<table name=\"");
    out.write(tableName);
    out.write("\"");

    if(reset)
    {
        out.write(" reset=\"true\"");
    }

    out.write(">");
    out.write(lineSeparator);

    out.write("<headers>");

    for(int i = 0; i < theColumnLabels.length; i++)
    {
        out.write("<header name=\"");
```

```
            out.write(theColumnLabels[i]);
            out.write("\" fieldType=\"");
            out.write(theColumnTypes[i]);
            out.write("\" />");
            out.write(lineSeparator);
        }

        out.write("</headers>");
        out.write(lineSeparator);

        while(next())
        {

            String S;
            out.write("<row>");
            out.write(lineSeparator);

            for(int i = 0; i < theColumnLabels.length; i++)
            {
                out.write("<field name=\"");
                out.write(null==(S=theColumnLabels[i])?"":S);
                out.write("\">");
                out.write(null==(S=theColumnValues[i])?"":Misc.htmlEscape(S));
                out.write("</field>");
                out.write(lineSeparator);
            }

            out.write("</row>");
            out.write(lineSeparator);

        }

        out.write("</table>");
        out.write(lineSeparator);

    }


public void toXML() throws Exception
{

    String tableName = theEnv.getStr("tableName", "ROWENUM");
    String resetStr = theEnv.getStr("reset", "false");

    boolean reset = (new Boolean(resetStr)).booleanValue();

    Object out = theEnv.get("OutputWriter");

    if( null == out || !(out instanceof Writer) )
    {
        toXML(new PrintWriter(System.out),tableName,reset);
    }
    else
```

```
    {
        toXML((Writer)out,tableName,reset);
    }

}
```

toMail()

This method uses JavaMail material that we haven't yet covered, but most of it should be understandable, especially if you are willing to suspend your disbelief when you see things like `trans.sendMessage`. The method proceeds as follows:

❑ Obtain system properties

❑ Get an instance of the `Session` class, using `System` properties

❑ From `Session`, obtain an instance of `Transport`, with SMTP as protocol

❑ Get the SMTP host from `Env` and connect to it

❑ For each element of `RowSeq`, create a `Message` object, fill it in from `Env`, and send

All of these will become quite familiar after we go over the main bean and the JavaMail API.

```
public void toMail()throws Exception
{

    // the RowSeq must define "msgtoaddr","msgfromaddr", "smtphost",
    // "msgsubject", and "msgcontent", but these need not be actual
    // columns; they just have to be defined in the Env
    // produced by getRow();

    java.util.Properties props = System.getProperties();
    Session sess = Session.getInstance(props, null);
    Transport trans = sess.getTransport("smtp");
    String smtphost = theEnv.getStr("smtphost");

    while(next())
    {
      MimeMessage mess = new MimeMessage(sess);
      String fromaddr = theEnv.getStr("msgfromaddr");
      String toaddr = theEnv.getStr("msgtoaddr");
      String subject = theEnv.getStr("msgsubject");
      String content = theEnv.getStr("msgcontent");
      mess.setFrom(new InternetAddress(fromaddr));
      mess.addRecipient(Message.RecipientType.TO,
              new InternetAddress(toaddr));
      mess.setSubject(subject);
      mess.setText(content);
      trans.sendMessage(mess, mess.getAllRecipients());
    }

    trans.close();

}
```

What About Sequence Methods?

We have reached the end of RowSeq that claims to implement an abstract lazily-evaluated sequence, and yet we have not seen the methods that retrieve the current element of a sequence or advance us to the next one. The reason is that RowSeq is an abstract class, and so it does not really have to define them, as long as they are defined in derived classes.

Still, a skeleton implementation of one, and a declaration of the other, are in order:

```
public Env getRow()
{
    return theEnv;
}

public abstract boolean next();
```

The getRow() method is useful as is, but next() has to be overridden in derived classes that know the content of the RowSeq and where it is coming from. Time to look at the derived classes.

DBRowSequence

As we said, the old RowSequence class has been rearranged so that much of its functionality is now in the abstract RowSeq class (specifically, in the toDB() method), and the remaining functionality is in its derivative, DBRowSequence. DBRowSequence can be described as a RowSeq with an additional ResultSet variable; all it does is serve the ResulSet as a RowSeq.

The class consists of imports, constructors and re-implementations of next(), shallowClone(), and close().

Imports and Constructors

The imports are exactly what you would expect:

```
import java.sql.*;
import java.util.Hashtable;
import MyNa.utils.*;
```

There are two constructors: one takes a ResultSet and an Env object with query information in it; the other takes a ResultSet only and creates a new Env (later initialized in some way):

```
public class DBRowSequence extends RowSeq
{
    ResultSet theResultSet;

    public DBRowSequence(ResultSet R, Env queryInfo)
            throws SQLException,Exception
    {
        super();
```

```
        theResultSet = R;
        theEnv = queryInfo;

        if(R == null)
        {
            theColumnLabels = null;
            theColumnTypes = null;
            theColumnValues = null;
            theNumberOfColumns = 0;
        }
        else
        {
            theColumnLabels = MiscDB.resultSetLabels(R);  // general utility
            theColumnTypes = MiscDB.resultSetTypes(R);    // general utility
            theEnv.put("theColumnLabels", theColumnLabels);
            theEnv.put("theColumnTypes", theColumnTypes);
            setInitEnv();                                 // defined in RowSeq
        }

    }

    public DBRowSequence(ResultSet R) throws SQLException
    {
        this(R, new Env());
    }
```

The two general utilities from MiscDB extract column labels and data types from the ResultSet using the metadata facilities of JDBC:

```
public static String [] resultSetLabels(ResultSet R)
        throws SQLException
{
    ResultSetMetaData rsmd = R.getMetaData();
    String S [] = new String[rsmd.getColumnCount()];
    for(int i = 0; i < S.length; i++)
    {
        S[i] = rsmd.getColumnLabel(i+1);
    }
    return S;
}

public static int resultSetColumnCount(ResultSet R)
        throws SQLException
{
    ResultSetMetaData rsmd = R.getMetaData();
    return rsmd.getColumnCount();
}

public static String [] resultSetTypes(ResultSet R)
        throws SQLException
{
```

```
        ResultSetMetaData rsmd = R.getMetaData();
        String S [] = new String[rsmd.getColumnCount()];

        for(int i = 0; i < S.length; i++)
        {
            S[i] = rsmd.getColumnTypeName(i+1);
        }

        return S;


    }
```

Overridden Methods

These are the methods that need to be overridden, to work specifically with a `ResultSet`:

```
public boolean next()
{

    if(theResultSet == null)
    {
        return false;
    }


    try
    {

        if(!theResultSet.next())
        {
            theResultSet.close();
            theResultSet = null;
            return false;
        }

        for(int i = 0; i < theNumberOfColumns; i++)
        {
            String S = theResultSet.getString(i+1);
            if(S == null)
            {
                S = "";
            }
            theColumnValues[i] = S;
            theEnv.put(theColumnLabels[i], S);
            theEnv.put(theFieldValueNum[i], S);
        }

        return true;

    }

    catch(Exception ex)
    {
        ex.printStackTrace();
```

```
        }

        return false;

    }

    public void close()
    {
        try
        {
            theResultSet.close();
            theResultSet = null;
        }
        catch(Exception ex)
        {
            ex.printStackTrace();
        }
    }
```

shallowClone() now has to copy a reference to the ResultSet. Before copying, the argument has to be cast to DBRowSequence:

```
    public void shallowClone(RowSeq re)
    {
        // a shallow copy
        super.shallowClone(re);
        if(re instanceof DBRowSequence)
        {
          this.theResultSet = ((DBRowSequence)re).theResultSet;
        }
    }

} // end of DBRowSequence class
```

MailSequence

MailSequence has the same structure as DBRowSequence: additional variables for working with a specific source of row data, two constructors (one with, the other without, an Env argument), and overridden methods. At this level of detail, the code is immediately understandable. However, the actual details of working with data use JavaMail constantly. We will therefore postpone MailSequence until after we become familiar with that API.

Filter and Map

Two more derived classes are not for *specific* data but for producing derived sequences of *any* data. One of these classes filters the original sequence by using a predicate on each row and passing through only those rows that conform. The other applies a function to each row of the original sequence and outputs the sequence of results. Just as with the EndHandlers of the SAXMiniLanguage, in many other programming languages we would just override the next() method giving it a function argument that does the required mappping or filtering; in Java we can achieve the same effect with derived classes, as shown below. There are two other possibilities but they involve major costs, either in design clumsiness (using extra interface definitions and name constraints), or in performance (using reflection).

In our approach, in order to obtain classes that both know their specific data and how to filter it, we derive a data-specific class from `FilterRowSeq`, rather than `RowSeq`. The same is true for mapping.

FilterRowSeq

The constructor of `FilterRowSeq` receives an "original" `RowSeq` that needs to be filtered. A reference to that original is stored as a local variable, and a shallow clone is produced. The class contains an `isOkRow()` predicate that has to be overridden in derived classes of specific filtering needs:

```java
import java.util.*;
import java.io.*;
import MyNa.utils.*;

public class FilterRowSeq extends RowSeq
{
    RowSeq innerRows;

    public FilterRowSeq(RowSeq re)throws Exception
    {
        super();
        innerRows = re;
        shallowClone(re);
    }

    public boolean isOkRow()
    {
        return true; // override
    }

    public boolean next()
    {
        boolean gotRow = innerRows.next();
        while (gotRow && !isOkRow())
        {
            gotRow = innerRows.next();
        }
        return gotRow;
    }

} // end FilterRowSeq
```

MapRowSeq

This class is a little longer because it provides a more substantive default: a mapping function that, in each row, sets a specific field to a specific value. There are more local variables and an extra constructor, to support that default. If the default is adequate, the class can be used as is; otherwise, `mapFunction()` needs to be overridden in a derived class:

```java
public class MapRowSeq extends RowSeq
{
    RowSeq innerRows;
    String fieldName;
```

```
    int fieldNum;
    String val;

    // used in most common case, in which a field
    // is set to be a particular value. May be
    // used for other purposes with mapFunction
    // overridden.

    public MapRowSeq(RowSeq re) throws Exception
    {
        super();
        innerRows = re;
        shallowClone(re);
        fieldName = null;
        fieldNum = -1;
        val = null;
    }

    public MapRowSeq(String field, String val, RowSeq re)
            throws Exception
    {

        super();
        innerRows = re;
        shallowClone(re);
        fieldName = field;
        this.val = val;

        if(theColumnLabels != null)
        {
            for(int i = 0; i < theColumnLabels.length; i++)
            {
                if(theColumnLabels[i].equals(field))
                {
                    fieldNum = i;
                    return;
                }
            }
        }

    }

    public void mapFunction()
    {
        // applied to each Env
        if(fieldNum >= 0)
        {
            theColumnValues[fieldNum] = val;
        }
        theEnv.put(fieldName, val);
    }

    public boolean next()
    {
```

```
        if(!innerRows.next())
        {
            return false;
        }
        mapFunction();
        return true;
    }

} // end MapRowSeq
```

This concludes our discussion of RowSeq and its children. As you will recall from the diagram of the application, our sub-beans (those that are sources of data) are not themselves RowSeqs: they contain a reference to a RowSeq and present a re-settable and editable view of it. In terms of software relationships, these sub-beans implement the RowViewSource interface. This is our next subsystem.

RowViewSource

A RowViewSource object should be able to:

- ❑ open a connection to (initialize a session with) a data source
- ❑ receive data from a source
- ❑ send data to a variety of destinations
- ❑ set its properties from an XML file or HTML form
- ❑ modify its data by deleting rows and perhaps (if enough information is given) adding rows
- ❑ search and delete within its data using some pattern expressions
- ❑ close its data source

The methods declared by the interface are divided by comments into those categories. As you read through the code, remember that all RowViewSources can be initialized from an XML file and further customized by user input from an HTML form. So, all the setXXX() methods that you see will have their arguments coming from those sources.

The declarations of RowViewSource try to be very generic in how they describe its sources and destinations of data: all that is assumed is that there are rows and fields, labels on fields, and data types associated with fields. It may help in getting the right feel for the code to remember that in this particular application the source is either a database or an email folder. Here we go:

```
package MyNa.xml;
import MyNa.utils.*;

public interface RowViewSource
{
    // open session with a database or mailhost or whatever
    // all necessary information is in the Env
    public void initSession(Env E) throws Exception;
```

```
    // get data, as a RowSeq, from the source
    public RowSeq getRowList();              // columnLabels view
    public RowSeq getAllColumnsRowList(); // wider view
    public Env getRow(int N);                // specific row, by number
    public RowSeq getFilteredRowList(String field,String pat);
    // get a selection of Rows by pattern; not yet implemented


    // send data to a destination
    public void sendTo(String destType, String destName);
    // e.g., sendTo("mail", "joe@email.addr.com");
    // or sendTo("db", "INBOX");
    // or sendTo("file", "/C:/MyNa/msgs.xml");
    // other options can be added; e.g. sendTo("socket", "56789")
    // or sendTo("string", "StringName");
    public void sendTo(Env E);// Env has destType, destName


    // setXXX() methods
    public void setDbUser(String dbUser);
    public void setDbPwd(String dbPwd);
    public void setDbName(String dbname); // db table or mail folder "INBOX"
    // jdbc driver or mail protocol (POP, IMAP); mail server requires port
    public void setDbDriver(String dbDriver);
    // database or mail server (or a socket) jdbc:odbc:PHONEBOOK;cs.colgate.edu
    public void setDbSource(String sourceName);
    // set column labels and types, either from comma-delimited sting or array
    public void setColumnLabels(String columnLabels);
    public void setColumnLabels(String [] columnLabels);
    public void setColumnTypes(String columnTypes);
    public void setColumnTypes(String [] columnTypes);
    public void setRowNum(int N); // e.g., to number email messages


    // getXXX() methods
    public String[] getColumnLabels();
    public String[] getColumnTypes();
    public int getNumberOfColumns();
    public int getRowNum();


    // delete and add rows
    public void delRow(int N);
    public void delRows(String[] fieldNames, String[] vals);
    // deletes rows in which each of those fieldnames
    // has exactly the corresponding value, apart from case
    public void delRowRange(int start, int end);
    public void delRowSearch(String field, String pat);
    // deletes rows selected by pattern; not yet implemented

    public void addRow(String[] fieldNames, String[] vals);
    // adds row in which each of those fieldnames has the corresponding value
    // may do nothing


    public void close();

/*
```

```
    The last group of declarations has to do with error handling; think of them as
    equivalent to, and replaceable by, exception handling.  Instead of exceptions,
    what we do here is a somewhat old-fashioned (or "traditional style") string-based
    system.
*/

    public boolean hasError();
    public String getErrorMessage(); // empty string signifies no error
    public String getErrorType();

} // end of RowViewSource
```

The New and Better Env

All sub-beans, whether `ViewSources` or not, are configurable by XML. Speaking again in terms of software relationships, they all implement the `XmlConfig` interface, either directly or by extending `XmlConfigBase` (which implements `XmlConfig`). A crucial role in the configuration process belongs to the `Env` class; as the diagram below shows, the process is channeled through an `Env`. So, our next adventure (before we get to `XmlConfig`) is a new and vastly improved `Env` class.

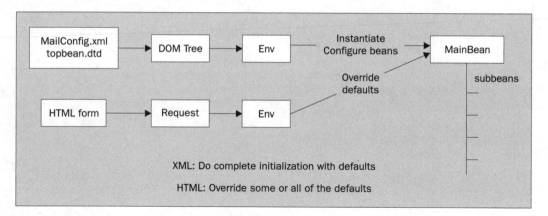

The main addition to `Env` is that it is recursive: it can contain a reference to a sub-`Env` which, in turn, may contain a reference to a sub-`Env`, and so on. The result is that a structure of embedded `Env`s can mirror both the structure of embedded sub-beans and the structure of an XML file – the XML file that initializes both the tree-structured `Env` and the tree-structured bean.

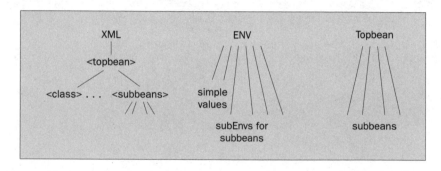

We will first present the additions that support the recursive Env structure, then other miscellaneous additions.

Recursive Env

A non-recursive Env associates a value with a string key. A recursive Env, in addition, can associate a value with an array of strings, such that all the elements of the array except the last one retrieve a sub-Env of the preceding Env. The last element of the array is a key that retrieves the actual value from the deepest-embedded Env. To support this feature, we have to overload the get() method and provide a matching put() method.

New get() and put() Methods

Here are the new get() and put() methods:

```
public Object get(String[] keys)
{

    if(null == keys || 0 == keys.length)
    {
        return null;
    }

    Env E = this;
    int lastIndex = keys.length - 1;

    for(int i = 0; i < lastIndex; i++)
    {
        Object ob = E.get(keys[i]);

        if( null == ob || !(ob instanceof Env) )
        {
            return null;
        }

        E = (Env)ob;

    }

    return E.get( keys[lastIndex] );

}


public void put(String[] keys, Object val)
{

    // put(["subEnv", "subsubEnv", "subSubSubEnv", "key"], "val"), so that
    // this.getEnv("subEnv").getEnv("subsubEnv").get("key") == "val"

    if(null == keys || 0 == keys.length)
    {
```

```
        return;
    }

    Env E = this;
    int lastIndex = keys.length - 1;

    for(int i = 0; i < lastIndex; i++)
    {
        Object ob = E.get(keys[i]);

        if( null == ob || !(ob instanceof Env) )
        {
            ob = new Env();
            E.put(keys[i], ob);
        }

        E = (Env)ob;

    }

    E.put(keys[lastIndex], val);

}
```

getSplit(), putSplit() and getEnv()

We also want to be able to access or create sub-Envs using a single underscore-separated string submitted from an HTML form: a string like "subEnv_subsubEnv_key" will be split at underscores, converted into an array and given as an argument to get():

```
public Object getSplit(String key)
{

    if(null == key)
    {
        return null;
    }

    if(key.indexOf('_') < 0)
    {
        return get(key);
    }

    return get(Misc.stringSplit(key,'_'));

}


public void putSplit(String key, Object val)
{

    if(null == key)
    {
```

```
        return;
    }

    if(key.indexOf('_') < 0)
    {
        put(key, val);
    }
    else
    {
        put(Misc.stringSplit(key,'_'), val);
    }

}
```

Sometimes, we simply want to retrieve an Env (or null), so here is getEnv(), similar to getStr():

```
public Env getEnv(String key)
{
    Object ob = get(key);
    if(ob == null || !(ob instanceof Env))
    {
        return null;
    }
    return (Env)ob;
}
```

New getStr()

Our getStr() has to add one more branch to behave appropriately if it comes up with an Env: what we want it to do is to call the toString() method that is defined to call getStr(), so getStr() becomes a recursive procedure:

```
public String getStr(String key)
{
    Object ob = this.get(key);

    if(ob == null)
    {
        return null;
    }
    else
    {
        if(ob instanceof String)
        {
            return (String)ob;
        }
    }
    else
    {
        if(ob instanceof String[])
        {
```

```
            return Misc.stringArrayJoin((String[])ob, ", ");
        }
    }
    else
    {
        if(ob instanceof Env)
        {
            return "[" + ((Env)ob).toString() + "]";
        }
    }
    else
    {
        return null;
    }
}
```

toStringRec()

With `getStr()` so redefined, we have to make sure that Env's `toString()` method does not go into an infinite loop when it has to write out an Env that contains cyclical references within its sub-Envs. (There are such references in this application because the main bean contains references to its sub-beans, and every sub-bean has a reference to its parent bean.) So we have a `toStringRec()` (recursive) that can write out to a string an arbitrary network of beans. Those familiar with graph traversal algorithms will recognize a depth-first traversal with a stack:

```
public String toStringRec()
{
    // use if subEnvs might be cyclic
    StringBuffer sB = new StringBuffer();
    tSS(this, new Stack(), sB);
    return sB.toString();
}

public void tSS(Env E, Stack eS, StringBuffer sB)
{
    // tostring subfunction for safe recursive Envs

    if(0 <= eS.search(E))
    {
        sB.append("***CYCLIC ENV***\n");
        return;
    }

    eS.push(E);
    Enumeration k = E.keys();

    while(k.hasMoreElements())
    {

        String key = (String)k.nextElement();

        for(int i = 0; i < eS.size(); i++)
        {
            sB.append("  ");
        }
```

```
            sB.append(key);
            sB.append("=");

            Object ob = E.get(key);

            if(null == ob)
            {
                sB.append("null;\n");
            }

            else
            {
                if(ob instanceof String)
                {
                    sB.append((String)ob);
                    sB.append(";\n");
                }
            }

            else
            {
                if(ob instanceof String[])
                {
                    sB.append( Misc.stringArrayJoin( (String[])ob, ", ") );
                    sB.append(";\n");
                }
            }

            else
            {

                if(ob instanceof Env)
                {
                    sB.append("[\n");
                    tSS((Env)ob, eS, sB);

                    for(int i = 0; i <= eS.size(); i++)
                    {
                        sB.append("  ");
                    }

                    sB.append("]\n");
                }

            }

            else
            {
                sB.append("??\n");
            }

    } //end of while loop

    eS.pop();

}
```

getStr() with a Default

Finally, we now have a version of getStr() that provides a default value to return if the key comes up empty:

```
public String getStr(String key, String dflt)
{
    Object ob = this.get(key);

    if(ob == null)
    {
        return dflt;
    }

    if(ob instanceof String)
    {
        return (String)ob;
    }

    else
    {
        if(ob instanceof String[])
        {
            return Misc.stringArrayJoin((String[])ob,", ");
        }
    }

    else
    {
        return dflt;
    }

}
```

With a recursive Env structure in hand, we can proceed to XML initialization/configuration.

XML Configuration

In this section, we will work through that part of the overall diagram that has to do with initializing the beans from an XML document. We repeat here an earlier diagram.

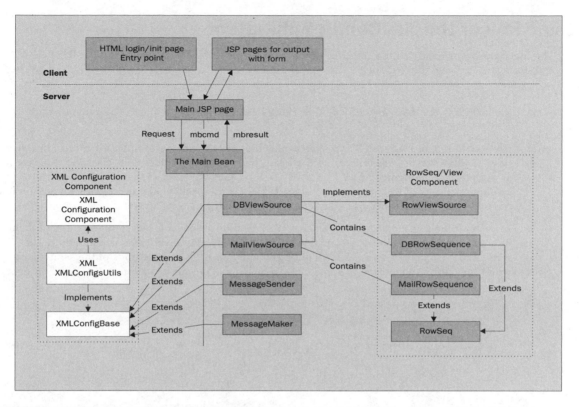

This is a nuts-and-bolts section that describes the basic plumbing of the system; you don't have to get every detail on first reading, as long as you understand the main concept and the overall structure of the code. These ideas are presented in the next two subsections.

The Main Concept: Three Recursive Data Structures

The main concept is this: we want to build a recursive structure of beans that can contain sub-beans that can contain sub-beans, and so on. All these beans and sub-beans have to be defined at compile time but they can be instantiated and configured dynamically at run time. That's what this section is about: how to instantiate and initialize a recursive structure of beans on the basis of a (recursively structured) XML document. The way we do this is by using a recursive structure of Envs as an intermediary: an XML document is mapped to an Env object that contains sub-Envs that may contain further sub-Envs, and so on.

The reason we do it this way is because we may, in some other systems, have Envs coming from sources other than an XML file. For instance, we can have an Env made out of a Request object that contains data submitted by an HTML form. As you remember, initialization is a layered process: the XML configuration builds the overall structure and provides defaults that can be overwritten by user input from an HTML form. (This especially concerns user authentication.) In general an initialization by Envs is equivalent to one by DOM trees, except that the DOM tree is more easily checked for validity whereas the Envs are more easily generated, e.g. by HTML forms. As the diagram above shows, we channel DOM initialization through an Env object, so we only have to provide one set of bean instantiation routines.

Overview of the XmlConfig Subsystem

The mechanism for configuring a structure of beans from an XML document consists of the `XmlConfig` interface, the `XmlConfigUtils` class, and the `XmlConfigBase` class. This is how they work together:

❑ `XmlConfig` declares the methods that every bean and sub-bean must implement, including `initFromEnv()` and `initFromDomTree()`.

❑ We would like to have `XmlConfig` as a class that provides default implementations, but we have to allow for the possibility that the beans have to extend some other class. So we leave it as an interface implemented by `XmlConfigBase`, an abstract class that provides default implementations of `XmlConfig` methods. If beans in a specific bean-sub-bean structure do not have to extend something else, they can simply extend `XmlConfigBase`.

❑ In order to help in implementing `XmlConfig` methods, we factor out common parts of them into static methods of the `XmlConfigUtils` class (which is never to be instantiated). The static `XmlConfigUtils` methods will be called by `XmlConfig` methods of the same name when they are implemented in some class or another. They are so called in `XmlConfigBase`.

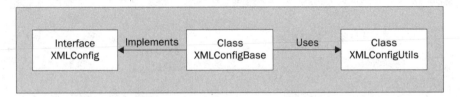

Although the names of the interface and two classes emphasize the XML connection, initialization from `Env`s is also implemented and constitutes a completely separable path through the system. (See the preceding diagram.) So, the material of this section can be seen either as organized into an interface and two classes, as in the diagram, or as developing two initialization paths, from `Env`s and from XML. We will switch between the two views as appropriate, in our unending effort to smooth the reader's learning curve.

Let us start working though an example: the configuration file for the `SimpleMailBean` of our application.

mailConfig.xml and the Env it Defines

Here is the overall structure of `mailConfig.xml`; it should be viewed in conjunction with the application diagram at the beginning of the chapter:

```xml
<?xml version="1.0" encoding="utf-8"?>
<!DOCTYPE topbean SYSTEM "topbean.dtd">
<topbean>
<mailertop>
  <class>simpleMail.SimpleMailBean</class>
  <sub-beans>
    <mailSource>
       ...
```

```
        </mailSource>
        <dbaseSource>
          ...
        </dbaseSource>
        <msgComposer>
          ...
        </msgComposer>
        <msgSender>
          ...
        </msgSender>
      </sub-beans>
      <rowViewSourceName>mailSource</rowViewSourceName>
      <messageMakerName>msgComposer</messageMakerName>
      <messageSenderName>msgSender</messageSenderName>
      <mbcmd>login</mbcmd>
      <mbresult>miscError</mbresult>
      <errorMessage>No Activity Yet</errorMessage>
    </mailertop>
  </topbean>
```

The `<topbean>` element is not really necessary: it corresponds to a class that does the actual work of instantiating the beans, so by the time the configuration file is processed that class already exists. We include it so the entire structure of the `SimpleMail` bean and sub-beans can be included in a larger application.

Leaving `<topbean>` aside, we have a single `<mailertop>` element whose first two children are `<class>` and `<sub-beans>`. This structure can repeat recursively at the sub-bean level: if, for instance, the `<mailSource>` sub-bean had further sub-beans, its first two children would be `<class>` and `<sub-beans>`. As it happens, it does not have sub-beans, so it only has `<class>` as the first child, followed by sub-bean-specific material. Here is the beginning of the document without omissions:

```
<?xml version="1.0" encoding="utf-8"?>
<!DOCTYPE topbean SYSTEM "topbean.dtd">
<topbean>
<mailertop>
  <class>simpleMail.SimpleMailBean</class>
  <sub-beans>
    <mailSource>
      <class>MyNa.xml.MailViewSource</class>
      <useclass>MyNa.xml.RowViewSource</useclass>
      <dbDriver>pop3</dbDriver>
      <dbName>mail.dreamscape.com</dbName>
      <dbUser>JohnSmith</dbUser>
      <dbPwd>hArd-tO-gUEss?</dbPwd>
      <dbSource>INBOX</dbSource>
      <columnLabels>msgsubject,msgdate,msgflags,msgfromaddr</columnLabels>
      <port>-1</port>
      <verbose>true</verbose>
      <debug>true</debug>
      <expunge>true</expunge>
    </mailSource>
    <dbSource>
      ...
```

This XML opening will create a DOM structure that is equivalent to an Env object defined by the following fragment of an HTML form:

```
<input type=hidden name="beanName" value="mailerTop">
<input type=hidden name="class" value="simpleMail.SimpleMailBean">
<input type=hidden name=mailSource_beanName value="mailSource">
<input type=hidden name=mailSource_class value="MyNa.xml.MailViewSource">
<input type=hidden name=mailSource_useclass value="MyNa.xml.RowViewSource">
<input type=hidden name=mailSource_dbDriver value="pop3">
...
```

The names and values of these input fields become the names and values in an Env object (via a Request object). In the process, the names containing underscores will be split into an array (see above the putSplit() method of the new Env object), and a sub-Env called mailSource will be created, corresponding to the <mailSource> sub-bean.

Time now to take a look at XmlConfig and its friends.

XmlConfig

This interface declares methods for creating recursive bean-sub-bean structures from two kinds of inputs, DOM trees and Env objects. In both cases, there is a "top" method, for starting the process and creating a recursive structure of Nodes or Env objects, and a "recursive" method for creating recursive structures of beans from a recursive structure of Node-with-sub-Nodes or Env-with-sub-Env objects.

```
package MyNa.xml;
import org.w3c.dom.Node;
import org.w3c.dom.NamedNodeMap;
import org.w3c.dom.DocumentType;
import org.w3c.dom.Attr;
import org.w3c.dom.Element;

import org.xml.sax.SAXParseException;
import org.xml.sax.InputSource;
import org.xml.sax.SAXException;
import com.sun.xml.parser.Resolver;
import com.sun.xml.tree.XmlDocument;

import MyNa.utils.Env;

public interface XmlConfig
{

    public String initFromTopEnv(Env E);
    // init using values from the Env,
    // with keys of the form xxx_yyy_zzz to refer to sub-bean locations
    // use putSplit() to create subEnvs

    public String initFromEnv(Env E);
    // init using values from the Env,
    // use subEnvs for sub-beans
```

```
        public String initFromTopDomTree(String fileName, boolean validate, Env E);
        // top level: construct tree, call Node version.

        public String initFromDomTree(Node node, Env E);
        // init from Node; use subNodes for sub-beans

    }


        // setters and getters
        public void setBeanName(String S);
        public void setVerbose(String S);
        public void setDebug(String S);
        public String getBeanName();

        public void setString(String strName, String val);
        // usually of the form
        // if(strName==null)return;
        // if(strName.equals("debug"))setDebug(val);
        // else if(strName.equals("verbose"))setVerbose(val);
        // and so forth.

        public String getString(String strName);
        // same idea as setString
```

Instead of looking at XmlConfigBase in its entirety, we are going to trace how initialization from Envs is implemented in XmlConfigBase and XmlConfigUtils; then we'll look at initialization from DOM trees, before we look, finally, at those classes in their entirety.

Creating Beans from Envs

XmlConfigBase is quite small. It provides a minimal implementation of XmlConfig, and even within a minimal implementation, it relegates most of the work to the static methods of XmlConfigUtils.

The XmlConfigBase implementations all follow the same pattern: they call the appropriate method of XmlConfigUtils to create a generic structure, and then call the local method to put in the finishing touches:

```
public String initFromTopEnv(Env E)
{

    // init using values from the Env,
    // with keys of the form xxx_yyy_zzz to refer to sub-bean locations.

    String S = XmlConfigUtils.initFromTopEnv(E);

    if(S.length() > 0)
    {
        return S; // something is wrong: non-empty error message
    }

    return initFromEnv(E);      // call the recursive version
```

```
    }

public String initFromEnv(Env E)
{
    // init using values from Env that includes subEnvs for sub-beans
    String S = XmlConfigUtils.initFromEnv(E);

    if(S.length() > 0)
    {
        return S; // something is wrong: non-empty error message
    }

    useEnv(E);
    return "";

}
```

XmlConfigUtils Methods

We will look at useEnv() in a moment, but first let's take the mystery out of what the XmlConfigUtils are doing. We are now in that class; assume that all the necessary packages have been imported. The "top" method, initFromTopEnv(), does only one thing: it modifies its Env argument by running putSplit() on those keys that contain the underscore character:

```
public static String initFromTopEnv(Env E)
{

    Enumeration keys = E.keys();

    while(keys.hasMoreElements())
    {
        String key = (String)keys.nextElement();

        if(key.indexOf('_') < 0)  // no underscores in key
        {
            continue;
        }

        E.putSplit(key, E.get(key));
        E.remove(key);

    }

    return "";  // no errors reported in this version.

}
```

The recursive initFromEnv() does considerably more work. Its main loop goes through the values of its Env argument looking for embedded Envs. If one is found, and it is a sub-bean-defining Env, a reference to its parent is put into it, and a check to see whether it has been instantiated yet is made. If not, then we go through the process of creating an instance of it and filling in its essential properties. Here is the code:

```
public static String initFromEnv(Env E)
{
    String msg = "";      // string to return; empty string means success

    try
    {

        Enumeration keys = E.keys();

        while(keys.hasMoreElements() && msg.length() == 0)
        {

            String key = (String)keys.nextElement();
            if(key.equals("theBeanParentEnv"))
            {
                // parent Env, already done
                continue;
            }

            Object ob = E.get(key);
            if(!(ob instanceof Env))
            {
                // not an Env, skip to next key
                continue;
            }

            Env beanEnv = (Env)ob;
            String beanName = beanEnv.getStr("beanName");
            String beanClass = beanEnv.getStr("class");

            if(null == beanName || null == beanClass)
            {
                // not the right kind of Env
                continue;
            }

            beanEnv.put("theBeanParentEnv", E); // store reference to parent

            if(null == beanEnv.get("theBeanItself"))
            {
                // not yet initialized
                msg = initBean(beanEnv, beanClass);
                if(msg.length() > 0)
                    return msg;
            }

            // if we're here, bean has been initialized
            XmlConfig xc = (XmlConfig) beanEnv.get("theBeanItself");
            msg = xc.initFromEnv(beanEnv);
            // indirect recursive call via XmlConfig method

        }// end of main while loop

    } // end of try
```

```
        catch(Exception e)
        {
            msg += e;
        }

        return msg;

    }
```

Note that in order to call `initFromEnv()` recursively with the newly-discovered sub-`Env`, we retrieve "the bean itself", cast it to `XmlConfig` (which they all implement, either directly or indirectly) and call its `initFromEnv()` method, which eventually will make the recursive call on the static of `XmlConfigUtils`.

What's inside `initBean()`? Basically, we use the standard Java tools to obtain the bean's class; given the class, we use reflection to obtain its null constructor (which a bean must have), and finally we use the constructor to obtain an instance of the bean:

```
public static String initBean(Env beanEnv, String beanClass)
{
    try
    {

        Class C = Class.forName(beanClass);
        Class[] paramTypes = {};
        Object[] paramVals = {};
        Constructor cons = C.getConstructor(paramTypes);
        Object theBean = cons.newInstance(paramVals);

        if(!(theBean instanceof XmlConfig))
        {
            return "class " + beanClass + " is not an XmlConfig";
        }

        beanEnv.put("theBeanItself", theBean);

    }

    catch(Exception E)
    {
        return "" + E;
    }

    return "";

}
```

Back to XmlConfigBase: useEnv()

We call useEnv() in the initFromEnv() method of the XmlConfigBase class, after we return from a call to XmlConfigUtils.initFromEnv() with an empty string. By that time, we have a recursive structure of Envs in place, with references to beans and sub-beans filled in. We now want to do two things. One is to provide a hook for saving this structure. We call the hook setInitDefs() and leave it to the derived classes to implement it. The other is to go through all the keys and values in the Env and, for each value that is a String, call a setString() method with the key and the value as arguments. The implementation of setString() is left to the derived class; you will see how it is used in SimpleBean when we get to it:

```
public void useEnv(Env E)
{
    setInitDefs(E); // override in derived classes
    Enumeration keys = E.keys();

    while(keys.hasMoreElements())
    {

        String key = (String)keys.nextElement();
        Object val = E.get(key);

        if(val instanceof String)
        {
            setString(key, (String)val);
        }

    }

}
```

This completes the initialization-from-Envs path through XmlConfig and its supporting classes. Let us look at the initialization-from-XML path.

Creating Beans from XML Documents

This path is structured somewhat differently from the Env path. There are still two methods in XmlConfigBase, a "top" method and a recursive one, but they receive different inputs. The "top" method, initFromXmlFile() receives a file and parses it – or rather asks XmlConfigUtils to do so. The recursive method receives a node in a DOM tree and initializes from the sub-tree underneath that node, again relegating all the real work to the corresponding static method of XmlConfigUtils. Note that the "top" method does not call the recursive method in this case.

The Methods of XmlConfigBase

The "top" method receives an XML file that needs to be parsed, a boolean that specifies either a validating or a non-validating parser, and an Env object in which the results of the parse will be stored. The parsing itself is done in the corresponding method of XmlConfigUtils. If everything is fine, we pass on the Env to the already familiar initFromEnv():

```
public String initFromXmlFile(String fileName, boolean validate, Env E)
{

    // top level; construct tree, call Node version.
    String S = XmlConfigUtils.initFromXmlFile(fileName, validate, E);

    if(S.length() > 0)
    {
        // non-empty error message
        return S;
    }

    return initFromEnv(E);

}
```

The "recursive" version, in this case, is not really recursive; it just passes control to a recursive method of `XmlConfigUtils` and gets a modified `Env` back (in the `Env` path, there was an indirect recursion between the two methods):

```
public String initFromDomTree(Node node, Env E)
{

    // init from Node; use subtrees for sub-beans
    String S = XmlConfigUtils.initFromDomTree(node, E);

    if(S.length() > 0)
    {
        // non-empty error message
        return S;
    }

    return initFromEnv(E);

}
```

The Methods of XmlConfigUtils

There are three methods here: `initFromXmlFile()`, `initFromTopDomTree()` and the recursive method `initFromDomTree()`. The first parses the file, builds a DOM tree and calls the second. The second finds the right place to start and calls the third. The third and longest one constructs the beans.

initFromXmlFile()

We are back in the familiar territory of XML parsers and input sources. The code hardly needs commenting:

```
public static String initFromXmlFile(String fileName, boolean validate, Env E)
{
    InputSource input;
    XmlDocument doc;
```

```
        if(null == fileName)
        {
            return "null fileName for xml initialization";
        }

        try
        {

            if(fileName.startsWith("http:"))
            {
                // local file or URL?
                input = Resolver.createInputSource(new URL(fileName), true);
            }
            else
            {
                input = Resolver.createInputSource(new File(fileName));
            }

            doc = XmlDocument.createXmlDocument (input, validate);
            return initFromTopDomTree(doc, E);

        }


        catch (SAXParseException err)
        {
            return "** Parsing error: line " + err.getLineNumber() + err;
        }

        catch (SAXException e)
        {
            return "" + e;
        }

        catch (IOException t)
        {
            return "" + t;
        }

    }
```

InitFromTopDomTree()

To understand this method, you have to remember the top-level structure of the XML configuration file. Here is the file's beginning:

```
<?xml version="1.0" encoding="utf-8"?>
<!DOCTYPE topbean SYSTEM "topbean.dtd">
<topbean>
<mailertop>
  <class>simpleMail.SimpleMailBean</class>
  <sub-beans>
  ...
```

The first thing that initFromTopDomTree() does is use com.sun.xml.tree.TreeWalker to find the <topbean> node. (We need a TreeWalker because we don't know how many other nodes the configurer inserted before it.) Once the <topbean> node is found, we take its first and only child and start the recursive process on it:

```
public static String initFromTopDomTree(Node theNode, Env E)
{
     // E is output.

    if(null == theNode)
    {
        return "no tree for initialization";
    }

    theNode = (new TreeWalker(theNode)).getNextElement("topbean");

    if(null == theNode)
    {
        return "no topbean node in initialization tree";
    }

    theNode = theNode.getFirstChild();
    return initFromDomTree(theNode, E);

}
```

At this point we cannot delay the real hard work any longer. The remaining method is long and rather involved. It is also quite general and may be useful in other contexts: it performs the task of mapping a DOM tree of bean descriptions to a recursive Env structure from which those beans can be instantiated and configured. So we will start a whole new (large) section for it, with a subsection for the DTD that defines the DOM.

From DOM to Env

In order to follow the code, we have to have the structure of the DOM tree clear in our minds. We will show that structure from two perspectives:

❑ as an outline of the XML file

❑ as a DTD

Outline of mailconfig.xml and its DTD

This outline is repeated in modified and shortened form from an earlier section:

```
<?xml version="1.0" encoding="utf-8"?>
<!DOCTYPE topbean SYSTEM "topbean.dtd">
<topbean>
<mailertop>
  <class>simpleMail.SimpleMailBean</class>
```

```
        <sub-beans><!-- four children corresponding to four sub-beans -->
          <mailSource><class>...</class><useclass>...</useclass>
            ...
          </mailSource>
          <databaseSource><class>...</class><useclass>...</useclass>
            ...
          </databaseSource>
          <msgComposer><class>...</class><useclass>...</useclass>
            ...
          </msgComposer>
          <msgSender><class>...</class><useclass>...</useclass>
            ...
          </msgSender>
        </sub-beans>

        <!-- several elements for topbean properties that are not sub-beans -->
        ...
      </mailertop>
    </topbean>
```

This is how the outline is reflected in the DTD (file `topbean.dtd`):

```
<!ELEMENT topbean (mailertop)>

<!ENTITY % beancommon "class,useclass?,sub-beans?">
<!ENTITY % mailerspecs "rowViewSourceName,messageMakerName,messageSenderName">
<!ENTITY % cmds "mbcmd,mbresult,errorMessage">

<!ELEMENT mailertop (%beancommon;,%mailerspecs;,%cmds;)>

<!ELEMENT sub-beans (mailSource,databaseSource,msgComposer,msgSender)>

<!-- define components of sub-beans as entities -->
<!ENTITY % srccommon "dbDriver,dbName,dbUser,dbPwd,dbSource,expunge">
<!ENTITY % flags "verbose,debug">
<!ENTITY % mailsrcspecs "columnLabels,port">
<!ENTITY % dbspecs "dbQuery">
<!ENTITY % composerspecs
             "msgsubject,msgtoaddr,msgfromaddr,msgcontent,msgcc,msgbcc">
<!ENTITY % senderspecs "smtphost,mailerName">

<!-- define sub-beans: all have beancommon and flags; sources have srccommon -->
<!ELEMENT mailSource      (%beancommon;,%srccommon;,%mailsrcspecs;,%flags;)>
<!ELEMENT databaseSource  (%beancommon;,%srccommon;,%dbspecs;,%flags;)>
<!ELEMENT msgComposer     (%beancommon;,%composerspecs;,%flags;)>
<!ELEMENT msgSender       (%beancommon;,%senderspecs;,%flags;)>

<!-- the rest of the DTD defines all remaining elements as #PCDATA -->
```

The Role of <class> and <useclass> Elements

As you can see from the XML file and the DTD, both the top bean (<mailertop>) and the sub-beans have, as their first child, a required element of type <class>. In addition, some sub-beans have, as their second child, an optional element of type <useclass>. The value of both <class> and <useclass> elements is a fully qualified Java class name.

As you will see from reading the code, the <class> element supplies the name of the class to give as an argument to Class.forName(). The class element that is a child of <mailerbean> is not used that way in our code but it can be, if the top bean is itself instantiated at runtime within another application.

Although we provide the <usebean> element in the mailconfig.xml, our application does not use it. In future applications (yes, we do intend to use this framework in real life applications beyond the confines of this book), we are going to use that element for data checking and debugging. The intent is to have the <usebean> class (i.e. the class whose name is the value of the <usebean> element) such that the <class> class (whose name is the value of the <class> element) can be cast to it. In other words, the <useclass> class has to be an ancestor class to the <class> class or an interface that the <class> class implements. For instance, in mailconfig.xml we have:

```
<class>MyNa.xml.MailViewSource</class>
<useclass>MyNa.xml.RowViewSource</useclass>
```

where RowViewSource is an interface implemented by MailViewSource.

Finally, we are ready to tackle the complexities of initFromDomTree().

initFromDomTree()

Actually, after all the preparation we have done, this method is not that complex. Basically, it checks to make sure that a child <class> node is there, and performs the appropriate action for the <useclass> and sub-beans nodes. Otherwise, for all the nodes that have only #PCDATA content (including <class> and <useclass> nodes), it saves the name of the node and its text value in the Env. This last action is performed by setNodeNameVal(); if you start it up on:

```
<class>MyNa.xml.MailViewSource</class>
```

then it will end up doing Env.put("class", "MyNa.xml.MailViewSource"), just as we did in Chapter 9 with the SAXMiniLanguage defaults. The function reads as follows:

```java
public static void setNodeNameVal(Env E, Node N)
{

    if(null == N)
    {
        return;
    }

    String name = N.getNodeName();
    N = N.getFirstChild(); // nodeName=#text, nodeValue=text
```

```
        if(null == N)
        {
            return;
        }

        String val = N.getNodeValue();

        if(null != val)
        {
            E.put(name, val);
        }

    }
```

Now, what is the correct action for sub-beans nodes? Simple: go through its children and recursively call yourself with a sub-bean element and a new Env. Here is the method in its entirety:

```
public static String initFromDomTree(Node theNode, Env E)
{

    // E is output
    // in this method, we depend on your DTD for correctness
    // or on your being careful, if you don't use a DTD

    if(null == theNode)
    {
        return "null node at start of initFromDomTree";
    }

    String beanName = theNode.getNodeName();
    E.put("beanName", beanName);

    theNode = firstKid(theNode); // has to be <class>xxx.yyy.zzz</class>

    if(null == theNode || !"class".equals(theNode.getNodeName()))
    {
        return "no class specified under " + beanName;
    }

    setNodeNameVal(E, theNode);
    theNode = nextSib(theNode);

    if(null == theNode)
    {
        return " bean def ends with class node for " + beanName;
    }

    if("useclass".equals(theNode.getNodeName()))
    {

        // save and move on
        setNodeNameVal(E, theNode); // put (Node name,Node text) in Env
        theNode = nextSib(theNode);  // skip to next element
```

```
            if(null == theNode)
            {
                return "bean def ends with useclass node for " + beanName;
            }

        } // end if"useclass"...

        String S = "";

        if("sub-beans".equals(theNode.getNodeName()))
        {

            Node sub = firstKid(theNode);

            while(null != sub && S.length() == 0)
            {
                String subName = sub.getNodeName();
                Env subEnv = new Env();
                E.put(subName, subEnv);
                S = initFromDomTree(sub, subEnv); // recursive call
                sub = nextSib(sub);
            }

            theNode = nextSib(theNode);

        } // end if("sub-beans")...; sub-beans done; now properties

        while(null != theNode)
        {
            setNodeNameVal(E, theNode);
            theNode = nextSib(theNode);
        }

    return S; // return empty if no error message.

}
```

This concludes the second path through the XML configuration system, the one that starts from an XML file and a DOM tree. We can now take a look at the complete text of `XmlConfigBase.java` and `XmlConfigUtils.java`. We will skip the definitions of those methods we have covered, but there are still important and instructive details we have not yet seen.

XmlConfigBase.java

The imports consist of general Java classes, JavaMail classes (including Bean Activation Framework), a DOM `Node` class, and, of course, `MyNa.utils`:

```
package MyNa.xml;
import java.util.*;
import java.io.*;
import javax.mail.*;
import javax.mail.internet.*;
```

```
import javax.activation.*;
import org.w3c.dom.Node;
import MyNa.utils.*;

public abstract class XmlConfigBase implements XmlConfig
{
```

Next, a null constructor, variables and set/get methods:

```
public XmlConfigBase(){}

String beanName = "topBean";
boolean verbose = true;
boolean debug = true;

public String getBeanName()
{
    return beanName;
}

public void setBeanName(String S)
{
    beanName = S;
}

public void setVerbose(String S)
{
    try
    {
        verbose = (new Boolean(S)).booleanValue();
    }
    catch(Exception ex)
    {
        verbose = true;
    }
}

public void setDebug(String S)
{
    // exactly the same as setVerbose()
    ...
}

public void setInitDefs(Env E)
{
    // no implementation; implement in derived class; probably save the Env
}

// the remaining methods have been thoroughly discussed; only declarations

public void useEnv(Env E){}
public String initFromTopEnv(Env E){}
public String initFromEnv(Env E){}
```

```
        public String initFromXmlFile(String fileName, boolean validate, Env E){}
        public String initFromDomTree(Node nd, Env E){}

}// end of XmlConfigBase
```

XmlConfigUtils.java

The imports reflect the complex pedigree of this class; apart from `MyNa.utils`, it needs:

- ❑ Java `io` and `net` classes for an input source to the XML parser
- ❑ `java.langClass` and `java.lang.reflect.Constructor` for bean instantiation
- ❑ DOM, SAX and `com.sun.xml` classes for XML files and DOM trees

```
package MyNa.xml;
import MyNa.utils.Env;
import java.util.Enumeration;

import java.net.URL;
import java.io.File;
import java.io.IOException;

import java.lang.Class;
import java.lang.reflect.Constructor;

import org.w3c.dom.Element;
import org.w3c.dom.Node;
import org.w3c.dom.NamedNodeMap;
import org.w3c.dom.DocumentType;
import org.w3c.dom.Attr;
import org.xml.sax.SAXParseException;
import org.xml.sax.InputSource;
import org.xml.sax.SAXException;
import com.sun.xml.parser.Resolver;
import com.sun.xml.tree.XmlDocument;
import com.sun.xml.tree.TreeWalker;

public class XmlConfigUtils
{
```

The class has no constructor, only static public methods. Here is a complete listing (declarations only):

```
// the XML-DOM path
public static String initFromXmlFile(String fileName, boolean validate, Env E)
public static String initFromTopDomTree(Node theNode, Env E)
public static String initFromDomTree(Node theNode, Env E)

// the Env path
public static String initFromTopEnv(Env E)
public static String initFromEnv (Env E)

// instantiate and initialize bean
```

```
public static String initBean(Env beanEnv, String beanClass)

// store Node name, text value as name-value pair in Env
public static void setNodeNameVal (Env E, Node N)

// app-specific DOM utilities
public static Node firstKid(Node theNode)
public static Node nextSib(Node theNode)
```

We have covered all of these except the last two; here they are, to complete the picture:

```
// get next sibling that is not a text node
public static Node nextSib(Node theNode)
{

    if(null == theNode)
    {
        return null;
    }

    Node nxt = theNode.getNextSibling();
    while(null != nxt && nxt.getNodeType() == Node.TEXT_NODE)
    {
        nxt = nxt.getNextSibling();
    }

  return nxt;

}


// get the first child element that is not a text node
public static Node firstKid(Node theNode)
{

    if(null == theNode)
    {
        return null;
    }


    Node nxt = theNode.getFirstChild();

    while(null != nxt && nxt.getNodeType() == Node.TEXT_NODE)
    {
        nxt = nxt.getNextSibling();
    }

    return nxt;

}
```

Now, it's time to look at the beans, which we shall do in the next chapter.

Conclusions

In this chapter, we presented an outline of a larger system, broke it into subsystems, and presented three of the subsystems: `RowSeq` and its derivatives, `RowViewSources`, and XML configuration that uses an improved `Env` class. While `RowSeq` and `RowViewSources` elaborate on earlier ideas, XML configuration is new and important. We now conceive of an application as a dynamically configured collection of JavaBeans that can be described by an XML document. This is very real meta-programming: we are using a simple declarative language (an XML mini-language) to construct an application out of prefabricated pieces (JavaBeans).

The instantiate-and-use relation between beans that we have implemented in this chapter imposes a tree structure on those beans, closely mirroring the tree structure of the XML document. However, it does not have to be so. Since we define `XmlConfig` in such a way as to give each bean access to an environment that contains a link to the parent environment, it is also possible for any bean to find its siblings (by name) or even search the `Env` tree to find other relatives. If the beans run in their own threads, we can now have a multiprogramming environment. We will elaborate on these ideas in the conclusions to the next chapter, after we have seen and tasted the beans.

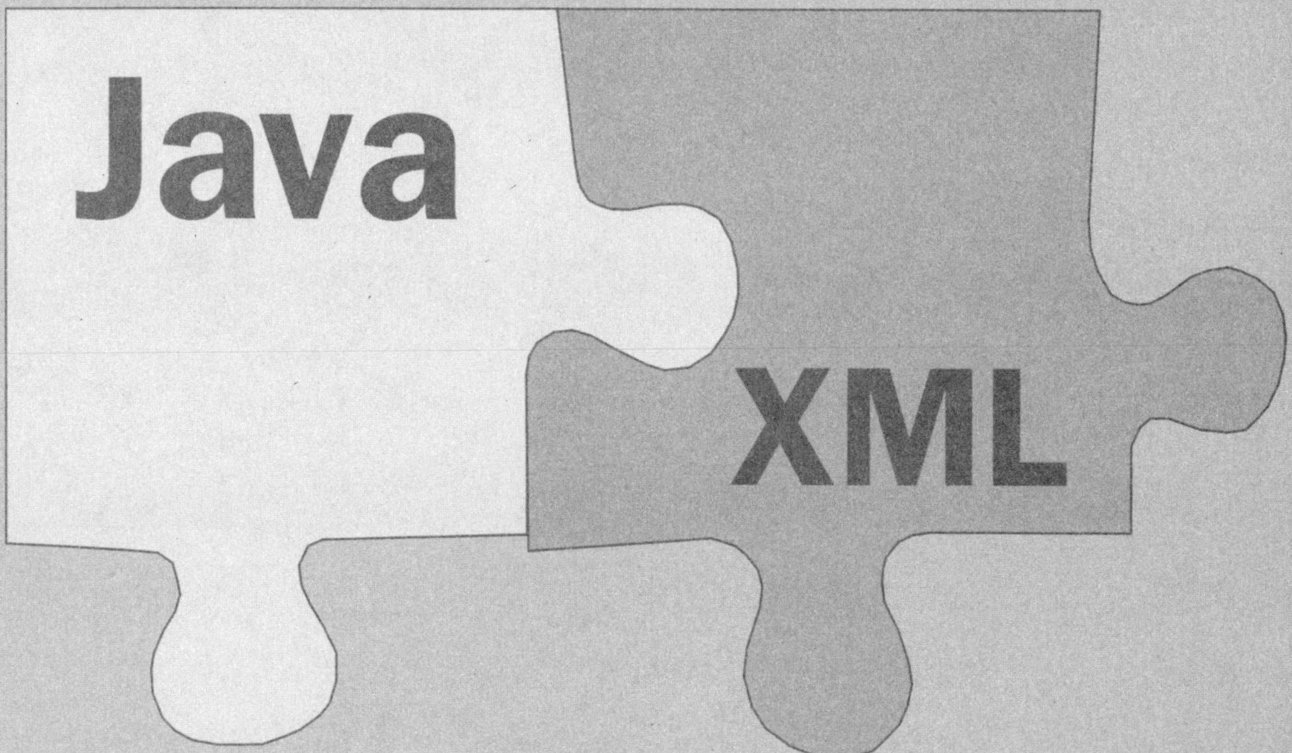
Java
XML

12

Toward a Many-Legged System: Specific Constructions

In this chapter, we continue and complete the tour of `XmlMail`. If Chapter 11 built generic data-flow and configuration tools for a fairly wide range of systems, this chapter will show specific HTML, JSP, and supporting beans for the system. We've tried to write these (especially our two `RowViewSource` classes) in a way that promotes reuse, but they are written specifically for `XmlMail`.

In outline, this chapter will proceed as follows:

- ❑ From the client to the main JSP page
- ❑ The main bean
- ❑ The two smaller beans: `MailSender` and `MailMaker`
- ❑ Another overview of the JavaMail API
- ❑ `RowViewSource` 1: `MailViewSource`
- ❑ `RowViewSource` 2: `DBViewSource`

Our main purpose throughout is to bring out the main structural theme of the application, which is a cooperation of several data sources, configurable by XML, that can both produce and consume XML data, as well as send e-mail and communicate with a database.

From the Client to the Main JSP page

The best way to start is to remind ourselves of the general view of the system again:

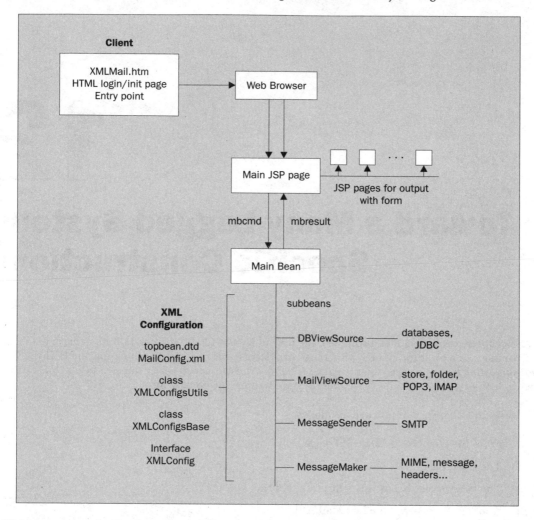

This time, instead of being analytical about it and taking the system apart, we'll trace the story (or a "use case"), beginning with the entry point.

The HTML Entry Point

The HTML file is deliberately simple, and has a small stylesheet (showing that these need not be anything too complex). The body of the page is primarily a form (some parts of that form are repeated in the JSP files for output). The only field that has to have a value is the hidden field for the initial value of mbcmd, which is "login" – the rest are optional overrides of the defaults provided in the XML file. Apart from the name of the XML configuration file, they fall into two groups: a table of "labels" (mostly text boxes but also a couple of SELECT elements), and a group of checkboxes for message lists.

Two considerations should be kept in mind as you read through the list of fields. First, if a field name contains an underscore, its value will go into a sub-Env of the Env created from Request, and so eventually that value will end up in the appropriate sub-bean. Second, a RowViewSource sub-bean can be either a MailViewSource or a DBViewSource; the HTML form doesn't know or care, but provides input fields for both. In this version of the program, only one view source can be open at a time (and so there is only one set of login/password input fields), but they can switched dynamically by the user.

Here is the code. Refer back to Chapter 11 for a screen shot of this output:

```
<!--
  http://localhost:8080/examples/jsp/xmlMail/xmlMail.htm
-->
<html>
<head><title>XmlMail</title>
<style>
  .errormessage {color:red}
  .msgdate {color:blue}
  .msgfromaddr {font:courier;color:pink}
  .msgtoaddr {font:courier;color:green}
  .msgsubject {font:arial;color:blue}
  .msgcontent {font:arial;color:black}
  .label {color:green}
</style></head>

<body bgcolor="white">
<h1>Opening page for xmlMail sample JSP</h1>
<p>
We read in an XML configuration file and set up the application with the defaults
it specifies. The fields below will override defaults.
</p>
 <form name="theForm" method="post" action="xmlmail.jsp" >
 <input type=hidden name=mbcmd value="login">
 <input type=text size=60 name="xmlInitFile"
          value="/C:/jswdk-1.0/examples/jsp/xmlMail/dbConfig.xml">

<table>
 <tr><td><p class="label">user</td>
     <td><input type=text name=rowViewSource_dbUser value="tmyers">
     </td>
     <td> userID may be the same for mail and dbase</td>
</tr>
 <tr><td><p class="label">password</td>
     <td><input type=text name=rowViewSource_dbPwd value="">
     </td>
</tr>
 <tr><td><p class="label">host</td>
     <td><input type=text name=rowViewSource_dbName value="">
     </td>
     <td>e.g. mailhost.yourserver.com for mail, jdbc:odbc:PHONEBOOK for db </td>
</tr>
 <tr><td><p class="label">mbox</td>
     <td><input type=text name=rowViewSource_dbSource value="">
```

```
          </td>
          <td>INBOX only for pop3, foldername for imap, tablename for db </td>
  </tr>
   <tr><td><p class="label">protocol</td>
          <td><input type=text name=rowViewSource_dbDriver value="">
          </td>
          <td>e.g. pop3 or imap for mail, or sun.jdbc.odbc.JdbcOdbcDriver for db </td>
   </tr>
   <tr><td><p class="label">smtphost</td>
          <td><input type=text name=messageSender_smtphost value="none.colgate.edu">
          </td>
          <td> in case you send any actual outgoing mail </td>
  </tr>
   <tr><td><p class="label">retaddr</td>
          <td><input type=text name=messageMaker_msgfromaddr value="">
          </td>
  </tr>
   <tr><td><p class="label">port</td>
          <td><input type=text name=rowViewSource_port value="">
          </td>
          <td>port number for mail connection; not used by db</td>
  </tr>
   <tr><td><p class="label">verbose</td>
          <td><select name=verbose size="1">
      <option value="true">true</option>;
      <option selected value="false">false</option>;
   </select>
          </td>
  </tr>
   <tr><td><p class="label">debug</td>
          <td><select name=debug size="1">
            <option selected value="true">true</option>;
            <option value="false">false</option>;
            </select>
          </td>
  </tr>
  </table><br>

Fields for message list:<br>
<input type=checkbox name=columnLabels value="msgfromaddr" checked>from
<input type=checkbox name=columnLabels value="msgtoaddr">to
<input type=checkbox name=columnLabels value="msgdate" checked>date
<input type=checkbox name=columnLabels value="msgsubject" checked>subject
<input type=checkbox name=columnLabels value="msgsize">size
<input type=checkbox name=columnLabels value="msgflags">flags
<input type=checkbox name=columnLabels value="msgxmailer">xmailer
<br>
<input type=submit value="Submit">
</form></body></html>
```

When submitted, this form goes to `xmlMail.jsp`.

Main JSP Page

The main JSP page is very similar to the one you saw in the `Birthdays` application in Chapter 9. The main difference is that, in `Birthdays`, we copied the `Request` object to the properties of the bean directly, by saying:

```
<jsp:setProperty name="bbean" property="*" />
```

This time around, we wrap the `Request` into a (recursive) `Env` and give it to the `doCommand()` method:

```
<% mailbean.doCommand(new MyNa.utils.Env(request)); %>
```

The first time around, when the value of `mbcmd` is "login", this line of code instantiates and initializes the beans. Every time this line of code is called, it triggers a sequence of actions, one of which sets the value of the `mbresult` property of the main bean.

Continuing with the structure of the main JSP page, we have now completed the bean initialization part and can begin with the HTML output template. To avoid clutter, we have moved all of the fixed material of the `<head>` element and the very beginning of the `<body>` into an included file, `header.jsp`. It is followed by two lines of code that retrieve the value of `mbresult` and report it to the user on-screen:

```
<%    String cmd=mailbean.getMbresult();    %>
The bean result was <%= cmd %>.<br>
```

The rest of `xmlMail.jsp` is an `if...else` statement that produces different output depending on the value of `mbresult`. In most cases, the output comes from an included file. The first two branches of the `if...else` deal with possible errors; the third branch is "logout". The rest of the branches include an output file that opens the input form and proceeds to include a common file, `continue.jsp`, that completes the form.

Here is `xmlMail.jsp` in total:

```
<!--
  http://localhost:8080/examples/jsp/xmlMail/xmlmail.jsp
-->
<%@ page import = "MyNa.utils.Env"  errorPage="errorpage.jsp" %>
<%@ page import = "MyNa.xml.RowSeq" %>

<jsp:useBean id="mailbean"
     class="xmlMail.XmlMailBean" scope="session"/>

<% mailbean.doCommand(new MyNa.utils.Env(request)); %>

<%@ include file="header.jsp" %>
```

```
<%
    String cmd=mailbean.getMbresult();
%>
The bean result was <%= cmd %> <br>
<%
    if (null==cmd){cmd="miscError";}
%>

<% if (cmd.equals("loginError")) { %>
  There was something wrong with your login;   please back up and try again. The
error message was
    <span class="errormessage">
    <xmp>
    <%= mailbean.getErrorMessage() %>
    </xmp></span>

<% } else if (cmd.equals("miscError")) { %>
  There's something wrong. The error message is
    <span class="errormessage">
      <xmp>
    <%= mailbean.getErrorMessage() %>
    </xmp></span>

<% } else if (cmd.equals("logout")) { %>

<%
HttpSession sess=request.getSession(false);
if(null!=sess){
%>
  Ending Session : <%=sess.getId()%>
<%
  sess.invalidate(); }
%>

<br>  goodbye, come again soon.

<% } else if (cmd.equals("msgShow")) { %>

<%@ include file="msg.jsp" %>

<% } else if (cmd.equals("msgList")) { %>

<%@ include file="msglist.jsp" %>

<% } else if (cmd.equals("msgDelete")) { %>

<%@ include file="msgdel.jsp" %>

<% } else if (cmd.equals("messageSent")) { %>

<%@ include file="msgsent.jsp" %>

<% } else if (cmd.equals("msgListSave2XML")) { %>
```

```
XML output:
<%@ include file="msgsent.jsp" %>
<% } else if (cmd.equals("msgListOutput")) { %>
XML output into message:
<%@ include file="msgsent.jsp" %>

<% } else if (cmd.equals("msgForward")) { %>
mail output (for the list):
<%@ include file="msgsent.jsp" %>

<% } else if (cmd.equals("msgListSave2DB")) { %>
Database output:
<%@ include file="msgsent.jsp" %>

<% } else { %>
  Unimplemented command: &quot;<span style="color:red"><%= cmd %></span>&quot;
  Please report this to system support.
<% } %>
</body></html>
```

JSP Pages for Output

To repeat, most conditional branches of the main page include an output file that opens the input form and proceeds to include a common file, continue.jsp, that completes the form. To illustrate, here is the shortest output page, msgsent.jsp:

```
The message was sent successfully.
  <form name="theForm" method="post" action="xmlmail.jsp">
  <%@ include file="continue.jsp" %>
```

The included continue.jsp page looks like this:

```
<select name=mbcmd size="1">
  <option selected value="msgList">show message list</option>
  <option value="msgShow">show message</option>
  <option value="msgDelete">delete message</option>
  <option value="msgSend">send message</option>
  <option value="logout">logout</option>
  <option value="msgListSendForward">
    send message list to 'to:' address</option>
  <option value="msgListOutputXML">
    send message list as XML in message</option>
  <option value="msgListSave2XML">
    send message list as XML to 'to:' file</option>
  <option value="msgListSave2DB">
    save message list to 'to:' db table</option>
</select>
<input type=submit value="Submit"><br>

<span class="msgtoaddr">to: </span>
  <input type=text name=messageMaker_msgtoaddr size=20><br>
<span class="msgsubject">re: </span>
  <input type=text name=messageMaker_msgsubject size=20><br>
```

```
<span class="msgsubject">message number: </span>
  <input type=text name=rowViewSource_rownum
         value="<%= mailbean.getRowNum() %>"><br>

<!-- text area for displaying and editing message content-->
<textarea name=messageMaker_msgcontent rows="10" cols="40">
  <%= mailbean.getMsgcontent() %>
</textarea><br>

</form>
```

The remaining JSP files for output are quite straightforward: they mix JSP tags with HTML tags to produce the desired output. We find them easy to use but less satisfactory than the SUBST mini-language templates because JSP pages have more semantic levels exposed simultaneously, and because their error messages are outside our control: a "typo", for example, may result in a `javac` error message dealing with one large file constructed from several JSP pages.

It is now time to move deeper inside, towards the hard core of the system.

The Main Bean

The main bean is a complex creature of many methods and over 400 lines of code. We will only review its main structural points:

- ❑ the imports, class level variables and the constructor
- ❑ `doLogin()` and initialization, including `initAliases()`
- ❑ `doCommand()`
- ❑ output methods (to e-mail, to XML documents in memory, to XML files, to a database) and the connection-related methods used by them
- ❑ methods to display, send and delete a message
- ❑ overridden methods of `XmlConfigBase`

The Imports, Class Level Variables and the Constructor

The imports reflect the bean's double interest in databases and e-mail. Class-level variables are commented to help your understanding; their role will become clear as we go through the code. The constructor initializes some of them:

```
package xmlMail;

import java.util.*;
import java.io.*;
import java.sql.*;
import javax.mail.*;
import javax.mail.internet.*;
```

```
import javax.activation.*;
import MyNa.utils.*;
import MyNa.xml.*;

public class XmlMailBean  extends XmlConfigBase
{
    Env beanEnv;        // contains subEnvs for sub-beans, including
                        // RowViewSources, MessageSender, MessageMaker
    Env requestEnv;     // given by main JSP page
    String className;   // should be xmlMail.XmlMailBean

    RowSeq rowSeq;      // result from rowViewSource
    RowViewSource rowViewSource; // local reference
    String rowViewSourceName;
    MessageMaker messageMaker;    // local reference
    String messageMakerName;
    MessageSender messageSender; // local reference
    String messageSenderName;

    String mbcmd;        // command sent from main JSP page
    String mbresult;     // command sent to main JSP page
    String errorMessage; // sent to main JSP page in case of error

    RowSeq messageList;  // filled by msgList()
    Env currentMessage;  // filled by msgShow()

    Connection dbConnection; // for saving messages to database
    boolean dbDriverHasBeenInitialized = false;

public XmlMailBean()
{
    // the constructor

    beanEnv = new Env();
    requestEnv = new Env();
    currentMessage = new Env();
    setMsgcontent("");
}
```

Note that currentMessage is an Env that holds all the properties of a given message, including its content. We start with a new message whose content is set to an empty string (so it is not null).

This is the condition of the bean after the <jsp:usebean .../> action is performed. What happens next is login and initialization.

doLogin() and Initialization

As you will recall, the entry-point HTML page set the initial command to "login". Channeled through the Request object, the main JSP page, and the doCommand() method of the mail bean, this results in a call to doLogin(). This is where the sub-beans are instantiated and configured:

```
public void doLogin()
{
    try
    {
        initBeanTree();      // XML configuration

        if(hasError())
        {
            return;
        }

        rowViewSource.initSession(beanEnv);
        checkRVErr();

        if(hasError())
        {
            return;
        }

        msgList();
    }

    catch(Exception E)
    {
        setMiscError("error in Login: " + E);
    }
}
```

As you can see, `doLogin()` makes two initialization calls. The first is to `initBeanTree()` that sets up `beanEnv` and performs the XML configuration. As a result, the `rowViewSource` variable is initialized, and we call its `initSession()` method. This is the second initialization call: it does different things depending on whether `rowViewSource` is a mail folder or a database. After each initialization call, we check to see whether the string variable that accumulates error messages is empty or not and, if it is not empty, we return it. Finally, we call `msgList()`, to see what data, if any, has arrived in our `RowSeq` variable as a result of the `initSession()` method call. (For instance, if there are new mail messages on the server, they will have been transferred to our bean.)

Let's look at the methods involved in detail.

initBeanTree()

You may want to review `initFromXmlFile()` and `initFromTopEnv()` in the preceding chapter because `initBeanTree()` calls these methods:

```
public void initBeanTree()
{

    // from requestEnv

    String xmlFileName = requestEnv.getStr("xmlInitFile", "mailConfig.xml");
    // i.e., get value of "xmlInitFile" from requestEnv;
    // if null, use the default "mailConfig.xml"

    String S = initFromXmlFile(xmlFileName, false, beanEnv);

    if(S.length() > 0)
    {
        setMiscError(S);
    }

    if(hasError())
    {
        // check the length of errrorString
        return;
    }

    // if we get here, bean structure has been initialized with defaults;
    // now we can override/extend defaults with html form info
    initFromTopEnv(requestEnv);           // first simple strings
    setStringArraysFromEnv(requestEnv);   // then arrays of strings

    // give messageMaker a reference to messageSender
    messageMaker.setMessageSender(messageSender);

    // initialize generic local aliases for beans
    initAliases(requestEnv);

    // have messageSender start a session; put reference in beanEnv
    messageSender.startSession();
    beanEnv.put("msgSession", messageSender.getSession());

}
```

Two items here merit further discussion: `setStringArraysFromEnv()` and `initAliases()`. We'll do the second one first, naturally.

initAliases()

As a result of `initFromXmlFile()` and `initFromTopEnv()`, the beans have been instantiated and configured. However, at this point, the main bean can only refer to the `RowViewSource` sub-bean by its "real" name, either as a `DBViewSource` or as a `MailViewSource`. However, we want to be able to refer to them generically, as a `RowViewSource`. In other words, we want a local and more generic alias for that sub-bean. Once we set up a local alias for one sub-bean, we can just as well set up aliases for all of them, in case future extensions of the program will allow more than one `MessageSender` or `MessageComposer`. This is what `initAliases()` does. It initializes three local variables (since at any given moment there are three sub-beans in operation) to refer to the sub-beans by names that can be different from the names that they received in the process of instantiation and initialization:

```
public void initAliases(Env E)
{
    Env subEnv = E.getEnv("rowViewSource");

    if(null != subEnv && null != rowViewSource)
    {
        ((XmlConfig)rowViewSource).initFromEnv(subEnv);
    }

    subEnv = E.getEnv("messageSender");

    if(null != subEnv && null != messageSender)
    {
        ((XmlConfig)messageSender).initFromEnv(subEnv);
    }

    subEnv = E.getEnv("messageMaker");

    if(null != subEnv && null != messageMaker)
    {
        ((XmlConfig)messageMaker).initFromEnv(subEnv);
    }
}
```

setStringArraysFromEnv()

This method immediately follows initFromTopEnv(requestEnv). In that call, those Request properties that are strings have been copied to the properties of the bean. However, there are HTML form fields that produce a string array, such as multiple-option SELECT elements and a group of non-mutually-exclusive checkboxes. If we simply copy such a value by an assignment statement, we'll get a new reference to the same array rather than a "real" copy, which is what we want. In our case here, we do have a group of checkboxes for columnLabels, so we provide a special (and admittedly a bit *ad hoc*) method to deal with it:

```
public void setStringArraysFromEnv(Env E)
{
    // at the moment, we are only concerned with columnLabels.

    Object ob = E.get("columnLabels");

    if(null == ob || !(ob instanceof String[]))
    {
        return;
    }

    setColumnLabels((String[])ob);
}
```

Note that the setColumnLabels() method of the main bean simply calls a RowViewSource method of the same name:

```
public void setColumnLabels(String[] A)
{
    rowViewSource.setColumnLabels(A);
}
```

The actual implementation, both in `MailRowSequence` and in `DBRowSequence`, copies the array:

```
public void setColumnLabels(String[]A)
{
    columnLabels = A;
    int N = 0;

    if(columnTypes == null ||
            columnTypes.length != (N = columnLabels.length))
    {
        columnTypes = new String[N];

        for(int i = 0; i < N; i++)
        {
            columnTypes[i]="VARCHAR";
        }
    }
}
```

This completes the first initialization call of `doLogin()`. The second initialization call (`initSession()`) takes place in `rowViewSources` and we'll look at this when we get to the sub-beans involved. The last thing that `doLogin()` does is call `msgList()`. This is a typical `doXXX()` method that produces output: on the first line, it sets the `mbresult` variable that is returned to the JSP page; its middle part consists of just one line that retrieves the contents of `rowViewSource` and places them in `rowSeq`; and then, finally, it checks for errors:

```
public void msgList()
{
    setMbresult("msgList");
    rowSeq = rowViewSource.getRowList();
    checkRVErr();
}
```

This concludes the activities of the `doLogin()` method. What other commands are there? Let's look at the `doCommand()` method that lists them all.

doCommand()

`doCommand()` is run every time a new request comes in. (The bean has session scope.) It reinitializes the beans from `requestEnv`, retrieves `mbcmd`, and calls the method specified by `mbcmd`:

```
public void doCommand(Env requestEnv)
{
    try
    {
        setErrorMessage(null);
        setRequestEnv(requestEnv);
        initFromTopEnv(requestEnv);
        initAliases(requestEnv);
        setMbcmd(requestEnv.getStr("mbcmd"));

        if(null == mbcmd)
            setMiscError("no mailbean command given");
        else
            if("login".equals(mbcmd))
                doLogin();
        else
            if("logout".equals(mbcmd))
                doLogout();
        else
            if("msgList".equals(mbcmd))
                msgList();
        else
            if("msgListSendForward".equals(mbcmd))
                msgListSendForward();
        else
            if("msgListOutputXML".equals(mbcmd))
                msgListOutputXML();
        else
            if("msgListSave2XML".equals(mbcmd))
                msgListSave2XMLFile();
        else
            if("msgListSave2DB".equals(mbcmd))
                msgListSave2DB();
        else
            if("msgShow".equals(mbcmd))
                msgShow();
        else
            if("msgSend".equals(mbcmd))
                msgSend();
        else
            if("msgDelete".equals(mbcmd))
                msgDelete();
        else
            setMiscError("unknown mailbean command [" + mbcmd + "]");
    }

    catch(Exception E)
    {
        setMiscError("ERROR: " + E);
    }
}
```

With all the commands listed for us by doCommand(), we can classify them into groups and briefly characterize each group:

- ❑ doLogin() and doLogout(): we have already seen doLogin(); doLogout() is a three-liner that sets up mbresult, closes up and exits

- ❑ msgList commands: you have already seen msgList(); the remaining four msgListXXX() methods forward or save the contents of RowSeq to various destinations

- ❑ msg commands: the three msgXXX() commands display, send, or delete the current message

We can move on to the msgList commands and msg commands.

msgList Commands

There are four of them:

- ❑ msgListSendForward()
- ❑ msgListOutputXML()
- ❑ msgListSave2XMLFile()
- ❑ msgListSave2DB()

What they all have in common is that they take a "message list" (which may be a list of rows in a database) and send it somewhere. All of them use one of the sendTo() methods of rowViewSource.

msgListSendForward()

This is the shortest of the four. It follows the familiar pattern of setting mbresult, performing its set task, and checking for rowViewSource errors:

```
public void msgListSendForward()
{
    setMbresult("msgForward");
    rowViewSource.sendTo("mail", messageMaker.getMsgtoaddr());
    checkRVErr();
}
```

This version of sendTo() takes two arguments, the type of destination and its name, and uses a more specialized method (sendToMail() in this case) to send the list of rows to the named destination.

msgListOutputXML() and msgListSave2XMLFile()

These two methods are nearly identical, except that one uses a StringWriter and the other a FileWriter. Both use outputTarget() to find the name of the target to send their output to. Both end up calling the toXml() method of RowSeq, with three arguments: the stream, the target name, and the Boolean value of reset. (See Chapter 11 for the reset parameter of RowSeq.) Note that the RowSeq object is obtained from rowViewSource using the getAllColumnsRowList() method: all the fields of the underlying table are thus retrieved.

```java
public void msgListOutputXML()
{
    String target = outputTarget();

    try
    {
        setMbresult("msgListOutput");
        StringWriter sw = new StringWriter();
        RowSeq rE = rowViewSource.getAllColumnsRowList();
        checkRVErr();

        if(hasError())
        {
            return;
        }

        rE.toXML(sw, target, false);
        setMsgcontent(sw.toString());
    }

    catch(Exception ex)
    {
        setMiscError("can't save XML to message " + target + "\n" + ex);
    }
}

public void msgListSave2XMLFile()
{
    String target = outputTarget();

    try
    {

        setMbresult("msgListSave2XML");
        RowSeq rE = rowViewSource.getAllColumnsRowList();
        checkRVErr();

        if(hasError())
        {
            return;
        }

        FileWriter fw = new FileWriter(new File(target));
        rE.toXML(fw, target, false);
        fw.close();
    }
```

```
    catch(Exception ex)
    {
        setMiscError("can't save XML to file " + target + "\n" + ex);
    }
}
```

msgListSave2DB()

Finally, to save to the database, we have to get a connection. Within RowSeq, we now call toDB() rather than toXml():

```
public void msgListSave2DB()
{
    String target = outputTarget();
    setMbresult("msgListSave2DB");

    try
    {
        boolean reset = false;
        RowSeq rE = rowViewSource.getAllColumnsRowList();
        checkRVErr();

        if(hasError())
        {
            return;
        }

        findDbConnection();
        rE.toDB(dbConnection, target, reset);
        freeDbConnection();
        checkRVErr();
    }

    catch(Exception ex)
    {
        setMiscError ("can't save XML to DB table " +
                target + "\n" + ex);
    }
}
```

We will cover connection-related methods in a moment, but first let us look at outputTarget().

outputTarget()

The first choice for the output target method is the to: address of MessageMaker. If it turns out to be null or empty, we call getDbSource() which retrieves the dbSource field of rowViewSource:

```
public String outputTarget()
{
    String target = messageMaker.getMsgtoaddr();

    if(target == null || target.length() == 0)
    {
        target = getDbSource();
    }

    return target;
}
```

findDbConnection(), freeDbConnection()

Now the connection methods. Properly done, the application should maintain a pool of connections, and then allocate connections from that pool. We take the easy route of creating a fresh connection for each call on `msgListSave2DB()` and then destroying it when done:

```
public void findDbConnection() throws Exception
{
    Env theEnv = beanEnv.getEnv("databaseSource");
    // databaseSource may or may not be the same
    // as the current rowViewSource of the application

    String dbDriver = theEnv.getStr("dbDriver",
            "sun.jdbc.odbc.JdbcOdbcDriver");
    String dbUrl = theEnv.getStr("dbUrl", "jdbc:odbc:PHONEBOOK");
    String dbUser = theEnv.getStr("dbUser", "JohnSmith");
    String dbPwd = theEnv.getStr("dbPwd", "password");

    if(!dbDriverHasBeenInitialized)
    {
        Class.forName(dbDriver);
        dbDriverHasBeenInitialized = true;
    }

    dbConnection=DriverManager.getConnection(dbUrl,dbUser,dbPwd);
}

public void freeDbConnection()throws Exception
{
    dbConnection.close();
}
```

Methods to Display, Send and Delete a Message

These methods are:

- ❑   msgShow()
- ❑   msgSend()
- ❑   msgDelete()

They follow the familiar pattern: set mbresult, perform a set task, and then check for errors. Ultimately, this work gets done in sub-beans. Note in particular this line from the msgSend() method:

```
try
{
    messageSender.sendMessage(messageMaker.getMessage());
}
```

On a first look, it is completely clear what's going on here: we get a message from messageMaker and simply give it to messageSender to send. As always, there is more to it and for a more satisfactory level of clarity, we'll have to wait until we get to the later sections on those two sub-beans. Similarly, see the ViewSource sub-beans for the workings of the getRow() and getRowNum() methods that these methods use:

```
public void msgShow()
{
    setMbresult("msgShow");
    currentMessage = rowViewSource.getRow(rowViewSource.getRowNum());
    checkRVErr();
}

public void msgSend()
{
    setMbresult("messageSent");
    try
    {
        messageSender.sendMessage(messageMaker.getMessage());
    }
    catch(Exception E)
    {
        setMiscError("failed to send msg; " + E);
    }
}

public void msgDelete()
{
    setMbresult("msgDelete");
    rowViewSource.delRow(rowViewSource.getRowNum());
    checkRVErr();
}
```

We are almost ready to abandon the main bean and move over to the sub-beans. In preparation for that move, we are going to review those methods that are shared by them all.

Overridden Methods of XmlConfigBase

All of the beans in this program implement `XmlConfig` by extending `XmlConfigBase` and overriding some of its methods. In particular, all of them override `setInitDefs()` and `setString()`.

setInitDefs()

This method adds the name-value pairs of its `Env` argument to the appropriate `Env` of the bean it belongs to. In the case of the main bean, the `Env` is `beanEnv`:

```
public void setInitDefs(Env E)
{
    beanEnv.addHashtable(E);
}
```

setString()

This method takes two arguments, a key-value pair, and uses the key to call the appropriate `setXXX()` method of the bean it is in. The selection of possibilities depends on the bean, but the structure of the method is the same in all of them:

```
public void setString(String key, String val)
{
if(key == null)
        return;

    if(key.equals("verbose"))
        setVerbose(val);
    else
        if(key.equals("debug"))
            setDebug(val);
    else
        if(key.equals("messageSenderName"))
            setMessageSenderName(val);
    else
        if(key.equals("messageMakerName"))
            setMessageMakerName(val);
    else
        if(key.equals("rowViewSourceName"))
            setRowViewSourceName(val);
    else
        if(key.equals("columnLabels"))
            setColumnLabels(val);
    else
        if(key.equals("mbcmd"))
            setMbcmd(val);
    else
        if(key.equals("class"))
            className=val;
}
```

In Conclusion

This concludes our discussion of the main bean. As you can imagine, there are a number of get/set methods and other supporting cast, but we have covered only the key components. Please, review and experiment with the entire code as found at the book's web site (http://www.wrox.com).

We now have four sub-beans to discuss. Two of them are RowViewSources; the other two are smaller, and specialized for composing and sending email. We'll start with a discussion of the smaller ones, and in the process, develop a better understanding of the JavaMail API (but you may want to review the two-page introduction to it found near the beginning of Chapter 11).

The Smaller Beans

The MessageSender and MessageMaker classes have a lot in common. They are similar in what they import, what variables they declare, and what methods of the parent class they override. We'll start with MessageSender and give it fairly detailed coverage, allowing a much briefer treatment of MessageMaker. In both cases, we'll make detours into JavaMail.

MessageSender

This is a really small class, less than eighty lines of code. In addition to the standard get/set methods, it clearly divides into:

- ❏ imports
- ❏ class-level variables and the constructor
- ❏ methods that use JavaMail
- ❏ methods that override XmlConfigBase

Imports

Both MessageSender and MessageMaker import JavaMail packages, along with other classes that JavaMail needs in order to function properly:

```
import MyNa.utils.*;
import javax.mail.*;
import javax.mail.internet.*;
import javax.activation.*;
import java.util.Properties;
```

The activation package is needed to support different MIME data types. Since a mail message can bring with it data of arbitrary MIME type, we have to be able to respond to it by dynamically activating the appropriate bean to handle the data on the basis of its MIME type. It is just this functionality that is supplied by the activation package.

The Properties class is needed to set some system properties that JavaMail uses. Refer back to Chapter 3 for examples and explanations on how it is used, or just read on: the Properties class has a very intuitive interface. It extends a very familiar Hashtable class.

Variables and the Constructor

Some variables are common to all beans; others correspond to child elements of the `msgSender` element in `mailconfig.xml`. Let's place the variables and the XML element next to each other:

```
/*  <msgSender>
      <class>MyNa.xml.MessageSender</class>
      <smtphost>mailhost.msn.com</smtphost>
      <mailerName>Simple Mail Bean 0.1</mailerName>
      <verbose>true</verbose>
      <debug>true</debug>
    </msgSender>
*/

public class MessageSender extends XmlConfigBase
{

    // MessageSender specific: name of SMTP host that does the sending
    // obtained from the XML config file or user input from HTML form
    String smtphost;    //e.g. cs.colgate.edu
    String mailerName;  // the name of the mailing program: XmlMailBean

    // common to many beans
    Env beanEnv;
    String errorMessage;
    String errorType;

    Session session; // essential JavaMail object

    public MessageSender()
    {
        beanEnv = new Env();
        errorMessage = "";
    }
}
```

As you may remember from the main bean, it's the `MailSender` that manages the session object that is used by other beans as well.

Sending Mail Using JavaMail

We have already seen how a session object is created: one of the options of the `doCommand()` method of the main bean is "login". In response:

- ❑ the bean calls its `doLogin()` method
- ❑ `doLogin()` calls `initBeanTree()`
- ❑ `initBeanTree()` creates the sub-beans, including `MessageSender`
- ❑ `initBeanTree()` then calls its `startSession()` method, which creates the session

```
public void startSession()
{
    // a method of MessageSender bean
    Properties props = System.getProperties();
    props.put("mail.smtp.host", getSmtphost());
    session = Session.getDefaultInstance(props, null);
    session.setDebug(debug);
}
```

Once a session object is created, sending mail is magically easy:

```
public void sendMessage(MimeMessage msg)
{
    try
    {
        Transport.send(msg);
    }
    catch(Exception E)
    {
        setMiscError("fail to send " + E);
    }
}
```

What's going on here? Obviously, there is a `Transport` class, and it has a public static method called `send()` that takes a message and sends it – but to where? And from where? All that information is contained within the message and system properties, and if something goes wrong, the method will throw an exception.

Other Methods for Sending Mail

Another public static method of the same name takes as its second argument an array of e-mail addresses and sends the message to all of them. There is also an instance method, `sendMessage()`, with this signature:

```
public abstract void sendMessage(Message msg, Address[] addresses)
        throws MessagingException
```

This method gives you additional control over what happens because you can register `TransportListeners` on this `Transport` object, and an appropriate `TransportEvent` indicating the delivery status will be delivered to those listeners.

This is all there is to sending mail using JavaMail. The remaining methods of `MailSender` fall into two groups: setters/getters, and redefined methods of `XmlConfigBase`. We will only comment on the latter.

Overriding the Methods of XmlConfigBase

The way `MessageSender` overrides `setInitDefs()`, `setString()` and `getString()` is typical of other beans as well:

```
public void setInitDefs(Env E)
{
    // add the argument to beanEnv
    beanEnv.addHashtable(E);
}

public void setString(String key, String val)
{
    if(key == null)
        return;
    else
        if(key.equals("verbose"))
            setVerbose(val);
    else
        if(key.equals("debug"))
            setDebug(val);
    else
        if(key.equals("beanName"))
            setBeanName(val);
    else
        if(key.equals("smtphost"))
            setSmtphost(val);
    else
        if(key.equals("mailerName"))
            setMailerName(val);
}


public String getString(String key)
{
    // return mailerName or null

    if(null == key)
    {
        return null;
    }

    if(key.equals("mailerName"))
    {
        return getMailerName();
    }

    return null;
}
```

The rest of MessageSender consists of set/get methods that are completely trivial.

MessageMaker

Just as with `MessageSender`, it is useful to review the XML element; if nothing else, it will give us an idea of the class-level variables of `MessageMaker`:

```
<class>MyNa.xml.MessageMaker</class>
<msgsubject> </msgsubject>
<msgtoaddr> </msgtoaddr>
<msgfromaddr> </msgfromaddr>
<msgcontent> </msgcontent>
<msgcc> </msgcc>
<msgbcc> </msgbcc>
<verbose>true</verbose>
<debug>true</debug>
```

You see the same variables in `setString()`, which `MessageMaker` overrides in exactly the same way as `MessageSender`:

```
public void setString(String key, String val)
{
    if(key == null)
        return;

    if(key.equals("verbose"))
        setVerbose(val);
    else
        if(key.equals("debug"))
            setDebug(val);
    else
        if(key.equals("beanName"))
            setBeanName(val);
    else
        if(key.equals("msgsubject"))
            setMsgsubject(val);
    else
        if(key.equals("msgtoaddr"))
            setMsgtoaddr(val);
    else
        if(key.equals("msgfromaddr"))
            setMsgfromaddr(val);
    else
        if(key.equals("msgcontent"))
            setMsgcontent(val);
    else
        if(key.equals("msgcc"))
            setMsgcc(val);
    else
        if(key.equals("msgbcc"))
            setMsgbcc(val);
    else
        System.out.println("(MessageMaker) no such setstring: "
                            + key + "!=" + val);

}
```

Note that `setInitDefs()` here is exactly the same as in `MessageSender`; the constructor trivially initializes `beanEnv`, and the set/get methods are simple one-liners. The only method of interest is `getMessage()`, which we look at next.

getMessage() and the MimeMessage Class

Both `getMessage()` and the `sendMessage()` method of `MessageSender` are used in a single line of the main bean:

```
messageSender.sendMessage(messageMaker.getMessage());
```

Neither message needs parameters; these are all stored in the variables of the class by `setXXX()` methods that ultimately get their arguments from the XML configuration file and the `Request` object. We can see how it all comes together from the code of the `getMessage()` method:

```
public MimeMessage getMessage()
        throws MessagingException
{
    // MessageSender has the session
    Session session = msgSender.getSession();
    MimeMessage msg = new MimeMessage(session);
    msg.setFrom(new InternetAddress(msgfromaddr));
    msg.setRecipients(Message.RecipientType.TO,
            InternetAddress.parse(msgtoaddr, false));

    if(msgcc != null && msgcc.length() > 0)
    {
        msg.setRecipients(Message.RecipientType.CC,
                InternetAddress.parse(msgcc, false));
    }

    if(msgbcc != null && msgbcc.length() > 0)
    {
        msg.setRecipients(Message.RecipientType.BCC,
                InternetAddress.parse(msgbcc, false));
    }

    msg.setSubject(msgsubject);
    msg.setHeader("X-Mailer", msgSender.getMailerName());
    msg.setText(msgcontent);
    msg.setSentDate(new Date());

    return msg;

}
```

A lot of action here is performed by the `setXXX()` methods of `MimeMessage` and the public static `parse()` method of `InternetAddress`. Isn't JavaMail wonderful? It does a lot of work for us in a clear and intuitive way. We will see more of it in the `MailViewSource` class.

RowViewSource 1: MailViewSource

Just as the two smaller e-mail sub-beans are similar in structure, so are the two larger ones that both implement the `RowViewSource` interface. They diverge in the source-specific code (e-mail store vs. database tables). Since databases have been with us since the start of the book, we will spend more time with `MailViewSource` (picking up more details of JavaMail in the process) and give `DBViewSource` a more cursory treatment.

Main Subdivisions

As with the main bean, this class is so big that meaningful subdivisions can be found:

- ❑ Introductory: imports, class-level variables, constructor, `setString()`
- ❑ Methods for working with JavaMail classes: `Store`, `Folder`, `FetchProfile`, `Message`
- ❑ Methods for getting messages
- ❑ Methods for deleting messages and message ranges
- ❑ Methods for output to XML, mail and database
- ❑ get/set methods

This list will serve as an outline for the rest of this section.

Imports, Variables, Constructor, and setString()

The imports fall into familiar groups. Note that we need the `sql` and `dom` packages for output methods:

```
package MyNa.xml;
import MyNa.utils.*;

import java.util.*;
import java.io.*;

import javax.mail.*;
import javax.mail.internet.*;
import javax.activation.*;

import org.w3c.dom.Node;
import java.sql.*;
```

Hidden within our "home-grown" `MyNa.xml` package is a new class, `MessageData`, which we use in both `MailViewSource` and `DBViewSource`. It is a convenient class that provides useful access methods; in effect, it makes a message look like a JDBC row with a `getString(String columnLabel)` method:

```
public class MailViewSource extends XmlConfigBase
        implements RowViewSource
{
    Env msgEnv;         // for an individual message

    String protocol;    // pop3, imap
    int port;           // -1 is fine
    String host;        // x.y.com, mail source
    String dbUser;      // userId for mail
    String dbPwd;
    String retaddr;
    String mbox;        // current mailbox name; INBOX only for pop3
    boolean expunge;    // if true, deletions are purged
    int rownum;         // for extraction/deletion of individual messages

    String[] columnLabels;
    String[] columnTypes;

    String errorType;
    String errorMessage;

    Session session;
    Store store;
    Folder folder;
    FetchProfile fp;

    // constructor: initialize variables
    public MailViewSource()
    {
        msgEnv = new Env();
        columnLabels = MessageData.getDefaultLabels();
        errorType = null;
        errorMessage = null;
        session = null;
        store = null;
        folder = null;
    }
```

The only new item here is the getDefaultLabels() method that returns the static string array defaultLabels from MessageData:

```
static String[] defaultLabels =
        {"msgfromaddr", "msgtoaddr", "msgdate", "msgsubject",
         "msgsize", "msgflags","msgxmailer"};
```

A number of variables can also be seen in the overridden setString() method:

```
public void setString(String name, String val)
{
    if(name == null)
        return;
```

```
        if(name.equals("dbDriver"))
            setDbDriver(val);
        else
            if(name.equals("dbName"))
                setDbName(val);
        else
            if(name.equals("dbUser"))
                setDbUser(val);
        else
            if(name.equals("dbPwd"))
                setDbPwd(val);
        else
            if(name.equals("dbSource"))
                setDbSource(val);
        else
            if(name.equals("expunge"))
                setExpunge(val);
        else
            if(name.equals("rownum"))
                setRowNum(val);
        else
            if(name.equals("verbose"))
                setVerbose(val);
        else
            if(name.equals("debug"))
                setDebug(val);
        else
            if(name.equals("retaddr"))
                setRetaddr(val);
        else
            if(name.equals("port"))
                setPort(val);
        else
            if(name.equals("columnLabels"))
                setColumnLabels(val);
        else
            if(name.equals("beanName"))
                setBeanName(val);
        else
            System.out.println("(MailViewSource) no such setString: "
                               + name + "!=" + val);

    }
```

As before, there are a number of set/get methods that we ask you to take for granted.

Methods for JavaMail

In order to retrieve messages, you need `Session`, `Store`, `FetchProfile`, and open `Folder` objects; then you can use the `getMessage()` and `getMessages()` methods of the `Folder` class. The methods of this group set it all up. They are:

- ❑ `initSession()`
- ❑ `initFetchProfile()`
- ❑ `initFolder()`
- ❑ `enterFolder()`
- ❑ `checkFolder()`
- ❑ and `close()`

It all starts with `initSession()` and ends with `close()`. The main bean calls both of these methods, and it's the main bean's responsibility to make sure that both events happen.

initSession()

By the time we get to `initSession()`, the main bean has already created a session (or, rather, asked `MessageSender` to do so) and placed it in its `beanEnv` object. That `beanEnv` of the main bean is the argument to `initSession()`, from which the session is retrieved on its first call. Since `initSession()` gets called from other places as well (from `initFolder()`, for example), we check to make sure that the `Env` has a non-null session in it:

```
public void initSession(Env E) throws Exception
{
    Session sess = (Session) E.get("msgSession");

    if(null != sess)
        setSession(sess);

    store = session.getStore(protocol);
    // if session is null, exception is thrown

    store.connect(host, port, dbUser, dbPwd);
    initFetchProfile();
}
```

You will notice that `session` gets you a `store` with the appropriate protocol, and `store` connects to the specified host on the specified `port`. If `port` is `-1`, the default `port` is used. The last thing that `initSession()` does is create and configure a `FetchProfile` object.

initFetchProfile()

`FetchProfile` is an optimization class for those stores (like IMAP) that support batch retrieval of messages in one request. As the documentation explains:

> "Messages obtained from a Folder are light-weight objects that typically start off as empty references to the actual messages."

When you go to such a message and ask it for its Subject (for instance), the Subject field is retrieved "on-demand". Suppose you have retrieved an array of "light-weight" messages and now want to retrieve their Subject fields in a batch operation. This is what `FetchProfiles` are for: you create a `FetchProfile` object, and use its `add()` method to indicate the fields that you want batch-retrieved. Arguments to `add()` may be individual fields or pre-packaged collections of fields wrapped into objects of the sub-classes of the inner class `ITEM`. The possible items are `ENVELOPE`, `FLAGS` and `CONTENT-INFO`. (There's some very clever Java programming here that uses inner classes with protected constructors to create, in effect, an enumerated list of values, as in C/C++ `enum`.)

Here is an example from the documentation that shows how `FetchObject` is instantiated and used:

```
Message[] msgs = folder.getMessages(); // retrieve an array of messages

FetchProfile fp = new FetchProfile();  // create a FetchProfile
fp.add(FetchProfile.Item.ENVELOPE);    // add an ENVELOPE object
fp.add("X-mailer");                    // add another field
folder.fetch(msgs, fp);                // retrieve fields for all messages
```

In our code, the `FetchProfile` object is created and configured in the `initFetchProfile()` method; it is used in `getMessages()` later:

```
public void initFetchProfile()
{
    fp = new FetchProfile();
    fp.add(FetchProfile.Item.ENVELOPE);
    fp.add(FetchProfile.Item.FLAGS);
}
```

initFolder(), enterFolder() and checkFolder()

The `initFolder()` method gets you to the default folder. Once there, you can enter a named folder of your choice, assuming that your server protocol supports multiple folders:

```
public boolean initFolder()
{
    try
    {
        if(null != folder && folder.isOpen())
        {
            folder.close(expunge);
            // reset; purge deleted msgs if expunge == true
        }
```

```
            if(null == store)
            {
                // bad session somehow
                initSession(msgEnv);
                if(hasError())
                {
                    return false;
                }
            }

            folder = store.getDefaultFolder();
            return true;
        }

        catch(Exception E)
        {
            setMiscError("MVS initFolder: " + E);
            return false;
        }
    }

public boolean enterFolder()
{
    // set to mbox name
    try
    {
        if(null == folder)
        {
            if(!initFolder())
            {
                return false;
            }
        }
    }

    catch(Exception E)
    {
        folder = null;
        setMiscError("enterFolder failed to get default for "
                + mbox + "\n" + E);
        return false;
    } // if we got here, folder is default folder.

    try
    {
        folder = folder.getFolder(mbox);
        folder.open(Folder.READ_WRITE);
    }

    catch(MessagingException E)
    {
```

```
                setMiscError("enter folder failed: " + mbox + "\n" + E);
                return false;
        }

        return true;
}
```

The methods for looking at messages or deleting them run `checkFolder()`. It does a good deal of work the first time it's called but normally does nothing thereafter:

```
public boolean checkFolder()
{
    try
    {
        if(folder != null)
        {
            return true;
        }

        if(!initFolder())
        {
            return false;
        }

        if(!enterFolder())
        {
            return false;
        }

        return true; // if we got here, the folder is open.
    }

    catch (Exception ex)
    {
        setMiscError("check folder error: " + mbox + "\n" + ex);
    }

    return false;
}
```

close()

The `close()` method (surprise, surprise) closes the `folder` and `store`, and sets `session` to null:

```
public void close()
{
    try
    {
```

```
        if(null != folder)
        {
            folder.close(expunge);
        }
        if(null != store)
        {
            store.close();
        }
        session = null;
    }

    catch(Exception E)
    {
        setMiscError("closing error " + E);
    }
}
```

We now have all the machinery in place to retrieve, forward, store and delete messages. We start with retrieval.

Methods for Getting Messages

We can retrieve an individual message by its number as an Env object, or we can retrieve a message list as a RowSeq. There are a couple of things to keep in mind:

- ❑ This bean has a msgEnv variable; that's the Env that is returned by this method
- ❑ The beanEnv has a columnLabels property that specifies the fields to be retrieved by getRowList()
- ❑ MessageData (our utility class) has a constructor that takes a Message object and a columnLabels parameter, to specify the kind of access to the Message object
- ❑ MessageData also has a static getAllLabels() method that returns all the available labels

With these reminders in place, we can easily read the methods of this group, getRow(), getRowList() and getAllColumnsRowList().

getRow()

We get the message from the folder and wrap it in MessageData for ease of use. We use MessageData to add the properties of the message to msgEnv; adding the content of the message requires a separate line of code. Finally, we return msgEnv:

```
public Env getRow(int N)
{
    if(N <=0 || !checkFolder())
    {
        return msgEnv; // miscError set.
    }
```

```
    rownum = N;

    try
    {
        Message m = folder.getMessage(rownum);
        MessageData md = new MessageData(m, columnLabels);
        md.addToEnv(msgEnv); // transfer columnLabels properties
        msgEnv.put("msgcontent", md.getContentString()); // add content
    }

    catch (IndexOutOfBoundsException iex)
    {
        setMiscError("getRow: Message number " + rownum
                + " is out of range");
    }

    catch (Exception ex)
    {
        setMiscError("getRow error: " + ex);
    }

    return msgEnv;

}
```

getRowList() and getAllColumnsRowList()

All the real work of getRowList() is done by a call on the MailSequence constructor. We have, of course, seen that constructor in Chapter 11, but it was a long time ago, and besides, at that time we didn't know much about Folders and FetchProfiles, so after we go through getRowList(), we'll make another pass over the constructor, to see how it all works together.

Note that getRowList() itself does very little: it adds columnLabels to msgEnv and calls the constructor. The rest is exception handling:

```
public RowSeq getRowList()
{
    // with columnLabels as in msgEnv
    try
    {
        if(!checkFolder())
        {
            return null;
        }
        msgEnv.put("columnLabels", columnLabels);
        return new MailSequence(folder, fp, msgEnv);
    }
    catch(MessagingException ex)
    {
        setMiscError("MVS.getRowList(): failed to get message list: " + ex);
        return null;
    }
```

```
        catch(Exception E)
        {
            setMiscError("MVS.getRowList(): err in getting MailSequence: " + E);
            return null;
        }
    }
```

MailSequence Constructor

The `MailSequence` constructor was covered in Chapter 11, but we need to look it over again in context. In particular, note that there are class-level variables with ponderous names like `theColumnLabels` or `theNumberOfColumns` that get filled in during the preparatory stage of the constructor. When the preparatory stage is finally over, we get the messages from the folder into a `Message` array (`theMessages`), set the current message index to zero, and use the `FetchProfile` to retrieve the properties of the messages in the array:

```
public MailSequence(Folder folder, FetchProfile fp, Env seqInfo)
        throws MessagingException, Exception
{
    super(seqInfo);

    if(null==theColumnLabels || theColumnLabels.length == 0)
    {
        theColumnLabels = seqInfo.getStrSeq("columnLabels");
    }

    if(null == theColumnLabels)
    {
        theColumnLabels = defaultLabels;
        seqInfo.put("columnLabels", theColumnLabels);
    }

    theNumberOfColumns = theColumnLabels.length;
    theColumnValues = new String[theNumberOfColumns];
    theColumnTypes = new String[theNumberOfColumns];

    for(int i = 0; i < theNumberOfColumns; i++)
    {
        theColumnTypes[i]="VARCHAR";
    }

    seqInfo.put("columnTypes", theColumnTypes);

    try
    {
        setInitEnv();
    }

    catch(Exception E)
    {
        throw new Exception("MailSequence error in setInitEnv:" + E);
    }
```

```
    if(null == folder)
    {
        throw new Exception("null folder has no messages!");
    }

    // end of preparatory stage; get the messages and fetch
    // their properties using the FetchProfile
    theMessages = folder.getMessages();
    current = 0;
    folder.fetch(theMessages, fp);
}
```

getAllColumnsRowList()

This method uses the preceding one, after setting `columnLabels` to contain all the labels:

```
public RowSeq getAllColumnsRowList()
{
    // use all column labels;
    String[] cL = columnLabels;
    columnLabels = MessageData.getAllLabels();
    RowSeq rE = getRowList();
    columnLabels = cL;
    return rE;
}
```

Methods for Deleting Messages and Message Ranges

Here we have `delRow()` and `delRowRange()`; both call `delMessageRange()`:

```
public void delRow(int N)
{
    if(!checkFolder())
    {
        return;
    }

    try
    {
        deleteMessageRange(N, N);
    }

    catch(MessagingException e)
    {
        setMiscError("" + e);
    }
}

public void delRowRange(int start, int end)
```

```
{
    if(!checkFolder())
    {
        return;
    }

    try
    {
        deleteMessageRange(start, end);
    }

    catch(Exception E)
    {
        setMiscError("error in deletion: " + E);
    }
}
```

The `deleteMessageRange()` method does the actual deletions. In the process, it uses the `Flags` class of JavaMail, because to delete a message means to set its `DELETED` flag to true. The final physical deletion takes place in the `close()` method, providing the `expunge` Boolean is set to true.

The Flags Class of JavaMail

There are predefined flags and user-defined flags. Predefined flags are, as with `FetchProfile`, objects of an inner class with a protected constructor, the `FLAG` class. User-defined flags are just case-insensitive `Strings`.

Both `Folder` and `Message` have flag-related methods. `Folder` has `getPermanentFlags()` and three versions of `setFlags()`, one of which we use. (The other two use an array of integers and a start-end pair of integers as the first argument to indicate the messages affected.) `Message` has a `getFlags()`/`setFlags()` pair to work with the `Flags` object associated with a message; a `getFlag()`/`setFlag()` pair to work with an individual flag, and an `isSet()` method to check an individual flag. The expunged flag has its own special `setExpunge()` method.

deleteMessageRange()

The code for this method should now be quite self-explanatory:

```
public boolean deleteMessageRange(int start, int end)
        throws MessagingException
{
    Message[] msgs = folder.getMessages(start, end);
    setMiscError("can't delete messages " + start + ".." + end);

    if(msgs.length == 0)
    {
        return false;
    }

    folder.setFlags(msgs, new Flags(Flags.Flag.DELETED), true);
```

```
    for(int i = 0; i < msgs.length; i++)
    {
        if(!msgs[i].isSet(Flags.Flag.DELETED))
        {
            return false;
        }
    }

    unsetError();
    return true;
}
```

Methods for Output

Methods for output are numerous but they follow a general pattern and bear a strong resemblance to the output methods of the main bean, so they should make easy reading. The methods are:

- ❑ sendTo() (two versions)
- ❑ sendToMail()
- ❑ sendToXmlString()
- ❑ sendToXmlFile()
- ❑ sendToXml()
- ❑ and sendToDB() (two verisions)

The general pattern of these methods is to obtain the RowSeq that contains the data to be sent, and then to use an output method of RowSeq. It might be useful to review the section of Chapter 11 that discusses those methods; their names, as you remember, are simply toDB(), toXML() and toMail().

sendTo()

This is a dispatch method that receives two arguments: the type and the name of the destination. Depending upon type, it calls a more specialized output method.

Note that although the arguments have to do with destinations, we call them sourceType and sourceName. This is because each destination is also a possible source of data; this is one of the main design principles of the framework we are developing:

```
public void sendTo(String sourceType, String sourceName)
{
    if("mail".equalsIgnoreCase(sourceType))
        sendToMail(sourceName);
    else
        if("db".equalsIgnoreCase(sourceType))
            sendToDB(sourceName);
    else
        if("file".equalsIgnoreCase(sourceType))
            sendToXMLFile(sourceName);
```

```
    else
        if("string".equalsIgnoreCase(sourceType))
            sendToXMLString(sourceName); // result is stored in msgEnv
    else
        setMiscError("unknown sourceType " + sourceType + " for sendTo");
}
```

The other version of sendTo() takes an Env argument and retrieves the destination type and name from it. The default is to send e-mail to the current value of retaddr:

```
public void sendTo(Env E)
{
    sendTo(msgEnv.getStr("sourceType", "mail"),
            msgEnv.getStr("sourceName", retaddr));
}
```

Now for more specific methods, beginning with sendToMail().

sendToMail() and forwardMessageList()

This method gets an address and tries to send the data to it:

```
public void sendToMail(String msgtoaddr)
{
    try
    {
        forwardMessageList(msgtoaddr);
    }
    catch(Exception E)
    {
        setMiscError("can't mail to " + msgtoaddr + ": " + E);
    }
}
```

The forwardMessageList() method does what we described as the general pattern of the output methods: it obtains the RowSeq and uses its toMail() method. However, before that method can be used, the to: address of each method has to be set to the new value. Mapping this action over the message list does this; in Java, to do such a mapping, you create a MapRowSeq object that gives the constructor the necessary data. (Please review the section on mapping over RowSeqs in Chapter 11.)

```
public void forwardMessageList(String msgtoaddr)throws Exception
{
    RowSeq msgs = getAllColumnsRowList();
    if(hasError())
    {
        return;
    }
    msgs = new MapRowSeq("msgtoaddr", msgtoaddr, msgs);
    msgs.toMail();
}
```

sendToXMLFile(), sendToXMLString() and sendToXML()

The methods for `File` and `String` obtain the appropriate `Writer` object, and call the generic `sendToXML()` method with that `Writer` as an argument:

```
public void sendToXMLFile(String fileName)
{
    try
    {
        Writer out = new BufferedWriter(new FileWriter(new File(fileName)));
        sendToXML(out);
        out.close();
    }

    catch(Exception E)
    {
        setMiscError("can't save to " + fileName + ": " + E);
    }
}

public void sendToXMLString(String name)
{
    try
    {
        StringWriter sw = new StringWriter();
        sendToXML(sw);
        msgEnv.put(name, sw.toString());
    }

    catch(Exception ex)
    {
        msgEnv.put(name, "MVS.sendToXMLString error: " + ex);
    }
}
```

The `sendToXML()` method obtains a `RowSeq` object and uses its `toXML()` method:

```
public void sendToXML(Writer out)throws Exception
{
    msgEnv.put("OutputWriter", out);
    msgEnv.put("tableName", mbox);
    RowSeq rE = getAllColumnsRowList();
    if(!hasError() && rE != null)
    {
        rE.toXML();
    }
}
```

toDB()

The commonly used version of `toDB()` follows the general pattern:

```java
public void sendToDB(Connection conn, String tableName, boolean reset)
      throws Exception
{
    RowSeq rE = getAllColumnsRowList();
    if(!hasError() && rE! = null)
    {
        rE.toDB(conn,tableName,reset);
    }
}
```

As a fallback, for those cases when the connection is not yet established, we provide a version that extracts all the necessary information from `msgEnv` and opens the connection itself:

```java
public void sendToDB(String mailboxName)
{
    // won't normally be used...fallback.
    Connection conn = null;
    try
    {
        String dbDriver = msgEnv.getStr("jdbcDriver",
                "sun.jdbc.odbc.JdbcOdbcDriver");
        String dbUrl = msgEnv.getStr("jdbcUrl", "jdbc:odbc:MAIL");
        String user = msgEnv.getStr("jdbcUser", dbUser);
        String pwd = msgEnv.getStr("jdbcPwd", dbPwd);
        Class.forName(dbDriver);
        conn = DriverManager.getConnection(dbUrl, dbUser, dbPwd);
        sendToDB(conn, mailboxName, false);
    }

    catch(Exception E)
    {
        setMiscError("can't save to db box " + mailboxName + ": " + E);
    }

    finally
    {
        try
        {
            if(null != conn)
            {
                conn.close();
            }
        }
        catch(Exception e)
        {
        }
    }
}
```

This concludes all of the essential components for `MailViewSource`. The rest are set/get methods that are by now very familiar. We proceed to `DBViewSource` whose material falls into very much the same subdivisions as those of `MailViewSource`.

RowViewSource 2: DBViewSource

`DBViewSource`, as we said, is very similar to `MailViewSource`. We will illustrate their similarities and differences by comparing the corresponding elements of the XML configuration file, the imports to the two classes, and their class-level variables and constructors. After that, we will cover those aspects of `DBViewSource` that distinguish it from `MailViewSource`.

The mailSource and databaseSource Elements

One good way to bring out the similarities and differences is to compare the two corresponding elements of the `mailConfig.xml` file:

```
<mailSource>
    <class>MyNa.xml.MailViewSource</class>
    <useclass>MyNa.xml.RowViewSource</useclass>
    <dbDriver>pop3</dbDriver>
    <dbName>mail.dreamscape.com</dbName>
    <dbUser>JohnSmith</dbUser>
    <dbPwd>hArd-tO-gUEss?</dbPwd>
    <dbSource>INBOX</dbSource>
    <columnLabels>msgsubject,msgdate,msgflags,msgfromaddr</columnLabels>
    <port>-1</port>
    <verbose>true</verbose>
    <debug>true</debug>
    <expunge>true</expunge>
</mailSource>

<databaseSource>
    <class>MyNa.xml.DBViewSource</class>
    <useclass>MyNa.xml.RowViewSource</useclass>
    <dbDriver>sun.jdbc.odbc.JdbcOdbcDriver</dbDriver>
    <dbName>jdbc:odbc:PHONEBOOK</dbName>
    <dbUser>JohnSmith</dbUser>
    <dbPwd>hArd-tO-gUEss?</dbPwd>
    <dbSource>INBOX</dbSource>
    <dbQuery>
      SELECT |columnLabels| FROM |dbSource| ORDER BY msgdate,msgfromaddr;
    </dbQuery>
    <verbose>true</verbose>
    <debug>true</debug>
    <expunge>true</expunge>
</databaseSource>
```

As you can see, while the text contents of their children are different, the names of the children are almost identical: the one difference is that `mailSource` has `port` while `databaseSource` has `dbQuery`. Note that the content of `dbQuery` uses the `|` character to delimit some strings. This does *not* mean that we are using the `SUBST` mini-language here; the delimited strings are simply used as keys to retrieve the corresponding value from the appropriate `Env` object. This is done by `Misc.stringDelimSubst()`, a static utility method, in the `MyNa.utils` package.

Imports, Variables and the Constructor

The imports to the two classes are identical, so we won't bother to repeat them here. The variables are also quite similar, except that `DBViewSource` needs a `DBHandler` and a `dbQuery` string, and does not need any of the mail-specific variables, such as `port` or `store`. (It does need a `retaddr` string, though, to use as a default in its `sendTo()` method.)

```
public class DBViewSource extends XmlConfigBase
        implements RowViewSource
{
    MyNa.xml.DBHandler dbHandler;
    String dbQuery;

    Env msgEnv;
    String dbDriver, dbName, dbUser, dbPwd;
    String dbSource;
    String retaddr;
    boolean expunge; // if true, deletions stay gone.

    int rownum;  // used for individual extraction/deletion
    String[] columnLabels;
    String[] columnTypes;
    String errorType;
    String errorMessage;
```

The constructor initializes some of the variables. Note how the initial value of `dbQuery` uses the `|` character again:

```
public DBViewSource()
{
    msgEnv = new Env();
    dbHandler = null;
    dbQuery = "SELECT |columnLabels| FROM |dbSource| ORDER BY
            msgdate,msgfromaddr";
    errorType = null;
    errorMessage = null;
}
```

Comparative Outline

What else is there? Let's repeat the outline of `MailViewSource` and see what changes need to be made:

- ❑ Introductory: imports, class-level variables, constructor, `setString()`
- ❑ Methods for working with JavaMail classes: `Store`, `Folder`, `FetchProfile`, `Message`
- ❑ Methods for getting messages
- ❑ Methods for deleting messages and message ranges
- ❑ Methods for output to XML, mail and database
- ❑ get/set methods

For `DBViewSource`, the outline becomes:

- ❑ Introductory: imports, class-level variables, constructor, `setString()`
- ❑ *Initialization methods: `initSession()`, `setQueries()`, `initDBHandler()`*
- ❑ Methods for getting *rows*
- ❑ Methods for deleting *rows* and *row* ranges
- ❑ Methods for output to XML, mail and database
- ❑ get/set methods

Even though we have not said anything about `setString()`, we are done with the first item in this outline because the text of this method is identical to `MailViewSource`: it sets the same strings. We are also done with methods for output because they are also identical in both classes. As before, we are not going to list the predictable get/set methods.

We are left with three items of importance: initialization methods, methods for getting rows and methods for deleting rows (which have been italicized in the above list to show the differences from `MailViewSource`).

initSession(), setQueries(), initDBHandler()

`initSession()`, which, you remember, is called from the main bean with its `beanEnv` as argument, puts all the necessary data into its `Env` argument and calls the `setQueries()` and `initDBHandler()` methods, in that order:

```
public void initSession(Env E) throws Exception
{
    if(null == E)
    {
        throw new Exception("null Env for DBViewSource.initSession");
    }
```

```
        E.put("dbSource", dbSource);
        E.put("dbDriver", dbDriver);
        E.put("dbName", dbName);
        E.put("dbUser", dbUser);
        E.put("dbPwd", dbPwd);
        setQueries(E);

        try
        {
            initDBHandler(E);
        }
        catch(Exception ex)
        {
            throw new Exception("DBViewSource.initSession: " + ex);
        }

    }
```

In order to understand what `setQueries()` is doing, remember that the XML configuration file sets the value of `dbQueries` as follows:

```
<dbQuery>
    SELECT |columnLabels| FROM |dbSource| ORDER BY msgdate,msgfromaddr;
</dbQuery>
```

`setQueries()` sets up name-value pairs in the `Env` that will be used by the `DBHandler` to initialize its `Query` objects. Four pairs need to be set up: one for the list of three queries and three more for the queries themselves:

```
public void setQueries(Env E)
{
    if(null == E)
    {
        return;
    }

    E.put("dbQueries", "getTable,getAllColumnsTable,delRow");

    E.put("columnLabels", MessageData.getAllLabels());
    E.put("getAllColumnsTable", Misc.stringDelimSubst(dbQuery, "|", E));

    E.put("columnLabels", columnLabels);
    E.put("getTable", Misc.stringDelimSubst(dbQuery, "|", E));

    // construct qStr = delete from inbox where msgsubject=? AND msgcontent=?
    String qStr = "DELETE FROM " + dbSource
            + " WHERE " + columnLabels[0] + "=?";

    for(int i = 1; i < columnLabels.length; i++)
    {
        qStr += " AND " + columnLabels[i] + "=?";
    }
```

```
        qStr += ";";
        E.put("delRow", qStr);

    }
```

Once the queries are set, initializing the `dbHandler` is a one-line affair:

```
public void initDBHandler(Env E) throws Exception
{
    dbHandler = new DBHandler(E);
}
```

With the `DBHandler` ready, we can use its queries to retrieve and delete rows. A general problem here is that we want to create a uniform interface for working with database rows and e-mail messages; however, e-mail messages are naturally numbered in a folder, while database rows are content-selectable and can be ordered in different ways. Our solution is always to use a query that imposes an ordering, and to loop through the result counting rows as we go. We should mention that JDBC 2.0 supports scrollable result sets, which would provide a more elegant and efficient solution to the problem, as long as we can keep result sets around for the lifetime of an HTTP session.

Methods for Getting Rows

These are the same three methods that you saw in `MailViewSource`; they just operate a little differently, in predictable ways.

The `getRowList()` and `getAllColumnsRowList()` methods do the same thing: they put the appropriate `dbOperation` into `msgEnv` and give it as an argument to `dbHandler.getQueryRows()`:

```
public RowSeq getRowList()
{
    // with columnLabels as in msgEnv
    if(null == dbHandler)
    {
        return null;
    }

    msgEnv.put("dbOperation", "getTable");

    try
    {
        return (RowSeq)dbHandler.getQueryRows(msgEnv);
    }
    catch(Exception ex)
    {
        setMiscError("dbVS.getRowList: \n" + ex);
        return null;
    }

}
```

```
public RowSeq getAllColumnsRowList()
{
    // with columnLabels as in msgEnv
    if(null == dbHandler)
    {
        return null;
    }

    msgEnv.put("dbOperation", "getAllColumnsTable");

    try
    {
        return (RowSeq)dbHandler.getQueryRows(msgEnv);
    }
    catch(Exception ex)
    {
        String S = "dbVS.getAllColumnsRowList: \n" + ex;
        setMiscError(S);
        return null;
    }

}
```

The getRow() method is a bit tricky because of the way you get to the Nth row in a RowSeq: we start at the beginning and count from N down, hoping to get to zero:

```
public Env getRow(int N)
{
    RowSeq rE = getAllColumnsRowList();

    if(null == rE)
    {
        setMiscError("failure to get row list");
        return msgEnv;
    }

    if(N<=0)
      // return header info and other RowSeq info from Row 0
      return rE.getRow();
    int lim=N;
    while(lim>0 && rE.next())
      lim--;
    if(lim>0)
      setMiscError("no item "+N+" available");
    Env row= rE.getRow();
    rE.close();
    return row;

}
```

Methods for Deleting Rows

Ultimately, the work of deleting is done by the delRows() method. It sets up msgEnv with parameters to put into the PreparedStatement of DBHandler and calls DBHandler.getQueryRows():

```
/*
    deletes rows in which
    each of the fieldnames has exactly the corresponding value,
    apart from case (nulls match each other)
*/

public void delRows(String[] fieldNames, String[] vals)
{
    try
    {
        for(int i = 1; i <= vals.length; i++)
        {
            msgEnv.put("Parameter" + i, vals[i-1]);
        }

        msgEnv.put("ParameterMax", "" + vals.length);
        msgEnv.put("dbOperation", "delRow");
        dbHandler.getQueryRows(msgEnv);
        msgEnv.put("ParameterMax", "0");
    }

    catch(Exception ex)
    {
        setMiscError("dbVS.delRows():\n" + ex);
    }
}


public void delRow(int N)
{
    if(N <= 0)
    {
        return;
    }

    RowSeq rE = getRowList();
    int lim = N;

    while(lim > 0 && rE.next())
    {
        lim--;
    }

    if(lim != 0)
    {
        setMiscError("no item " + N + " available");
    }

    delRows(rE.getColumnLabels(), rE.getColumnValues());
}
```

To delete a row range, we just call `delRow()` in a loop:

```
public void delRowRange(int start, int end)
{
    for(int i = start; i < end; i++)
    {
        delRow(i);
    }
}
```

This concludes our discussion of `DBViewSource` and the entire journey through `XmlMail` that we started in Chapter 11. To review all the places we have visited, take one final look at the diagram showing the entire application:

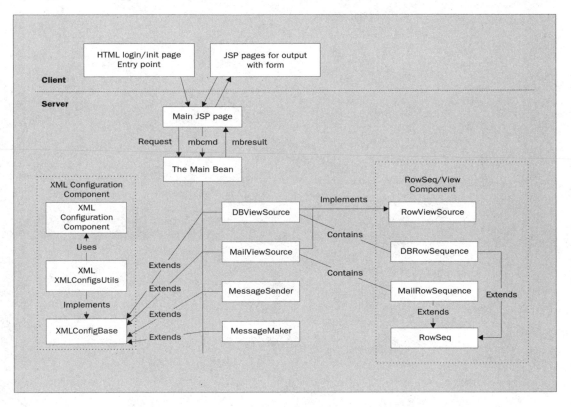

Conclusions

Let us recapitulate the main structural ideas of this application.

Overall, as a JSP application, it repeats the design of the much smaller `Birthdays` program of Chapter 9. We believe that it is a good design for JSP applications that successfully separates the main dispatcher from the computational logic (confined to beans) and templates for output (confined mostly to included JSP files). Other designs are possible; our point is not to push our design but to suggest that JSPs by themselves do not impose or even suggest a design, and a separate architectural organization must be layered on top of "plain JSP". It is possible that when the `taglib` mechanism of version 1.1 is available, it will become a major tool for constructing that architectural layer.

A major new idea of this application is to have the computational component configured by an XML file. We have developed a DTD for configuring a recursive structure of beans that form a network of "configure and use" relationships. In support of this feature, we have re-defined the `Env` class so that its object can recursively contain sub-`Env`s. Our application constructs a recursive structure of `Env`s from a recursive sub-bean element of the XML configuration file, and then uses this structure of `Env`s to instantiate and configure the network of beans.

Another idea we consider important is that the beans of the application work to connect a variety of uniformly represented data sources. The "data source" beans can receive data either from a database or a mail store and send it to a database, an XML file, an XML string, or to an e-mail address. It would not be hard, since we already have it in a `Writer`, to send it over a socket as well. As you saw in our `SAXMinilanguage` chapter, this is fairly easy to do.

In terms of the interfaces and classes involved, a data source bean extends `XmlConfigBase` (because it is XML-configurable) and implements the `RowViewSource` interface that contains methods to initialize a source of data and to direct data to all the output types we have just mentioned. As a `RowViewSource`, a data source bean contains a `RowSeq` object that is the source of the actual data.

Finally, as a specific application (rather than as a demonstration of several design ideas) `XmlMail` is a web-based mail client that also supports some database operations. As a mail client, it uses the JavaMail API, and we have used this opportunity to present this rather amazing API that does an extremely good job of hiding the complexities of the underlying protocols behind an abstraction layer of Java classes.

In summary, `XmlMail` can be evaluated from two angles: as a specific mail client application, and as framework for creating XML-configurable networks of data sources. As a mail client, it should probably remain a toy: Eudora, for example, does the job far better, although the ability to dump e-mail messages to a database table is something that other mail clients might consider. As a framework, it does, we believe, show promise and can (and will) be further developed beyond the confines of this book.

To repeat from the conclusions of Chapter 11, we are using XmlConfig as a mini-language in which we define an application as the result of "applying" a bean not only to its parameters but to (recursively defined) sub-applications. This is very real meta-programming. In this application, the instantiate-and-use relation between beans imposes a tree structure on them, closely mirroring the tree structure of the XML document. However, it does not have to be so. Since we define XmlConfig in such a way as to give each bean access to an environment which contains a link to the parent environment, it is also possible for any bean to find its siblings (by name) or even search the Env tree to find other relatives. If the beans run in their own threads, we can now have a multiprogramming environment.

Consider, for example, that MessageMaker and MessageSender need not be controlled from above: the manager bean passes the basic message data on to MessageMaker, which passes it along to MessageSender, and the manager bean does not even know that MessageSender exists. If they communicate through PipedOutputStreams feeding into PipedInputStreams, then XmlConfig is basically setting up a network with no center. The extension of XmlConfig to standardize such connections, with a list of <inputs> and a list of <outputs> to come just after the list of <subbeans>, is just a little bit outside the scope of this book; but if you think of each bean as an N-legged octopus (an N-topus), then you're already pretty close.

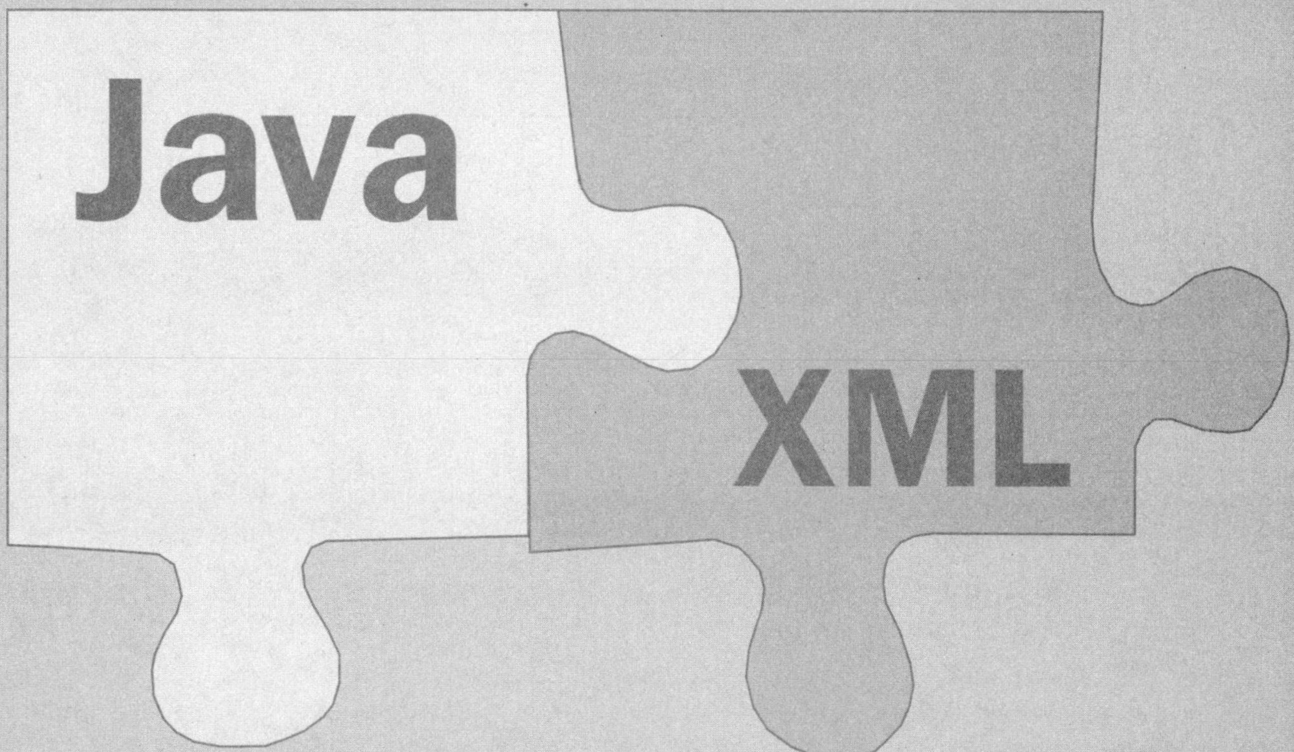
Java
XML

13

XSLT and XPath

Introduction

This chapter covers the **eXtensible Stylesheet Language for Transformations** (XSLT) and a related language, XPath, and shows how they can be used in a distributed application. We use the standard versions of both, released as Recommendations on November 16, 1999.

XSLT is different from most other technologies we have presented in that its intended users are not programmers, but rather that category of people whom we call Competent Users, i.e. people who have gotten used to SQL and may or may not be comfortable with Excel Basic but generally prefer declarative languages. XSLT is quite powerful, and it can do fairly sophisticated things for you, like number items in a list or sort a table in numeric or lexicographic order (with lexicographic order possibly being that of Katakana or Old Slavic or classical Greek, or other language). Still, in essence it is a mini-language, and its main importance for you may be the following: if you can frame solutions to your customers' problems in XSLT, they are going to find those solutions more valuable than if the same solutions were framed in JSP or as Java servlets. In particular, if you generate your output through a stylesheet, they will probably have a lot more flexibility in customizing that stylesheet to suit their needs than if you use a JSP page that performs the same tasks. We will return to this comparison towards the end of the chapter.

As we said, XSLT is quite large, and it would be impossible for us – nor is it our purpose – to put a detailed tutorial in the remainder of this book. Instead, we'll aim to create a conceptual framework (into which you can later fit a multitude of details) and provide a very selective sample of XSLT topics that we feel will be the most relevant to you. In particular, after a very brief overview of XSLT, we will:

❑   show you how to install and configure the XT processor and XT servlet so that they work with Sun's XML parser (or any other SAX parser) and jswdk

❑   show you how an XSLT stylesheet can be used to do generic SQL-like search and retrieval from XML documents that conform to our `dbdata.dtd` of earlier chapters

❑   show you how to use Java code from within a stylesheet using the extension mechanism built into XT

❑   show you how to do "algorithmic" programming with XSLT: loops, nested loops and recursion. The idea is that the role of programmers is to write this sort of complex XSLT templates for non-programmers to use in their stylesheets

XSLT Overview

After a brief historical introduction, we present a quick summary of XSLT. We also introduce XPath, a supporting language for both XSLT and XPointer (a specification for hypertext links – see below). XPath proper is a little like a common parent class with generic functionality that gets differently extended in XSLT and XPointer. When we go over those areas of XSLT that use and extend XPath, we will point out the XPath features.

History of Ideas

The history of XSL has been brief but eventful. Consider this: work on XSL started in 1997, but the two specifications we discuss and use in this chapter (because they have become Recommendations) did not exist as independent projects until fairly late in 1999. As the XSL project unfolded, different parts of it grew at different speeds, and their relative importance and state of preparedness were constantly changing. Eventually, XSLT and XPath got carved out into separate products and completed, while the formatting part is still in the Working Draft stage, even though initially it was the formatting that was the main rationale for XSL.

That a style sheet language was needed for XML to function was obvious from the beginning: if users can define their own elements, they have to be able to specify how those elements will look when displayed in the browser window or other media. Also from the beginning, the intent was to make the style sheet language more powerful than Cascading Style Sheets (CSS). CSS has a good deal of control over *how* different elements are displayed, but very little control over *what* gets displayed and in what order. (About the only tool CSS has for controlling output content is `display:none`.) XSL was intended to be able to add, remove and re-order the elements of the document tree, so, for instance, the style sheet could handle multiple reports from a database table, showing different fields and sorting records in different ways.

Initially, the tree-transformation part of XSL was meant to be an aid to the formatting part, but several factors conspired to bring it to greater prominence. One of the factors was that it was easier to deal with and build a consensus about XSL. Another one was a changing in the understanding of the role of XML. As XML's role was evolving from a tool for document markup to (also being) a tool for data interchange between applications and components of applications, the transformation "module" was developing an independent significance, totally unrelated to formatting and display. At some point, these forces brought about a split between XSL for Formatting and XSL for Transformation (XSLT). The XSLT part was taken over by James Clark who brought it to a swift completion while at the same time producing a fully compliant reference implementation of the XSLT processor (see *Appendix B* for references).

An essential feature of a tree transformation language is the ability to refer to tree paths, both in absolute terms (starting from the root) and relative to the current position in the tree. As work on XSLT unfolded, this "sub-language" was naturally growing in size and sophistication. At some point, it was realized that exactly the same sub-language is needed for XLink/XPointer, a specification for hypertext links between XML documents and parts of documents. Here again, the idea was to make the linking facility more powerful and flexible than HTML's <A> or <LINK> tags, so that both the source and the target(s) of a link can be specified in structural terms. The result was that the sub-language for tree path description became separated from both XSLT and XLink/XPointer and assumed independent existence under the name of XPath. XPath was also brought to a swift completion, on the same date as XSLT, by James Clark and Steve DeRose, representing the XSL and the XML-Linking Working Groups, respectively.

To the best of our knowledge, this book is the first to describe the stable "Recommendation" versions of XSLT and XPath, and to use a fully compliant processor, the November 5, 1999 version of James Clark's XT.

A Quick Summary

In this section we will use multiple quotes from the Abstract and Introduction sections of the XSLT Recommendation, interspersed with our comments and explanations, and broken into subsections for clarity. The references in square brackets that appear within the quotes are hypertext links either to sections of the same specification or to another W3C document.

Definition

"XSLT is a language for transforming XML documents into other XML documents". (Abstract). This definition is not quite accurate: while an input to an XSLT stylesheet does have to be a well-formed XML document, you can tweak XSLT to produce plain text or other formats as the output. By-and-large (and in all our examples), the output will be well-formed XML.

Relationship to XSL

"XSLT is designed for use as part of XSL, which is a stylesheet language for XML. In addition to XSLT, XSL includes an XML vocabulary for specifying formatting. XSL specifies the styling of an XML document by using XSLT to describe how the document is transformed into another XML document that uses the formatting vocabulary.

XSLT is also designed to be used independently of XSL. However, XSLT is not intended as a completely general-purpose XML transformation language. Rather it is designed primarily for the kinds of transformations that are needed when XSLT is used as part of XSL". (Abstract) A text written in XSLT is called a stylesheet "because, in the case when XSLT is transforming into the XSL formatting vocabulary, the transformation functions as a stylesheet". (Introduction)

Where does XSLT Happen?

There are basically three scenarios. The first is for a browser to come equipped with both an XML parser and an XSLT processor working together. This is currently only (December 1999) true of Internet Explorer 5.0 whose processor is gravely out of date. The second is for an XML parser and an XSLT processor, working together, to produce an HTML (or XHTML) file and send it to the browser. Finally, a parser and a processor, working together, can produce an arbitrary XML text, or, in fact, any other kind of text, and send to another piece of software to do something with it. Either the parser or the processor or both can be integrated with the server in some way. In this chapter, we give three very simple examples that can be displayed in Internet Explorer 5.0, then switch to using a parser (Sun's, as before) and a processor (the XT package).

The XT processor can be used in two ways, either from the command line or as a servlet. The command-line usage is as follows. Suppose you have two files, greeting.xml and greeting.xsl, and all the .jars are in the right places (see *Appendix A* for what those places are). Then the line below (yes, it must be a single line even if it wraps on the book page) will generate an HTML file:

```
java -Dcom.jclark.xsl.sax.parser=com.sun.xml.parser.Parser
com.jclark.xsl.sax.Driver greeting.xml greeting.xsl greeting.htm
```

To save yourself a bit (quite a bit) of typing, you can define an xsl.bat file (in Windows; a one-line shell script in Unix) with this one line in it (it again wraps on the book page):

```
java -Dcom.jclark.xsl.sax.parser=com.sun.xml.parser.Parser
com.jclark.xsl.sax.Driver %1 %2 %3
```

If you do that, you can produce the same HTML file with:

```
xsl greeting.xml greeting.xsl greeting.htm
```

If you want to send the same content to standard output, omit the last argument:

```
xsl greeting.xml greeting.xsl
```

If we additionally arrange to have both of those files in the xslrules directory and tell jswdk how to find them (see instructions later in this chapter) then

```
http://localhost:8080/xslgreet/xslrules/greeting
```

will display the output in the browser window (XT provides the .xml extension).

An XSLT Stylesheet is an XML Document

Syntactically, an XSLT stylesheet is a well-formed XML document that uses Namespaces. The start tag of the root element of a stylesheet looks like this:

```
<xsl:stylesheet version="1.0" xmlns:xsl="http://www.w3.org/1999/XSL/Transform">
```

"XSLT-defined elements are distinguished by belonging to a specific XML namespace..., which is referred to in this specification as the XSLT namespace. Thus this specification is a definition of the syntax and semantics of the XSLT namespace." (Introduction) The prefix associated with XSLT elements is `xsl`, but it can be associated with any namespace. The standard is as shown above, but Internet Explorer 5.0 insists on a namespace associated with an older Working Draft.

The XSLT Recommendation does not specify how to associate a stylesheet with an XML document, but the processors expect the conventions of the W3C Recommendation *Associating Style Sheets with XML documents* (see Chapter 5 and Internet Explorer 5.0 examples below) to be followed. If you are using a parser and a processor, you specify the stylesheet to be used *explicitly* and you don't have to mention the stylesheet in the XML file at all.

Source Tree, Result Tree, Patterns and Templates

Semantically, an XSLT stylesheet expresses a **transformation** of a **source tree** into a **result tree**. "The transformation is achieved by associating **patterns** with **templates**. A pattern is matched against elements in the source tree. A template is instantiated to create part of the result tree. The result tree is separate from the source tree. The structure of the result tree can be completely different from the structure of the source tree. In constructing the result tree, elements from the source tree can be filtered and reordered, and arbitrary structure can be added." (Introduction.)

Top-Level Elements and Instruction Elements

As we said, an XSLT stylesheet is an XML document whose root element is `<xsl:stylesheet>`. The children of the root are called **top-level elements**. Here is a complete list of them, from Section 2.2 of the Recommendation; syntactic summaries of use are from it's Appendix B:

Element	Typical use
`xsl:import`	`<xsl:import href="..."/>`
`xsl:include`	`<xsl:include href="..."/>`
`xsl:strip-space`	`<xsl:strip-space elements="..."/>`
`xsl:preserve-space`	`<xsl:preserve-space elements="..."/>`
`xsl:output`	`<xsl:output method="..."/>`
`xsl:key`	`<xsl:key name="..." match="..." use="..."/>`
`xsl:decimal-format`	`<xsl:decimal-format name="..."/>`
`xsl:namespace-alias`	`<xsl:namespace-alias stylesheet-prefix="..." result-prefix="..."/>`
`xsl:attribute-set`	`<xsl:attribute-set name="..."> ... </xsl:attribute-set>`
`xsl:variable`	`<xsl:variable name="...">...</xsl:variable>`
`xsl:param`	`<xsl:param name="...">...</xsl:param>`
`xsl:template`	`<xsl:template match="..."> ... </xsl:template>`
	`<xsl:template name="..."> ... </xsl:template>`

In the course of this chapter, you will see what strip-space, output, param and template can do; you will have to refer to the *Recommendation* for what the rest of them can do for you. By far the most important of them is xsl:template; it would be a rare stylesheet indeed that did not use it. It is within template elements that instruction elements make their appearance.

Instruction elements are too numerous for us to list all of them here. The ones you will see in this chapter are:

Element	Typical use

xsl:apply-templates	`<xsl:apply-templates`
	`  select = `**`node-set-expression mode = qname>`**`...`
	`</xsl:apply-templates>`

xsl:call-template	`<xsl:call-template`
	`  name = `**`qname>`**
	`  <!-- Content: xsl:with-param* -->`
	`</xsl:call-template>`

xsl:for-each	`<xsl:for-each`
	`  select = `**`node-set-expression>`**
	`  <!-- Content: (xsl:sort*, template) -->`
	`</xsl:for-each>`

xsl:if	`<xsl:if`
	`  test = `**`boolean-expression>`**
	`  <!-- Content: template -->`
	`</xsl:if>`

xsl:output	`<xsl:output` ` method = "xml"	"html"	"text"	`**`qname-but-not-ncname`** ` ... />`

xsl:variable	`<xsl:variable`
	`  name = `**`qname`**
	`  select = `**`expression>`**
	`  <!-- Content: template -->`
	`</xsl:variable>`

xsl:param	See the table above.

xsl:with-param	`<xsl:with-param`
	`  name = `**`qname`**
	`  select = `**`expression>`**
	`  <!-- Content: template -->`
	`</xsl:with-param>`

xsl:template	See the table above.
xsl:value-of	`<xsl:value-of` `  select = `**`string-expression`** ` disable-output-escaping = "yes"	"no" />`

xsl:when	`<xsl:when`
	`  test = `**`boolean-expression>`**
	`  <!-- Content: template -->`
	`</xsl:when>`

You will notice that xsl:template and xsl:param can appear both at the top level and as a processing instruction with xsl:template. You will see how it works as we go through the examples.

Template Rules and the Processing Model

"A stylesheet contains a set of template rules. A template rule has two parts: a **pattern** which is matched against nodes in the source tree and a **template** which can be instantiated to form part of the result tree. This allows a stylesheet to be applicable to a wide class of documents that have similar source tree structures. ... The result tree is constructed by finding the template rule for the root node and instantiating its template." (Introduction.) This may and usually does trigger further template rules.

There may be more than one template rule applicable to a node, in which case precedence rules are used to determine which template rule to apply. "A node is processed by finding all the template rules with patterns that match the node, and choosing the best amongst them; the chosen rule's template is then instantiated with the node as the current node and with the list of source nodes as the current node list. A template typically contains instructions that select an additional list of source nodes for processing. ... A list of source nodes is processed by appending the result tree structure created by processing each of the members of the list in order." (5.1)

Here is the processing model in summary. At any given time, there is a list of source nodes, usually found by matching a pattern. A result tree fragment is created by processing that list; "processing" usually means instantiating a template associated with the pattern. In the course of that processing, new source nodes can be added to the list, usually by the `<xsl:apply-templates/>` element. The transformation process begins by processing a list containing just the root node. The transformation process ends when the source node list is empty. This picture is a bit over-simplified, but adequate for now. Let's work though a couple of examples to get a feel for what it's like to program in XSLT.

IE5 Examples

All examples in this section are intended to be used with Internet Explorer 5.0. For this reason, the value of the `xmlns` attribute in every stylesheet is `http://www.w3.org/TR/WD-xsl`; otherwise, their XSL text is in conformance with the *Recommendation*.

Example 1: Boiler-Plate Output

In our first example, we'll have no recursion, only a template rule that matches the root. The stylesheet, `ms1.xsl`, looks like this:

```
<?xml version="1.0"?>
<xsl:stylesheet xmlns:xsl="http://www.w3.org/TR/WD-xsl">
  <xsl:template match="/">
    <html><head><title>Boiler Plate</title></head>
    <body><h1 align="center">Boiler-Plate Output</h1>
       <p>No matter what you give me, I produce the same output</p>
    </body></html>
  </xsl:template>
</xsl:stylesheet>
```

If your XML file is like this:

```
<?xml version="1.0" encoding="utf-8"?>
<?xml-stylesheet type="text/xsl" href="ms1.xsl"?>
<!-- any well-formed xml whatsoever -->
```

your output will always be:

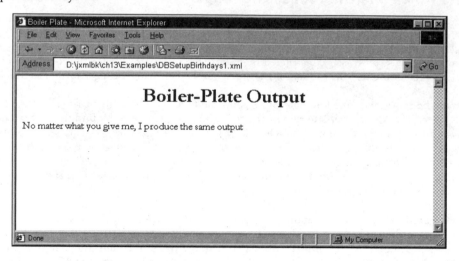

Example 2: the Value of the Root

In the second example, we will produce an output that is not the same for all documents, but is still generic, in the sense that the stylesheet does not mention any specific tags. We'll do something very simple: ask the stylesheet to output the value of the root node. This will run all the text content of the document together, without any structure to it. Here is the template rule to replace the one in `ms1.xsl`; the rest of the stylesheet is the same:

```
<xsl:template match="/">
  <html><head><title>List contents</title></head>
  <body><h1 align="center">List Contents as Value-of Root</h1>
   <xsl:value-of select="."/>
  </body></html>
</xsl:template>
```

We are using an `xsl:value-of` element that has a select attribute. The values of that attribute are XPath expressions. The "." refers to "the currently-matched node", in this case the root.

Let's attach this stylesheet to a `DBSetup` page that conforms to our `dbdata.dtd` of Chapter 10. For instance, `DBSetupBirthdays.xml` looks like this:

```
<?xml version="1.0" encoding="utf-8"?>
<!DOCTYPE dbdata SYSTEM "dbdata.dtd">
<dbdata>
<jdbc_info driver="sun.jdbc.odbc.JdbcOdbcDriver"
   db_url="jdbc:odbc:PHONEBOOK" />
<user-info>
  <uname>JoeSchmoe</uname>
  <upass>orgleborgle</upass>
</user-info>
<table name="Birthdays" reset="true">
```

```
   <headers>
     <header name="Who"    fieldType="VARCHAR" />
     <header name="When"   fieldType="DATE" />
     <header name="Addr"   fieldType="VARCHAR" />
   </headers>
   <row>
     <field name="Who">Joseph Conrad</field>
     <field name="When">12/3/1857</field>
     <field name="Addr">tom.myers@worldnet.att.net</field>
   </row>
<!-- many more rows -->
</table></dbdata>
```

With Internet Explorer 5.0's default stylesheet, the file looks like this:

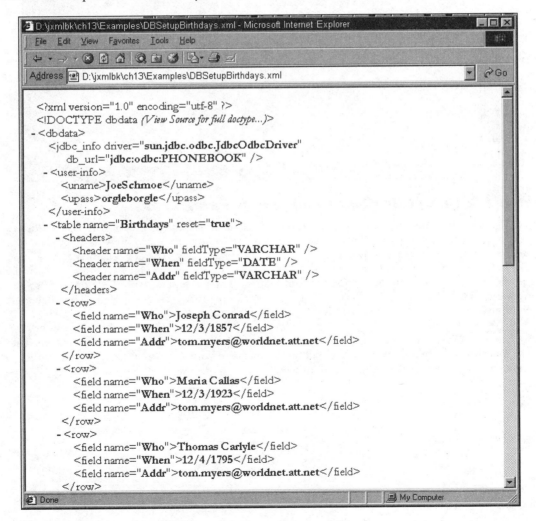

With our `ms2.xsl` spreadsheet, the output will look like this:

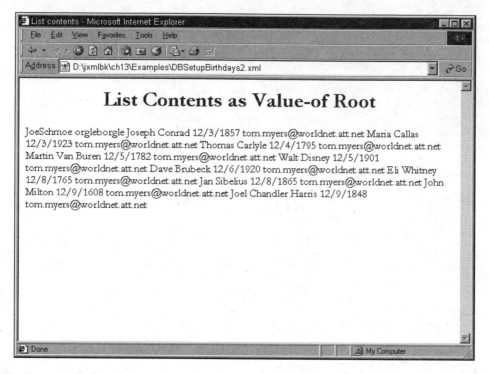

Example 3: Output Attributes and Text as Paragraphs

Usually, you don't just process the root but recursively descend into its children and its children's children, selecting those you want to use and specifying what you want to do with them. The mechanism for this recursive processing is the `<xsl:apply-templates/>` element placed inside the `<xsl:template>` element. In our last Internet Explorer 5.0 example, for each node that has a child that is a text node, we will output the value of that text node as a paragraph. If that node also has an attribute whose name is "`name`", we will output the value of that attribute as well. (To match an attribute node, use the "`@`" character followed by the name of the attribute.)

So, our stylesheet will have two template rules. The first will match the root node, as before. The second will match any node, and its template will be "the value of your '`name`' attribute, if any, followed by the value of the text node that is a child of yours". Here is the stylesheet:

```
<xsl:template match="/">
  <html><head><title>copy as paragraphs</title></head>
  <body style="background-color:lightblue">
    <h1 align="center">Output text nodes as paragraphs</h1>
    <xsl:apply-templates/>
  </body>
  </html>
</xsl:template>
```

```
<xsl:template match="node()">
  <p>
    <xsl:value-of select="@name"/><!-- a reference to attribute node -->
    <xsl:value-of select="./text()"/><!-- a function expression -->
  </p>
  <xsl:apply-templates/>
</xsl:template>
```

With this stylesheet, the same `DBSetupBirthdays.xml` will look like this:

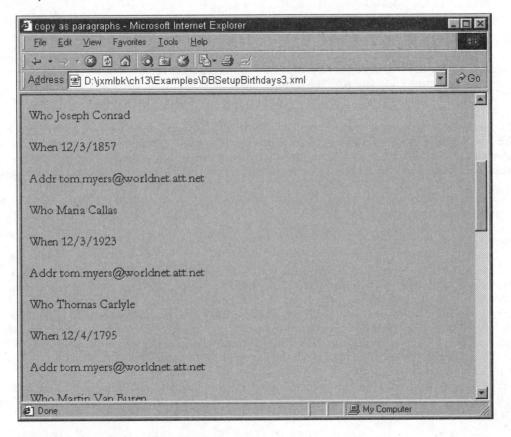

A Comment on the Role of XPath

As you can see, XSLT makes frequent use of match and select attributes. Their values are quoted strings that specify both the pattern that selects a set of nodes to be processed and the values to use in instantiating the template. **These quoted strings are expressions written in XPath language.** XPath expressions have an elaborate syntax for specifying node sets, and they also can use a number of functions that return values of other data types: strings, numbers and booleans. For instance, there is a function to take a sub-string of a string, and there are functions for arithmetic operations on numbers. We will have a section on XPath later in the chapter; for now, just be aware that as you read the values of match and select attributes, you are learning XPath.

Farewell to IE5

We are going to make a jump now from very simple examples to fairly sophisticated ones. To avoid bumping into Internet Explorer 5.0 incompatibilities, we are going to switch to XT and Sun's XML parser jointly producing HTML files. You may want to make a brief detour into that section of *Appendix A* that describes how to install xt, but here's how you would configure it to be used with either XP or Sun's XML parser. With either parser, you can use XT from the command line or as an XSLServlet; we could only make it work as a servlet with jswdk-1.0 but not with JRun 2.3 where `ServletConfig.getResource()` returns null. (It would be fairly easy to modify James Clark's code to pull the XSL file from wherever needed without using `getResource()`.)

Configuring XT

Configuring XT to be used from the command line is trivial: all you need to do is make sure that everything is on the classpath. Use the command line and options given in `xt.htm` that comes with the XT distribution; you can specify either XP or Sun's parser or any other SAX parser to work with XT.

Configuring for servlet use is more involved. There are two issues involved: how to specify the parser and how to make the servlet known to the server. For the parser, go into `startserver.bat` (or the equivalent Unix file) in the jswdk root directory. The classpath is specified in that file, and the java processor is called explicitly. Put the same `-D` option that you use on the command line into that file.

Regarding the servlet-server connection, the "Servlet Usage" section of `xt.htm` that comes with the XT distribution, states:

"Servlet Usage

XT can be used as a servlet. This requires a servlet engine that implements at least version 2.1 of the Java Servlet API. The servlet class is `com.jclark.xsl.sax.XSLServlet`. The servlet requires an `init` parameter stylesheet; the value is the path of the stylesheet in a form suitable to be passed to `ServletContext.getResource`. The translated path gives the XML document to be transformed. An extension of `.xml` will be automatically added to the translated path if necessary. (Some browsers assume that a URL ending in `.xml` is an XML document.) Parameters from the query part of the URL are passed in as parameters to the stylesheet. The stylesheet is cached on initialization."

This is how it works out in the case of jswdk. Suppose you have an XML file, `greeting.xml`, and a stylesheet to go with it, `greeting.xsl`. You want to be able to invoke the stylesheet on the file from a browser by saying:

```
http://localhost:8080/xslgreet/xslrules/greeting
```

Here, `xslgreet` is a virtual path and `xslrules` is a real directory. (Note that you don't want to put `.xml` in the end because "some browsers" will then assume that you just want the XML file with the browser's default stylesheet rather than the result of the servlet running your stylesheet on it.) In order to have this usage available, you follow these steps:

1. Create an `xslrules` subdirectory of the default directory for Web pages, such as `C:/jswdk-1.0/webpages`; put the XML file and the stylesheet into that directory

2. In the `mappings.properties` file, include this line:

```
/xslgreet=xslgreet
```

3. In the `servlets.properties` file, include these two lines:

```
xslgreet.code=com.jclark.xsl.sax.XSLServlet
xslgreet.initparams=stylesheet=/xslrules/greeting.xsl
```

Now you are all set. To use a different stylesheet, say `innerloop.xsl`, on the same XML file, you would put another virtual path in the `mappings.properties` file, e.g. `xslnest`:

```
/xslnest=xslnest
```

and in `servlets.properties`:

```
xslnest.code=com.jclark.xsl.sax.XSLServlet
xslnest.initparams=stylesheet=/xslrules/innerloop.xsl
```

Furthermore, if `innerloop.xsl` has a top-level parameter called `tablesize` (these are explained shortly) then you can set this parameter to 8 from the browser by typing the following into the location window:

```
http://localhost:8080/xslnest/xslrules/greeting.xml?tablesize=8
```

Or you can use an HTML form. This is really quite convenient. The only problem is that, as `xt.htm` tells us, "[t]he stylesheet is cached on initialization", and so this setup is not good for debugging.

Three Extended Examples

All the multiple uses of XSLT can be roughly divided into three categories:

- reformatting documents
- processing data
- doing some programming

We are going to look at three examples, one from each category, explaining their XSLT features as they come along. The document example is adopted from the first example of Appendix D of the *Recommendation*; the other two are our own.

Apart from two explanatory comments in square brackets inserted in the middle of the stylesheet, everything in the next section is quoted verbatim from Appendix D, section D1, of the *XSLT Recommendation*.

Document Example

This example is a stylesheet for transforming documents that conform to a simple DTD into XHTML. The DTD is:

```
<!ELEMENT doc (title, chapter*)>
<!ELEMENT chapter (title, (para|note)*, section*)>
<!ELEMENT section (title, (para|note)*)>
<!ELEMENT title    (#PCDATA|emph)*>
<!ELEMENT para     (#PCDATA|emph)*>
<!ELEMENT note     (#PCDATA|emph)*>
<!ELEMENT emph     (#PCDATA|emph)*>
```

The stylesheet is:

```
<xsl:stylesheet version="1.0"
                xmlns:xsl="http://www.w3.org/1999/XSL/Transform"
                xmlns="http://www.w3.org/TR/xhtml1/strict">

<xsl:strip-space elements="doc chapter section"/>
```

[Explanation (see also 3.4): After the tree for a source document or stylesheet document has been constructed, but before it is otherwise processed by XSLT, some text nodes that contain only whitespace are stripped. This is particularly helpful if the document is processed by a non-validating parser.]

```
<xsl:output
    method="xml"
    indent="yes"
    encoding="iso-8859-1"
/>
```

[Explanation (see also 16): The method attribute of the <xsl:output> element specifies how the result tree should be output. The value of the method attribute can be "html", "xml", "text", or any Qualified Name (i.e. a name with a namespace prefix). For the three non-qualified values, an XSLT processor **should** output the result tree as specified by the <xsl:output> element; however, it is not required to do so.

If there is no <xsl:output> element or its method attribute is not specified, then a default is used If the root element of the result tree has a child that says <html> (in any capitalization pattern) then the default method is "html"; otherwise it's "xml". In our case here, we want "xml" (XHTML), so we need to override the default to produce the right declarations at the top of the resulting document – see the example at the end of this section.

The rest of the stylesheet is fairly straightforward templates that do not require explanations.]

```xsl
<xsl:template match="doc">
 <html>
   <head>
     <title>
       <xsl:value-of select="title"/>
     </title>
   </head>
   <body>
     <xsl:apply-templates/>
   </body>
 </html>
</xsl:template>

<xsl:template match="doc/title">
  <h1>
    <xsl:apply-templates/>
  </h1>
</xsl:template>

<xsl:template match="chapter/title">
  <h2>
    <xsl:apply-templates/>
  </h2>
</xsl:template>

<xsl:template match="section/title">
  <h3>
    <xsl:apply-templates/>
  </h3>
</xsl:template>

<xsl:template match="para">
  <p>
    <xsl:apply-templates/>
  </p>
</xsl:template>

<xsl:template match="note">
  <p class="note">
    <b>NOTE: </b>
    <xsl:apply-templates/>
  </p>
</xsl:template>

<xsl:template match="emph">
  <em>
    <xsl:apply-templates/>
  </em>
</xsl:template>

</xsl:stylesheet>
```

With the following input document:

```
<!DOCTYPE doc SYSTEM "doc.dtd">
<doc>
<title>Document Title</title>
<chapter>
<title>Chapter Title</title>
<section>
<title>Section Title</title>
<para>This is a test.</para>
<note>This is a note.</note>
</section>
<section>
<title>Another Section Title</title>
<para>This is <emph>another</emph> test.</para>
<note>This is another note.</note>
</section>
</chapter>
</doc>
```

The stylesheet would produce the following result:

```
<?xml version="1.0" encoding="iso-8859-1"?>
<html xmlns="http://www.w3.org/TR/xhtml1/strict">
<head>
<title>Document Title</title>
</head>
<body>
<h1>Document Title</h1>
<h2>Chapter Title</h2>
<h3>Section Title</h3>
<p>This is a test.</p>
<p class="note">
<b>NOTE: </b>This is a note.</p>
<h3>Another Section Title</h3>
<p>This is <em>another</em> test.</p>
<p class="note">
<b>NOTE: </b>This is another note.</p>
</body>
</html>
```

[Explanation: Note that the first two lines of the result are produced on the basis of the stylesheet declaration and the value of the method attribute of `<xsl:output>`.]

Programming Example: Countdown

Although data processing usage is much more common, we are going to put a programming example first, because it is simpler and introduces some features that the data example will also use. The example will ignore the XML document that invokes it and output a one-row table that counts down from a given parameter value to 1: if the parameter value is "4", the table will show 4 3 2 1.

The new XSLT features of this stylesheet are:

❑ named templates: you can give a template rule a name and call it from another template using the `<xsl:call-template>` element.

❑ template parameters: you can give a template a parameter, e.g. `counter`, and refer to it as `$counter` (remember, this is XPath syntax)

❑ arithmetic operations: you can do arithmetic with parameter values; XPath will automatically convert strings to numbers and back

❑ conditional execution: you can test a condition with an `<xsl:if>` element and instantiate or not instantiate the element's content depending on the test.

Here is the stylesheet:

```
<xsl:stylesheet xmlns:xsl="http://www.w3.org/1999/XSL/Transform"
                version="1.0">
<!-- testing a simple loop -->
<xsl:template match="/">
  <html><head><title>Simple Loop Test</title></head>
    <body>
     <h3>We will now call on "count-down". </h3>
     <table border="1">
     <tr>
       <xsl:call-template name="count-down">
          <xsl:with-param name="counter" select="8"/>
       </xsl:call-template>
     </tr></table>
```

This XSL stylesheet completely ignores its input; all it does is generate a 1-row table that counts down from the initial parameter value (8 in this example) for the "count-down" template.

```
    </body></html>
</xsl:template>

<xsl:template name="count-down">
   <xsl:param name="counter" select="4"/>  <!-- this value is overridden -->
   <td>
     <xsl:value-of select="$counter"/>      <!-- parameter reference -->
   </td>
   <xsl:if test="$counter>1">
     <xsl:call-template name="count-down"><!-- recursive call -->
       <xsl:with-param
           name="counter"
           select="($counter)-1"/>          <!-- XPath arithmetic expression -->
     </xsl:call-template>
   </xsl:if>
 </xsl:template>

</xsl:stylesheet>
```

This stylesheet produces the following HTML file (white space reformatted):

```
<html><head><title>Simple Loop Test</title></head>

<body>
<h3>We will now call on "count-down". </h3>
<table border="1">
<tr>
<td>8</td><td>7</td><td>6</td><td>5</td><td>4</td><td>3</td><td>2</td><td>1</td>
</tr>
</table>

This XSL stylesheet completely ignores its input; all it does is generate a 1-row
table that counts down from the initial parameter value (8 in this example) for
the "count-down" template.

</body></html>
```

Although this example has the initial parameter value hard-wired into its code, a minor modification would make it possible to set that value in an HTML form and pass it as a parameter to the stylesheet. All we'd need to do is create a top-level `<xsl:param>` element and use an XSLServlet. The next example shows this usage.

The Data Example: SQL to XSL

Although brief, this example illustrates two important ideas. One has just been mentioned: a stylesheet can have top-level `<xsl:param>` elements that are settable from an HTML form. The other has to do with our generic `dbdata.dtd` that describes both a database connection and the content of a database table as the content of an XML document. Combining the two ideas, we have an HTML form that configures an XSLT stylesheet that expresses a SQL query addressed to an arbitrary `dbdata` document (that can be obtained from the database specified in the same HTML form).

The DTD and the XML Document

The `dbdata.dtd` that we used in `Xml2DBTables` is repeated here for ease of reference:

```
<!ELEMENT dbdata (jdbc_info, user-info, table*)>
<!ELEMENT jdbc_info EMPTY>
<!ATTLIST jdbc_info
  driver    CDATA "com.sun.jdbc.odbc"
  db_url    CDATA "YourFavoriteDB"
>
<!ELEMENT user-info (uname, upass)>
<!ELEMENT uname (#PCDATA)>
<!ELEMENT upass (#PCDATA)>

<!ELEMENT table (headers, row*)>
<!ATTLIST table
  name CDATA #REQUIRED
  reset (true|false) "false" >

<!ELEMENT headers (header+)>
<!ELEMENT header EMPTY>
<!ATTLIST header
  name CDATA #REQUIRED
```

```
    fieldType
(CHAR|VARCHAR|LONGVARCHAR|NUMERIC|DECIMALBIT|TINYINT|SMALLINT|INTEGER|BIGINT|
REAL|FLOAT|DOUBLE|BINARY|VARBINARY|LONGVARBINARY|DATE|TIME|TIMESTAMP)
        "VARCHAR" >

<!ELEMENT row (field*)> <!-- number of field <= number of headers -->
<!ELEMENT field (#PCDATA)>
<!ATTLIST field
  name CDATA #REQUIRED
>
```

We create an example `dbdata` document and display it as an HTML table using a stylesheet. The stylesheet is, in effect, a translation of an SQL query into XSLT. Here is the document:

```
<?xml version="1.0" encoding="utf8"?>
<!DOCTYPE dbdata SYSTEM "dbdata.dtd">
<dbdata>
<jdbc_info driver="sun.jdbc.odbc.JdbcOdbcDriver"
   db_url="jdbc:odbc:BIRTHDAYS"/>
<user-info>
  <uname>JoeSchmoe</uname>
  <upass>hArd2guEss</upass>
</user-info>
<table name="Birthdays" reset="true">
  <headers>
    <header name="Who" fieldType="VARCHAR"/>
    <header name="When" fieldType="DATE"/>
    <header name="Addr" fieldType="VARCHAR"/>
  </headers>
  <row>
    <field name="Who">Joseph Conrad</field>
    <field name="When">12/3/1857</field>
    <field name="Addr">tom.myers@worldnet.att.net</field>
  </row>
  <!-- many more rows -->
  <row>
    <field name="Who">Joel Chandler Harris</field>
    <field name="When">12/9/1848</field>
    <field name="Addr">tom.myers@worldnet.att.net</field>
  </row>
 </table>
</dbdata>
```

The Stylesheet and the SQL Query

The stylesheet will express the following SQL query (with some XPath syntax thrown in):

```
SELECT * FROM $table WHERE $field LIKE $target;
```

Here, `$table`, `$field` and `$target` are references to `<xsl:param>` elements that get their values from the table, field and target input elements of an HTML form. For instance, if the user enters "Birthdays", "Who" and " C" as the values, the stylesheet will produce all the records that contain the string " C" in their Who field.

Given a SQL query, a Competent User can easily construct both the appropriate XSLT stylesheet and the HTML form to go with it, and thus enable the end-user to submit instantiated queries and receive result sets back. With a little JavaScript, the HTML form can be made completely generic, soliciting both the names of the table fields and their values from the end-user.

Because of the linguistic mismatch between SQL and XPath, the stylesheet cannot express the SQL concept of LIKE precisely; we translate it as the XPath function contains() (as in "string A contains string B"). Before we show the stylesheet, we introduce the new XSLT/XPath features in the stylesheet first.

New XSLT/XPath Features

We have seen that XPath is used within XSLT for two distinct purposes. One is to express a pattern that identifies source tree nodes that we want to process or use the values of, as in:

```
<xsl:template match="section/title">
```

The other is to create numeric or string (or boolean) expressions whose values we want to use either in constructing the result tree or for other programming needs, as in:

```
<xsl:if test="$counter>1">
<xsl:with-param name="counter" select="($counter)-1"/>
```

These are indeed the two main uses of XPath, and in the next stylesheet we will see more involved examples of both. We will also see some new XSLT elements.

Node Set Expressions with Boolean Conditions on Nodes

We have seen simple node set expressions in which nodes are identified by their tag name, as in

```
<xsl:template name="tabletop" match="table">
<xsl:variable name="headers" select="headers"/>
```

Now we want to select not just any field nodes but only those whose name attribute is the same as the value of the stylesheet parameter "field". We attach this boolean condition, in brackets, to the simple node set expression. (Remember that @name refers to the value of the name attribute, and $field refers to the value of the field parameter.)

```
<xsl:variable name="rowval" select="field[@name=$field]"/>
```

XPath Functional Expressions

We have already seen an XPath expression that looked like a function call with no arguments: the node() expression in ms2.xsl that selected all nodes. There are more recognizable function expressions in XPath that take arguments and return numeric, string or boolean values. For instance, the function contains() takes two string arguments and returns a boolean:

```
<xsl:if test="contains($rowval,$target)">
```

This expression returns true if the value of the rowval variable contains the value of the target parameter. What's the difference between a variable and a parameter? This is a good XSLT question.

Variables and Parameters in XSLT

Both `<xsl:variable>` and `<xsl:param>` can establish a binding; both can appear at the top level and within a template. "The difference is that the value specified on the `xsl:param` variable is only a default value for the binding; when the template or stylesheet within which the `xsl:param` element occurs is invoked, parameters may be passed that are used in place of the default values." (11) For instance, as we saw in the countdown example, if you say, within a named template:

```
<xsl:param name="counter" select="4"/><!-- '4' is default value -->
```

but invoke the template as:

```
<xsl:call-template name="count-down">
  <xsl:with-param name="counter" select="8"/>
```

the default value gets overridden. There is no such mechanism for overriding defined values of variables; you can only redefine them using the `xsl:variable` element.

Loops in XSLT with xsl:for-each

You can use the `xsl:for-each` element to run a loop. The following template rule will output the headers of the Birthdays table as the headeings row of the HTML table:

```
<xsl:template match="headers">
 <tr>
  <xsl:for-each select="header">
    <th>
      <xsl:value-of select="@name"/>:<xsl:value-of select="@fieldType"/>
    </th>
  </xsl:for-each>
  </tr>
</xsl:template>
```

Note that `xsl:for-each` elements can be nested, as in the template rule named `"tabletop"` in `dbdata.xsl`.

dbdata.xsl

Here is the stylesheet in its entirety:

```
<xsl:stylesheet xmlns:xsl="http://www.w3.org/1999/XSL/Transform"
                version="1.0">
<xsl:output method="html"/>
<xsl:param name="table" select="'Birthdays'"/>
<xsl:param name="field" select="'Who'"/>
<xsl:param name="target" select="'C'"/>

<!-- SELECT * FROM $table WHERE $field %LIKE% $target; -->

<xsl:template match="/">
  <xsl:apply-templates/>
</xsl:template>
```

```
<xsl:template match="dbdata">

<html><head><title>Simple SQL in XSL</title></head>
<body>
<p>
   This is an example of generating HTML from an XML data table, using XSL to
select and format relevant rows. We are looking for table
   '<xsl:value-of select="$table"/>',
and presenting just those rows where field
   '<xsl:value-of select="$field"/>'
contains the string
   '<xsl:value-of select="$target"/>',
whether as the whole field-value or as a substring.
</p>
<xsl:apply-templates select="table[@name=$table]"/>

</body></html>
</xsl:template>

<xsl:template name="tabletop" match="table">
  <h3>Table name: <xsl:value-of select="@name"/></h3>
  <xsl:variable name="headers" select="headers"/>
  <table border="true">
  <xsl:apply-templates select="headers"/>
  <xsl:for-each select="row">                  <!-- outer loop -->

     <xsl:variable name="rowval" select="field[@name=$field]"/>
     <xsl:if test="contains($rowval,$target)">
       <tr>
          <xsl:for-each select="field">   <!-- inner loop -->
            <td><xsl:value-of select="."/></td>
          </xsl:for-each>
        </tr>
     </xsl:if>
  </xsl:for-each>
   </table>
</xsl:template>

<xsl:template match="headers">
 <tr>
  <xsl:for-each select="header">
    <th>
      <xsl:value-of select="@name"/>:<xsl:value-of select="@fieldType"/>
    </th>
  </xsl:for-each>
  </tr>
</xsl:template>

</xsl:stylesheet>
```

XSLT and XPath in More Detail

We cannot possibly give an adequate coverage to XSLT in the remainder of this chapter, but we can summarize it as best we can. In order to use XSLT effectively, three things need to be understood:

❑   XSLT Data Model

❑   XSLT Processing Model

❑   The role of XPath

Beyond this general understanding, you just have to learn XSLT elements and their attributes, and the syntax of XPath expressions. In this section, we will bring together the observations we have made in connection with our examples and try to arrange them in some sort of a system. We will also present the extension mechanism built into XT that makes it possible to use Java code from within an XSLT stylesheet.

XSLT Data Model

XSLT thinks of a document, very much the way DOM does, as forming a tree of nodes. However, the node types of XSLT are somewhat different from DOM's, and so are their string values. A summary below is culled from the XPath Recommendation Section 5, because the XSLT Data Model is just copied from XPath but with minor additions that need not concern us. The reason Data Model is defined in XPath and copied to XSLT is because it is the XPath expressions that select the node sets in XSLT stylesheets. Here is the summary:

XPath models an XML document as a tree of nodes. There are seven types of node:

❑   root nodes

❑   element nodes

❑   text nodes

❑   attribute nodes

❑   namespace nodes

❑   processing instruction nodes

❑   comment nodes

Much of the XPath/XSLT Data Model should be familiar from DOM. There is one root node per document, and the root of the element tree is a child of the root node. There is an element node for each XML element within a document. The character data of an element node is placed in a text node that is a child of that element node. (This does not happen with the character data of attribute, processing instruction or comment nodes.) Namespace nodes are tricky (for instance, they are not children of their parents) and outside the scope of this chapter.

For every type of node, there is a way of determining a string-value for a node of that type:

❏ for text, attribute, processing instruction and comment nodes, the string-value is part of the node

❏ for root and element nodes, the string-value is computed from the string-value of descendant nodes by concatenating all their text values together

> This is where XPath/XSLT differ from DOM: for element nodes and root nodes, the string-value of a node is not the same as the string returned by DOM's `nodeValue()` method.

XSLT Processing Model

We have already presented the Processing Model of XSLT in an earlier section. We repeat the basics here:

❏ At any given time, there is a list of source nodes, usually found by matching a pattern.

❏ A result tree fragment is created by processing that list; "processing" usually means instantiating a template associated with the pattern.

❏ In the course of that processing, new source nodes can be added to the list, usually by the `<xsl:apply-templates/>` element.

❏ The transformation process begins by processing a list containing just the root node.

❏ The transformation process ends when the source node list is empty.

An Overview of XPath

As the examples show, XPath is used very heavily in XSLT: every time you state `match="..."` or `select="..."  "`, what you put inside those quotes is an XPath expression. XPath also defines many operators and core functions that are used to output parts of the result tree.

XPath is an Expression Language

XPath is a language that consists of **expressions**. There are several kinds of expressions, the most important of which is **path expressions** (also known as location paths). The value of a path expression is a node-set. For instance, "`/`" is a path expression that matches a node-set that consists of a single node, the root. It is path expressions of the XPath language that are used in the pattern part of an XSLT template rule. Other expressions evaluate to boolean, numeric or string values; there are four data types in XPath altogether.

XPath Data Model

"XPath models an XML document as a tree of nodes. There are different types of nodes, including element nodes, attribute nodes and text nodes." (Introduction.) At our level of detail, the data models of XSLT and XPath are identical, although in actual fact, the XSLT data model has a few minor extensions summarized in the *Recommendation*.

XPath Expression Types

The most important type is **location path** expressions that evaluate to node-sets. Otherwise, there are arithmetic, boolean and string expressions. They can be either primary (variable reference, literal, function call), or compound expressions that use operators. There is a modest set of arithmetic operations (no shifts, no ternary operator), the standard boolean operators (and, or – not() is a function), and relational operators. There are type conversion functions boolean(), string() and number(), but there are no objects that can be converted to node-sets: the only way to obtain a node-set is to use a location path expression. In many situations, data type conversion is performed automatically: 4>"3" returns the boolean value true.

Location Path Expressions

The same location path expressions are used in XSLT and XPointer/XLink. In XSLT, location paths are used to select a node set for processing. In XPointer/XLink, when they are ready, location paths will be used to specify hypertext links. As you can see, the idea is that, unlike HTML links, XML links will point precisely to structural components of documents, and a single link may point to more than one target. In this chapter we only discuss how location path expressions are used in XSLT.

Location path expressions can be absolute or relative. Absolute expressions start with "/", just like absolute directory paths in Unix; the "/" alone refers to the root of the tree. Both absolute and relative expressions are evaluated relative to a starting point, which is the root for absolute expressions and the context node for relative ones.

There are two versions of path expression syntax: verbose and abbreviated. Just as the *Recommendation* does, we will use verbose syntax to illustrate the key concepts of location path and location step before switching to abbreviated syntax. (Only abbreviated syntax was used in examples above, so you've already seen quite a bit of it.)

Here is an example of verbose syntax that we are going to use for illustrations:

```
/child::doc/child::chapter[position()=5]/child::section[attribute::title="XX"]
```

This is an absolute location path. Stepping through it left to right, we first arrive at the "doc" element that is a child of the root, then at the fifth chapter element that is also a child of "doc", and finally at that section element that is a child of the fifth chapter and has a "title" attribute whose value is "XX". In other words, this location path selects the XX section of the fifth chapter of the doc element that is a child of the root.

Location Steps and Their Components

A location path consists of one or more **location steps** separated by a "/". There are three location steps in our example. A location step consists of three parts:

- ❏ axis – in what direction are we going

- ❏ node test – what nodes are we selecting while going in that direction

- ❏ additional predicate (optional) – further conditions on nodes to be selected

Axes

The best way to understand XPath is to think of the starting point of evaluation as radiating several "axes", such as child, parent, preceding-sibling, attribute, and so on. Here is a complete list of axes, from Production 6 of the *XPath Recommendation*:

```
[6]    AxisName    ::=
      'ancestor'
   | 'ancestor-or-self'
   | 'attribute'
   | 'child'
   | 'descendant'
   | 'descendant-or-self'
   | 'following'
   | 'following-sibling'
   | 'namespace'
   | 'parent'
   | 'preceding'
   | 'preceding-sibling'
   | 'self'
```

Most of these are self-explanatory. The namespace axis is a bit tricky (because namespace nodes are tricky) and outside the scope of this chapter. The rest have to do either with attribute nodes (the attribute axis) or element nodes (the rest of them). We say that an attribute node is the **principal node type** for the attribute axis and that an element node is the principal node type for the remaining axes (except the namespace axis).

Node Tests

A node test is, for most practical purposes, the name of an element or attribute node. So, for instance, `child::chapter` selects all the children of the context node that are chapter elements. There are several node tests that select in more generic ways (2.3):

"A node test * is true for any node of the principal node type. For example, `child::*` will select all element children of the context node, and `attribute::*` will select all attributes of the context node.

The node test `text()` is true for any text node. For example, `child::text()` will select the text node children of the context node. Similarly, the node test `comment()` is true for any comment node, and the node test `processing-instruction()` is true for any processing instruction. A node test `node()` is true for any node of any type whatsoever".

Additional predicates

Additional predicates are XPath boolean expressions in square brackets.

Examples

Here are a few examples, borrowed or adapted from the *XPath Recommendation* Section 2, of location paths in verbose syntax so location steps are easy to see:

```
child::chapter/child::section[position()=last()-1] selects the next to last
section grandchild of the context node

/child::doc/child::chapter[position()=5]/child::section[position()=2] selects the
second section of the fifth chapter of the doc document element

child::para[attribute::type="warning"] selects all para children of the context
node that have a type attribute with value warning
```

Abbreviated Syntax for Location Path Expressions

The most important abbreviation is that `::child` is a default axis: if no axis is specified, child is assumed. Other abbreviations include:

Abbreviation	Meaning	Example
@	::attribute	[@type="warning]
//	::descendant	.//para
[number]	[position()=number]	chapter[5]
.	self::node()	./chapter[5]
..	parent::node()	../chapter[5]

The above examples of verbose syntax come out abbreviated as follows:

```
chapter/section[last()-1]
/doc/chapter[5]/section[2]
para[@type="warning"]
```

See the *XPath Recommendation* Section 2 for many more examples and explanations.

XPath Core Function Library

All implementations of XPath, such as those in XSLT and XPointer, must implement its core function library, described in Section 4 of the *XPath Recommendation*. In addition, an implementation may add functions of its own. XSLT additional functions are described in Section 12 of the *XSLT Recommendation*.

By and large, learning XPath boils down to learning the abbreviated syntax of location path expressions and the functions of the core library.

This concludes our brief and necessarily selective overview of XSLT and XPath. The rest, we hope, can be learned from consulting documentation and reading code.

Extensions to XSLT

What happens if you want to do something that is beyond the capabilities of XSLT? Here is what the Introduction to the *Recommendation* states: "XSLT provides two 'hooks' for extending the language, one hook for extending the set of instruction elements used in templates and one hook for extending the set of functions used in XPath expressions. These hooks are both based on XML namespaces. This version of XSLT does not define a mechanism for implementing the hooks. See [14 Extensions].

NOTE: The XSL Working Group intends to define such a mechanism in a future version of this specification or in a separate specification."

While a standard mechanism is still lacking, James Clark's XT distribution comes with a "hook of the second kind", a mechanism for extending XPath functions with Java methods. The mechanism is quite powerful; here is how it works (we quote from `xt.htm` in the XT distribution of November 5, 1999):

"A call to a function `ns:foo` where `ns` is bound to a namespace of the form

```
http://www.jclark.com/xt/java/className
```

is treated as a call of the static method `foo` of the class with fully-qualified name `className`. Hyphens in method names are removed with the character following the hyphen being upper-cased. Overloading based on number of parameters is supported; overloading based on parameter types is not. A non-static method is treated like a static method with the `this` object as an additional first argument. A constructor is treated like a static method named `new`. Extension functions can return objects of arbitrary types which can then be passed as arguments to other extension functions or stored in variables.

For example, the following

```
<xsl:stylesheet
  version="1.0"
  xmlns:xsl="http://www.w3.org/1999/XSL/Transform"
  xmlns:date="http://www.jclark.com/xt/java/java.util.Date">

<xsl:template match="/">
  <html>
    <xsl:if test="function-available('date:to-string') and
                  function-available('date:new')">
      <p><xsl:value-of select="date:to-string(date:new())"/></p>
    </xsl:if>
  </html>
</xsl:template>

</xsl:stylesheet>
```

will print out the current date."

As you can see, the set of XPath function is extended to include `function-available()` that returns a boolean, and all the methods and constructors of the imported Java class. There is also a general mechanism for importing Java classes using the syntax of Namespace declarations.

More Advanced Programming Examples

In conclusion, we present a series of three more advanced programming examples. They build on the countdown example earlier in the chapter and demonstrate progressively more involved uses of recursion. The examples include a nested loop and permutations, and culminate in the well-known "8 Queens" problem (a rather interesting puzzle about placing Queens on a chessboard – see the section devoted to it later). This last example was inspired by Oren Ben-Kiki's contribution to the XSL list at mulberrytech.com (`http://www.mulberrytech.com/xsl/xsl-list/archive/msg05056.html`).

Although programming is more advanced, we will not need to learn much more XSLT or XPath. We use parameters and named templates often, and introduce some new string functions of XPath: `concat()`, `substring()`, `substring-before()` and `substring-after()`, all easily understandable in context.

Nested Loops

The countdown example showed how to do a loop in XSLT using a recursive call on a named template. Here we extend that example to show a loop that prints a square two-dimensional table. We also add a top-level `xsl:param` element so that the size of the table can be set from an HTML page:

```
<xsl:stylesheet xmlns:xsl="http://www.w3.org/1999/XSL/Transform"
                version="1.0">
<!-- testing a nested loop -->
<xsl:param name="tablesize" select="4"/><!-- override from HTML -->

<xsl:template match="/">
  <html><head><title>Nested Loop Test</title></head>
  <body>
     <h3>We will now call on "outer-loop".</h3>
     <table border="1">
     <xsl:call-template name="outer-loop">
       <xsl:with-param name="i" select="$tablesize"/>
     </xsl:call-template>
     </table></body>
  </html>
</xsl:template>

<xsl:template name="outer-loop">
  <xsl:param name="i" select="0"/>
  <xsl:if test="$i>0">
    <tr>
    <xsl:call-template name="inner-loop">
      <xsl:with-param name="i" select="$i"/>
      <xsl:with-param name="j" select="$tablesize"/>
    </xsl:call-template>
    </tr>
    <xsl:call-template name="outer-loop">
      <xsl:with-param name="i" select="($i)-1"/>
    </xsl:call-template>
  </xsl:if>
</xsl:template>

<xsl:template name="inner-loop">
   <xsl:param name="i" select="0"/>
   <xsl:param name="j" select="0"/>
   <xsl:if test="$j>0">
     <td>
       <xsl:value-of select="$i"/>,<xsl:value-of select="$j"/>
     </td>
     <xsl:call-template name="inner-loop">
       <xsl:with-param name="i" select="$i"/>
       <xsl:with-param name="j" select="($j)-1"/>
     </xsl:call-template>
   </xsl:if>
 </xsl:template>

</xsl:stylesheet>
```

If you install this stylesheet as a servlet "xslnest" through XT's XSLServlet mechanism, you can change the `tablesize` through the query:

```
http://localhost:8080/xslnest/xslrules/greeting.xml?tablesize=8
```

The stylesheet will produce a table of size 8 x 8, even though the default size is 4. You can use any existing XML file instead of `greeting.xml` because the stylesheet ignores the file in generating its output.

Permutations

This stylesheet produces a table in which each row is a permutation of numbers from 1 to `$permlimit`. Most of the work is done in the template called `shuffle` that constructs the body of the table:

```
<xsl:stylesheet xmlns:xsl="http://www.w3.org/1999/XSL/Transform"
                version="1.0">
<xsl:output method="html"/>
<!-- testing fairly tortuous recursion -->
<xsl:param name="permlimit" select="4"/>

<xsl:template match="/">

<html><head><title>Permutation Test</title></head>
<body>
   <table border="1">
   <xsl:call-template name="shuffle"/>
   </table>
</body></html>

</xsl:template>
```

`shuffle` produces each permutation as a string of numbers separated by commas. This "internal representation" is convenient for testing whether a given number is already in the emerging permutation or not. Once a permutation is constructed, it is given to the `outperm` template to output as `<td>` elements. That template uses two XPath string functions, `substring-before()` and `substring-after()`, to split off the number before the first comma, and the remaining string after the first comma:

```
<xsl:template name="outperm">
  <xsl:param name="list" select="''"/>
  <xsl:if test="contains($list,',')">
    <td>
     <xsl:value-of select="substring-before($list,',')"/>
    </td>
    <xsl:call-template name="outperm">
      <xsl:with-param name="list" select="substring-after($list,',')"/>
    </xsl:call-template>
  </xsl:if>
</xsl:template>
```

Now we only have to understand how `shuffle` builds each row. It does so with the help of two other named templates, `shuffletry` and `addifnew`. It uses three parameters:

❑ `list` is a string in which the permutation is built

❑ `listlen` is a number that is the current length of the list (by length we mean the number of items separated by commas)

❑ `lim` is a number which is the limit on list length and also the largest number to use in permutations; it is the value of `$permlimit`

Initially, list is `","` and `listlen` is 0. When `listlen` becomes equal to `lim`, `shuffle` outputs `<tr>...</tr>` and calls `outperm` in the middle to produce another row. (Since the string that `shuffle` builds begins with a comma, it sends `outperm` a sub-string starting with the second character.) As long as `listlen` is less than `lim`, `shuffle` calls `shuffletry`:

```
<xsl:template name="shuffle">
  <xsl:param name="lim" select="$permlimit"/>
  <xsl:param name="list" select="','"/>
  <xsl:param name="listlen" select="0"/>
  <xsl:if test="$lim>$listlen">
    <xsl:call-template name="shuffletry">
      <xsl:with-param name="lim" select="$lim"/>
      <xsl:with-param name="list" select="$list"/>
      <xsl:with-param name="listlen" select="$listlen"/>
    </xsl:call-template>
  </xsl:if>
  <xsl:if test="$listlen>=$lim">
    <tr>
    <xsl:call-template name="outperm">
      <xsl:with-param name="list" select="substring($list,2)"/>
    </xsl:call-template>
    </tr>
  </xsl:if>
</xsl:template>
```

In addition to the three parameters that `shuffletry` receives from `shuffle`, it has a fourth called `val` that always starts out as 1. As long as `val` is less than `lim`, `shuffletry` calls two named templates:

❑ One is `addifnew`; it checks to see whether `val` (surrounded by commas) is in the list already, and if not, it appends `val` (followed by a comma) to the list, and sends the augmented list to `shuffle`, thus completing the recursive loop.

❑ The other named template that `shuffletry` calls is `shuffletry` itself, with `val` incremented by 1. This is the other recursive loop that is needed to generate all possible values in a given position in a permutation.

Together, `shuffletry` and `addifnew` implement what is known as a **generate-and-test algorithm**: one serves as a generator of possible ways to proceed, the other tests the generated suggestions. Here are `shuffletry` and `addifnew`:

```xsl
<xsl:template name="shuffletry">
  <xsl:param name="val" select="1"/>
  <xsl:param name="lim" select="$permlimit"/>
  <xsl:param name="list" select="','"/>
  <xsl:param name="listlen" select="0"/>
  <xsl:if test="$lim>=$val" >
    <xsl:call-template name="addifnew">
        <xsl:with-param name="val" select="$val"/>
        <xsl:with-param name="lim" select="$lim"/>
        <xsl:with-param name="list" select="$list"/>
        <xsl:with-param name="listlen" select="$listlen"/>
    </xsl:call-template>
    <xsl:call-template name="shuffletry">
        <xsl:with-param name="val" select="1+$val"/>
        <xsl:with-param name="lim" select="$lim"/>
        <xsl:with-param name="list" select="$list"/>
        <xsl:with-param name="listlen" select="$listlen"/>
    </xsl:call-template>
  </xsl:if>
</xsl:template>

<xsl:template name="addifnew">
  <xsl:param name="val" select="1"/>
  <xsl:param name="lim" select="$permlimit"/>
  <xsl:param name="list" select="','"/>
  <xsl:param name="listlen" select="0"/>
  <xsl:variable name="valcomma"
          select="concat(',',$val,',')"/>
  <xsl:if test="not(contains($list,$valcomma))">
    <xsl:call-template name="shuffle">
        <xsl:with-param name="lim" select="$lim"/>
        <xsl:with-param name="list"
                select="concat($list,substring($valcomma,2))"/>
        <xsl:with-param name="listlen" select="1+$listlen"/>
    </xsl:call-template>
  </xsl:if>
</xsl:template>
```

We have seen all the pieces of the stylesheet; all together it looks like this:

```xsl
<xsl:stylesheet xmlns:xsl="http://www.w3.org/1999/XSL/Transform" version="1.0">
<xsl:output method="html"/>
<xsl:param name="permlimit" select="4"/>

<xsl:template match="/">

<html><head><title>Permutation Test</title></head>
```

```
<body>
   <table border="1">
   <xsl:call-template name="shuffle"/>
   </table>
</body>
</html>
</xsl:template>

<xsl:template name="shuffle">
...
</xsl:template>

<xsl:template name="shuffletry">
...
</xsl:template>

<xsl:template name="addifnew">
...
</xsl:template>

<xsl:template name="outperm">
...
</xsl:template>
</xsl:stylesheet>
```

With `tablesize=4`, the first few lines of the HTML output look like this:

```
<html>
<head>
<title>Permutation Test</title>
</head>
<body>
<table border="1">
<tr>
<td>1</td><td>2</td><td>3</td><td>4</td>
</tr>
<tr>
<td>1</td><td>2</td><td>4</td><td>3</td>
</tr>
<tr>
<td>1</td><td>3</td><td>2</td><td>4</td>
</tr>
```

The next problem might look much more difficult than permutations, but the solution is, to a surprising degree, similar.

8 Queens Puzzle

Our task is to find all possible ways to place 8 Queens on an 8 x 8 chessboard in such a way that they don't threaten each other. As you can imagine, the trickiest part is to make sure that they don't threaten each other diagonally. For this reason, we need two extra parameters passed around, upd and downd (for up-diagonal and down-diagonal); otherwise, the composition of the stylesheet is very much the same.

First, let's establish the internal representation of the solution: each solution will be a sequence of eight numbers. The position of a number represents the row of the board, and the value of each number represents the column number in which a queen is placed on that number's row. So, a solution

```
<tr>
<td>1</td><td>5</td><td>8</td><td>6</td><td>3</td><td>7</td><td>2</td><td>4</td>
</tr>
```

indicates that the first queen goes into row 1, column 1, the second queen goes into row 2, column 5, and so on, up until row 8, column 4. We internally represent sequences of numbers as comma-separated lists, themselves represented as character strings; so the above solution is first built as a string "1,5,8,6,3,7,2,4" and then sent to outperm for output.

Here is how it all looks in outline:

```
<xsl:stylesheet xmlns:xsl="http://www.w3.org/1999/XSL/Transform" version="1.0">
<xsl:output method="html"/>
<xsl:param name="boardsize" select="8"/>

<xsl:template match="/">
<html><head><title>N Queens</title></head>
<body>
  <table border="1">
    <xsl:call-template name="queens"/>
  </table>
</body>
</html>
</xsl:template>

<xsl:template name="queens">
...
</xsl:template>

<xsl:template name="queenstry">
...
</xsl:template>

<xsl:template name="addifnew">
...
</xsl:template>

<xsl:template name="outperm">
...
</xsl:template>
</xsl:stylesheet>
```

The parameter name is `boardsize`, and the name of the "main template" is `queens`, but otherwise we're doing exactly the same thing as in the permutation example. The changes are in the named templates `queens`, `queenstry` and `addifnew`. Even there, although the details are different, the generate-and-test structure of the algorithm is exactly the same. We leave for your reading pleasure to trace down the recursive ways of the queens; you are also welcome to test the stylesheet with boards of different sizes. However, be aware that XSLT is not C or even LISP; it takes 6.70 seconds on a 450mhz Pentium with a lot of memory running Windows 98 to do a problem of `boardsize=8` (and that's using what seems to be the most efficient XSL processor).

```
<xsl:template name="queens">
  <xsl:param name="lim" select="$boardsize"/>
  <xsl:param name="list" select="','"/>
  <xsl:param name="upd" select="','"/>
  <xsl:param name="dnd" select="','"/>
  <xsl:param name="listlen" select="0"/>
  <xsl:if test="$lim>$listlen">
    <xsl:call-template name="queenstry">
      <xsl:with-param name="lim" select="$lim"/>
      <xsl:with-param name="list" select="$list"/>
      <xsl:with-param name="upd" select="$upd"/>
      <xsl:with-param name="dnd" select="$dnd"/>
      <xsl:with-param name="listlen" select="$listlen"/>
    </xsl:call-template>
  </xsl:if>
  <xsl:if test="$listlen>=$lim">
    <tr>
    <xsl:call-template name="outperm">
      <xsl:with-param name="list" select="substring($list,2)"/>
    </xsl:call-template>
    </tr>
  </xsl:if>
</xsl:template>

<xsl:template name="queenstry">
  <xsl:param name="val" select="1"/>
  <xsl:param name="lim" select="$boardsize"/>
  <xsl:param name="list" select="','"/>
  <xsl:param name="upd" select="','"/>
  <xsl:param name="dnd" select="','"/>
  <xsl:param name="listlen" select="0"/>
  <xsl:if test="$lim>=$val" >
    <xsl:call-template name="addifnew">
      <xsl:with-param name="val" select="$val"/>
      <xsl:with-param name="lim" select="$lim"/>
      <xsl:with-param name="list" select="$list"/>
      <xsl:with-param name="upd" select="$upd"/>
      <xsl:with-param name="dnd" select="$dnd"/>
      <xsl:with-param name="listlen" select="$listlen"/>
    </xsl:call-template>
    <xsl:call-template name="queenstry">
      <xsl:with-param name="val" select="1+$val"/>
      <xsl:with-param name="lim" select="$lim"/>
      <xsl:with-param name="list" select="$list"/>
      <xsl:with-param name="upd" select="$upd"/>
      <xsl:with-param name="dnd" select="$dnd"/>
      <xsl:with-param name="listlen" select="$listlen"/>
    </xsl:call-template>
  </xsl:if>
</xsl:template>
```

```
<xsl:template name="addifnew">
  <xsl:param name="val" select="1"/>
  <xsl:param name="lim" select="$boardsize"/>
  <xsl:param name="list" select="','"/>
  <xsl:param name="upd" select="','"/>
  <xsl:param name="dnd" select="','"/>
  <xsl:param name="listlen" select="0"/>
  <xsl:variable name="valcomma"
                select="concat(',',$val,',')"/>
  <xsl:variable name="valup"
                select="concat(',',($val+$listlen),',')"/>
  <xsl:variable name="valdn"
                select="concat(',',(($boardsize+$val)-$listlen),',')"/>
  <xsl:if
     test="not(contains($list,$valcomma)
               or contains($upd,$valup)
               or contains($dnd,$valdn))">
    <xsl:call-template name="queens">
      <xsl:with-param name="lim" select="$lim"/>
      <xsl:with-param name="list"
           select="concat($list,substring($valcomma,2))"/>
      <xsl:with-param name="upd"
           select="concat($upd,substring($valup,2))"/>
      <xsl:with-param name="dnd"
           select="concat($dnd,substring($valdn,2))"/>
      <xsl:with-param name="listlen" select="1+$listlen"/>
    </xsl:call-template>
  </xsl:if>
</xsl:template>
```

What's XSLT For?

We are rapidly approaching the summary and conclusions to this final chapter of the book. In the meantime, the main conclusion **about XSLT** that we hope you will draw from this chapter is this: XSLT is best described as a general-purpose mini-language, intended to make many common operations on XML documents easy to express and accessible to non-programmers. This understanding has frequently emerged as a desired characteristic of the language in discussions on xsl-list, and it is also expressed by the creator of the language in http://www.jclark.com/xml/xslt-talk.htm. The rationale for the language may be stated briefly thus:

❑ XSLT is not a general-purpose XML transformation language

❑ XML can represent arbitrary data of arbitrary complexity

❑ General-purpose XML transformation requires a general-purpose programming language

❑ What's the Point? Why not just use a general-purpose programming language?

❑ Allows non-programmers to do some transformations:
  – without tools, only simple things
  – with tools, more complex things

The main goal of this chapter has been to provide some ideas about how programmers can create additional tools in XSLT that will empower non-programmers to perform much more complicated tasks, thus freeing programmers to do even more complex and interesting things.

What XSLT is (and is not) Good For

As our 8-Queens example shows very clearly, it is easy to get carried away with XSLT and start using it for problems that it is ill-suited to solve. There is a fine line here between extending XSLT for a broader range of tasks and pushing it beyond its limits of usefulness. We would define the line as follows.

> **If you are pushing XSLT to its limit in order to solve an individual problem, then it's not a good idea. If you do it in order to create a generic tool that a non-programmer can use, then it might be a good idea, depending on how good the tool is.**

As a general guide on when to use XSLT vs. a general-purpose programming language to operate on the output of the XML parser, we cannot do much better than quote James Clark's contribution to xsl-list (XSL-List Digest V2 #247):

"There are many, real-world transformation problems for which XSLT is not the right tool. I would never claim that XSLT is the one true transformation language for XML. Whether it's a good choice for a particular transformation problem depends on a number of factors, including the following:

❑ XSLT is better at down translations than up translations; if your transformation is going from a less-structured form to a more-structured form, XSLT may not be a good choice

❑ XSLT is better at transformations on structure than transformations on content; if your transformation is doing complex transformations on the text content of the document, XSLT may not be a good choice

❑ XSLT is very tree-oriented; if the structure in the input or output document is not reflected in the XML tree structure, then XSLT may not be a good choice (this can happen with XML documents that encode data structures that are graphs rather than trees)

XSLT is powerful enough that you can push it to perform transformations for which a conventional programming language would be a much better tool. I would strongly encourage the XSL community *not* to do this. A key part of educating people about XSLT should be to educate them about when to use it and when not to use it."

XSLT vs. JSP

As of today, JSP is a tool for a programmer while XSLT is a tool for a Competent User who is NOT a programmer. However, imagine a not so distant future when XSLT has a standard mechanism for incorporating Java beans, while JSP becomes an XML language with a convenient mechanism for adding custom-designed tag libraries (`jsp:taglib`, to become functional in version 1.1). The line will begin to blur: both can be described as XML languages in which some tags are associated with custom-designed code in a general-purpose programming language. Most likely, there will be an area of overlap but they will remain separate entities, one better suited for imperative programming, the other providing a more declarative mode of expression, better suited for a mini-language. Identifying their appropriate spheres of influence and modes of cooperation will be an interesting subject for another book (or for a second edition of this one).

Summary

In this chapter, we have taken a very quick tour of XSLT and XPath, and provided examples of several levels of complexity. We have also stepped through the not-entirely-trivial procedure of setting up the XSLT processor to work with an XML parser of your choice, both as a command-line application and as a servlet. Here are the highlights of the chapter: we have learnt how to:

- ❑ configure XT to work with either XP or Sun's parser
- ❑ configure XSLServlet to work with jswdk
- ❑ put together simple stylesheets and view them in Internet Explorer 5.0
- ❑ use stylesheets for document processing, data processing and programming
- ❑ use a stylesheet to "run a SQL query" on an XML document representing a database table
- ❑ use stylesheets for sophisticated recursive programming, including generate-and-test algorithms

Our overviews of XSLT and XPath, although brief, summarize the main structural features of the two languages and provide a basis for steady accumulation of more detailed and advanced skills.

From Here...

This book is built around two "big ideas". One is organizational: the idea of a framework in which programmers like you can set up extremely configurable systems that seriously stretch what a competent user or administrator can do. The other is architectural: the idea of a distributed application that consists of processing nodes, all of them configurable by XML and capable of emitting and consuming XML data streams. In outline, Chapters 3 and 4 develop the first idea, while Chapters 11 and 12 develop both of them together in an integrated system; the remaining chapters build the necessary scaffolding. Some of you will perhaps find those remaining chapters the most valuable for your day-to-day work, and that's fine.

The technologies that make it all possible are Java and XML. Java is great because it has some truly wonderful tools for building and connecting distributed components, and because you can instantiate, load and configure those components at run time. XML is great because it is so versatile: you can use it on the back end both to encode data and to describe the configuration of your system; and you can use it on the front end, for user input. (For the time being, front-end capabilities are limited because the browsers have not quite caught up yet, so there is a layer of HTML-XML exchange there that will eventually go away.)

So, in more concrete terms, how do you build an application "configurable by XML"? You want an XML file that describes the application, and you want a processor that parses that file and interprets what it says as instructions to instantiate and configure a network of interconnected beans. The XML configuration component of Chapter 11, with its `XmlConfig` interface and `topbean` DTD, should give you an idea of how to go about doing that.

Once you have an XML-configurable system, you have a number of options for constructing its user interfaces, both for the system administrator and for the end user. In all of those options, you will probably want to insert another processing level between the user and the configuration files because, even though the configuration files are XML and can be validated against a DTD, their XML language is too technical: it talks about beans and sub-beans, and classes to use, and so forth. You want to give the user a simpler mini-language that will enable the user to "configure the configuration files". You also want to give the user a mini-language to describe desired output. You can design those mini-languages in plain XML with a custom processor, or you can use XSLT to transform user input into configuration files, or you can use JSP pages. We have not done all of this in the book, but you have seen enough of all those technologies to continue on your own. Just remember the main unifying idea of everything we've said so far: you design XML languages to solve problems. You design the syntax of the language (its tags and attributes) with a specific user in mind, and, if you want the syntax checked, you write a DTD for it. You then provide the interpretation and semantic checking for your syntax by writing Java code, or constructing the necessary code out of large building blocks, such as JSPs. **The central notion is a formal language that is given an interpretation.**

The book has made a fair progress towards its big visions, but they are not quite complete. Some parts are missing because the technologies are not quite there yet: the browsers cannot really show XML, and JSP engines cannot yet do custom-designed tag libraries. Some other parts, or connections between parts, are missing because there is only so much you can put in a book. For instance, if you go back to the XmlMail application of Chapters 11-12, you will notice that they can write to an XML string or an XML file, but not to a data-driven XML sequence that can be submitted to a SAX processor. (We can, of course, write XML to file and open that file, but this would be too much like DOS.) So, this is one connection that is missing.

Another good connection to have is between chained servlets, including the XSLServlet. Servlets and JSP can always output XML, and it would be good to be able to chain that output to the XSLServlet to apply a stylesheet to it, or to any other servlet that is outfitted with a SAX processor. More generally, it should be very easy to send XML data, from whatever source, to a cached stylesheet that is modifiable by a Competent User. This would create a nice clean interface, with very powerful and yet intuitive tools, between programmers and competent users. Remember that, ideally, there should be just one place for the competent user to make each necessary decision. With XML and XSLT, you can design a mini-language for QShell applications such that both the initialization files and the HTML output files are generated from the same XML source. XSLT is a great tool for doing that.

We hope that you will think about those missing parts and connections as opportunities for you to pursue. It doesn't mean that you have to share our vision in order to make use of this book. The multiple technologies it presents can be used separately, or combined in different ways for completely different kinds of systems. You can read this book simply as an analytical description of several technologies, with extended examples of how they can be used.

As we said in the Introduction, we have been fortunate to write this book when the technologies it describes have all been released in stable versions, so its code is likely to remain in good working condition for a while. At the same time, the technologies are rapidly evolving (with a clear commitment to backward compatibility), so that there are many exciting new possibilities clearly visible in the near and mid-range future: possibilities for constructing ever more powerful, elegant and useful applications. We very much look forward to trying them out, and we hope that, after reading this book, you do too.

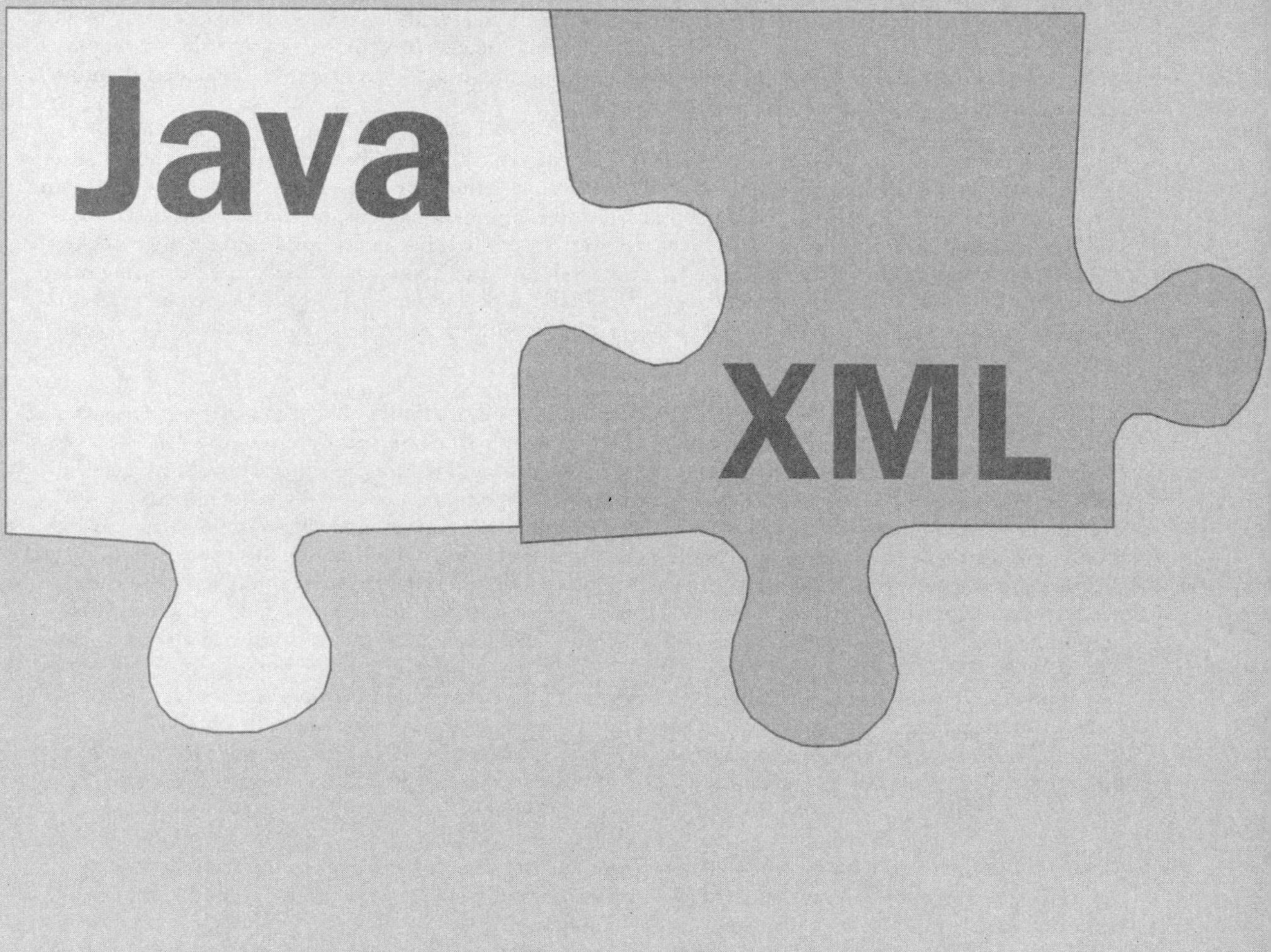
Java
XML

A Brief Installation Guide

The software you need falls into two parts: our own code, and its supporting cast of downloads. In this appendix we give instructions on how to download and install all of it.

Our Code

All our code comes in one file: `MyNa.zip`. It contains the source files (Java, XML, XSL, and configuration files) for every program you see in the book, including those that are only briefly mentioned and not covered in detail. These files are spread out over several directory sub-trees in a way which will, we hope, make usage easier. We recommend that you expand the whole zip file, e.g. into a "Downloads" directory, and move them where you want them. (We'll tell you where you might want them in a moment.) We don't include the compiled files; you should be able to re-create them all with a few "`javac`" commands.

Other Software: Downloads

In order to work with our code, we suggest the following downloads (free, as of the beginning of December 1999; you may of course prefer to substitute commercial packages for some):

Sun

Java 1.2 SDK
> `http://java.sun.com/products/jdk/1.2/`

JavaServer Web Development Kit, jswdk-1.0
> `http://java.sun.com/products/servlet/index.html`

Project X xml-tr2
> `http://java.sun.com/products/xml/index.html`

JavaMail
> `http://java.sun.com/products/javamail/index.html`
> (the POP3 provider is a separate download on the same page)

Java Activation Framework (required for JavaMail)
> `http://java.sun.com/beans/glasgow/jaf.html`

JRun (you don't need JRun Pro to start development)
    http://www.allaire.com/products/Jrun/

James Clark
XT and XP
    http://www.jclark.com/xml/

Apache
Element Construction Kit (ECS)
    http://java.apache.org/

You don't have to do these all at once:

- ❏ Chapters 1-4 depend only on the JSDK, ECS, and JRun (or some other servlet engine)

- ❏ Chapters 5-9 depend, in addition, on Sun's TR-2 (or some other conformant XML processor)

- ❏ Chapters 10-12 depend, instead of JRun, on jswdk-1.0 (or some other servlet-and-JSP engine)

- ❏ Chapter 13 depends, in addition, on XT (or some other conformant XSLT processor)

On Servlet Engines

As you can see, we are using two servlet engines. Until things settle down, we suggest that for development purposes you should have more than one; it's often inexplicably easy to do something on platform X which is inexplicably hard to do with platform Y, but then the next day the difficulty-levels are reversed. We could have used JSWDK throughout (although JRun has features, such as servlet chaining, which are not supported by jswdk-1.0). If we'd used JRun exclusively, that would have been fine except for Chapter 13 (where we couldn't get JRun's ServletConfig.getResource() method to return a non-null, and even then we could have programmed around it). As soon as Apache releases a stable version of Jakarta, we are going to try it and, if successful, update this file with additional instructions.

Windows and Other Installations

We'll focus on the Windows installation, but the software is not dependent on Windows; there should be no problem translating to other platforms.

Begin by installing the JSDK from Sun. (If you're re-installing, be careful to uninstall the old before installing the new.) This installs the full System Development Kit, by default in C:\jdk1.2.2 for Windows users, but it also includes the re-distributable Runtime Engine as a separate system; the result is that you have different "java.exe" files and possible values for JAVA_HOME, and therefore you will have different possible substitutes for CLASSPATH usage: you have to decide whether to drop jar files into

    C:\jdk1.2.2\jre\lib\ext
or

    C:\Program Files\JavaSoft\JRE\1.2\lib\ext

or, after installing JRun, even

    C:\JRun\jre\lib\ext

Each of those is the right place for the corresponding java.exe (or javaw.exe, which does not display an MSDOS window). Make sure this part works; use the demos, if nothing else.

Now install your servlet-runner; for JRun, you get a choice of which JVM you want to use and a choice of what web server to connect to. The "weakest" configuration is probably the MS Personal Web Server, and even that works fine. For the JVM, we suggest the JavaSoft\JRE because jswdk-1.0 will want to use that one. Again, test with the included demos.

Now "install" ECS by dropping `ecs.jar` into whichever `ext` directory corresponds to the JVM you'll be using, or putting it on your `CLASSPATH`. If you already downloaded the other packages, do the same with

- ❏ `mail.jar`, `pop3.jar`, `activation.jar`, `xml.jar` and `webserver.jar` from Sun

- ❏ `xt.jar` and possibly `xp.jar` from James Clark

- ❏ `servlet.jar` from Sun (jswdk-1.0) or from JRun

Do any testing you feel like for any of those systems. They all come with installation instructions and demos for testing.

We have had no problem using both JRun and jswdk-1.0, but if you do (or don't want to risk it) then you can simply assign one JVM to each situation, or make sure that the `CLASSPATH` is correctly set when you run. As a debugging aid, we strongly suggest frequent checks of `System.getProperties()`, e.g. by saying:

```
System.out.println("properties: " + System.getProperties());
```

This will tell you which JVM you're running, what the `CLASSPATH` is, and a host of other things that you may have forgotten to check for.

Installing Our Code

Ready for `MyNa`? Unzip `MyNa.zip` into a folder somewhere, and look at the resulting directory tree. It's set up as follows:

- ❏ Servlets in the JRun default servlets directory

- ❏ JSP pages and their beans in the default jswdk-1.0 directories for those purposes

- ❏ Three `MyNa` directories:

- ❏ `C:\JRun\jsm-default\MyNa` containing the configuration files for the early servlets

- ❏ `C:\JRun\jsm-default\classes\MyNa`, containing the two packages we use for tools, `MyNa.utils` (unaware of XML) and `MyNa.xml`

- ❏ `C:\MyNa\xml` containing the starting HTML pages for servlets

The first `MyNa` sub-tree, configuration, needs to go in the default directory for whichever servlet engine you use for the early servlets.

The second `MyNa` sub-tree just needs to be on the `CLASSPATH`. (Servlets themselves should not be on the `CLASSPATH`; the servlet loader is not the same as the class loader.)

The third `MyNa` sub-tree can go wherever you like, but we find it useful to tell the web server about the xml subdirectory; thus we set up PWS to reach `C:\MyNa\xml` as `http://localhost/xmlTst`.

That should be it – enjoy.

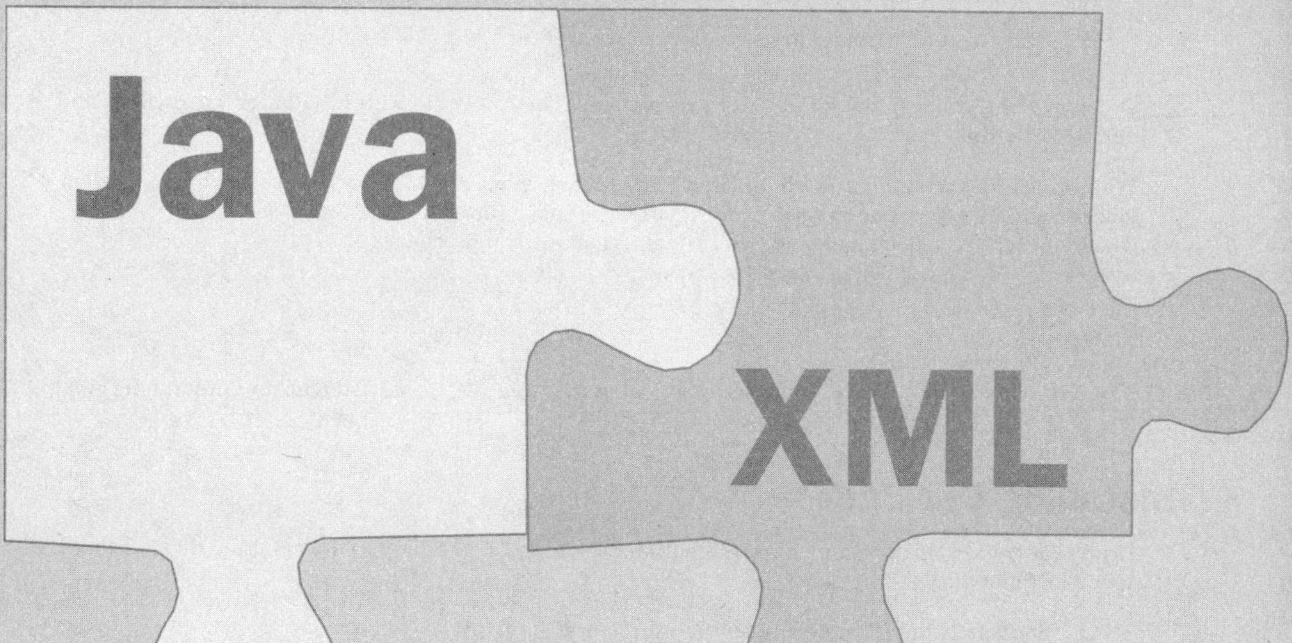
Java
XML

B

Resources

The following URLs and resources include valuable information about all the technologies covered in this book. We've arranged them into four categories: Basic Java Resources; Java non-XML resources; Java XML resources, and XML/XSL resources.

Basic Java Resources

`http://java.sun.com/`
Java's home page. An index of the documentation available can be found at
`http://developer.java.sun.com/developer/infodocs/index.shtml.`

`http://java.sun.com/docs/books/tutorial/`
Sun's own Java tutorial; useful. There are many more available on the web.

`http://java.sun.com/docs/faqindex.html`
The full list of all the Sun Java FAQs.

`http://java.sun.com/aboutJava/newsgroups.html`
The full list of comp.lang.java.X newsgroups.

Java and related Resources

http://java.sun.com/j2ee/
Enterprise edition APIs and product information.

http://www.ibm.com/developer/java/
IBM developerWorks, providing links to some useful white papers, and some interesting case studies.

http://www.gjt.org/pkgdoc/tree/index:html
Giant Java Tree is a great repository for Java code.

http://www.gnu.org/software/java/java-software.html
GNU Java programs – open source Java code for Unix platforms.

JDBC

http://java.sun.com/products/jdbc/
The core pages for JDBC.

http://java.sun.com/products/jdbc/drivers.html
Provides a list and links to most of the major JDBC driver vendors.

JSP

http://java.sun.com/products/jsp/
Sun's JSP home page, with links to documentation, downloads and FAQs

http://jakarta.apache.org/
Jakarta project, home of the Tomcat Apache-based implementation of Servlets 2.2 and JSP 1.1.

http://www.esperanto.org.nz/jsp/jspfaq.html
Thorough JSP FAQ

http://www.klomp.org/gnujsp/
GNUJSP home page

http://www.bitmechanic.com/
GNU Server Pages

Servers

http://www.tagtraum.com/
Java server-side support, including JSPExecutor

http://www.allaire.com/products/jrun/
JRUN servlet engine, the engine we use in this book.

http://www.newatlanta.com/
ServletExec from NewAtlanta

Servlets

http://java.sun.com/products/servlet/
Sun's servlet home page, including links to resources, FAQs, and tutorials.

http://jakarta.apache.org/
Jakarta project, home of the Tomcat Apache-based implementation of Servlets 2.2 and JSP 1.1.

http://www.ericsson.com/WAP/developer/
Servlet classes and resources for developers interested in the **Wireless Application Protocol** (**WAP**)

Java XML Resources

http://java.sun.com/xml/
The official java/XML site. Tutorials, documentation and downloads. Also includes the Java/XML
mailing list, **xml-interest@java.sun.com.**

http://xml.apache.org/
XML for Apache; good resources and links.

XML/XSL Resources

http://www.w3.org
The World Wide Web Consortium's home page, and the home site for almost all the specifications
discussed in the book. The first place to go for technical information about XML or XSL.

http://www.ucc.ie/xml
Home of a good, general XML FAQ.

http://www.oasis-open.org/cover
Robin Cover's personal XML & SGML pages, containing a huge range of articles, information and links
to other resources.

http://www.xml.com
O'Reilly sponsored (but otherwise excellent) source of XML news and articles.

http://www.megginson.com
David Megginson's site, again with a range of resources, tutorials, and some excellent FAQs.

The most important XML discussion group is the XML-DEV newsgroup. To subscribe to the digest,
mailed on Monday of each week, send email to <majordomo@ic.ac.uk> with the message line
'subscribe xml-dev-digest'.

The archives are held at http://www.lists.ic.ac.uk/hypermail/xml-dev/

Microsoft Sites

Although we've not examined Microsoft's approach to XML in any depth, the following URLs provide
more information regarding Redmond's implementations:

http://msdn.microsoft.com/xml/
http://www.biztalk.org/

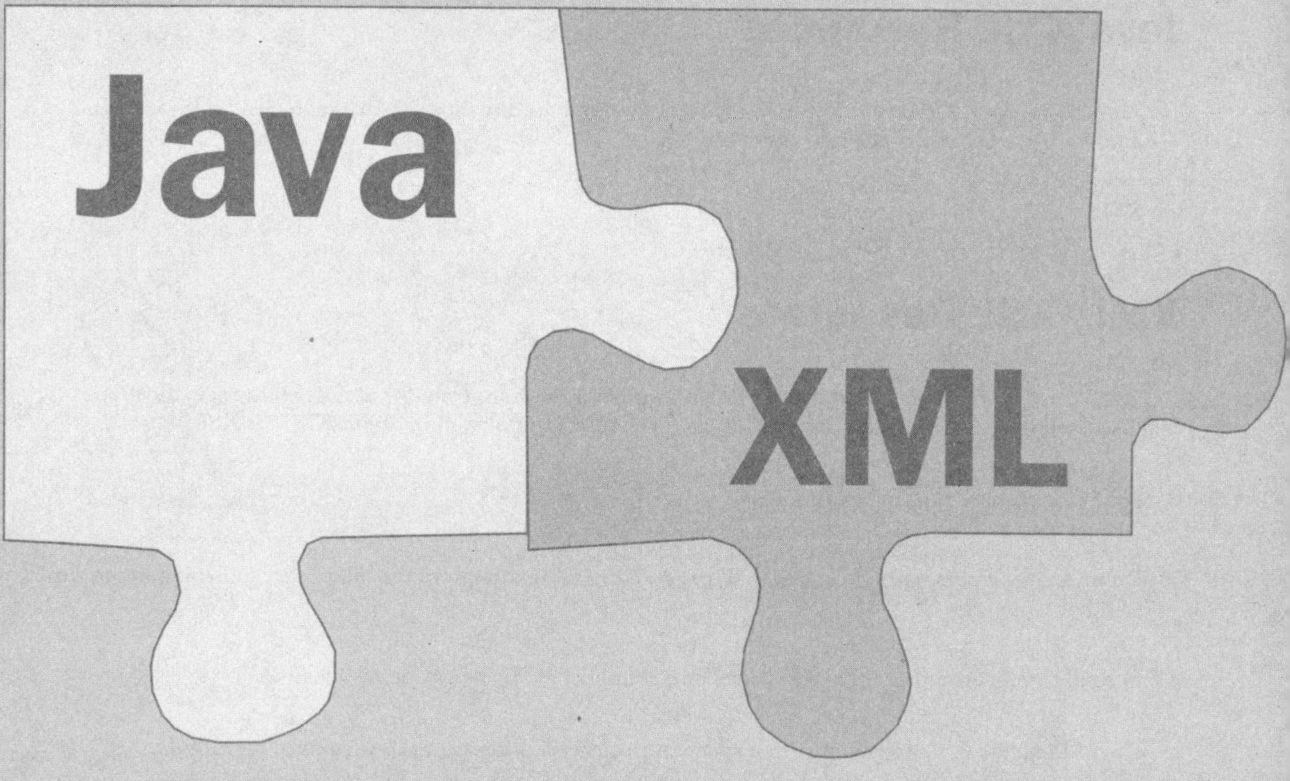
Java
XML

C

HTTP

The Hypertext Transfer Protocol (HTTP) is an application-level protocol for distributed hypermedia information systems. It is a generic, stateless protocol, which can be used for many tasks beyond its use for hypertext. A feature of HTTP is the typing and negotiation of data representation, allowing systems to be built independently of the data being transferred.

The first version of HTTP, referred to as HTTP/0.9, was a simple protocol for raw data transfer across the Internet. HTTP/1.0, as defined by RFC 1945 improved the protocol by allowing messages to be in a MIME-like format, containing meta-information about the data transferred and modifiers on the request/response semantics. The current version HTTP/1.1, made performance improvements by making all connections persistent and supporting absolute URLs in requests.

HTTP communication usually takes place over TCP/IP connections. The default port is TCP 80, but other ports can be used. This does not preclude HTTP from being implemented on top of any other protocol on the Internet, or on other networks. HTTP only presumes a reliable transport; any protocol that provides such guarantees can be used.

URIs, URLs, and URNs

A **Uniform Resource Identifier** (**URI**) is a means of unambiguously locating a resource on the Internet. The resources can be files, email addresses, programs, services, or something else. There are two types of URIs; **Uniform Resource Locators** (**URLs**), and **Uniform Resource Names** (**URNs**).

A URL is a pointer to a particular resource on the internet at a particular location, for example `http://www.wrox.com` and `ftp://ftp.wrox.com/pub/examples`. A URL specifies the protocol used to access the server, the name of the server and the location of the resource on the server. For example, the URL `http://www.wrox.com/index.html` specifies http as the protocol, `www.wrox.com` as the server location and `/index.html` as that path of the resource.

URNs are intended to serve as persistent, location-independent, resource identifiers. Given a URN a client will be able to retrieve it from any server that has the resource. HTTP exclusively deals with URLs.

Overall Operation

The HTTP protocol is a request/response protocol. A client sends a request to the server in the form of a request method, URI, and protocol version, followed by a MIME-like message containing request modifiers, client information, and possible body content over a connection with a server. The server responds with a status line, including the message's protocol version and a success or error code, followed by a MIME-like message containing server information, entity meta-information, and possible entity-body content.

Most HTTP communications are initiated by a **user agent**, which is the client which initiates a request.

User agents are typically browsers, editors, spiders or other end-user tools. The communication consists of a request to be applied to a resource on a server. In the simplest case, this may be accomplished via a single connection between the user agent and the HTTP server as shown in the figure below.

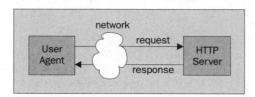

A more complicated situation occurs when one or more intermediaries are present in the request/response chain. There are three common forms of intermediary: **proxy, gateway**, and **tunnel**. A proxy is a forwarding agent, receiving requests for a URI in its absolute form, rewriting all or part of the message, and forwarding the reformatted request toward the server identified by the URI. A gateway is a receiving agent, acting as a layer above some other server(s) and, if necessary, translating the requests to the underlying server's protocol. A tunnel acts as a relay point between two connections without changing the messages; tunnels are used when the communication needs to pass through an intermediary (such as a firewall) even when the intermediary cannot understand the contents of the messages. The server where the actual request URI resides is called the **origin server**. The figure below illustrates a HTTP communication when intermediaries are present.

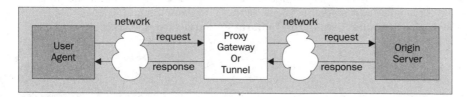

Any party to the communication that is not acting as a tunnel may employ an internal cache for handling requests. The effect of a **cache** is that the request/response chain is shortened if one of the participants along the chain has a cached response applicable to that request. Not all responses are usefully cacheable, and some requests may contain modifiers that place special requirements on cache behavior

HTTP Basics

Each HTTP client request and server response has three parts: the request or response line, a header section and the entity body.

Client Request

The client initiates the transaction as follows.

The client connects to a HTTP based server at a designated port (by default, 80) and sends a request by specifying an HTTP command called a method, followed by a document address, and an HTTP version number. The format of the request line is

```
Method          Request-URI     Protocol
```

For example,

```
GET  /index.html     HTTP/1.0
```

uses the GET method to request the document /index.html using version 1.0 of the protocol.

Next, the client sends optional header information to the server about its configuration and the document formats it will accept. All header information is sent line by line, each with a header name and value in the form

```
Keyword: Value
```

For example,

```
User-Agent:     Lynx/2.4 libwww/5.1k
Accept:         image/gif, image/x-xbitmap, image/jpeg, */*
```

The **User-Agent** keyword lets the server determine what browser is being used. This allows the server to send files optimized for the particular browser type. The **Accept** keyword will inform the server what kinds of data the client can handle. The request line and the subsequent header lines are all terminated by a carriage return/linefeed (\r\n) sequence. The client sends a blank line to end the headers.

Finally, after sending the request and headers the client may send additional data. This data is mostly used by CGI programs using the POST method. This additional information is called request entity. Finally a blank line (\r\n\r\n) terminates the request. A complete request might look like the following:

```
GET /index.html HTTP/1.0
Accept: */*
Connection: Keep-Alive
Host: www.w3.org
User-Agent: Generic
```

Server Response

The HTTP response also contains 3 parts.

Firstly, the server replies with status line containing three fields: the HTTP version, status code, and description of status code in the following format.

```
Protocol    Status-code       Description
```

For example, the status line

```
HTTP/1.0 200  OK
```

indicates that the server uses version 1.0 of the HTTP in its response. A status code of 200 means that the client request was successful.

After the response line, the server sends header information to the client about itself and the requested document. All header information is sent line by line, each with a header name and value of the form

```
Keyword: Value
```

For example,

```
HTTP/1.1 200 OK
Date: Wed, 19 May 1999 18:20:56 GMT
Server: Apache/1.3.6 (Unix) PHP/3.0.7
Last-Modified: Mon, 17 May 1999 15:46:21 GMT
ETag: "2da0dc-2870-374039cd"
Accept-Ranges: bytes
Content-Length: 10352
Connection: close
Content-Type: text/html; charset=iso-8859-1
```

The **Server** keyword lets the browser know what server is being used. The **date** header will inform the client the time of the response (in terms of server time zone). The **Last-Modified** header will let the browser know the last time this document was modified and finally the **Content-type** and **Content-length** will inform the browser the properties of the document that is being sent. The response line and the subsequent header lines are all terminated by a carriage return/linefeed (\r\n) sequence. The server sends a blank line to end the headers.

If the client's request if successful, the requested data is sent. This data may be a copy of a file, or the response from a CGI program. This result is called a response entity. If the client's request could not be fulfilled, additional data sent may be a human-readable explanation of why the server could not fulfill the request. The properties (type and length) of this data are sent in the headers. Finally a blank line (\r\n\r\n) terminates the response.

A complete request might look like the following:

```
HTTP/1.1 200 OK
Date: Wed, 19 May 1999 18:20:56 GMT
Server: Apache/1.3.6 (Unix) PHP/3.0.7
Last-Modified: Mon, 17 May 1999 15:46:21 GMT
ETag: "2da0dc-2870-374039cd"
Accept-Ranges: bytes
Content-Length: 10352
Connection: close
Content-Type: text/html; charset=iso-8859-1

<!DOCTYPE HTML PUBLIC "-//W3C//DTD HTML 4.0 Transitional//EN"
"http://www.w3.org/TR/REC-html40/loose.dtd">
<html>
  ...
</body>
</html>
```

In HTTP/1.0, after the server has finished sending the response, it disconnects from the client and the transaction is over unless the client sends a `Connection: KeepAlive` header. In HTTP/1.1, however the connection is maintained so that the client can make additional requests unless the client had sent and explicit `Connection: close header`. Since many HTML documents embed other documents as inline images, applets, frames and so on, this persistent connection feature of HTTP/1.1 protocol will save the overhead of the client having to repeatedly connect to the same server just to retrieve a single page.

Entity

Request and response messages may transfer an entity if not otherwise restricted by the request method or response status code. An entity consists of entity-header fields and an entity-body, although some responses will only include the entity-headers. For example, in the above server response the following are the entity-headers:

```
Last-Modified: Mon, 17 May 1999 15:46:21 GMT
ETag: "2da0dc-2870-374039cd"
Content-Length: 10352
Content-Type: text/html; charset=iso-8859-1
```

Request Methods

The first line of a request contains command, request-URI, and protocol components. The HTTP command is called the method. The method tells the server the purpose of the client's request. There are many methods defined for HTTP, but three of them, GET, HEAD, and POST are widely used.

GET

```
GET        Request-URI      Protocol
```

The GET method is used to retrieve whatever information (in the form of an entity) is identified by the Request-URI. GET is the most commonly used method by browsers. When you type http://www.w3.org in your browser, the browser sends the following GET command to the server www.w3.org:

```
GET / HTTP/1.0
Accept: */*
Connection: Keep-Alive
Host: www.w3.org
User-Agent: Generic
```

If the Request-URI refers to a data-producing process such as a CGI program, it is the produced data that will be returned as the entity in the response rather than the source text of the process, unless that text is the output of the process. **The entity body portion of the GET request is always empty**. The GET method can also be used to send limited amount of input to programs like CGI through form tags. When a HTML form tag specifies the method=GET attribute, the key-value pairs representing the form input are appended to the URL following a question mark (?). Pairs are separated by ampersands. For example

```
GET /cgi/sendGreeting.pl?"name=krishna"&email=krishnav@valicert.com
HTTP/1.0
```

The length of the GET Request-URI will be limited to the input-buffer sizes on various machines. This limits the amount of data that can be sent to the server through HTML form tags. To send large amounts of data usually POST method is used.

The GET method may also have two other meanings. If the request message contains a Range header field then only part of the entity is transferred. This allows partially retrieved entities to be fully retrieved without the transfer of data already held by the client, and so is known as a "partial GET". If the request message contains an If-Modified-Since, If-Unmodified-Since, If-Match, If-None-Match, or If-Range header field, then the request is a "conditional GET" and the entity will only be transferred if the conditions in these header fields are fulfilled. Both the partial GET and conditional GET methods are intended to reduce unnecessary network usage by making sure data already held by the client is not transferred again.

HEAD

```
HEAD       Request-URI      Protocol
```

The HEAD and GET methods are identical except that the server will not return a message-body in the response to the HEAD method. The information contained in the HTTP headers in the response to a HEAD request will be identical to that sent in response to a GET request, and so the method can be used to obtaining information about the entity implied by the request without actually transferring the entity-body itself. This method is often used to check that a hypertext link is valid, or when a link was last modified.

For example the following HEAD request for the same GET Request-URI,

```
HEAD / HTTP/1.0
Accept: */*
Connection: Keep-Alive
Host: www.w3.org
User-Agent: Generic
```

Produces the same response without the entity body.

```
HTTP/1.1 200 OK
Date: Thu, 20 May 1999 16:21:35 GMT
Server: Apache/1.3.6 (Unix) PHP/3.0.7
Last-Modified: Mon, 17 May 1999 15:46:21 GMT
ETag: "2da0dc-2870-374039cd"
Accept-Ranges: bytes
Content-Length: 10352
Keep-Alive: timeout=15
Connection: Keep-Alive
Content-Type: text/html; charset=iso-8859-1
```

POST

```
POST          Request-URI       Protocol
Headers
...
<newline>
<entitydata>
```

The Request-URI in POST methods usually refers to a data-producing process like a CGI program, it is the produced data that will be returned as the entity in the response and not the source text of the process, unless that text happens to be the output of the process. **The entity body portion of the POST request is always non-empty**. The POST method is used to send any amount of input to programs like CGI through form tags. When a HTML form tag specifies the method=POST attribute, the key-value pairs representing the form are sent in the entity body of the POST request, with pairs separated by an ampersand. For example:

```
POST /cgi/sendGreetins.pl HTTP/1.0
Accept: */*
Connection: Keep-Alive
Host: tcl.ooha.com
User-Agent: Generic

name=krishna&email=krishnav@valicert.com
```

Since GET can only send a limited amount of data to the server, the POST method is used to send any amount of data to the server in a client request. POST is designed to cover functions such as posting a message to a newsgroup or mailing list, submitting forms to a data-handling process or adding entries to a database.

The function performed by the POST method is determined by the server and usually depends on the Request-URI. The posted entity is subordinate to that URI, just as a file is subordinate to the directory it is in, and a news article is subordinate to the newsgroup it is posted to. The action that the POST method performs may result in a resource that cannot be identified by a URI, in which case the response from the server should be 200 (OK) if the response includes an entity describing the result or 204 (No Content) otherwise. If a resource has been created on the origin server, the response will be 201 (Created) and will contain an entity describing the status of the request and referring to the new resource.

PUT

PUT	Request-URI	Protocol

The PUT method requests that the origin server stores the entity enclosed with the request under the supplied Request-URI. If the Request-URI refers to an already existing resource, then the enclosed entity is considered to be a modified version of this resource. If it refers to a resource that doesn't exist, then the origin server will create a resource with that URI if the requesting user agent is able to define that URI as a new resource. If the origin server creates a new resource, it will inform the user agent with a 201 (Created) response. If an existing resource is modified, the origin server should respond with a 200 (OK) or 204 (No Content) response to indicate that the request was successfully completed. If the resource referred to by the supplied URI could not be created or modified, an appropriate error response should be returned.

OPTIONS

OPTIONS	*	Protocol

The OPTIONS method allows a client to request information about the communication options available on a server for the Request-URI. It allows the client to determine what options and requirements are associated with a resource without retrieving the resource or performing an action upon it. It also allows the client to examine the capabilities of the server. For example, the following request

```
OPTIONS / HTTP/1.0
Accept: */*
Connection: Keep-Alive
Host: www.w3.org
User-Agent: Generic
```

will result in the response given below, giving the operations allowed by the destination server.

```
HTTP/1.1 200 OK
Date: Wed, 19 May 1999 19:38:46 GMT
Server: Apache/1.3.6 (Unix) PHP/3.0.7
Content-Length: 0
Allow: GET, HEAD, POST, PUT, DELETE, CONNECT, OPTIONS, PATCH,
PROPFIND, PROPPATC\
H, MKCOL, COPY, MOVE, LOCK, UNLOCK, TRACE
Keep-Alive: timeout=15
Connection: Keep-Alive
```

DELETE

```
DELETE          Request-URI      Protocol
```

The DELETE method requests that the server deletes the resource that is identified by the supplied Request-URI. This request for deletion may be overridden on the origin server, either by human intervention or by some other means. The client has no guarantee that the deletion has been carried out, even if the status code returned from the origin server indicates that the action has been completed successfully. However, the server should not indicate a successful deletion to the client unless it intends to carry out the request.

TRACE

```
TRACE           Request-URI      Protocol
```

The TRACE method is used to invoke a server loop-back of the request message. The final recipient of the request will reflect the received message back to the client as the entity-body of a 200 (OK) response. A TRACE request will not include an entity. Using the TRACE method allows the client to see what is being received at the other end of the request chain and then use that data for either testing or diagnostic purposes. For example, the following trace request

```
TRACE / HTTP/1.0
Accept: /
Connection: Keep-Alive
Host: www.w3.org
UserAgent: Generic
X_Fwd_IP_Addr: 63.65.221.2
```

will result in the response

```
HTTP/1.1 200 OK
Date: Wed, 19 May 1999 19:31:35 GMT
Server: Apache/1.3.6 (Unix) PHP/3.0.7
Connection: close
Content-Type: message/http
```

CONNECT

This is a method name reserved for future use. CONNECT will be used with a proxy that can dynamically switch to being a tunnel.

Server Response Codes

The HTTP server reply status line contains three fields: HTTP version, status code, and description in the following format. Status is given with a three-digit server response code. Status codes are grouped as follows:

Code Range	Meaning
100-199	Informational
200-299	Client request successful
300-399	Client request redirected, further action necessary
400-499	Client request incomplete
500-599	Server errors

Informational 1XX

This class of status code consists only of the Status-Line and optional headers, terminated by an empty line. HTTP/1.0 did not define any 1xx status codes.

Name	Text	Description
100	Continue	The client should continue with its request. This is an interim response that is used to inform the client that the initial part of the request has been received and has not yet been rejected by the server. The client should send the rest of the request or ignore this response if the request has already completed. The server sends a final response when the request is fully completed.
101	Switching Protocols	The server understands the client's request for a change in the application protocol being used on this connection, and is willing to comply with it.

Client Request Successful 2XX

These status codes indicate that the client's request was successfully received, understood, and accepted.

Code	Text	Description
200	OK	The request has succeeded. The server's response contains the requested data.
201	Created	The request has been carried out and a new resource has been created. The URI(s) returned in the entity of the response can be used to reference the newly created resource.

Code	Text	Description
202	Accepted	The request has been accepted but not yet fully processed. The request may or may not eventually be acted upon, since it might be disallowed when the processing actually takes place.
203	Non-Authoritative Information	The returned information in the entity-header is not the definitive set coming from the origin server, but instead comes from a local or a third-party copy.
204	No Content	The server has carried out the request but does not need to return an entity-body. Browsers should not update their document view upon receiving this response. This is useful code for an image-map handler to return when the user clicks on the useless or blank areas of the image.
205	Reset Content	The browser should clear the form that caused the request to be sent. This response is intended to allow the user to input actions via a form, followed by the form being cleared so the user can input further actions.
206	Partial Content	The server has carried out a partial GET request for the resource. This is used in response to a request specifying a Range header. The server must specify the range included in the response with the Content-Range header

Redirection   3XX

These codes indicate that the user agent needs to take further actions for the request to be successfully carried out.

Code	Text	Description
300	Multiple Choices	The requested URI corresponds to any one of a set of representations; for example, the URI could refer to a document that has been translated into many languages. Agent-driven negotiation information is provided to the user agent so that the preferred representation can be selected and the user agent's request redirected to that location.
301	Moved Permanently	The requested resource has been assigned a new permanent URI, and any future references to this resource should use one of the returned URIs in the Location header.
302	Found	The requested resource resides temporarily under a different URI. The Location header points to the new location. The client should use the new URI to resolve the request but the old URI should be used for future requests, since the redirection may not be permanent.

Code	Text	Description
303	See Other	The response to the request can be found at a different URI that is specified in the Location header, and should be retrieved using a GET method on that resource.
304	Not Modified	The client has performed a conditional GET request using If-Modified-Since header, but the document has not been modified. The entity body is not sent and the client should use its local copy
305	Use Proxy	The requested resource must be accessed through a proxy whose URI is given in the Location field.

Client Request Incomplete   4xx

The 4xx class of status code is intended for cases where the client seems to have made an error.

Code	Text	Description
400	Bad Request	The request could not be understood by the server due to badly formed syntax.
401	Unauthorized	The result code is given along with the WWW-Authenticate header to indicate that the request lacked proper authorization, and the client should supply proper authentication when the requesting the same URI again.
402	Payment Required	This code is reserved for future use.
403	Forbidden	The server understood the request, but is refusing to fulfill it. The request should not be repeated.
404	Not Found	The server has not found anything matching the Request-URI. If the server knows that this condition is permanent then code 410 (Gone) should be used instead.
405	Method Not Allowed	The method specified in the Request-Line is not allowed for the resource identified by the Request-URI.
406	Not Acceptable	The resource identified by the request can only generate response entities which have content characteristics incompatible with the accept headers sent in the request.

Code	Text	Description
407	Proxy Authentication Required	This code is indicates that the client must first authenticate itself with the proxy, using the `Proxy-Authenticate` header.
408	Request Timeout	The client did not produce a request within the time that the server was prepared to wait.
409	Conflict	The request could not be completed because of a conflict with the current state of the resource.
410	Gone	The requested resource is no longer available at the server and no forwarding address is known.
411	Length Required	The server is refusing to accept the request without a defined `Content-Length from the client.`
412	Precondition Failed	The precondition given in one or more of the `IF` request-header fields evaluated to false when it was tested on the server.
413	Request Entity Too Large	The request entity is larger than the server is willing or able to process.
414	Request-URI Too Long	The `Request-URI` is longer than the server is willing to interpret
415	Unsupported Media Type	The entity body of the request is in a format not supported.

Server Error   5xx

These response status codes indicate cases in which the server is aware that it has made an error or cannot perform the request.

Code	Text	Description
500	Internal Server Error	The server encountered an unexpected condition, which prevented it from fulfilling the request.
501	Not Implemented	The server does not support the functionality required to fulfill the request.
502	Bad Gateway	The server, while acting as a gateway or a proxy, received an invalid response from the upstream server it accessed while trying to carry out the request.
503	Service Unavailable	The server is unable to handle the request at the present time due to a temporary overloading or maintenance of the server.

Code	Text	Description
504	Gateway Timeout	The server, while acting as a gateway or proxy, did not receive a response from the upstream server within the time it was prepared to wait.
505	HTTP Version Not Supported	The server does not (or refuses to) support the HTTP protocol version that was used in the request message.

HTTP Headers

HTTP headers are used to transfer information between the client and server. There are four categories of headers:

General	Information that is not related to the client, server or HTTP protocol
Request	Preferred document formats and server parameters
Response	Information about the server
Entity	Information on the data that is being sent between the client and server.

General and Entity headers are same for both client and servers. All headers follow the "Name:value" format. Header names are case insensitive. In HTTP/1.1, the value of headers can extend over multiple lines by preceding each extra line with at least one space or tab. All headers are terminated by a carriage-return newline sequence (\r\n).

General Headers

These header fields have general applicability for both request and response messages, but do not apply to the entity being transferred. These header fields apply only to the message being transmitted.

Cache-Control: Directives

Caching directives are specified in a comma-separated list. They fall into 2 categories, request-based and response-based. The following tables list the allowed directives.

Request

Request Directives	Description
no-cache	Do not cache the information.
no-store	Remove the information from volatile storage as soon as possible after forwarding it.
Max-age = seconds	The client is willing to accept a response no older than the specified time in seconds.

Request Directives	Description
Max-stale [= seconds]	If max-stale is assigned a value, then the client is willing to accept a response that has exceeded its expiration time by no more than the specified number of seconds. The client will accept a stale response of any age if no value is assigned.
Min-fresh = seconds	Indicates that the client is willing to accept a response that will still be fresh for the specified time in seconds.
only-if-cached	This directive is used if a client wants a cache to return only those responses that it currently has stored, and not to reload or revalidate with the origin server.

Response

Response Directives	Description
No-transform	Caches that convert data to different formats to save space or reduce traffic should not do so if they see this directive.
cache-extension	Cache extension tokens are interpreted by individual applications and ignored by the applications that don't understand them.
Public	Indicates that the response may be cached by any cache.
Private	Indicates that all or part of the response message is intended for a single user and must not be cached by a shared cache.
must-revalidate	A cache must not use an entry after it becomes stale to respond to a subsequent request, without first revalidating it with the origin server.
proxy-revalidate	The proxy-revalidate directive has the same meaning as the must-revalidate directive, except for private client caches.
Max-age = seconds	This directive may be used by an origin server to specify the expiry time of an entity.

Connection: options

The header allows the sender to specify options that are to be used for a particular connection and must not be communicated by proxies over further connections. HTTP/1.1 defines the "close" connection option to allow the sender to signal that the connection will be closed after the response has been completed.

Header	Options	Description
Date:	date-in-rfc1123-format	Represents the date and time at which the message was originated. The field value is sent in RFC 1123 -date format. An example is Date: Tue, 15 Nov 1994 08:12:31 GMT

Header	Options	Description
`Pragma:`	`no-cache`	When a request message contains the `no-cache` directive, an application should forward the request to the origin server even if it has a cached copy of what is being requested.
`Trailer:`	`header-fields`	This header indicates that the given set of header fields is present in the trailer of a message encoded with chunked transfer-coding.
`Transfer-Encoding:`	`encoding-type`	Transfer-coding values are used to indicate an encoding transformation that has been, can be, or may need to be applied to an entity-body in order to ensure "safe transport" through the network.
`Upgrade:`	`protocol/version`	This header allows the client to specify to the server what additional communication protocols it supports and would like to use. If the server finds it appropriate to switch protocols, it will use this header within a 101 (Switching Protocols) response.
`Via:`	`protocol receiver-by-host [comment]`	This header must be used by gateways and proxies to indicate the intermediate protocols and recipients between both the user agent and the server on requests, and the origin server and the client on responses
`Warning:`	`warn-code warn-agent warn-text`	This header carries extra information about the status or transformation of a message that might not be present in the message.

Request Headers

These header fields allow the client to pass additional information about the request, and about the client itself, to the server.

Header	Options	Description
`Accept:`	`type/subtype [; q=value]`	This header specifies which media types are acceptable for the response. `Accept` headers can be used to indicate that the request is limited to a small set of specific types, as in the case of a request for an in-line image. The `q=value` parameter ranges from 0 to 1 (with 1 being the default) and is used to indicate a relative preference for that type. For example, `Accept: text/plain; q=0.5, text/htm; q=0.8`

Header	Options	Description
Accept-Charset:	charset [; q=value]	This header is used to indicate which character sets are acceptable for the response. The q=value parameter represents the user's preference for that particular character set.
Accept-Encoding:	encoding-types [; q=value]	This header restricts the content-codings that are acceptable in the response. The q=value parameter allows the user to express a preference for a particular type of encoding.
Accept-Language:	language [; q=value]	This header restricts the set of natural languages that are preferred as a response to the request. Each language may be given an associated preference with the q=value parameter.
Authorization:	credentials	This provides the client's authorization to access the URI. When a requested URI requires authorization, the server responds with a WWW-Authenticate header describing the type of authorization required. The client then repeats the request with proper authorization information.
Expect:	100-continue | expectation	This header indicates that particular server behaviors are required by the client. A server that cannot understand or comply with any of the expectation values in the Expect field of a request will respond with an appropriate error status.
From:	email	This header contains an Internet e-mail address for the human controlling the requesting user agent.
Host:	host [: port]	This header specifies the Internet host and port number of the resource being requested.

Header	Options	Description
If-Match:		A client that has previously obtained one or more entities from the resource can include a list of their associated entity tags in this header field to verify that one of those entities is current.
If-Modified-Since:	datein-rfc1123-format	This header specifies that the URI data should be sent only if it has been modified since the date given.
If-None-Match:	entity-tags	This header is similar to the If-Match header, but is used to verify that none of those entities previously obtained by the client is current.
If-Range:	entity-tag | date	If a client has a partial copy of an entity in its cache, it can use this header to retrieve the rest of the entity if it is unmodified, or the whole entity if it has changed.
If-Unmodified-Since:	date-in-rfc1123-format	This specifies that the URI data should only be sent if it has not been modified since the given date.
Max-Forwards:	number	This header limits the number of proxies and gateways that can forward the request.
Proxy-Authorization:	credentials	The Proxy-Authorization request-header field allows the client to identify itself (or its user) to a proxy that requires authentication.
Range:	bytes= n-m	Using this header with a conditional or unconditional GET allows the retrieval of one or more sub-ranges of an entity, rather than the entire entity.
Referer:	url	The Referer request-header field allows the client to specify, the URI of the resource from which the Request-URI was obtained.

Header	Options	Description
TE:	transfer-encoding [; q = val]	The TE request-header field indicates which extension transfer-codings the client is willing to accept in the response. If the keyword "trailers" is present then the client is willing to accept trailer fields in a chunked transfer-coding.
User-Agent:	product | comment	This header contains information about the user agent originating the request. This allows the server to automatically recognize user agents and tailoring its responses to avoid particular user agent limitations.

Response Headers

The response-header fields allow the server to pass additional information about the response that cannot be placed in the Status-Line. These header fields give information about the server and about further access to the resource identified by the Request-URI.

Header	Options	Description
Accept-Ranges:	range-unit | none	This header allows the server to indicate its acceptance of range requests for a resource.
Age:	seconds	This header contains the sender's estimate of the amount of time since the response was generated at the origin server.
Etag:	entity-tag	This header provides the current value of the requested entity tag.
Location:	URI	This is used to redirect the recipient to a location other than the Request-URI to complete the request.
Proxy-Authenticate:	scheme realm	This header indicates the authentication scheme and parameters applicable to the proxy for this Request-URI.
Retry-After:	date | seconds	This is used by the server to indicate how long the service is expected to be unavailable to the requesting client.

Header	Options	Description
Server:	string	The Server header contains information about the software that the origin server used to handle the request.
Vary:	*	headers	This header specifies that the entity has multiple sources and may therefore vary according to specified list of request headers. Multiple headers can be listed separated by commas. An asterisk means another factor other than the request headers may affect the response that is returned.
WWW-Authenticate: scheme realm		This header is used with the 401 response code to indicate to the client that the requested URI needs authentication. The value specifies the authorization scheme and the realm of authority required from the client.

Entity Headers

Entity-header fields define meta-information about the entity-body or, if no body is present, about the resource identified by the request.

Header	Options	Description
Allow:	methods	This header is used to inform the recipient of valid methods associated with the resource.
Content-Encoding:	encoding	This header indicates what additional content encodings have been applied to the entity-body, and hence what decoding must be carried out in order to obtain the media-type referenced by the Content-Type header field.
Content-Language:	languages	The Content-Language header describes the natural language(s) of the intended audience for the enclosed entity.
Content-Length:	n	This header indicates the size of the entity-body. Due to the dynamic nature of some requests, the content-length is sometimes unknown and this header is omitted.
Content-Location:	uri	The Content-Location header supplies the resource location for the entity enclosed in the message when that entity may be accessed from a different location to the requested resource's URI.

Header	Options	Description
Content-MD5:	digest	This header contains an MD5 digest of the entity-body that is used to provide an end-to-end message integrity check (MIC) of the entity-body. See RFC 1864 for more details.
Content-Range:	bytes n-m/length	The Content-Range header is sent with a partial entity-body to specify where in the full entity-body the partial body should come from.
Content-Type:	type/subtype	This header describes the media type of the entity-body sent to the recipient. In the case of the HEAD method, it describes the media type that would have been sent had the request been a GET.
Expires: RFC-1123-	date	The Expires header gives the date and time after which the response is considered stale.
Last-Modified:	RFC-1123-date	This header indicates the date and time at which the origin server believes the variant was last modified.

References

- ❑ "Hypertext Transfer Protocol - HTTP/1.1" specification: (http://www.w3.org/Protocols/HTTP/1.1/draft-ietf-http-v11-spec-rev-06.txt)

- ❑ MIME (Multipurpose Internet Mail Extensions): (http://www.faqs.org/rfcs/rfc1341.html)

- ❑ Date and Time specifications: RFC 1123:(http://www.faqs.org/rfcs/rfc1123.html)

- ❑ The Content-MD5 header field: RFC 1864: (http://www.faqs.org/rfcs/rfc1864.html)

- ❑ Standard for Interchange of USENET Messages: (http://www.faqs.org/rfcs/rfc850.html)

- ❑ World Wide Web Consortium: (http://www.w3.org)

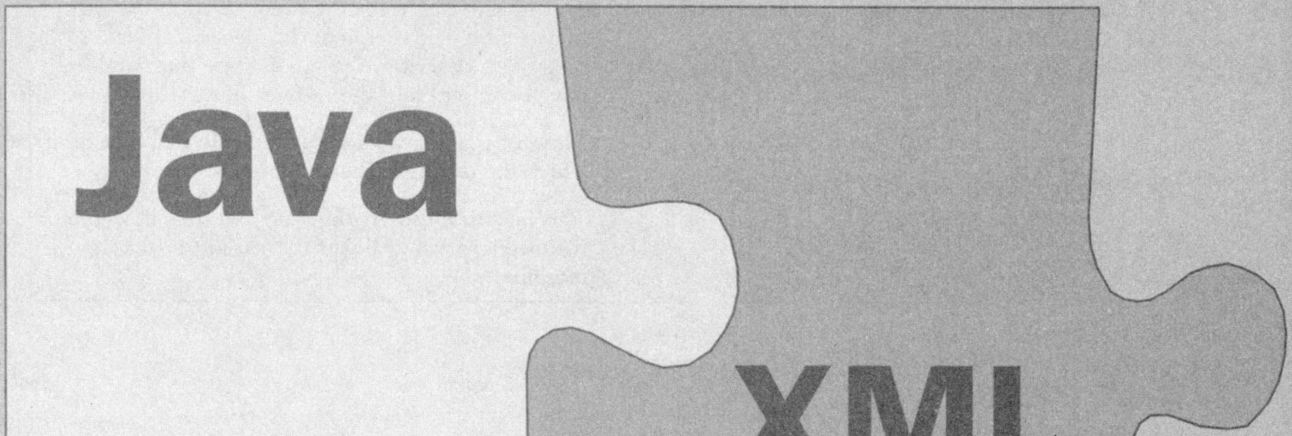
Java
XML

JDBC API Reference

Key

Within this API Reference, the following conventions are used:

- ❑ Interface, Class and Exception names within the APIs listed are all written in **bold**.
- ❑ Interface, Class and Exception names not within the APIs listed are all written in *italics*.
- ❑ Method and Class names are written in `Courier Bold`.

Package java.sql

The Java Data Base Connectivity API contains one core package, **java.sql**, and one extension package, **javax.sql**, which is not covered in this appendix. The core package enables the use and execution of SQL queries and operations within Java applications. It also provides support for the retrieval of results and their manipulation. Note that this appendix covers version 2.0 of the JDBC API which became available with the release of Java 2.

Interfaces

public abstract interface	**Array**		
public abstract interface	**Blob**		
public abstract interface	**CallableStatement**	extends	*java.sql.***PreparedStatement**
public abstract interface	**Clob**		
public abstract interface	**Connection**		
public abstract interface	**DatabaseMetaData**		
public abstract interface	**Driver**		
public abstract interface	**PreparedStatement**	extends	*java.sql.***Statement**
public abstract interface	**Ref**		
public abstract interface	**ResultSet**		
public abstract interface	**ResultSetMetaData**		
public abstract interface	**SQLData**		
public abstract interface	**SQLInput**		
public abstract interface	**SQLOutput**		
public abstract interface	**Statement**		
public abstract interface	**Struct**		

Classes

public class	**Date**	extends	*java.util.***Date**
public class	**DriverManager**		
public class	**DriverPropertyInfo**		
public class	**Time**	extends	java.util.**Date**
public class	**TimeStamp**	extends	java.util.**Date**
public class	**Types**		

Exceptions

public class	**BatchUpdateException**	extends	*java.sql.***SQLException**
public class	**DataTruncation**	extends	*java.sql.***SQLWarning**
public class	**SQLException**	extends	*java.lang.Exception*
public class	**SQLWarningException**	extends	*java.sql.***SQLException**

Interface java.sql.Array

```
public abstract interface Array
```

Corresponds to the SQL **Array** type.

Methods

public *java.lang.Object*	**getArray**	()
	throws	*java.sql.***SQLException**
public *java.lang.Object*	**getArray**	(*java.util.Map* map)
	throws	*java.sql.***SQLException**
public *java.lang.Object*	**getArray**	(long index,
		int count)
	throws	*java.sql.***SQLException**
public *java.lang.Object*	**getArray**	(long index,
		int count,
		java.util.Map map)
	throws	*java.sql.***SQLException**
public int	**getBaseType**	()
	throws	*java.sql.***SQLException**
public *java.lang.String*	**getBaseTypeName**	()
	throws	*java.sql.***SQLException**
public *java.sql.***ResultSet**	**getResultSet**	()
	throws	*java.sql.***SQLException**
public *java.sql.***ResultSet**	**getResultSet**	(*java.util.Map*)
	throws	*java.sql.***SQLException**
public *java.sql.***ResultSet**	**getResultSet**	(long index,
		int count)
	throws	*java.sql.***SQLException**
public *java.sql.***ResultSet**	**getResultSet**	(long index,
		int count,
		java.util.Map map)
	throws	*java.sql.***SQLException**

Interface java.sql.Blob

```
public abstract interface Blob
```

Corresponds to the SQL **Blob** type.

Methods

public *java.io.InputStream*	**getBinaryStream**	()
	throws	*java.sql.***SQLException**
public *java.lang.Byte[]*	**getBytes**	(long pos,
		int length)
	throws	*java.sql.***SQLException**
public long	**length**	()
	throws	*java.sql.***SQLException**

public long	**position**	(*java.lang.Byte*[] pattern, long start)
	throws	*java.sql*.**SQLException**
public long	**position**	(*java.sql*.Blob pattern, long start)
	throws	*java.sql*.**SQLException**

Interface java.sql.CallableStatement

```
public abstract interface CallableStatement
```

Extends *java.sql*.**PreparedStatement**. **CallableStatement** executes stored SQL procedures. Some methods have been deprecated.

Methods

public *java.sql*.**Array**	**getArray**	(int i)
	throws	*java.sql*.**SQLException**
public *java.math.BigDecimal*	**getBigDecimal**	(int parameterIndex)
	throws	*java.sql*.**SQLException**
public *java.sql*.Blob	**getBlob**	(int i)
	throws	*java.sql*.**SQLException**
public boolean	**getBoolean**	(int parameterIndex,)
	throws	*java.sql*.**SQLException**
public *java.lang.Byte*	**getByte**	(int parameterIndex)
	throws	*java.sql*.**SQLException**
public *java.lang.Byte*[]	**getBytes**	(int parameterIndex)
	throws	*java.sql*.**SQLException**
public *java.sql*.Clob	**getClob**	(int i)
	throws	*java.sql*.**SQLException**
public *java.sql*.Date	**getDate**	(int parameterIndex, *java.util.Calendar* cal)
	throws	*java.sql*.**SQLException**
public double	**getDouble**	(int parameterIndex)
	throws	*java.sql*.**SQLException**
public float	**getFloat**	(int parameterIndex)
	throws	*java.sql*.**SQLException**
public int	**getInt**	(int parameterIndex)
	throws	*java.sql*.**SQLException**
public long	**getLong**	(int parameterIndex)
	throws	*java.sql*.**SQLException**
public *java.lang.Object*	**getObject**	(int parameterIndex)
	throws	*java.sql*.**SQLException**
public *java.lang.Object*	**getObject**	(int i, *java.util.Map* map)
	throws	*java.sql*.**SQLException**
public *java.sql*.Ref	**getRef**	(int i)
	throws	*java.sql*.**SQLException**
public short	**getShort**	(int parameterIndex)
	throws	*java.sql*.**SQLException**
public *java.lang.String*	**getString**	(int parameterIndex)
	throws	*java.sql*.**SQLException**
public *java.sql*.Time	**getTime**	(int parameterIndex)
	throws	*java.sql*.**SQLException**
public *java.sql*.Time	**getTime**	(int parameterIndex, *java.util.Calendar* cal)
	throws	*java.sql*.**SQLException**
public *java.sql*.Timestamp	**getTimeStamp**	(int parameterIndex)
	throws	*java.sql*.**SQLException**
public *java.sql*.Timestamp	**getTimeStamp**	(int parameterIndex, *java.util.Calendar* cal)
	throws	*java.sql*.**SQLException**
public void	**registerOutParameter**	(int parameterIndex, int sqlType)
	throws	*java.sql*.**SQLException**

public void	**registerOutParameter**	(int parameterIndex, int sqlType, int scale)
	throws	*java.sql.***SQLException**
public void	**registerOutParameter**	(int paramIndex, int sqlType, *java.lang.String* typeName)
	throws	*java.sql.***SQLException**
public boolean	**wasNull**	()
	throws	*java.sql.***SQLException**

Inherited from *java.sql.***PreparedStatement**:

    addBatch, clearParameters, execute, executeQuery, executeUpdate,getMetaData, setArray, setAsciiStream, setBigDecimal, setBinaryStream,setBlob, setBoolean, setByte, setBytes, setCharacterStream, setClob, setDate, setDate, setDouble, setFloat, setInt, setLong, setNull, setNull, setObject, setObject, setObject, setRef, setShort, setString, setTime, setTime, setTimestamp, setTimestamp, setUnicodeStream

Inherited from *java.sql.***Statement**:

    addBatch, cancel, clearBatch, clearWarnings, close, execute,executeBatch, executeQuery, executeUpdate, getConnection, getFetchDirection, getFetchSize, getMaxFieldSize, getMaxRows, getMoreResults, getQueryTimeout, getResultSet, getResultSetConcurrency, getResultSetType, getUpdateCount, getWarnings, setCursorName, setEscapeProcessing, setFetchDirection, setFetchSize, setMaxFieldSize, setMaxRows, setQueryTimeout

Deprecated Methods

public *java.math.BigDecimal*	**getBigDecimal**	(int parameterIndex, int scale)
	throws	*java.sql.***SQLException**

Interface java.sql.Clob

    public abstract interface Clob

Corresponds to the SQL **Clob** type.

Methods

public *java.io.InputStream*	**getAsciiStream**	()
	throws	*java.sql.***SQLException**
public *java.io.Reader*	**getCharacterString**	()
	throws	*java.sql.***SQLException**
public *java.lang.String*	**getSubString**	(long pos, int length)
	throws	*java.sql.***SQLException**
public long	**length**	()
	throws	*java.sql.***SQLException**
public long	**position**	(*java.lang.String* searchstr, long start)
	throws	*java.sql.***SQLException**
public long	**position**	(*java.sql.***Clob** searchstr, long start)
	throws	*java.sql.***SQLException**

Interface java.sql.Connection

```
public abstract interface Connection
```

Connection provides a connection(session) with a database, within which SQL statements may be executed and the results read.

Field Constants

public final static int	**TRANSACTION_NONE**
public final static int	**TRANSACTION_READ_COMMITTED**
public final static int	**TRANSACTION_READ_UNCOMMITTED**
public final static int	**TRANSACTION_REPEATABLE_READ**
public final static int	**TRANSACTION_SERIALIZABLE**

Methods

public void	**clearWarnings**	()
	throws	*java.sql.***SQLException**
public void	**close**	()
	throws	*java.sql.***SQLException**
public void	**commi**	()
	throws	*java.sql.***SQLException**
public *java.sql.***Statement**	**createStatement**	()
	throws	*java.sql.***SQLException**
public *java.sql.***Statement**	**createStatement**	(int resultSetType, int resultSetConcurrency)
	throws	*java.sql.***SQLException**
public boolean	**getAutoCommit**	()
	throws	*java.sql.***SQLException**
public *java.lang.String*	**getCatalog**	()
	throws	*java.sql.***SQLException**
public *java.sql.***DatabaseMetaData**	**getMetaData**	()
	throws	*java.sql.***SQLException**
public int	**getTransactionIsolation**	()
	throws	*java.sql.***SQLException**
public *java.util.Map*	**getTypeMap**	()
	throws	*java.sql.***SQLException**
public *java.sql.***SQLWarning**	**getWarnings**	()
	throws	*java.sql.***SQLException**
public boolean	**isClosed**	()
	throws	*java.sql.***SQLException**
public boolean	**isReadOnly**	()
	throws	*java.sql.***SQLException**
public *java.lang.String*	**nativeSQL**	(*java.lang.String* sql)
	throws	*java.sql.***SQLException**
public *java.sql.***CallableStatement**	**prepareCall**	(*java.lang.string* sql, int resultSetType, int resultSetConcurrency)
	throws	*java.sql.***SQLException**
public *java.sql.***CallableStatement**	**prepareCall**	(*java.lang.string* sql)
	throws	*java.sql.***SQLException**
public *java.sql.***PreparedStatement**	**prepareStatement**	(*java.lang.string* sql, int resultSetType, int resultSetConcurrency)
	throws	*java.sql.***SQLException**
public *java.sql.***PreparedStatement**	**prepareStatement**	(*java.lang.string* sql)
	throws	*java.sql.***SQLException**
public void	**rollback**	()
	throws	*java.sql.***SQLException**
public void	**setAutoCommit**	(boolean autoCommit)
	throws	*java.sql.***SQLException**
public void	**setCatalog**	(*java.lang.String* catalog)
	throws	*java.sql.***SQLException**
public void	**setReadOnly**	(boolean readOnly)
	throws	*java.sql.***SQLException**

public void	setTransactionIsolation	(int level)
	throws	*java.sql.***SQLException**
public void	setTypeMap	(*java.util.Map* map)
	throws	*java.sql.***SQLException**

Interface java.sql.DatabaseMetaData

```
public abstract interface DatabaseMetaData
```

DatabaseMetaData provides information about the full database.

Field Constants

public static final int	bestRowNotPseudo
public static final int	bestRowPseudo
public static final int	bestRowSession
public static final int	bestRowTemporary
public static final int	bestRowTransaction
public static final int	bestRowUnknown
public static final int	columnNoNulls
public static final int	columnNullable
public static final int	columnNullableUnknown
public static final int	importedKeyCascade
public static final int	importedKeyInitiallyDeferred
public static final int	importedKeyInitiallyImmediate
public static final int	importedKeyNoAction
public static final int	importedKeyNotDeferrable
public static final int	importedKeyRestrict
public static final int	importedKeySetDefault
public static final int	importedKeySetNull
public static final int	procedureColumnIn
public static final int	procedureColumnInOut
public static final int	procedureColumnOut
public static final int	procedureColumnResult
public static final int	procedureColumnReturn
public static final int	procedureColumnUnknown
public static final int	procedureNoNulls
public static final int	procedureNoResult
public static final int	procedureNullable
public static final int	procedureNullableUnknown
public static final int	procedureResultUnknown
public static final int	procedureReturnsResult
public static final short	tableIndexClustered
public static final short	tableIndexHashed
public static final short	tableIndexOther
public static final short	tableIndexStatistic
public static final int	typeNoNulls
public static final int	typeNullable
public static final int	typeNullableUnknown
public static final int	typePredBasic
public static final int	typePredChar
public static final int	typePredNone
public static final int	typeSearchable
public static final int	versionColumnNotPseudo
public static final int	versionColumnPseudo
public static final int	versionColumnUnknown

Methods

public boolean	allProceduresAreCallable	()
	throws	*java.sql.***SQLException**
public boolean	allTablesAreSelectable	()
	throws	*java.sql.***SQLException**
public boolean	dataDefinitionCausesTransactionCommit	()
	throws	*java.sql.***SQLException**
public boolean	dataDefinitionIgnoredInTransactions	()
	throws	*java.sql.***SQLException**
public boolean	deletesAreDetected	(int type)
	throws	*java.sql.***SQLException**

public boolean	**doesMaxRowSizeIncludeBlobs**	()
	throws	*java.sql.***SQLException**
public *java.sql.*ResultSet	**getBestRowIdentifier**	(*java.lang.String* catalog,
		java.lang.String schema,
		java.lang.String table,
		int scope,
		boolean nullable)
	throws	*java.sql.***SQLException**
public *java.sql.*ResultSet	**getCatalogs**	()
	throws	*java.sql.***SQLException**
public *java.lang.String*	**getCatalogSeparator**	()
	throws	*java.sql.***SQLException**
public *java.lang.String*	**getCatalogTerm**	()
	throws	*java.sql.***SQLException**
public *java.sql.*ResultSet	**getColumnPrivileges**	(*java.lang.String* catalog,
		java.lang.String schema,
		java.lang.String table,
		java.lang.String columnNamePattern)
	throws	*java.sql.***SQLException**
public *java.sql.*ResultSet	**getColumns**	(*java.lang.String* catalog,
		java.lang.String schemaPattern,
		java.lang.String tableNamePattern,
		java.lang.String columnNamePattern)
	throws	*java.sql.***SQLException**
public *java.sql.*Connection	**getConnection**	()
	throws	*java.sql.***SQLException**
public *java.sql.*ResultSet	**getCrossReference**	(*java.lang.String* primaryCatalog,
		java.lang.String primarySchema,
		java.lang.String primaryTable,
		java.lang.String foreignCatalog,
		java.lang.String foreignSchema,
		java.lang.String foreignTable)
	throws	*java.sql.***SQLException**
public *java.lang.String*	**getDatabaseProductName**	()
	throws	*java.sql.***SQLException**
public *java.lang.String*	**getDatabaseProductVersion**()	
	throws	*java.sql.***SQLException**
public int	**getDefaultTransactionIsolation**	()
	throws	*java.sql.***SQLException**
public int	**getDriverMajorVersion**	()
	throws	*java.sql.***SQLException**
public int	**getDriverMinorVersion**	()
	throws	*java.sql.***SQLException**
public *java.lang.String*	**getDriverName**	()
	throws	*java.sql.***SQLException**
public *java.lang.String*	**getDriverVersion**	()
	throws	*java.sql.***SQLException**
public *java.sql.*ResultSet	**getExportedKeys**	(*java.lang.String* catalog,
		java.lang.String schema,
		java.lang.String table)
	throws	*java.sql.***SQLException**
public *java.lang.String*	**getExtraNameCharacters**	()
	throws	*java.sql.***SQLException**
public *java.lang.String*	**getIdentifierQuoteString**	()
	throws	*java.sql.***SQLException**
public *java.sql.*ResultSet	**getImportedKeys**	(*java.lang.String* catalog,
		java.lang.String schema,
		java.lang.String table)
	throws	*java.sql.***SQLException**
public *java.sql.*ResultSet	**getIndexInfo**	(*java.lang.String* catalog,
		java.lang.String schema,
		java.lang.String table,
		boolean unique,
		boolean approximate)
	throws	*java.sql.***SQLException**

public int	`getMaxBinaryLiteralLength()`	
	throws	*java.sql.*SQLException
public int	`getMaxCatalogNameLength`	()
	throws	*java.sql.*SQLException
public int	`getMaxCharLiteralLength`	()
	throws	*java.sql.*SQLException
public int	`getMaxColumnNameLength`	()
	throws	*java.sql.*SQLException
public int	`getMaxColumnsInGroupBy`	()
	throws	*java.sql.*SQLException
public int	`getMaxColumnsInIndex`	()
	throws	*java.sql.*SQLException
public int	`getMaxColumnsInOrderBy`	()
	throws	*java.sql.*SQLException
public int	`getMaxColumnsInSelect`	()
	throws	*java.sql.*SQLException
public int	`getMaxColumnsInTable`	()
	throws	*java.sql.*SQLException
public int	`getMaxConnections`	()
	throws	*java.sql.*SQLException
public int	`getMaxCursorNameLength`	()
	throws	*java.sql.*SQLException
public int	`getMaxIndexLength`	()
	throws	*java.sql.*SQLException
public int	`getMaxProcedureNameLength`	()
	throws	*java.sql.*SQLException
public int	`getMaxRowSize`	()
	throws	*java.sql.*SQLException
public int	`getMaxSchemaNameLength`	()
	throws	*java.sql.*SQLException
public int	`getMaxStatementLength`	()
	throws	*java.sql.*SQLException
public int	`getMaxStatements`	()
	throws	*java.sql.*SQLException
public int	`getMaxTableNameLength`	()
	throws	*java.sql.*SQLException
public int	`getMaxTablesInSelect`	()
	throws	*java.sql.*SQLException
public int	`getMaxUserNameLength`	()
	throws	*java.sql.*SQLException
public *java.lang.String*	`getNumericFunctions`	()
	throws	*java.sql.*SQLException
public *java.sql.*ResultSet	`getPrimaryKeys`	(*java.lang.String* catalog, *java.lang.String* schema, *java.lang.String* table)
	throws	*java.sql.*SQLException
public *java.sql.*ResultSet	`getProcedureColumns`	(*java.lang.String* catalog, *java.lang.String* schemaPattern, *java.lang.String* procedureNamePattern, *java.lang.String* columnNamePattern)
	throws	*java.sql.*SQLException
public *java.sql.*ResultSet	`getProcedures`	(*java.lang.String* catalog, *java.lang.String* schemaPattern, *java.lang.String* procedureNamePattern)
	throws	*java.sql.*SQLException
public *java.lang.String*	`getProcedureTerm`	()
	throws	*java.sql.*SQLException
public *java.sql.*ResultSet	`getSchemas`	()
	throws	*java.sql.*SQLException
public *java.lang.String*	`getSchemaTerm`	()
	throws	*java.sql.*SQLException
public *java.lang.String*	`getSearchStringEscape`	()
	throws	*java.sql.*SQLException
public *java.lang.String*	`getSQLKeywords`	()
	throws	*java.sql.*SQLException

public *java.lang.String*	`getStringFunctions`	()
	throws	*java.sql.***SQLException**
public *java.lang.String*	`getSystemFunctions`	()
	throws	*java.sql.***SQLException**
public *java.sql.*ResultSet	`getTablePrivileges`	(*java.lang.String* catalog,
		java.lang.String schemaPattern,
		java.lang.String tableNamePattern)
	throws	*java.sql.***SQLException**
public *java.sql.*ResultSet	`getTables`	(*java.lang.String* catalog,
		java.lang.String schemaPattern,
		java.lang.String tableNamePattern,
		java.lang.String[] types)
	throws	*java.sql.***SQLException**
public *java.sql.*ResultSet	`getTableTypes`	()
	throws	*java.sql.***SQLException**
public *java.lang.String*	`getTimeDateFunctions`	()
	throws	*java.sql.***SQLException**
public *java.sql.*ResultSet	`getTypeInfo`	()
	throws	*java.sql.***SQLException**
public *java.sql.*ResultSet	`getUDTs`	(*java.lang.String* catalog,
		java.lang.String schemaPattern,
		java.lang.String typeNamePattern,
		int[] types)
	throws	*java.sql.***SQLException**
public *java.lang.String*	`getURL`	()
	throws	*java.sql.***SQLException**
public *java.lang.String*	`getUserName`	()
	throws	*java.sql.***SQLException**
public *java.sql.*ResultSet	`getVersionColumns`	(*java.lang.String* catalog,
		java.lang.String schema,
		java.lang.String table)
	throws	*java.sql.***SQLException**
public boolean	`insertsAreDetected`	(int type)
	throws	*java.sql.***SQLException**
public boolean	`isCatalogAtStart`	()
	throws	*java.sql.***SQLException**
public boolean	`isReadOnly`	()
	throws	*java.sql.***SQLException**
public boolean	`nullPlusNonNullIsNull`	()
	throws	*java.sql.***SQLException**
public boolean	`nullsAreSortedAtEnd`	()
	throws	*java.sql.***SQLException**
public boolean	`nullsAreSortedAtStart`	()
	throws	*java.sql.***SQLException**
public boolean	`nullsAreSortedHigh`	()
	throws	*java.sql.***SQLException**
public boolean	`nullsAreSortedLow`	()
	throws	*java.sql.***SQLException**
public boolean	`othersDeletesAreVisible`	(int type)
	throws	*java.sql.***SQLException**
public boolean	`othersInsertsAreVisible`	(int type)
	throws	*java.sql.***SQLException**
public boolean	`othersUpdatesAreVisible`	(int type)
	throws	*java.sql.***SQLException**
public boolean	`ownDeletesAreVisible`	(int type)
	throws	*java.sql.***SQLException**
public boolean	`ownInsertsAreVisible`	(int type)
	throws	*java.sql.***SQLException**
public boolean	`ownUpdatesAreVisible`	(int type)
	throws	*java.sql.***SQLException**
public boolean	`storesLowerCaseIdentifiers`	()
	throws	*java.sql.***SQLException**
public boolean	`storesLowerCaseQuotedIdentifiers`	()
	throws	*java.sql.***SQLException**
public boolean	`storesMixedCaseIdentifiers`	()
	throws	*java.sql.***SQLException**

public boolean	storesMixedCaseQuotedIdentifiers	()
	throws	*java.sql.*SQLException
public boolean	storesUpperCaseIdentifiers	()
	throws	*java.sql.*SQLException
public boolean	storesUpperCaseQuotedIdentifiers	()
	throws	*java.sql.*SQLException
public boolean	supportsAlterTableWithAddColumn	()
	throws	*java.sql.*SQLException
public boolean	supportsAlterTableWithDropColumn	()
	throws	*java.sql.*SQLException
public boolean	supportsANSI92EntryLevelSQL	()
	throws	*java.sql.*SQLException
public boolean	supportsANSI92FullSQL	()
	throws	*java.sql.*SQLException
public boolean	supportsANSI92IntermediateSQL	()
	throws	*java.sql.*SQLException
public boolean	supportsBatchUpdates	()
	throws	*java.sql.*SQLException
public boolean	supportsCatalogsInDataManipulation	()
	throws	*java.sql.*SQLException
public boolean	supportsCatalogsInIndexDefinitions	()
	throws	*java.sql.*SQLException
public boolean	supportsCatalogsInPrivilegeDefinitions	()
	throws	*java.sql.*SQLException
public boolean	supportsCatalogsInProcedureCalls	()
	throws	*java.sql.*SQLException
public boolean	supportsCatalogsInTableDefinitions	()
	throws	*java.sql.*SQLException
public boolean	supportsColumnAliasing	()
	throws	*java.sql.*SQLException
public boolean	supportsConvert	()
	throws	*java.sql.*SQLException
public boolean	supportsConvert	(int fromType, int toType)
	throws	*java.sql.*SQLException
public boolean	supportsCoreSQLGrammar	()
	throws	*java.sql.*SQLException
public boolean	supportsCorrelatedSubqueries	()
	throws	*java.sql.*SQLException
public boolean	supportsDataDefinitionAndDataManipulationTransactions	()
	throws	*java.sql.*SQLException
public boolean	supportsDataManipulationTransactionsOnly	()
	throws	*java.sql.*SQLException
public boolean	supportsDifferentTableCorrelationNames	()
	throws	*java.sql.*SQLException
public boolean	supportsExpressionsInOrderBy	()
	throws	*java.sql.*SQLException
public boolean	supportsExtendedSQLGrammar	()
	throws	*java.sql.*SQLException
public boolean	supportsFullOuterJoins	()
	throws	*java.sql.*SQLException
public boolean	supportsGroupBy	()
	throws	*java.sql.*SQLException
public boolean	supportsGroupByBeyondSelect	()
	throws	*java.sql.*SQLException
public boolean	supportsGroupByUnrelated	()
	throws	*java.sql.*SQLException
public boolean	supportsIntegrityEnhancementFacility	()
	throws	*java.sql.*SQLException
public boolean	supportsLikeEscapeClause	()
	throws	*java.sql.*SQLException

public boolean	supportsLimitedOuterJoins()	
	throws	*java.sql.*SQLException
public boolean	supportsMinimumSQLGrammar()	
	throws	*java.sql.*SQLException
public boolean	supportsMixedCaseIdentifiers	
	throws	()
		*java.sql.*SQLException
public boolean	supportsMixedCaseQuotedIdentifiers	
	throws	()
		*java.sql.*SQLException
public boolean	supportsMultipleResultSets	
	throws	()
		*java.sql.*SQLException
public boolean	supportsMultipleTransactions	
	throws	()
		*java.sql.*SQLException
public boolean	supportsNonNullableColumns	
	throws	()
		*java.sql.*SQLException
public boolean	supportsOpenCursorsAcrossCommit	
	throws	()
		*java.sql.*SQLException
public boolean	supportsOpenCursorsAcrossRollback	
	throws	()
		*java.sql.*SQLException
public boolean	supportsOpenStatementsAcrossCommit	
	throws	()
		*java.sql.*SQLException
public boolean	supportsOpenStatementsAcrossRollback	
	throws	()
		*java.sql.*SQLException
public boolean	supportsOrderByUnrelated	
	throws	()
		*java.sql.*SQLException
public boolean	supportsOuterJoins	
	throws	()
		*java.sql.*SQLException
public boolean	supportsPositionedDelete	
	throws	()
		*java.sql.*SQLException
public boolean	supportsPositionedUpdate	
	throws	()
		*java.sql.*SQLException
public boolean	supportsResultSetConcurrency	(int type,
		int concurrency)
	throws	*java.sql.*SQLException
public boolean	supportsResultSetType	(int type)
	throws	*java.sql.*SQLException
public boolean	supportsSchemasInDataManipulation	
	throws	()
		*java.sql.*SQLException
public boolean	supportsSchemasInIndexDefinitions	
	throws	()
		*java.sql.*SQLException
public boolean	supportsSchemasInPrivilegeDefinitions	
	throws	()
		*java.sql.*SQLException
public boolean	supportsSchemasInProcedureCalls	
	throws	()
		*java.sql.*SQLException
public boolean	supportsSchemasInTableDefinitions	
	throws	()
		*java.sql.*SQLException
public boolean	supportsSelectForUpdate	
	throws	()
		*java.sql.*SQLException
public boolean	supportsStoredProcedures	
	throws	()
		*java.sql.*SQLException
public boolean	supportsSubqueriesInComparisons	
	throws	()
		*java.sql.*SQLException
public boolean	supportsSubqueriesInExists	
	throws	()
		*java.sql.*SQLException
public boolean	supportsSubqueriesInIns	
	throws	()
		*java.sql.*SQLException
public boolean	supportsSubqueriesInQuantifieds	
	throws	()
		*java.sql.*SQLException
public boolean	supportsTableCorrelationNames	
	throws	()
		*java.sql.*SQLException
public boolean	supportsTransactionIsolationLevel	(int level)
	throws	*java.sql.*SQLException
public boolean	supportsTransactions	
	throws	()
		*java.sql.*SQLException
public boolean	supportsUnion	
	throws	()
		*java.sql.*SQLException

public boolean	supportsUnionAll	()
	throws	*java.sql.***SQLException**
public boolean	updatesAreDetected	(int type)
	throws	*java.sql.***SQLException**
public boolean	usesLocalFilePerTable	()
	throws	*java.sql.***SQLException**
public boolean	usesLocalFiles	()
	throws	*java.sql.***SQLException**

Interface java.sql.Driver

```
public abstract interface Driver
```

Driver is the basic interface which must be implemented by every driver class.

Methods

public boolean	acceptsURL	(*java.lang.String* url)
	throws	*java.sql.***SQLException**
public *java.sql.***Connection**	connect	(*java.lang.String* url,
		java.util.Properties info)
	throws	*java.sql.***SQLException**
public int	getMajorVersion	()
public int	getMinorVersion	()
public *java.sql.***DriverPropertyInfo**[]	getPropertyInfo	(*java.lang.String* url,
		java.util.Properties info)
	throws	*java.sql.***SQLException**
public boolean	jdbcCompliant	()

Interface java.sql.PreparedStatement

```
public abstract interface PreparedStatement
```

```
Extends java.sql.Statement
```
PreparedStatement represents a compiled SQL statement. Some methods are deprecated.

Methods

public void	addBatch	()
	throws	*java.sql.***SQLException**
public void	clearParameters	()
	throws	*java.sql.***SQLException**
public boolean	execute	()
	throws	*java.sql.***SQLException**
public *java.sql.*ResultSet	executeQuery	()
	throws	*java.sql.***SQLException**
public int	executeUpdate	()
	throws	*java.sql.***SQLException**
public *java.sql.*ResultSetMetaData	getMetaData	()
	throws	*java.sql.***SQLException**
public void	setArray	(int i
		*java.sql.*Array x)
	throws	*java.sql.***SQLException**
public void	setAsciiStream	(int parameterIndex,
		java.io.InputStream x,
		int length)
	throws	*java.sql.***SQLException**
public void	setBigDecimal	(int parameterIndex,
		java.math.BigDecimal x)
	throws	*java.sql.***SQLException**
public void	setBinaryStream	(int parameterIndex,
		java.io.InputStream x,
		int length)
	throws	*java.sql.***SQLException**

public void	setBlob	(int i
		java.sql.Blob x)
	throws	*java.sql*.**SQLException**
public void	setBoolean	(int parameterIndex,
		boolean x)
	throws	*java.sql*.**SQLException**
public void	setByte	(int parameterIndex,
		byte x)
	throws	*java.sql*.**SQLException**
public void	setBytes	(int parameterIndex, byte[] x)
	throws	*java.sql*.**SQLException**
public void	setCharacterStream	(int parameterIndex,
		java.io.Reader reader,
		int length)
	throws	*java.sql*.**SQLException**
public void	setClob	(int i,
		java.sql.Clob x)
	throws	*java.sql*.**SQLException**
public void	setDate	(int parameterIndex,
		java.sql.Date x)
	throws	*java.sql*.**SQLException**
public void	setDate	(int parameterIndex,
		java.sql.Date x,
		java.util.Calendar cal)
	throws	*java.sql*.**SQLException**
public void	setDouble	(int parameterIndex,
		double x)
	throws	*java.sql*.**SQLException**
public void	setFloat	(int parameterIndex,
		float x)
	throws	*java.sql*.**SQLException**
public void	setInt	(int parameterIndex,
		int x)
	throws	*java.sql*.**SQLException**
public void	setLong	(int parameterIndex,
		long x)
	throws	*java.sql*.**SQLException**
public void	setNull	(int parameterIndex,
		int sqlType)
	throws	*java.sql*.**SQLException**
public void	setNull	(int paramIndex,
		int sqlType,
		java.lang.String typeName)
	throws	*java.sql*.**SQLException**
public void	setObject	(int parameterIndex,
		java.lang.Object x,
		int targetSqlType,
		int scale)
	throws	*java.sql*.**SQLException**
public void	setObject	(int parameterIndex,
		java.lang.Object x,
		int targetSqlType)
	throws	*java.sql*.**SQLException**
public void	setObject	(int parameterIndex,
		java.lang.Object x)
	throws	*java.sql*.**SQLException**
public void	setRef	(int i
		java.sql.Ref x)
	throws	*java.sql*.**SQLException**
public void	setShort	(int parameterIndex,
		short x)
	throws	*java.sql*.**SQLException**
public void	setString	(int parameterIndex,
		java.lang.String x)
	throws	*java.sql*.**SQLException**

public void	**setTime**	(int parameterIndex, *java.sql.*Time x)
	throws	*java.sql.***SQLException**
public void	**setTime**	(int parameterIndex, *java.sql.*Time x, *java.util.*Calendar cal)
	throws	*java.sql.***SQLException**
public void	**setTimestamp**	(int parameterIndex, *java.sql.*TimeStamp x)
	throws	*java.sql.***SQLException**
public void	**setTimestamp**	(int parameterIndex, *java.sql.*TimeStamp x, *java.util.Calendar* cal)
	throws	*java.sql.***SQLException**

Inherited from *java.sql.*Statement:
addBatch, cancel, clearBatch, clearWarnings, close, execute, executeBatch, executeQuery, executeUpdate, getConnection, getFetchDirection, getFetchSize, getMaxFieldSize, getMaxRows, getMoreResults, getQueryTimeout, getResultSet, getResultSetConcurrency, getResultSetType, getUpdateCount, getWarnings, setCursorName, setEscapeProcessing, setFetchDirection, setFetchSize, setMaxFieldSize, setMaxRows, setQueryTimeout

Deprecated Methods

public void	**setUnicodeStream**	(int parameterIndex, *java.io.InputStream* x, int length)

Interface java.sql.Ref

```
public abstract interface Ref
```

Ref is a reference to an SQL structured type value.

Methods

public *java.lang.String*	**getBaseTypeName**	()
	throws	*java.sql.***SQLException**

Interface java.sql.ResultSet

```
public abstract interface ResultSet
```

ResultSet allows access to a table of data. Some methods are deprecated.

Methods

public boolean	**absolute**	(int row)
	throws	*java.sql.***SQLException**
public void	**afterLast**	()
	throws	*java.sql.***SQLException**
public void	**beforeFirst**	()
	throws	*java.sql.***SQLException**
public void	**cancelRowUpdates**	()
	throws	*java.sql.***SQLException**
public void	**clearWarnings**	()
	throws	*java.sql.***SQLException**
public void	**close**	()
	throws	*java.sql.***SQLException**
public void	**deleteRow**	()
	throws	*java.sql.***SQLException**

public int	**findColumn**	(*java.lang.String* columnName)
	throws	*java.sql*.**SQLException**
public boolean	**first**	()
	throws	*java.sql*.**SQLException**
public *java.sql*.Array	**getArray**	(int i)
	throws	*java.sql*.**SQLException**
public *java.sql*.Array	**getArray**	(*java.lang.String* colName)
	throws	*java.sql*.**SQLException**
public *java.io.InputStream*	**getAsciiStream**	(int columnIndex)
	throws	*java.sql*.**SQLException**
public *java.io.InputStream*	**getAsciiStream**	(*java.lang.String* columnIndex)
	throws	*java.sql*.**SQLException**
public *java.math.BigDecimal*	**getBigDecimal**	(int columnIndex)
	throws	*java.sql*.**SQLException**
public *java.math.BigDecimal*	**getBigDecimal**	(*java.lang.String* columnName)
	throws	*java.sql*.**SQLException**
public *java.io.InputStream*	**getBinaryStream**	(int columnIndex)
	throws	*java.sql*.**SQLException**
public *java.io.InputStream*	**getBinaryStream**	(*java.lang.String* columnIndex)
	throws	*java.sql*.**SQLException**
public *java.sql*.Blob	**getBlob**	(int i)
	throws	*java.sql*.**SQLException**
public *java.sql*.Blob	**getBlob**	(*java.lang.String* colName)
	throws	*java.sql*.**SQLException**
public boolean	**getBoolean**	(int columnIndex)
	throws	*java.sql*.**SQLException**
public boolean	**getBoolean**	(*java.lang.String* columnIndex)
	throws	*java.sql*.**SQLException**
public byte	**getByte**	(int columnIndex)
	throws	*java.sql*.**SQLException**
public byte	**getByte**	(*java.lang.String* columnIndex)
	throws	*java.sql*.**SQLException**
public byte[]	**getBytes**	(int columnIndex)
	throws	*java.sql*.**SQLException**
public byte[]	**getBytes**	(*java.lang.String* columnIndex)
	throws	*java.sql*.**SQLException**
public *java.io.Reader*	**getCharacterStream**	(int columnIndex)
	throws	*java.sql*.**SQLException**
public *java.io.Reader*	**getCharacterStream**	(*java.lang.String* columnName)
	throws	*java.sql*.**SQLException**
public *java.sql*.Clob	**getClob**	(int i)
	throws	*java.sql*.**SQLException**
public *java.sql*.Clob	**getClob**	(*java.lang.String* colName)
	throws	*java.sql*.**SQLException**
public int	**getConcurrency**	()
	throws	*java.sql*.**SQLException**
public *java.lang.String*	**getCursorName**	()
	throws	*java.sql*.**SQLException**
public *java.sql*.Date	**getDate**	(int columnIndex)
	throws	*java.sql*.**SQLException**
public *java.sql*.Date	**getDate**	(*java.lang.String* columnIndex)
	throws	*java.sql*.**SQLException**
public *java.sql*.Date	**getDate**	(int columnIndex,
		java.util.Calendar cal)
	throws	*java.sql*.**SQLException**
public *java.sql*.Date	**getDate**	(*java.lang.String* columnName
		java.util.Calendar cal)
	throws	*java.sql*.**SQLException**
public double	**getDouble**	(int columnIndex)
	throws	*java.sql*.**SQLException**
public double	**getDouble**	(*java.lang.String* columnIndex)
	throws	*java.sql*.**SQLException**
public int	**getFetchDirection**	()
	throws	*java.sql*.**SQLException**
public int	**getFetchSize**	()
	throws	*java.sql*.**SQLException**

public float	**getFloat**	(int columnIndex)
	throws	*java.sql.***SQLException**
public float	**getFloat**	(*java.lang.String* columnIndex)
	throws	*java.sql.***SQLException**
public int	**getInt**	(int columnIndex)
	throws	*java.sql.***SQLException**
public int	**getInt**	(*java.lang.String* columnIndex)
	throws	*java.sql.***SQLException**
public long	**getLong**	(int columnIndex)
	throws	*java.sql.***SQLException**
public long	**getLong**	(*java.lang.String* columnIndex)
	throws	*java.sql.***SQLException**
public *java.sql.*ResultSetMetaData	**getMetaData**	()
	throws	*java.sql.***SQLException**
public *java.lang.Object*	**getObject**	(int columnIndex)
	throws	*java.sql.***SQLException**
public *java.lang.Object*	**getObject**	(*java.lang.String* columnName)
	throws	*java.sql.***SQLException**
public *java.lang.Object*	**getObject**	(*java.lang.String* colName,
		java.util.Map map)
	throws	*java.sql.***SQLException**
public *java.lang.Object*	**getObject**	(int i
		java.util.Map map)
	throws	*java.sql.***SQLException**
public *java.sql.*Ref	**getRef**	(*java.lang.String* colName)
	throws	*java.sql.***SQLException**
public *java.sql.*Ref	**getRef**	(int i)
	throws	*java.sql.***SQLException**
public int	**getRow**	()
	throws	*java.sql.***SQLException**
public short	**getShort**	(int columnIndex)
	throws	*java.sql.***SQLException**
public short	**getShort**	(*java.lang.String* columnIndex)
	throws	*java.sql.***SQLException**
public *java.sql.*Statement	**getStatement**	()
	throws	*java.sql.***SQLException**
public *java.lang.String*	**getString**	(int columnIndex)
	throws	*java.sql.***SQLException**
public *java.lang.String*	**getString**	(*java.lang.String* columnIndex)
	throws	*java.sql.***SQLException**
public *java.sql.*Time	**getTime**	(int columnIndex)
	throws	*java.sql.***SQLException**
public *java.sql.*Time	**getTime**	(*java.lang.String* columnIndex)
	throws	*java.sql.***SQLException**
public *java.sql.*Time	**getTime**	(int columnIndex
		java.util.Calendar cal)
	throws	*java.sql.***SQLException**
public *java.sql.*Time	**getTime**	(*java.lang.String* columnName,
		java.util.Calendar cal)
	throws	*java.sql.***SQLException**
public *java.sql.*Timestamp	**getTimestamp**	(int columnIndex)
	throws	*java.sql.***SQLException**
public *java.sql.*Timestamp	**getTimestamp**	(*java.lang.String* columnIndex)
	throws	*java.sql.***SQLException**
public *java.sql.*Timestamp	**getTimestamp**	(int columnIndex
		java.util.Calendar cal)
	throws	*java.sql.***SQLException**
public *java.sql.*Timestamp	**getTimestamp**	(*java.lang.String* columnName,
		java.util.Calendar cal)
	throws	*java.sql.***SQLException**
public int	**getType**	()
	throws	*java.sql.***SQLException**
public *java.sql.*SQLWarning	**getWarnings**	()
	throws	*java.sql.***SQLException**

public void	**insertRow**	()
	throws	*java.sql.***SQLException**
public boolean	**isAfterLast**	()
	throws	*java.sql.***SQLException**
public boolean	**isBeforeFirst**	()
	throws	*java.sql.***SQLException**
public boolean	**isFirst**	()
	throws	*java.sql.***SQLException**
public boolean	**isLast**	()
	throws	*java.sql.***SQLException**
public boolean	**last**	()
	throws	*java.sql.***SQLException**
public void	**moveToInsertRow**	()
	throws	*java.sql.***SQLException**
public void	**moveToCurrentRow**	()
	throws	*java.sql.***SQLException**
public boolean	**next**	()
	throws	*java.sql.***SQLException**
public boolean	**previous**	()
	throws	*java.sql.***SQLException**
public void	**refreshRow**	()
	throws	*java.sql.***SQLException**
public boolean	**relative**	(int rows)
	throws	*java.sql.***SQLException**
public boolean	**rowDeleted**	()
	throws	*java.sql.***SQLException**
public boolean	**rowInserted**	()
	throws	*java.sql.***SQLException**
public boolean	**rowUpdated**	()
	throws	*java.sql.***SQLException**
public void	**setFetchDirection**	(int direction)
	throws	*java.sql.***SQLException**
public void	**setFetchSize**	(int rows)
	throws	*java.sql.***SQLException**
public void	**updateAsciiStream**	(int columnIndex, *java.io.InputStream* x, int length)
	throws	*java.sql.***SQLException**
public void	**updateAsciiStream**	(*java.lang.String* columnName, *java.io.InputStream* x, int length)
	throws	*java.sql.***SQLException**
public void	**updateBigDecimal**	(int columnIndex, *java.math.BigDecimal* x)
	throws	*java.sql.***SQLException**
public void	**updateBigDecimal**	(*java.lang.String* columnName, *java.math.BigDecimal* x)
	throws	*java.sql.***SQLException**
public void	**updateBinaryStream**	(int columnIndex, *java.io.InputStream* x, int length)
	throws	*java.sql.***SQLException**
public void	**updateBinaryStream**	(*java.lang.String* columnName, *java.io.InputStream* x, int length)
	throws	*java.sql.***SQLException**
public void	**updateBoolean**	(int columnIndex, boolean x)
	throws	*java.sql.***SQLException**
public void	**updateBoolean**	(*java.lang.String* columnName, boolean x)
	throws	*java.sql.***SQLException**
public void	**updateByte**	(int columnIndex, byte x)
	throws	*java.sql.***SQLException**

public void	**updateByte**	(*java.lang.String* columnName, byte x)
	throws	*java.sql.***SQLException**
public void	**updateBytes**	(int columnIndex, byte[] x)
	throws	*java.sql.***SQLException**
public void	**updateBytes**	(*java.lang.String* columnName, byte[] x)
	throws	*java.sql.***SQLException**
public void	**updateCharacterStream**	(int columnIndex, *java.io.Reader* x, int length)
	throws	*java.sql.***SQLException**
public void	**updateCharacterStream**	(*java.lang.String* columnName, *java.io.Reader* reader, int length)
	throws	*java.sql.***SQLException**
public void	**updateDate**	(int columnIndex, *java.sql.*Date x)
	throws	*java.sql.***SQLException**
public void	**updateDate**	(*java.lang.String* columnName, *java.sql.*Date date)
	throws	*java.sql.***SQLException**
public void	**updateDouble**	(int columnIndex, double x)
	throws	*java.sql.***SQLException**
public void	**updateDouble**	(*java.lang.String* columnName, double x)
	throws	*java.sql.***SQLException**
public void	**updateFloat**	(int columnIndex, float x)
	throws	*java.sql.***SQLException**
public void	**updateFloat**	(*java.lang.String* columnName, float x)
	throws	*java.sql.***SQLException**
public void	**updateInt**	(int columnIndex, int x)
	throws	*java.sql.***SQLException**
public void	**updateInt**	(*java.lang.String* columnName, int x)
	throws	*java.sql.***SQLException**
public void	**updateLong**	(int columnIndex, long x)
	throws	*java.sql.***SQLException**
public void	**updateLong**	(*java.lang.String* columnName, long x)
	throws	*java.sql.***SQLException**
public void	**updateNull**	(int columnIndex) (*java.lang.String* columnName)
	throws	*java.sql.***SQLException**
public void	**updateObject**	(int columnIndex, *java.lang.Object* x, int scale)
	throws	*java.sql.***SQLException**
public void	**updateObject**	(int columnIndex, *java.lang.Object* x)
	throws	*java.sql.***SQLException**
public void	**updateObject**	(*java.lang.String* columnName, *java.lang.Object* x, int scale)
	throws	*java.sql.***SQLException**
public void	**updateObject**	(*java.lang.String* columnName, *java.lang.Object* x)
	throws	*java.sql.***SQLException**

public void	updateRow	()
	throws	*java.sql*.**SQLException**
public void	updateShort	(int columnIndex,
		short x)
	throws	*java.sql*.**SQLException**
public void	updateShort	(*java.lang.String* columnName,
		short x)
	throws	*java.sql*.**SQLException**
public void	updateString	(int columnIndex,
		java.lang.String x)
	throws	*java.sql*.**SQLException**
public void	updateString	(*java.lang.String* columnName,
		java.lang.String x)
	throws	*java.sql*.**SQLException**
public void	updateTime	(int columnIndex,
		java.sql.Time x)
	throws	*java.sql*.**SQLException**
public void	updateTime	(*java.lang.String* columnName,
		java.sql.Time time)
	throws	*java.sql*.**SQLException**
public void	updateTimestamp	(int columnIndex,
		java.sql.Timestamp x)
	throws	*java.sql*.**SQLException**
public void	updateTimestamp	(*java.lang.String* columnName,
		java.sql.Timestamp x)
	throws	*java.sql*.**SQLException**
public boolean	wasNull	()
	throws	*java.sql*.**SQLException**

Deprecated Methods

public *java.math.BigDecimal*	getBigDecimal	(int columnIndex,
		int scale)
public *java. math.BigDecimal*	getBigDecimal	(*java.lang.String* columnName,
		int scale)
public *java.io.InputStream*	getUnicodeStream	(int columnIndex)
public *java.io.InputStream*	getUnicodeStream	(*java.lang.String* columnName)

Fields

public static final int	CONCUR_READ_ONLY
public static final int	CONCUR_UPDATABLE
public static final int	FETCH_FORWARD
public static final int	FETCH_REVERSE
public static final int	FETCH_UNKNOWN
public static final int	TYPE_FORWARD_ONLY
public static final int	TYPE_SCROLL_INSENSITIVE
public static final int	TYPE_SCROLL_SENSITIVE

Interface java.sql.ResultSetMetaData

```
public abstract interface ResultSetMetaData
```

ResultSetMetaData allows access to types and properties of ResultSet columns.

Methods

public *java.lang.String*	getCatalogName	(int column)
	throws	*java.sql*.**SQLException**
public *java.lang.String*	getColumnClassName	(int column)
	throws	*java.sql*.**SQLException**
public int	getColumnCount	()
	throws	*java.sql*.**SQLException**

public int	**getColumnDisplaySize**	(int column)
	throws	*java.sql.***SQLException**
public *java.lang.String*	**getColumnLabel**	(int column)
	throws	*java.sql.***SQLException**
public *java.lang.String*	**getColumnName**	(int column)
	throws	*java.sql.***SQLException**
public int	**getColumnType**	(int column)
	throws	*java.sql.***SQLException**
public *java.lang.String*	**getColumnTypeName**	(int column)
	throws	*java.sql.***SQLException**
public int	**getPrecision**	(int column)
	throws	*java.sql.***SQLException**
public int	**getScale**	(int column)
	throws	*java.sql.***SQLException**
public *java.lang.String*	**getSchemaName**	(int column)
	throws	*java.sql.***SQLException**
public *java.lang.String*	**getTableName**	(int column)
	throws	*java.sql.***SQLException**
public boolean	**isAutoIncrement**	(int column)
	throws	*java.sql.***SQLException**
public boolean	**isCaseSensitive**	(int column)
	throws	*java.sql.***SQLException**
public boolean	**isCurrency**	(int column)
	throws	*java.sql.***SQLException**
public boolean	**isDefinitelyWritable**	(int column)
	throws	*java.sql.***SQLException**
public int	**isNullable**	(int column)
	throws	*java.sql.***SQLException**
public boolean	**isSearchable**	(int column)
	throws	*java.sql.***SQLException**
public boolean	**isSigned**	(int column)
	throws	*java.sql.***SQLException**
public boolean	**isReadOnly**	(int column)
	throws	*java.sql.***SQLException**
public boolean	**isWritable**	(int column)
	throws	*java.sql.***SQLException**

Fields

public static final int	**columnNoNulls**
public static final int	**columnNullable**
public static final int	**columnNullableUnknown**

Interface java.sql.SQLData

```
public abstract interface SQLData
```

SQLData provides customizable mapping in Java for SQL user-defined types.

Methods

public *java.lang.String*	**getSQLTypeName**	()
	throws	*java.sql.***SQLException**
public void	**readSQL**	(*java.sql.***SQLInputstream**,
		java.lang.String typeName)
	throws	*java.sql.***SQLException**
public long	**writeSQL**	(*java.sql.***SQLOutputstream**)
	throws	*java.sql.***SQLException**

Interface java.sql.SQLInput

```
public abstract interface SQLInput
```

SQLInput represents an instance of an SQL structured or distinct type as a stream of values.

Methods

public *java.sql.***Array**	**readArray**	()
	throws	*java.sql.***SQLException**
public *java.io.InputStream*	**readAsciiStream**	()
	throws	*java.sql.***SQLException**
public *java.math.BigDecimal*	**readBigDecimal**	()
	throws	*java.sql.***SQLException**
public *java.io.InputStream*	**readBinaryStream**	()
	throws	*java.sql.***SQLException**
public *java.sql.***Blob**	**readBlob**	()
	throws	*java.sql.***SQLException**
public boolean	**readBoolean**	()
	throws	*java.sql.***SQLException**
public byte	**readByte**	()
	throws	*java.sql.***SQLException**
public byte[]	**readBytes**	()
	throws	*java.sql.***SQLException**
public *java.io.Reader*	**readCharacterStream**	()
	throws	*java.sql.***SQLException**
public *java.sql.***Clob**	**readClob**	()
	throws	*java.sql.***SQLException**
public *java.sql.***Date**	**readDate**	()
	throws	*java.sql.***SQLException**
public double	**readDouble**	()
	throws	*java.sql.***SQLException**
public float	**readFloat**	()
	throws	*java.sql.***SQLException**
public int	**readInt**	()
	throws	*java.sql.***SQLException**
public long	**readLong**	()
	throws	*java.sql.***SQLException**
public *java.lang.Object*	**readObject**	()
	throws	*java.sql.***SQLException**
public *java.sql.***Ref**	**readRef**	()
	throws	*java.sql.***SQLException**
public short	**readShort**	()
	throws	*java.sql.***SQLException**
public *java.lang.String*	**readString**	()
	throws	*java.sql.***SQLException**
public *java.sql.***Time**	**readTime**	()
	throws	*java.sql.***SQLException**
public *java.sql.***TimeStamp**	**readTimeStamp**	()
	throws	*java.sql.***SQLException**
public boolean	**wasNull**	()
	throws	*java.sql.***SQLException**

Interface java.sql.SQLOutput

```
public abstract interface SQLOutput
```

SQLOutput represents an instance of an SQL structured or distinct type as a stream of values.

Methods

public void	**writeArray**	(*java.sql.***Array** x)
	throws	*java.sql.***SQLException**
public void	**writeAsciiStream**	(*java.io.InputStream* x)
	throws	*java.sql.***SQLException**
public void	**writeBigDecimal**	(*java.math.BigDecimal* x)
	throws	*java.sql.***SQLException**
public void	**writeBinaryStream**	(*java.io.InputStream* x)
	throws	*java.sql.***SQLException**
public void	**writeBlob**	(*java.sql.***Blob** x)
	throws	*java.sql.***SQLException**

public void	writeBoolean	(boolean x)
	throws	*java.sql*.**SQLException**
public void	writeByte	(byte x)
	throws	*java.sql*.**SQLException**
public void	writeBytes	(byte[] x)
	throws	*java.sql*.**SQLException**
public void	writeCharacterStream	(*java.io.Reader* x)
	throws	*java.sql*.**SQLException**
public void	writeClob	(*java.sql*.**Clob** x)
	throws	*java.sql*.**SQLException**
public void	writeDate	(*java.sql*.**Date** x)
	throws	*java.sql*.**SQLException**
public void	writeDouble	(double x)
	throws	*java.sql*.**SQLException**
public void	writeFloat	(float x)
	throws	*java.sql*.**SQLException**
public void	writeInt	(int x)
	throws	*java.sql*.**SQLException**
public void	writeLong	(long x)
	throws	*java.sql*.**SQLException**
public void	writeObject	(*java.sql*.**SQLData** x)
	throws	*java.sql*.**SQLException**
public void	writeRef	(*java.sql*.**Ref** x)
	throws	*java.sql*.**SQLException**
public void	writeShort	(short x)
	throws	*java.sql*.**SQLException**
public void	writeString	(*java.lang.String* x)
	throws	*java.sql*.**SQLException**
public void	writeStruct	(*java.sql*.**Struct** x)
	throws	*java.sql*.**SQLException**
public void	writeTime	(*java.sql*.**Time** x)
	throws	*java.sql*.**SQLException**
public void	writeTimeStamp	(*java.sql*.**TimeStamp** x)
	throws	*java.sql*.**SQLException**

Interface java.sql.Statement

```
public abstract interface Statement
```

Statement executes a static SQL statement and reads the results (given in a resultset).

Methods

public void	addBatch	(*java.lang.String* sql)
	throws	*java.sql*.**SQLException**
public void	cancel	()
	throws	*java.sql*.**SQLException**
public void	clearBatch	()
	throws	*java.sql*.**SQLException**
public void	clearWarnings	()
	throws	*java.sql*.**SQLException**
public void	close	()
	throws	*java.sql*.**SQLException**
public boolean	execute	(*java.lang.String* sql)
	throws	*java.sql*.**SQLException**
public int[]	executeBatch	()
	throws	*java.sql*.**SQLException**
public *java.sql*.**ResultSet**	executeQuery	(*java.lang.String* sql)
	throws	*java.sql*.**SQLException**
public int	executeUpdate	(*java.lang.String* sql)
	throws	*java.sql*.**SQLException**
public *java.sql*.**Connection**	getConnection	()
	throws	*java.sql*.**SQLException**
public int	getFetchDirection	()
	throws	*java.sql*.**SQLException**

public int	**getFetchSize**	()
	throws	*java.sql.***SQLException**
public int	**getMaxFieldSize**	()
	throws	*java.sql.***SQLException**
public int	**getMaxRows**	()
	throws	*java.sql.***SQLException**
public boolean	**getMoreResults**	()
	throws	*java.sql.***SQLException**
public int	**getQueryTimeout**	()
	throws	*java.sql.***SQLException**
public *java.sql.***ResultSet**	**getResultSet**	()
	throws	*java.sql.***SQLException**
public int	**getResultSetConcurrency**	()
	throws	*java.sql.***SQLException**
public int	**getResultSetType**	()
	throws	*java.sql.***SQLException**
public int	**getUpdateCount**	()
	throws	*java.sql.***SQLException**
public *java.sql.***SQLWarning**	**getWarnings**	()
	throws	*java.sql.***SQLException**
public void	**setCursorName**	(*java.lang.String* name)
	throws	*java.sql.***SQLException**
public void	**setEscapeProcessing**	(boolean enable)
	throws	*java.sql.***SQLException**
public void	**setFetchDirection**	(int direction)
	throws	*java.sql.***SQLException**
public void	**setFetchSize**	(int rows)
	throws	*java.sql.***SQLException**
public void	**setMaxFieldSize**	(int max)
	throws	*java.sql.***SQLException**
public void	**setMaxRows**	(int max)
	throws	*java.sql.***SQLException**
public void	**setQueryTimeout**	(int seconds)
	throws	*java.sql.***SQLException**

Interface *java.sql.Struct*

```
public abstract interface Struct
```

Struct represents standard mapping for an SQL structured type.

Methods

public *java.lang.Object*[]	**getAttributes**	()
	throws	*java.sql.***SQLException**
public *java.lang.Object*[]	**getAttributes**	(*java.util.***Map** map)
	throws	*java.sql.***SQLException**
public *java.lang.String*	**getSQLTypeName**	()
	throws	*java.sql.***SQLException**

Class *java.sql.Date*

```
public class Date
extends java.util.Date
```

Date represents a date in milliseconds since 1/1/1970:00:00:00 GMT, stored as a long. Some methods and constructors have been deprecated.

Constructor Method

public	**Date**	(long date)

Deprecated Constructor Method

public	Date	(int year,
		int month,
		int day)

Methods

public void	setTime	(long date)
public static *java.sql*.Date	valueOf	(*java.lang.String* s)
public *java.lang.String*	toString	()

Inherited from *java.util*.Date:

```
after, before, clone, compareTo, compareTo, equals, getDate, getDay,
getMonth, getTime, getTimezoneOffset, getYear, hashCode, parse,
setDate, setMonth, setYear, toGMTString, toLocaleString, UTC
```

Inherited from *java.lang.Object*:

```
finalize, getClass, notify, notifyAll, wait, wait, wait
```

DeprecatedMethods

public int	getHours	()
public int	getMinutes	()
public int	getSeconds	()
public void	setHours	()
public void	setMinutes	()
public void	setSeconds	()

Class java.sql.DriverManager

```
public class DriverManager
```

DriverManager manages a set of JDBC drivers. Some methods have been deprecated.

Methods

public static void	deregisterDriver	(*java.sql*.Driver driver)
	throws	*java.sql*.**SQLException**
public static *java.sql*.Connection	getConnection	(*java.lang.String* url,
		java.util.Properties info)
	throws	*java.sql*.**SQLException**
public static *java.sql*.Connection	getConnection	(*java.lang.String* url,
		java.lang.String user,
		java.lang.String password)
	throws	*java.sql*.**SQLException**
public static *java.sql*.Connection	getConnection	(*java.lang.String* url)
	throws	*java.sql*.**SQLException**
public static *java.sql*.Driver	getDriver	(*java.lang.String* url)
	throws	*java.sql*.**SQLException**
public static *java.util*.Enumeration	getDrivers	()
public static int	getLoginTimeout	()
public static *java.io.PrintWriter*	getLogWriter	()
public static void	println	(*java.lang.String* message)
public static void	registerDriver	(*java.sql*.Driver driver)
	throws	*java.sql*.**SQLException**
public static void	setLoginTimeout	(int seconds)
public static void	setLogWriter	(*java.io.PrintStream* out)

Inherited from *java.lang.Object*:

```
clone, equals, finalize, getClass, hashCode, notify, notifyAll, toString, wait,
wait, wait
```

Deprecated Methods

public static *java.io.PrintStream*	`getLogStream`	()
public static int	`setLogStream`	(*java.lang.String* url)

Class java.sql.DriverPropertyInfo

```
public class DriverPropertyInfo
```

DriverPropertiesInfo contains the driver properties used in creating connections.

Constructor Method

public	`DriverPropertyInfo`	(*java.lang.String* name, *java.lang.String* value)

Methods

Inherited from *java.lang.Object*:
`clone, equals, finalize, getClass, hashCode, notify, notifyAll, toString, wait, wait, wait`

Fields

public *java.lang.String*[]	`choices`
public *java.lang.String*	`description`
public *java.lang.String*	`name`
public boolean	`required`
public *java.lang.String*	`value`

Class java.sql.Time

```
public class Time
extends java.sql.Date
```

Adds to the *java.util.Date* class the ability to parse and work with the JDBC escape syntax for time values. Also equates *java.util.Date* with SQL TIME values.

Constructor Methods

public	`Time`	(int hour, int minute, int second)
public	`Time`	(long time)

Methods

public void	`setTime`	(long time)
public *java.lang.String*	`toString`	()
public static *java.sql.*Time	`valueOf`	(*java.lang.String* s)

Inherited from *java.util.Date*:
`after, before, clone, compareTo, compareTo, equals, getHours, getMinutes, getSeconds, getTime, getTimezoneOffset, hashCode, parse, setHours, setMinutes, setSeconds, toGMTString, toLocaleString, UTC`

Inherited from *java.lang.Object*:
`finalize, getClass, notify, notifyAll, wait, wait, wait`

Deprecated Methods

public int	getDate	()
public int	getDay	()
public int	getMonth	()
public int	getYear	()
public void	setDate	(int i)
public void	setMonth	(int i)
public void	setYear	(int i)

Class java.sql.Timestamp

```
public class Timestamp
extends java.util.Date
```

Timestamp represents an SQL TIMESTAMP value. Some methods and constructors have been deprecated.

Constructor Methods

public	**Timestamp**	(long time)

Deprecated Constructor Methods

public	**Time**	(int year, int month, int date, int hour, int minute, int second, int nano)

Methods

public boolean	after	(*java.sql.*Timestamp ts)
public boolean	before	(*java.sql.*Timestamp ts)
public boolean	equals	(*java.sql.*Timestamp ts)
public boolean	equals	(*java.lang.Object* ts)
public int	getNanos	()
public void	setNanos	(int n)
public *java.lang.String*	toString	()
public static **Timestamp**	valueOf	(*java.lang.String* s)

Inherited from *java.util.*Date:
after, before, clone, compareTo, compareTo, getDate, getDay, getHours, getMinutes, getMonth, getSeconds, getYear, hashCode, parse, setDate, setHours, setMinutes, setMonth, setSeconds, setTime, setYear, toGMTString, toLocaleString, UTC

Inherited from *java.lang.Object*:
finalize, getClass, notify, notifyAll, wait, wait, wait

Class java.sql.Types

```
public class Types
```

Types defines the constants used to identify generic SQL types.

Methods

Inherited from *java.lang.Object*:
clone, equals, finalize, getClass, hashCode, notify, notifyAll, toString, wait, wait, wait

Fields

public static final int	ARRAY
public static final int	BIGINT
public static final int	BINARY
public static final int	BIT
public static final int	BLOB
public static final int	CHAR
public static final int	CLOB
public static final int	DATE
public static final int	DECIMAL
public static final int	DISTINCT
public static final int	DOUBLE
public static final int	FLOAT
public static final int	INTEGER
public static final int	JAVA_OBJECT
public static final int	LONGVARBINARY
public static final int	LONGVARCHAR
public static final int	NULL
public static final int	NUMERIC
public static final int	OTHER
public static final int	REAL
public static final int	REF
public static final int	SMALLINT
public static final int	STRUCT
public static final int	TIME
public static final int	TIMESTAMP
public static final int	TINYINT
public static final int	VARBINARY
public static final int	VARCHAR

Class java.sql.BatchUpdateException

```
public class BatchUpdate
extends java.sql.SQLException
```

Thrown when an error occurs during a batch update operation.

Constructor Methods

public	BatchUpdateException	()
public	BatchUpdateException	(int[] updateCounts)
public	BatchUpdateException	(*java.lang.String* reason, int[] updateCounts)
public	BatchUpdateException	(*java.lang.String* reason, *java.lang.String* SQLState, int[] updateCounts)
public	BatchUpdateException	(*java.lang.String* reason, *java.lang.String* SQLState, int vendorCode, int[] updateCounts)

Methods

public int[]	getUpdateCounts	()

Inherited from *java.sql.*SQLException:
> getErrorCode, getNextException, getSQLState, setNextException

Inherited from *java.lang.Throwable*:
> fillInStackTrace, getLocalizedMessage, getMessage, printStackTrace, printStackTrace, printStackTrace, toString

Inherited from *java.lang.Object*:
> clone, equals, finalize, getClass, hashCode, notify, notifyAll, wait, wait, wait

Class java.sql.DataTruncation

```
public class DataTruncation
extends java.sql.SQLWarning
```

DataTruncation is thrown when JDBC truncates a data value during a write, or reports a warning when JDBC truncates a data value during a read.

Constructor Methods

public	DataTruncation	(int index,
		boolean parameter,
		boolean read,
		int dataSize,
		int transferSize)

Methods

public int	getDataSize	()
public int	getIndex	()
public boolean	getParameter	()
public boolean	getRead	()
public int	getTransferSize	()

Inherited from *java.sql.*SQLWarning:
  `getNextWarning, setNextWarning`

Inherited from *java.sql.*SQLException:
  `getErrorCode, getNextException, getSQLState, setNextException`

Inherited from *java.lang.Throwable*:
  `fillInStackTrace, getLocalizedMessage, getMessage, printStackTrace,`
  `printStackTrace, printStackTrace, toString`

Inherited from *java.lang.Object*:
  `clone, equals, finalize, getClass, hashCode, notify, notifyAll, wait, wait,`
  `wait`

Class java.sql.SQLException

```
public class DataTruncation
extends java.lang.SQLException
```

SQLException is thrown following a database access error, returning information about it.

Constructor Methods

public	SQLException	()
public	SQLException	(*java.lang.String* reason)
public	SQLException	(*java.lang.String* reason,
		java.lang.String SQLState)
public	SQLException	(*java.lang.String* reason,
		java.lang.String SQLState,
		int vendorCode)

Methods

public int	getErrorCode	()
public *java.sql*.SQLException	getNextException	()
public *java.lang.String*	getSQLState	()
public void	setNextException	(*java.lang*.SQLException)

Inherited from *java.lang.Throwable*:

```
fillInStackTrace, getLocalizedMessage, getMessage, printStackTrace,
printStackTrace, printStackTrace, toString
```

Inherited from *java.lang.Object*:

```
clone, equals, finalize, getClass, hashCode, notify, notifyAll, wait, wait,
wait
```

Class java.sql.SQLWarning

```
public class SQLWarning
                    extends                          java.sql.SQLException
```

SQLWarning returns information about database access warnings, attached to the object invoking the warning.

Constructor Methods

public	SQLWarning	()
public	SQLWarning	(*java.lang.String* reason)
public	SQLWarning	(*java.lang.String* reason, *java.lang.String* SQLState)
public	SQLWarning	(*java.lang.String* reason, *java.lang.String* SQLState, int vendorCode)

Methods

public *java.sql*.SQLWarning	getNextWarning	()
public void	setNextWarning	(*java.sql*.SQLWarning w)

Inherited from *java.sql*.SQLException:

```
getErrorCode, getNextException, getSQLState, setNextException
```

Inherited from *java.lang.Throwable*:

```
fillInStackTrace, getLocalizedMessage, getMessage, printStackTrace,
printStackTrace, printStackTrace, toString
```

Inherited from *java.lang.Object*:

```
clone, equals, finalize, getClass, hashCode, notify, notifyAll, wait, wait,
wait
```

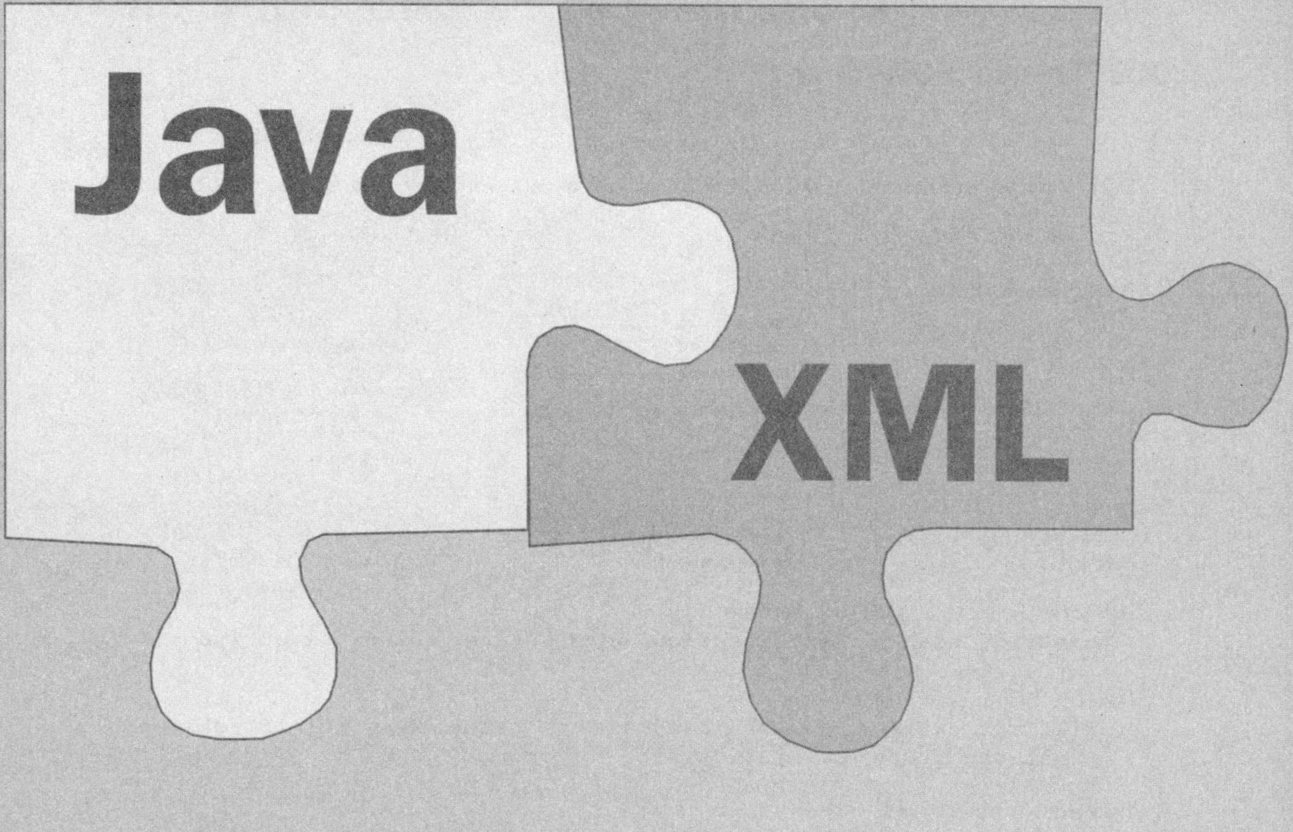
Java
XML

JSDK API Reference

Key

Within this API Reference, the following conventions are used:

- ❑ Interface, Class and Exception names within the APIs listed are all written in **bold**.
- ❑ Interface, Class and Exception names not within the APIs listed are all written in *italics*.
- ❑ Method names are all written in `Courier Bold`.

Package javax.servlet

javax.servlet is found in the Java Servlet Development Kit. This package contains classes and interfaces for developing generic servlets.

Interfaces

public abstract interface	**RequestDispatcher**
public abstract interface	**Servlet**
public abstract interface	**ServletConfig**
public abstract interface	**ServletContext**
public abstract interface	**ServletRequest**
public abstract interface	**ServletResponse**
public abstract interface	**SingleThreadModel**

Classes

public abstract class	**GenericServlet**	implements	*javax.servlet.***Servlet**, *javax.servlet.***ServletConfig**, *java.io.Serializable*
public abstract class	**ServletInputStream**	extends	java.io.InputStream
public abstract class	**ServletOutputStream**	extends	java.io.OutputStream

Exceptions

public class	ServletException	extends	*java.lang.exception*
public class	UnavailableException	extends	javax.servlet.**ServletException**

Interface javax.servlet.RequestDispatcher

```
public abstract interface RequestDispatcher
```

Appears in JSDK 2.1 only. RequestDispatcher defines an object that receives requests from a client and `forwards` them to any resource (such as a servlet, HTML file, or JSP file) on the server.

Methods in JSDK 2.1

public void	forward	`	(**ServletRequest** request, **ServletResponse** response)
	throws		*javax.servlet.***ServletException**, *java.io.IOException*;
public void	include		(**ServletRequest** request, **ServletResponse** response)
	throws		*javax.servlet.***ServletException**, *java.io.IOException*;

Interface javax.servlet.Servlet

```
public abstract interface Servlet
```

Appears in JSDK 2.0, 2.1. **Is implemented by** *javax.servlet*.GenericServlet. Servlet defines the methods that all servers must implement. In its life-cycle, a servlet is created and `initialized`, `services` any requests it receives and is then **destroy**ed.

Methods in JSDK 2.0 and 2.1

public void	init	(**ServletConfig** config)
	throws	*javax.servlet.***ServletException***;*
public void	service	(**ServletRequest** request, **ServletResponse** response)
	throws	*javax.servlet.***ServletException**, *java.io.IOException*;
public void	destroy	();
public **ServletConfig**	getServletConfig	();
public *java.lang.String*	getServletInfo	();

Interface javax.servlet.ServletConfig

```
public abstract interface ServletConfig
```

Appears in JSDK 2.0, 2.1. Is implemented by javax.servlet.**GenericServlet**. ServletConfig defines an object holding the configuration information necessary to initialize a servlet.

Methods in JSDK 2.0 and 2.1

public *java.lang.String*	getInitParameter	(*java.lang.String* name);
public *java.util.Enumeration*	getInitParameterNames	();
public **ServletContext**	getServletContext	();

Interface javax.servlet.ServletContext

```
public abstract interface ServletContext
```

Appears in JSDK 2.0, 2.1 though the method set varies between the two. Some methods have been deprecated. ServletContext defines a set of methods that servlet uses to find out about the server that it is running on and other servlets that are also running on the server besides itself.

Methods new in JSDK 2.1

public *java.util.Enumeration*	**getAttributeNames**	();
public **ServletContext**	**getContext**	(*java.lang.String* name);
public int	**getMajorVersion**	();
public int	**getMinorVersion**	();
public **RequestDispatcher**	**getRequestDispatcher**	(*java.lang.String* urlPath);
public *java.net.URL*	**getResource**	(*java.lang.String* path);
public *java.io.InputStream*	**getResourceAsStream**	(*java.lang.String* path);
public void	**log**	(*java.lang.String* message, *java.lang.Throwable* throwable);
public void	**removeAttribute**	(*java.lang.String* name);
public void	**setAttribute**	(*java.lang.String* name, *java.lang.Object* object);

Methods in JSDK 2.0 and 2.1

public *java.lang.Object*	**getAttribute**	(*java.lang.String* name);
public *java.lang.String*	**getMimeType**	(*java.lang.String* file);
public *java.lang.String*	**getRealPath**	(*java.lang.String* path);
public *java.lang.String*	**getServerInfo**	();
public *void*	**log**	(*java.lang.String* msg);

Deprecated Methods

public **Servlet**	**getServlet** throws	(*java.lang.String* name) *javax.servlet.***ServletException**;
public *java.util.Enumeration*	**getServletNames**	();
public *java.util.Enumeration*	**getServlets**	();
public void	**log**	(*java.lang.Exception* exception, *java.lang.String* msg);

Interface javax.servlet.ServletRequest

```
public abstract interface ServletRequest
```

Appears in JSDK 2.0, 2.1 though the method set varies between the two. Some methods have been deprecated. **Is extended by**: *javax.servlet.http.***HttpServletRequest**. ServletRequest defines the object that servlet engines use to pass (information about) client requests onto servlets.

Methods new in JSDK 2.1

public *java.util.Enumeration*	**getAttributeNames**	();
public void	**setAttribute**	(*java.lang.String* key, *java.lang.Object* o);

Methods in JSDK 2.0 and 2.1

public *java.lang.Object*	getAttribute	(*java.lang.String* name);
public *java.lang.string*	getCharacterEncoding	();
public int	getContentLength	();
public *java.lang.String*	getContentType	();
public **ServletInputStream**	getInputStream	()
throws		*java.io.IOException*;
public *java.lang.String*	getParameter	(*java.lang.String* name);
public *java.util.Enumeration*	getParameterNames	();
public *java.lang.String[]*	getParameterValues	(*java.lang.String* name);
public *java.lang.String*	getProtocol	();
public *java.io.BufferedReader*	getReader	()
throws		*java.io.IOException*;
public *java.lang.String*	getRemoteAddr	();
public *java.lang.String*	getRemoteHost	();
public *java.lang.String*	getScheme	();
public *java.lang.String*	getServerName	();
public int	getServerPort	();

Deprecated Methods

public *java.lang.String*	getRealPath	(*java.lang.String* path);

Interface javax.servlet.ServletResponse

```
public abstract interface ServletResponse
```

Appears in JSDK 2.0, 2.1. **Is extended by:** *javax.servlet.http.***HttpServletResponse**. ServletResponse objects are passed by servlet engines as arguments to a servlet's `service` method. The servlet uses it to send MIME-encoded data back to the client.

Methods in JSDK 2.0 and 2.1

public *java.lang.String*	getCharacterEncoding	();
public **ServletOutputStream**	getOutputStream	()
throws		*java.io.IOException*;
public *java.io.PrintWriter*	getWriter	()
throws		*java.io.IOException*;
public void	setContentLength	(int len);
public void	setContentType	(*java.lang.String* type);

Interface javax.servlet.SingleThreadModel

```
public abstract interface SingleThreadModel
```

Appears in JSDK 2.0, 2.1. SingleThreadModel is used to ensure that servlets handle only one request at a time. If a servlet implements this interface, you are guaranteed that no two threads will execute concurrently in the servlet's `service` method.

SingleThreadModel has no methods.

Class javax.servlet.GenericServlet

```
public abstract class GenericServlet
```

implements *javax.servlet.***Servlet**, *javax.servlet.***ServletConfig**, *java.io.Serializable*

Appears in JSDK 2.0, 2.1 though the method set varies between the two. **Is extended by** *javax.servlet.http.***HttpServlet**. GenericServlet defines a generic, protocol-independent servlet. To write an HTTP servlet to use with a Web site, you must extend **HttpServlet**. To write a generic servlet, you need only override the service method.

Constructor Method

public	GenericServlet	();

Methods new in JSDK 2.1

public void	init	()
	throws	*javax.servlet.***ServletException**;
public void	log	(*java.lang.String* message,
		java.lang.Throwable t)

Methods in JSDK 2.0 and 2.1

public void	log	(*java.lang.String* message);

Specified by *javax.servlet.***Servlet**
init, service, destroy, getServletConfig, getServletInfo

Specified by *javax.servlet.***ServletConfig**
getInitParameter, getInitParameternames, getServletContext

Inherited from *java.lang.object*
clone, equals, finalize, getClass, hashCode, notify, notifyAll, toString, wait, wait, wait

Class javax.servlet.ServletInputStream

```
public abstract class ServletInputStream
```

extends *java.io.InputStream*

Appears in JSDK 2.0, 2.1. ServletInputStream must be implemented by all servlet engines as it provides an input stream for reading binary data from a client request. Any subclasses of this class must implement the *java.io.InputStream.*read method.

Constructor Method

protected	ServletInputStream	();

Methods in JSDK 2.0 and 2.1

public int	readLine	(byte[] b,
		int off, int len)
	throws	*java.io.IOException*;

Inherited from *java.io.InputStream*
available, close, mark, markSupported, read, read, read, reset, skip

Inherited from *java.lang.object*
```
clone, equals, finalize, getClass, hashCode, notify, notifyAll, toString, wait,
wait, wait
```

Class javax.servlet.ServletOutputStream

```
public abstract class ServletOutputStream
```

extends *java.io.OutputStream*

Appears in JSDK 2.0, 2.1. ServletOutputStream provides servlet engines with an output stream to send binary data back to the client. Therefore engines usually extend and define it. Any subclasses of this class must implement the java.io.OutputStream.write(int) method.

Constructor Method

protected	`ServletOutputStream`	();

Methods in JSDK 2.0 and 2.1

public void	`print`	(long l)
	throws	*java.io.IOException*;
public void	`print`	(float f)
	throws	*java.io.IOException*;
public void	`print`	(double d)
	throws	*java.io.IOException*;
public void	`print`	(int i)
	throws	java.io.IOException;
public void	`print`	(*java.lang.String* s)
	throws	java.io.IOException;
public void	`print`	(boolean b)
	throws	java.io.IOException;
public void	`print`	(char c)
	throws	java.io.IOException;
public void	`println`	()
	throws	*java.io.IOException*;
public void	`println`	(long l)
	throws	*java.io.IOException*;
public void	`println`	(float f)
	throws	*java.io.IOException*;
public void	`println`	(double d)
	throws	*java.io.IOException*;
public void	`println`	(int i)
	throws	*java.io.IOException*;
public void	`println`	(*java.lang.String* s)
	throws	*java.io.IOException*;
public void	`println`	(boolean b)
	throws	*java.io.IOException*;
public void	`println`	(char c)
	throws	*java.io.IOException*;

Inherited from *java.io.OutputStream*
```
close, flush, write, write, write
```

Inherited from *java.lang.object*
```
clone, equals, finalize, getClass, hashCode, notify, notifyAll, toString, wait,
wait, wait
```

Class javax.servlet.ServletException

```
public class ServletException
```

extends *java.lang.Exception*

Appears in JSDK 2.0, 2.1 though the method set varies between the two. Is extended by *javax.servlet.***UnavailableException**. ServletException defines the general exception a servlet throws when it encounters difficulty.

Constructor Methods (JSDK 2.1 only)

| public | `ServletException` | (*java.lang.Throwable* rootCause); |
| public | `ServletException` | (*java.lang.String* message, *java.lang.Throwable* rootCause); |

Constructor Methods (JSDK 2.0 and 2.1)

| public | `ServletException` | (); |
| public | `ServletException` | (*java.lang.String* message); |

Methods in JSDK 2.1 only

| public *java.lang.Throwable* | `getRootCause` | (); |

Methods in JSDK 2.0 and 2.1

Inherited from *java.lang.Throwable*
`fillInStackTrace, getLocalizedMessage, getMessage, printStackTrace, printStackTrace, printStackTrace, toString`

Inherited from *java.lang.object*
`clone, equals, finalize, getClass, hashCode, notify, notifyAll, toString, wait, wait, wait`

Class javax.servlet.UnavailableException

```
public class UnavailableException
```

extends *javax.servlet.***ServletException**

Appears in JSDK 2.0, 2.1. UnavailableException defines the specific exception a servlet throws to indicate that it is either temporarily or permanently available.

Constructor Method

| public | `UnavailableException` | (*javax.servlet.***Servlet** servlet, *java.lang.String* msg); |
| public | `UnavailableException` | (int seconds, *javax.servlet.***Servlet** servlet, *java.lang.String* msg); |

Methods in JSDK 2.1 only

Inherited from javax.servlet.**ServletException**
`getRootCause`

Methods in JSDK 2.0 and 2.1

public boolean	`isPermanent`	();
public **Servlet**	`getServlet`	();
public int	`getUnavailableSeconds`	();

Inherited from *java.lang. Throwable*
`fillInStackTrace, getLocalizedMessage, getMessage, printStackTrace, printStackTrace, printStackTrace, toString`

Inherited from *java.lang.object*
`clone, equals, finalize, getClass, hashCode, notify, notifyAll, toString, wait, wait, wait`

Package javax.servlet.http

javax.servlet is found in the Java Servlet Development Kit. This package contains classes and interfaces for writing servlets that work with the HTTP protocol used by web servers.

Interfaces

public abstract interface	**HttpServletRequest**	extends	*javax.servlet.***ServletRequest**
public abstract interface	**HttpServletResponse**	extends	*javax.servlet.***ServletResponse**
public abstract interface	**HttpSession**		
public abstract interface	**HttpSessionBindingListener**	extends	*java.util.**EventListener*

Classes

public class	**Cookie**	implements	*java.lang.Cloneable*
public abstract class	**HttpServlet**	extends	*javax.servlet.***GenericServlet**
		implements	*java.io.Serializable*
public class	**HttpSessionBindingEvent**	extends	*java.util.EventObject*
public class	**HttpUtils**		

Deprecated

public abstract interface   **HttpSessionContext**

Interface javax.servlet.http.HttpServletRequest

`public abstract interface HttpServletRequest`

extends *javax.servlet.***ServletRequest**

Appears in JSDK 2.0, 2.1 though the method set varies between the two. Some methods have been deprecated. HttpServletRequest is a specialization of *javax.servlet.***ServletRequest** providing additional functionality for the request object that is passed to an HTTP servlet.

Methods new in JSDK 2.1

public boolean	`isRequestedSessionIdFromURL`	();
public **HttpSession**	`getSession`	();

Inherited from *javax.servlet.***ServletRequest**
`getAttributeNames, setAttribute`

Methods in JSDK 2.0 and 2.1

public *java.lang.String*	getAuthType	();
public **Cookie**[ ]	getCookies	();
public long	getDateHeader	(*java.lang.String* name);
public *java.lang.String*	getHeader	(*java.lang.String* name);
public *java.lang.Enumeration*	getHeaderNames	();
public int	getIntHeader	(*java.lang.String* name);
public *java.lang.String*	getMethod	();
public *java.lang.String*	getPathInfo	();
public *java.lang.String*	getPathTranslated	();
public *java.lang.String*	getQueryString	();
public *java.lang.String*	getRemoteUser	();
public *java.lang.String*	getRequestedSessionId	();
public *java.lang.String*	getRequestURI	();
public *java.lang.String*	getServletPath	();
public **HttpSession**	getSession	(boolean create);
public boolean	isRequestedSessionIdFromCookie	();
public boolean	isRequestedSessionIdValid	();

Inherited from *javax.servlet*.**ServletRequest**
getAttribute, getCharacterEncoding, getContentLength, getContentType,
getInputStream, getParameter, getParameterNames, getParameterValues,
getProtocol, getReader, getRemoteAddr, getRemoteHost, getScheme, getServerName,
getServerPort

Deprecated Methods

public boolean	isRequestedSessionIdFromUrl	();

Interface javax.servlet.http.HttpServletResponse

```
public abstract interface HttpServletResponse
```

extends *javax.servlet*.**ServletResponse**

Appears in JSDK 2.0, 2.1 though the method set varies between the two. Some
methods have been deprecated. HttpServletResponse is implemented by an HTTP
servlet engine to allow a servlet's service method to access HTTP headers and
return data to its client.

Methods new in JSDK 2.1

public *java.lang.String*	encodeRedirectURL	(*java.lang.String* url);
public *java.lang.String*	encodeURL	(*java.lang.String* url);

Methods in JSDK 2.0 and 2.1

public void	addCookie	(*javax.servlet.http*.**Cookie** cookie);
public boolean	containsHeader	(*java.lang.String* name);
public void	sendError	(int sc)
	throws	java.*io.IOException*;
public void	sendError	(int sc,
		java.lang.String msg)
	throws	java.*io.IOException*;
public void	sendRedirect	(*java.lang.String* location)
	throws	java.*io.IOException*;

public void	setDateHeader	(*java.lang.String* name, long date);
public void	setHeader	(*java.lang.String* name, *java.lang.String* value);
public void	setIntHeader	*java.lang.String* name, int value);
public void	setStatus	(int sc);

Inherited from *javax.servlet.***ServletResponse**
`getCharacterEncoding, getOutputStream, getWriter, setContentLength, setContentType`

Deprecated Methods

public *java.lang.String*	encodeRedirectUrl	(*java.lang.String* url);
public *java.lang.String*	encodeUrl	(*java.lang.String* url);
public void	setStatus	(int sc, *java.lang.String* sm);

Field Constants

public final static int	SC_ACCEPTED;
public final static int	SC_BAD_GATEWAY;
public final static int	SC_BAD_REQUEST;
public final static int	SC_CONFLICT;
public final static int	SC_CONTINUE;
public final static int	SC_CREATED;
public final static int	SC_FORBIDDEN;
public final static int	SC_GATEWAY_TIMEOUT;
public final static int	SC_GONE;
public final static int	SC_HTTP_VERSION_NOT_SUPPORTED;
public final static int	SC_INTERNAL_SERVER_ERROR;
public final static int	SC_LENGTH_REQUIRED;
public final static int	SC_METHOD_NOT_ALLOWED;
public final static int	SC_MOVED_PERMANENTLY;
public final static int	SC_MOVED_TEMPORARILY;
public final static int	SC_MULTIPLE_CHOICES;
public final static int	SC_NO_CONTENT;
public final static int	SC_NON_AUTHORITATIVE_INFORMATION;
public final static int	SC_NOT_ACCEPTABLE;
public final static int	SC_NOT_FOUND;
public final static int	SC_NOT_IMPLEMENTED;
public final static int	SC_NOT_MODIFIED;
public final static int	SC_OK;
public final static int	SC_PARTIAL_CONTENT;
public final static int	SC_PAYMENT_REQUIRED;
public final static int	SC_PRECONDITION_FAILED;
public final static int	SC_PROXY_AUTHENTICATION_REQUIRED;
public final static int	SC_REQUEST_ENTITY_TOO_LARGE;
public final static int	SC_REQUEST_TIMEOUT;
public final static int	SC_REQUEST_URI_TOO_LONG;
public final static int	SC_RESET_CONTENT;
public final static int	SC_SEE_OTHER;
public final static int	SC_SERVICE_UNAVAILABLE;
public final static int	SC_SWITCHING_PROTOCOLS;
public final static int	SC_UNAUTHORIZED;
public final static int	SC_UNSUPPORTED_MEDIA_TYPE;
public final static int	SC_USE_PROXY;

Interface javax.servlet.http.HttpSession

```
public abstract interface HttpSession
```

Appears in JSDK 2.0, 2.1 though the method set varies between the two. Some methods have been deprecated. HttpSession provides a concept of state and user identification across more than one page request or visit to a web site.

Methods new in JSDK 2.1

public int	getMaxInactiveInterval	();
public void	setMaxInactiveInterval	(int interval);

Methods in JSDK 2.1 and 2.0

public long	getCreationTime	();
public *java.lang.String*	getId	();
public long	getLastAccessedTime	();
public *java.lang.String*[ ]	getValueNames	();
public *java.lang.Object*	getValue	(*java.lang.String* name);
public void	invalidate	();
public boolean	isNew	();
public void	putValue	(*java.lang.String* name, *java.lang.Object* value);
public void	removeValue	(*java.lang.String* name);

Deprecated Methods

public **HttpSessionContext**	getSessionContext	();

Interface javax.servlet.http.HttpSessionBindingListener

```
public abstract interface HttpSessionBindingListener
```

extends *java.util.EventListener*

Appears in JSDK 2.0, 2.1. Causes an object to be notified when it is bound to or unbound from a session. The object is notified by an HttpSessionBindingEvent object.

Methods in JSDK 2.1 and 2.0

public void	valueBound	(*javax.servlet.http.***HttpSessionBindingEvent** event);
public void	valueUnbound	(*javax.servlet.http.***HttpSessionBindingEvent** event);

Class javax.servlet.http.Cookie

```
public class Cookie
```

implements *java.lang.Cloneable*

Appears in JSDK 2.0, 2.1. Represents a cookie which is used to store information on a client's computer.

Constructor Method

public	Cookie	(*java.lang.String* name, *java.lang.String* value);

Methods in JSDK 2.0 and 2.1

public *java.lang.Object*	`clone`	();
public *java.lang.String*	`getComment`	();
public *java.lang.String*	`getDomain`	();
public int	`getMaxAge`	();
public *java.lang.String*	`getName`	();
public *java.lang.String*	`getPath`	();
public boolean	`getSecure`	();
public *java.lang.String*	`getValue`	();
public int	`getVersion`	();
public void	`setComment`	(*java.lang.String* purpose);
public void	`setDomain`	(*java.lang.String* pattern);
public void	`setMaxAge`	(int expiry);
public void	`setPath`	(*java.lang.String* uri);
public void	`setSecure`	(boolean flag);
public void	`setValue`	(*java.lang.String* newValue);
public void	`setVersion`	(int v);

Class *javax.servlet.http.HttpServlet*

```
public abstract class HttpServlet
```

extends   *javax.servlet.***GenericServlet**
implements *java.io.Serializable*

Appears in JSDK 2.0, 2.1 though the method set varies between the two. Provides an abstract class to create an HTTP servlet which then responds to and receives information from a web site.

Constructor Method

public	`HttpServlet`	();

Methods new in JSDK 2.1

Inherited from *javax.servlet.***GenericServlet**
`init`, `log`

Methods in JSDK 2.0 and 2.1

protected void	`doDelete`	(**HttpServletRequest** req, **HttpServletResponse** resp)
	throws	java.*servlet.***ServletException**, *java.io.IOException*;
protected void	`doGet`	(**HttpServletRequest** req, **HttpServletResponse** resp)
	throws	java.*servlet.***ServletException**, *java.io.IOException*;
protected void	`doOptions`	(**HttpServletRequest** req, **HttpServletResponse** resp)
	throws	java.*servlet.***ServletException**, *java.io.IOException*;
protected void	`doPost`	(**HttpServletRequest** req, **HttpServletResponse** resp)
	throws	java.*servlet.***ServletException**, *java.io.IOException*;
protected void	`doPut`	(**HttpServletRequest** req, **HttpServletResponse** resp)
	throws	java.*servlet.***ServletException**, *java.io.IOException*;
protected void	`doTrace`	(**HttpServletRequest** req, **HttpServletResponse** resp)
	throws	java.*servlet.***ServletException**, *java.io.IOException*;

protected long	getLastModified	(**HttpServletRequest** req);
protected void	service	(**HttpServletRequest** req,
		HttpServletResponse resp)
	throws	java.*servlet*.**ServletException**,
		java.*io.IOException*;
public void	service	(*javax.servlet*.**ServletRequest** req,
		javax.servlet.**ServletResponse** resp)
	throws	java.*servlet*.**ServletException**,
		java.*io.IOException*;

Inherited from *javax.servlet*.**GenericServlet**
```
init, service, destroy, getServletConfig, getServletInfo, log
```

Inherited from *java.lang.Object*
```
clone, equals, finalize, getClass, hashCode, notify, notifyAll, toString, wait,
wait, wait
```

Class *javax.servlet.http.HttpSessionBindingEvent*

```
public class HttpSessionBindingEvent
```

extends *java.util.EventObject*

Appears in JSDK 2.0, 2.1. Represents the message to an object telling it that it has been bound to or unbound from the session.

Constructor Method

| public | HttpSessionBindingEvent | (**HttpSession** session, |
| | | *java.lang.String* name) |

Methods in JSDK 2.0 and 2.1

| public *java.lang.String* | getName | (); |
| public **HttpSession** | getSession | (); |

Inherited from *java.util.EventObject*
```
getSource, toString
```

Inherited from *java.lang.Object*
```
clone, equals, finalize, getClass, hashCode, notify, notifyAll, toString, wait,
wait, wait
```

Class *javax.servlet.http.HttpUtils*

```
public class HttpUtils
```

Appears in JSDK 2.0, 2.1. Adds a few methods useful for writing servlets with.

Constructor Method

| public | HttpUtils | (); |

Methods in JSDK 2.0 and 2.1

public static *java.lang.StringBuffer*	getRequestURL	(**HttpServletRequest** req);
public static *java.util.Hashtable*	parsePostData	(int len,
		ServletInputStream in);
public static *java.util.Hashtable*	parseQueryString	(*java.lang.String* s)

Inherited from *java.lang.object*
```
clone, equals, finalize, getClass, hashCode, notify, notifyAll, toString, wait,
wait, wait
```

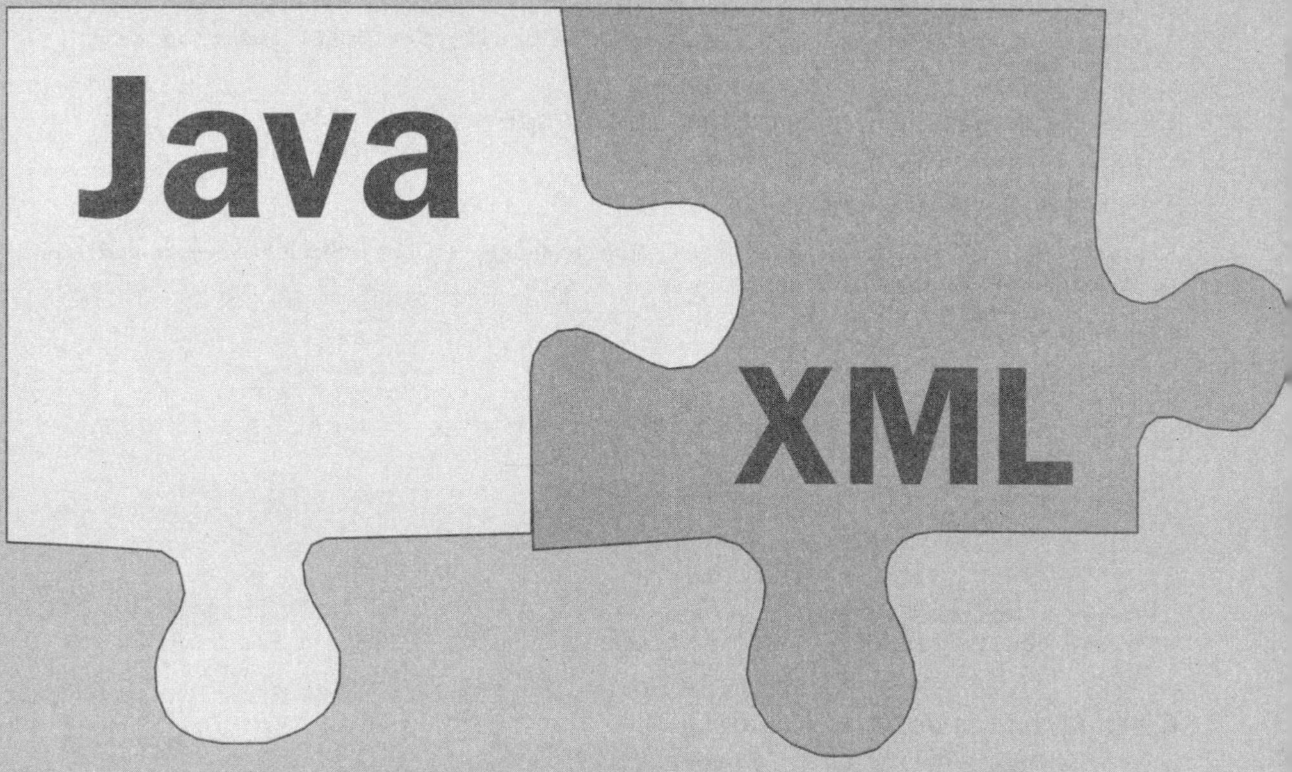
Java
XML

JavaServer Pages Syntax Summary

This appendix provides a quick guide to the syntax of JavaServer Pages. A complete reference to the core JSP 1.1 syntax can be obtained at `http://java.sun.com/products/jsp/docs.html`

Comments

Comments can be embedded in a JSP page in two different ways. A HTML comment is sent to the browser, whilst a JSP comment is removed and does not appear in the final HTML page.

An HTML comment is embedded in the usual way:

```
<!-- This is an HTML comment -->
```

A JSP comment is embedded as follows:

```
<%-- This is a JSP comment  -->
```

Directives

Directives give the JSP engine information for the page that follows. The general syntax of a JSP directive is `<%@ directive { attribute="value" } %>`, where the directive may have a number of (optional) attributes. The possible directives in JSP 1.1 are `page`, `include` and `taglib`.

Page Directive

```
<%@ page
    { language = "java" }
    { extends = "package.class" }
    { import = "{package.class | package.*},..." }
    { session = "true|false" }
    { buffer = "none|8kb|sizekb" }
    { autoFlush="true|false" }
    { isThreadSafe="true|false" }
    { info="text" }
    { errorPage="pathToErrorPage" }
    { isErrorPage="true|false" }
    { contentType="text/html;charset=ISO-8859-1" }
%>
```

The page directive defines attributes that apply to an entire JSP page. There are many possible attributes, but specifying them is optional as the mandatory ones have default values.

Attribute and possible values	Description
language="java"	The language variable tells the server what language will be used in the file. Java is the only supported syntax for a JSP in the current specification.
	Support for other scripting languages is available at http://www.plenix.org/polyjsp and http://www.caucho.com (JavaScript).
extends="package.class"	The extends variable defines the parent class of the generated servlet. It isn't normally necessary to use anything other than the provided base classes.
import="{package.class| package.*},..."	The import variable is similar to the first section of any Java program. As such, it should always be placed at the top of the JSP file. The value of the import variable should be a comma-separated list of the packages and classes that you wish to import.
session="true|false"	By default, the session variable is true, meaning that session data is available to a page.
buffer="none|8kb|sizekb"	Determines if the output stream is buffered. By default it is set to 8kb. Use with autoFlush
autoFlush="true|false"	If set to true, flushes the output buffer when it's full, rather than raising an exception.

Attribute and possible values	Description
isThreadSafe="true|false"	By default this is set true, signaling to the JSP engine that that multiple client requests can be dealt with at once. It's the JSP author's job to synchronize shared state, so that the page really is thread safe.
	If isThreadSafe is set to false, the single thread model will be used, controlling client access to the page.
	This doesn't let you off the hook, however, as servers may, at their discretion, have multiple instances of the page running to deal with the client request load. And there's no guarantee that consecutive requests from the same client will be directed to the same instance of the JSP page. Any resources or state that are shared between page requests must therefore be synchronized.
info="text"	Information on the page that can be accessed through the page's Servlet.getServletInfo() method.
errorPage="pathToErrorPage"	Gives the relative path to the JSP page that will handle unhandled exceptions. That JSP page will have isErrorPage set to true
isErrorPage="true|false"	Marks the page as an error page. We'll see this in action later.
contentType="text/html;charset=ISO-8859-1"	The mime type and character set of the JSP and the final page. This information must come early in the file, before any non-Latin-1 characters appear in the file.

Include Directive

```
<%@ include file="pathToIncludedFile" %>
```

The include directive inserts a file into a JSP page verbatim. If the included file contains any JSP elements, they are processed by the JSP engine.

Taglib Directive

```
<%@ taglib uri="uriToTaglibLibrary" prefix="tagPrefix" %>
```

The taglib directive allows you to define a tag library and prefix for any custom tags that you are using in a page. More details on how to create custom tags can be found in the JavaServer Pages 1.1 specifiction.

Declarations

```
<%! declaration %>
```

A JSP declaration can be thought of as the definition of class-level variables and methods that are to be used throughout the page. For example:

```
<%! String var1 = "x";
    int count = 0;

    private void incrementCount() {
        count++;
    }
%>
```

Note that you put semi-colons after each variable declaration, just as if you were writing it in a class.

Scriptlets

```
<% code fragment %>
```

Scriptlets are defined as any block of valid Java code that resides between `<%` and `%>` tags. The Java code will be executed when the page is requested.

This code will be placed in the generated servlet's `_jspService()` method. Code that is defined within a scriptlet can access any variable and any beans that have been declared. There are a host of implicit objects available to a scriptlet from the servlet environment.

Implicit Objects	Description
request	The client's request. This is usually a subclass of `HttpServletRequest`. This has the parameter list if there is one.
response	The JSP page's response, a subclass of `HttpServletResponse`.
pageContext	Page attributes and implicit objects (essentially what makes up the server environment in which the JSP runs) need to be accessible through a uniform API, to allow the JSP engine to compile pages. But each server will have specific implementations of these attributes and objects.
	The solution to this problem is for the JSP engine to compile in code that uses a factory class to return the server's implementation of the `PageContext` class. That `PageContext` class has been initialized with the `request` and `response` objects and some of the attributes from the page directive (`errorpage`, `session`, `buffer` and `autoflush`) and provides the other implicit objects for the page request. We'll see more on this in a moment.
session	The HTTP session object associated with the request.

Implicit Objects	Description
application	The servlet context returned by a call to `getServletConfig().getContext()`
out	The object representing the output stream.
config	The `ServletConfig` object for the page.
page	The page's way of referring to itself (as an alternative to `this` in any Java code).
exception	The uncaught subclass of `Throwable` that is passed to the errorpage URL.

Expressions

```
<%= expression %>
```

A JSP expression allows you to embed values within your HTML code. Anything between `<%=` and `%>` tags will be evaluated, converted to a string, and then displayed. Conversion from a primitive type to a string is handled automatically.

```
The current price of item A100 is <%= request.getParameter("price") %>
```

Note that the expression doesn't end with a semi-colon, because the JSP engine puts the expression into an `out.println()` call for you.

JSP

These elements perform a custom JSP-specific functions when a page is requested. The syntax of these tags is based on that of the tag-library syntax in the JavaServer Pages 1.1 specification.

forward

```
<jsp:forward page="pathToPageToBeForwarded" />
```

This tag is used to forward a client request to another file. The file receiving the request can be a HTML file, a JSP file or a servlet.

getProperty

```
<jsp:getProperty  name="beanName" property"propertyName" />
```

This tag is used to get the value of a Bean property. This property value may then be displayed in a JSP page.

include

```
<jsp:include page="pathToPageToBeIncluded" {<jsp:param
name="paramName" value ="paramValue"/>} />
```

The `jsp:include` element allows you to include files in a JSP file. The `include` directive discussed previously only allows you to include *static* files, whereas this element allows either *static* or *dynamic* files to be included. The content of a static file is included in the JSP page. If a file is dynamic, it will act on the request (using the parameters in the `jsp:param` element), and the result of this request will be returned and included in the JSP page.

plugin

```
<jsp:plugin type="bean|applet" code="className" codebase="classDir"
/>
```

This element allows you to execute an applet or a Bean. If necessary, it downloads a Java plug-in to execute it.

setProperty

```
<jsp:setProperty  name="beanName" property"propertyName" />
```

The `setProperty` element allows you to set property values in a Bean. The Bean must be declared with the `jsp:useBean` element before using this element to set its properties.

useBean

```
<jsp:useBean {attr="value"} />
```

The `jsp:useBean` element first searches for a bean instance that matches the scope and class. If it can't find one it instantiates the named class, using its public, no-args constructor. If there are any initialization time properties you need to set, you can place the appropriate tags between `<jsp:useBean>` and `</jsp:useBean>` - these are only executed when a new instance is created. The attributes associated with this element are described in the table below.

useBean Attributes	Description
id="name"	The name by which the instance of the bean can be referenced in the page. Other Bean tags use name to refer to it, so do note the difference
scope="page"	The scope over which the bean can be called. More below.
class="package.class"	Fully qualified name of the bean class. Because this needs to be the full name, you don't need to import these classes in the page directive.

useBean Attributes	Description
beanName="name"	This allows you to specify a serialized bean (.ser file) or a bean's name that can be passed to the instantiate() method from the java.beans.Beans. Needs an associated type tag rather than class.
type="package.class"	A synonym for class that is used for beanName.

The scope on a JSP page is described below:

Scope	Description
page	This is the scope of the PageContext object we saw earlier. It lasts until the page completes, and there is no storage of state.
	Page wasn't implemented in the EA1 reference version of JSP 1.0.
request	The bean instance lasts for the client request. The named bean instance is available as an attribute of the ServletRequest object, so it follows the request to another servlet / JSP if control is forwarded.
session	The bean lasts as long as the client session. A reference is available through HttpSession.getValue(name).
	Don't use this scope level if you have declared the page directive session false.
application	The bean instance is created with the application and remains in use until the application ends. It's an attribute of the ServletContext object.

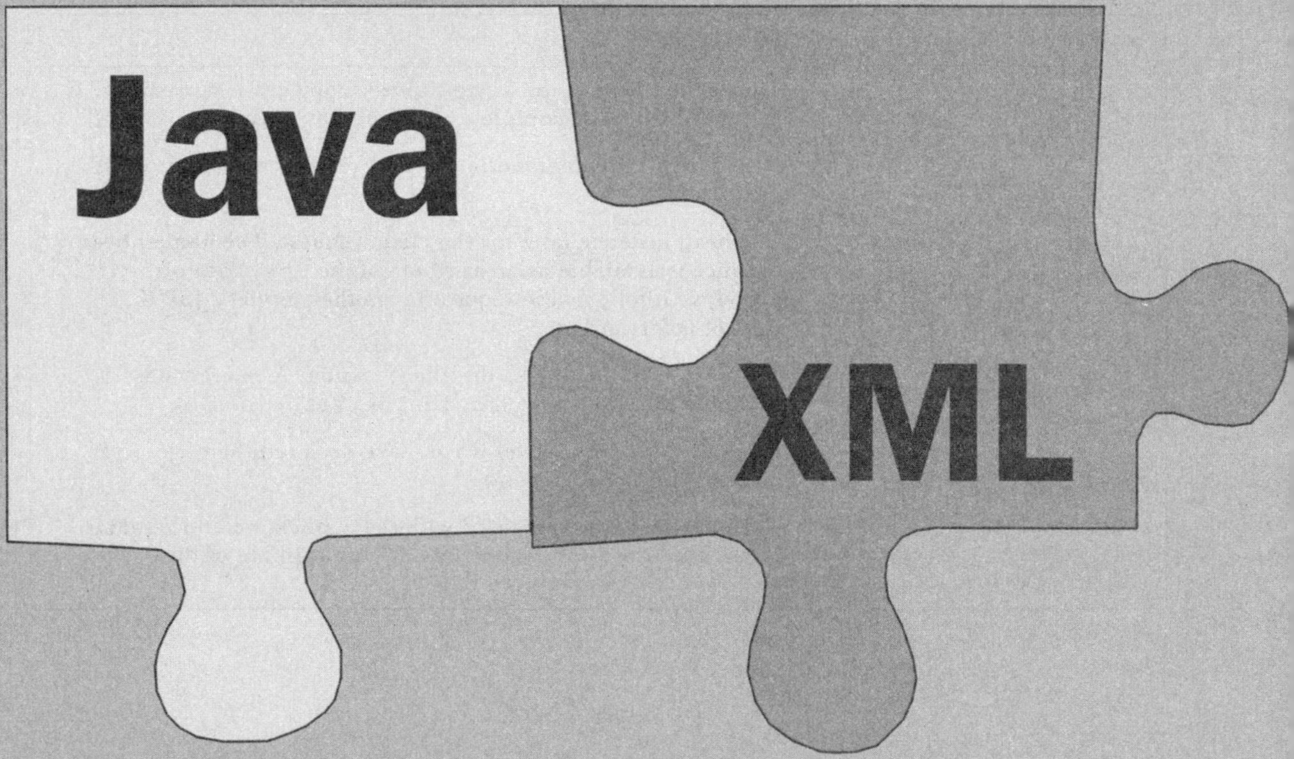
Java
XML

Core JavaMail / JAF API Reference

Key

Within this API Reference, the following conventions are used:
- ❑ Interface, Class and Exception names within the APIs listed are all written in **bold**.
- ❑ Interface, Class and Exception names not within the APIs listed are all written in *italics*.
- ❑ Method names are all written in `Courier Bold`.

The core JavaMail API package, **javax.mail,** provides a set of classes and interfaces that model a mail system and is implemented as a Java platform standard extension. The current version of the JavaMail API at time of going to press is 1.1.2.

In order for JavaMail to run correctly, you also need the JavaBeans Activation Framework which is currently at version 1.0.1. Thus the JAF API (**javax.activation**) is detailed first.

Package javax.activation

javax.activation is the single package that contains the Java Activation Framework (JAF) standard extension. The JAF is a component registry that maintains a list of JavaBeans that can perform named actions (such as "edit" and "print") on specified MIME data types.

Interfaces

```
public abstract interface        CommandObject;
public abstract interface        DataContentHandler;
public abstract interface        DataContentHandlerFactory;
public abstract interface        DataSource;
```

Classes

public class	**ActivationDataFlavor**	extends	*java.awt.datatransfer.DataFlavor*;
public class	**CommandInfo**;		
public abstract class	**CommandMap**;		
public class	**DataHandler**	implements	*java.awt.datatransfer.Transferable*;
public class	**FileDataSource**	implements	*javax.activation.DataSource*;
public abstract class	**FileTypeMap**;		
public class	**MailcapCommandMap**	extends	*javax.activation.CommandMap*;
public class	**MimeType**	implements	*java.io.Externalizable*;
public class	**MimeTypeParameterList**;		
public class	**MimetypesFileTypeMap**	extends	*javax.activation.FileTypeMap*;
public class	**URLDataSource**	implements	*javax.activation.DataSource*;

Exceptions

public class	**MimeTypeParseException**	extends	*java.lang.Exception*;
public class	**UnsupportedDataTypeException**	extends	*java.io.IOException*;

Interface javax.activation.CommandObject

```
public abstract interface CommandObject
```

CommandObject provides JavaBeans with what they're being asked to do and where to find the data they should be operating on.

Methods

public abstract void	setCommandContext	(*java.lang.String* verb,
		javax.activation.**DataHandler** dh)
	throws	*java.io.IOException*;

Interface javax.activation.DataContentHandler

```
public abstract interface DataContentHandler
```

Generally called indirectly through the equivalent methods in *javax.activation.***DataHandler**, **DataContentHandler** is used to extend the JAF to convert streams into objects and write objects to streams.

Methods

public java.lang.Object	getContent	(javax.activation.**DataSource** ds)
	throws	*java.io.IOException*;
public java.lang.Object	getTransferData	(java.awt.datatransfer.DataFlavor df,
		javax.activation.**DataSource** ds)
	throws	java.awt.datatransfer.UnsupportedFlavorException,
		java.io.IOException;
public java.awt.datatransfer.DataFlavor[ ]		
	getTransferDataFlavors	();
public void	writeTo	(*java.lang.Object* obj,
		java.lang.string mimeType,
		java.io.OutputStream os)
	throws	*java.io.IOException*;

Interface javax.activation.DataContentHandlerFactory

```
public abstract interface DataContentHandlerFactory
```

DataContentHandlerFactory defines a factory for **DataContentHandlers**. Authors writing implementations of this interface should map a MIME type into an instance of **DataContentHandler.**

Methods

public **DataContentHandler**	`createDataContentHandler`	(*java.lang.String* mimeType);

Interface javax.activation.DataSource

```
public abstract interface DataSource
```

Is implemented by *javax.activation.***FileDataSource** and *javax.activation.***URLDataSource**. DataSource acts as a locator and descriptor of an arbitrary collection of data, giving it a type and access routes through *InputStream*s and *Outputstream*s.

Methods

public *java.lang.String*	`getContentType`	();
public *java.io.InputStream*	`getInputStream`	()
	throws	*java.io.IOException*;
public *java.lang.String*	`getName`	();
public *java.io.OutputStream*	`getOutputStream`	()
	throws	*java.io.IOException*;

Class javax.activation.ActivationDataFlavor

```
public class ActivationDataFlavor
```

```
extends java.awt.datatransfer.DataFlavor
```

ActivationDataFlavor is a special subclass of *java.awt.datatransfer.DataFlavor* with the exception that it can also set the three values used in the *DataFlavor* class with its methods which override those in *DataFlavor*.

Constructor Methods

public **ActivationDataFlavor**	(*java.lang.String* mimeType, *java.lang.String* humanPresentableName);
public **ActivationDataFlavor**	(*java.lang.Class* representationClass, *java.lang.String* humanPresentableName);
public **ActivationDataFlavor**	(*java.lang.Class* representationClass, *java.lang.string* mimeType, *java.lang.String* humanPresentableName);

Methods

public boolean	`equals`	(*java.awt.datatransfer.DataFlavor* dataFlavor);
public *java.lang.String*	`getHumanPresentableName`	();
public *java.lang.String*	`getMimeType`	();
public *java.lang.Class*	`getRepresentationClass`	();
public boolean	`isMimeTypeEqual`	(*java.lang.String* mimeType);
protected *java.lang.String*	`normalizeMimeType`	(*java.lang.String* mimeType);
protected *java.lang.String*	`normalizeMimeTypeParameter`	(*java.lang.String* parameterName, *java.lang.String* parameterValue);
public void	`setHumanPresentableName`	(*java.lang.String* humanPresentableName);

Inherited from java.awt.datatransfer.DataFlavor
```
clone, equals, equals, getParameter, getPrimaryType, getSubType,
isFlavorJavaFileListType,
isFlavorRemoteObjectType, isFlavorSerializedObjectType, isMimeTypeEqual,
isMimeTypeSerializedObject,
isRepresentationClassInputStream, isRepresentationClassRemote,
isRepresentationClassSerializable,
readExternal, tryToLoadClass, writeExternal
```

Inherited from java.lang.object
```
clone, equals, finalize, getClass, hashCode, notify, notifyAll, toString, wait,
wait, wait
```

Fields

Inherited from java.awt.datatransfer.DataFlavor
```
javaFileListFlavor, javaJVMLocalObjectMimeType, javaRemoteObjectMimeType,
javaSerializedObjectMimeType,
plainTextFlavor, stringFlavor
```

Class javax.activation.CommandInfo

```
public class CommandInfo
```

CommandInfo is used by (*javax.activation.*)**CommandMap** implementations to describe the results of command requests. NB. The `getCommandClass` method may return NULL depending on how it was called. Do not depend on this method returning a valid value.

Constructor Method

public	CommandInfo	(*java.lang.String* verb, *java.lang.String* className);

Methods

public *java.lang.String*	getCommandClass	();
public *java.lang.String*	getCommandName	();
public *java.lang.Object*	getCommandObject	(*javax.activation.*DataHandler dh, *java.lang.ClassLoader* loader)
	throws	*java.io.IOException*, *java.lang.ClassNotFoundException*;

Inherited from java.lang.object
```
clone, equals, finalize, getClass, hashCode, notify, notifyAll, toString, wait,
wait, wait
```

Class javax.activation.CommandMap

```
public abstract class CommandMap
```

Is extended by *javax.activation.*MailcapCommandMap. **CommandMap** provides a way to access a registry of command objects available in the system.

Constructor Method

public	CommandMap	();

Methods

public abstract **DataContentHandler**	createDataContentHandler	(*java.lang.String* mimeType);
public abstract **CommandInfo**[ ]	getAllCommands	(*java.lang.String* mimeType);
public abstract **CommandInfo**	getCommand	(*java.lang.String* mimeType, *java.lang.String* cmdName);
public static **CommandMap**	getDefaultCommandMap	();
public abstract **CommandInfo**[ ]	getPreferredCommands	(*java.lang.String* mimeType);
public static void	setDefaultCommandMap	(*javax.activation.*CommandMap commandMap);

Inherited from java.lang.object

```
clone, equals, finalize, getClass, hashCode, notify, notifyAll, toString, wait,
wait, wait
```

Class *javax.activation.DataHandler*

```
public class DataHandler
```

implements *java.awt.datatransfer.Transferable*

DataHandler acts as a consistent interface to any set of data, whichever format it is in. It implements *java.awt.datatransfer.Transferable* to be able to handle operations like cut, paste and drag and drop.

Constructor Methods

public	DataHandler	(*javax.activation.***DataSource** ds);
public	DataHandler	(*java.net.URL* url);
public	DataHandler	(*java.lang.Object* obj,
		java.lang.String mimeType);

Methods

public **CommandInfo**[ ]	getAllCommands	();
public *java.lang.Object*	getBean	(*javax.activation.***CommandInfo** cmdinfo);
public **CommandInfo**	getCommand	(*java.lang.String* cmdName);
public *java.lang.Object*	getContent	()
	throws	*java.io.IOException*;
public *java.lang.String*	getContentType	();
public **DataSource**	getDataSource	();
public *java.io.InputStream*	getInputStream	()
	throws	*java.io.IOException*;
public *java.lang.String*	getName	();
public *java.io.OutputStream*	getOutputStream	()
	throws	*java.io.IOException*;
public **CommandInfo**[ ]	getPreferredCommands	();
public *java.lang.Object*	getTransferData	(*java.awt.datatransfer.DataFlavor* flavor)
	throws	*java.awt.datatransfer.UnsupportedFlavorException*,
		java.io.IOException;
public *java.awt.datatransfer.DataFlavor*[ ]	getTransferDataFlavors	();
public boolean	isDataFlavorSupported	(*java.awt.datatransfer.DataFlavor* flavor);
public void	setCommandMap	(*javax.activation.***CommandMap** commandMap);
public static void	setDataContentHandlerFactory	
		(*javax.activation.***DataContentHandlerFactory** newFactory);
public void	writeTo	(*java.io.OutputStream* os)
	throws	*java.io.IOException*;

Inherited from java.lang.object

```
clone, equals, finalize, getClass, hashCode, notify, notifyAll, toString, wait,
wait, wait
```

Class *javax.activation.FileDataSource*

```
public class FileDataSource
```

implements *javax.activation.***DataSource**

FileDataSource implements *javax.activation.***DataSource** to represent a file. Of those methods in FileDataSource, four methods are actually specified in *javax.activation.***DataSource**: `getContentType, getName, getInputStream, getOutputStream`.

Constructor Methods

public	FileDataSource	(*java.lang.String* name);
public	FileDataSource	(*java.io.File* File);

Methods

public *java.lang.String*	getContentType	();
public *java.io.File*	getFile	();
public *java.lang.String*	getName	();
public void	setFileTypeMap	(*javax.activation.***FileTypeMap** map);
public *java.io.InputStream*	getInputStream	()
	throws	*java.io.IOException*;
public *java.io.OutputStream*	getOutputStream	()
	throws	*java.io.IOException*;

Inherited from java.lang.object
```
clone, equals, finalize, getClass, hashCode, notify, notifyAll, toString, wait,
wait, wait
```

Class javax.activation.FileTypeMap

```
public abstract class FileTypeMap
```

Is extended by *javax.activation.***MimetypesFileMap**. **FileTypeMap** is an abstract class that provides a data typing interface for files.

Constructor Method

public	FileTypeMap	();

Methods

public abstract *java.lang.String*	getContentType	(*java.io.File* file);
public abstract *java.lang.String*	getContentType	(*java.lang.String* filename);
public static **FileTypeMap**	getDefaultFileTypeMap	();
public static void	setDefaultFileTypeMap	(*javax.activation.***FileTypeMap** map);

Inherited from java.lang.object
```
clone, equals, finalize, getClass, hashCode, notify, notifyAll, toString, wait,
wait, wait
```

Class javax.activation.MailcapCommandMap

```
public class MailcapCommandMap
```

extends *javax.activation.***CommandMap**

MailcapCommandMap extends the *javax.activation.***CommandMap** class to create a map that conforms to the mailcap specification as laid down in RFC 1524. All the non-constructor methods except **addMailcap** override those laid out in **CommandMap**.

Constructor Methods

public	MailcapCommandMap	();
public	MailcapCommandMap	(*java.io.InputStream* is);
public	MailcapCommandMap	(*java.lang.String* fileName)
throws	*java.io.IOException*;	

Methods

public void	addMailcap	(*java.lang.String* mail_cap);
public **DataContentHandler**	createDataContentHandler	(*java.lang.String* mimeType);
public **CommandInfo**[ ]	getAllCommands	(*java.lang.String* mimeType);
public **CommandInfo**	getCommand	(*java.lang.String* mimeType, *java.lang.String* cmdName);
public **CommandInfo**[ ]	getPreferredCommands	(*java.lang.String* mimeType);

Class javax.activation.MimeType

```
public class MimeType
```

implements java.io.*Externalizable*

MimeType represents a Multipurpose Internet Mail Extension (MIME) type, as defined in RFCs 2045 and 2046.

Constructor Methods

public	MimeType	();
public	MimeType	(*java.lang.String* rawdata)
	throws	*javax.activation.***MimeTypeParseException**;
public	MimeType	(*java.lang.String* primary, *java.lang.String* sub)
	throws	*javax.activation.***MimeTypeParseException**;

Methods

public *java.lang.String*	getBaseType	();
public *java.lang.string*	getParameter	(*java.lang.String* name);
public **MimeTypeParameterList**	getParameters	();
public *java.lang.String*	getPrimaryType	();
public *java.lang.String*	getSubType	();
public boolean	match	(*java.lang.String* rawdata)
	throws	*javax.activation.***MimeTypeParseException**;
public boolean	match	(*javax.activation.***MimeType** type);
public void	readExternal	(*java.io.ObjectInput* in)
	throws	*java.io.IOException,* *java.lang.ClassNotFoundException*;
public void	removeParameter	(*java.lang.String* name);
public void	setParameter	(*java.lang.String* name, *java.lang.String* value);
public void	setPrimaryType	(*java.lang.String* primary)
	throws	*javax.activation.***MimeTypeParseException**;
public void	setSubType	(*java.lang.String* sub)
	throws	*javax.activation.***MimeTypeParseException**;
public *java.lang.String*	toString	();
public void	writeExternal	(*java.io.ObjectOutput* out)
	throws	*java.io.IOException*;

Inherited from java.lang.object
```
clone, equals, finalize, getClass, hashCode, notify, notifyAll, wait, wait, wait
```

Class javax.activation.MimeTypeParameterList

```
public class MimeTypeParameterList
```

Represents the parameter list of a Mime type as specified in RFCs 2045 and 2046. The Primary type of the object must already be stripped off.

Constructor Methods

public	MimeTypeParameterList	();
public	MimeTypeParameterList	(*java.lang.String* parameterList)
	throws	*javax.activation.***MimeTypeParseException**;

Methods

public boolean	isEmpty	();
public *java.util.Enumeration*	getNames	();
public *java.lang.string*	get	(*java.lang.String* name);
public void	remove	(*java.lang.String* name);
public void	set	(*java.lang.String* name,
		java.lang.String value);
public int	size	();
protected void	parse	(*java.lang.String* parameterList)
	throws	*javax.activation.***MimeTypeParseException**;
public *java.lang.String*	toString	();

Inherited from *java.lang.object*
clone, equals, finalize, getClass, hashCode, notify, notifyAll, wait, wait, wait

Class javax.activation.MimetypesFileTypeMap

public class MimetypesFileTypeMap

extends *javax.activation.***FileTypeMap**

MimetypesFileTypeMap provides a file typing system by checking a file's extension against available Mime type lists. It uses the **.mime.types** format.

Constructor Methods

public	MimetypesFileTypeMap	();
public	MimetypesFileTypeMap	(*java.lang.String* mimeTypeFileName)
	throws	*java.io.IOException*;
public	MimetypesFileTypeMap	(*java.io.InputStream* is);

Methods

public void	addMimeTypes	(*java.lang.String* mime_types);
public *java.lang.String*	getContentType	(*java.io.File* f);
public *java.lang.String*	getContentType	(*java.lang.String* filename);

Inherited from *javax.activation.***FileTypeMap**
getDefaultFileTypeMap, setDefaultFileTypeMap

Inherited from *java.lang.object*
clone, equals, finalize, getClass, hashCode, notify, notifyAll, toString, wait, wait, wait

Class javax.activation.URLDataSource

public class URLDataSource

implements *javax.activation.***DataSource**

If a data source is specified by a URL, **URLDataSource** provides an object to wrap that URL in a **DataSource** interface. NB: The **DataHandler** object creates a **URLDataSource** internally, when it is constructed with a URL.

Constructor Method

public	URLDataSource	(*java.net.URL* url);

Methods

public *java.lang.String*	getContentType	();
public *java.io.InputStream*	getInputStream	()
throws	*java.io.IOException*;	
public *java.lang.String*	getName	();
public *java.io.OutputStream*	getOutputStream	()
throws	*java.io.IOException*;	
public *java.net.URL*	getURL	();

Inherited from *java.lang.object*

```
clone, equals, finalize, getClass, hashCode, notify, notifyAll, toString, wait,
wait, wait
```

Class javax.activation.MimeTypeParseException

```
public class MimeTypeParseException
```

extends *java.lang.Exception*

An exception class to cover MimeType parsing related exceptions.

Constructor Methods

public	MimeTypeParseException	();
public	MimeTypeParseException	(*java.lang.String* s);

Methods

Inherited from java.lang.Throwable

```
fillInStackTrace, getLocalizedMessage, getMessage, printStackTrace,
printStackTrace, printStackTrace, toString
```

Inherited from *java.lang.object*

```
clone, equals, finalize, getClass, hashCode, notify, notifyAll, wait, wait, wait
```

Class javax.activation.UnsupportedDataTypeException

```
public class UnsupportedDataTypeException
```

extends *java.io.IOException*

An exception class signalling that the requested operation does not support the requested data type.

Constructor Methods

public	UnsupportedDataTypeException	();
public	UnsupportedDataTypeException	(*java.lang.String* s);

Methods

Inherited from java.lang.Throwable

```
fillInStackTrace, getLocalizedMessage, getMessage, printStackTrace,
printStackTrace, printStackTrace, toString
```

Inherited from *java.lang.object*

```
clone, equals, finalize, getClass, hashCode, notify, notifyAll, wait, wait, wait
```

Package javax.mail

javax.mail implements the JavaMail standard extension and contains the high-level classes and interfaces necessary for working with electronic mail.

Interfaces

public abstract interface	**MessageAware**;		
public abstract interface	**MultipartDataSource**	extends	*javax.activation.***DataSource**;
public abstract interface	**Part**;		
public abstract interface	**UIDFolder**;		

Classes

public abstract class	**Address** ;		
public abstract class	**Authenticator** ;		
public abstract class	**BodyPart**	implements	*javax.mail.***Part**;
public class	**FetchProfile**;		
public static class	**FetchProfile.Item**;		
public class	**Flags**	implements	*java.lang.Cloneable*;
public static final class	**Flags.Flag**;		
public abstract class	**Folder**;		
public class	**Header**;		
public abstract class	**Message**	implements	*javax.mail.***Part**;
public static class	**Message.RecipientType**;		
public class	**MessageContext**;		
public abstract class	**Multipart**;		
public final class	**PasswordAuthentication**;		
public class	**Provider**;		
public static class	**Provider.Type**;		
public abstract class	**Service**;		
public abstract class	**Store**	extends	*javax.mail.***Service**;
public abstract class	**Transport**	extends	*javax.mail.***Service**;
public final class	**Session**;		
public static class	**UIDFolder.FetchProfileItem**	extends	*javax.mail.***FetchProfile.Item**;
public class	**URLName**;		

Exceptions

public class	**AuthenticationFailedException**	extends	*javax.mail.***MessagingException** ;
public class	**FolderClosedException**	extends	*javax.mail.***MessagingException** ;
public class	**FolderNotFoundException**	extends	*javax.mail.***MessagingException** ;
public class	**IllegalWriteException**	extends	*javax.mail.***MessagingException** ;
public class	**MessageRemovedException**	extends	*javax.mail.***MessagingException** ;
public class	**MessagingException**	extends	*java.lang.Exception*;
public class	**MethodNotSupportedException**	extends	*javax.mail.***MessagingException** ;
public class	**NoSuchProviderException**	extends	*javax.mail.***MessagingException** ;
public class	**SendFailedException**	extends	*javax.mail.***MessagingException** ;
public class	**StoreClosedException**	extends	*javax.mail.***MessagingException** ;

Interface javax.mail.MessageAware

```
public abstract interface MessageAware
```

Is implemented by javax.mail.**MimePartDataSource**. Supplies information to a (*javax.activation.*)**DataContentHandler** about the message context in which the data content object is running.

Methods

public abstract **MessageContext**	getMessageContext	();

Interface javax.mail.MultipartDataSource

`public abstract interface MultipartDataSource`

extends *javax.activation.***DataSource**

MultipartDataSource acts as the interface to data sources such as mail messages which have multiple body parts to them. It contains the appropriate methods to access the individual body parts.

Methods

public **BodyPart**	getBodyPart	(int index)
	throws	*javax.mail.***MessagingException**;
public int	getCount	();

Inherited from *javax.activation.***DataSource**
`getContentType, getInputStream, getName, getOutputStream`

Interface javax.mail.Part

`public abstract interface Part`

Is extended by *javax.mail.internet.MimePart.* Is implemented by *javax.mail.***BodyPart** and *javax.mail.***Message**. Part is the common base interface for Messages and BodyParts.

Methods

public void	addHeader	(*java.lang.* header_name, *java.lang.String* header_value)
	throws	*javax.mail.***MessagingException**;
public *java.util.Enumeration*	getAllHeaders	()
	throws	*javax.mail.***MessagingException**;
public *java.lang.*Object	getContent	()
	throws	*java.io.IOException,*
		*javax.mail.***MessagingException**;
public *java.lang.String*	getContentType	()
	throws	*javax.mail.***MessagingException**;
public **DataHandler**	getDataHandler	()
	throws	*javax.mail.***MessagingException**;
public *java.lang.String*	getDescription	()
	throws	*javax.mail.***MessagingException**;
public *java.lang.String*	getDisposition	()
	throws	*javax.mail.***MessagingException**;
public *java.lang.String*	getFileName	()
	throws	*javax.mail.***MessagingException**;
public *java.io.InputStream*	getInputStream	()
	throws	*java.io.IOException,*
		*javax.mail.***MessagingException**;
public int	getLineCount	()
	throws	*javax.mail.***MessagingException**;
public *java.lang.String*[ ]	getHeader	(*java.lang.String* header_name)
	throws	*javax.mail.***MessagingException**;
public *java.util.Enumeration*	getMatchingHeaders	(*java.lang.String*[ ] header_names)
	throws	*javax.mail.***MessagingException**;
public *java.util.Enumeration*	getNonMatchingHeaders	(*java.lang.String*[ ] header_names)
	throws	*javax.mail.***MessagingException**;

public int	**getSize**	()
	throws	*javax.mail.***MessagingException**;
public boolean	**isMimeType**	(*java.lang.String* mimeType)
	throws	*javax.mail.***MessagingException**;
public void	**removeHeader**	(*java.lang.String* header_name)
	throws	*javax.mail.***MessagingException**;
public void	**setContent**	(*javax.mail.***Multipart** mp)
	throws	*javax.mail.***MessagingException**;
public void	**setContent**	(*java.lang.Object* obj,
		java.lang.String type)
	throws	*javax.mail.***MessagingException**;
public void	**setDataHandler**	(*javax.activation.***DataHandler** dh)
	throws	*javax.mail.***MessagingException**;
public void	**setDescription**	(*java.lang.String* description)
	throws	*javax.mail.***MessagingException**;
public void	**setDisposition**	(*java.lang.String* disposition)
	throws	*javax.mail.***MessagingException**;
public void	**setFileName**	(*java.lang.String* filename)
	throws	*javax.mail.***MessagingException**;
public void	**setHeader**	(*java.lang.String* header_name,
		java.lang.String header_value)
	throws	*javax.mail.***MessagingException**;
public void	**setText**	(*java.lang.String* text)
	throws	*javax.mail.***MessagingException**;
public void	**writeTo**	(java.io.OutputStream os)
	throws	*java.io.IOException*,
		*javax.mail.***MessagingException**;

Fields

| public static final *java.lang.String* | **ATTACHMENT**; |
| public static final *java.lang.String* | **INLINE**; |

Interface javax.mail.UIDFolder

```
public abstract interface UIDFolder
```

UIDFolder is implemented by (mail) folders that can operate 'offline' - disconnected from the mail server. It does this by providing unique IDs for messages in the folder.

Inner Class

| public static class | **UIDFolder.FetchProfileItem** | extends | **FetchProfile.Item** ; |

Methods

public **Message**	**getMessageByUID**	(long uid)
	throws	*javax.mail.***MessagingException**;
public **Message[ ]**	**getMessagesByUID**	(long[ ] uids)
	throws	*javax.mail.***MessagingException**;
public **Message[ ]**	**getMessagesByUID**	(long start,
		long end)
	throws	*javax.mail.***MessagingException**;
public long	**getUID**	(*javax.mail.***Message** message)
	throws	*javax.mail.***MessagingException**;
public long	**getUIDValidity**	()
	throws	*javax.mail.***MessagingException**;

Field

| public static final long | **LASTUID**; |

Class Javax.mall.Address

```
public abstract class Address
```

Is extended by *javax.mail.internet.InternetAddress* and *javax.mail.internet.NewsAddress*. Represents the addresses in the message. Its subclasses provide specific implementations.

Constructor Method

public	Address	();

Methods

public abstract *java.lang.String*	getType	();
public abstract boolean	equals	(*java.lang.Object* address);
public abstract *java.lang.String*	toString	();

Inherited from *java.lang.object*
clone, finalize, getClass, hashCode, notify, notifyAll, wait, wait, wait

Class javax.mall.Authenticator

Represents the (method of obtaining) authentication required for a network connection.

Constructor Method

public	Authenticator	();

Methods

protected final *java.lang.String*	getDefaultUserName	();
protected **PasswordAuthentication**	getPasswordAuthentication	();
protected final int	getRequestingPort	();
protected final *java.lang.String*	getRequestingPrompt	();
protected final *java.lang.String*	getRequestingProtocol	();
protected final *java.net.InetAddress*	getRequestingSite	();

Inherited from *java.lang.object*
clone, equals, finalize, getClass, hashCode, notify, notifyAll, toString, wait, wait, wait

Class javax.mall.BodyPart

```
public abstract class BodyPart
```

```
implements javax.mail.Part
```

Is extended by *javax.mail.internet.MimeBodyPart.* This class models a message part within a MultiPart message. Subclasses of this abstract class provide the actual implementations.

Constructor Method

public	BodyPart	();

Methods

public **Multipart**   `getParent`   `();`

Inherited from *java.lang.object*
```
clone, equals, finalize, getClass, hashCode, notify, notifyAll, toString, wait,
wait, wait
```

Fields

protected **Multipart**   `parent;`

Class javax.mail.FetchProfile

```
public class FetchProfile
```

Used to list the (*javax.mail.*)**Message** attributes that clients wish to prefetch before downloading the full message.

Inner Class

public static class   **FetchProfile.Item**;

Constructor Method

public   `FetchProfile`   `();`

Methods

public void	`add`	(*java.lang.String* headerName);
public void	`add`	(*javax.mail.***FetchProfile.Item** item);
public boolean	`contains`	(*java.lang.String* headerName);
public boolean	`contains`	(*javax.mail.***FetchProfile.Item** item);
public *java.lang.String*[ ]	`getHeaderNames`	();
public **FetchProfile.Item**[ ]	`getItems`	();

Inherited from *java.lang.object*
```
clone, equals, finalize, getClass, hashCode, notify, notifyAll, toString, wait,
wait, wait
```

Class javax.mail.FetchProfile.Item

```
public static class FetchProfile.Item
```

This inner class is the base class of all items that can be requested in a **FetchProfile**. The items currently defined here are **ENVELOPE**, **CONTENT_INFO** and **FLAGS**. The **UIDFolder** interface defines the UID Item as well. Note that this class only has a protected constructor, thereby restricting new Item types to either this class or subclasses. This effectively implements an enumeration of allowed Item types.

Constructor Method

protected   `FetchProfile.Item`   (*java.lang.String* name);

Methods

Inherited from *java.lang.object*
```
clone, equals, finalize, getClass, hashCode, notify, notifyAll, toString, wait,
wait, wait
```

Fields

public final static **FetchProfile.Item**	CONTENT_INFO;	
public final static **FetchProfile.Item**	ENVELOPE;	
public final static **FetchProfile.Item**	FLAGS;	

Class javax.mail.Flags

```
public class Flags
```

implements *java.lang.Cloneable*

Represents the set of flags on a Message.

Inner Class

public static final class	**Flags.Flag**

Constructor Methods

public	**Flags**	();
public	**Flags**	(*javax.mail.***Flags.Flag** flag);
public	**Flags**	(*java.lang.String* flag);
public	**Flags**	(*javax.mail.***Flags** flags);

Methods

public void	**add**	(*javax.mail.***Flags.Flag** flag);
public void	**add**	(*java.lang.String* flag);
public void	**add**	(*javax.mail.***Flags** flags);
public *java.lang.Object*	**clone**	();
public boolean	**contains**	(*javax.mail.***Flags.Flag** flag);
public boolean	**contains**	(*java.lang.String* flag);
public boolean	**contains**	(*javax.mail.***Flags** flags);
public boolean	**equals**	(*java.lang.Object* obj);
public **Flags.Flag**[ ]	**getSystemFlags**	();
public *java.lang.String*[ ]	**getUserFlags**	();
public int	**hashCode**	();
public void	**remove**	(*javax.mail.***Flags.Flag** flag);
public void	**remove**	(*java.lang.String* flag);
public void	**remove**	(*javax.mail.***Flags** flags);

Inherited from *java.lang.object*
```
finalize, getClass, notify, notifyAll, toString, wait, wait, wait
```

Class javax.mail.Flags.Flag

```
public static final class Flags.Flag
```

This inner class represents the set of predefined standard system flags.

Methods

Inherited from *java.lang.object*
```
clone, equals, finalize, getClass, hashCode, notify, notifyAll, toString, wait,
wait, wait
```

Fields

public final static **Flags.Flag**	ANSWERED;	
public final static **Flags.Flag**	DELETED;	
public final static **Flags.Flag**	DRAFT;	
public final static **Flags.Flag**	FLAGGED;	
public final static **Flags.Flag**	RECENT;	
public final static **Flags.Flag**	SEEN;	
public final static **Flags.Flag**	USER;	

Class javax.mail.Folder

```
public abstract class Folder
```

Represents a mail folder (in an information store). Subclasses of Folder represent protocol specific folders.

Constructor Method

protected	**Folder**	(*javax.mail*.**Store** store);

Methods

public void	**addConnectionListener**	(*javax.mail.event.ConnectionListener* l);
public void	**addFolderListener**	(*javax.mail.event.FolderListener* l);
public void	**addMessageChangedListener**	(*javax.mail.event.MessageChangedListener* l);
public void	**addMessageCountListener**	(*javax.mail.event.MessageCountListener* l);
public abstract void	**appendMessages**	(*javax.mail*.**Message**[ ] msgs)
	throws	*javax.mail*.**MessagingException**;
public abstract void	**close**	(boolean expunge)
	throws	*javax.mail*.**MessagingException**;
public void	**copyMessages**	(*javax.mail*.**Message**[ ] msgs,
		javax.mail.**Folder** folder)
	throws	*javax.mail*.**MessagingException**;
public abstract boolean	**create**	(int type)
	throws	*javax.mail*.**MessagingException**;
public abstract boolean	**delete**	(boolean recurse)
	throws	*javax.mail*.**MessagingException**;
public abstract boolean	**exists**	()
	throws	*javax.mail*.**MessagingException**;
public abstract **Message**[ ]	**expunge**	()
	throws	*javax.mail*.**MessagingException**;
public void	**fetch**	(*javax.mail*. **Message**[ ] msgs,
		javax.mail.**FetchProfile** fp)
	throws	*javax.mail*.**MessagingException**;
protected void	**finalize**	()
	throws	*java.lang.Throwable*;
public abstract **Folder**	**getFolder**	(*java.lang.String* name)
	throws	*javax.mail*.**MessagingException**;
public abstract *java.lang.String*	**getFullName**	();
public abstract Message	**getMessage**	(int msgnum)
	throws	*javax.mail*.**MessagingException**;
public abstract int	**getMessageCount**	()
	throws	*javax.mail*.**MessagingException**;
public **Message**[ ]	**getMessages**	()
	throws	*javax.mail*.**MessagingException**;
public **Message**[ ]	**getMessages**	(int[ ] msgnums)
	throws	*javax.mail*.**MessagingException**;
public **Message**[ ]	**getMessages**	(int start,
		int end)
	throws	*javax.mail*.**MessagingException**;
public int	**getMode**	();
public abstract *java.lang.String*	**getName**	();
public int	**getNewMessageCount**	()
	throws	*javax.mail*.**MessagingException**;
public abstract **Folder**	**getParent**	()
	throws	*javax.mail*.**MessagingException**;

public abstract **Flags**	getPermanentFlags	();
public abstract char	getSeparator	()
	throws	*javax.mail.***MessagingException**;
public **Store**	getStore	();
public abstract int	getType	()
	throws	*javax.mail.***MessagingException**;
public int	getUnreadMessageCount	()
	throws	*javax.mail.***MessagingException**;
public **URLName**	getURLName	()
	throws	*javax.mail.***MessagingException**;
public abstract boolean	hasNewMessages	()
	throws	*javax.mail.***MessagingException**;
public abstract boolean	isOpen	();
public boolean	isSubscribed	();
public **Folder**[ ]	list	()
	throws	*javax.mail.***MessagingException**;
public abstract **Folder**[ ]	list	(*java.lang.String* pattern)
	throws	*javax.mail.***MessagingException**;
public **Folder**[ ]	listSubscribed	()
	throws	*javax.mail.***MessagingException**;
public **Folder**[ ]	listSubscribed	(*java.lang.String* pattern)
	throws	*javax.mail.***MessagingException**;
protected void	notifyConnectionListeners	(int type);
protected void	notifyFolderListeners	(int type);
protected void	notifyFolderRenamedListeners	(*javax.mail.***Folder** folder);
protected void	notifyMessageAddedListeners	(*javax.mail.***Message**[ ] msgs);
protected void	notifyMessageChangedListeners	(int type,
		*javax.mail.***Message** msg);
protected void	notifyMessageRemovedListeners	(boolean removed,
		*javax.mail.***Message**[ ] msgs);
public abstract void	open	(int mode)
	throws	*javax.mail.***MessagingException**;
public void	removeConnectionListener	(*javax.mail.event.ConnectionListener* l);
public void	removeFolderListener	(*javax.mail.event.FolderListener* l);
public void	removeMessageChangedListener	(*javax.mail.event.MessageChangedListener* l);
public void	removeMessageCountListener	(*javax.mail.event.MessageCountListener* l);
public abstract boolean	renameTo	(*javax.mail.***Folder** f)
	throws	*javax.mail.***MessagingException**;
public **Message**[ ]	search	(*javax.mail.search.SearchTerm* term)
throws	*javax.mail.***MessagingException**;	
public **Message**[ ]	search	(*javax.mail.search.SearchTerm* term,
		*javax.mail.***Message**[ ] msgs)
	throws	*javax.mail.***MessagingException**;
public void	setFlags	(*javax.mail.***Message**[ ] msgs,
		*javax.mail.***Flags** flag,
		boolean value)
	throws	*javax.mail.***MessagingException**;
public void	setFlags	(int[ ] msgnums,
		*javax.mail.***Flags** flag,
		boolean value)
	throws	*javax.mail.***MessagingException**;
public void	setFlags	(int start,
		int end,
		*javax.mail.***Flags** flag,
		boolean value)
	throws	*javax.mail.***MessagingException**;
public void	setSubscribed	(boolean subscribe)
	throws	*javax.mail.***MessagingException**;
public *java.lang.String*	toString	();

Inherited from *java.lang.object*
clone, equals, getClass, hashCode, notify, notifyAll, wait, wait, wait

Fields

public final static int	HOLDS_FOLDERS;
public final static int	HOLDS_MESSAGES;
public final static int	READ_ONLY;
public final static int	READ_WRITE;
protected int	mode;
protected **Store**	store;

Class javax.mail.Header

```
public class Header
```

Represents a mail header as a name - value pair.

Constructor Method

public	**Header**	(*java.lang.string* name, *java.lang.string* value);

Methods

public *java.lang.String*	getName	();
public *java.lang.String*	getValue	();

Inherited from *java.lang.object*
```
clone, equals, finalize, getClass, hashCode, notify, notifyAll, toString, wait,
wait, wait
```

Class javax.mail.Message

```
public abstract class Message
```

implements *javax.mail.***Part**

Is extended by *javax.mail.***MimeMessage**. This abstract class represents an email message. Its subclasses represent actual types of message.

Inner Class

public static final class	**Message.RecipientType**

Constructor Methods

protected	**Message**	();
protected	**Message**	(*javax.mail.***Session** session);
protected	**Message**	(*javax.mail.***Folder** folder, int msgnum);

Methods

public abstract void	**addFrom**	(*javax.mail.Address*[ ] addresses)
	throws	*javax.mail.***MessagingException**;
public void	**addRecipient**	(*javax.mail.***Message.RecipientType** type, *javax.mail.***Address** addresses)
	throws	*javax.mail.***MessagingException**;
public abstract void	**addRecipients**	(*javax.mail.***Message.RecipientType** type, *javax.mail.***Address**[ ] addresses)
	throws	*javax.mail.***MessagingException**;
public **Address**[ ]	**getAllRecipients**	()
	throws	*javax.mail.***MessagingException**;
public abstract **Flags**	**getFlags**	()

public **Folder**	getFolder	();
public abstract **Address**[ ]	getFrom	()
	throws	*javax.mail*.**MessagingException**;
public int	getMessageNumber	();
public abstract *java.util.Date*	getReceivedDate	()
	throws	*javax.mail*.**MessagingException**;
public abstract **Address**[ ]	getRecipients	(*javax.mail*.**Message.RecipientType** type)
	throws	*javax.mail*.**MessagingException**;
public **Address**[ ]	getReplyTo	()
	throws	*javax.mail*.**MessagingException**;
public abstract *java.util.Date*	getSentDate	()
	throws	*javax.mail*.**MessagingException**;
public abstract *java.lang.String*	getSubject	()
	throws	*javax.mail*.**MessagingException**;
public boolean	isExpunged	();
public boolean	isSet	(*javax.mail*.**Flags.Flag** flag)
	throws	*javax.mail*.**MessagingException**;
public boolean	match	(*javax.mail.search.SearchTerm* term)
	throws	*javax.mail*.**MessagingException**;
public abstract **Message**	reply	(boolean replyToAll)
	throws	*javax.mail*.**MessagingException**;
public abstract void	saveChanges	()
	throws	*javax.mail*.**MessagingException**;
protected void	setExpunged	(boolean expunged);
public void	setFlag	(*javax.mail*.**Flags.Flag** flag, boolean set)
	throws	*javax.mail*.**MessagingException**;
public abstract void	setFlags	(*javax.mail*.**Flags** flag, boolean set)
	throws	*javax.mail*.**MessagingException**;
public abstract void	setFrom	()
	throws	*javax.mail*.**MessagingException**;
public abstract void	setFrom	(*javax.mail*.**Address** address)
	throws	*javax.mail*.**MessagingException**;
protected void	setMessageNumber	(int msgnum);
public void	setReplyTo	(*javax.mail*.**Address**[ ] addresses)
	throws	*javax.mail*.**MessagingException**;
public abstract void	setSentDate	(*java.util.Date* date)
	throws	*javax.mail*.**MessagingException**;
public abstract void	setSubject	(*java.lang.String* subject)
	throws	*javax.mail*.**MessagingException**;
public void	setRecipient	(*javax.mail*.**Message.RecipientType** type, *javax.mail*.**Address** addresses)
	throws	*javax.mail*.**MessagingException**;
public abstract void	setRecipients	(*javax.mail*.**Message.RecipientType** type, *javax.mail*.**Address**[ ] addresses)
	throws	*javax.mail*.**MessagingException**;

Inherited from *java.lang.object*
```
clone, equals, finalize, getClass, hashCode, notify, notifyAll, toString, wait,
wait, wait
```

Fields

protected boolean	expunged;
protected **Folder**	folder;
protected int	msgnum;
protected **Session**	session;

631

Class javax.mail.Message.RecipientType

```
public abstract class Message.RecipientType
```

Is extended by javax.mail.internet.*MimeMessage.RecipientType*. Defines the recipient fields allowed by the Message class.

Constructor Methods

protected	`Message.RecipientType`	(*java.lang.String* type);

Methods

Inherited from *java.lang.object*
`clone, equals, finalize, getClass, hashCode, notify, notifyAll, toString, wait, wait, wait`

Fields

public final static **Message.RecipientType**	`BCC;`
public final static **Message.RecipientType**	`CC;`
public final static **Message.RecipientType**	`TO;`
protected *java.lang.String*	`type;`

Class javax.mail.MessageContext

```
public class MessageContext
```

Represents the context under which a piece of Message content, regarded as a data source, is being kept. For example, which part of the message, which session, etc.

Constructor Methods

public	`MessageContext`	(*javax.mail.***Part** part);

Methods

public **Message**	`getMessage`	`();`
public **Part**	`getPart`	`();`
public **Session**	`getSession`	`();`

Inherited from *java.lang.object*
`clone, equals, finalize, getClass, hashCode, notify, notifyAll, toString, wait, wait, wait`

Class javax.mail.Multipart

```
public abstract class Multipart
```

Is extended by *javax.mail.internet.MimeMultipart.* Represents a many-parted body of a message.

Constructor Method

protected	`Multipart`	`();`

Methods

public void	**addBodyPart**	(*javax.mail.***BodyPart** part)
	throws	*javax.mail.***MessagingException**;
public void	**addBodyPart**	(*javax.mail.***BodyPart** part,
		int index)
	throws	*javax.mail.***MessagingException**;
public **BodyPart**	**getBodyPart**	(int index)
	throws	*javax.mail.***MessagingException**;
public *java.lang.String*	**getContentType**	();
public int	**getCount**	()
	throws	*javax.mail.***MessagingException**;
public **Part**	**getParent**	();
public boolean	**removeBodyPart**	(*javax.mail.***BodyPart** part)
	throws	*javax.mail.***MessagingException**;
public void	**removeBodyPart**	(int index)
	throws	*javax.mail.***MessagingException**;
protected void	**setMultipartDataSource**	(*javax.mail.***MultipartDataSource** mp)
	throws	*javax.mail.***MessagingException**;
public void	**setParent**	(*javax.mail.***Part** parent);
public abstract void	**writeTo**	(*java.io.OutputStream* os)
	throws	*java.io.IOException*,
		*javax.mail.***MessagingException**;

Inherited from *java.lang.object*
```
clone, equals, finalize, getClass, hashCode, notify, notifyAll, toString, wait,
wait, wait
```

Fields

protected *java.lang.String*	**contentType**;
protected **Part**	**parent**;
protected java.util.Vector	**parts**;

Class javax.mail.PasswordAuthentication

```
public final class PasswordAuthentication
```

Holds for a password and user id for use by *javax.mail.***Authenticator**

Constructor Method

public	**PasswordAuthentication**	(*java.lang.String* userName,
		java.lang.String password);

Methods

public *java.lang.String*	**getPassword**	();
public *java.lang.String*	**getUserName**	();

Inherited from *java.lang.object*
```
clone, equals, finalize, getClass, hashCode, notify, notifyAll, toString, wait,
wait, wait
```

Class javax.mail.Provider

```
public class Provider
```

Describes the implementation of a protocol. It uses the values given in the *javamail.providers* and *javamail.default.providers* resource files.

633

Inner Class

public static class	**Provider.Type**	

Methods

public *java.lang.String*	getClassName	();
public *java.lang.String*	getProtocol	();
public **Provider.Type**	getType	();
public *java.lang.String*	getVendor	();
public *java.lang.String*	getVersion	();
public *java.lang.String*	toString	();

Class javax.mail.Provider.Type

```
public static class Provider.Type
```

Defines the type of protocol being implemented. Currently, this is limited to either **STORE** or **TRANSPORT**.

Methods

Inherited from *java.lang.object*
clone, equals, finalize, getClass, hashCode, notify, notifyAll, toString, wait, wait, wait

Fields

public static final **Provider.Type**	STORE;
public static final **Provider.Type**	TRANSPORT;

Class javax.mail.Service

```
public abstract class Service
```

Is extended by *javax.mail.***Store** and *javax.mail.***Transport**. Abstract class holding the standard functionality common to messaging systems.

Constructor Method

protected	Service	(*javax.mail.*Session, *javax.mail.*URLName urlname);

Methods

public void	addConnectionListener	(*javax.mail.event.ConnectionListener* l);
public void	close	()
	throws	*javax.mail.*MessagingException;
public void	connect	()
	throws	*javax.mail.*MessagingException;
public void	connect	(*java.lang.String* host, *java.lang.string* user, *java.lang.string* password)
	throws	*javax.mail.*MessagingException;
public void	connect	(*java.lang.String* host, int port, *java.lang.string* user, *java.lang.string* password)
	throws	*javax.mail.*MessagingException;
protected void	finalize	()
	throws	*java.lang.Throwable*;

public **URLName**	getURLName	();
public boolean	isConnected	();
protected void	notifyConnectionListeners	(int type);
protected boolean	protocolConnect	(*java.lang.String* host,
		int port,
		java.lang.string user,
		java.lang.string password)
	throws	*javax.mail.***MessagingException**;
protected void	queueEvent	(*javax.mail.event.MailEvent* event,
		java.util.Vector vector);
public void	removeConnectionListener	(*javax.mail.event.ConnectionListener* l);
protected void	setConnected	(boolean connected);
protected void	setURLName	(*javax.mail.***URLName** url);
public *java.lang.String*	toString	();

Inherited from *java.lang.object*

```
clone, equals, getClass, hashCode, notify, notifyAll, wait, wait, wait
```

Fields

protected boolean	debug;
protected **Session**	session;
protected **URLName**	url;

Class *javax.mail.Session*

```
public final class Session
```

Represents a mail session which can be shared among many applications. Holds settings and defaults as used by the mail APIs.

Methods

public boolean	getDebug	();
public static **Session**	getDefaultInstance	(*java.util.Properties* props,
		*javax.mail.***Authenticator** authenticator);
public static **Session**	getInstance	(*java.util.Properties* props,
		*javax.mail.***Authenticator** authenticator);
public **Folder**	getFolder	(*javax.mail.***URLName** url)
	throws	*javax.mail.***MessagingException**;
public **PasswordAuthentication**	getPasswordAuthentication	(*javax.mail.***URLName** url);
public *java.util.Properties*	getProperties	();
public *java.lang.string*	getProperty	(*java.lang.string* name);
public **Provider**	getProvider	(*java.lang.String* protocol)
	throws	*javax.mail.***NoSuchProviderException**;
public **Provider**[ ]	getProviders	();
public **Store**	getStore	()
	throws	*javax.mail.***NoSuchProviderException**;
public **Store**	getStore	(*javax.mail.***Provider** provider)
	throws	*javax.mail.***NoSuchProviderException**;
public **Store**	getStore	(*java.lang.String* protocol)
	throws	*javax.mail.***NoSuchProviderException**;
public **Store**	getStore	(*javax.mail.***URLName** url)
	throws	*javax.mail.***NoSuchProviderException**;
public **Transport**	getTransport	()
	throws	*javax.mail.***NoSuchProviderException**;
public **Transport**	getTransport	(*javax.mail.***Provider** provider)
	throws	*javax.mail.***NoSuchProviderException**;
public **Transport**	getTransport	(*javax.mail.Address* address)
	throws	*javax.mail.***NoSuchProviderException**;
public **Transport**	getTransport	(*javax.mail.***URLName** url)
	throws	*javax.mail.***NoSuchProviderException**;

public **Transport**	getTransport	(*java.lang.String* protocol)
	throws	*java.mail.***NoSuchProviderException**;
public **PasswordAuthentication**	requestPasswordAuthentication	(*java.net.InetAddress* addr,
		int port,
		java.lang.string protocol,
		java.lang.string prompt,
		java.lang.String defaultUserName);
public void	setDebug	(boolean debug);
public void	setProvider	(*javax.mail.***Provider** provider)
	throws	*javax.mail.***NoSuchProviderException**;
public void	setPasswordAuthentication	(*javax.mail.***URLName** url,
		*javax.mail.***PasswordAuthentication** pw);

Inherited from *java.lang.object*
clone, equals, finalize, getClass, hashCode, notify, notifyAll, toString, wait, wait, wait

Class javax.mail.Store

```
public abstract class Store
```

extends *javax.mail.***Service**

Abstract class representing a message store. Actual implementations are covered by subclasses.

Constructor Method

protected	Store	(*javax.mail.***Session** session,
		*javax.mail.***URLName** urlname);

Methods

public void	addFolderListener	(*javax.mail.event.FolderListener* l);
public void	addStoreListener	(*javax.mail.event.StoreListener* l);
public abstract **Folder**	getDefaultFolder	()
	throws	*javax.mail.***MessagingException**;
public abstract **Folder**	getFolder	(*javax.mail.***URLName** url)
	throws	*javax.mail.***MessagingException**;
public abstract **Folder**	getFolder	(*java.lang.String* name)
	throws	*javax.mail.***MessagingException**;
protected void	notifyFolderListeners	(int type,
		*javax.mail.***Folder** folder);
protected void	notifyFolderRenamedListeners	(*javax.mail.***Folder** oldF,
		*javax.mail.***Folder** newF);
protected void	notifyStoreListeners	(int type,
		java.lang.string message);
public void	removeFolderListener	(*javax.mail.event.FolderListener* l);
public void	removeStoreListener	(*javax.mail.event.StoreListener* l);

Inherited from *javax.mail.***Service**
addConnectionListener, close, connect, connect, connect, finalize, getURLName, isConnected, notifyConnectionListeners, protocolConnect, queueEvent, removeConnectionListener, setConnected, setURLName, toString

Inherited from *java.lang.object*
clone, equals, getClass, hashCode, notify, notifyAll, wait, wait, wait

Fields

Inherited from *javax.mail.***Service**
debug, session, url

Class *javax.mail.Transport*

```
public abstract class Transport
```

extends *javax.mail.***Service**

Abstract class representing a message transport mechanism. Actual implementations are covered by subclasses.

Constructor Method

public	`Transport`	(*javax.mail.***Session** session, *javax.mail.***URLName** urlname);

Methods

public void	`addTransportListener`	(*javax.mail.event.TransportListener* l);
protected void	`notifyTransportListeners`	(int type, *javax.mail.***Address**[ ] validSent, *javax.mail.***Address**[ ] validUnsent, *javax.mail.***Address**[ ] invalid, *javax.mail.***Message** msg);
public static void	`send`	(*javax.mail.***Message** msg)
public static void	`send`	(*javax.mail.***Message** msg, *javax.mail.***Address**[ ] addresses)
	throws	*javax.mail.***MessagingException**;
public abstract void	`sendMessage`	(*javax.mail.***Message** msg, *javax.mail.***Address**[ ] addresses)
	throws	*javax.mail.***MessagingException**;
public void	`removeTransportListener`	(*javax.mail.event.TransportListener* l);

Inherited from *javax.mail.***Service**
```
addConnectionListener, close, connect, connect, connect, finalize, getURLName,
isConnected, notifyConnectionListeners, protocolConnect, queueEvent,
removeConnectionListener, setConnected, setURLName, toString
```

Inherited from *java.lang.object*
```
clone, equals, getClass, hashCode, notify, notifyAll, wait, wait, wait
```

Fields

Inherited from *javax.mail.***Service**
```
debug, session, url
```

Class *javax.mail.UIDFolder.FetchProfileItem*

```
public static class UIDFolder.FetchProfileItem
```

extends *javax.mail.***FetchProfile.Item**

An inner class of *javax.mail.***FetchProfile.Item,** this represents a way to add new FetchProfile.Item types specific to UIDFolders.

Constructor Method

protected	`UIDFolder.FetchProfileItem`	(*java.lang.String* name);

Methods

Inherited from *java.lang.object*
```
clone, equals, finalize, getClass, hashCode, notify, notifyAll, toString, wait,
wait, wait
```

Fields

public final static **UIDFolder.FetchProfileItem**
```
                       UID;
```

Inherited from *javax.mail.***FetchProfile.Item**
```
CONTENT_INFO, ENVELOPE, FLAGS
```

Class javax.mail.URLName

```
public class URLName
```

Represents a URL name and also provides the basic parsing functionality to parse most internet standard URL schemes.

Constructor Methods

public	URLName	(*java.net.URL* url);
public	URLName	(*java.lang.String* url);
public	URLName	(*java.lang.String* protocol,
		java.lang.string host,
		int port,
		java.lang.string file,
		java.lang.string username,
		java.lang.string password);

Methods

public boolean	equals	(*java.lang.Object* obj);
public *java.lang.String*	getFile	();
public *java.lang.String*	getHost	();
public *java.lang.String*	getPassword	();
public int	getPort	();
public *java.lang.String*	getProtocol	();
public *java.lang.String*	getRef	();
public *java.net.URL*	getURL	()
	throws	*java.net.MalformedURLException*;
public *java.lang.String*	getUsername	();
public int	hashCode	();
protected void	parseString	(*java.lang.String* url);
public *java.lang.String*	toString	();

Inherited from *java.lang.object*
```
clone, finalize, getClass, notify, notifyAll, wait, wait, wait
```

Fields

protected *java.lang.String*   `fullURL;`

Class javax.mail.AuthenticationFailedException

```
public class AuthenticationFailedException
```

extends *javax.mail.***MessagingException**

Represents the exception thrown when a user is not authenticated when connecting to a (*javax.mail.*)**Store** or (*javax.mail.*)**Transport** object.

Constructor Methods

public	AuthenticationFailedException	( );
public	AuthenticationFailedException	(*java.lang.String* message);

Methods

Inherited from *javax.mail.***MessagingException**
getMessage, getNextException, setNextException

Inherited from *java.lang.Throwable*
fillInStackTrace, getLocalizedMessage, printStackTrace, printStackTrace,
printStackTrace, toString

Inherited from *java.lang.object*
clone, equals, finalize, getClass, hashCode, notify, notifyAll, wait, wait, wait

Class *javax.mail.FolderClosedException*

public class FolderClosedException

extends *javax.mail.***MessagingException**

Represents the exception thrown when a method is run on a messaging object in a folder that has 'died' for some reason.

Constructor Methods

public	FolderClosedException	(*javax.mail.***Folder** folder);
public	FolderClosedException	(*javax.mail.***Folder** folder, *java.lang.String* message);

Methods

public **Folder**	getFolder	();

Inherited from *javax.mail.***MessagingException**
getMessage, getNextException, setNextException

Inherited from *java.lang.Throwable*
fillInStackTrace, getLocalizedMessage, printStackTrace, printStackTrace,
printStackTrace, toString

Inherited from *java.lang.object*
clone, equals, finalize, getClass, hashCode, notify, notifyAll, wait, wait, wait

Class *javax.mail.FolderNotFoundException*

public class FolderNotFoundException

extends *javax.mail.***MessagingException**

Represents the exception thrown when a method is run on a messaging object in a folder that does not exist.

639

Constructor Methods

| public | FolderNotFoundException | (); |
| public | FolderNotFoundException | (*java.lang.String* s, *javax.mail.***Folder** folder); |

Methods

| public **Folder** | getFolder | (); |

Inherited from *javax.mail.***MessagingException**
`getMessage, getNextException, setNextException`

Inherited from *java.lang.Throwable*
`fillInStackTrace, getLocalizedMessage, printStackTrace, printStackTrace, printStackTrace, toString`

Inherited from *java.lang.object*
`clone, equals, finalize, getClass, hashCode, notify, notifyAll, wait, wait, wait`

Class javax.mail.IllegalWriteException

`public class IllegalWriteException`

extends *javax.mail.***MessagingException**

Represents the exception thrown when a write method is called upon a read-only object.

Constructor Methods

| public | IllegalWriteException | (); |
| public | IllegalWriteException | (*java.lang.String* s); |

Methods

Inherited from *javax.mail.***MessagingException**
`getMessage, getNextException, setNextException`

Inherited from *java.lang.Throwable*
`fillInStackTrace, getLocalizedMessage, printStackTrace, printStackTrace, printStackTrace, toString`

Inherited from *java.lang.object*
`clone, equals, finalize, getClass, hashCode, notify, notifyAll, wait, wait, wait`

Class javax.mail.MessageRemovedException

`public class MessageRemovedException`

extends *javax.mail.***MessagingException**

Represents the exception thrown when an invalid method is called upon a message that has been removed.

Constructor Methods

| public | MessageRemovedException | (); |
| public | MessageRemovedException | (*java.lang.String* s); |

Methods

Inherited from *javax.mail*.**MessagingException**
`getMessage, getNextException, setNextException`

Inherited from *java.lang.Throwable*
`fillInStackTrace, getLocalizedMessage, printStackTrace, printStackTrace, printStackTrace, toString`

Inherited from *java.lang.object*
`clone, equals, finalize, getClass, hashCode, notify, notifyAll, wait, wait, wait`

Class javax.mail.MessagingException

`public class MessagingException`

Is extended by **AuthenticationFailedException, FolderClosedException, FolderNotFoundException, IllegalWriteException, MessageRemovedException, MethodNotSupportedException, NoSuchProviderException, ParseException, SearchException, SendFailedException, StoreClosedException.** This is the base class for all the other messaging exception classes in the **javax.mail** package.

Constructor Methods

public	`MessagingException`	();
public	`MessagingException`	(*java.lang.String* s);
public	`MessagingException`	(*java.lang.string* s, java.lang.Exception e);

Methods

public *java.lang.String*	`getMessage`	();
public *java.lang.Exception*	`getNextException`	();
public boolean	`setNextException`	(*java.lang.Exception* ex);

Inherited from *java.lang.Throwable*
`fillInStackTrace, getLocalizedMessage, printStackTrace, printStackTrace, printStackTrace, toString`

Inherited from *java.lang.object*
`clone, equals, finalize, getClass, hashCode, notify, notifyAll, wait, wait, wait`

Class javax.mail.MethodNotSupportedException

`public class MethodNotSupportedException`

extends *javax.mail*.**MessagingException**

Represents the exception thrown when a method is called that is not incorporated into the implementation.

Constructor Methods

public	`MethodNotSupportedException`	();
public	`MethodNotSupportedException`	(*java.lang.String* s);

Methods

Inherited from *javax.mail.***MessagingException**
`getMessage, getNextException, setNextException`

Inherited from *java.lang.Throwable*
`fillInStackTrace, getLocalizedMessage, printStackTrace, printStackTrace,`
`printStackTrace, toString`

Inherited from *java.lang.object*
`clone, equals, finalize, getClass, hashCode, notify, notifyAll, wait, wait, wait`

Class javax.mail.NoSuchProviderException

`public class NoSuchProviderException`

`extends` *javax.mail.***MessagingException**

Represents the exception thrown when a mail Session attempts to instantiate a Provider that has not been defined.

Constructor Methods

public	`NoSuchProviderException`	();
public	`NoSuchProviderException`	(*java.lang.String* message);

Methods

Inherited from *javax.mail.***MessagingException**
`getMessage, getNextException, setNextException`

Inherited from *java.lang.Throwable*
`fillInStackTrace, getLocalizedMessage, printStackTrace, printStackTrace,`
`printStackTrace, toString`

Inherited from *java.lang.object*
`clone, equals, finalize, getClass, hashCode, notify, notifyAll, wait, wait, wait`

Class javax.mail.SendFailedException

`public class SendFailedException`

`extends` *javax.mail.***MessagingException**

Represents the exception thrown when a mail message cannot be sent.

Constructor Methods

public	`SendFailedException`	();
public	`SendFailedException`	(*java.lang.String* s);
public	`SendFailedException`	(*java.lang.String* s, *java.lang.Exception* e);
public	`SendFailedException`	(*java.lang.String* s, *java.lang.Exception* e, *javax.mail.***Address**[ ] validSent, *javax.mail.***Address**[ ] validUnsent, *javax.mail.***Address**[ ] invalid);

Methods

public **Address**[ ]	`getInvalidAddresses`	`();`
public **Address**[ ]	`getValidSentAddresses`	`();`
public **Address**[ ]	`getValidUnsentAddresses`	`();`

Inherited from *javax.mail.***MessagingException**
`getMessage, getNextException, setNextException`

Inherited from *java.lang.Throwable*
`fillInStackTrace, getLocalizedMessage, printStackTrace, printStackTrace,`
`printStackTrace, toString`

Inherited from *java.lang.object*
`clone, equals, finalize, getClass, hashCode, notify, notifyAll, wait, wait, wait`

Fields

protected transient **Address**[ ]	`invalid;`
protected transient **Address**[ ]	`validSent;`
protected transient **Address**[ ]	`validUnsent;`

Class javax.mail.StoreClosedException

`public class StoreClosedException`

extends *javax.mail.***MessagingException**

Represents the exception thrown when a method is run on a messaging object in a store that has 'died' for some reason. This should be treated as a fatal error.

Constructor Methods

public	`StoreClosedException`	(*javax.mail.***Store** store);
public	`StoreClosedException`	(*javax.mail.***Store** store, *java.lang.String* message);

Methods

public **Store**	`getStore`	`();`

Inherited from *javax.mail.***MessagingException**
`getMessage, getNextException, setNextException`

Inherited from *java.lang.Throwable*
`fillInStackTrace, getLocalizedMessage, printStackTrace, printStackTrace,`
`printStackTrace, toString`

Inherited from *java.lang.object*
`clone, equals, finalize, getClass, hashCode, notify, notifyAll, wait, wait, wait`

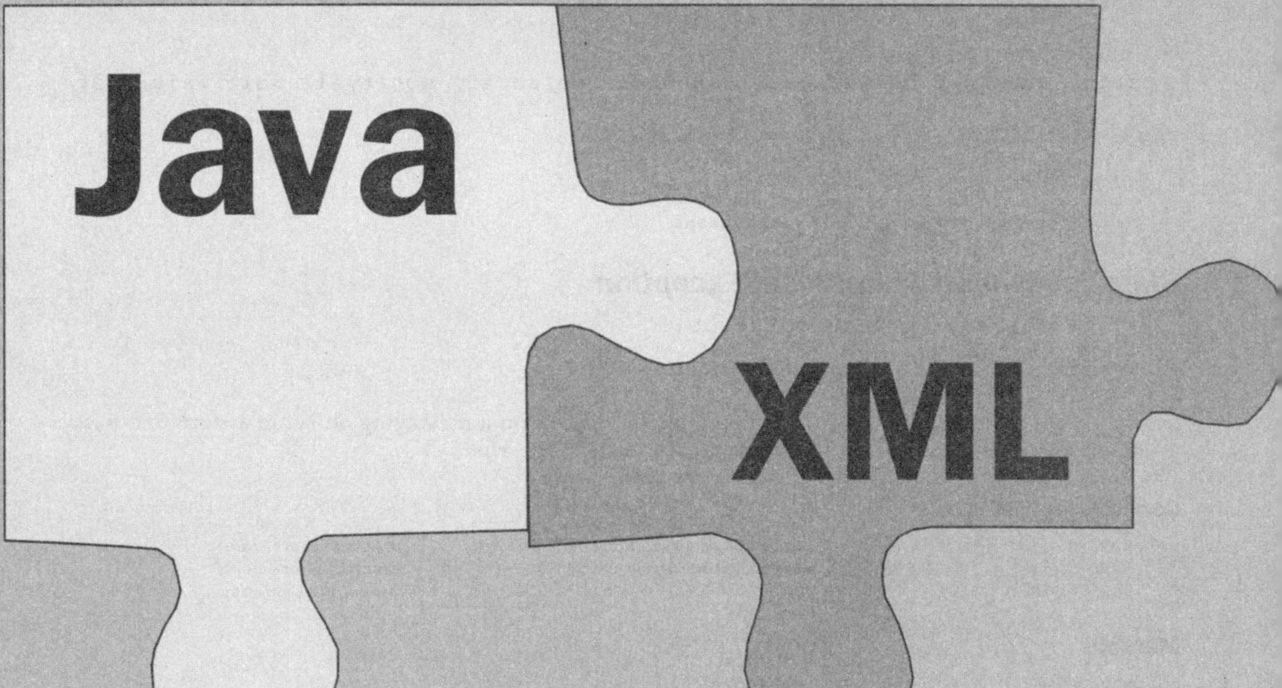
Java
XML

Extensible Markup Language (XML) 1.0 Specification

Rec-xml-19980210
World Wide Web Consortium 10-February-1998

This appendix is taken from the W3C Recommendation at
http://www.w3.org/TR/REC-xml

A list of known errors in this specification is available at
http://www.w3.org/XML/xml-19980210-errata

Copyright Notice

Status of this Document

This document has been reviewed by W3C Members and other interested parties and has been endorsed by the Director as a W3C Recommendation. It is a stable document and may be used as reference material or cited as a normative reference from another document. W3C's role in making the Recommendation is to draw attention to the specification and to promote its widespread deployment. This enhances the functionality and interoperability of the Web.

This document specifies a syntax created by subsetting an existing, widely used international text processing standard (Standard Generalized Markup Language, ISO 8879:1986(E) as amended and corrected) for use on the World Wide Web. It is a product of the W3C XML Activity, details of which can be found at `http://www.w3.org/XML`. A list of current W3C Recommendations and other technical documents can be found at `http://www.w3.org/TR`.

This specification uses the term URI, which is defined by Berners-Lee et al. (1997), a work in progress expected to update IETF RFC1738 and IETF RFC1806.

Editors

Tim Bray (Textuality and Netscape)   `tbray@textuality.com`
Jean Paoli (Microsoft)   `jeanpa@microsoft.com`
C. M. Sperberg-McQueen
    (University of Illinois at Chicago)   `cmsmcq@uic.edu`

Abstract

The Extensible Markup Language (XML) is a subset of SGML that is completely described in this document. Its goal is to enable generic SGML to be served, received, and processed on the Web in the way that is now possible with HTML. XML has been designed for ease of implementation and for interoperability with both SGML and HTML.

Extensible Markup Language (XML) 1.0

Table of Contents

Appendices

1. Introduction

Extensible Markup Language, abbreviated XML, describes a class of data objects called XML documents and partially describes the behavior of computer programs which process them. XML is an application profile or restricted form of SGML, the Standard Generalized Markup Language [ISO 8879]. By construction, XML documents are conforming SGML documents.

XML documents are made up of storage units called entities, which contain either parsed or unparsed data. Parsed data is made up of characters, some of which form character data, and some of which form markup. Markup encodes a description of the document's storage layout and logical structure. XML provides a mechanism to impose constraints on the storage layout and logical structure.

A software module called an **XML processor** is used to read XML documents and provide access to their content and structure. It is assumed that an XML processor is doing its work on behalf of another module, called the **application**. This specification describes the required behavior of an XML processor in terms of how it must read XML data and the information it must provide to the application.

1.1 Origin and Goals

XML was developed by an XML Working Group (originally known as the SGML Editorial Review Board) formed under the auspices of the World Wide Web Consortium (W3C) in 1996. It was chaired by Jon Bosak of Sun Microsystems with the active participation of an XML Special Interest Group (previously known as the SGML Working Group) also organized by the W3C. The membership of the XML Working Group is given in an appendix. Dan Connolly served as the WG's contact with the W3C. The design goals for XML are:

1.   XML shall be straightforwardly usable over the Internet.
2.   XML shall support a wide variety of applications.
3.   XML shall be compatible with SGML.
4.   It shall be easy to write programs which process XML documents.
5.   The number of optional features in XML is to be kept to the absolute minimum, ideally zero.
6.   XML documents should be human-legible and reasonably clear.
7.   The XML design should be prepared quickly.
8.   The design of XML shall be formal and concise.
9.   XML documents shall be easy to create.
10.   Terseness in XML markup is of minimal importance.

This specification, together with associated standards (Unicode and ISO/IEC 10646 for characters, Internet RFC 1766 for language identification tags, ISO 639 for language name codes, and ISO 3166 for country name codes), provides all the information necessary to understand XML Version 1.0 and construct computer programs to process it.

This version of the XML specification may be distributed freely, as long as all text and legal notices remain intact.

1.2 Terminology

The terminology used to describe XML documents is defined in the body of this specification. The terms defined in the following list are used in building those definitions and in describing the actions of an XML processor:

may

Conforming documents and XML processors are permitted to but need not behave as described.

must

Conforming documents and XML processors are required to behave as described; otherwise they are in error.

error

A violation of the rules of this specification; results are undefined. Conforming software may detect and report an error and may recover from it.

fatal error

An error which a conforming XML processor must detect and report to the application. After encountering a fatal error, the processor may continue processing the data to search for further errors and may report such errors to the application. In order to support correction of errors, the processor may make unprocessed data from the document (with intermingled character data and markup) available to the application. Once a fatal error is detected, however, the processor must not continue normal processing (i.e., it must not continue to pass character data and information about the document's logical structure to the application in the normal way).

at user option

Conforming software may or must (depending on the modal verb in the sentence) behave as described; if it does, it must provide users a means to enable or disable the behavior described.

validity constraint

A rule which applies to all valid XML documents. Violations of validity constraints are errors; they must, at user option, be reported by validating XML processors.

well-formedness constraint

A rule which applies to all well-formed XML documents. Violations of well-formedness constraints are fatal errors.

match

(Of strings or names:) Two strings or names being compared must be identical. Characters with multiple possible representations in ISO/IEC 10646 (e.g. characters with both precomposed and base+diacritic forms) match only if they have the same representation in both strings. At user option, processors may normalize such characters to some canonical form. No case folding is performed.

(Of strings and rules in the grammar:) A string matches a grammatical production if it belongs to the language generated by that production. (Of content and content models:) An element matches its declaration when it conforms in the fashion described in the constraint "Element Valid".

for compatibility

A feature of XML included solely to ensure that XML remains compatible with SGML.

for interoperability

A non-binding recommendation included to increase the chances that XML documents can be processed by the existing installed base of SGML processors which predate the WebSGML Adaptations Annex to ISO 8879.

2. Documents

A data object is an **XML document** if it is well-formed, as defined in this specification. A well-formed XML document may in addition be valid if it meets certain further constraints.

Each XML document has both a logical and a physical structure. Physically, the document is composed of units called entities. An entity may refer to other entities to cause their inclusion in the document. A document begins in a "root" or document entity. Logically, the document is composed of declarations, elements, comments, character references, and processing instructions, all of which are indicated in the document by explicit markup. The logical and physical structures must nest properly, as described in "4.3.2 Well-Formed Parsed Entities".

2.1 Well-Formed XML Documents

A textual object is a well-formed XML document if:

1. Taken as a whole, it matches the production labeled **document**.
2. It meets all the well-formedness constraints given in this specification.
3. Each of the parsed entities which is referenced directly or indirectly within the document is well-formed.

Document
[1]   document   ::=   prolog element Misc*

Matching the **document** production implies that:

1. It contains one or more elements.
2. There is exactly one element, called the **root**, or document element, no part of which appears in the content of any other element. For all other elements, if the start-tag is in the content of another element, the end-tag is in the content of the same element. More simply stated, the elements, delimited by start- and end-tags, nest properly within each other.

As a consequence of this, for each non-root element C in the document, there is one other element P in the document such that C is in the content of P, but is not in the content of any other element that is in the content of P. P is referred to as the **parent** of C, and C as a **child** of P.

2.2 Characters

A parsed entity contains **text**, a sequence of characters, which may represent markup or character data. A **character** is an atomic unit of text as specified by ISO/IEC 10646 [ISO/IEC 10646]. Legal characters are tab, carriage return, line feed, and the legal graphic characters of Unicode and ISO/IEC 10646. The use of "compatibility characters", as defined in section 6.8 of [Unicode], is discouraged.

Character Range		
[2] Char ::=	#x9 | #xA | #xD | [#x20-#xD7FF] | [#xE000-#xFFFD] | [#x10000-#x10FFFF]	/*any Unicode character, excluding the surrogate blocks, FFFE, and FFFF. */

The mechanism for encoding character code points into bit patterns may vary from entity to entity. All XML processors must accept the UTF-8 and UTF-16 encodings of 10646; the mechanisms for signaling which of the two is in use, or for bringing other encodings into play, are discussed later, in "4.3.3 Character Encoding in Entities".

2.3 Common Syntactic Constructs

This section defines some symbols used widely in the grammar.

S (white space) consists of one or more space (#x20) characters, carriage returns, line feeds, or tabs.

White Space	
[3] ::=	(#x20 | #x9 | #xD | #xA)+

Characters are classified for convenience as letters, digits, or other characters. Letters consist of an alphabetic or syllabic base character possibly followed by one or more combining characters, or of an ideographic character. Full definitions of the specific characters in each class are given in "B. Character Classes".

A **Name** is a token beginning with a letter or one of a few punctuation characters, and continuing with letters, digits, hyphens, underscores, colons, or full stops, together known as name characters. Names beginning with the string "**xml**", or any string which would match ((`'X'`|`'x'`) (`'M'`|`'m'`) (`'L'`|`'l'`)), are reserved for standardization in this or future versions of this specification.

Note: The colon character within XML names is reserved for experimentation with name spaces. Its meaning is expected to be standardized at some future point, at which point those documents using the colon for experimental purposes may need to be updated. (There is no guarantee that any name-space mechanism adopted for XML will in fact use the colon as a name-space delimiter.)

In practice, this means that authors should not use the colon in XML names except as part of name-space experiments, but that XML processors should accept the colon as a name character.

An **Nmtoken** (name token) is any mixture of name characters.

Names and Tokens			
[4]	**NameChar**	::=	Letter | Digit | '.' | '-' | '_' | ':' | CombiningChar | Extender
[5]	**Name**	::=	(Letter | '_' | ':') (NameChar)*
[6]	**Names**	::=	Name (S Name)*
[7]	**Nmtoken**	::=	(NameChar)+
[8]	**Nmtokens**	::=	Nmtoken (S Nmtoken)*

Literal data is any quoted string not containing the quotation mark used as a delimiter for that string. Literals are used for specifying the content of internal entities (**EntityValue**), the values of attributes (**AttValue**), and external identifiers (**SystemLiteral**). Note that a **SystemLiteral** can be parsed without scanning for markup.

Literals			
[9]	**EntityValue**	::=	'"' ([^%&"] | PEReference | Reference)* '"'
			| "'" ([^%&'] | PEReference | Reference)* "'"
[10]	**AttValue**	::=	'"' ([^<&"] | Reference)* '"'
			| "'" ([^<&'] | Reference)* "'"
[11]	**SystemLiteral**	::=	('"' [^"]* '"') | ("'" [^']* "'")
[12]	**PubidLiteral**	::=	'"' PubidChar* '"' | "'" (PubidChar - "'")* "'"
[13]	**PubidChar**	::=	#x20 | #xD | #xA | [a-zA-Z0-9] | [-'()+,./:=?;!*#@$_%]

2.4 Character Data and Markup

Text consists of intermingled character data and markup. **Markup** takes the form of start-tags, end-tags, empty-element tags, entity references, character references, comments, CDATA section delimiters, document type declarations, and processing instructions.

All text that is not markup constitutes the **character data** of the document.

The ampersand character (&) and the left angle bracket (<) may appear in their literal form *only* when used as markup delimiters, or within a comment, a processing instruction, or a CDATA section. They are also legal within the literal entity value of an internal entity declaration; see "4.3.2 Well-Formed Parsed Entities". If they are needed elsewhere, they must be escaped using either numeric character references or the strings "&" and "<" respectively.

The right angle bracket (>) may be represented using the string ">", and must, for compatibility, be escaped using ">" or a character reference when it appears in the string "]]>" in content, when that string is not marking the end of a CDATA section.

In the content of elements, character data is any string of characters which does not contain the start-delimiter of any markup. In a CDATA section, character data is any string of characters not including the CDATA-section-close delimiter, "]]>".

To allow attribute values to contain both single and double quotes, the apostrophe or single-quote character (') may be represented as "'", and the double-quote character (") as """.

Character Data
[14]   CharData   ::=   [^<&]* - ([^<&]* ']]>' [^<&]*)

2.5 Comments

Comments may appear anywhere in a document outside other markup; in addition, they may appear within the document type declaration at places allowed by the grammar. They are not part of the document's character data; an XML processor may, but need not, make it possible for an application to retrieve the text of comments. For compatibility, the string "--" (double-hyphen) must not occur within comments.

Comments
[15]   Comment   ::=   '<!--' ((Char - '-') | ('-' (Char - '-')))* '-->'

An example of a comment:

```
<!-- declarations for <head> & <body> -->
```

2.6 Processing Instructions

Processing instructions (PIs) allow documents to contain instructions for applications.

Processing Instructions
[16]   PI   ::=   '<?' PITarget (S (Char* - (Char* '?>' Char*)))? '?>'
[17]   PITarget ::=   Name - (('X' | 'x') ('M' | 'm') ('L' | 'l'))

PIs are not part of the document's character data, but must be passed through to the application. The PI begins with a target (**PITarget**) used to identify the application to which the instruction is directed. The target names "XML", "xml", and so on are reserved for standardization in this or future versions of this specification. The XML Notation mechanism may be used for formal declaration of PI targets.

2.7 CDATA Sections

CDATA sections may occur anywhere character data may occur; they are used to escape blocks of text containing characters which would otherwise be recognized as markup. CDATA sections begin with the string "`<![CDATA[`" and end with the string "`]]>`":

CDATA Sections			
[18]	`CDSect`	`::=`	CDStart CData CDEnd
[19]	`CDStart`	`::=`	`'<![CDATA['`
[20]	`CData`	`::=`	(Char* - (Char* `']]>'` Char*))
[21]	`CDEnd`	`::=`	`']]>'`

Within a CDATA section, only the CDEnd string is recognized as markup, so that left angle brackets and ampersands may occur in their literal form; they need not (and cannot) be escaped using "`&lt;`" and "`&amp;`". CDATA sections cannot nest.

An example of a CDATA section, in which "`<greeting>`" and "`</greeting>`" are recognized as character data, not markup:

```
<![CDATA[<greeting>Hello, world!</greeting>]]>
```

2.8 Prolog and Document Type Declaration

XML documents may, and should, begin with an **XML declaration** which specifies the version of XML being used. For example, the following is a complete XML document, well-formed but not valid:

```
<?xml version="1.0"?>
<greeting>Hello, world!</greeting>
```

and so is this:

```
<greeting>Hello, world!</greeting>
```

The version number "`1.0`" should be used to indicate conformance to this version of this specification; it is an error for a document to use the value "`1.0`" if it does not conform to this version of this specification. It is the intent of the XML working group to give later versions of this specification numbers other than "`1.0`", but this intent does not indicate a commitment to produce any future versions of XML, nor if any are produced, to use any particular numbering scheme. Since future versions are not ruled out, this construct is provided as a means to allow the possibility of automatic version recognition, should it become necessary. Processors may signal an error if they receive documents labeled with versions they do not support.

The function of the markup in an XML document is to describe its storage and logical structure and to associate attribute-value pairs with its logical structures. XML provides a mechanism, the document type declaration, to define constraints on the logical structure and to support the use of predefined storage units. An XML document is **valid** if it has an associated document type declaration and if the document complies with the constraints expressed in it.

The document type declaration must appear before the first element in the document.

Prolog			
[22]	prolog	::=	XMLDecl? Misc* (doctypedecl Misc*)?
[23]	XMLDecl	::=	'<?xml' VersionInfo EncodingDecl? SDDecl? S? '?>'
[24]	VersionInfo	::=	S 'version' Eq (' VersionNum ' | " VersionNum ")
[25]	Eq	::=	S? '=' S?
[26]	VersionNum	::=	([a-zA-Z0-9_.:] | '-')+
[27]	Misc	::=	Comment | PI | S

The XML **document type declaration** contains or points to markup declarations that provide a grammar for a class of documents. This grammar is known as a document type definition, or **DTD**. The document type declaration can point to an external subset (a special kind of external entity) containing markup declarations, or can contain the markup declarations directly in an internal subset, or can do both. The DTD for a document consists of both subsets taken together.

A **markup declaration** is an element type declaration, an attribute-list declaration, an entity declaration, or a notation declaration. These declarations may be contained in whole or in part within parameter entities, as described in the well-formedness and validity constraints below. For fuller information, see "4. Physical Structures".

Document Type Definition				
[28]	doctypedecl	::=	'<!DOCTYPE' S Name (S ExternalID)? S? ('[' (markupdecl | PEReference | S)* ']' S?)? '>'	[VC: Root Element Type]
[29]	markupdecl	::=	elementdecl | AttlistDecl | EntityDecl | NotationDecl | PI | Comment	[VC: Proper Declaration/PE Nesting]
				[WFC: PEs in Internal Subset]

The markup declarations may be made up in whole or in part of the replacement text of parameter entities. The productions later in this specification for individual nonterminals (**elementdecl**, **AttlistDecl**, and so on) describe the declarations *after* all the parameter entities have been included.

Validity Constraint: Root Element Type

The **Name** in the document type declaration must match the element type of the root element.

Validity Constraint: Proper Declaration/PE Nesting

Parameter-entity replacement text must be properly nested with markup declarations. That is to say, if either the first character or the last character of a markup declaration (**markupdecl** above) is contained in the replacement text for a parameter-entity reference, both must be contained in the same replacement text.

Well-Formedness Constraint: PEs in Internal Subset

In the internal DTD subset, parameter-entity references can occur only where markup declarations can occur, not within markup declarations. (This does not apply to references that occur in external parameter entities or to the external subset.)

Like the internal subset, the external subset and any external parameter entities referred to in the DTD must consist of a series of complete markup declarations of the types allowed by the non-terminal symbol **markupdecl**, interspersed with white space or parameter-entity references. However, portions of the contents of the external subset or of external parameter entities may conditionally be ignored by using the conditional section construct; this is not allowed in the internal subset.

External Subset			
[30]	extSubset	::=	TextDecl? extSubsetDecl
[31]	extSubsetDecl	::=	(markupdecl | conditionalSect | PEReference | S)*

The external subset and external parameter entities also differ from the internal subset in that in them, parameter-entity references are permitted *within* markup declarations, not only *between* markup declarations.

An example of an XML document with a document type declaration:

```
<?xml version="1.0"?>
<!DOCTYPE greeting SYSTEM "hello.dtd">
<greeting>Hello, world!</greeting>
```

The system identifier "**hello.dtd**" gives the URI of a DTD for the document.

The declarations can also be given locally, as in this example:

```
<?xml version="1.0" encoding="UTF-8" ?>
<!DOCTYPE greeting [
  <!ELEMENT greeting (#PCDATA)>
]>
<greeting>Hello, world!</greeting>
```

If both the external and internal subsets are used, the internal subset is considered to occur before the external subset. This has the effect that entity and attribute-list declarations in the internal subset take precedence over those in the external subset.

2.9 Standalone Document Declaration

Markup declarations can affect the content of the document, as passed from an XML processor to an application; examples are attribute defaults and entity declarations. The standalone document declaration, which may appear as a component of the XML declaration, signals whether or not there are such declarations which appear external to the document entity.

Standalone Document Declaration		
[32] SDDecl ::=	S 'standalone' Eq (("'" ('yes' | 'no') "'") | ('"' ('yes' | 'no') '"'))	[VC: Standalone Document Declaration]

In a standalone document declaration, the value "**yes**" indicates that there are no markup declarations external to the document entity (either in the DTD external subset, or in an external parameter entity referenced from the internal subset) which affect the information passed from the XML processor to the application. The value "**no**" indicates that there are or may be such external markup declarations. Note that the standalone document declaration only denotes the presence of external *declarations*; the presence, in a document, of references to external *entities*, when those entities are internally declared, does not change its standalone status.

If there are no external markup declarations, the standalone document declaration has no meaning. If there are external markup declarations but there is no standalone document declaration, the value "**no**" is assumed.

Any XML document for which **standalone="no"** holds can be converted algorithmically to a standalone document, which may be desirable for some network delivery applications.

Validity Constraint: Standalone Document Declaration

The standalone document declaration must have the value "**no**" if any external markup declarations contain declarations of:

❑ attributes with default values, if elements to which these attributes apply appear in the document without specifications of values for these attributes, or

❑ entities (other than **amp**, **lt**, **gt**, **apos**, **quot**), if references to those entities appear in the document, or

❑ attributes with values subject to normalization, where the attribute appears in the document with a value which will change as a result of normalization, or

❑ element types with element content, if white space occurs directly within any instance of those types.

An example XML declaration with a standalone document declaration:

```
<?xml version="1.0" standalone='yes'?>
```

2.10 White Space Handling

In editing XML documents, it is often convenient to use "white space" (spaces, tabs, and blank lines, denoted by the nonterminal **S** in this specification) to set apart the markup for greater readability. Such white space is typically not intended for inclusion in the delivered version of the document. On the other hand, "significant" white space that should be preserved in the delivered version is common, for example in poetry and source code.

An XML processor must always pass all characters in a document that are not markup through to the application. A validating XML processor must also inform the application which of these characters constitute white space appearing in element content.

A special attribute named **xml:space** may be attached to an element to signal an intention that in that element, white space should be preserved by applications. In valid documents, this attribute, like any other, must be declared if it is used. When declared, it must be given as an enumerated type whose only possible values are "**default**" and "**preserve**". For example:

```
<!ATTLIST poem   xml:space (default|preserve) 'preserve'>
```

The value "**default**" signals that applications' default white-space processing modes are acceptable for this element; the value "**preserve**" indicates the intent that applications preserve all the white space. This declared intent is considered to apply to all elements within the content of the element where it is specified, unless overriden with another instance of the **xml:space** attribute.

The root element of any document is considered to have signaled no intentions as regards application space handling, unless it provides a value for this attribute or the attribute is declared with a default value.

2.11 End-of-Line Handling

XML parsed entities are often stored in computer files which, for editing convenience, are organized into lines. These lines are typically separated by some combination of the characters carriage-return (#xD) and line-feed (#xA).

To simplify the tasks of applications, wherever an external parsed entity or the literal entity value of an internal parsed entity contains either the literal two-character sequence "#xD#xA" or a standalone literal #xD, an XML processor must pass to the application the single character #xA. (This behavior can conveniently be produced by normalizing all line breaks to #xA on input, before parsing.)

2.12 Language Identification

In document processing, it is often useful to identify the natural or formal language in which the content is written. A special attribute named **xml:lang** may be inserted in documents to specify the language used in the contents and attribute values of any element in an XML document. In valid documents, this attribute, like any other, must be declared if it is used. The values of the attribute are language identifiers as defined by [IETF RFC 1766], "Tags for the Identification of Languages":

Language Identification			
[33]	LanguageID	::=	Langcode ('-' Subcode)*
[34]	Langcode	::=	ISO639Code | IanaCode | UserCode
[35]	ISO639Code	::=	([a-z] | [A-Z]) ([a-z] | [A-Z])
[36]	IanaCode	::=	('i' | 'I') '-' ([a-z] | [A-Z])+
[37]	UserCode	::=	('x' | 'X') '-' ([a-z] | [A-Z])+
[38]	Subcode	::=	([a-z] | [A-Z])+

The Langcode may be any of the following:

❑ a two-letter language code as defined by [ISO 639], "Codes for the representation of names of languages"

❑ a language identifier registered with the Internet Assigned Numbers Authority [IANA]; these begin with the prefix "**i-**" (or "**I-**")

❑ a language identifier assigned by the user, or agreed on between parties in private use; these must begin with the prefix "**x-**" or "**X-**" in order to ensure that they do not conflict with names later standardized or registered with IANA

There may be any number of **Subcode** segments; if the first subcode segment exists and the Subcode consists of two letters, then it must be a country code from [ISO 3166], "Codes for the representation of names of countries." If the first subcode consists of more than two letters, it must be a subcode for the language in question registered with IANA, unless the **Langcode** begins with the prefix "**x-**" or "**X-**".

It is customary to give the language code in lower case, and the country code (if any) in upper case. Note that these values, unlike other names in XML documents, are case insensitive.

For example:

```
<p xml:lang="en">The quick brown fox jumps over the lazy dog.</p>
<p xml:lang="en-GB">What colour is it?</p>
<p xml:lang="en-US">What color is it?</p>
<sp who="Faust" desc='leise' xml:lang="de">
<l>Habe nun, ach! Philosophie,</l>
```

```
<l>Juristerei, und Medizin</l>
<l>und leider auch Theologie</l>
<l>durchaus studiert mit heißem Bemüh'n.</l>
</sp>
```

The intent declared with **xml:lang** is considered to apply to all attributes and content of the element where it is specified, unless overridden with an instance of **xml:lang** on another element within that content.

A simple declaration for **xml:lang** might take the form

```
xml:lang  NMTOKEN  #IMPLIED
```

but specific default values may also be given, if appropriate. In a collection of French poems for English students, with glosses and notes in English, the **xml:lang** attribute might be declared this way:

```
<!ATTLIST poem    xml:lang NMTOKEN 'fr'>
<!ATTLIST gloss   xml:lang NMTOKEN 'en'>
<!ATTLIST note    xml:lang NMTOKEN 'en'>
```

3. Logical Structures

Each XML document contains one or more **elements**, the boundaries of which are either delimited by start-tags and end-tags, or, for empty elements, by an empty-element tag. Each element has a type, identified by name, sometimes called its "generic identifier" (GI), and may have a set of attribute specifications. Each attribute specification has a name and a value.

Element		
[39] element ::= EmptyElemTag		
	| STag content ETag	[**WFC:** Element Type Match]
		[**VC:** Element Valid]

This specification does not constrain the semantics, use, or (beyond syntax) names of the element types and attributes, except that names beginning with a match to (('X' \| 'x') ('M' \| 'm') ('L' \| 'l')) are reserved for standardization in this or future versions of this specification.

Well-Formedness Constraint: Element Type Match

The **Name** in an element's end-tag must match the element type in the start-tag.

Validity Constraint: Element Valid

An element is valid if there is a declaration matching **elementdecl** where the **Name** matches the element type, and one of the following holds:

1. The declaration matches **EMPTY** and the element has no content.
2. The declaration matches **children** and the sequence of child elements belongs to the language generated by the regular expression in the content model, with optional white space (characters matching the nonterminal **S**) between each pair of child elements.
3. The declaration matches **Mixed** and the content consists of character data and child elements whose types match names in the content model.
4. The declaration matches **ANY**, and the types of any child elements have been declared.

3.1 Start-Tags, End-Tags, and Empty-Element Tags

The beginning of every non-empty XML element is marked by a **start-tag**.

Start-tag				
[40]	STag	::=	`'<' Name (S Attribute)* S? '>'`	[WFC: Unique Att Spec]
[41]	Attribute	::=	`Name Eq AttValue`	[VC: Attribute Value Type]
				[WFC: No External Entity References]
				[WFC: No < in Attribute Values]

The **Name** in the start- and end-tags gives the element's **type**. The **Name-AttValue** pairs are referred to as the **attribute specifications** of the element, with the **Name** in each pair referred to as the **attribute name** and the content of the **AttValue** (the text between the ' or " delimiters) as the **attribute value**.

Well-Formedness Constraint: Unique Att Spec

No attribute name may appear more than once in the same start-tag or empty-element tag.

Validity Constraint: Attribute Value Type

The attribute must have been declared; the value must be of the type declared for it. (For attribute types, see "3.3 Attribute-List Declarations".)

Well-Formedness Constraint: No External Entity References

Attribute values cannot contain direct or indirect entity references to external entities.

Well-Formedness Constraint: No < in Attribute Values

The replacement text of any entity referred to directly or indirectly in an attribute value (other than "<") must not contain a <.

An example of a start-tag:

```
<termdef id="dt-dog" term="dog">
```

The end of every element that begins with a start-tag must be marked by an **end-tag** containing a name that echoes the element's type as given in the start-tag:

End-tag
[42]   ETag   ::=   '</' Name S? '>'

An example of an end-tag:

```
</termdef>
```

The text between the start-tag and end-tag is called the element's **content**:

Content of Elements
[43]   content   ::=   (element | CharData | Reference | CDSect | PI | Comment)*

If an element is **empty**, it must be represented either by a start-tag immediately followed by an end-tag or by an empty-element tag. An **empty-element tag** takes a special form:

Tags for Empty Elements	
[44] EmptyElemTag ::= '<' Name (S Attribute)* S? '/>'	[WFC: Unique Att Spec]

Empty-element tags may be used for any element which has no content, whether or not it is declared using the keyword **EMPTY**. For interoperability, the empty-element tag must be used, and can only be used, for elements which are declared **EMPTY**.

Examples of empty elements:

```
<IMG align="left"
 src="http://www.w3.org/Icons/WWW/w3c_home" />
<br></br>
<br/>
```

3.2 Element Type Declarations

The element structure of an XML document may, for validation purposes, be constrained using element type and attribute-list declarations. An element type declaration constrains the element's content.

Element type declarations often constrain which element types can appear as children of the element. At user option, an XML processor may issue a warning when a declaration mentions an element type for which no declaration is provided, but this is not an error.

An **element type declaration** takes the form:

Element Type Declaration				
[45]	`elementdecl`	`::=`	`'<!ELEMENT' S Name S` `contentspec S? '>'`	[VC: Unique Element Type Declaration]
[46]	`contentspec`	`::=`	`'EMPTY' | 'ANY' | Mixed` `| children`	

where the **Name** gives the element type being declared.

Validity Constraint: Unique Element Type Declaration

No element type may be declared more than once.

Examples of element type declarations:

```
<!ELEMENT br EMPTY>
<!ELEMENT p (#PCDATA|emph)* >
<!ELEMENT %name.para; %content.para; >
<!ELEMENT container ANY>
```

3.2.1 Element Content

An element type has **element content** when elements of that type must contain only child elements (no character data), optionally separated by white space (characters matching the nonterminal **S**). In this case, the constraint includes a content model, a simple grammar governing the allowed types of the child elements and the order in which they are allowed to appear. The grammar is built on content particles (**cps**), which consist of names, choice lists of content particles, or sequence lists of content particles:

Element-content Models			
[47]	`children ::= (choice | seq) ('?' | '*' | '+')?`		
[48]	`cp        ::= (Name | choice | seq) ('?' | '*' | '+')?`		
[49]	`choice    ::= '(' S? cp ( S? '|' S? cp )* S? ')'`	[VC: Proper Group/PE Nesting]	
[50]	`seq       ::= '(' S? cp ( S? ',' S? cp )* S? ')'`	[VC: Proper Group/PE Nesting]	

where each **Name** is the type of an element which may appear as a child. Any content particle in a choice list may appear in the element content at the location where the choice list appears in the grammar; content particles occurring in a sequence list must each appear in the element content in the order given in the list. The optional character following a name or list governs whether the element or the content particles in the list may occur one or more (**+**), zero or more (*****), or zero or one times (**?**).

The absence of such an operator means that the element or content particle must appear exactly once. This syntax and meaning are identical to those used in the productions in this specification.

The content of an element matches a content model if and only if it is possible to trace out a path through the content model, obeying the sequence, choice, and repetition operators and matching each element in the content against an element type in the content model. For compatibility, it is an error if an element in the document can match more than one occurrence of an element type in the content model. For more information, see "E. Deterministic Content Models".

Validity Constraint: Proper Group/PE Nesting
Parameter-entity replacement text must be properly nested with parenthetized groups. That is to say, if either of the opening or closing parentheses in a **choice**, **seq**, or **Mixed** construct is contained in the replacement text for a parameter entity, both must be contained in the same replacement text. For interoperability, if a parameter-entity reference appears in a **choice**, **seq**, or **Mixed** construct, its replacement text should not be empty, and neither the first nor last non-blank character of the replacement text should be a connector (I or ,).

Examples of element-content models:

```
<!ELEMENT spec (front, body, back?)>
<!ELEMENT div1 (head, (p | list | note)*, div2*)>
<!ELEMENT dictionary-body (%div.mix; | %dict.mix;)*>
```

3.2.2 Mixed Content

An element type has **mixed content** when elements of that type may contain character data, optionally interspersed with child elements. In this case, the types of the child elements may be constrained, but not their order or their number of occurrences:

Mixed-content Declaration	
[51] **Mixed** ::= '(' S? '#PCDATA' (S? 'I' S? Name)* S? ')*'	
I '(' S? '#PCDATA' S? ')'	[VC: Proper Group/PE Nesting]
	[VC: No Duplicate Types]

where the Names give the types of elements that may appear as children.

Validity Constraint: No Duplicate Types

The same name must not appear more than once in a single mixed-content declaration.

Examples of mixed content declarations:

```
<!ELEMENT p (#PCDATA|a|ul|b|i|em)*>
<!ELEMENT p (#PCDATA | %font; | %phrase; | %special; | %form;)* >
<!ELEMENT b (#PCDATA)>
```

3.3 Attribute-List Declarations

Attributes are used to associate name-value pairs with elements. Attribute specifications may appear only within start-tags and empty-element tags; thus, the productions used to recognize them appear in "3.1 Start-Tags, End-Tags, and Empty-Element Tags". Attribute-list declarations may be used:

❑ To define the set of attributes pertaining to a given element type.

❑ To establish type constraints for these attributes.

❑ To provide default values for attributes.

Attribute-list declarations specify the name, data type, and default value (if any) of each attribute associated with a given element type:

Attribute-list Declaration
[52] `AttlistDecl` ::= `'<!ATTLIST'` S Name AttDef* S? `'>'`
[53] `AttDef` ::= S Name S AttType S DefaultDecl

The `Name` in the `AttlistDecl` rule is the type of an element. At user option, an XML processor may issue a warning if attributes are declared for an element type not itself declared, but this is not an error. The `Name` in the `AttDef` rule is the name of the attribute.

When more than one `AttlistDecl` is provided for a given element type, the contents of all those provided are merged. When more than one definition is provided for the same attribute of a given element type, the first declaration is binding and later declarations are ignored. For interoperability, writers of DTDs may choose to provide at most one attribute-list declaration for a given element type, at most one attribute definition for a given attribute name, and at least one attribute definition in each attribute-list declaration. For interoperability, an XML processor may at user option issue a warning when more than one attribute-list declaration is provided for a given element type, or more than one attribute definition is provided for a given attribute, but this is not an error.

3.3.1 Attribute Types

XML attribute types are of three kinds: a string type, a set of tokenized types, and enumerated types. The string type may take any literal string as a value; the tokenized types have varying lexical and semantic constraints, as noted:

Attribute Types		
[54] `AttType` ::= StringType | TokenizedType | EnumeratedType		
[55] `StringType` ::= `'CDATA'`		
[56] `TokenizedType` ::= `'ID'`	[VC: ID]	

Attribute Types		
		[VC: One ID per Element Type]
		[VC: ID Attribute Default]
	| 'IDREF'	[VC: IDREF]
	| 'IDREFS'	[VC: IDREF]
	| 'ENTITY'	[VC: Entity Name]
	| 'ENTITIES'	[VC: Entity Name]
	| 'NMTOKEN'	[VC: Name Token]
	| 'NMTOKENS'	[VC: Name Token]

Validity Constraint: ID

Values of type **ID** must match the **Name** production. A name must not appear more than once in an XML document as a value of this type; i.e., ID values must uniquely identify the elements which bear them.

Validity Constraint: One ID per Element Type

No element type may have more than one ID attribute specified.

Validity Constraint: ID Attribute Default

An ID attribute must have a declared default of **#IMPLIED** or **#REQUIRED**.

Validity Constraint: IDREF

Values of type **IDREF** must match the **Name** production, and values of type **IDREFS** must match **Names**; each **Name** must match the value of an ID attribute on some element in the XML document; i.e. **IDREF** values must match the value of some ID attribute.

Validity Constraint: Entity Name

Values of type **ENTITY** must match the **Name** production, values of type **ENTITIES** must match **Names**; each **Name** must match the name of an unparsed entity declared in the DTD.

Validity Constraint: Name Token

Values of type **NMTOKEN** must match the **Nmtoken** production; values of type **NMTOKENS** must match **Nmtokens**.

Enumerated attributes can take one of a list of values provided in the declaration. There are two kinds of enumerated types:

Enumerated Attribute Types			
[57]	EnumeratedType ::=	NotationType | Enumeration	
[58]	NotationType ::=	'NOTATION' S '(' S? Name (S? '|' S? Name)* S? ')'	[VC: Notation Attributes]
[59]	Enumeration ::=	'(' S? Nmtoken (S? '|' S? Nmtoken)* S? ')'	[VC: Enumeration]

A **NOTATION** attribute identifies a notation, declared in the DTD with associated system and/or public identifiers, to be used in interpreting the element to which the attribute is attached.

Validity Constraint: Notation Attributes

Values of this type must match one of the notation names included in the declaration; all notation names in the declaration must be declared.

Validity Constraint: Enumeration

Values of this type must match one of the **Nmtoken** tokens in the declaration.

For interoperability, the same **Nmtoken** should not occur more than once in the enumerated attribute types of a single element type.

3.3.2 Attribute Defaults

An attribute declaration provides information on whether the attribute's presence is required, and if not, how an XML processor should react if a declared attribute is absent in a document.

Attribute Defaults	
[60] DefaultDecl ::=	'#REQUIRED' | '#IMPLIED'
	| (('#FIXED' S)? AttValue) [VC: Required Attribute]
	[VC: Attribute Default Legal]
	[WFC: No < in Attribute Values]
	[VC: Fixed Attribute Default]

In an attribute declaration, **#REQUIRED** means that the attribute must always be provided, **#IMPLIED** that no default value is provided. If the declaration is neither **#REQUIRED** nor **#IMPLIED**, then the **AttValue** value contains the declared **default** value; the **#FIXED** keyword states that the attribute must always have the default value. If a default value is declared, when an XML processor encounters an omitted attribute, it is to behave as though the attribute were present with the declared default value.

Validity Constraint: Required Attribute

If the default declaration is the keyword **#REQUIRED**, then the attribute must be specified for all elements of the type in the attribute-list declaration.

Validity Constraint: Attribute Default Legal

The declared default value must meet the lexical constraints of the declared attribute type.

Validity Constraint: Fixed Attribute Default

If an attribute has a default value declared with the **#FIXED** keyword, instances of that attribute must match the default value.

Examples of attribute-list declarations:

```
<!ATTLIST termdef
          id      ID       #REQUIRED
          name    CDATA    #IMPLIED>
<!ATTLIST list
          type    (bullets|ordered|glossary)   "ordered">
<!ATTLIST form
          method  CDATA    #FIXED "POST">
```

3.3.3 Attribute-Value Normalization

Before the value of an attribute is passed to the application or checked for validity, the XML processor must normalize it as follows:

- ❑ a character reference is processed by appending the referenced character to the attribute value

- ❑ an entity reference is processed by recursively processing the replacement text of the entity

- ❑ a whitespace character (#x20, #xD, #xA, #x9) is processed by appending #x20 to the normalized value, except that only a single #x20 is appended for a "#xD#xA" sequence that is part of an external parsed entity or the literal entity value of an internal parsed entity

- ❑ other characters are processed by appending them to the normalized value

If the declared value is not CDATA, then the XML processor must further process the normalized attribute value by discarding any leading and trailing space (#x20) characters, and by replacing sequences of space (#x20) characters by a single space (#x20) character.

All attributes for which no declaration has been read should be treated by a non-validating parser as if declared **CDATA**.

3.4 Conditional Sections

Conditional sections are portions of the document type declaration external subset which are included in, or excluded from, the logical structure of the DTD based on the keyword which governs them.

Conditional Section		
[61] conditionalSect	::=	includeSect | ignoreSect
[62] includeSect	::=	`'<![' S? 'INCLUDE' S? '[' extSubsetDecl ']]>'`
[63] ignoreSect	::=	`'<![' S? 'IGNORE' S? '[' ignoreSectContents* ']]>'`
[64] ignoreSectContents	::=	Ignore `('<![' ignoreSectContents ']]>' Ignore)*`
[65] Ignore	::=	`Char* - (Char* ('<![' | ']]>') Char*)`

Like the internal and external DTD subsets, a conditional section may contain one or more complete declarations, comments, processing instructions, or nested conditional sections, intermingled with white space.

If the keyword of the conditional section is **INCLUDE**, then the contents of the conditional section are part of the DTD. If the keyword of the conditional section is **IGNORE**, then the contents of the conditional section are not logically part of the DTD. Note that for reliable parsing, the contents of even ignored conditional sections must be read in order to detect nested conditional sections and ensure that the end of the outermost (ignored) conditional section is properly detected. If a conditional section with a keyword of **INCLUDE** occurs within a larger conditional section with a keyword of **IGNORE**, both the outer and the inner conditional sections are ignored.

If the keyword of the conditional section is a parameter-entity reference, the parameter entity must be replaced by its content before the processor decides whether to include or ignore the conditional section.

An example:

```
<!ENTITY % draft 'INCLUDE' >
<!ENTITY % final 'IGNORE' >

<![%draft;[
<!ELEMENT book (comments*, title, body, supplements?)>
]]>
<![%final;[
<!ELEMENT book (title, body, supplements?)>
]]>
```

4. Physical Structures

An XML document may consist of one or many storage units. These are called **entities**; they all have **content** and are all (except for the document entity, see below, and the external DTD subset) identified by **name**. Each XML document has one entity called the document entity, which serves as the starting point for the XML processor and may contain the whole document.

Entities may be either parsed or unparsed. A **parsed entity's** contents are referred to as its replacement text; this text is considered an integral part of the document.

An **unparsed entity** is a resource whose contents may or may not be text, and if text, may not be XML. Each unparsed entity has an associated notation, identified by name. Beyond a requirement that an XML processor make the identifiers for the entity and notation available to the application, XML places no constraints on the contents of unparsed entities.

Parsed entities are invoked by name using entity references; unparsed entities by name, given in the value of **ENTITY** or **ENTITIES** attributes.

General entities are entities for use within the document content. In this specification, general entities are sometimes referred to with the unqualified term *entity* when this leads to no ambiguity. Parameter entities are parsed entities for use within the DTD. These two types of entities use different forms of reference and are recognized in different contexts. Furthermore, they occupy different namespaces; a parameter entity and a general entity with the same name are two distinct entities.

4.1 Character and Entity References

A **character reference** refers to a specific character in the ISO/IEC 10646 character set, for example one not directly accessible from available input devices.

Character Reference		
[66] `CharRef   ::=    '&#' [0-9]+ ';'`		
`| '&#x' [0-9a-fA-F]+ ';'`		[WFC: Legal Character]

Well-Formedness Constraint: Legal Character

Characters referred to using character references must match the production for Char.

If the character reference begins with "**&#x**", the digits and letters up to the terminating **;** provide a hexadecimal representation of the character's code point in ISO/IEC 10646. If it begins just with "**&#**", the digits up to the terminating **;** provide a decimal representation of the character's code point.

An **entity reference** refers to the content of a named entity. References to parsed general entities use ampersand (**&**) and semicolon (**;**) as delimiters. **Parameter-entity references** use percent-sign (**%**) and semicolon (**;**) as delimiters.

Entity Reference		
[67] `Reference ::= EntityRef	CharRef`		
[68] `EntityRef    ::=    '&' Name ';'`		[WFC: Entity Declared]
		[VC: Entity Declared]
		[WFC: Parsed Entity]

Entity Reference	
	[WFC: No Recursion]
[69] **PEReference** ::= '%' Name ';'	[VC: Entity Declared]
	[WFC: No Recursion]
	[WFC: In DTD]

Well-Formedness Constraint: Entity Declared

In a document without any DTD, a document with only an internal DTD subset which contains no parameter entity references, or a document with "standalone='yes'", the **Name** given in the entity reference must match that in an entity declaration, except that well-formed documents need not declare any of the following entities: **amp**, **lt**, **gt**, **apos**, **quot**. The declaration of a parameter entity must precede any reference to it. Similarly, the declaration of a general entity must precede any reference to it which appears in a default value in an attribute-list declaration. Note that if entities are declared in the external subset or in external parameter entities, a non-validating processor is not obligated to read and process their declarations; for such documents, the rule that an entity must be declared is a well-formedness constraint only if **standalone='yes'**.

Validity Constraint: Entity Declared

In a document with an external subset or external parameter entities with "standalone='no'", the **Name** given in the entity reference must match that in an entity declaration. For interoperability, valid documents should declare the entities **amp**, **lt**, **gt**, **apos**, **quot**, in the form specified in "4.6 Predefined Entities". The declaration of a parameter entity must precede any reference to it. Similarly, the declaration of a general entity must precede any reference to it which appears in a default value in an attribute-list declaration.

Well-Formedness Constraint: Parsed Entity

An entity reference must not contain the name of an unparsed entity. Unparsed entities may be referred to only in attribute values declared to be of type **ENTITY** or **ENTITIES**.

Well-Formedness Constraint: No Recursion

A parsed entity must not contain a recursive reference to itself, either directly or indirectly.

Well-Formedness Constraint: In DTD

Parameter-entity references may only appear in the DTD.

Examples of character and entity references:

```
Type <key>less-than</key> (&#x3C;) to save options.
This document was prepared on &docdate; and
is classified &security-level;.
```

Example of a parameter-entity reference:

```
<!-- declare the parameter entity "ISOLat2"... -->
<!ENTITY % ISOLat2
         SYSTEM "http://www.xml.com/iso/isolat2-xml.entities" >
<!-- ... now reference it. -->
%ISOLat2;
```

4.2 Entity Declarations

Entities are declared thus:

Entity Declaration			
[70]	**EntityDecl**	::=	GEDecl | PEDecl
[71]	**GEDecl**	::=	'**<!ENTITY**' S Name S EntityDef S? '**>**'
[72]	**PEDecl**	::=	'**<!ENTITY**' S '**%**' S Name S PEDef S? '**>**'
[73]	**EntityDef**	::=	EntityValue | (ExternalID NDataDecl?)
[74]	**PEDef**	::=	EntityValue | ExternalID

The **Name** identifies the entity in an entity reference or, in the case of an unparsed entity, in the value of an **ENTITY** or **ENTITIES** attribute. If the same entity is declared more than once, the first declaration encountered is binding; at user option, an XML processor may issue a warning if entities are declared multiple times.

4.2.1 Internal Entities

If the entity definition is an **EntityValue**, the defined entity is called an **internal entity**. There is no separate physical storage object, and the content of the entity is given in the declaration. Note that some processing of entity and character references in the literal entity value may be required to produce the correct replacement text: see "4.5 Construction of Internal Entity Replacement Text".

An internal entity is a parsed entity.

Example of an internal entity declaration:

```
<!ENTITY Pub-Status "This is a pre-release of the
  specification.">
```

4.2.2 External Entities

If the entity is not internal, it is an **external entity**, declared as follows:

External Entity Declaration			
[75]	**ExternalID**	::=	'**SYSTEM**' S SystemLiteral

External Entity Declaration	
	| `'PUBLIC'` S PubidLiteral S SystemLiteral
[76] `NDataDecl` `::=` S `'NDATA'` S Name	**[VC:** Notation Declared **]**

If the `NDataDecl` is present, this is a general unparsed entity; otherwise it is a parsed entity.

Validity Constraint: Notation Declared

The `Name` must match the declared name of a notation.

The `SystemLiteral` is called the entity's **system identifier**. It is a URI, which may be used to retrieve the entity. Note that the hash mark (#) and fragment identifier frequently used with URIs are not, formally, part of the URI itself; an XML processor may signal an error if a fragment identifier is given as part of a system identifier. Unless otherwise provided by information outside the scope of this specification (e.g. a special XML element type defined by a particular DTD, or a processing instruction defined by a particular application specification), relative URIs are relative to the location of the resource within which the entity declaration occurs. A URI might thus be relative to the document entity, to the entity containing the external DTD subset, or to some other external parameter entity.

An XML processor should handle a non-ASCII character in a URI by representing the character in UTF-8 as one or more bytes, and then escaping these bytes with the URI escaping mechanism (i.e., by converting each byte to %HH, where HH is the hexadecimal notation of the byte value).

In addition to a system identifier, an external identifier may include a **public identifier**. An XML processor attempting to retrieve the entity's content may use the public identifier to try to generate an alternative URI. If the processor is unable to do so, it must use the URI specified in the system literal. Before a match is attempted, all strings of white space in the public identifier must be normalized to single space characters (#x20), and leading and trailing white space must be removed.

Examples of external entity declarations:

```
<!ENTITY open-hatch
         SYSTEM "http://www.textuality.com/boilerplate/OpenHatch.xml">
<!ENTITY open-hatch
         PUBLIC "-//Textuality//TEXT Standard open-hatch boilerplate//EN"
         "http://www.textuality.com/boilerplate/OpenHatch.xml">
<!ENTITY hatch-pic
         SYSTEM "../grafix/OpenHatch.gif"
         NDATA gif >
```

4.3 Parsed Entities

4.3.1 The Text Declaration

External parsed entities may each begin with a **text declaration**.

Text Declaration
[77]   `TextDecl` `::=`   `'<?xml'` VersionInfo? EncodingDecl S? `'?>'`

The text declaration must be provided literally, not by reference to a parsed entity. No text declaration may appear at any position other than the beginning of an external parsed entity.

4.3.2 Well-Formed Parsed Entities

The document entity is well-formed if it matches the production labeled **document**. An external general parsed entity is well-formed if it matches the production labeled **extParsedEnt**. An external parameter entity is well-formed if it matches the production labeled **extPE**.

Well-Formed External Parsed Entity
[78]   `extParsedEnt` `::=`   TextDecl? content
[79]   `extPE`   `::=`   TextDecl? extSubsetDecl

An internal general parsed entity is well-formed if its replacement text matches the production labeled **content**. All internal parameter entities are well-formed by definition.

A consequence of well-formedness in entities is that the logical and physical structures in an XML document are properly nested; no start-tag, end-tag, empty-element tag, element, comment, processing instruction, character reference, or entity reference can begin in one entity and end in another.

4.3.3 Character Encoding in Entities

Each external parsed entity in an XML document may use a different encoding for its characters. All XML processors must be able to read entities in either UTF-8 or UTF-16.

Entities encoded in UTF-16 must begin with the Byte Order Mark described by ISO/IEC 10646 Annex E and Unicode Appendix B (the ZERO WIDTH NO-BREAK SPACE character, #xFEFF). This is an encoding signature, not part of either the markup or the character data of the XML document. XML processors must be able to use this character to differentiate between UTF-8 and UTF-16 encoded documents.

Although an XML processor is required to read only entities in the UTF-8 and UTF-16 encodings, it is recognized that other encodings are used around the world, and it may be desired for XML processors to read entities that use them. Parsed entities which are stored in an encoding other than UTF-8 or UTF-16 must begin with a text declaration containing an encoding declaration:

Encoding Declaration
[80]   `EncodingDecl` `::=`   S `'encoding'` Eq (`'"'` EncName `'"'` | `"'"` EncName `"'"`)

Encoding Declaration		
[81] EncName ::=	`[A-Za-z] ([A-Za-z0-9._]` `| '-')*`	/*Encoding name contains only Latin characters */

In the document entity, the encoding declaration is part of the XML declaration. The **EncName** is the name of the encoding used.

In an encoding declaration, the values "**UTF-8**", "**UTF-16**", "**ISO-10646-UCS-2**", and "**ISO-10646-UCS-4**" should be used for the various encodings and transformations of Unicode / ISO/IEC 10646, the values "**ISO-8859-1**", "**ISO-8859-2**", ... "**ISO-8859-9**" should be used for the parts of ISO 8859, and the values "**ISO-2022-JP**", "**Shift_JIS**", and "**EUC-JP**" should be used for the various encoded forms of JIS X-0208-1997. XML processors may recognize other encodings; it is recommended that character encodings registered (as *charset*s) with the Internet Assigned Numbers Authority [IANA], other than those just listed, should be referred to using their registered names. Note that these registered names are defined to be case-insensitive, so processors wishing to match against them should do so in a case-insensitive way.

In the absence of information provided by an external transport protocol (e.g. HTTP or MIME), it is an error for an entity including an encoding declaration to be presented to the XML processor in an encoding other than that named in the declaration, for an encoding declaration to occur other than at the beginning of an external entity, or for an entity which begins with neither a Byte Order Mark nor an encoding declaration to use an encoding other than UTF-8. Note that since ASCII is a subset of UTF-8, ordinary ASCII entities do not strictly need an encoding declaration.

It is a fatal error when an XML processor encounters an entity with an encoding that it is unable to process.

Examples of encoding declarations:

```
<?xml encoding='UTF-8'?>
<?xml encoding='EUC-JP'?>
```

4.4 XML Processor Treatment of Entities and References

The table below summarizes the contexts in which character references, entity references, and invocations of unparsed entities might appear and the required behavior of an XML processor in each case. The labels in the leftmost column describe the recognition context:

Reference in Content

as a reference anywhere after the start-tag and before the end-tag of an element; corresponds to the nonterminal **content**.

Reference in Attribute Value

as a reference within either the value of an attribute in a start-tag, or a default value in an attribute declaration; corresponds to the nonterminal **AttValue**.

Occurs as Attribute Value

as a **Name**, not a reference, appearing either as the value of an attribute which has been declared as type **ENTITY**, or as one of the space-separated tokens in the value of an attribute which has been declared as type **ENTITIES**.

Reference in Entity Value

as a reference within a parameter or internal entity's literal entity value in the entity's declaration; corresponds to the nonterminal **EntityValue**.

Reference in DTD

as a reference within either the internal or external subsets of the DTD, but outside of an **EntityValue** or **AttValue**.

	Entity Type				Character
	Parameter	Internal General	External Parsed General	Unparsed	
Reference in Content	Not recognized	Included	Included if validating	Forbidden	Included
Reference in Attribute Value	Not recognized	Included in literal	Forbidden	Forbidden	Included
Occurs as Attribute Value	Not recognized	Forbidden	Forbidden	Notify	Not recognized
Reference in EntityValue	Included in literal	Bypassed	Bypassed	Forbidden	Included
Reference in DTD	Included as PE	Forbidden	Forbidden	Forbidden	Forbidden

4.4.1 Not Recognized

Outside the DTD, the **%** character has no special significance; thus, what would be parameter entity references in the DTD are not recognized as markup in **content**. Similarly, the names of unparsed entities are not recognized except when they appear in the value of an appropriately declared attribute.

4.4.2 Included

An entity is **included** when its replacement text is retrieved and processed, in place of the reference itself, as though it were part of the document at the location the reference was recognized. The replacement text may contain both character data and (except for parameter entities) markup, which must be recognized in the usual way, except that the replacement text of entities used to escape markup delimiters (the entities **amp**, **lt**, **gt**, **apos**, **quot**) is always treated as data. (The string

"**AT&T;**" expands to "**AT&T;**" and the remaining ampersand is not recognized as an entity-reference delimiter.) A character reference is **included** when the indicated character is processed in place of the reference itself.

4.4.3 Included If Validating

When an XML processor recognizes a reference to a parsed entity, in order to validate the document, the processor must include its replacement text. If the entity is external, and the processor is not attempting to validate the XML document, the processor may, but need not, include the entity's replacement text. If a non-validating parser does not include the replacement text, it must inform the application that it recognized, but did not read, the entity.

This rule is based on the recognition that the automatic inclusion provided by the SGML and XML entity mechanism, primarily designed to support modularity in authoring, is not necessarily appropriate for other applications, in particular document browsing. Browsers, for example, when encountering an external parsed entity reference, might choose to provide a visual indication of the entity's presence and retrieve it for display only on demand.

4.4.4 Forbidden

The following are forbidden, and constitute fatal errors:

- ❏ the appearance of a reference to an unparsed entity.
- ❏ the appearance of any character or general-entity reference in the DTD except within an **EntityValue** or **AttValue**.
- ❏ a reference to an external entity in an attribute value.

4.4.5 Included in Literal

When an entity reference appears in an attribute value, or a parameter entity reference appears in a literal entity value, its replacement text is processed in place of the reference itself as though it were part of the document at the location the reference was recognized, except that a single or double quote character in the replacement text is always treated as a normal data character and will not terminate the literal. For example, this is well-formed:

```
<!ENTITY % YN '"Yes"' >
<!ENTITY WhatHeSaid "He said &YN;" >
```

while this is not:

```
<!ENTITY EndAttr "27'" >
<element attribute='a-&EndAttr;>
```

4.4.6 Notify

When the name of an unparsed entity appears as a token in the value of an attribute of declared type **ENTITY** or **ENTITIES**, a validating processor must inform the application of the system and public (if any) identifiers for both the entity and its associated notation.

4.4.7 Bypassed

When a general entity reference appears in the `EntityValue` in an entity declaration, it is bypassed and left as is.

4.4.8 Included as PE

Just as with external parsed entities, parameter entities need only be included if validating. When a parameter-entity reference is recognized in the DTD and included, its replacement text is enlarged by the attachment of one leading and one following space (#x20) character; the intent is to constrain the replacement text of parameter entities to contain an integral number of grammatical tokens in the DTD.

4.5 Construction of Internal Entity Replacement Text

In discussing the treatment of internal entities, it is useful to distinguish two forms of the entity's value. The **literal entity value** is the quoted string actually present in the entity declaration, corresponding to the non-terminal `EntityValue`. The **replacement text** is the content of the entity, after replacement of character references and parameter-entity references.

The literal entity value as given in an internal entity declaration (`EntityValue`) may contain character, parameter-entity, and general-entity references. Such references must be contained entirely within the literal entity value. The actual replacement text that is included as described above must contain the *replacement text* of any parameter entities referred to, and must contain the character referred to, in place of any character references in the literal entity value; however, general-entity references must be left as-is, unexpanded. For example, given the following declarations:

```
<!ENTITY % pub    "&#xc9;ditions Gallimard" >
<!ENTITY   rights "All rights reserved" >
<!ENTITY   book   "La Peste: Albert Camus,
&#xA9; 1947 %pub;. &rights;" >
```

then the replacement text for the entity "**book**" is:

```
La Peste: Albert Camus,
© 1947 Éditions Gallimard. &rights;
```

The general-entity reference "`&rights;`" would be expanded should the reference "`&book;`" appear in the document's content or an attribute value.

These simple rules may have complex interactions; for a detailed discussion of a difficult example, see "D. Expansion of Entity and Character References".

4.6 Predefined Entities

Entity and character references can both be used to **escape** the left angle bracket, ampersand, and other delimiters. A set of general entities (**amp**, **lt**, **gt**, **apos**, **quot**) is specified for this purpose. Numeric character references may also be used; they are expanded immediately when recognized and must be treated as character data, so the numeric character references "`&#60;`" and "`&#38;`" may be used to escape < and & when they occur in character data.

All XML processors must recognize these entities whether they are declared or not. For interoperability, valid XML documents should declare these entities, like any others, before using them. If the entities in question are declared, they must be declared as internal entities whose replacement text is the single character being escaped or a character reference to that character, as shown below.

```
<!ENTITY lt     "&#38;#60;">
<!ENTITY gt     "&#62;">
<!ENTITY amp    "&#38;#38;">
<!ENTITY apos   "&#39;">
<!ENTITY quot   "&#34;">
```

Note that the < and & characters in the declarations of "lt" and "amp" are doubly escaped to meet the requirement that entity replacement be well-formed.

4.7 Notation Declarations

Notations identify by name the format of unparsed entities, the format of elements which bear a notation attribute, or the application to which a processing instruction is addressed.

Notation declarations provide a name for the notation, for use in entity and attribute-list declarations and in attribute specifications, and an external identifier for the notation which may allow an XML processor or its client application to locate a helper application capable of processing data in the given notation.

Notation Declarations		
[82] **NotationDecl** ::=	'**<!NOTATION**' S Name S (ExternalID | PublicID) S? '**>**'	
[83] **PublicID** ::=	'**PUBLIC**' S PubidLiteral	

XML processors must provide applications with the name and external identifier(s) of any notation declared and referred to in an attribute value, attribute definition, or entity declaration. They may additionally resolve the external identifier into the system identifier, file name, or other information needed to allow the application to call a processor for data in the notation described. (It is not an error, however, for XML documents to declare and refer to notations for which notation-specific applications are not available on the system where the XML processor or application is running.)

4.8 Document Entity

The **document entity** serves as the root of the entity tree and a starting-point for an XML processor. This specification does not specify how the document entity is to be located by an XML processor; unlike other entities, the document entity has no name and might well appear on a processor input stream without any identification at all.

5. Conformance

5.1 Validating and Non-Validating Processors

Conforming XML processors fall into two classes: validating and non-validating.

Validating and non-validating processors alike must report violations of this specification's well-formedness constraints in the content of the document entity and any other parsed entities that they read.

Validating processors must report violations of the constraints expressed by the declarations in the DTD, and failures to fulfill the validity constraints given in this specification. To accomplish this, validating XML processors must read and process the entire DTD and all external parsed entities referenced in the document.

Non-validating processors are required to check only the document entity, including the entire internal DTD subset, for well-formedness. While they are not required to check the document for validity, they are required to **process** all the declarations they read in the internal DTD subset and in any parameter entity that they read, up to the first reference to a parameter entity that they do *not* read; that is to say, they must use the information in those declarations to normalize attribute values, include the replacement text of internal entities, and supply default attribute values. They must not process entity declarations or attribute-list declarations encountered after a reference to a parameter entity that is not read, since the entity may have contained overriding declarations.

5.2 Using XML Processors

The behavior of a validating XML processor is highly predictable; it must read every piece of a document and report all well-formedness and validity violations. Less is required of a non-validating processor; it need not read any part of the document other than the document entity. This has two effects that may be important to users of XML processors:

❑ Certain well-formedness errors, specifically those that require reading external entities, may not be detected by a non-validating processor. Examples include the constraints entitled Entity Declared, Parsed Entity, and No Recursion, as well as some of the cases described as forbidden in "4.4 XML Processor Treatment of Entities and References".

❑ The information passed from the processor to the application may vary, depending on whether the processor reads parameter and external entities. For example, a non-validating processor may not normalize attribute values, include the replacement text of internal entities, or supply default attribute values, where doing so depends on having read declarations in external or parameter entities.

For maximum reliability in interoperating between different XML processors, applications which use non-validating processors should not rely on any behaviors not required of such processors. Applications which require facilities such as the use of default attributes or internal entities which are declared in external entities should use validating XML processors.

6. Notation

The formal grammar of XML is given in this specification using a simple Extended Backus-Naur Form (EBNF) notation. Each rule in the grammar defines one symbol, in the form

```
symbol ::= expression
```

Symbols are written with an initial capital letter if they are defined by a regular expression, or with an initial lower case letter otherwise. Literal strings are quoted.

Within the expression on the right-hand side of a rule, the following expressions are used to match strings of one or more characters:

#xN

where **N** is a hexadecimal integer, the expression matches the character in ISO/IEC 10646 whose canonical (UCS-4) code value, when interpreted as an unsigned binary number, has the value indicated. The number of leading zeros in the **#xN** form is insignificant; the number of leading zeros in the corresponding code value is governed by the character encoding in use and is not significant for XML.

[a-zA-Z], [#xN-#xN]

matches any character with a value in the range(s) indicated (inclusive).

[^a-z], [^#xN-#xN]

matches any character with a value *outside* the range indicated.

[^abc], [^#xN#xN#xN]

matches any character with a value not among the characters given.

"string"

matches a literal string matching that given inside the double quotes.

'string'

matches a literal string matching that given inside the single quotes.

These symbols may be combined to match more complex patterns as follows, where **A** and **B** represent simple expressions:

(expression)

expression is treated as a unit and may be combined as described in this list.

A?

matches **A** or nothing; optional **A**.

A B

matches **A** followed by **B**.

A | B

matches **A** or **B** but not both.

A - B

matches any string that matches **A** but does not match **B**.

A+

matches one or more occurrences of **A**.

A*

matches zero or more occurrences of **A**.

Other notations used in the productions are:

/* ... */

comment.

[wfc: ...]

well-formedness constraint; this identifies by name a constraint on well-formed documents associated with a production.

[vc: ...]

validity constraint; this identifies by name a constraint on valid documents associated with a production.

Appendices

A. References

A.1 Normative References

IANA

(Internet Assigned Numbers Authority) *Official Names for Character Sets*, ed. Keld Simonsen et al. See ftp://ftp.isi.edu/in-notes/iana/assignments/character-sets.

IETF RFC 1766

IETF (Internet Engineering Task Force). *RFC 1766: Tags for the Identification of Languages*, ed. H. Alvestrand. 1995.

ISO 639

(International Organization for Standardization). *ISO 639:1988 (E). Code for the representation of names of languages.* [Geneva]: International Organization for Standardization, 1988.

ISO 3166

(International Organization for Standardization). *ISO 3166-1:1997 (E). Codes for the representation of names of countries and their subdivisions -- Part 1: Country codes* [Geneva]: International Organization for Standardization, 1997.

ISO/IEC 10646

ISO (International Organization for Standardization). *ISO/IEC 10646-1993 (E). Information technology -- Universal Multiple-Octet Coded Character Set (UCS) -- Part 1: Architecture and Basic Multilingual Plane.* [Geneva]: International Organization for Standardization, 1993 (plus amendments AM 1 through AM 7).

Unicode

The Unicode Consortium. *The Unicode Standard, Version 2.0.* Reading, Mass.: Addison-Wesley Developers Press, 1996.

A.2 Other References

Aho/Ullman

Aho, Alfred V., Ravi Sethi, and Jeffrey D. Ullman. *Compilers: Principles, Techniques, and Tools.* Reading: Addison-Wesley, 1986, rpt. corr. 1988.

Berners-Lee et al.

Berners-Lee, T., R. Fielding, and L. Masinter. *Uniform Resource Identifiers (URI): Generic Syntax and Semantics.* 1997. (Work in progress; see updates to RFC1738.)

Brüggemann-Klein

Brüggemann-Klein, Anne. *Regular Expressions into Finite Automata.* Extended abstract in I. Simon, Hrsg., LATIN 1992, S. 97-98. Springer-Verlag, Berlin 1992. Full Version in Theoretical Computer Science 120: 197-213, 1993.

Brüggemann-Klein and Wood

Brüggemann-Klein, Anne, and Derick Wood. *Deterministic Regular Languages.* Universität Freiburg, Institut für Informatik, Bericht 38, Oktober 1991.

Clark

James Clark. Comparison of SGML and XML. See `http://www.w3.org/TR/NOTE-sgml-xml-971215`.

IETF RFC1738

IETF (Internet Engineering Task Force). *RFC 1738: Uniform Resource Locators (URL)*, ed. T. Berners-Lee, L. Masinter, M. McCahill. 1994.

IETF RFC1808

IETF (Internet Engineering Task Force). *RFC 1808: Relative Uniform Resource Locators*, ed. R. Fielding. 1995.

IETF RFC2141

IETF (Internet Engineering Task Force). *RFC 2141: URN Syntax*, ed. R. Moats. 1997.

ISO 8879

ISO (International Organization for Standardization). *ISO 8879:1986(E). Information processing -- Text and Office Systems -- Standard Generalized Markup Language (SGML).* First edition -- 1986-10-15. [Geneva]: International Organization for Standardization, 1986.

ISO/IEC 10744

ISO (International Organization for Standardization). *ISO/IEC 10744-1992 (E). Information technology -- Hypermedia/Time-based Structuring Language (HyTime).* [Geneva]: International Organization for Standardization, 1992. *Extended Facilities Annexe.* [Geneva]: International Organization for Standardization, 1996.

B. Character Classes

Following the characteristics defined in the Unicode standard, characters are classed as base characters (among others, these contain the alphabetic characters of the Latin alphabet, without diacritics), ideographic characters, and combining characters (among others, this class contains most diacritics); these classes combine to form the class of letters. Digits and extenders are also distinguished.

Characters

[84]	**Letter**	::=	BaseChar | Ideographic

```
[#x0041-#x005A] | [#x0061-#x007A] | [#x00C0-
#x00D6] | [#x00D8-#x00F6] | [#x00F8-#x00FF]
| [#x0100-#x0131] | [#x0134-#x013E]
| [#x0141-#x0148] | [#x014A-#x017E]
| [#x0180-#x01C3] | [#x01CD-#x01F0]
| [#x01F4-#x01F5] | [#x01FA-#x0217]
| [#x0250-#x02A8] | [#x02BB-#x02C1] | #x0386
| [#x0388-#x038A] | #x038C | [#x038E-#x03A1]
| [#x03A3-#x03CE] | [#x03D0-#x03D6] | #x03DA
| #x03DC | #x03DE | #x03E0 | [#x03E2-#x03F3]
| [#x0401-#x040C] | [#x040E-#x044F]
| [#x0451-#x045C] | [#x045E-#x0481]
| [#x0490-#x04C4] | [#x04C7-#x04C8]
| [#x04CB-#x04CC] | [#x04D0-#x04EB]
| [#x04EE-#x04F5] | [#x04F8-#x04F9]
| [#x0531-#x0556] | #x0559 | [#x0561-#x0586]
| [#x05D0-#x05EA] | [#x05F0-#x05F2]
| [#x0621-#x063A] | [#x0641-#x064A]
| [#x0671-#x06B7] | [#x06BA-#x06BE]
| [#x06C0-#x06CE] | [#x06D0-#x06D3] | #x06D5
| [#x06E5-#x06E6] | [#x0905-#x0939] | #x093D
| [#x0958-#x0961] | [#x0985-#x098C]
| [#x098F-#x0990] | [#x0993-#x09A8]
| [#x09AA-#x09B0] | #x09B2 | [#x09B6-#x09B9]
```

[85]	**BaseChar**	::=	

```
| [#x09DC-#x09DD] | [#x09DF-#x09E1]
| [#x09F0-#x09F1] | [#x0A05-#x0A0A]
| [#x0A0F-#x0A10] | [#x0A13-#x0A28]
| [#x0A2A-#x0A30] | [#x0A32-#x0A33]
| [#x0A35-#x0A36] | [#x0A38-#x0A39]
| [#x0A59-#x0A5C] | #x0A5E | [#x0A72-#x0A74]
| [#x0A85-#x0A8B] | #x0A8D | [#x0A8F-#x0A91]
| [#x0A93-#x0AA8] | [#x0AAA-#x0AB0]
| [#x0AB2-#x0AB3] | [#x0AB5-#x0AB9] | #x0ABD
| #x0AE0 | [#x0B05-#x0B0C] | [#x0B0F-#x0B10]
| [#x0B13-#x0B28] | [#x0B2A-#x0B30]
| [#x0B32-#x0B33] | [#x0B36-#x0B39] | #x0B3D
| [#x0B5C-#x0B5D] | [#x0B5F-#x0B61]
| [#x0B85-#x0B8A] | [#x0B8E-#x0B90]
| [#x0B92-#x0B95] | [#x0B99-#x0B9A] | #x0B9C
| [#x0B9E-#x0B9F] | [#x0BA3-#x0BA4]
| [#x0BA8-#x0BAA] | [#x0BAE-#x0BB5]
| [#x0BB7-#x0BB9] | [#x0C05-#x0C0C]
| [#x0C0E-#x0C10] | [#x0C12-#x0C28]
| [#x0C2A-#x0C33] | [#x0C35-#x0C39]
| [#x0C60-#x0C61] | [#x0C85-#x0C8C]
| [#x0C8E-#x0C90] | [#x0C92-#x0CA8]
| [#x0CAA-#x0CB3] | [#x0CB5-#x0CB9] | #x0CDE
| [#x0CE0-#x0CE1] | [#x0D05-#x0D0C]
| [#x0D0E-#x0D10] | [#x0D12-#x0D28]
```

```
                                    |  [#x0D2A-#x0D39]  |  [#x0D60-#x0D61]
                                    |  [#x0E01-#x0E2E]  |  #x0E30  |  [#x0E32-#x0E33]
                                    |  [#x0E40-#x0E45]  |  [#x0E81-#x0E82]  |  #x0E84
                                    |  [#x0E87-#x0E88]  |  #x0E8A  |  #x0E8D
                                    |  [#x0E94-#x0E97]  |  [#x0E99-#x0E9F]
                                    |  [#x0EA1-#x0EA3]  |  #x0EA5  |  #x0EA7
                                    |  [#x0EAA-#x0EAB]  |  [#x0EAD-#x0EAE]  |  #x0EB0
                                    |  [#x0EB2-#x0EB3]  |  #x0EBD  |  [#x0EC0-#x0EC4]
                                    |  [#x0F40-#x0F47]  |  [#x0F49-#x0F69]
                                    |  [#x10A0-#x10C5]  |  [#x10D0-#x10F6]  |  #x1100
                                    |  [#x1102-#x1103]  |  [#x1105-#x1107]  |  #x1109
                                    |  [#x110B-#x110C]  |  [#x110E-#x1112]  |  #x113C
                                    |  #x113E  |  #x1140  |  #x114C  |  #x114E  |  #x1150
                                    |  [#x1154-#x1155]  |  #x1159  |  [#x115F-#x1161]
                                    |  #x1163  |  #x1165  |  #x1167  |  #x1169
                                    |  [#x116D-#x116E]  |  [#x1172-#x1173]  |  #x1175
                                    |  #x119E  |  #x11A8  |  #x11AB  |  [#x11AE-#x11AF]
                                    |  [#x11B7-#x11B8]  |  #x11BA  |  [#x11BC-#x11C2]
                                    |  #x11EB  |  #x11F0  |  #x11F9  |  [#x1E00-#x1E9B]
                                    |  [#x1EA0-#x1EF9]  |  [#x1F00-#x1F15]
                                    |  [#x1F18-#x1F1D]  |  [#x1F20-#x1F45]
                                    |  [#x1F48-#x1F4D]  |  [#x1F50-#x1F57]  |  #x1F59
                                    |  #x1F5B  |  #x1F5D  |  [#x1F5F-#x1F7D]
                                    |  [#x1F80-#x1FB4]  |  [#x1FB6-#x1FBC]  |  #x1FBE
                                    |  [#x1FC2-#x1FC4]  |  [#x1FC6-#x1FCC]
                                    |  [#x1FD0-#x1FD3]  |  [#x1FD6-#x1FDB]
                                    |  [#x1FE0-#x1FEC]  |  [#x1FF2-#x1FF4]
                                    |  [#x1FF6-#x1FFC]  |  #x2126  |  [#x212A-#x212B]
                                    |  #x212E  |  [#x2180-#x2182]  |  [#x3041-#x3094]
                                    |  [#x30A1-#x30FA]  |  [#x3105-#x312C]
                                    |  [#xAC00-#xD7A3]
```

```
[86]    Ideographic    ::=    [#x4E00-#x9FA5] | #x3007 | [#x3021-#x3029]
```

```
                                   [#x0300-#x0345]  |  [#x0360-#x0361]  |  [#x0483-
                                   #x0486]  |  [#x0591-#x05A1]  |  [#x05A3-#x05B9]
                                   |  [#x05BB-#x05BD]  |  #x05BF  |  [#x05C1-#x05C2]
                                   |  #x05C4  |  [#x064B-#x0652]  |  #x0670
                                   |  [#x06D6-#x06DC]  |  [#x06DD-#x06DF]
                                   |  [#x06E0-#x06E4]  |  [#x06E7-#x06E8]
                                   |  [#x06EA-#x06ED]  |  [#x0901-#x0903]  |  #x093C
                                   |  [#x093E-#x094C]  |  #x094D  |  [#x0951-#x0954]
                                   |  [#x0962-#x0963]  |  [#x0981-#x0983]  |  #x09BC
                                   |  #x09BE  |  #x09BF  |  [#x09C0-#x09C4]
                                   |  [#x09C7-#x09C8]  |  [#x09CB-#x09CD]  |  #x09D7
                                   |  [#x09E2-#x09E3]  |  #x0A02  |  #x0A3C  |  #x0A3E
                                   |  #x0A3F  |  [#x0A40-#x0A42]  |  [#x0A47-#x0A48]
                                   |  [#x0A4B-#x0A4D]  |  [#x0A70-#x0A71]
[87]    Combining      |  [#x0A81-#x0A83]  |  #x0ABC  |  [#x0ABE-#x0AC5]
        Char   ::=    |  [#x0AC7-#x0AC9]  |  [#x0ACB-#x0ACD]
                                   |  [#x0B01-#x0B03]  |  #x0B3C  |  [#x0B3E-#x0B43]
                                   |  [#x0B47-#x0B48]  |  [#x0B4B-#x0B4D]
                                   |  [#x0B56-#x0B57]  |  [#x0B82-#x0B83]
                                   |  [#x0BBE-#x0BC2]  |  [#x0BC6-#x0BC8]
                                   |  [#x0BCA-#x0BCD]  |  #x0BD7  |  [#x0C01-#x0C03]
                                   |  [#x0C3E-#x0C44]  |  [#x0C46-#x0C48]
                                   |  [#x0C4A-#x0C4D]  |  [#x0C55-#x0C56]
                                   |  [#x0C82-#x0C83]  |  [#x0CBE-#x0CC4]
                                   |  [#x0CC6-#x0CC8]  |  [#x0CCA-#x0CCD]
                                   |  [#x0CD5-#x0CD6]  |  [#x0D02-#x0D03]
                                   |  [#x0D3E-#x0D43]  |  [#x0D46-#x0D48]
                                   |  [#x0D4A-#x0D4D]  |  #x0D57  |  #x0E31
                                   |  [#x0E34-#x0E3A]  |  [#x0E47-#x0E4E]  |  #x0EB1
                                   |  [#x0EB4-#x0EB9]  |  [#x0EBB-#x0EBC]
```

			`| [#x0EC8-#x0ECD]	[#x0F18-#x0F19]	#x0F35` `| #x0F37	#x0F39	#x0F3E	#x0F3F` `| [#x0F71-#x0F84]	[#x0F86-#x0F8B]` `| [#x0F90-#x0F95]	#x0F97	[#x0F99-#x0FAD]` `| [#x0FB1-#x0FB7]	#x0FB9	[#x20D0-#x20DC]` `| #x20E1	[#x302A-#x302F]	#x3099	#x309A`
[88]	`Digit`	`::=`	`[#x0030-#x0039]	[#x0660-#x0669]	[#x06F0-` `#x06F9]	[#x0966-#x096F]	[#x09E6-#x09EF]` `	[#x0A66-#x0A6F]	[#x0AE6-#x0AEF]` `	[#x0B66-#x0B6F]	[#x0BE7-#x0BEF]` `	[#x0C66-#x0C6F]	[#x0CE6-#x0CEF]` `	[#x0D66-#x0D6F]	[#x0E50-#x0E59]` `	[#x0ED0-#x0ED9]	[#x0F20-#x0F29]`
[89]	`Extender`	`::=`	`#x00B7	#x02D0	#x02D1	#x0387	#x0640` `	#x0E46	#x0EC6	#x3005	[#x3031-#x3035]` `	[#x309D-#x309E]	[#x30FC-#x30FE]`

The character classes defined here can be derived from the Unicode character database as follows:

❑ Name start characters must have one of the categories Ll, Lu, Lo, Lt, Nl.

❑ Name characters other than Name-start characters must have one of the categories Mc, Me, Mn, Lm, or Nd.

❑ Characters in the compatibility area (i.e. with character code greater than #xF900 and less than #xFFFE) are not allowed in XML names.

❑ Characters which have a font or compatibility decomposition (i.e. those with a "compatibility formatting tag" in field 5 of the database -- marked by field 5 beginning with a "<") are not allowed.

❑ The following characters are treated as name-start characters rather than name characters, because the property file classifies them as Alphabetic: [#x02BB-#x02C1], #x0559, #x06E5, #x06E6.

❑ Characters #x20DD-#x20E0 are excluded (in accordance with Unicode, section 5.14).

❑ Character #x00B7 is classified as an extender, because the property list so identifies it.

❑ Character #x0387 is added as a name character, because #x00B7 is its canonical equivalent.

❑ Characters ':' and '_' are allowed as name-start characters.

❑ Characters '-' and '.' are allowed as name characters.

C. XML and SGML (Non-Normative)

XML is designed to be a subset of SGML, in that every valid XML document should also be a conformant SGML document. For a detailed comparison of the additional restrictions that XML places on documents beyond those of SGML, see Clark.

D. Expansion of Entity and Character References (Non-Normative)

This appendix contains some examples illustrating the sequence of entity- and character-reference recognition and expansion, as specified in "4.4 XML Processor Treatment of Entities and References".

If the DTD contains the declaration

```
<!ENTITY example "<p>An ampersand (&#38;#38;) may be escaped
numerically (&#38;#38;#38;) or with a general entity
```

then the XML processor will recognize the character references when it parses the entity declaration, and resolve them before storing the following string as the value of the entity "**example**":

```
<p>An ampersand (&#38;) may be escaped
numerically (&#38;#38;) or with a general entity
(&amp;amp;).</p>
```

A reference in the document to "**&example;**" will cause the text to be reparsed, at which time the start- and end-tags of the "**p**" element will be recognized and the three references will be recognized and expanded, resulting in a "**p**" element with the following content (all data, no delimiters or markup):

```
An ampersand (&) may be escaped
numerically (&#38;) or with a general entity
(&amp;).
```

A more complex example will illustrate the rules and their effects fully. In the following example, the line numbers are solely for reference.

```
1 <?xml version='1.0'?>
2 <!DOCTYPE test [
3 <!ELEMENT test (#PCDATA) >
4 <!ENTITY % xx '&#37;zz;'>
5 <!ENTITY % zz '&#60;!ENTITY tricky "error-prone" >' >
6 %xx;
7 ]>
8 <test>This sample shows a &tricky; method.</test>
```

This produces the following:

- in line 4, the reference to character 37 is expanded immediately, and the parameter entity "**xx**" is stored in the symbol table with the value "**%zz;**". Since the replacement text is not rescanned, the reference to parameter entity "**zz**" is not recognized. (And it would be an error if it were, since "**zz**" is not yet declared.)

- in line 5, the character reference "**<**" is expanded immediately and the parameter entity "**zz**" is stored with the replacement text "**<!ENTITY tricky "error-prone" >**", which is a well-formed entity declaration.

- in line 6, the reference to "**xx**" is recognized, and the replacement text of "**xx**" (namely "**%zz;**") is parsed. The reference to "**zz**" is recognized in its turn, and its replacement text ("**<!ENTITY tricky "error-prone" >**") is parsed. The general entity "**tricky**" has now been declared, with the replacement text "**error-prone**".

- in line 8, the reference to the general entity "**tricky**" is recognized, and it is expanded, so the full content of the "**test**" element is the self-describing (and ungrammatical) string *This sample shows a error-prone method.*

E. Deterministic Content Models (Non-Normative)

For compatibility, it is required that content models in element type declarations be deterministic. SGML requires deterministic content models (it calls them "unambiguous"); XML processors built using SGML systems may flag non-deterministic content models as errors.

For example, the content model `((b, c) | (b, d))` is non-deterministic, because given an initial **b** the parser cannot know which **b** in the model is being matched without looking ahead to see which element follows the **b**. In this case, the two references to **b** can be collapsed into a single reference, making the model read `(b, (c | d))`. An initial **b** now clearly matches only a single name in the content model. The parser doesn't need to look ahead to see what follows; either **c** or **d** would be accepted.

More formally: a finite state automaton may be constructed from the content model using the standard algorithms, e.g. algorithm 3.5 in section 3.9 of Aho, Sethi, and Ullman [Aho/Ullman]. In many such algorithms, a follow set is constructed for each position in the regular expression (i.e., each leaf node in the syntax tree for the regular expression); if any position has a follow set in which more than one following position is labeled with the same element type name, then the content model is in error and may be reported as an error.

Algorithms exist which allow many but not all non-deterministic content models to be reduced automatically to equivalent deterministic models; see Brüggemann-Klein 1991 [Brüggemann-Klein].

F. Autodetection of Character Encodings (Non-Normative)

The XML encoding declaration functions as an internal label on each entity, indicating which character encoding is in use. Before an XML processor can read the internal label, however, it apparently has to know what character encoding is in use--which is what the internal label is trying to indicate. In the general case, this is a hopeless situation. It is not entirely hopeless in XML, however, because XML limits the general case in two ways: each implementation is assumed to support only a finite set of character encodings, and the XML encoding declaration is restricted in position and content in order to make it feasible to autodetect the character encoding in use in each entity in normal cases. Also, in many cases other sources of information are available in addition to the XML data stream itself. Two cases may be distinguished, depending on whether the XML entity is presented to the processor without, or with, any accompanying (external) information. We consider the first case first.

Because each XML entity not in UTF-8 or UTF-16 format *must* begin with an XML encoding declaration, in which the first characters must be '`<?xml`', any conforming processor can detect, after two to four octets of input, which of the following cases apply. In reading this list, it may help to know that in UCS-4, '`<`' is "`#x0000003C`" and '`?`' is "`#x0000003F`", and the Byte Order Mark required of UTF-16 data streams is "`#xFEFF`".

- ❑ `00 00 00 3C`: UCS-4, big-endian machine (1234 order)

- ❑ `3C 00 00 00`: UCS-4, little-endian machine (4321 order)

- ❑ `00 00 3C 00`: UCS-4, unusual octet order (2143)

- ❑ `00 3C 00 00`: UCS-4, unusual octet order (3412)

- ❑ `FE FF`: UTF-16, big-endian

- ❑ `FF FE`: UTF-16, little-endian

- ❑ `00 3C 00 3F`: UTF-16, big-endian, no Byte Order Mark (and thus, strictly speaking, in error)

- ❑ `3C 00 3F 00`: UTF-16, little-endian, no Byte Order Mark (and thus, strictly speaking, in error)

- ❑ `3C 3F 78 6D`: UTF-8, ISO 646, ASCII, some part of ISO 8859, Shift-JIS, EUC, or any other 7-bit, 8-bit, or mixed-width encoding which ensures that the characters of ASCII have their normal positions, width, and values; the actual encoding declaration must be read to detect which of these applies, but since all of these encodings use the same bit patterns for the ASCII characters, the encoding declaration itself may be read reliably

- ❑ `4C 6F A7 94`: EBCDIC (in some flavor; the full encoding declaration must be read to tell which code page is in use)

- ❑ other: UTF-8 without an encoding declaration, or else the data stream is corrupt, fragmentary, or enclosed in a wrapper of some kind

This level of autodetection is enough to read the XML encoding declaration and parse the character-encoding identifier, which is still necessary to distinguish the individual members of each family of encodings (e.g. to tell UTF-8 from 8859, and the parts of 8859 from each other, or to distinguish the specific EBCDIC code page in use, and so on).

Because the contents of the encoding declaration are restricted to ASCII characters, a processor can reliably read the entire encoding declaration as soon as it has detected which family of encodings is in use. Since in practice, all widely used character encodings fall into one of the categories above, the XML encoding declaration allows reasonably reliable in-band labeling of character encodings, even when external sources of information at the operating-system or transport-protocol level are unreliable.

Once the processor has detected the character encoding in use, it can act appropriately, whether by invoking a separate input routine for each case, or by calling the proper conversion function on each character of input.

Like any self-labeling system, the XML encoding declaration will not work if any software changes the entity's character set or encoding without updating the encoding declaration. Implementors of character-encoding routines should be careful to ensure the accuracy of the internal and external information used to label the entity.

The second possible case occurs when the XML entity is accompanied by encoding information, as in some file systems and some network protocols. When multiple sources of information are available, their relative priority and the preferred method of handling conflict should be specified as part of the

higher-level protocol used to deliver XML. Rules for the relative priority of the internal label and the MIME-type label in an external header, for example, should be part of the RFC document defining the text/xml and application/xml MIME types. In the interests of interoperability, however, the following rules are recommended.

- ❑ If an XML entity is in a file, the Byte-Order Mark and encoding-declaration PI are used (if present) to determine the character encoding. All other heuristics and sources of information are solely for error recovery.

- ❑ If an XML entity is delivered with a MIME type of text/xml, then the **charset** parameter on the MIME type determines the character encoding method; all other heuristics and sources of information are solely for error recovery.

- ❑ If an XML entity is delivered with a MIME type of application/xml, then the Byte-Order Mark and encoding-declaration PI are used (if present) to determine the character encoding. All other heuristics and sources of information are solely for error recovery.

These rules apply only in the absence of protocol-level documentation; in particular, when the MIME types text/xml and application/xml are defined, the recommendations of the relevant RFC will supersede these rules.

G. W3C XML Working Group (Non-Normative)

This specification was prepared and approved for publication by the W3C XML Working Group (WG). WG approval of this specification does not necessarily imply that all WG members voted for its approval. The current and former members of the XML WG are:

Jon Bosak, Sun (Chair); James Clark (Technical Lead); Tim Bray, Textuality and Netscape (XML Co-editor); Jean Paoli, Microsoft (XML Co-editor); C. M. Sperberg-McQueen, U. of Ill. (XML Co-editor); Dan Connolly, W3C (W3C Liaison); Paula Angerstein, Texcel; Steve DeRose, INSO; Dave Hollander, HP; Eliot Kimber, ISOGEN; Eve Maler, ArborText; Tom Magliery, NCSA; Murray Maloney, Muzmo and Grif; Makoto Murata, Fuji Xerox Information Systems; Joel Nava, Adobe; Conleth O'Connell, Vignette; Peter Sharpe, SoftQuad; John Tigue, DataChannel

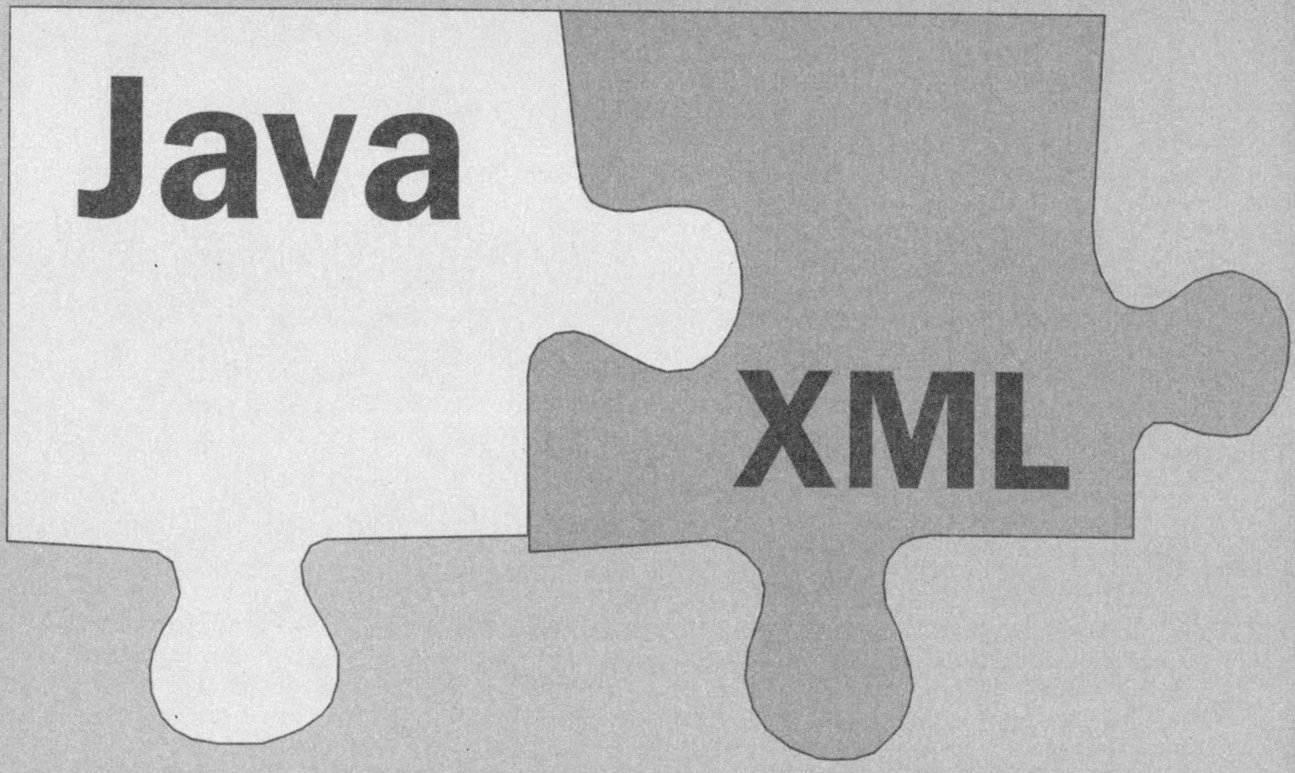
Java
XML

Namespaces in XML

Rec-xml-names-19990114
World Wide Web Consortium 14-January-1999

This appendix is taken from the W3C Recommendation at
`http://www.w3.org/TR/REC-xml-names`

Incorporates the list of known errors in this specification available at
`http://www.w3.org/XML/xml-names-19990114-errata`

Status of this Document
This document has been reviewed by W3C Members and other interested parties and has been endorsed by the Director as a W3C Recommendation. It is a stable document and may be used as reference material or cited as a normative reference from another document. W3C's role in making the Recommendation is to draw attention to the specification and to promote its widespread deployment. This enhances the functionality and interoperability of the Web.

Editors
Tim Bray (Textuality)   tbray@textuality.com
Dave Hollander (Hewlett-Packard Company)   dmh@corp.hp.com
Andrew Layman (Microsoft)   andrewl@microsoft.com

Abstract

XML namespaces provide a simple method for qualifying element and attribute names used in Extensible Markup Language documents by associating them with namespaces identified by URI references.

Table of Contents

Appendices

1. Motivation and Summary

We envision applications of Extensible Markup Language (XML) where a single XML document may contain elements and attributes (here referred to as a "markup vocabulary") that are defined for and used by multiple software modules. One motivation for this is modularity; if such a markup vocabulary exists which is well-understood and for which there is useful software available, it is better to re-use this markup rather than re-invent it.
Such documents, containing multiple markup vocabularies, pose problems of recognition and collision. Software modules need to be able to recognize the tags and attributes which they are designed to process, even in the face of "collisions" occurring when markup intended for some other software package uses the same element type or attribute name.

These considerations require that document constructs should have universal names, whose scope extends beyond their containing document. This specification describes a mechanism, *XML namespaces*, which accomplishes this.

[Definition:] An **XML namespace** is a collection of names, identified by a URI reference [RFC2396], which are used in XML documents as element types and attribute names. XML namespaces differ from the "namespaces" conventionally used in computing disciplines in that the XML version has internal structure and is not, mathematically speaking, a set. These issues are discussed in "A. The Internal Structure of XML Namespaces".

[Definition:] URI references which identify namespaces are considered **identical** when they are exactly the same character-for-character. Note that URI references which are not identical in this sense may in fact be functionally equivalent. Examples include URI references which differ only in case, or which are in external entities which have different effective base URIs.

Names from XML namespaces may appear as qualified names, which contain a single colon, separating the name into a namespace prefix and a local part. The prefix, which is mapped to a URI reference, selects a namespace. The combination of the universally managed URI namespace and the document's own namespace produces identifiers that are universally unique. Mechanisms are provided for prefix scoping and defaulting.

URI references can contain characters not allowed in names, so cannot be used directly as namespace prefixes. Therefore, the namespace prefix serves as a proxy for a URI reference. An attribute-based syntax described below is used to declare the association of the namespace prefix with a URI reference; software which supports this namespace proposal must recognize and act on these declarations and prefixes.

1.1 A Note on Notation and Usage

Note that many of the nonterminals in the productions in this specification are defined not here but in the XML specification. ??? put in http When nonterminals defined here have the same names as nonterminals defined in the XML specification, the productions here in all cases match a subset of the strings matched by the corresponding ones there.

In this document's productions, the NSC is a "Namespace Constraint", one of the rules that documents conforming to this specification must follow.

Note that all Internet domain names used in examples, with the exception of w3.org, are selected at random and should not be taken as having any import.

2. Declaring Namespaces

[Definition:] A namespace is **declared** using a family of reserved attributes. Such an attribute's name must either be xmlns or have xmlns: as a prefix. These attributes, like any other XML attributes, may be provided directly or by default.

Attribute Names for Namespace Declaration	
[1]	NSAttName ::= PrefixedAttName	DefaultAttName
[2]	PrefixedAttName ::= 'xmlns' NCName
[3]	DefaultAttName ::= 'xmlns'
[4]	NCName ::= (Letter | '_') (NCNameChar)* [An XML Name, minus the ":" */]
[5]	NCNameChar ::= Letter	Digit	'.'	'-'	'_'	CombiningChar	Extender

[Definition:] The attribute's value, a URI reference, is the **namespace name** identifying the namespace. The namespace name, to serve its intended purpose, should have the characteristics of uniqueness and persistence. It is not a goal that it be directly usable for retrieval of a schema (if any exists). An example of a syntax that is designed with these goals in mind is that for Uniform Resource Names [RFC2141]. However, it should be noted that ordinary URLs can be managed in such a way as to achieve these same goals.

[Definition:] If the attribute name matches PrefixedAttName, then the NCName gives the **namespace prefix**, used to associate element and attribute names with the namespace name in the attribute value in the scope of the element to which the declaration is attached. In such declarations, the namespace name may not be empty.

[Definition:] If the attribute name matches DefaultAttName, then the namespace name in the attribute value is that of the **default namespace** in the scope of the element to which the declaration is attached. In such a default declaration, the attribute value may be empty. Default namespaces and overriding of declarations are discussed in "5. Applying Namespaces to Elements and Attributes".

An example namespace declaration, which associates the namespace prefix `edi` with the namespace name `http://ecommerce.org/schema`:

```
<x xmlns:edi='http://ecommerce.org/schema'>
    <!-- the "edi" prefix is bound to http://ecommerce.org/schema
         for the "x" element and contents -->
</x>
```

Namespace Constraint: Leading "XML"

Prefixes beginning with the three-letter sequence x, m, l, in any case combination, are reserved for use by XML and XML-related specifications.

3. Qualified Names

[Definition:] In XML documents conforming to this specification, some names (constructs corresponding to the nonterminal Name) may be given as **qualified names**, defined as follows:

Qualified Name	
[6]	QName ::= (Prefix ':')? LocalPart
[7]	Prefix ::= NCName
[8]	LocalPart ::= NCName

The Prefix provides the namespace prefix part of the qualified name, and must be associated with a namespace URI reference in a namespace declaration.

[Definition:] The LocalPart provides the **local part** of the qualified name.

Note that the prefix functions *only* as a placeholder for a namespace name. Applications should use the namespace name, not the prefix, in constructing names whose scope extends beyond the containing document.

4. Using Qualified Names

In XML documents conforming to this specification, element types are given as qualified names, as follows:

Element Types
[9]   STag ::= '<' QName (S Attribute)* S? '>'
[10]   ETag ::= '</' QName S? '>'
[11]   EmptyElemTag ::= '<' QName (S Attribute)* S? '/>'

An example of a qualified name serving as an element type:

```
<x xmlns:edi='http://ecommerce.org/schema'>
    <!-- the 'price' element's namespace is http://ecommerce.org/schema -->
    <edi:price units='Euro'>32.18</edi:price>
</x>
```

Attributes are either namespace declarations or their names are given as qualified names:

Attribute
[12]   Attribute ::= NSAttName Eq AttValue| QName Eq AttValue

An example of a qualified name serving as an attribute name:

```
<x xmlns:edi='http://ecommerce.org/schema'>
    <!-- the 'taxClass' attribute's namespace is http://ecommerce.org/schema -->
    <lineItem edi:taxClass="exempt">Baby food</lineItem>
</x>
```

Namespace Constraint: Prefix Declared

The namespace prefix, unless it is xml or xmlns, must have been declared in a namespace declaration attribute in either the start-tag of the element where the prefix is used or in an an ancestor element (i.e. an element in whose content the prefixed markup occurs). The prefix xml is by definition bound to the namespace name http://www.w3.org/XML/1998/namespace. The prefix xmlns is used only for namespace bindings and is not itself bound to any namespace name.

This constraint may lead to operational difficulties in the case where the namespace declaration attribute is provided, not directly in the XML document entity, but via a default attribute declared in an external entity. Such declarations may not be read by software which is based on a non-validating XML processor. Many XML applications, presumably including namespace-sensitive ones, fail to require validating processors. For correct operation with such applications, namespace declarations must be provided either directly or via default attributes declared in the internal subset of the DTD.

Element names and attribute types are also given as qualified names when they appear in declarations in the DTD:

Qualified Names in Declarations	
[13]	doctypedecl ::= '<!DOCTYPE' S QName (S ExternalID)? S? ('[' (markupdecl | PEReference | S)* ']' S?)? '>'
[14]	elementdecl ::= '<!ELEMENT' S QName S contentspec S? '>'
[15]	cp ::= (QName | choice | seq) ('?' | '*' | '+')?
[16]	Mixed ::= '(' S? '#PCDATA' (S? '|' S? QName)* S? ')*' | '(' S? '#PCDATA' S? ')'
[17]	AttlistDecl ::= '<!ATTLIST' S QName AttDef* S? '>'
[18]	AttDef ::= S (QName | NSAttName) S AttType S DefaultDecl

5. Applying Namespaces to Elements and Attributes

5.1 Namespace Scoping

The namespace declaration is considered to apply to the element where it is specified and to all elements within the content of that element, unless overridden by another namespace declaration with the same NSAttName part:

```
<?xml version="1.0"?>
<!-- all elements here are explicitly in the HTML namespace -->
<html:html xmlns:html='http://www.w3.org/TR/REC-html40'>
    <html:head><html:title>Frobnostication</html:title></html:head>
    <html:body><html:p>Moved to
        <html:a href='http://frob.com'>here.</html:a></html:p></html:body>
</html:html>
```

Multiple namespace prefixes can be declared as attributes of a single element, as shown in this example:

```
<?xml version="1.0"?>
<!-- both namespace prefixes are available throughout -->
<bk:book xmlns:bk='urn:loc.gov:books'
         xmlns:isbn='urn:ISBN:0-395-36341-6'>
    <bk:title>Cheaper by the Dozen</bk:title>
    <isbn:number>1568491379</isbn:number>
</bk:book>
```

5.2 Namespace Defaulting

A default namespace is considered to apply to the element where it is declared (if that element has no namespace prefix), and to all elements with no prefix within the content of that element. If the URI reference in a default namespace declaration is empty, then unprefixed elements in the scope of the declaration are not considered to be in any namespace. Note that default namespaces do not apply directly to attributes.

```
<?xml version="1.0"?>
<!-- elements are in the HTML namespace, in this case by default -->
<html xmlns='http://www.w3.org/TR/REC-html40'>
    <head><title>Frobnostication</title></head>
    <body><p>Moved to
        <a href='http://frob.com'>here</a>.</p></body>
</html>
```

```
<?xml version="1.0"?>
<!-- unprefixed element types are from "books" -->
<book xmlns='urn:loc.gov:books'
      xmlns:isbn='urn:ISBN:0-395-36341-6'>
    <title>Cheaper by the Dozen</title>
    <isbn:number>1568491379</isbn:number>
</book>
```

A larger example of namespace scoping:

```
<?xml version="1.0"?>
<!-- initially, the default namespace is "books" -->
<book xmlns='urn:loc.gov:books'
      xmlns:isbn='urn:ISBN:0-395-36341-6'>
    <title>Cheaper by the Dozen</title>
    <isbn:number>1568491379</isbn:number>
    <notes>
        <!-- make HTML the default namespace for some commentary -->
        <p xmlns='urn:w3-org-ns:HTML'>
            This is a <i>funny</i> book!
        </p>
    </notes>
</book>
```

The default namespace can be set to the empty string. This has the same effect, within the scope of the declaration, of there being no default namespace.

```
<?xml version='1.0'?>
<Beers>
    <!-- the default namespace is now that of HTML -->
    <table xmlns='http://www.w3.org/TR/REC-html40'>
        <th><td>Name</td><td>Origin</td><td>Description</td></th>
        <tr>
            <!-- no default namespace inside table cells -->
            <td><brandName xmlns="">Huntsman</brandName></td>
            <td><origin xmlns="">Bath, UK</origin></td>
            <td>
                <details xmlns=""><class>Bitter</class><hop>Fuggles</hop>
                    <pro>Wonderful hop, light alcohol, good summer beer</pro>
                    <con>Fragile; excessive variance pub to pub</con>
                </details>
            </td>
        </tr>
    </table>
</Beers>
```

5.3 *Uniqueness of Attributes*

In XML documents conforming to this specification, no tag may contain two attributes which:

❑ have identical names, or

❑ have qualified names with the same local part and with prefixes which have been bound to namespace names that are identical.

For example, each of the bad start-tags is illegal in the following:

```
<!-- http://www.w3.org is bound to n1 and n2 -->
<x xmlns:n1="http://www.w3.org"
   xmlns:n2="http://www.w3.org" >
  <bad a="1" a="2" />
  <bad n1:a="1" n2:a="2" />
</x>
```

However, each of the following is legal, the second because the default namespace does not apply to attribute names:

```
<!-- http://www.w3.org is bound to n1 and is the default -->
<x xmlns:n1="http://www.w3.org"
   xmlns="http://www.w3.org" >
  <good a="1" b="2" />
  <good a="1" n1:a="2" />
</x>
```

6. Conformance of Documents

In XML documents which conform to this specification, element types and attribute names must match the production for QName and must satisfy the "Namespace Constraints".

An XML document conforms to this specification if all other tokens in the document which are required, for XML conformance, to match the XML production for Name, match this specification's production for NCName.

The effect of conformance is that in such a document:

❑ All element types and attribute names contain either zero or one colon.

❑ No entity names, PI targets, or notation names contain any colons.

Strictly speaking, attribute values declared to be of types ID, IDREF(S), ENTITY(IES), and NOTATION are also Names, and thus should be colon-free. However, the declared type of attribute values is only available to processors which read markup declarations, for example validating processors. Thus, unless the use of a validating processor has been specified, there can be no assurance that the contents of attribute values have been checked for conformance to this specification.

Appendices

A. The Internal Structure of XML Namespaces (Non-Normative)

A.1 The Insufficiency of the Traditional Namespace

In the computing disciplines, the term "namespace" conventionally refers to a *set* of names, i.e. a collection containing no duplicates. However, treating the names used in XML markup as such a namespace would greatly impair their usefulness. The primary use of such names in XML documents is to enable identification of logical structures in documents by software modules such as query processors, stylesheet-driven rendering engines, and schema-driven validators. Consider the following example:

```
<section><title>Book-Signing Event</title>
<signing>
    <author title="Mr" name="Vikram Seth" />
    <book title="A Suitable Boy" price="$22.95" /></signing>
<signing>
    <author title="Dr" name="Oliver Sacks" />
    <book title="The Island of the Color-Blind" price="$12.95" /></signing>
</section>
```

In this example, there are three occurrences of the name `title` within markup, and the name alone clearly provides insufficient information to allow correct processing by a software module.

Another problematic area comes from the use of "global" attributes, as illustrated by this example, a fragment of an XML document which is to be displayed using a CSS stylesheet:

```
<RESERVATION>
  <NAME HTML:CLASS="largeSansSerif">Layman, A</NAME>
  <SEAT CLASS="Y" HTML:CLASS="reallyImportant">33B</SEAT>
  <DEPARTURE>1997-05-24T07:55:00+1</DEPARTURE></RESERVATION>
```

In this case, the `CLASS` attribute, which describes the fare basis and takes values such as "J", "Y", and "C", is distinct at all semantic levels from the `HTML:CLASS` attribute, which is used to simulate syntactic richness in HTML, as a means of overcoming the limited element repertoire by subclassing.

XML 1.0 does not provide a built-in way to declare "global" attributes; items such as the HTML `CLASS` attribute are global only in their prose description and their interpretation by HTML applications. However, such attributes, an important distinguishing feature of which is that their names are unique, are commonly observed to occur in a variety of applications.

A.2 XML Namespace Partitions

In order to support the goal of making both qualified and unqualified names useful in meeting their intended purpose, we identify the names appearing in an XML namespace as belonging to one of several disjoint traditional (i.e. set-structured) namespaces, called namespace partitions. The partitions are:

❑ The All Element Types Partition

All element types in an XML namespace appear in this partition. Each has a unique local part; the combination of the namespace name and the local part uniquely identifies the element type.

❑ The Global Attribute Partition

This partition contains the names of all attributes which are defined, in this namespace, to be global. The only required characteristic of a global attribute is that its name be unique in the global attribute partition. This specification makes no assertions as to the proper usage of such attributes. The combination of the namespace name and the attribute name uniquely identifies the global attribute.

❑ The Per-Element-Type Partitions

Each type in the All Element Types Partition has an associated namespace in which appear the names of the unqualified attributes that are provided for that element. This is a traditional namespace because the appearance of duplicate attribute names on an element is forbidden by XML 1.0. The combination of the attribute name with the element's type and namespace name uniquely identifies each unqualified attribute.

In XML documents conforming to this specification, the names of all qualified (prefixed) attributes are assigned to the global attribute partition, and the names of all unqualified attributes are assigned to the appropriate per-element-type partition.

A.3 Expanded Element Types and Attribute Names

For convenience in specifying rules and in making comparisons, we define an expanded form, expressed here in XML element syntax, for each element type and attribute name in an XML document.

[Definition:] An **expanded element type** is expressed as an empty XML element of type `ExpEType`. It has a required `type` attribute which gives the type's LocalPart, and an optional `ns` attribute which, if the element is qualified, gives its namespace name.

[Definition:] An **expanded attribute name** is expressed as an empty XML element of type `ExpAName`. It has a required `name` attribute which gives the name. If the attribute is global, it has a required `ns` attribute which gives the namespace name; otherwise, it has a required attribute `eltype` which gives the type of the attached element, and an optional attribute `elns` which gives the namespace name, if known, of the attached element.

Slight variations on the examples given above will illustrate the working of expanded element types and attribute names. The following two fragments are each followed by a table showing the expansion of the names:

```
<!-- 1 --> <section xmlns='urn:com:books-r-us'>
<!-- 2 -->     <title>Book-Signing Event</title>
<!-- 3 -->     <signing>
<!-- 4 -->         <author title="Mr" name="Vikram Seth" />
<!-- 5 -->         <book title="A Suitable Boy" price="$22.95" />
           </signing>
       </section>
```

The names would expand as follows:

Line	Name	Expanded
1	section	`<ExpEType type="section" ns="urn:com:books-r-us" />`
2	title	`<ExpEType type="title" ns="urn:com:books-r-us" />`
3	signing	`<ExpEType type="signing" ns="urn:com:books-r-us" />`
4	author	`<ExpEType type="author" ns="urn:com:books-r-us" />`
4	title	`<ExpAName name='title' eltype="author" elns="urn:com:books-r-us" />`
4	name	`<ExpAName name='name' eltype="author" elns="urn:com:books-r-us" />`
5	book	`<ExpEType type="book" ns="urn:com:books-r-us" />`
5	title	`<ExpAName name='title' eltype="book" elns="urn:com:books-r-us" />`
5	price	`<ExpAName name='price' eltype="book" elns="urn:com:books-r-us" />`

```
<!-- 1 --> <RESERVATION xmlns:HTML="http://www.w3.org/TR/REC-html40">
<!-- 2 --> <NAME HTML:CLASS="largeSansSerif">Layman, A</NAME>
<!-- 3 --> <SEAT CLASS="Y" HTML:CLASS="largeMonotype">33B</SEAT>
<!-- 4 --> <HTML:A HREF='/cgi-bin/ResStatus'>Check Status</HTML:A>
<!-- 5 --> <DEPARTURE>1997-05-24T07:55:00+1</DEPARTURE></RESERVATION>
```

705

1	RESERVATION	<ExpEType type="RESERVATION" />
2	NAME	<ExpEType type="NAME" />
2	HTML:CLASS	<ExpAName name="CLASS" ns=http://www.w3.org/TR/REC-html40 />
3	SEAT	<ExpEType type="SEAT" />
3	CLASS	<ExpAName name="CLASS" eltype="SEAT"/>
3	HTML:CLASS	<ExpAName name="CLASS" ns="http://www.w3.org/TR/REC-html40" />
4	HTML:A	<ExpEType type="A" ns="http://www.w3.org/TR/REC-html40" />
4	HREF	<ExpAName name="HREF" eltype="A" elns="http://www.w3.org/TR/REC-html40" />
5	DEPARTURE	<ExpEType type="DEPARTURE" />

A.4 Unique Expanded Attribute Names

The constraint expressed by "5.3 Uniqueness of Attributes" above may straightforwardly be implemented by requiring that no element have two attributes whose expanded names are equivalent, i.e. have the same attribute-value pairs.

B. Acknowledgements (Non-Normative)

This work reflects input from a very large number of people, including especially the members of the World Wide Web Consortium XML Working Group and Special Interest Group and the participants in the W3C Metadata Activity. The contributions of Charles Frankston of Microsoft were particularly valuable.

C. References

RFC2141
    IETF (Internet Engineering Task Force) *RFC 2141: URN Syntax*, ed. R. Moats. May 1997.
RFC2396
    IETF (Internet Engineering Task Force) *RFC 2396: Uniform Resource Identifiers (URI): Generic Syntax*, eds. T. Berners-Lee, R. Fielding, L. Masinter. August 1998.
XML
    Extensible Markup Language (XML) 1.0, eds. Tim Bray, Jean Paoli, and C. M. Sperberg-McQueen. 10 February 1998. Available at http://www.w3.org/TR/REC-xml.

W3C® Copyright Document Notice and License

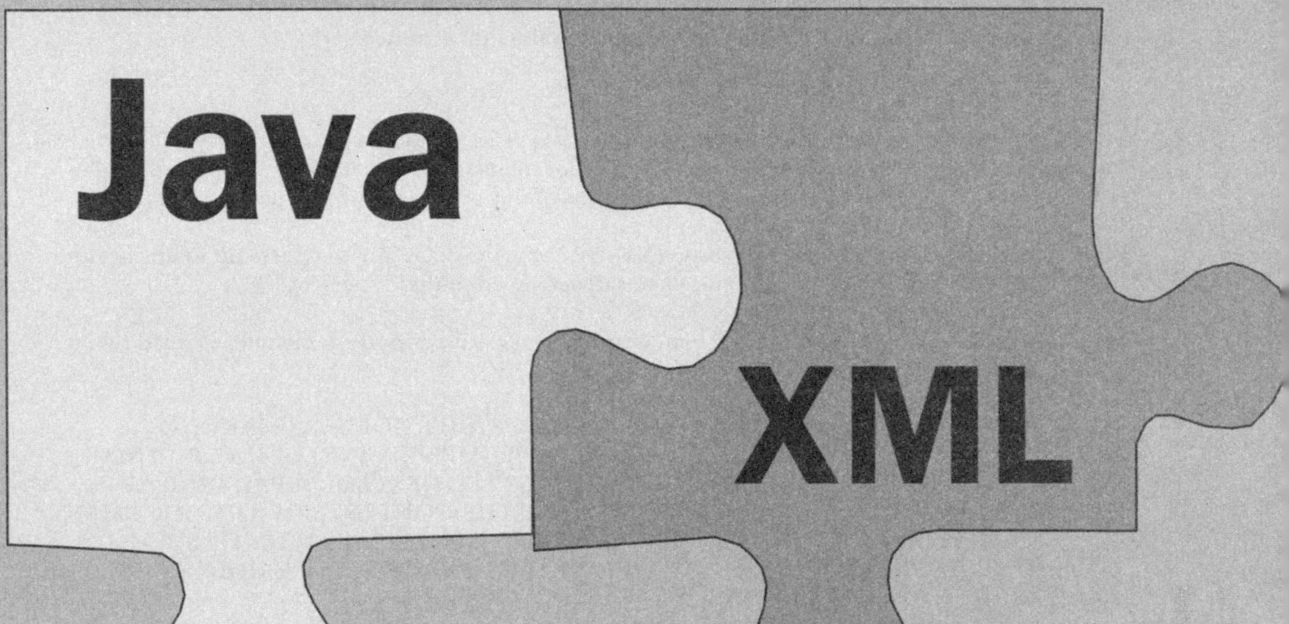
Java
XML

DOM 1 Core: IDL and Java Language Binding

This appendix is taken from the W3C DOM Object Model (DOM) Level 1 Specification, the full text of which may be found at `http://www.w3.org/TR/REC-DOM-Level-1`.

Status of the full DOM Level 1 Specification

This document has been reviewed by W3C Members and other interested parties and has been endorsed by the Director as a W3C Recommendation. It is a stable document and may be used as reference material or cited as a normative reference from another document. W3C's role in making the Recommendation is to draw attention to the specification and to promote its widespread deployment. This enhances the functionality and interoperability of the Web.

IDL Definitions

This section contains the OMG IDL definitions for the interfaces in the Core Document Object Model specification.

exception DOMException

```
exception DOMException {
    unsigned short    code;
};

// ExceptionCode
const unsigned short    INDEX_SIZE_ERR    = 1;
const unsigned short    DOMSTRING_SIZE_ERR = 2;
const unsigned short    HIERARCHY_REQUEST_ERR = 3;
const unsigned short    WRONG_DOCUMENT_ERR = 4;
const unsigned short    INVALID_CHARACTER_ERR = 5;
const unsigned short    NO_DATA_ALLOWED_ERR = 6;
const unsigned short    NO_MODIFICATION_ALLOWED_ERR = 7;
const unsigned short    NOT_FOUND_ERR    = 8;
const unsigned short    NOT_SUPPORTED_ERR = 9;
const unsigned short    INUSE_ATTRIBUTE_ERR = 10;

// ExceptionCode
const unsigned short    INDEX_SIZE_ERR    = 1;
const unsigned short    DOMSTRING_SIZE_ERR = 2;
const unsigned short    HIERARCHY_REQUEST_ERR = 3;
const unsigned short    WRONG_DOCUMENT_ERR = 4;
const unsigned short    INVALID_CHARACTER_ERR = 5;
const unsigned short    NO_DATA_ALLOWED_ERR = 6;
const unsigned short    NO_MODIFICATION_ALLOWED_ERR = 7;
const unsigned short    NOT_FOUND_ERR    = 8;
const unsigned short    NOT_SUPPORTED_ERR = 9;
const unsigned short    INUSE_ATTRIBUTE_ERR = 10;
```

interface DOMImplementation

```
interface DOMImplementation {
    boolean                hasFeature(in DOMString feature,
                                      in DOMString version);
};
```

interface DocumentFragment : Node

```
interface DocumentFragment : Node {
};
```

interface Document : Node

```
interface Document : Node {
  readonly attribute  DocumentType          doctype;
  readonly attribute  DOMImplementation     implementation;
  readonly attribute  Element               documentElement;
  Element                      createElement(in DOMString tagName)
                                            raises(DOMException);
  DocumentFragment             createDocumentFragment();
  Text                         createTextNode(in DOMString data);
  Comment                      createComment(in DOMString data);
  CDATASection                 createCDATASection(in DOMString data)
                                            raises(DOMException);
  ProcessingInstruction        createProcessingInstruction(
in DOMString target,
in DOMString data)
raises(DOMException);
  Attr                         createAttribute(in DOMString name)
                                            raises(DOMException);
  EntityReference              createEntityReference(in DOMString name)
                                            raises(DOMException);
  NodeList                     getElementsByTagName(in DOMString tagname);
};
```

interface Node

```
interface Node {
  // NodeType
  const unsigned short    ELEMENT_NODE        = 1;
  const unsigned short    ATTRIBUTE_NODE      = 2;
  const unsigned short    TEXT_NODE           = 3;
  const unsigned short    CDATA_SECTION_NODE = 4;
  const unsigned short    ENTITY_REFERENCE_NODE = 5;
  const unsigned short    ENTITY_NODE         = 6;
  const unsigned short    PROCESSING_INSTRUCTION_NODE = 7;
  const unsigned short    COMMENT_NODE        = 8;
  const unsigned short    DOCUMENT_NODE       = 9;
  const unsigned short    DOCUMENT_TYPE_NODE = 10;
  const unsigned short    DOCUMENT_FRAGMENT_NODE = 11;
  const unsigned short    NOTATION_NODE       = 12;

  readonly attribute  DOMString          nodeName;
           attribute  DOMString          nodeValue;
                                            // raises(DOMException) on
setting
                                            // raises(DOMException) on
retrieval
  readonly attribute unsigned short       nodeType;
  readonly attribute Node                 parentNode;
  readonly attribute NodeList             childNodes;
  readonly attribute Node                 firstChild;
  readonly attribute Node                 lastChild;
  readonly attribute Node                 previousSibling;
  readonly attribute Node                 nextSibling;
```

```
       readonly attribute   NamedNodeMap          attributes;
       readonly attribute   Document              ownerDocument;
       Node                  insertBefore(in Node newChild,
                                          in Node refChild)
                                       raises(DOMException);
       Node                  replaceChild(in Node newChild,
                                          in Node oldChild)
                                       raises(DOMException);
       Node                  removeChild(in Node oldChild)
                                       raises(DOMException);
       Node                  appendChild(in Node newChild)
                                       raises(DOMException);
       boolean               hasChildNodes();
       Node                  cloneNode(in boolean deep);
};
```

interface NodeList

```
   interface NodeList {
     Node                  item(in unsigned long index);
     readonly attribute  unsigned long        length;
   };
```

interface NamedNodeMap

```
   interface NamedNodeMap {
     Node                  getNamedItem(in DOMString name);
     Node                  setNamedItem(in Node arg)
                                          raises(DOMException);
     Node                  removeNamedItem(in DOMString name)
                                       raises(DOMException);
     Node                  item(in unsigned long index);
     readonly attribute  unsigned long        length;
   };
```

interface CharacterData : Node

```
   interface CharacterData : Node {
           attribute  DOMString          data;
                              // raises(DOMException) on setting
                              // raises(DOMException) on retrieval
     readonly attribute  unsigned long        length;
     DOMString             substringData(in unsigned long offset,
                                         in unsigned long count)
                                       raises(DOMException);
     void                  appendData(in DOMString arg)
                                       raises(DOMException);
     void                  insertData(in unsigned long offset,
                                      in DOMString arg)
                                       raises(DOMException);
     void                  deleteData(in unsigned long offset,
                                      in unsigned long count)
                                       raises(DOMException);
     void                  replaceData(in unsigned long offset,
                                       in unsigned long count,
```

712

```
                                            in DOMString arg)
                                    raises(DOMException);
    };
```

interface Attr : *Node*

```
    interface Attr : Node {
      readonly attribute  DOMString         name;
      readonly attribute  boolean           specified;
               attribute  DOMString          value;
    };
```

interface Element : *Node*

```
    interface Element : Node {
      readonly attribute  DOMString            tagName;
      DOMString               getAttribute(in DOMString name);
      void                    setAttribute(in DOMString name,
                                           in DOMString value)
                                        raises(DOMException);
      void                    removeAttribute(in DOMString name)
                                        raises(DOMException);
      Attr                    getAttributeNode(in DOMString name);
      Attr                    setAttributeNode(in Attr newAttr)
                                        raises(DOMException);
      Attr                    removeAttributeNode(in Attr oldAttr)
                                        raises(DOMException);
      NodeList                getElementsByTagName(in DOMString name);
      void                    normalize();
    };
```

interface Text : *CharacterData*

```
    interface Text : CharacterData {
      Text                    splitText(in unsigned long offset)
                                    raises(DOMException);
    };
```

interface Comment : *CharacterData*

```
    interface Comment : CharacterData {
    };
```

interface CDATASection : *Text*

```
    interface CDATASection : Text {
    };
```

interface DocumentType : *Node*

```
interface DocumentType : Node {
  readonly attribute  DOMString          name;
  readonly attribute  NamedNodeMap       entities;
  readonly attribute  NamedNodeMap       notations;
};
```

interface Notation : *Node*

```
interface Notation : Node {
  readonly attribute  DOMString          publicId;
  readonly attribute  DOMString          systemId;
};
```

interface Entity : *Node*

```
interface Entity : Node {
  readonly attribute  DOMString          publicId;
  readonly attribute  DOMString          systemId;
  readonly attribute  DOMString          notationName;
};
```

interface EntityReference : *Node*

```
interface EntityReference : Node {
};
```

interface ProcessingInstruction : *Node*

```
interface ProcessingInstruction : Node {
  readonly attribute  DOMString          target;
           attribute  DOMString          data;
                                   // raises(DOMException) on setting
};
```

Java Language Binding

This section contains the Core definitions of the Java Binding for the Level 1 Document Object Model

class DOMException

```
public abstract class DOMException extends RuntimeException {
  public DOMException(short code, String message) {
    super(message);
    this.code = code;
  }
  public short   code;
  // ExceptionCode
  public static final short          INDEX_SIZE_ERR       = 1;
```

```
        public static final short        DOMSTRING_SIZE_ERR   = 2;
        public static final short        HIERARCHY_REQUEST_ERR = 3;
        public static final short        WRONG_DOCUMENT_ERR   = 4;
        public static final short        INVALID_CHARACTER_ERR = 5;
        public static final short        NO_DATA_ALLOWED_ERR  = 6;
        public static final short        NO_MODIFICATION_ALLOWED_ERR = 7;
        public static final short        NOT_FOUND_ERR        = 8;
        public static final short        NOT_SUPPORTED_ERR    = 9;
        public static final short        INUSE_ATTRIBUTE_ERR  = 10;

    }

    // ExceptionCode
    public static final short        INDEX_SIZE_ERR       = 1;
    public static final short        DOMSTRING_SIZE_ERR   = 2;
    public static final short        HIERARCHY_REQUEST_ERR = 3;
    public static final short        WRONG_DOCUMENT_ERR   = 4;
    public static final short        INVALID_CHARACTER_ERR = 5;
    public static final short        NO_DATA_ALLOWED_ERR  = 6;
    public static final short        NO_MODIFICATION_ALLOWED_ERR = 7;
    public static final short        NOT_FOUND_ERR        = 8;
    public static final short        NOT_SUPPORTED_ERR    = 9;
    public static final short        INUSE_ATTRIBUTE_ERR  = 10;

    }
```

interface DOMImplementation

```
    public interface DOMImplementation {
      public boolean              hasFeature(String feature,
                                             String version);
    }
```

interface DocumentFragment

```
    public interface DocumentFragment extends Node {
    }
```

interface Document

```
    public interface Document extends Node {
      public DocumentType       getDoctype();
      public DOMImplementation  getImplementation();
      public Element            getDocumentElement();
      public Element            createElement(String tagName)
                                         throws DOMException;
      public DocumentFragment   createDocumentFragment();
      public Text               createTextNode(String data);
      public Comment            createComment(String data);
      public CDATASection       createCDATASection(String data)
                                         throws DOMException;
      public ProcessingInstruction createProcessingInstruction(
String target,

                                         String data)
                                         throws DOMException;
```

```
        public Attr               createAttribute(String name)
                                                  throws DOMException;
        public EntityReference    createEntityReference(String name)
                                                  throws DOMException;
        public NodeList           getElementsByTagName(String tagname);
    }
```

interface Node

```
    public interface Node {
        // NodeType
        public static final short         ELEMENT_NODE            = 1;
        public static final short         ATTRIBUTE_NODE          = 2;
        public static final short         TEXT_NODE               = 3;
        public static final short         CDATA_SECTION_NODE      = 4;
        public static final short         ENTITY_REFERENCE_NODE   = 5;
        public static final short         ENTITY_NODE             = 6;
        public static final short         PROCESSING_INSTRUCTION_NODE = 7;
        public static final short         COMMENT_NODE            = 8;
        public static final short         DOCUMENT_NODE           = 9;
        public static final short         DOCUMENT_TYPE_NODE      = 10;
        public static final short         DOCUMENT_FRAGMENT_NODE  = 11;
        public static final short         NOTATION_NODE           = 12;
    public String              getNodeName();
        public String              getNodeValue()
                                                  throws DOMException;
        public void                setNodeValue(String nodeValue)
                                                  throws DOMException;
        public short               getNodeType();
        public Node                getParentNode();
        public NodeList            getChildNodes();
        public Node                getFirstChild();
        public Node                getLastChild();
        public Node                getPreviousSibling();
        public Node                getNextSibling();
        public NamedNodeMap        getAttributes();
        public Document            getOwnerDocument();
        public Node                insertBefore(Node newChild,
                                        Node refChild)
                                                  throws DOMException;
        public Node                replaceChild(Node newChild,
                                        Node oldChild)
                                                  throws DOMException;
        public Node                removeChild(Node oldChild)
                                                  throws DOMException;
        public Node                appendChild(Node newChild)
                                                  throws DOMException;
        public boolean             hasChildNodes();
        public Node                cloneNode(boolean deep);
    }
```

interface NodeList

```
public interface NodeList {
    public Node              item(int index);
    public int               getLength();
}
```

interface NamedNodeMap

```
public interface NamedNodeMap {
    public Node              getNamedItem(String name);
    public Node              setNamedItem(Node arg)
                                     throws DOMException;
    public Node              removeNamedItem(String name)
                                     throws DOMException;
    public Node              item(int index);
    public int               getLength();
}
```

interface CharacterData

```
public interface CharacterData extends Node {
    public String            getData()
                                 throws DOMException;
    public void              setData(String data)
                                 throws DOMException;
    public int               getLength();
    public String            substringData(int offset,
                                       int count)
                                           throws DOMException;
    public void              appendData(String arg)
                                     throws DOMException;
    public void              insertData(int offset,
                                    String arg)
                                         throws DOMException;
    public void              deleteData(int offset,
                                    int count)
                                     throws DOMException;
    public void              replaceData(int offset,
                                     int count,
                                     String arg)
                                     throws DOMException;
}
```

interface Attr

```
public interface Attr extends Node {
    public String            getName();
    public boolean           getSpecified();
    public String            getValue();
    public void              setValue(String value);
}
```

public interface Element

```
public interface Element extends Node {
   public String          getTagName();
   public String          getAttribute(String name);
   public void            setAttribute(String name,
                                       String value)
                                       throws DOMException;
   public void            removeAttribute(String name)
                                                throws DOMException;
   public Attr            getAttributeNode(String name);
   public Attr            setAttributeNode(Attr newAttr)
                                                throws DOMException;
   public Attr            removeAttributeNode(Attr oldAttr)
                                                throws DOMException;
   public NodeList        getElementsByTagName(String name);
   public void            normalize();
}
```

interface Text

```
public interface Text extends CharacterData {
   public Text            splitText(int offset)
                                           throws DOMException;
}
```

interface Comment

```
public interface Comment extends CharacterData {
}
```

interface CDATASection

```
public interface CDATASection extends Text {
}
```

interface DocumentType

```
public interface DocumentType extends Node {
   public String          getName();
   public NamedNodeMap    getEntities();
   public NamedNodeMap    getNotations();
}
```

interface Notation

```
public interface Notation extends Node {
   public String          getPublicId();
   public String          getSystemId();
}
```

interface Entity

```
public interface Entity extends Node {
   public String            getPublicId();
   public String            getSystemId();
   public String            getNotationName();
}
```

interface EntityReference

```
public interface EntityReference extends Node {
}
```

interface ProcessingInstruction

```
public interface ProcessingInstruction extends Node {
   public String            getTarget();
   public String            getData();
   public void              setData(String data)
                                         throws DOMException;

}
```

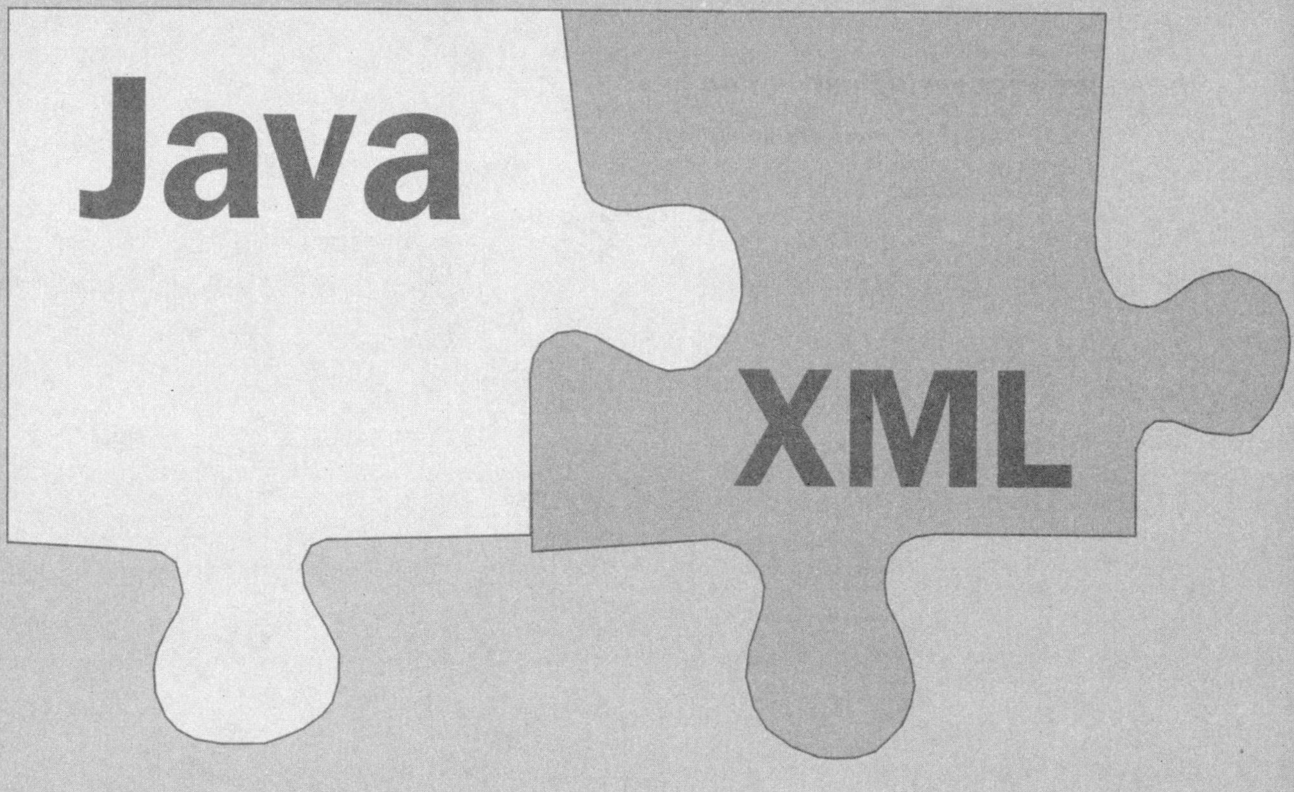
Java
XML

SAX API Reference

Key

Within this API Reference, the following conventions are used:

- ❑ Interface, Class and Exception names within the APIs listed are all written in **bold**.
- ❑ Interface, Class and Exception names not within the APIs listed are all written in *italics*.
- ❑ Method and Class names are written in `Courier Bold`.

Package org.xml.sax

The SAX API for Java contains one core package, **org.xml.sax**, and one extension package, **org.xml.sax.helpers**, which contains 3 Java-specific helper classes. Both of these packages are covered in this appendix. More complete documentation on the SAX API can be found at `http://www.megginson.com/SAX/index.html`, along with other useful information such as bug reports and details of parsers and applications that support the SAX API.

Interfaces

public interface	**AttributeList**
public interface	**DTDHandler**
public interface	**DocumentHandler**
public interface	**EntityResolver**
public interface	**ErrorHandler**
public interface	**Locator**
public interface	**Parser**

Classes

public class	**HandlerBase**	extends	*java.lang.***Object**
public class	**InputSource**	extends	*java.lang.***Object**

Exceptions

public class	**SAXException**	extends	*java.lang.***Exception**
public class	**SAXParseException**	extends	*java.lang.***Exception**

Interface org.xml.sax.AttributeList

```
public interface AttributeList
```

This is the interface for the attribute specifications of an element.

Methods

public abstract int	**getLength**	()
public abstract String	**getName**	(int i)
public abstract String	**getType**	(int i)
public abstract String	**getType**	(String name)
public abstract int	**getValue**	(int i)
public abstract int	**getValue**	(String name)

Interface org.xml.sax.DTDHandler

```
public interface DTDHandler
```

This interface receives notification of basic DTD-related events.

Methods

public abstract void	**notationDecl**	(String name, String publicId, String systemId)
	throws **SAXException**	
public abstract void	**unparsedEntityDecl**	(String name, String publicId, String systemId, String notationName)
	throws **SAXException**	

Interface org.xml.sax.DocumentHandler

```
public interface DocumentHandler
```

This interface receives notification of general document events.

Methods

```
public abstract void    characters          (char ch[],
                                              int start,
                                              int length)
                            throws SAXException

public abstract void    endDocument         ()
                            throws SAXException

public abstract void    endElement          (String name)
                            throws SAXException

public abstract void    ignorableWhitespace (char ch[],
                                              int start,
                                              int length)
                            throws SAXException

public abstract void    processingInstruction    (String target,
                                                   String data)
                            throws SAXException

public abstract void    setDocumentocator   (Locator locator)
                            throws SAXException

public abstract void    startDocument       ()
                            throws SAXException

public abstract void    startElement        (String name,
                                             AttributeList atts)
                            throws SAXException
```

Interface org.xml.sax.EntityResolver

```
public interface EntityResolver
```

This is the basic interface for resolving entities.

Methods

```
public abstract InputSource    resolveEntity    (String publicId,
                                                  String systemId)
                            throws SAXException
```

Interface org.xml.sax.ErrorHandler

```
public interface ErrorHandler
```

This is the basic interface for error handling in a SAX application.

Methods

```
public abstract void    error       (SAXParseException exception)
                            throws SAXException

public abstract void    fatalError       (SAXParseException exception)
                            throws SAXException
```

```
public abstract void        warning                 (SAXParseException exception)
                                throws SAXException
```

Interface org.xml.sax.Locator

```
public interface Locator
```

This is the interface that associates a SAX event with a document location.

Methods

```
public abstract int     getColumnNumber             ()

public abstract int     getLineNumber               ()

public abstract String  getPublicId                 ()

public abstract String  getSystemId                 ()
```

Interface org.xml.sax.Parser

```
public interface Parser
```

This is the basic interface that all SAX parsers must implement.

Methods

```
public abstract void    parse                   (InputSource source)
                            throws SAXException, IOException

public abstract void    parse                   (String systemId)
                            throws SAXException, IOException

public abstract void    setDocumentHandler      (DocumentHandler handler)

public abstract void    setDTDHandler           (DTDHandler handler)

public abstract void    setEntityResolver       (EntityResolver resolver)

public abstract void    setErrorHandler         (ErrorHandler handler)

public abstract void    setLocale               (Locale locale)
                            throws SAXException
```

Class org.xml.sax.HandlerBase

```
public class HandlerBase
extends java.lang.Object
implements EntityResolver, DTDHandler, DocumentHandler, ErrorHandler
```

This is the default base class for handlers.

Constructor

```
public      HandlerBase             ()
```

Methods

```
public void        characters          (char ch[],
                                        int start,
                                        int length)
                       throws SAXException

public void        endDocument          ()
                       throws SAXException

public void        endElement          (String name)
                       throws SAXException

public void        error          (SaxParseException e)
                       throws SAXException

public void        fatalError          (SaxParseException e)
                       throws SAXException

public void        ignorableWhitespace          (char ch[],
                                        int start,
                                        int length)
                       throws SAXException

public void        notationDecl          (String name,
                                        String publicId,
                                        String systemId)

public void        processingInstruction          (String target,
                                        String data)
                       throws SAXException

public InputSource resolveEntity          (String publicId,
                                        String systemId)
                       throws SAXException

public void        setDocumentLocator          (Locator locator)

public void        startDocument          ()
                       throws SAXException

public void        startElement          (String name,
                                        AttributeList attributes)
                       throws SAXException

public void        unparsedEntityDecl          (String name,
                                        String publicId,
                                        String systemId,
                                        String notationName)

public void        warning          (SaxParseException e)
                       throws SAXException
```

Class org.xml.sax.InputSource

```
public class InputSource
extends java.lang.Object
```

This class allows information about an input source to be enapsulated in a single object.

Constructors

```
public      InputSource      ()
public      InputSource      (String systemId)
public      InputSource      (InputStream byteStream)
public      InputSource      (Reader characterStream)
```

Methods

```
public InputStream    getByteStream        ()

public Reader         getCharacterStream   ()

public String         getEncoding          ()

public String         getPublicId          ()

public String         getSystemId          ()

public void           setByteStream        (InputStream byteStream)

public void           setCharacterStream   (Reader characterStream)

public void           setEncoding          (String encoding)

public void           setPublicId          (String publicId)

public void           setSystemId          (String systemId)
```

Class org.xml.sax.SAXException

```
public class
extends java.lang.Exception
```

This class encapsulates general SAX errors or warnings.

Constructors

```
public      SAXException      (String message)

public      SAXException      (Exception e)

public      SAXException      (String message,
                               Exception e)
```

Methods

```
public Exception getException       ()

public String    getMessage         ()

public String    toString           ()
```

Class org.xml.sax.SAXParseException

```
public class SAXPArseException
extends org.xml.sax.SAXException
```

This class encapsulates errors or warnings occurring during XML parsing.

Constructors

```
public     SAXParseException         (String message,
                                       Locator locator)

public     SAXParseException         (String message,
                                       Locator locator,
                                       Exception e)

public     SAXParseException         (String message,
                                       String publicId,
                                       String systemId,
                                       int lineNumber,
                                       int columnNumber)

public     SAXParseException         (String message,
                                       String publicId,
                                       String systemId,
                                       int lineNumber,
                                       int columnNumber,
                                       Exception e)
```

Methods

```
public int       getColumnNumber     ()

public int       getLineNumber       ()

public String    getPublicId         ()

public String    getSystemId         ()
```

Package org.xml.sax.helpers

This package is an extension to the org.xml.sax core package, and contains 3 Java-specific helper classes.

Classes

```
public class   AttributListImpl      extends   java.lang.Object
public class   LocatorImpl           extends   java.lang.Object
public class   ParserFactory         extends   java.lang.Object
```

Class org.xml.sax.helpers.AttributeListImpl

```
public class AttributeListImpl
extends java.lang.Object
implements AttributeList
```

This is a convenience implementation for AttributeList.

Constructors

```
public      AttributeListImpl    ()

public      AttributeListImpl    (AttributeList atts)
```

Methods

```
public void      addAttribute        (String name,
                                       String type,
                                       String value)

public void      clear               ()

public int       getLength           ()

public String    getName             (int i)

public String    getType             (int i)

public String    getType             (String name)

public String    getValue            (int i)

public String    getValue            (String name)

public void      removeAttribute     (String name)

public void      setAttributeList    (AttributeList atts)
```

Class org.xml.sax.helpers.LocatorImpl

```
public class LocatorImpl
extends java.lang.Object
implements Locator
```

This is an optional convenience implementation for Locator.

Constructors

```
public      LocatorImpl         ()

public      LocatorImpl         (Locator locator)
```

Methods

public int	**getColumnNumber**	()
public int	**getLineNumber**	()
public String	**getPublicId**	()
public String	**getSystemId**	()
public void	**setColumnNumber**	(int columnNumber)
public void	**setLineNumber**	(int lineNumber)
public void	**setPublicId**	(String publicId)
public void	**setSystemId**	(String systemId)

Class org.xml.sax.helpers.ParserFactory

```
public class ParserFactory
extends java.lang.Object
```

This is a class for dynamically loading SAX parsers that is specific to Java.

Constructor

public	**ParserFactory**	()

Methods

```
public static Parser    makeParser          ()
            throws ClassNotFoundException, IllegalAccessException,
                   InstaniationException, NullPointerException,
                   ClassCastException

public static Parser    makeParser          (String className)
            throws ClassNotFoundException, IllegalAccessException,
                   InstantiationException, ClassCastException
```

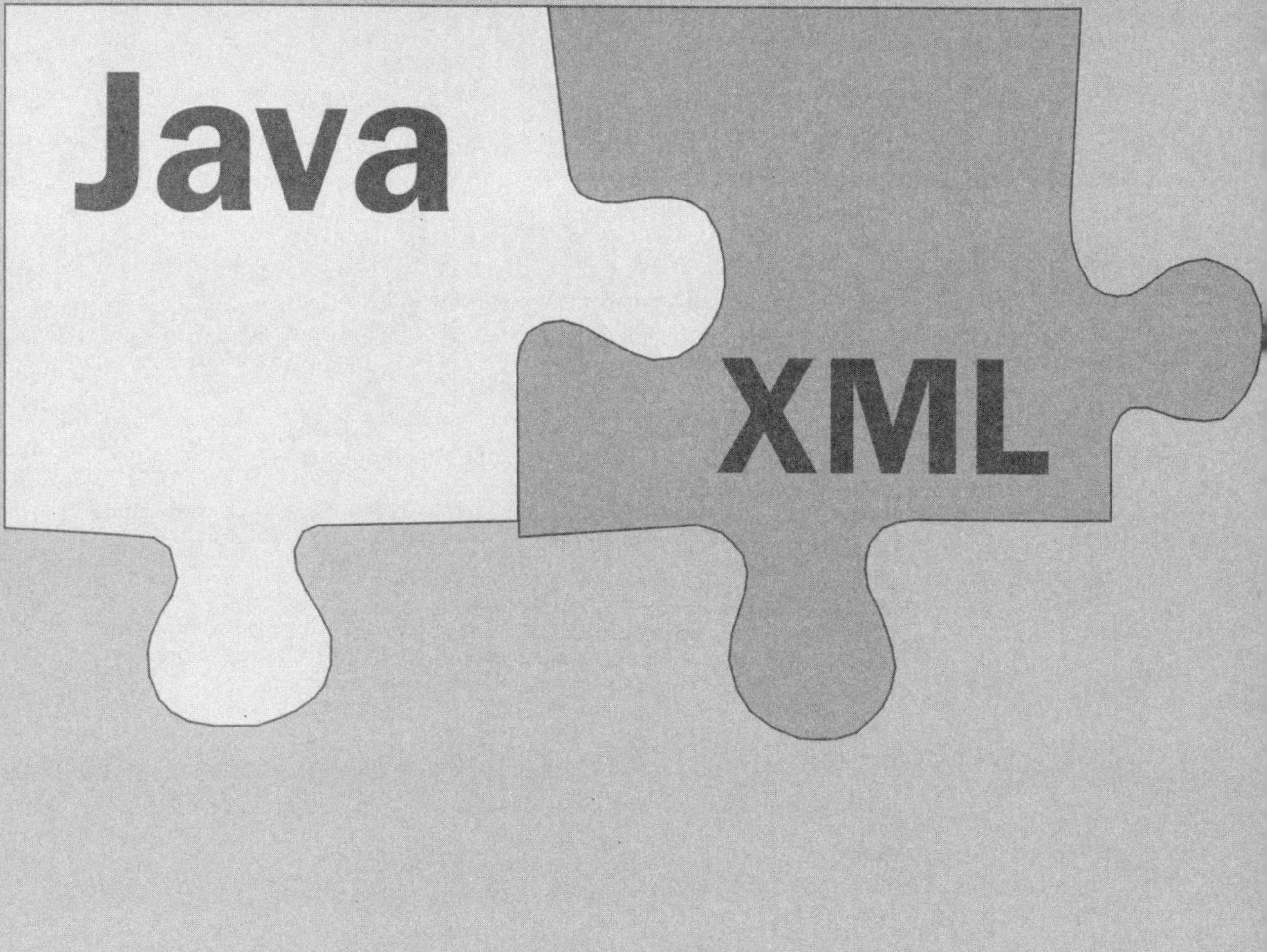
Java
XML

Regular Expressions

The Language of Regular Expressions

Regular expressions are written in a special language. The purpose of the language is to describe patterns of characters. The main operation is matching; the main activity is to find a pattern (a regular expression) that matches exactly the set of strings that we want to do something with, or to, or about. The pattern-matching activity always takes place in the context of some operation, such as find-and-replace. Once the pattern is found, the operation is carried out.

Just as string literals are delimited by a pair of quotes, RE literals are delimited by a pair of slash characters. The second slash can be followed by the letters "i" or "g" or both. The letter "g" (as in "global") means "find all the strings that match the pattern, not just the first one, which is the default." The letter "i" means "make your match case-insensitive."

Regular Expressions used for substitutions

Regular expressions are frequently used to find and replace substrings of a string. In Javascript, you can say:

```
var s = "floating boats";
var t = s.replace(/oat/gi,"ee"); t;
```

This says: "Replace all occurrences of "oat", globally and case-insensitively, with "ee". The result will be "fleeing bees".

Alphanumeric Characters, Sequences and Grouping

A very simple RE pattern is /ab/. It matches the string "ab". This is rule 1 of RE matching: alphanumeric characters match themselves. The rule is simple but not very helpful because for every pattern there's only one sequence of characters that matches it. We want our patterns to be both precise and concise, so that every pattern can match a lot of different strings, very precisely described. That's what the RE language is for.

We can group characters into classes such that the class matches any one character in it. Square brackets [] are used for that purpose. Suppose you always use the letters i, j and k to name your integer variables. You can match them all by the pattern /[ijk]/. Then you may notice that these letters form a sequence (come together in the alphabet and the Latin-1 encoding), and abbreviate your pattern to /[i-k]/. This is not much of an abbreviation, but consider /[a-z]/ (matches any lowercase letter) and /[0-9]/ (matches any digit). The pattern /[a-z][0-9]/ then matches any identifier that consists of a lower-case letter followed by a digit. That's getting better; one little pattern matches 260 precisely specified strings.

Negated Classes

Actually, we cheated a little in the last paragraph: the pattern /[ijk]/ will match not only single-letter identifiers but **any** occurrence of those three letters anywhere. To catch only the identifiers, you want to say: "find any one of those letters preceded and followed by a non-identifier character." What's a non-identifier character? Suppose identifiers have to start with a letter or underscore, and may continue with letters or digits. The pattern /[_A-Za-z0-9]/ matches any legitimate identifier character. To match anything that is not in this class, put the ^ character right after the opening square bracket. The entire pattern for our identifiers becomes:

```
/[^_A-Z a-z 0-9][ijk][^_A-Z a-z 0-9]/
```

This is rather a mouthful; can't we write it more concisely? The sequence A-Za-z0-9 seems to repeat often. The answer is yes; we'll get to abbreviations for popular classes soon.

Repetition

We can now pose ourselves a real-life problem: write a regular expression that matches all and only the legitimate identifiers of JavaScript. Something like this regular expression is sitting inside the JavaScript interpreter in the bowels of your browser and finds identifier tokens in your program.

As we were just reminded, an identifier has to start with a letter or an underscore. So the beginning is easy: /[_A-Za-z]. This can be followed by the same set, plus digits, repeated any number of times, including 0 times. How do we express that? Remarkably easily. We just put together the expression we want repeated and put an * after it. The entire pattern is:

```
/[_A-Za-z][_A-Za-z0-9]*/
```

Note that we don't have to add anything after the * character because of the "maximal match" principle. The pattern will try to find the maximal possible expression it matches, and will stop only when it comes across a non-identifier character.

There are other frequent repetition patterns. Suppose you need more than three integer variables and you've started using names like i2 or k7. In other words, you want to match i, j, k followed by 0 or 1 digits. Easy: use the ? instead of the *:

```
/[ijk][0-9]?/
```

Finally, the + sign means "repeat one or more times." The pattern /[ijk][0-9]+/ will match j23 or k29856 but not just j or k. That's good, but what if we want something repeated specifically 2 or 3 or 4 times, and not any other number of times. The most precise way to indicate repetition is by using braces, as follows:

```
/a{3}/                    // matches aaa and nothing else
/a{2,4}/                  // matches 2 or 3 or 4 a's
/a{2,}/                   // matches 2 or more a's
```

Now you can see that +,* and ? are just abbreviations for the most common braced intervals: + means {1,}, * means {0,}, and ? means {0,1}.

Alternation and Grouping

We know how to express the idea "match this OR that" with respect to individual characters: /[ijk]/ matches i or j or k. What if we want to match this string OR that string? In that case, we have to use an explicit OR character, which is the vertical bar. To match either "ab" or "bc" you say: /ab|bc/. Now the next question is: how do you match "ab" or "bc" followed by "ef"? This is ambiguous; the two interpretations are:

```
"ab" or ("bc" followed by "ef")
("ab" or "bc") followed by "ef"
```

To disambiguate we need parentheses, used exactly the same way in English and in RE.

```
/(ab|bc)ef/                                     // the second interpretation
```

Special Characters

By now we have accumulated quite a few characters that have specialized meaning in RE. Let's review them all before we proceed:

Character(s)	Meaning
/	mark beginning and end of pattern
[...]	match any character in the class
[^...]	match any character not in the class
.	match any character other than new line
−	match any character in a range
* + ? {..}	repetitions of various kinds
( )	parentheses for grouping
|	alternation: match this or that

What if we wanted to match one of those special characters literally, letting them escape their specialized meaning? You can probably guess the answer: use the same "\" escape character.

Alphabetical Characters with Special Meaning

For non-alphabetical characters, you use the escape character to have them interpreted literally. With alphabetical characters it's the other way around: you use the escape character to give them a special meaning. Some of them are the familiar escapees from string literals: \f, \n, \r, \t, \v, meaning Formfeed, Newline, Return, Tab, and Vertical tab, respectively. These are collectively known as whitespace. A very special case is the backspace character: to match it, you have to make it into a single-character class [\b]. You'll see why in a moment.

Another big set of escaped letter characters contains abbreviations for popular character classes:

Character(s)	Meaning
\w	Any word character. Same as [A-Za-z0-9]
\W	Any non-word character. Same as [^A-Za-z0-9]
\s	Any whitespace character. Same as [\f\n\r\t\v]
\S	Any non-whitespace character. Same as [^\f\n\r\t\v]
\d	Any digit. Same as [0-9]
\D	Any non-digit. Same as [^0-9]

We'd like to remind you here that there is also a non-alphabetic abbreviation for a character class. It is the . (dot) character which stands for "any character except Newline," or [^\n]. It is used unescaped in its special meaning, and has to be escaped to be used literally.

Anchoring the Match at a Specific Position

The dollar sign character has to be escaped if you want to match it literally, because unescaped it has a special meaning. The meaning is unusual. The dollar sign doesn't match any particular character of group of characters. Rather, it stipulates that the preceding pattern has to be found at the end of the string, or, in a multi-line string, at the end of a line. For instance, the pattern /!$/ matches all and only lines that end with the exclamation point. We can say that the dollar sign **anchors** the match to a specific position in the text, or we can say that it matches a position in the text.

To anchor the match at the beginning of a line, the ^ character is called into duty again. To find the next occurrence of a digit at the beginning of a line you'd use the pattern /^[0-9]/. You can also anchor the match at the word boundary, i.e., at a position between \w, a word character and \W, a non-word character. That anchor is performed by the b character, escaped. This explains why the backspace character can only be matched by [\b]:the reason is that \b by itself is used as an anchor. The \B pattern matches any position that is not a word boundary.

And Much More...

Regular expressions form a large topic, and there are whole books written about them, but what we have described in this Appendix is sufficient for very vigorous pattern matching.

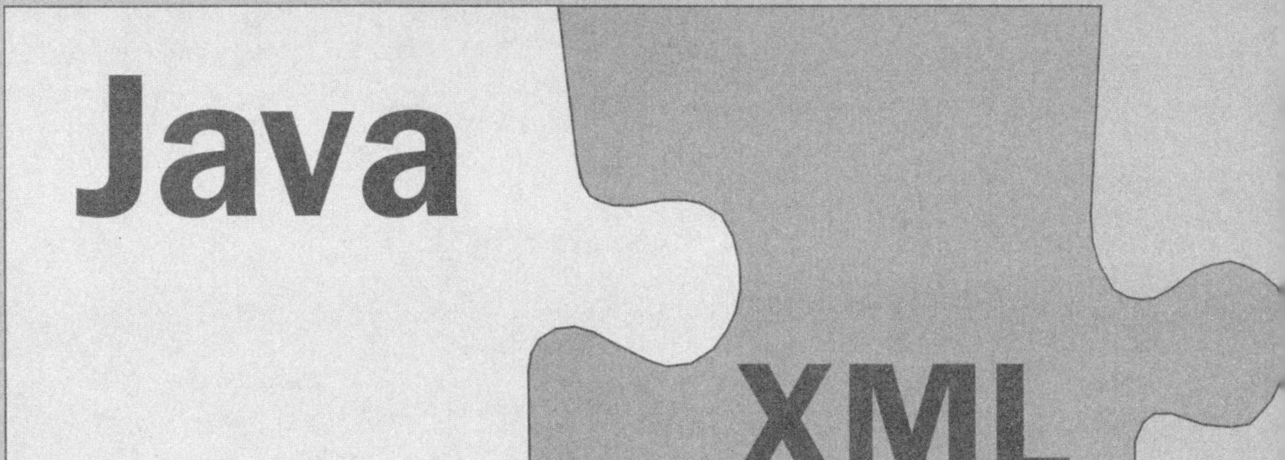
Java
XML

Support and Errata

One of the most irritating things about any programming book is when you find that bit of code you've just spent an hour typing simply doesn't work. You check it a hundred times to see if you've set it up correctly and then you notice the spelling mistake in the variable name on the book page. Of course, you can blame the authors for not taking enough care and testing the code, the editors for not doing their job properly, or the proofreaders for not being eagle-eyed enough, but this doesn't get around the fact that mistakes do happen.

We try hard to ensure no mistakes sneak out into the real world, but we can't promise that this book is 100% error free. What we can do is offer the next best thing by providing you with immediate support and feedback from experts who have worked on the book and try to ensure that future editions eliminate these gremlins. The following section will take you step by step through the process of posting errata to our web site to get that help. The sections that follow, therefore, are:

- ❏ Wrox Developers Membership
- ❏ Finding a list of existing errata on the web site

There is also a section covering how to e-mail a question for technical support. This comprises:

- ❏ What your e-mail should include
- ❏ What happens to your e-mail once it has been received by us

So that you only need view information relevant to yourself, we ask that you register as a Wrox Developer Member. This is a quick and easy process, that will save you time in the long run. If you are already a member, just update membership to include this book.

Wrox Developer's Membership

To get your FREE Wrox Developer's Membership click on Membership in the navigation bar of our home site – `http://www.wrox.com`. This is shown in the following screenshot:

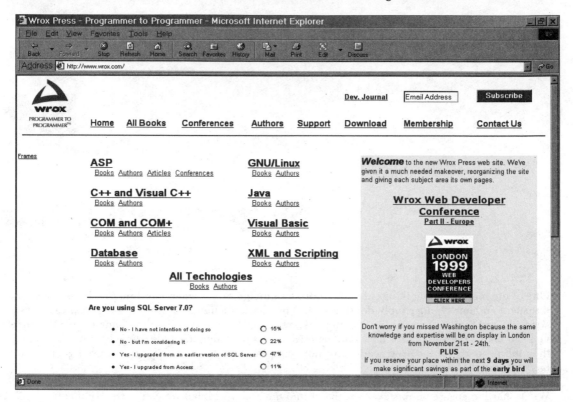

Then, on the next screen (not shown), click on New User. This will display a form. Fill in the details on the form and submit the details using the Register button at the bottom. Go back to the main Membership page, enter your details and select Logon. Before you can say 'The best read books come in Wrox Red' you will get the following screen:

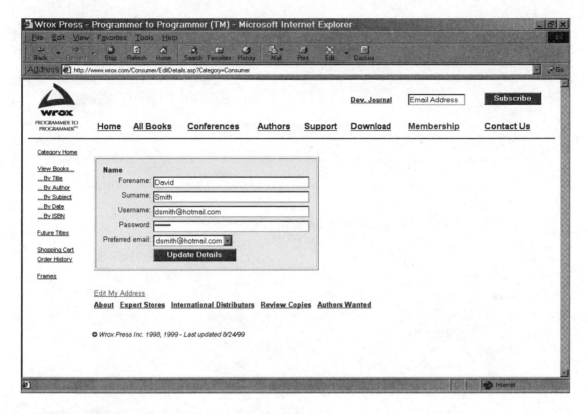

Finding an Errata on the Web Site

Before you send in a query, you might be able to save time by finding the answer to your problem on our web site – http:\\www.wrox.com.

Each book we publish has its own page and its own errata sheet. You can get to any book's page by clicking on Support from the top navigation bar.

From this page you can locate any book's errata page on our site. Select your book from the pop-up menu and click on it.

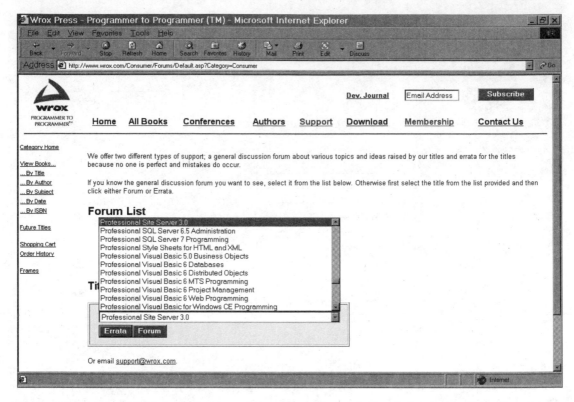

Then click on Errata. This will take you to the errata page for the book. Select the criteria by which you want to view the errata, and click the Apply criteria… button. This will provide you with links to specific errata. For an initial search, you are advised to view the errata by page numbers. If you have looked for an error previously, then you may wish to limit your search using dates. We update these pages daily to ensure that you have the latest information on bugs and errors.

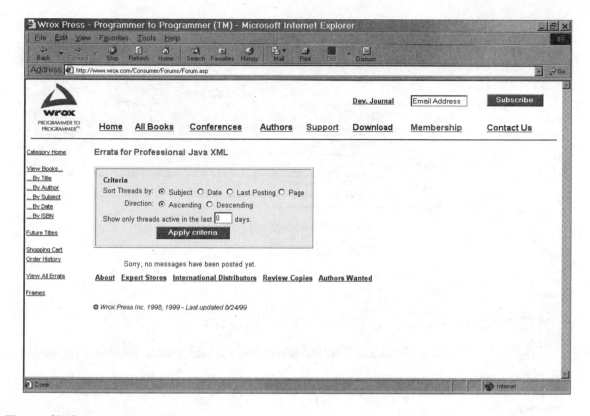

E-mail Support

If you wish to directly query a problem in the book with an expert who knows the book in detail then e-mail support@wrox.com, with the title of the book and the last four numbers of the ISBN in the subject field of the e-mail. A typical email should include the following things:

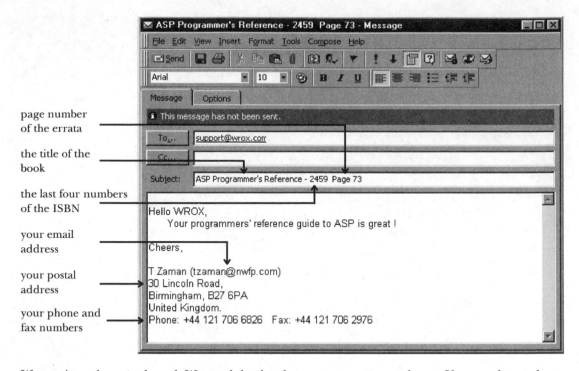

page number of the errata

the title of the book

the last four numbers of the ISBN

your email address

your postal address

your phone and fax numbers

We won't send you junk mail. We need the details to save your time and ours. If we need to replace a disk or CD we'll be able to get it to you straight away. When you send an e-mail it will go through the following chain of support:

Customer Support

Your message is delivered to one of our customer support staff who are the first people to read it. They have files on most frequently asked questions and will answer anything general immediately. They answer general questions about the book and the web site.

Editorial

Deeper queries are forwarded to the technical editor responsible for that book. They have experience with the programming language or particular product and are able to answer detailed technical questions on the subject. Once an issue has been resolved, the editor can post the errata to the web site.

The Authors

Finally, in the unlikely event that the editor can't answer your problem, s/he will forward the request to the author. We try to protect the author from any distractions from writing. However, we are quite happy to forward specific requests to them. All Wrox authors help with the support on their books. They'll mail the customer and the editor with their response, and again all readers should benefit.

What We Can't Answer

Obviously with an ever-growing range of books and an ever-changing technology base, there is an increasing volume of data requiring support. While we endeavor to answer all questions about the book, we can't answer bugs in your own programs that you've adapted from our code. So, while you might have loved the help desk systems in our Active Server Pages book, don't expect too much sympathy if you cripple your company with a live adaptation you customized from Chapter 12. However, do tell us if you're especially pleased with the routine you developed with our help.

How to Tell Us Exactly What You Think

We understand that errors can destroy the enjoyment of a book and can cause many wasted and frustrated hours, so we seek to minimize the distress that they can cause.

You might just wish to tell us how much you liked or loathed the book in question. Or you might have ideas about how this whole process could be improved, in which case you should e-mail feedback@wrox.com. You'll always find a sympathetic ear, no matter what the problem is. Above all you should remember that we do care about what you have to say and we will do our utmost to act upon it.

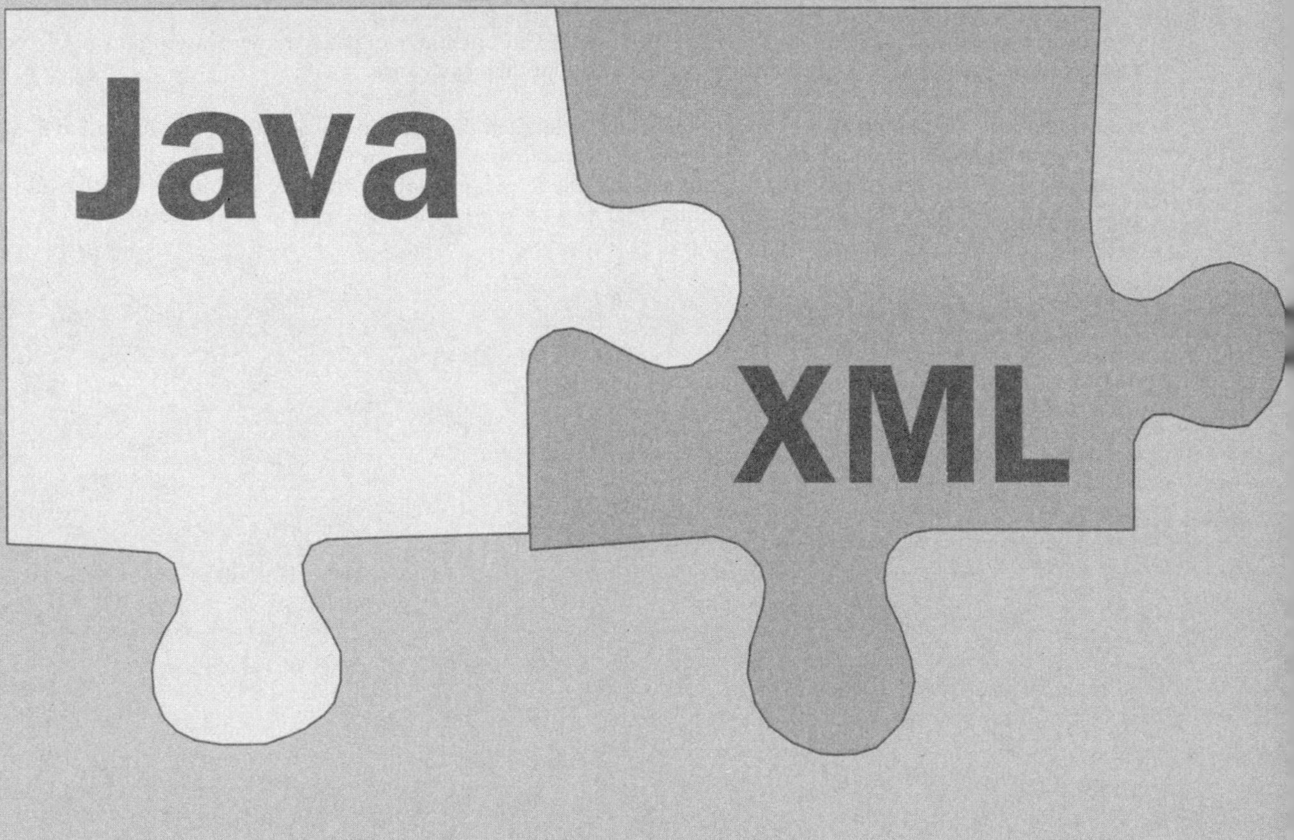
Java
XML

Index

C

Index

Index

Y

wrox

PROGRAMMER TO PROGRAMMER™

Wrox writes books for you. Any suggestions, or ideas about how you want information given in your ideal book will be studied by our team.
Your comments are always valued at Wrox.

Free phone in USA 800-USE-WROX
Fax (312) 893 8001

UK Tel. (0121) 687 4100   Fax (0121) 687 4101

Programming with Servlets and JSP - Registration Card

Name _____

Address _____

_____

_____

City _____ State/Region _____

Country _____ Postcode/Zip _____

E-mail _____

Occupation _____

How did you hear about this book? _____

☐ Book review (name) _____

☐ Advertisement (name) _____

☐ Recommendation _____

☐ Catalog _____

☐ Other _____

Where did you buy this book? _____

☐ Bookstore (name) _____ City _____

☐ Computer Store (name) _____

☐ Mail Order _____

☐ Other _____

What influenced you in the
purchase of this book?

☐ Cover Design

☐ Contents

☐ Other (please specify) _____

How did you rate the overall
contents of this book?

☐ Excellent   ☐ Good

☐ Average   ☐ Poor

What did you find most useful about this book? _____

_____

What did you find least useful about this book? _____

_____

Please add any additional comments. _____

_____

What other subjects will you buy a computer

book on soon? _____

_____

What is the best computer book you have used this year?

_____

Note: This information will only be used to keep you updated about new Wrox Press titles and will not be used for any other purpose or passed to any other third party.

Check here if you DO NOT want to receive support for this book ☐

wrox
PROGRAMMER TO PROGRAMMER™

NB. If you post the bounce back card below in the UK, please send it to:

Wrox Press Ltd., Arden House, 1102 Warwick Road,
Acocks Green, Birmingham B27 6BH. UK.

———— *Computer Book Publishers* ————